The Correspondence of Henry Oldenburg

Volume IX
1672 - 1673

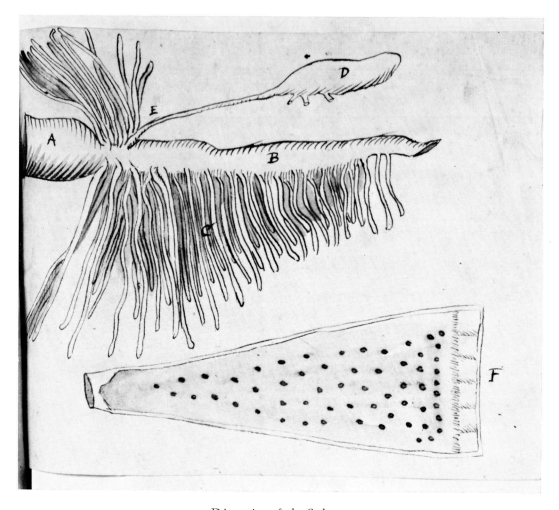

Dissection of the Salmon
By Swammerdam with Letter 2203

The
Correspondence
of
Henry Oldenburg

Edited and Translated by
A. RUPERT HALL & MARIE BOAS HALL

Volume IX
1672-1673

The University of Wisconsin Press

Published 1973
The University of Wisconsin Press
Box 1379, Madison, Wisconsin 53701

The University of Wisconsin Press, Ltd.
70 Great Russell St., London

First printing

Printed in the Netherlands

For LC CIP information, see the colophon
ISBN 0-299-06390-9

Contents

THE CORRESPONDENCE

List of Plates

This volume is dedicated to

George Boas

Philosopher and Historian

Preface

We have endeavored in this volume to follow precedents of style, printing, spelling, and so on adopted from time to time in previous volumes. In particular we have treated Antoni Leeuwenhoek's letters—of which the first appears here—in the same manner as we do those of Newton, printing only short summaries with comment, but for the full text relying upon the edition of his *Collected Letters*, which is complete for our period.

Certain mathematical letters in this volume were later regarded by Newton and John Collins as relevant to the claim for English priority over Leibniz in the invention of the calculus; they were therefore collected together for publication in *Commercium epistolicum*, 1713. The volume in the Royal Society into which were bound the manuscripts from which the book was printed is also known as Commercium epistolicum.

We are indebted, as on so many occasions, to various libraries and institutions which have permitted us to reproduce manuscripts in their possession, especially to the British Museum, Bibliothèque Nationale, Biblioteca Universitaria di Bologna, Bodleian Library, Cambridge University Library, the Kgl. Bibliotek in Copenhagen, the Königliche Bibliothek in Hannover, the Laurenziana Library in Florence, the Observatoire of Paris, the Rijksuniversiteit, Leiden, the Royal Society; and to the Hollandsche Maatschappij for permission to reprint the Huygens-Oldenburg correspondence.

For information tirelessly provided in answer to innumerable awkward questions we wish to thank a host of colleagues and friends. In particular, we have to thank Dr. K. Boratynski, John Shillcock, and Professor T. R. E. Southwood of Imperial College, John Peake of the British Museum of Natural History, and Dr. Edmund Burke of Newcastle University for help on zoological problems; Mrs. Sheila Francis for solution of a mycological one; Dr. J. E. Hofmann and Mr. A. Prag for invaluable assistance over Leibniz; Miss Diana Laurillard; Dr. M. P. Earles for pharmacological assistance; Dr. A. I. Sabra and Professor V. L. Ménage for Arabic assistance; Professor John Olmsted, Mrs. Gunnel Ingham, Mrs. Magda Whitrow, and the Librarians of the Wellcome Medical Library. Dr. A. Van Helden helped us much in transcription, and solved several Dutch riddles. Our patient secretary, Mrs. K. H. Fraser, once again typed the manuscript. Two particular debts remain to be acknowledged with especial pleasure: to Dr. D. T. Whiteside, who generously and patiently shared with us as much of his vast knowledge of seventeenth-century mathematics as we could assimilate and prevented many errors, and, in a different way, to the Librarian of the Royal Society and his assistants, who so kindly helped to make accessible much that is here printed. Finally we are indebted in a different way to the Wellcome Trust for a generous loan to the Wisconsin Press which made possible the publication of this volume.

A. RUPERT HALL
MARIE BOAS HALL

Imperial College
February 1972

Abbreviated Titles

Adelmann
   Howard B. Adelmann, *Marcello Malpighi and the Evolution of Embryology.* 5 vols.
   Ithaca, N.Y. 1966.

Baily
   Francis Baily, *An Account of the Revd. John Flamsteed.* London, 1835.

Birch, *Boyle*
   Thomas Birch (ed.), *The Life and Works of the Honourable Robert Boyle,* 2nd ed.
   6 vols. London, 1772.

Birch, *History*
   Thomas Birch, *The History of the Royal Society.* 4 vols. London, 1756–57.

B.M.
   British Museum

BN
   Bibliothèque Nationale, Paris (Lat. = Fonds Latin; Fr. = Fonds Français;
   N.a.L. = Nouvelles acquisitions Latines; N.a.f. = Nouvelles acquisitions françaises.)

Bologna
   Biblioteca Universitaria di Bologna.

Boncompagni
   *Bullettino di Bibliografia et di Storia delle Scienze Matematiche e Fisiche, pubblicato di
   B. Boncompagni,* Vol. XVII. Rome, 1884.

Brown
   Harcourt Brown, *Scientific Organizations in Seventeenth Century France.* Baltimore,
   1934.

Cole, *Comparative Anatomy*
F. J. Cole, *A History of Comparative Anatomy. From Aristotle to the Eighteenth Century*. London, 1949.

Copenhagen MSS.
Boll. Brevs. U⁴ in the Kgl. Bibliotek, Copenhagen.

C.S.P.D.
Calendar of State Papers Domestic.

CUL MS. Add.
Cambridge University Library, Additional Manuscript.

Denis, *Conférence*
Jean Denis, *1ᵉ–15ᵉ Conference, Presentee a Monseigneur Le Dauphin*. Paris, 1672–74.

Denis, *Mémoires*
Jean Denis (ed.), *Mémoires concernant les Arts & les Sciences*. Paris, 1672, 1673.

DSB
Dictionary of Scientific Biography. New York, 1970–

Duhamel
Jean Baptiste Duhamel, *Regiae scientiarum academiae historia*. Paris, 1698.

Gerhardt
C. J. Gerhardt (ed.), *Der Briefwechsel von Gottfried Wilhelm Leibniz mit Mathematikern*, I. Berlin, 1899.

Grew, *Musaeum*
Nehemiah Grew, *Musaeum Regalis Societatis. Or A Catalogue & Description of the Natural and Artificial Rarities belonging to the Royal Society and preserved at Gresham College*. London, 1681.

Hannover MSS.
Leibniz Briefe 695 in the Königliche Bibliothek, Hannover, Germany.

Hofmann, *Entwicklungsgeschichte*
J. E. Hofmann, *Die Entwicklungsgeschichte der Leibnizschen Mathematik während des Aufenthaltes in Paris (1672–1676)*. Leipzig, 1949.

Hofmann, *Prioritätstreites*

J. E. Hofmann, "Studien zur Vorgeschichte des Prioritätstreites zwischen Leibniz und Newton um die Entdeckung der höheren Analysis," *Abhandlungen der Preussischen [Deutsche] Akademie der Wissenschaften. Jahrgang 1943. Mathematischnaturwissenschaftliche* Klasse. No. 2. Berlin, 1943. Pp. 1–130.

Hooke, *Diary*

H. W. Robinson and W. Adams (eds.), *The Diary of Robert Hooke M.A., M.D., F.R.S. 1670–1680.* London, 1935.

Joecher

Christian Gottlieb Joecher, *Allgemeines Gelehrten-Lexicon.* 4 vols. Leipzig, 1750–1751.

Laurenziana

R. Biblioteca Mediceo-Laurenziana, Florence, collezione Ashburnham-Libri, Catal. Ashb. 1866.

Leeuwenhoek, *Letters*

The Collected Letters of Antoni van Leeuwenhoek. Amsterdam, 1939–

Leiden

The Library at the Rijksuniversiteit.

Newton, *Correspondence*

H. W. Turnbull *et al.* (eds.), *The Correspondence of Isaac Newton.* Cambridge, 1959–

Newton, *Mathematical Papers*

D. T. Whiteside (ed.), *The Mathematical Papers of Isaac Newton.* Cambridge, 1967–

Observatoire

Volumes VI to XII of the bound correspondence of Hevelius, preserved in the library of the Observatoire de Paris. These letters are numbered, not foliated.

Œuvres Complètes

Christiaan Huygens, *Œuvres Complètes.* The Hague, 1888–1950.

Olhoff

Johann Eric Olhoff, *Excerpta ex literis illustrium et clarissimorum virorum ad . . . Dominum Johannem Hevelium perscriptis.* Danzig, 1683.

Opera omnia
  Marcello Malpighi, *Opera omnia*. 2 vols. London, 1686.

Parkinson
  John Parkinson, *Theatrum Botanicum: The Theater of Plants. Or, an Herball of Large Extent*. London, 1640.

Philosophical Letters
  W. Derham (ed.), *Philosophical Letters between the late Learned Mr. Ray and Several of his Ingenious Correspondents . . . To which are added those of Francis Willughby Esq*. London, 1718.

Phil. Trans.
  Henry Oldenburg (ed.), *Philosophical Transactions: giving some Accompt of the present Undertakings, Studies and Labours of the Ingenious in many considerable parts of the World*. London and Oxford, 1665–77.

Pizzoli
  Ugo Pizzoli, *Marcello Malpighi e l'opere sua*. Milan, 1897.

P.R.O.
  Public Record Office, London.

Raven, *Ray*
  Charles E. Raven, *John Ray Naturalist: His Life and Works*. Cambridge, 1950.

Rigaud
  [Stephen Jordan Rigaud], *Correspondence of Scientific Men of the Seventeenth Century . . . in the Collection of . . . the Earl of Macclesfield*. 2 vols. Oxford, 1851.

Schierbeek, *Swammerdam*
  A. Schierbeek, *Jan Swammerdam 1637–80. His Life and Works*. Amsterdam, 1967.

Sprat, *History*
  Thomas Sprat, *The History of the Royal Society of London, for the Improving of Natural Knowledge* [1667], 3rd ed. London, 1722.

Turnbull, *Gregory*
  H. W. Turnbull, *James Gregory Tercentenary Memorial Volume*. London, 1939.

Introduction

The letters in this volume, which covers the period from the beginning of April 1672 to the end of May 1673, are more numerous than usual, nearly three hundred in all. They are addressed to sixty-six correspondents, of whom only a third were living in England. (Eight English correspondents lived abroad.)

There are various explanations for this. One is a noticeable tendency on the part of both Oldenburg and many of his correspondents towards brevity, which in turn may be traceable to the lasting difficulties of transmission resulting from the continuance of the Anglo-Dutch War, which now involved France as well. For the same reason more letters than usual were lost in the post, their existence being known only from memoranda or reference; yet others have mysteriously vanished without obvious reason. We have also been able to include more letters because of our practice of abridging letters which have been fully edited and made available in English in recent times, here those of Newton and Leeuwenhoek.

All this is not to say that the level of scientific interest is lower than in previous volumes, for this is far from being the case. No volume could lack interest which contained comments upon Newton's first work in optics; there are in addition high points of interest in anatomy, zoology, astronomy, and above all in mathematics. Most notable is the fact that the Royal Society in war, as in peace, maintained its supreme importance in the eyes of Englishmen and foreigners alike. There were few new Fellows elected in this period, but they include two foreigners who earnestly sought the honor, and were extremely grateful for it, Cassini in 1672 and Leibniz in 1673. How well the Society had managed to sustain its reputation for impartiality is amply demonstrated by Swammerdam's tribute, which Oldenburg was to print in the *Philosophical Transactions*, "no one dares, or ought to dare, to resort in matters of natural philosophy to any other tribunal than the Royal Society," a precept he himself followed, as were to do other scientists from Holland, France, Denmark, Italy, and various parts of Germany. So Huygens, sending a dozen copies of *Horologium oscillatorium* for distribution in England, wrote, "I should be very pleased to learn what is said about it by all those learned geometers, who are more numerous in that country than in any other in Europe."

Swammerdam's comment is a tribute not only to the Royal Society, but to its ever-industrious secretary who managed the correspondence and the printing of a part of it with such tact as to remain on friendly terms with all parties at this stage. When it came to inclusion of material in the *Philosophical Transactions* Oldenburg tried, as he told Lister, to "manage, as to their publishing or keeping privat, as you shall direct" (Letter 2089). His own preference was naturally for publication, for the "knowledge of to ye philosophical and curious world," but he patiently forebore to publish, although not to urge publication, of those communications which their authors were reluctant to see in print. Thus he nursed Lister's work on snails for two years, before publication. He patiently and successfully managed to print without rancor the hydra-like controversy arising from Newton's first paper on light and colors (Letter 1891 in Vol. VIII), which involved communications from Hooke, Huygens, Pardies, and Newton himself—no easy task; in the end he resorted to the device of depersonalizing criticism by not printing the names of the controversialists. Similarly he managed to print the substance of the discussion between Huygens and Sluse on Alhazen's problem, and Sluse's "method of tangents," while just at the end of our period he printed Brouncker's work on the isochronism of the cycloid to establish his priority over work by Pardies, made relevant by the publication in 1673 of Huygens' *Horologium oscillatorium*. The importance of the *Philosophical Transactions* to the Continental world of learning is emphasized by the publication of the first six volumes in Latin by the Amsterdam printers, Henry and Theodor Boom. After the poor job made of the translation by John Sterpin (see Vol. VIII), they engaged a learned German, Christoph Sand, who was to cause Oldenburg considerable vexation in the early part of 1672/3 by a tedious correspondence over errors, and by his failure to make the printers stop ascribing the *Philosophical Transactions* to the Royal Society when it was, after all, Oldenburg's private venture and responsibility.

In this volume the network of correspondence grows increasingly complex, so that it is difficult to separate it into domestic and foreign in any strict sense. The supreme example is the case of Newton: there was never any question in the mind of Oldenburg, or of most of the active

Fellows of the Royal Society, of the supreme importance of Newton's optical work, and Oldenburg proceeded accordingly to spread word of it far and wide partly by letter, partly by publishing it as far as this was consistent with Newton's distaste for wrangling in public. Newton's work appeared in the *Philosophical Transactions* in an international context, along with comments on it by Hooke, Huygens, and Pardies, and Newton's replies to these comments—all this published in either English or Latin, but with Latin predominating. Similarly with Wallis: although much of his correspondence is concerned with domestic matters, his preoccupation with pneumatics in 1672, culminating with the publication of a Latin paper in the *Philosophical Transactions*, arose from work announced by Huygens; this provoked Wallis, in association with Brouncker, into experimental and theoretical expansion of work they had touched on earlier. Flamsteed again, although very English in his outlook, sceptical often of the work of foreigners, and with a poor command of Latin, yet provided lunar predictions and tables for all, and was beginning to exchange information with Cassini in Paris. He, like others, was much excited by Johannes Hecker's prediction of a transit of Mercury to be expected in 1674; Hecker had sent copies of his pamphlet to Oldenburg for distribution, another tribute to the Royal Society's rôle in the dissemination of information. Leibniz, having visited England in 1671/2, returned to Paris to send eager word of his ever-widening knowledge of events in the French scientific world, and to effect an exchange of mathematical discoveries.

Leibniz's news of books and events was the more welcome in the first half of 1673, as the invaluable Francis Vernon had left Paris in the late spring or early summer of 1672. No one replaced him as a source of general news. Justel presumably wrote, for although there are no surviving letters from him in this period there are frequent references to letters from him containing news from France and even Italy (as in Letter 2227), but Justel was an unreliable source of scientific news, although an eminent gossip. Many French scientists wrote, but their letters are confined to their own interests. From Paris, Charas and Denis wrote on medical matters, Cassini on astronomical ones; Pardies sent news of his own work, and commented upon Newton's, the only critic of Newton to be convinced by Newton's arguments; Huygens wrote as usual on Alhazen's problem (for Sluse), on pneumatics, on Newton's optical discoveries (which he failed to appreciate fully), and on his own affairs; Duhamel announced the appearance of his own books, and passed on the news of medical novelties; and Huet sent word of the Dauphin's education and of the world of classical learning.

From Caen there was news of provincial scientific and literary circles, and Martel revived an old acquaintanceship from Montauban.

Contact was not lost with Italy, even when Dodington was recalled from his post as English resident late in 1672, much to the regret of the Venetian government. Although parcels were difficult of transmission—Malpighi had to wait nearly two years for transmission of the printed copies of his *De formatione pulli in ovo*—letters traveled well to northern Italy either through Venice or through Paris. There are interesting glimpses of Magalotti's circle in Florence, both through Magalotti's own letters, now often enterprisingly written in English, or through the long account of Thomas Platt (Letter 2037), an English visitor who was admitted to intimacy with this circle. It was much more difficult to reach the south of Italy. Correspondence continued sporadically with Borelli, Cornelio, and Gornia (who was called upon for his medical judgment), but there was a copious exchange of news with Malpighi, whose claim to priority the Royal Society upheld against English contenders like Croone (in embryology) or Grew (in plant anatomy).

With Germany Oldenburg's correspondence was very lively. There were Hevelius and Hecker in Danzig writing on astronomical matters, and Christopher Kirkby writing on natural history. From Hamburg, Vogel continued to write on a great diversity of subjects, his interest in narcotics leading him to make continued demands upon English oriental scholars. As we have remarked before, the introduction of exotics to the European pharmacopoeia is an interesting facet of the history of medicine, in which it would seem Vogel deserves his place. Partly stimulated by the interests of Edward Bernard at Oxford, partly perhaps by Huet's work, partly by hints dropped by Vogel, Oldenburg tried somewhat inconclusively to establish connections with German classical scholars. And from time to time contributors to the *Miscellanea Curiosa* wrote news of the German medical world.

More interesting, and more unusual, was a lively correspondence with Denmark. Although Erasmus Bartholin had for some years been in slightly tenuous touch with the Royal Society, the presence of an English embassy at Copenhagen, among which was Thomas Henshaw, facilitated proper communication at last. Henshaw himself provided a great deal of information about Danish natural history and provided a link with others. Among many curious facts not the least curious were those he sent about the customs of lemmings.

Among English correspondents, besides Flamsteed and Wallis, Lister and Towneley figure most frequently. Lister was a fairly steady correspondent, and in this period produced important work on the classification of snails, on entomology, and on veins in plants. Towneley wrote intermittently with news of astronomical observations with Flamsteed, and of pneumatic experiments. Lister, Towneley, and Flamsteed were all badgered for information about longevity in the North, an old and inexplicable interest of Oldenburg's. John Beale wrote less frequently than in the past, although in the same rambling style as ever, and Richard Reed sent grafts and information about orchards from Herefordshire.

The chief English interest, however, centers around the figure of Newton, not here so much in his native context as in relation to the wider world of European science. Oldenburg had assiduously spread word abroad of Newton's new theory of light and colors; now—without encouragement from Newton himself—Oldenburg appears in a new rôle as the private disseminator of Newton's mathematical discoveries, a rôle in which he was assisted by that great mathematical gossip and magpie, John Collins. In this volume, other than the bare outline of Newton's method of tangents sent by Oldenburg to Sluse (see Letters 2136, 2204), Newton's accomplishments could only be hinted at darkly by Collins (Letters 2196, 2196a).

But the recipient of these hints was Leibniz, a man of great acuity even though his judgment was not always sound, and at this stage his education in contemporary mathematics was defective. Thus, in mathematical history, the journey of Leibniz to London in 1673 served as a prelude to his still more fateful visit there three years later. This earlier introduction to the Royal Society taught Leibniz to regard Oldenburg, a fellow German, as a friend; whereas he may well have sensed a certain unkindness in the English. How different from the warm encouragement that his mathematical researches received from Huygens was the chilly reception his proud claims elicited from Pell and Collins! As for Hooke, his behavior to a young foreign visitor seems no less inexplicable than indefensible (Letter 2165). The idea of a mechanical calculator was not new; nevertheless, Leibniz felt satisfaction in his elegant and practical design. In his claim to have anticipated Leibniz, in his promises of superior achievement for his own design, in his final assertion of the inferiority of mechanical calculators to computation and the use of tables, Hooke showed himself ungenerous, unimaginative, and perhaps unknowing (for the best answer to such a calculator as Leibniz's is of course the abacus). If any one feels strong admiration for the character of Robert Hooke, let him imagine himself in the position of Leibniz—who, in turn, by a strange and unjust irony of fate, was to find himself accused of false dealing.

There is perhaps no better illustration of the dangers of correspondence by letter than that of Leibniz with England, which we have now begun. It was unsatisfactory from Leibniz's point of view because he never received a full and open account of English mathematical thought, in which new ideas and methods were plainly described and frankly claimed, nor on the other hand did his own ideas ever receive serious criticism from the English. It was certainly unsatisfactory from Newton's point of view, since he did not control, perhaps did not even know, all that was communicated to Leibniz on his behalf by Collins and Oldenburg (who did not understand the subject matter anyway). Nor again were his own claims ever precisely stated. Inevitably such a correspondence created doubt, jealousy, anger. Newton grudged his praise of others, but he could be notably fair (in his admission about Sluse, for example, in Letter 2258 of Vol. X). One suspects that like Wallis, Hooke, and even Collins, Newton early formed a mistrust of Leibniz that was partly justifiable (in the sense that Leibniz was a philosopher, not a scientist, yet claimed to speak on scientific issues) and partly the consequence of mischievous circumstance.

As these new issues with a long shadow stretching into the future come over the horizon, so inevitably with the passage of years some correspondents vanish through death. The year 1672–73 was notably saddened for the scientific world by deaths of a number of eminent scientists. In the early summer of 1672 Oldenburg learned of the death of the German medical writer P. J. Sachs in the previous January. Later that summer Francis Willughby died at the age of 37, to the concern of his friends, a loss especially felt by those like Ray to whom he had been a helpful patron. The death of Wilkins in November of 1672 was a further loss to Ray and other naturalists, although it cannot have been totally unexpected, since he was 67 years of age. In the spring of 1673 Pardies died at the same age as Willughby, and equally mourned; he seems to have been a most sympathetic character. This volume also contains the last communication from De Graaf, who was to die at the age of only 32 in the summer of 1673. In the ten years since Oldenburg had become secretary to the Royal Society these men had all become friends as well as correspondents, and it is reasonable to assume that he truly regretted their loss.

At the other extreme, Oldenburg had reason to rejoice at the birth of his first child, in the summer of 1672, an event noted by Beale in Letter 2027. It seems reasonable to assume that this child was his son Rupert, the elder of the two children alive at his death. It is true that Birch in his obituary of Oldenburg (*History*, III, 355 and note c) says that he left "admonitions" to his son and daughter, the latter dated 16 October 1672; but Birch's account is highly inaccurate, and the only "admonitions" we have found are both undated and addressed to a son—these having once been in Birch's possession, since they are now in the Birch manuscripts in the British Museum, Additional MSS. 4458.

Oldenburg was ill in September, evidently at a somewhat critical state in his affairs. What the difficulty may have been is nowhere clear, except that it could be rectified by Sir Joseph Williamson, but it caused genuine concern to both Robert Boyle and Sir Robert Moray. On 17 September 1672 (P.R.O. MS. 29/316, no. 184 (1)) Boyle wrote to Moray as follows:

> If I had not been hinderd by a visit, just as I was goeing out, I had this morning waited on you, to put you in mind yt ye Affair of our threaten'd friend will grow ye more difficult, ye longer it remains undispatch'd; and therefore being not in a condition to come now to White hall my selfe, I must by this Paper beg you to renew our solicitations to Sr. J. W. who is so great a friend to ye Society in Generall, & has been so kind to ye Party in particular, yt I hope we shall not need all our Interest to prevail with him on this occasion, wherein I ye rather press expedition to you, because ye menaced Person is now by sickness confined to his house. And I know you would not expose at such a time to an avoidable melancholy a Person yt is so usefull to ye Society, & so much your servant.

This letter Moray sent to Williamson on 19 October 1672 (P.R.O. MS. S.P. 29/316, no. 184) with the following equally cryptic message:

> You will give me leave to apprehend that multitude of Business may have hindered you from doing what I desired you to do for our poor friend Mr Oldenb. in Mr Boiles name aswell as mine own, & so will not be displeased I have put you in minde of it, especially, seing I was to wait upon you at the office, & am this morning going out of Town a litle way for 3. or 4. dayes. You will see by the inclosed how much your favor imports to the Gentleman, how much it will please Mr Boile, & I do assure you it will very much oblige, My very worthy friend, your most humble real servant R. Moray. pray let Mr Oldenb. know what he may except.

There is no further direct reference to this matter, and all we know is that in February 1672/3 Oldenburg was hard at work at what was evidently a familiar task, the translating of intercepted letters for the State Paper

Office and the translating of printed papers to provide news for the *London Gazette*, evidently a recognized employment. As he wistfully remarked (in Letter 2199), "I hope it will be considered, that I have spent many a day, and sometimes a good part of the night too, in such work," that is, in translating material sent to him by Williamson. Clearly he hoped for more than the regular pay due to him for such duties, but we do not know what the expected preferment was to be.

    It is not difficult to see that Oldenburg was kept continually busy. From October to late June or early July there was a weekly meeting of the Council of the Royal Society, followed by a meeting of the Society itself. As Letter 2078 makes plain, Oldenburg normally met once a week with the President, Lord Brouncker, to discuss the Society's affairs and presumably to consider correspondence. He had his immense correspondence to maintain, and the *Philosophical Transactions* to edit. He still undertook a good deal of work for Boyle, and probably for others as well. It was scrappy work, and not well paid, but there was no doubt that it was useful and valuable. Oldenburg's importance to the learned world receives ample testimony throughout the letters printed here.

The Correspondence

1945
Flamsteed to Oldenburg
1 April 1672

From the original in Royal Society MS. F 1, no. 85

Derby Aprill 1. 1672

Mr Oldenburge
Sr

I send yu here two transits of Jove[1] so accurately observd especially ye last as I thinke I may say without boasteing you will find but few amongst all the observations hitherto made of this planet yu may communicate them unto whom you please yu will find yt ye Rudolphine places of Jove erre more yn ye Caroline of which I could wish Hevelius were enformd who esteemes them the best extant.[2] I had calculated ye place of Jove both from ye Philolaick & Brattish tables but can onely tell yu that they erred lesse then ye Caroline by much but not give yu ye places & latitudes I found for I can not find ye paper I made ye calculations upon else I have given them wth ye places I have derived from Streets tables & Heckers Ephemerides.[3] Last 19 and 27th of March I made severall observations of the greatest elongation of ye 4th satellit from Jupiter & found it at least 24½ semidiameters of Jupiter from him or 24¾ as Mr Townly stated it to mee, & not 23 as Cassini makes it[4] but I feare my last observations of him will interrupt the course of those I intend for holdeing my glasse over ye flame of a candle to smeare it as I used to doe frequently it cracked in a veine through ye middle & a bit of ye breadth of a great pins head burst from it. I have since tried it on ye moone and can not say yt it performes any worse then it did. but I dare not confide in any observations made by it for each of ye peeces will cast a distinct figure & if one slip from ye other it will distort & confuse ye appearance. I shall send monys to Mr Collins when my freind comes up to London & then I shall desire

3

either him or Mr Hooke to procure mee another for the same tube of 14 foot which is ye most convenient lenght & to which I have althings accomodated. but before then I may have an opportunity of writeing to yu againe & shall let yu know more of my mind about it.

My last trialls persuade mee so much of ye accuracy of this method of observeing which I use at present that I doubt not but if I had once ye opportunity of observeing any transit of Mars in or near his Achronicall appearance by any, tho unknowne, fixed star; I could determine something concerneing his & consequently ye earths distances a Sole[5] & parallaxes; better than as yet any one has, when I find any appearance fit for my purpose I shall send you notice, yt yu may informe Mr Hooke & if hee have leasure wee may expect his observations.

In ye letter I sent to yu which yu lost[6] wth ye note there were 3 admonitions for Joviall observations, one of these I have now observed, so there remaine but two to wait for which I have notified at ye foot of my observations which pray recommend to Mr Hooke. I forbore to answer yr note soone because I hoped yu would receave a letter wth an account of ye moons appulse to ye Pleiades in it which would satisfie till I had time for this desireing to heare what news from yu I rest

yr obliged freind & servant
John Flamsteed

ADDRESS
For Henry Oldenburg Esq
  at his house in ye middle of
    ye Pell mell these
        present

NOTES

1 With this letter Flamsteed sent his Latin notes of the close passage of Jupiter by a star in Virgo (see Vol. VIII, Letter 1918) and of another transit of the same planet past a star in Leo. The observations, made between 16 and 19 March, were printed in *Phil. Trans.*, no. 82 (22 April 1672), 4036–38.

2 Flamsteed refers to Kepler's *Tabulae Rudolphinae* (Ulm, 1627); Thomas Streete, *Astronomia Carolina* (London, 1661); Ismael Boulliaud, *Astronomia Philolaica* (Paris, 1645); and Vincent Wing, *Astronomia Britannica* (London, 1669).

3 Johannes Hecker, *Ephemerides motuum coelestium ab anno 1666 ad annum 1680* (Danzig, 1662).

4 In the margin Flamsteed has noted that Jupiter's diameter is 126 parts, and the satellite's distance 1614 parts, of his micrometer scale; this would make the distance exceed $25\frac{1}{2}$ semidiameters.

5 "from the sun."

6 See Letter 1918, note 1 (Vol. VIII).

1946
Pardies to Oldenburg

3 April 1672

From the original in Royal Society MS. P 1, no. 78

Paris 13. Avril 1672 [N.S.]

Monsieur

Je vous avois escrit un mot par le dernier courrier, mais j'ay appris que ma lettre s'est perdue par les chemins entre ici et la poste.[1] Je vous donnois avis que j'avois donné un pacquet à M. Justel pour vous, qu'un Gentilhomme devoit vous porter en partant d'ici dés le 2e de ce mois. Il ya dans ce pacquet 2. exemplaires d'un *discours dela connoissances des Bestes*,[2] Je vous priois d'en vouloir presenter un à M. Willis à moins que vous n'en voulussier disposer autrement, car c'est à vous que je les donne tous deux. J'y avois ajouté un autre livre qui est fort rare, car je ne pense pas qu'il l'en soit debité une vintaine. Il est fait contre la doctrine de M. Descartes et il ya la dedans des choses tres-fortes et tres-bien escrites contre cette doctrine. Celuy qui passe pour en estre autheur est tres-intelligent et de mes intimes amis. il enseigne la philosophie à Poitiers et se nomme le P. Rouchon.[3] Les Cartesiens ont fait courir le bruit que ce livre estoit supprimé par ordre du Roy de peur qu'il ne fist du bruit: mais cela n'est pas vray, et s'il ne paroit pas c'est parce que le libraire a este mis en prison pour des debtes et tous ses magazins scellez. ce livre s'est trouvé la dedans enveloppé avec les autres et il faut attendre que toutes ces affaires soient accomodées. Je vous remerciois de l'escrit qu'il vous a plu m'envoyer de la trompette, et des avis du scavant M. Wallis. Depuis ce temps j'ay lu dans vostre journal l'hypothese de M. Newton touchant la Lumiere et les couleurs. J'en ay fait une à ma facon dans un des livres de ma mechanique, qui ne scauroit subsister si cellecy de M. Newton est veritable, je vous en envoye quelques remarques que j'ay escrites en latin afin que vous puissiez les faire voir plus librement si vous le jugerez à propos.[4]

Si vos libraires n'ont point fait encore mon emplete de livres je vous priois de ne vous en mettre pas en peine parce que M. Jolly nous fera venir toutes choses. Je suis

Tout vostre
Pardies

ADDRESS
A Monsieur
    Monsieur Grubendol
        A Londres

TRANSLATION

Paris, 13 April 1672 [N.S.]

Sir,

I wrote you a line by the last messenger, but I have learned that my letter was lost in the streets between here and the post.[1] I told you that I had given Mr. Justel a packet for you, which a gentleman was to carry to you, having left here upon the second of this month. In this packet are two copies of a *Discours de la connoissance des Bêtes*.[2] I requested you kindly to present one to Mr. Willis, at least if you did not wish to dispose of it otherwise, for both copies I give to you. I added another book which is very rare; indeed I do not think that more than a score have been sold. It is written against the doctrine of Mr. Descartes, and contains very strong and well written arguments against this doctrine. The supposititious author is very intelligent and one of my intimate friends. He teaches philosophy at Poitiers and is called Père Rouchon.[3] The Cartesians have spread the rumor that this book has been suppressed by order of the King, for fear lest it make a stir, but this is not true, and if the book is not visible it is because the bookseller has been put in prison for debt and his stocks sealed. This book has found itself caught up there with the others and we must wait until all these matters are put in order. I thanked you for the account you were so kind as to send me about the trumpet, and for the opinion of the learned Mr. Wallis. Since then I have read in your journal Mr. Newton's hypothesis on light and colors. I have proposed one in my own fashion in one of the books of my *Mechanics*, which cannot hold good if this one of Mr. Newton's is true. I send you some remarks on it which I wrote in Latin so that you can show them more freely if you judge them suitable.[4]

If your booksellers have not yet made my purchase of books, I requested you not to take any trouble about it because Mr. Jolly will have everything conveyed to us. I am

Entirely yours,
Pardies

ADDRESS
Mr. Grubendol
    London

NOTES

1 Letter 1942 (Vol. VIII) in fact reached Oldenburg safely on 7 April and was perhaps read to the Society on 18 April 1672, although in view of the similarity of the two letters, it is possible that the present letter was the one produced at the Society's meeting.
2 Just published; see Letter 1942.
3 The book is *Lettre d'un philosophe à un Cartésien de ses amis* (Paris, 1672); see Letter 1942, note 4.
4 Letter 1946a.

1946a
Pardies's Commentary on Newton's
Theory of Light

Enclosure with Letter 1946
The original is Royal Society MS. P 1, no. 75
Printed in *Phil. Trans.*, no. 84 (17 June 1672), 4087–90
and in Newton, *Correspondence*, I, 130–34

TRANSLATION

I have read Newton's very ingenious hypothesis of light and colors.[1] And because I have devoted no little effort to reflection and the making of experiments on that subject, I write down a few points that come to mind concerning that new doctrine.

What that most learned man says of the very nature of light seems absolutely extraordinary, namely that light consists of an aggregation of an almost infinite number of rays, each of which carries and retains a color according to its nature and so is made fit to be refracted to a definite and individual extent, some more, some less. When rays of this kind are mingled together confusedly in open daylight they cannot by any means be detected, but are rather called pure white light; whereas in refraction individual rays of one color are separated from others of another and in this way what was hidden appears in its true natural hue. Those bodies appear of a certain color, for example red, which are suited to reflect or transmit only the red rays.

This so very extraordinary hypothesis which, as he remarks himself, overthrows the basis of dioptrics and renders useless the practical methods employed hitherto, is wholly founded on that experiment with the glass prism, in which the rays entering a dark chamber through a hole in the window [shutter] and then received on the wall or a sheet of paper did not form a round shape such as he seemed to expect following the received rules of optics, but appeared stretched out into an oblong shape. Whence he concluded that the oblong shape was caused by the fact that some rays were refracted more and others less, etc.

But it seems to me that in fact according to the ordinary and accepted laws of dioptrics the figure ought to be not round but oblong.[2] For as the rays proceeding from opposite parts of the sun's disk have a different inclination in their passage to the prism they ought to be refracted differently, so that as the inclination of some of them is at least 30′ greater than the inclination of others, their refraction should prove greater too. Thus these opposite rays emerging from the far side of the prism diverge and spread out more than they would if all had proceeded without infraction, or with equal infraction. Now that refraction of the rays only occurs in directions which may be supposed perpendicular to the axis of the prism and no inequality of refraction arises in directions parallel to its axis, as may easily be demonstrated; for the surfaces of two prisms may be thought of as parallel between themselves, taking into account the inclination of the axis, since each is parallel to its own axis. But no refraction can be computed from two parallel plane surfaces because the ray is as much bent back by the second surface as it was bent in the opposite direction by the first. Therefore since the solar rays transmitted from the hole through the prism are not refracted to either side they proceed onwards as though no surface of a prism stood in the way (that is, if as I say one considers only a sideways divergence); but in fact as the same rays are infracted upwards or downwards some more, some less, according as they are unequally inclined it is necessary that they diverge variously among themselves and so spread out into an oblong shape.

But to go through the calculation properly: as the lateral rays were found by Mr. Newton of such a breadth as to subtend an arc of 31′, corresponding to the diameter of the sun, there can be no doubt but that that height of the image which subtended 2° 49′ is also the very one corresponding to the same solar diameter after unequal refractions in that same instance.

And in fact supposing the prism to be ABC whose angle A is 60° and the ray DE making with the perpendicular EH an angle of 30° I find that when it emerges along FG it makes with the perpendicular FI an angle of 76° 22′. Now let there be another ray dE making an angle of 29° 30′ with the perpendicular EH. I find that when it emerges along fg it makes an angle of 78° 45′ with the perpendicular fi. Hence these two rays DE and dE which may be imagined as coming from opposite sides of the sun, make with each other an angle of 30′; when the same rays emerge along the lines FG and fg they diverge so as to make an angle of 2° 23′. If two other rays were considered nearer to the perpendicular EH (for example, rays making with it angles of 29° 30′ and 29°) then the emergent rays would diverge still more and make a great angle, sometimes slightly over 3°.

And besides this separation of the refracted rays is further increased because the two rays *DE* and *dE* meeting at *E* begin to diverge there and impinge upon two separate points of the other surface, that is, at *F* and *f*. For which reason it is not enough when making the calculation correctly to subtract the diameter of the hole at the window from the length of the image formed on the paper; for even supposing the hole *E* to be infinitesimal, there would still be formed as it were a broad hole in the other surface, *Ff*.

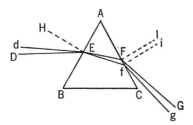

What the author calls the *experimentum crucis* also seems to me to square with the ordinary and accepted rules of refraction. For as I showed just now the solar rays that in meeting and converging form an angle of 30′ when they emerge (even from an infinitesimal hole) diverge at an angle of two or three degrees. For which reason it is not surprising if when these rays fall separately upon another prism through a very small aperture they are unequally refracted, as their inclination is unequal. Nor is it relevant whether those rays may be raised or depressed by rotating the first prism while keeping the second one motionless (which however cannot be done in every case), or whether keeping the first prism motionless the second may be moved so that it receives in succession the colored rays of the whole image, for either way the extreme rays, the red and the violet, must fall upon the second prism at unequal angles and so their refraction is unequal and hence the violet is the greater.

Since therefore a manifest cause may be brought forward to show why the shape of the rays is oblong, that cause springing from the very nature of refraction, it seems unnecessary to run after another hypothesis or to admit a diverse frangibility in those rays.

What the author next elaborates about colors indeed follows very well from the preceding hypothesis, yet that too is not without its difficulties. For when he says that where all the rays are promiscuously confused no color appears but rather whiteness this does not seem to agree with all phenomena. Doubtless those variations that are seen in the mixture of various bodies possessed of different colors may also be observed in the mixture of various rays also possessing different colors; and he himself has very correctly noticed that just as a yellow and a blue substance make green, so yellow and blue rays make green. So if all the rays of all the colors be mixed together according to this hypothesis the same color should actually appear, as is made by a mixture of all the pigments. But if this is done, that is, if red and yellow and blue and purple and all other possible ones are mixed and compounded no white, but a dark, deep color is produced. Therefore a similar color should appear in ordinary light, should it consist of a mixture of all colors.

Indeed, at the first glance nothing could be more ingenious or appropriate than what he says of the experiment of the very acute Hooke in which two fluids (the one red, the other blue), each transparent by itself, become opaque when they are mixed. For this, the famous Newton says, happens because one fluid can only transmit the red rays, and the other only the yellow; whence being mixed they transmit none. This I say seems at once to be very much to the point. Nevertheless it would seem from this that a similar opacity should be brought about by the mixture of fluids of any kind, if of different colors. Which is not true.

To Mr Grubendol,
London.

NOTES

Someone wrote "Paris April. 9. 1672 [N.S.]" at the head of these sheets, evidently supposing them to belong with Letter 1942 (Vol. VIII). This incorrect date was copied in Newton, *Correspondence*.

The criticism was sent by Oldenburg to Newton on 9 April, with Letter 1950, and read to the Royal Society on 18 April.

1 Letter 1891 (Vol. VIII) as printed in the *Phil. Trans.*, no. 80 (19 February 1671/2).

2 To understand this argument it may be helpful to remember that if the angle either of incidence or of emergence be large, and the other therefore small, the rates of change of their sines will be very unequal. But if, as Newton points out in his reply (Letter 1957a) the angles of incidence and emergence are equal, the rate of change of the sine in each is equal also. Hence rays slightly inclined to each other on entering the prism retain an almost identical inclination when emerging from it.

1947
Oldenburg to Grew
4 April 1672

Grew's Letter 1921 (Vol. VIII) is endorsed as received on 12 March and answered on 4 April.

1948
Oldenburg to Richard Towneley

6 April 1672

Mentioned in Towneley's reply, Letter 1958.

1949
Oldenburg to Huygens

8 April 1672

From *Œuvres Complètes*, VII, 168–69
Original in the Huygens Collection at Leiden

A londres le 8 Avril 1672

Monsieur,

Voicy le nombre 81 des Transactions, où vous trouverez presque tout ce qu'il m'a escrit touchant sa lunette:[1] Je dis *presque tout*, vû que depuis que i'avois envoyé la copie de cet Imprimé à la presse, i'ay receu quelque chose de plus, non seulement touchant les Apertures et les charges pour toutes sortes de longueurs, mais aussi sur le changement qui se pourra faire du miroir plat et oval en une autre figure et matiere: dont vous serez, peut estre, informez dans les Transactions, qui s'imprimeront pour ce mois d'Avril.[2]

Quand vous aurez consideré sa theorie des couleurs, vous nous obligerez de nous communiquer vos pensees là dessus. Je ne manqueray pas de faire voir à quelques uns de nos Philosophes et Mathematiciens ce que vous avez medité de nouveau sur le probleme d'Alhazen. Si vous ne me le defendez pas, ie pourray prendre la liberté d'inserer cy-apres dans mes Transactions, *et* la premiere construction, que vous nous en envoiastez il y a longtemps, avec l'abbregement que vous en avez trouvé depuis, et l'autre, que vous appelez la bonne, come ayant lieu dans tous les cas imaginables.[3] Je vous diray des nouvelles touchant les traitez de Kinkhuysen par ma prochaine.

À present ie n'ay rien a adjouster, si non que vous estes desiré d'examiner le discours latin de Monsieur Wallis touchant sa double methode des Tangens, inserée dans les Transactions;[4] et que ie suis Monsieur

Vostres treshumble et tres-obeissant serviteur
Oldenburg

ADDRESS

     A Monsieur
     Monsieur Christian Hugens de Zulechem
       a la Bibliotheque du Roy à
           Paris

TRANSLATION

London, 8 April 1672

Sir,

Here is number 81 of the *Transactions* where you will find almost everything that he has written to me about his telescope.[1] I say *almost everything*, seeing that since I sent the copy for this printed work to the press I have received something more, not only concerning the apertures and the diameters of the eyepiece for every variety of length, but also concerning the changes which can be effected in the flat and oval mirror by another shape and material; of this you will perhaps be informed in the *Transactions* which will be printed for this month, April.[2]

When you have thought about his theory of colors, you will oblige us by communicating your thoughts upon it to us. I shall not fail to show some of our philosophers and mathematicians what you have considered afresh about Alhazen's problem. If you do not forbid it, I may take the liberty later of inserting in my *Transactions both* the first construction which you sent us long ago with the abridgement you have since discovered, *and* the other one, which you call the good one since it holds in all imaginable cases.[3] I shall tell you the news about Kinckhuysen's treatise in my next.

For the present I have nothing more to add, except that you are requested to examine Mr. Wallis's Latin discourse upon his double method of tangents, inserted in the *Transactions*,[4] and that I am, Sir,

Your very humble and obedient servant,
Oldenburg

ADDRESS

     To Mr. Christiaan Huygens of Zulichem
       The King's Library
          Paris

NOTES

Reply to Letter 1944 (Vol. VIII).

1 *Phil. Trans.*, no. 81 (25 March 1672), pp. 4004–7, 4009–10, prints a description of Newton's telescope (see Letter 1866a in Vol. VIII) and extracts from Newton's Letters 1861, 1871, 1883, and 1928 (all in Vol. VIII).

2 Newton's Letters 1937 and 1941 (Vol. VIII) were both printed in *Phil. Trans.*, no. 82 (22 April 1672), 4032–35.

3 See *Phil. Trans.*, no. 97 (6 October 1673), 6119–26, which prints extracts from the solutions of both Huygens and Sluse.

4 Wallis's "Epitome binae methodi tangentium," dated 15 February 1671/2, is printed in *Phil. Trans.*, no. 81 (25 March 1672), 4010–16; in this Wallis makes it clear that he claims no new discoveries in the methods of drawing tangents to curves, but is summarizing succinctly what he had earlier published in *De cycloide, Arithmetica infinitorum, Mechanica* and elsewhere. The paper is addressed to Oldenburg, but there is no reference to it in the previous extant correspondence. Accordingly the circumstances in which Wallis compiled it are unknown; possibly Wallis was stimulated by the interest which the allusions to Sluse's method of tangents had evoked; such at least was Collins' opinion in March 1672 (Turnbull, *Gregory*, p. 224). For an explanation of Wallis's two methods, see Hofmann, *Prioritätstreites*, pp. 72–74. No manuscript of the paper exists.

1950
Oldenburg to Newton
9 April 1672

Printed in Newton, *Correspondence*, I, 135, from the original in CUL MS. Add. 3976, no. 4

This not only enclosed Pardies's Letter 1946a but also quoted the relevant sentences from Huygens' Letter 1944 (Vol. VIII), reported the reading of Newton's Letter 1941 (Vol. VIII) to the Royal Society, and requested Newton to finish his reply to Hooke for inclusion in an early number of the *Transactions*.

195 1

Vernon to Oldenburg

10 April 1672

From the original in Royal Society MS. V, no. 24

Paris Aprill 20 1672 [N.S.]

Sr

I have received severall oblidging letters from you to all wch I have suspended my answer. because in truth I am not a little hamperd in businesse. For my Lord is going away[1] & iudge you whether it bee possible to bee wthout. I have not seene Sigre Cassini of late butt at a Thesis of Pere Pardies about Comets.[2] Where I had not an opportunity of entring into discourses wth him about other notions. I have received the Pacquet sent mee by Monsr dela Peyrere[3] of five of Doctor Pococks bookes[4] of wch I shall give him an account & observe his orders very precisely.

The trumpet you send hither of Sr. Samuel Morelands to speake the truth doth not outdoe one wch Monsieur Denis caused to bee made here according to the best Idea hee could frame out of Sr Samuels description wch hee gives in his printed sheet—true it is both the Tube & the wide end of Doctor Denis's is much larger—& it is wound round having a good large circle in the middle. as Sr Samuel Moreland caused some of his to bee made though that send hither was streight. however all agree that sound is considerably improved by this Invention & that the voyce is carried much farther by this then any other way. there needs noe other testimonies then such as every ones eares can give him.

Mr Newtons Telescope is much applauded & much admired here. & noe body doubts butt the representation of objects at a distance is infinitely betterd by it. Mr Huygens hath made one, whose reflexive mirrorr is about 3. inches diameter & hee is sufficiently satisfied wth it & hath provided a plate of about a foot diameter & hopes to polish it much better & give it a truer figure then hee hath done his first & give a far greater clearnesse & largenesse to objects then yet hath beene given.[5] hee speakes of Mr Newton wth expressions full of esteeme & hopes that optiques by his meanes will see farther then ever they could doe yet. hee would gladly see the Treatise of Dioptriques wch hee understands hee intends to publish, & those notes on Kinhuysens algebra, because hee makes them.[6] hee conceives great hopes of them.

The Letter wch Doctor Wallis sent to Pere Quesnel[7] I deliverd not to himself because hee was gone to the Novitiat butt to one of the Fathers. who undertooke the delivery of it. & I doe not question butt hee will heare from him. only one thing I must advize as to the superscription. that hee is not de ordine minimorum[8] as Doctor Wallis styles him. butt Presbyter ex oratorio Jesu.[9] for hee is Pere del oratoir. who are very distinct from the Cordeliers both in habits & Customes & foundations.

The Journal of Mr Flamsteads predicitions of Lunar appulses to the fixed Starres[10] I have left wth Signre Cassini who intends to compare them wth his owne observations, & see how iustly they will agree.

There is scarce any thing of new here in matters of Philosophy. Le Pere Pardies his treatise dela Cognoissance des bestes because I supposed Monsr Justel sends to you I forbeare to doe it.

Monsr huygens his treatise de Cycloide et pendulo[11] is written faire & ready for the presse & hee intends the printing it with what expedition is possible. I doe not heare of any thing else coming out presently wch may bee worth your Reguard. my Respects & observances to those of your Society whom I have the honour to bee acquainted wth. I am, Deare Sr

your most obedient Servant
Francis Vernon

You write in your Last letter concerning Mr Newtons Telescope wch Monsr St Hilaire was sending over[12] what iudgement they might make of it here butt I cannot heare that it is arrived.

NOTES

The letters to which this is a reply have not been found.

1 If Vernon means the Ambassador, this was probably the first Duke of Montagu (1638?–1709); see Vol. V, p. 462, note.

2 The observations on the comet made at the Collège de Clermont (where Pardies taught) are reported in identical terms in Denis, *Mémoires*, the sixth, dated 1 April 1672 [N.S.], and the *Journal des Sçavans* for 11 April 1672 [N.S.]. According to the latter, the observations were made public on 28 March 1672 [N.S.].

3 Isaac de la Peyrère (1594–1676) was the librarian of the Prince de Condé.

4 See Letters 1833 and 1836 (Vol. VIII).

5 See Huygens' correspondence in *Œuvres Complètes*, VII, 151, 157, 159, etc. He had the small reflector made in March and was very satisfied with it, though neither mirror was perfect. He then had the artisan work on a 10- or 11-inch mirror of 12-foot focal length, which failed because the metal departed from a true spherical form in the polishing.

6 See Letter 1906, note 6 (Vol. VIII). Neither enterprise matured, but it is obvious that Newton's plans were widely known.

7   A copy of this letter of 6 February 1671/2, made by Oldenburg, is in Royal Society
    MS. W 2, no. 138. Pasquier Quesnel (1634–1719) was, as Vernon says below, an
    Oratorian Father. He was also a Jansenist. His best known work is *Reflexions morales*
    (Paris, 1671), a commentary on the New Testament, often enlarged and reprinted.
    From Wallis's letters it appears that he was known to Edward Bernard.
8   "Of the Minim Order."
9   "Priest of the oratory of Jesus."
10 Flamsteed's lists of appulses had been printed in *Phil. Trans.*, no. 77 (20 November
    1671) and no. 79 (22 January 1671/2); if neither of these was what Vernon meant,
    it must have been a manuscript list. See also Letter 1836 (Vol. VIII).
11 The future *Horologium oscillatorium*, published in the following year.
12 See Letter 1920 (Vol. VIII).

1952
Oldenburg to Sluse
11 April 1672

From the draft in Royal Society MS. O 2, no. 81

Illustrissimo Viro
Domino Renato Francisco Slusio Canonico Leodiensi
Henricus Oldenburg Prosperitatem

Quae deerant, Vir Amplissime, in postremis meis 4 Nonas Martij ad Te
datis,[1] Domini Hugenii de secundis tuis circa Alhazeni problema
meditatis sensa, ea nunc cum nuper ab ipso acceperim, quantocius tibi
impertiri non gravabor. Rem eadem que ipse scripsit, lingua sic accipe

Vide Epistolam ipsius Hugenij,
unde excerpta illa fuere quae hic indigitantur.[2]

Pervelim ea, quae et tu et ille de hoc argumento egregia dixistis, et
communicastis, luci publicae exponere, si quidem assensum tuum ex parte
tua non neges, urgent, ut id fiat, amici, qui utrumque vestrum magni-
faciunt, nec concedendum putant, ut haec cogitata vestra intercidant.[3]
Jungo hic, quam novam Doctissimus Newtonus noster de luce et
coloribus Theoriam excogitavit, quam sic satis te ex Anglico sermone
intellecturum spero.[4] Patebit inde tibi, Authorem statuere, lumen constare
ex aggregatione infinitorum propemodum radiorum, qui suapte indole
suum quisque colorem referant retineantque, atque adeo apti nati sint certa
quadam et peculiari ratione, plus alij, alij minus refringi. Radios ejusmodi

dum promiscue in aperto lumine confunduntur, nullatenus discerni, sed Candorem potius referri, in refractione vero singulos unius coloris ab aliis alterius coloris secerni, et hoc modo secretos, sub proprio et nativo colore apparere: ea corpora sub aliquo colore, v.g. rubro videri, quae apta sunt reflectere aut transmittere radios solummodo rubros.[5]

Ingeniosa certe videtur Hypothesis, at dispiciendum utique num omnibus Phaenomenis et Experimentis consonet. Tu nobis, Vir perspicacissime, tuam de re tota sententiam exponere dignaberis.

Adjicio Doctoris Wallisij binam de Tangentibus methodum, quam etiam ut subacto tuo judicio pervolvere ne graveris, impense rogamus.[6] Vale vir optime meque ex asse tuum crede. Dabam Londini d. 11. April 1672.

TRANSLATION

Henry Oldenburg wishes prosperity to the very illustrious Mr. René François de Sluse, Canon of Liège

I make it no trouble, Worthy Sir, to send you as soon as possible after I have received it from Mr. Huygens himself what was lacking from my last letter to you of 4 March,[1] that is, his opinion of your second thoughts about the Problem of Alhazen. Here it is in the same language in which he wrote it:

> See the letter of Huygens himself, whence extract that which is indicated here.[2]

I wish very much to publish the noteworthy things that you and he have said and communicated [to each other] on this subject; and if you will not withhold your consent on your side, there are friends who press for this to be done who praise both of you highly and think it cannot be allowed that these thoughts of yours should be lost.[3]

I here add the new theory of light and colors developed by our very learned Newton, which I hope you will understand well enough from the English text.[4] It will be evident to you from that, that the author postulates that light consists of an aggregation of an almost infinite number of rays each of which carries and retains a color according to its nature, and so is made fit to be refracted to a definite and individual extent, some more, some less. When rays of this kind are mingled together confusedly in open daylight they cannot by any means be detected but are rather called pure white light, whereas in refraction individual rays of one color are separated from others of another and in this way what was hidden appears in its own natural hue. Those bodies appear of a certain color, for example red, which are suited to reflect or transmit only the red rays.[5]

This hypothesis certainly seems ingenious, but assuredly it is yet to be discovered whether it agrees with all phenomena and experiments. You will be so good, Sir, as to expound to us your most clear-sighted opinion of the whole issue.

I add Dr. Wallis's double method of tangents, which also we earnestly beg you to submit to your acute judgment, if you will.[6] Farewell, excellent Sir, and believe me wholeheartedly yours. London, 11 April 1672.

NOTES

1 Letter 1916 (Vol. VIII).
2 The extract was to be taken from Letter 1944 (Vol. VIII). The instruction is to the amanuensis.
3 The correspondence was printed in *Phil. Trans.*, nos. 97 (6 October 1673) and 98 (17 November 1673), 6119–26, and 6140–46.
4 This was Letter 1891 (Vol. VIII), printed in *Phil. Trans.*, no. 80 (19 February 1671/2).
5 This passage is identical with one in Pardies's remarks on Newton (Letter 1946a); either, then, Oldenburg had used these same passages previously writing in Latin to Pardies, and now repeated them; or he found it convenient to borrow Pardies's Latin summary. The latter hypothesis is perhaps the more likely.
6 See Letter 1949, note 4.

1953
Dodington to Oldenburg

12 April 1672

From the original in Royal Society MS. D 1, no. 28

Honoured Sr

I have binn 2 dayes at Padoa, but had not time to see the Baths called Aponensia,[1] I shall howbeit perfect my observations there in 2 or 3 weekes since I purpose an expresse jornie thither for yt end.

I am to entreat ye favour of some 2 or 3 of our new Telescopes, Hyperbolic & Elyptic, if brought to perfection, as I heare they are, & I pray they may be with ye first.[2]

I brought out of Eng. a collection I had made of all yr monthly Transactions, wch I caused to be well bound, beginning from March 11. 1666. no. 23. fol. 409. & ending in 1668, no. 43. fol. 876. I would begg to have ye preceding & subsequent ones, if to be gott for love or mony, Heere is a worthy inquisitive studious friend of mine, who is resolved to translate & print them at Padoa incouraged to it by many hundreds who will contribute to ye Charge.[3] I hold it, a duty to man, & my Country, to promote ye Knowledge of ye one, & Honor of ye other.

on ye 14. Instant n.s. being Holy Thursday, most peeple in this Citty, who were not interrupted by other Accidents were notoriously sensible of an Earthquake wch then hapned about 5 of ye Clock, after noon. The next day I acquainted Sr Joseph Williamson therewith, adding, I expected an accompt of wt mischiefe it had done in other places, for heere it hath left no signs, of it's having binne amongst us. Accordingly we have now a sadd accompt of ye effects it produced at Pesaro Rimini Cesena and other adjacent places in ye Ecc[lesiastical] state.[4] I will only observe to you, the Time of it's progression. At the places above named it made it selfe observable neere about 3 of ye Clock. At Padoa, it was remarkd at 4 and heere not before 5. According to ye Solemnity of Holy Thursday the Bp and Clergy of Rimini were at service in ye domo[5] accompanyed by most of ye Citty, when ye Church fell in upon them, so as no one escaped. Report sayeth the Whole Citty is destroyed even to a howse & of above 11000 inhabitants 8 persons only are escaped. But I hope, fame is a lyar and that on a second accompt, things will appeare with more mirth & less mischiefe, though doubtlesse it is very sadd. It came from Abruzzo & otranto, I expect minute accompts of all ye needful circumstances to satisfye any curious inquisitor Many observed some few days before this hapned an unusual Fuscous dark Circle about ye Sun, wch cleared not up until about noon. And this is all I can yet say of it, until I have a more exact accompt. And so I rest

Sr yr most assured humble servant
John dodington

Venice Apr. 22. 1672. [N.S.]

ADDRESS

 For mr Henry oldenberg
  These
   In London

NOTES

1 See Letters 1919 and 1930 *ad fin* (Vol. VIII).
2 Dodington was—not surprisingly—confused.
3 We have not found such an edition.
4 That is, the Romagna. The center of the earthquake, which occurred at 4:48 P.M. on 14 April, N.S., was at Rimini, but it was also felt, although less violently, at Ravenna and Ancona. It was said that more than 1500 people were killed.
5 *Duomo,* "cathedral."

1954
Kirkby to Oldenburg
13 April 1672

From the original in Royal Society MS. K, no. 9

Dantzigk 23th Aprill 72 [N.S.]

Honored Sr

The Warr 'twixt us & holland Breakeing out soe soone;[1] & the Appre-hensions that it will bee vigourously prosecuted on both sijdes; have Deprived mee of an oppertunitij bij water to send Mr Ro. Boyle The in-closed observations about Colde Comunicated to mee by the Learned Doctor of physick Monsr Israel Conradt;[2] and not knoweing how to address any thing for him; but to yourselfe, I am bolde to give you this trouble, requesting the favour at your hands. After perusall to present the same together with my most humble service to That noble person, whom I dare not importune with a letter, feareing to Disturbe (even for a moment) his more serious studies;—

in my Last of the 20th Februarij I Requested the communication of The new invention for makeing of steele; (if a thing that may bee knowne) and should bee much rejoijced to heare from you That the Designe of shorten-ing glasses may have taken effect—I have heard a confused Rumor of a glass one foote long that should performe as much as one of 16; if true I wish the Experiment may hold a minorij in majus;[3] and prove practicable; them I hope should shortly see one heare; wherein you would much oblige mee; if you pleased to gett mee one of a foote Long Mr Sam. Lee[4] will receive it pay you the Costs and send send it mee; as I Doubt not but hee hath done for the glass plates, which I Expect per Mr Pennis:—

Monsr Hevelius is very much Busied, as I suppose hee hath given you an account himselfe (though not yett at Large) the observing the Comett and The getting his Designed Booke readij takeing up what time his publique affaires leave him free; haveing beene of late hindred from goeing much abroad, I have mist the oppertunitij to speake with him soe know not certainelij whether the Comett disappeare or not; nor am I capacitated to give you a further account of his Actions: & for others studij wanting Encouragement in These parts Little rare or observable happens. Except what occurrs to some physitian in his practise and then tis ten to one 'tis either neglected or supprest; but I Beg you Excuse and beseech you to beleive That I am happij in beeing Sr:

> your affectionate friend
> & humble servant
> *Chri Kirkbij*

ADDRESS

    A Monsieur
    Monsieur Grubendol
      presentement
      a
        Londres
    per post: Franco Anvers 5

NOTES

1 The war began officially on 7 March 1671/2; the first engagement was on the twelfth (see Letter 1931 in Vol. VIII, note 3).
2 The British Museum lists Israel Conradt, *Disputatio medica de febribus* (Leiden, 1659), obviously Conradt's doctoral thesis. In "The Publisher to the Reader" of the second edition of Boyle's *New Experiments and Observations touching Cold* (London, 1683) there is a quotation in praise of Boyle's experiments from a work by Conradt there called *Dissertatio medicophysica de frigoris natura et effectibus*. This is reputed to have been published in 1677.
3 "from the small scale to the large."
4 He was previously mentioned in Letters 1709 and 1838 (Vol. VIII).
5 "To Mr. Grubendol, promptly, at London. By post, franked to Antwerp."

1955
Vernon to Oldenburg
13 April 1672
From the original in Royal Society MS. V, no. 25

Paris Aprill 23. 1672 [N.S.]

Sr

It is some time since I writt you word that Signre Cassini had promised to send you a letter now I send you the performance of that promise, this enclosed pacquet is from him wch I suppose containes his desires to bee made a member of your Society wch hee infinitely honours & if You are pleased to admit him amongst you will esteeme him self honoured by it.[1] I, who am farre inferiour to him in merit & in an establisht fame & reputation in the world, wch is confirmd & approved by an uniform opinion, not only of different men, butt nations & princes yet in this I may vie wth him in a constant esteeme & an earnest zeale for the honour & interest of that Society to wch, though I can butt meanely contribute by any faculties of mine, yet those I have are soe sincerely devoted to its glory & greatnesse, that I shall alwaies thinke my self happy in the occasion wherin I can signalize my zeale in making it serviceable to its ends; & if that Learned assembly please to thinke it fitt to adde mee to their number,[2] I shall make it my designe & iudge it my duty, to make what additions I can, to their name & splendour, & in all circumstances of obedience expresse my self, Honoured Sr, both their's & your

Most devoted & oblidged Servant
Francis Vernon

NOTES

1 For the enclosure, see Letter 1956. For the reference to Cassini's intention, see Letter 1877 and its note 12 (Vol. VIII).
2 Oldenburg proposed Vernon as a candidate at the same time as Cassini, and they were both elected at the meeting on 22 May 1672.

1956
Cassini to Oldenburg

13 April 1672

From the original in Royal Society MS. C 1, no. 53

Clarissimo Viro
Domino Henrico Oldenburg regiae societatis Anglicae
a secretis
J. D. Cassinus S.P.D.

Mitto tibi, Vir Clarissime, meas observationes Jovis et Cometae nuperis diarijs insertas.[1] Quam mihi communicasti observationem lunaris eclipsis Hierapoli habitam, eam contuli cum Italicis quibusdam in quibus immersio et emersio ex umbra fuit observata[2] et in tempore a totali immersione ad initium recuperationis luminis quod ab ipsa ponitur h.1.41 non multum discrepat ab observatione Patavina Renaldini, idem tempus exhibente h.1.46. Sed mirum quantum harum utraque dissentiat ab observatione Bononiensi Montanarij observatoris diligentissimi, qui et ex altitudinibus Arcturi, et ex horologio collegit tempus a totali immersione ad initium emersionis minutorum tantummodo 46. notato etiam hac in re ingenti discrimine Tabularum ab observatione. Ex quo apparet collationes observationum lunarium Eclipsium non posse sine magna circumspectione utiliter adhiberi ad Meridianorum differentias colligendas. Certiores experimur observationes eclipsium satellitum Jovis aequalibus Telescopijs paris bonitatis institutas, quae eorundem meridianorum differentiam multoties per eas examinatam in eodem minuto plerumque largitae sunt. Quam ad rem multum conferet ars contrahendi Telescopia a vestris excogitata modo idoneos habeat artifices, quales vos habetis, nostri enim hactenus nihil visu dignum hac in re praestare potuerunt.

Quod tu mihi saepius per literas, et D. Vernonius coram significastis de regiae societatis vestrae in me voluntate, id magna animi submissione et reverentia excepi. Ego tantorum virorum caetum semper colui, Institutum vestrum artes scientiasque promovendi summe probavi. Utinam ipse talis essem qui eidem possem meis conatibus aliquid conferre. Qualiscumque sim, me Regiae Societati addictissimum exhibeo, si quid illa censet ex me posse proficisci quod ad eius philosophicum studium conferat, ex eius pendebo nutibus, et tum ipsius instituto, tum societatis ipsius gloriae pro viribus studebo. Vale Vir Clarissime, et has submissas animi mei significationes ipsi regiae societati, ubi opportunum videbitur, expone.

Parisijs die 23 Aprilis 1672 [N.S.]

TRANSLATION

J. D. Cassini sends many greetings to the famous Mr. Henry Oldenburg, Secretary of the English Royal Society

I send you, famous Sir, my observations of Jupiter and of the comet published in the recent *Journal*.[1] The observation you communicated to me of the lunar eclipse, made at Aleppo, I have compared with certain Italian ones in which the immersion into and emergence from the shadow were observed;[2] and in the time from the total immersion to the beginning of the recovery of the light (which is there to be 1hr. 41m.) it does not differ much from the observation of Renaldini at Padua, giving the same time of 1hr. 46m. But it is extraordinary how much both of these differ from the observation made at Bologna by Montanari, a most diligent observer, who from his clock and the altitude of Arcturus makes the time from the total immersion to the beginning of the emergence only 46 minutes. Notable also in this is the great discrepancy of the Tables from the observation. From which it is obvious that comparisons between the observations of lunar eclipses can only usefully be employed to derive differences of latitude with very great caution. We find more certain observations of the eclipses of Jupiter's satellites made with matched telescopes of similar quality, which have often furnished the difference between the same two meridians taken many times by this means down to the very same minute. The art of shortening telescopes that you people have devised may be very useful in this context, if only some outstanding craftsmen (such as you have) set about it, for ours have so far been able to accomplish nothing noteworthy in this matter.

The goodwill of your Society towards myself so often signified by you in letters and by Mr. Vernon in person I accept with great humbleness of spirit and respect. I have always looked up to an assembly of such distinguished men, and for your purpose of promoting the arts and sciences I have always felt the warmest approbation. Would that I were such a one, who could make some contribution by his own endeavors. Such as I am, I shall prove myself most devoted to the Royal Society if it judges that it can expect anything from me that can add to its own philosophical investigations; I shall wait upon its wishes, and work zealously towards its glory and its objects. Farewell, famous Sir, and convey these humble expressions of my mind to the Royal Society itself when opportunity serves.

Paris, 23 April 1672 [N.S.].

NOTES

Reply to Letter 1868 (Vol. VIII).

1 In the *Journal des Sçavans* of 21 March 1672 [N.S.] appeared Cassini's study of Jupiter's axial rotation based on observations of the great red spot; in the same journal for 11 April [N.S.] were published his observations and reflections on the recent comet. Both were presented to the Royal Society on 24 April, and (in English translation) were printed in *Phil. Trans.*, no. 82 (22 April 1672), 4039–50.

2 See Letter 1848 (Vol. VIII).

1957
Newton to Oldenburg

13 April 1672

Printed in Newton, *Correspondence*, I, 136–39, from the original in CUL MS. Add. 3976, no. 5

In this reply to Letter 1950, Newton enclosed his reply to the criticisms of Pardies (Letter 1957a). He thanks Oldenburg for communicating to him the comments and criticisms of others, and promises to send a reply to Hooke's objections. While accepting Huygens' comments, he insists that chromatic aberration arises not from the shape of the lens only, but from the nature of light. Newton then briefly touches on some experiments proposed by Moray; these, with the remainder of the letter, are printed in *Phil. Trans.*, no. 83 (20 May 1672), 4059–62; they were concerned with varying the conditions of Newton's prism experiment either by moving the prism or obscuring some faces or by attenuating the light. Newton reports having tried all these variations.

1957a
Newton's Commentary on Pardies's Letter 1946a

Enclosure with Letter 1957
The original is Royal Society MS. N 1, no. 38
Printed in *Phil. Trans.*, no. 84 (17 June 1672), 4091–93
and in Newton, *Correspondence*, I, 140–42

TRANSLATION

Trinity College, April 13, 1672.

Sir,

I have received the observations of Father Pardies upon my letter to yourself about the refractions of light, and colors, for which I confess myself much obliged to him, and I have written this in response in order to resolve the difficulties he has raised. He says in the first place that no other cause for the length of the solar image made by the refraction of the prism need be assigned than the different incidence of the rays coming from opposite parts of the sun's disk, and so it does not prove the different refrangibility of the various rays.[1] And in order to strengthen the truth of his assertion he describes a case in which from a difference in incidence of thirty minutes a difference in the refracted rays of 2° 23 minutes or even more may arise, just as my experiment demands. But the reverend father has missed the point. For he has made refractions on either side of the prism as unequal as possible while I saw to it that they were equal both in my experiments and in the calculations based on my experiments as may be seen in the above-mentioned letter.[2] Accordingly let *ABC* be the cross-section of a prism perpendicular to its axis, *FL* and *KG* two rays meeting at *X* (in the center of the [window] hole) and entering the prism at *G* and *L*; and let the refracted rays be *GH* and *LM*, or finally *HI* and *MN*. And as I had supposed the refractions at the side *AC* to be equal to the refractions at the side *BC*, more or less and if *AC*

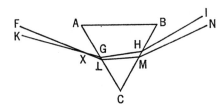

and *BC* are postulated equal, the inclination of the rays *GH* and *LM* to the base *AB* will be the same; and so $\angle CLM = \angle CHG$ and $\angle CML = \angle CGH$. For which reason also the refractions at *G* and *M* will be equal and also those at *L* and *H*; and so $\angle KGA = \angle NMB$ and $\angle FLA = \angle BHI$. Hence the inclination of the refracted rays *HI* and *MN* to each other is the same as the inclination of the incident rays *FL* and *KG*. Therefore let the angle *FXK* be 30′, equal to the sun's diameter, and the angle included between *HI* and *MN* will also be 30′, provided that the rays *FL* and *KG* are postulated as equally refrangible. But in my experiment the angle between the ray *HI* having a deep violet color and the ray *MN* having a blue[3] proved to be 2° 49′ roughly, and so those rays must be differently refrangible, or else it must necessarily be allowed that refractions obey an unequal law of the sines of incidence and refractions.

Moreover, the reverend father adds that it is not enough in making a correct calculation of the length of the image falling upon the paper to subtract the size of the hole in the window shutter, since even if that hole were infinitesimal, still there would be a wide quasi-hole on the far surface of the prism. Yet nothwith-standing this it seems to me that the refractions of the rays crossing on either the anterior or the posterior surface of the prism can be properly calculated from the principles stated. And if it were not so the breadth of the interval on the posterior surface, or quasi-hole, would scarcely make an error of two seconds, and in practice it is not worth while to pay attention to such minutiae.

The reverend father offers no objection against that other experiment, which I called crucial, when he argues that the unequal refractions of the rays endued with different colors were caused by different [angles of] incidence. For with the rays passing through two very small holes, fixed and distant from each other, as I arranged the experiment, the incidences were absolutely equal, while the refractions were plainly unequal. Should he be doubtful of our experiments, I beg him to measure the refractions of rays endued with different colors, the angles of incidence being equal, and he will find them to be unequal. If the method that I developed for his purpose does not please him (though none can be more excellent) it is easy to think of others, and I myself have attempted not a few others, with profit.

It is objected against the theory of colors that when powders of different colors are mixed they do not appear pure white, but of a dull grey color. To me it seems, indeed, that white, black, and all intermediate shades made by mixing white and black do not differ as to color but only in the quantity of [reflected] light. And since in a mixture of pigments the individual particles reflect only their own proper color, the better part of the incident light is suppressed and absorbed; the reflected light comes back as dark and as it were mingled with a duskiness so that it should exhibit not a bright white but some mixture of [white with] black, that is a grey.

Then it is objected that opacity should be produced equally by mingling fluids of different colors in the same vessel or by putting them in different vessels, which he says is not the case. But I do not see the consequence. For many fluids react upon each other, and unawares bring into existence a new contexture of their particles, whence they may become opaque, transparent, or endued with various colors in no way arising from the colors of the mixed substances. And for this reason I have always thought experiments of this sort less suitable for the drawing of conclusions. It is to be noted, however, that this experiment requires fluids endued with full and intense colors which transmit few rays other than those of their own color, such as are rarely to be met with, as may be seen by illuminating fluids in a dark room with various prismatic colors. For few can be found that appear pretty transparent in light of their own colors and opaque in other colors. Moreover the colors employed should be complementary, such as I take red and blue to be, or yellow and violet, or even green and that purple which is akin to kermes red. And some fluids of this sort (whose coloring parts do not coalesce) will perhaps become more opaque when mixed together. But I am not at all anxious about the outcome, both because the experiment is a better one when made with separated fluids and because that particular experiment (like the phenomena of the rainbow, the tincture of *lignum nephriticum*,[4] and other natural bodies) was proposed by me not as proving the theory but only in illustration of it.

That the reverend father should call our theory an hypothesis I accept in a friendly manner, since he does not regard it as established. Yet I had proposed it in a different frame of mind and it seemed [to me] to contain nothing but certain properties of light which I think it is not difficult to prove now that they are discovered, and which if I did not know them to be true I should rather prefer to repudiate as empty and useless speculation than to acknowledge as my hypothesis. How they deserve to be judged will appear more clearly from my reply to the remarks of our celebrated fellow countryman Hooke, which will perhaps be ready soon. Meanwhile farewell, and continue to love

Your most obliged,
Newton

NOTES

Reply to Letter 1946a. As with that letter, we have given a complete translation here since no modern English rendering of the letter is otherwise available.

1 Newton treated the formation of a circular solar image by homogeneous rays in *Lectiones opticae* (London, 1729), pp. 6–12.
2 That is, Letter 1891 (Vol. VIII); here Newton said, in the full text, that he arranged for the refractions on both sides of the prism to be nearly equal; in fact if (as Newton arranged it) the rays emerging from the prism be horizontal, the equal angles of incidence and emergence will each be equal to half the sum of the sun's altitude and the included angle of the prism, that is, in his experiment, to $54° 4'$.
3 Read: "red" (Newton's slip).
4 *Lignum nephriticum* is the wood of a Central American shrub or small tree (apparently either *Eysenhardtia polystacha* or *Pterocarpus amphymenium* DC) which, when infused in slightly acidulated water, yields a yellow solution which also gives a blue light by luminescence. Another *Pterocarpus* species from the Philippines behaves similarly. The effect was well known in the seventeenth century and was explained by G. G. Stokes in 1852. The wood received its name from its supposed value in the treatment of kidney disorders, first stated by Nicolas Monardes in 1565. (See J. R. Partington in *Annals of Science*, 11, 1955, 1–26.)

1958
Towneley to Oldenburg
15 April 1672

From the original in Royal Society MS. T, no. 22

Towneley Aprill. 15. 1672

Sr

'T was about ye 10th of Feb. last yt comeing home, I found 2 letters you did me ye honour to write unto mee, wch I answerd few days after,[1] but by your last of ye 6th instant (wch I onelie received on Saturday last by reason of my being abroad) I am sorrie to find yt it miscarried, since it not onelie contain'd my thanks for your favour, but was intended to beg my excuse to my Ld. Bruncar, assuring you yt if my former letter to you had in it ye word misterie, 'twas no ways intended to relate to my Ld, but to my owne not understanding his designe, and this right I hope you will doe mee to lett his Lp. know as much, with my most humble service.[2] That letter allso contain'd ye beginning of an experiment I intend God willing to trie a little further, what alteration as to heate and could our Colliers find underground for I caused a sealed Thermometer wch exactlie in my chamber kept touche with an other I had from Mr. Shortgrave,[3] to be placed so in a coal pitt, as not to be in ye way of ye currant of aire yt constantlie comes in at one shaft, and out at an other: where wee found yt from about ye 26 of Januarie, till ye 4 of Marche it kept at a constant station viz at 4|4, though during yt time, yt at home varied verie much, for it hath beene above 2 under nothing or o, and sometimes as warme as now about noone at 3|3. everie division is above 1. inche & subdivided into 10.[4] To my thanks for your former kindnesse I must now add those for your last and wish yt by ye meanes of Mr. Newtons invention, (wch I can not but hope to find admirable by what I have allreadie seene in yr. Transactions about his new discoveries about light and colours) I may be able to observe ye permanent spot you mention Sigr Cassini hath so well regulated:[5] but I can not yett understand how more yn verie grosselie ye Longitudes can be found by it since ye bodie of Jupiter appears to us too little to be divided into such exact parts as ye nicetie of yt businesse requires. but from these grave persons wee may hope for more then wee can have anie ways of ourselves imagine faisable. and tis for ye communication of them that wee are so particularlie obliged unto you, and for wch you shall ever have ye thanks of Sr

> your most humble servant
> *Rich. Towneley*

ADDRESS
> These
> For Mr. Henry Ouldenbourg at
>   his house in ye Pailmail
>   Westminster

NOTES

1 Neither Oldenburg's letters nor Towneley's February letter have survived.
2 Towneley was at this time in close correspondence with John Collins; from these letters it is clear that he was interested in Brouncker's method of applying a pendulum to a clock and regulating it.

3 Richard Shortgrave (d. 1676) was the Royal Society's operator, Hooke's assistant; he made, and presumably sold, alcohol thermometers graduated in "Hooke degrees" (= 2.4° C).

4 Since zero on Hooke's scale was the freezing temperature of water, 4.4° Hooke equals 10.6° C; −2° Hooke equals −4.8° C; and 3.3° Hooke equals 8° C, roughly.

5 See Letter 1956, note 1; this makes it obvious that Oldenburg had received the March *Journal* long before Cassini sent it, and had written about Cassini's article to Towneley.

1959
Vogel to Oldenburg
15 April 1672

From the original in Royal Society MS. F 1, no. 36

Viro Nobilissimo & Doctissimo
HENRICO OLDENBURGIO
S.P.D.
Martinus Fogelius

Ego vero, Vir Nobilissime, vos multo feliciores puto nobis, quibus paucorum Maecenatum opera Philosophiae studium promovere datum est, cum ne unum quidem hac in urbe invenire liceat, qui amore saltem in illud, si non opibus, nos ad capessendos alacrius labores similes excitet.

Thalii Catalogus Plantarum in montibus & locis vicinis Semanae Silvae, pridem distractus est, 1588 a Joachimo Camerario editus.[1] Quod si aliquo a me invenietur, tibi servabo.

Loencisii vero liber hoc anno iterum impressus est,[2] & Morisoni Plantorum Umbelliferarum Historia, aliisve libris[3] commutatus ad te mittetur, si modo pericula nostrorum Navigorum hac aestate carebit.

Rauvolfii itinerarum rarius hodie prostat, etiam inter veteres libros requirendum.[4] aliquoties tamen mihi occurrit. Scriptum est ab Auctore lingua Germanica. sed in Latinam etiam translatum reperitur. Dabo operam, ut accipias. Quod si quidem inde interea describi velis, meo exemplari hic tibi libens serviam.

Divisio Plantarum in 30 Genera Summa minus Logica est. Ego longe pauciora constituo, differentiasque a Floribus pro secondariis habeo. cujus rei argumentum jam in Doxoscopiis Jungii⁵ proposui. Velim, ut nitidum Exemplar mihi eligas.⁶

Relationem de Groenlandia brevi, spero, praelo subjiciemus.⁷

Prodiit nuper Gerkenij Experimentorum de Aere liber,⁸ & Muntingii de Plantis lingua Belgica.⁹ In hac Plantae quaedam, hactenus non satis distincte depictae, eleganter depinguntur.

Curiosi etiam nostrae Germaniae secundum Tomum ediderunt suarum Ephemeridum.

Siferus literas his adjecit, quas pridem mihi reddidit.¹⁰ Sed occupationibus impeditus nunc demum mitto. Eaedem etiam faciunt, ut hic finiam. Vale. Scribam Hamburgi 1672 d. 15 April.

Galilaei Vitam distincto charactere describi quam maxime opto. Iterum Vale.

ADDRESS
A Monsr
Monsr Grubendol

TRANSLATION

Martin Vogel presents many greetings to the very noble and learned Henry Oldenburg

Indeed I think that you, noble Sir, are much better off than we are, who enjoy the efforts of few patrons towards promoting the study of philosophy since not a single person can be found in this city who will incite us by love, let alone by money, to pursue our labors eagerly.

Thal's catalogue of the plants in the hills and woods neighboring the Thuringian forest was first published in 1588, as edited by Joachim Camerarius.¹ If I can find one it shall be at your service.

Lonicer's book has been printed again this year, in fact,² and may be sent to you in exchange for Morison's history of umbelliferous plants or other books,³ if only the dangers to our shipping will ease off this summer.

Rauwolff's *Itinerary* is rarely seen on sale today and is even sought for as an antiquarian book.⁴ Yet I sometimes come across it. It was written in German by the author. But it may be found in Latin translations. I will see to it that you get a copy. But if meanwhile you wish for something to be transcribed out of it, I will gladly make use of my own copy.

The division of plants into thirty principal classes is not at all logical. I have decided upon far fewer, and I take the differences between flowers to be merely

secondary. I have taken up this question already in the *Doxoscopiae* of Jungius.[5]
I hope that you will select a splendid copy for me.[6]

I hope that we may soon send the account of Greenland to the printer.[7]

There have recently appeared von Guericke's book[8] of experiments on the air and Munting's book on plants, in Dutch.[9] In this certain plants which have not so far been sufficiently clearly illustrated are elegantly portrayed.

The *curiosi* of our Germany have published the second volume of their miscellanies.

Sivers has added to this his own letter, which he delivered to me long ago;[10] but being obstructed by business I now send it at last. Business now calls me to a halt. Farewell.

Hamburg, 15 April 1672.

I very much hope that the life of Galileo will be copied out in a clear hand. Farewell again.

ADDRESS

     To Mr. Grubendol

NOTES

     Reply to Letter 1934 (Vol. VIII).
1 See Letter 1885, note 4 (Vol. VIII).
2 See Letter 1885, note 5 (Vol. VIII).
3 See Letter 1701, note 4 (Vol. VIII).
4 See Letter 1934, note 1 (Vol. VIII).
5 We have not found this title, though the *Phytoscopia* of Jungius has been several times mentioned before and perhaps this is what Vogel meant.
6 The whole paragraph seems to refer to Morison's botanical writings, of which the work on umbelliferous plants was planned as the thirtieth part. Presumably Vogel wanted a copy of this book (which was noticed in *Phil. Trans.*, no. 81 (25 March 1672), 4027–28).
7 See Letter 1885 (Vol. VIII).
8 See Letter 1799, note 9 (Vol. VIII).
9 Abraham Munting, *Waare oeffening der planten* (Amsterdam, 1672); see *Phil. Trans.*, no. 111 (22 February 1674/5), 247–52.
10 This letter is now missing. It may have been a reply to Letter 1935 (Vol. VIII), in which case Vogel's "pridem" is an exaggeration.

1960
Oldenburg to Pardies
22 April 1672

Oldenburg's endorsement on Letter 1942 (Vol. VIII) indicates that although it reached him on 7 April he did not reply to it until 22 April. He forwarded Newton's Letter 1957a, as mentioned below in Letter 1971.

1961
Oldenburg to Charas
22 April 1672

From the memorandum in Royal Society MS. C 1, no. 102

Peut estre, qu'il faut dans le climat de France une commotion des esprits pour faire l'effet, come il faut de la chaleur quelquefois artificielle pour causer la fermentation dans de la biere, qu'il nest pas dans des paix chauds; ou peut estre une superaddition empeschera la fermentation.

TRANSLATION

Perhaps in the climate of France a commotion of the spirits is required to produce the effect, as heat, sometimes artificial, is required to cause fermentation in beer, as it is not in hot countries; or perhaps a superaddition will hinder fermentation.

NOTE

Reply to Letter 1943 (Vol. VIII), which Oldenburg received on 8 April 1672.

1962

E. Bartholin to Oldenburg

23 April 1672

From the original in Royal Society MS. B 2, nos. 15 and 16

Nobilissime et Doctissime Domine

Non ignoro me nomine negligentiae suspectum esse debere, nisi excusatione varia officium supplere liceat. Nam et mole opprimor negotiorum et pauca hic occurrunt, quae tuae curiositati satisfacere possunt. Gratias ago maximas de honorifica mentione mei, atque experimentorum, in transactionibus Philosophicis,[1] ego vicissim tibi, atque honori tuo quavis occasione inserviam. Cometae observationes hic cum Domino Picarto habitas a Domino Fogelio haud dubie cognovisti, et exactius perspicies in actis nostris Academicis quae editurus est frater Thomas Bartholinus.[2] Tychonis Brahaei observationum impressionem ex mea recensione Parisijs nos molire, quaeso Domino Vallisio significes meoque nomine officiosissimam salutem nunties. Dominus Picart egregijs hic defunctus studijs observationum variarum coelestium ad suos redire instituit.

Vale, et me ut soles ama.

Haunia die 23 Aprilis An. 1672.

T.

E Bartholin

ADDRESS[3]

    Nobilissimo Atque Eximio Viro
        Domino Oldenburgio
           Londinum

TRANSLATION

Most noble and learned Sir,

I am not unaware that I should be suspected of negligence, were it not that I can offer a variety of occupations as my excuse. For I am indeed oppressed by a mass of business and there is little occurring here to satisfy your curiosity. I return you warm thanks for your honorific mention of myself and of my experiments in your *Philosophical Transactions*,[1] and in return I shall when opportunity serves make some service to you and your reputation. No doubt you already known of the observations of the comet made here with Mr. Picard from Mr. Vogel and you may see a more exact account of them in our *Academic Transactions* which will be published by my brother Thomas Bartholin.[2] I beg you to greet Mr. Wallis most zealously from me, and to let him know that we are trying to get my edition of the observations of Tycho Brahe printed at Paris. Having completed his remarkable application to a number of different observations in the heavens here Mr. Picard has decided to return home. Farewell, and love me as you do. Copenhagen, 23 April 1672.

Yours,

E. *Bartholin*

ADDRESS[3]

To the very noble and distinguished
Mr. Henry Oldenburg,
London.

NOTES

This reply to Letter 1907 (Vol. VIII) and perhaps also to Letter 1552 (Vol. VII) was not received until 24 June 1672.

1 In *Phil. Trans.*, no. 67 (16 January 1670/1), 2039–48, where Oldenburg printed a partial translation of Bartholin's Letter 1405 (Vol. VI) and a long summary of Bartholin's *Experimenta chrystalli Islandici dis-diaclastici* (Copenhagen, 1669).

2 Thomas Bartholin, *Acta medica et philosophica Ann. 1671 et 1672* (Copenhagen, 1673), no. 129, p. 222. Vogel does not appear to have written to Oldenburg about the comet, but it may be that Sivers did in a letter now lost (see Letter 1959, note 10). Oldenburg published nothing from Vogel about the comet.

3 The address is on MS. B 2, no. 16.

1963
Oldenburg to Mauritius

24 April 1672

From the copy in Royal Society MS. O 2, no. 109

Nobilissimo et Consultissimo Viro
Domino Erico Mauritio, Imp. Camerae Assessori
Henr. Oldenburg Salutem

Quod binis tuis litteris, 19 et 22 Martij datis, perhumaniter me com-
pellare, in ijsque uberem in Regiam societatem cultum et affectum
tuum depromere voluisti, habemus equidem amicissime; Tibique pro
tanto erga institutum illud philosophicum studio gratias quam maximas
reponimus. Voluptatem haud levem Caetus ille capit, quoties intelligit,
suos in excolendis scientijs conatus viris bonis et doctis probari, exindeque
ad labores suos gnaviter urgendos mirifice accenditur: Imprimis cum
sentit, aliarum gentium viros eruditos et solertes ad symbola sua curis et
studijs ipsius adjicienda certatim concurrere. In horum et Te merito censum
referimus, Vir Clarissime, qui tanta lubentia operam tuam nostrae socian-
dam offers. Amplectimur profecto, quod sponte tua largiris; et quaecunque
de Germaniae rebus, Historiam naturalem spectantibus, sive Acidulae et
Thermae, sive Fossilia sive Vegetabilia &c. illa fuerint, notatu digna
impertiri nobis volueris, in rem utique nostram et philosophicam, inque
nominis tui decus amplissimum vertere annitemur. Quae de nupero
Cometa perscripsisti, conferenda sunt cum ijs, quae insignes Astronomi,
Cassinus et Hevelius, observarunt.[1] Prior horum decem habuit observationes satis accuratas; ex quibus colligit, Cometam hunc eadem quasi
semita cum posteriore Anni 1665. cumque Tychonico Anni 1677 [*sic*],
incessisse quod easdem fere cum ipsis constellationes permeaverit, utut
paulo magis Boream versus abiverit, Eclipticamque 5. vel 6. gradibus
anterius illo, qui 1665. visus est, secuerit: unde conjectura mentem eius
subit, in illo Caeli loco quendam Cometas zodiacum obtinere.[2] Alter,
Hevelius inquam, hactenus non nisi pauca de eodem phaenomeno observata perscripsit. a quo tamen indies plura expectamus.

    Doctissimum Reicheltium,[3] Mathematicum Argentoratensem, pluri-
mum salvere jubeo, atque alia multa de penu ipsius philosophico mihi
promitto. Nescio, an viderit ille, quae Wallisius noster de Motu et Mecha-

nice; quaeque Barrovius de Optice et Geometria in lucem nuper emiserunt. Nec forte hactenus vobis innotuit, quid novi Newtonus, Mathematum professor Cantabrigiensis, de Luce et Coloribus, deque Telescopijs Cata-dioptricis, Vulgaria Tubo-specilla citra effecti fraudem mire contrahentibus, nuper invenit: quid item Eques noster Morelandus in auditu proferendo, Tubae suae Stentoro-phonicae beneficio, praestitit. Haec et similia in novissimis quibusdam Actis philosophicis, quorum Exemplaria nonnulla transmitti Hamburgum solent, fuse satis describuntur.

Per paucos ante dies hic prodiere, Domini Willisij de Brutorum Anima Exercitationes duae;[4] quarum prior Physiologica, eiusdem naturam, partes, potentias et affectiones tradit; altera Pathologica, morbos, ipsam et sedem eius primariam, cerebrum nempe et nervosum genus, afficientes, explicat, eorumque Therapeias instituit.

Brevi hunc excipiet Illustris Boylij de Gemmarum origine et Viribus Diatriba,[5] aliorumque e societate nostra eruditorum virorum scripta, varijs physicae partibus elucidandis accommodata. Praeterijssem fere Doctori Grewi libellum, Anglice nuper editum, de Anatome Plantorum; ubi multa nova et egregia panduntur; quibus concinit Malpighius Bononiensis, qui sua nobis in idem argumentum observata liberalissime communicavit;[6] juncta simul de Ovis, tum nondum incubatis, tum incubatis, Dissertatione limatissima, ubi Harvaei de Ovo doctrinam egregie provehit, inque Ovis fecundis, necdum incubatis, faetus rudimenta seu prima stamina detegit: que in re adstipulantem habet Medicum Anglum, etiam societatis nostrae consortem, Doctorem Croonium, qui idem plane, nil quicquam tamen de prioris investigatione compertum habens, deprehendit.[7]

Quid in Germania nostra in Physicis, Medicina et Mathesi nunc praes-tetur, quique in hisce studiis ibi nunc excellant, scire pervelim: Nolim omnino concives meos stare post principia, quin maxime in votis habeo, ut et studia sua in commune conferant, et hac ratione una cum Anglis, Gallis, aliisque humano generi prodesse satagant. Vale, Vir Amplissime, et me ama. Dabam Londini 24. April. 1672

TRANSLATION

Henry Oldenburg greets the very learned and wise Mr. Erich Mauritius, As-sessor of the Imperial Chamber

I take it as a most friendly act that you should address me so very kindly in your two letters of 19 and 22 March, and in them take the trouble to promise your copious goodwill and affection towards the Royal Society; we return you our warmest thanks for such great zeal on behalf of that philosophical institution. That philosophical assembly feels no little delight whenever it understands that its endeavors towards the promotion of the sciences are approved by good and learned men, and so is marvellously encouraged to pursue its labors energetically, especially when it feels that the learned and the skilful of other countries will unfailingly add their contributions to its activities and researches. We deservedly number you among them, famous Sir, who offer with so much satisfaction to combine your efforts with ours. We do indeed accept what you freely offer. We shall endeavor to turn everything you may send us concerning the natural history of Germany, its hot springs and spas, its vegetables and minerals, which you shall find notable enough to be imparted to us, both to the advantage of philosophy and the furtherance of your reputation.

What you wrote to us about the new comet is to be compared with what has been observed by those outstanding astronomers, Cassini and Hevelius.[1] The former of these has ten pretty accurate observations from which he has deduced that this comet has traced almost exactly the same path as the later comet of 1665, and Tycho's comet of 1577, "for they have pass'd through almost the same constellations; though this be more inclined North-ward, and cut the Ecliptique five or six degrees more forward than that of 1665," whence the conjecture comes to his mind "that in this place of the Heavens there is, at it were, a Zodiaque for comets."[2] The other, Hevelius I mean, has so far adduced only a few observations, but we daily expect more from him.

I send all good wishes to the very learned Reichelt,[3] the mathematician at Strasbourg, and I promise myself much more from his philosophical store. I do not know whether he will know what our countrymen Wallis and Barrow have recently published concerning, respectively, motion and mechanics, and optics and geometry. And perhaps you will not know what Newton, the professor of mathematics at Cambridge, has recently discovered to do with new properties of light and colors, and a catadioptrical telescope wonderfully shortening ordinary refracting telescopes without loss of effectiveness; as also what Sir [Samuel] Morland has achieved in the transmission of sound by means of his stentorophonic tube. These and similar matters are described pretty fully in some recent issues of our *Philosophical Transactions*, of which several copies are regularly sent to Hamburg.

A few days ago appeared Mr. Willis's two essays on the soul of animals,[4] of which the first, physiological, treats of their nature, parts, powers, and properties; the other, pathological, explains diseases affecting the head or of a nervous kind, both in themselves and in their primary seat, and establishes treatment for them.

There will soon follow the illustrious Boyle's essay on the origin and virtues of gems[5] and the writings of other learned Fellows of our Society, directed to the understanding of various branches of medicine. I almost forgot to mention Dr. Grew's book, recently published in English, on the anatomy of plants, where many new and remarkable things are set forth; Malpighi of Bologna concurs with these.[6] He has very freely communicated to us his observations on the same subject together with a most polished dissertation on eggs, both incubated and unincubated, in which he has advanced Harvey's teaching concerning the egg in a most remarkable manner, having detected the rudiments of the fetus or first living thread in fertilized eggs that have not yet been incubated. In this he has the concurrence of an English physician, Dr. Croone, also a Fellow of our Society, who has made a plain discovery of the same thing although quite ignorant of the former investigation.[7]

I long to know what is being done in my native Germany with respect to physics, medicine, and mathematics, and what persons now excel there in such investigations. I do very strongly hope that you will not suppose me a laggard in wishing with all my heart that its learning will be added to the common stock, and that in this way Germans will strive alongside the English, French, and other peoples to advance the human race. Farewell, most excellent Sir, and love me. London, 24 April 1672.

NOTES

Reply to Letters 1927, 1927a, and 1932 (Vol. VIII).
1 See Letters 1915 (Vol. VIII) and 1956, note 1.
2 From Oldenburg's English translation of Cassini's paper in the *Journal des Sçavans*, printed in *Phil. Trans.*, no. 82 (22 April 1672), 4050.
3 For Julius Reichelt (1637–1719), see Letter 1927, note 1.
4 Thomas Willis, *De anima brutorum* (Oxford, 1672).
5 Robert Boyle, *The Origine & Virtues of Gems* (London, 1672).
6 Nehemiah Grew, *The Anatomy of Vegetables Begun* (London, 1671); see Vol. VIII for Malpighi's work, esp. Letters 1805, note 2, and 1912, note 3.
7 See Letters 1879, notes 1 and 2, and 1908, note 2 (Vol. VIII).

1964
Oldenburg to De Graaf

24 April 1672

From the memorandum in Royal Society MS. G, no. 9

Acc. d. 2. April 72. resp. d. 24. April. per Dominum Timaeum[1] Scripsi, ut quod habet committat navi ordinariae, et curet ad Heythusen pro me, una cum Swammerdamio:[2] innui, quae Malpighius et Grew de Plantis quaeque Malpighius et Croone de ovis observavere.

TRANSLATION

Received 2 April 72, answered on 24 April by Mr. Timaeus.[1] I wrote that he should entrust what he has to the ordinary boat, along with Swammerdam, directed to Mr. Heythusen for myself.[2] I gave some hints of what Malpighi and Grew had observed with regard to plants, and Malpighi and Croone with respect to eggs.[3]

NOTES

Reply to Letter 1931 (Vol. VIII). The note contains many abbreviations, here expanded.
1 We have not been able to identify Timaeus or Heythusen. It appears from the next letter that the former was a traveler returning to the Continent, and the latter a merchant at Ostend.
2 See the next letter.
3 See Letter 1908 (Vol. VIII), note 2.

1965
Oldenburg to Swammerdam
24 April 1672
From the copy in Royal Society MS. O 2, no. 82

Clarissimo Viro
Domino Johanni Swammerdam Medici Doctori
Henricus Oldenburg
Felicitatem

Elegantissimum munus tuum, Vir Egregie, quo Societatem Regiam locupletare nuper voluisti, fronte adeo serena receptum ab ea fuit, ut quantocyus in mandatis mihi daret, maximas gratias tibi ut agerem, uberrimamque suam in te benevolentiam tibi confirmarem. Male interim nos habet, quod infestis hisce temporibus Matricem illam, reliquasque a Te in litteris tuis commemoratas Humani corporis partes non nisi difficulter consequi valeamus. Paravit et non nulla, nobis destinata doctissimus Dn. de Graaf, qui pariter de tuta transmittendi ratione ambigit. Putem tamen, si res illae, et tuae et suae, Mercatori cuidam Ostendano, Londinum nave quadam Flandrica transvehendae, commendarentur, ipsas citra periculum ad manus nostras esse perventuras. Idem per hunc ipsum Latorem dicto de Graaf suggessi, velimque omnino, si placeat, vos ambos ex condicto, quae transmittere nobis statuistis, duabus capsulis includere, easque navigio cuidam Ostendano per amicum committere. Hac ratione futurum omnino putaverim, ut res vestrae tuto ad me perferantur. Poteris igitur, si visum ita fuerit, hoc ipsum Domino de Graaf significare, et junctis cum eo consilijs sententiam meam in rem vertere—

Nescio, an tibi innotuerit, quid tunc Grewus nostras, Doctor Medicus, tunc eximius Malpighius, de Plantarum Anatome sunt commentati. Prior, observata et cogitata sua in lucem, sermone Anglico jam emisit, alter vero, Dominus Malpighius, hactenus non-nisi manuscripto, societati nostrae dicato, rem tamen eandem, mira observationum consonantia, exegit, arbitroque nostro Editionem ejus permisit.

Sed et idem Malpighius, vir sane cedro dignissimus, novissimis annis per-accuratum Ovorum non-incubatorum aeque ac Incubatorum examen instituit, solertissimasque de ijs observationes habuit, quas et ipsas ejusdem societatis judicio submittere non dubitavit. Eas hac aestate iterare decrevit, ijsque nonnulla, quae Galli Gallinacei Partes Spermaticas et Gallinarum Uterum Spectant, adjungere.[1] Mirum profecto, quam et in hoc argumento Doctissimus Croonius noster et Clarissimus Malpighius concurrant; cum tamen extra omne sit dubium, neutrum horum priusquam scripta eorum simul compararent, quicquam rescivisse ab altero, sed utrumque propria solertia et cura, observationes, quae innui, peregisse. Earum praecipua est, in Ovo faecundo, necdum tamen incubato, ambos illos Medicos ipsa faetus rudimenta, caput scilicet et appensae carinae stamina, deprehendisse. Habebunt exinde, ni fallor, alij, in quo porro industriam et sagacitatem suam exerceant, ad latentem hactenus veram generationis indolem pervestigandam eruendamque. Tu, Vir Doctissime, Symbolam porro tuam huc conferre non gravaberis, atque hac ratione, naturalium rerum scientiam adaugere. Vale, et me Tuum crede. Dabam Londini d. 24. April, 1672.

TRANSLATION

Henry Oldenburg wishes happiness to the very famous Mr. Jan Swammerdam, M.D.

The very elegant gift with which you recently decided to enrich the Royal Society, excellent Sir, was received by it with so much eagerness that I was at once instructed to send you the best thanks I could, and strengthen your sense of its warm goodwill towards yourself. However, we are disappointed because in these unfortunate times we cannot without difficulty obtain the uterus and other parts of the human body mentioned in your letter. The very learned Mr. De Graaf has also made ready several things for us, which are also held in suspense while there is doubt about a safe way of sending them. Yet I think that if those things, both yours and his, were entrusted to a certain Ostend merchant to be brought to London in some Flemish ship, they would come safely to our hands. By the actual bearer of this letter I have suggested the same thing to the said De Graaf, and I am very anxious that you should both, please, by agreement, put what you have decided to send to us into two boxes and entrust them to some Ostend sailor by a friend. In this way, I am quite sure, your objects will reach me safely. If you think fit, therefore, you can let Mr. De Graaf know of this scheme, and together with him inform me of your joint opinion in return.

I am not aware whether you will be familiar with what both our fellow-countryman Grew, a Doctor of Medicine, and the distinguished Malpighi have observed about the anatomy of plants. The former has already published his thoughts and observations in English; the latter, Mr. Malpighi, has completed [a work on] the very same subject marvelously agreeing in the observations, which is still in the form of a manuscript dedicated to the Royal Society, whose publication he has left at our disposition.

But further the same Malpighi, a man surely most deserving of immortal fame, has in recent years undertaken a very accurate investigation of the egg, both incubated and unincubated, and collected most skilful observations of them which he made no bones about submitting to the judgment of the same Society. He has decided to repeat them this summer and to combine with them some others concerning the spermatic parts of barnyard cocks and the uterine parts of hens.[1] It is very remarkable that our learned Dr. Croone concurs with the famous Malpighi in this business; yet as it is quite beyond doubt that neither of these had prior knowledge of the other's writings nor could have learned anything from him, each has made the observations I have mentioned by his own skill and attention. The chief of them is, that each of these medical men has discovered in the fertile but unincubated egg the actual rudiments of the embryo, that is to say its head and vestiges of its attached spine. Thence others, if I mistake not, will take that on further to exercise their own industry and intelligence, in order to investigate and elucidate the true nature of reproduction that has hitherto remained concealed. You yourself, learned Sir, will not scruple to add your contribution to further this end, and so increase our knowledge of nature. Farewell, and believe me to be yours. London, 24 April 1672.

NOTES

Reply to Letter 1938 (Vol. VIII); compare the preceding letter to De Graaf.
1 Compare Letter 1936 (Vol. VIII).

1966
Oldenburg to Malpighi

24 April 1672

From the original in Bologna MS. 2085, I, f. 86
Printed in *Opera omnia*, I, *De formatione pulli in ovo*, p. 16

Celeberrimo Viro
Domino Marcello Malpighio Phil. et Med. Bononiensi
Henr. Oldenburg S.

Perplacet Regiae Societati, Vir Clarissime, statutum Tibi esse, utramque tuam de Plantis et Ovis indaginem, Ipsi nuper, Epitomes forma, transmissam, hoc tempore verno revolvere, ac, si qua inibi obscura supersunt, elucidare. Hoc dum praestas, vere Philosophi imples mensuram, quidque ad genuinam Naturae historiam, solidae Philosophiae substernendam, requiratur, probe Te intelligere testaris.

Recte praeterea sentis, fieri saepe posse, viros rite philosophantes idem plane in Natura detegere et observare.[1] Aliquoties profecto sociis nostris contigit, quod non-nulli ex ipsis, locorum intercapedine disjuncti, nec quicquam alteri ab alteris, priusquam scripta eorum simul comparerent, resciscentes, eadem penitus Naturae arcana reserarunt. Cordate igitur agis, Vir Eximie, quod Nostratium Observationibus, tecum consonis, nequicquam obstantibus, investigationes et labores tuos circa Plantarum et Ovorum Anatomen jugiter urgere et proferre decrevisti. Eo firmiori stabunt talo, quae junctis hunc in modum ingeniis et operis, depromentur; eaque alios ad consimilia certatim audenda omni procul dubio suscitabunt.

Vix quidem, in oras vestras pervenisse ante annos aliquot promissum, nunc vero editum Regneri de Graaf Tractatum,[2] ut vocat, Novum, de Mulierum Organis generationi inservientibus concinnatum; in quo ostendere conatur Author, Homines caeteraque animalia omnia, quae Vivipara dicuntur, haud minus quam ovipara, ab Ovo originem ducere. Audacter asserit, Ova Quadrupedum e testibus[3] propulsa, perque Fallopianas tubas in uterum devecta, crebro semet conspexisse; atque indies idipsum demonstrare se posse affirmat.

Quid hac in re Tu, aliique in Italia vestra Anatomici observaveritis, scire perquam avemus. Vale, et me Doctrinae ac Virtutis tuae Cultorem studiosissimum crede. Dabam Londini d. 24. April. 1672.

TRANSLATION

Henry Oldenburg greets the very famous Mr. Marcello Malpighi, philosopher and physician of Bologna

It pleases the Royal Society very much that you have decided, famous Sir, to reconsider in this spring season your two investigations into plants and eggs that were formerly sent to it in summary form, and to clear up any difficulties that may remain in them. When you do this you show yourself a true philosopher, and you make it plain that you understand what is required for a genuine natural history, which will one day serve as a foundation for a sound philosophy of nature.

Further, I think that you rightly suppose that it must often happen that those who philosophize correctly must observe and disclose exactly the same things in Nature.[1] Sometimes, indeed, it has happened among our Fellows that some of them (separated by geography and knowing nothing of each other's activities until their writings were compared) have unraveled identical secrets of Nature. Therefore you are acting prudently, excellent Sir, in resolving to push on at once and continue your researches and efforts concerning the anatomy of plants and eggs, notwithstanding the observations made by our countrymen here which agree with your own. Whatever results from such a union of minds and labors will be the more solidly based, and doubtless will encourage others to dare attempt the like.

The new treatise (so called) of Regnier de Graaf,[2] announced a few years ago and now actually published, dealing with the female organs of generation, can scarcely have reached your part of the world yet. In it the author seeks to show that men and all other animals described as viviparous originate from eggs no less than the ovipara. He has boldly asserted that he has often observed the eggs of quadrupeds expelled from the testes[3] and carried down to the uterus through the Fallopian tubes, and declares that he can demonstrate this very fact at any time.

We are very eager to know what you yourself and other anatomists in your native Italy have observed as to this matter. Farewell, and believe me a most zealous admirer of your learning and virtues. London, 24 April 1672.

NOTES

Reply to Letter 1936, which had been read to the Society on 18 April. Oldenburg was then instructed, it seems, to prepare a suitable reply, which was approved by the Society at its next meeting, on 24 April.

1 This is an obvious allusion to the studies of Grew and Croone, already hinted at by Oldenburg in earlier letters to Malpighi. (For the publication of the former's book, see Letter 1963, note 6, and compare Letter 1969; on the latter, see Letter 1908, note 2, in vol. VIII.)

2 *Regneri de Graaf de mulierum organis generationi inservientibus tractatus novus* (Leiden, 1672) was reviewed in *Phil. Trans.*, no. 82 (22 April 1672), 4052–54; there is a brief allusion to the work on embryology of Malpighi and Croone at the end of this account.

3 As noted before, this word was commonly applied to the female gonads, subsequently recognized and named ovaries. De Graaf never observed the true mammalian egg, but its follicle; however, his notions were essentially correct.

1967
Oldenburg to Cornelio
24 April 1672
From the draft in Royal Society MS. O 2, no. 84

Clarissimo Viro
Domino Thomae Cornelio, Philosopho et Medico Neapolitano
Henr. Oldenburg Salutem

Vidit Societas Regia, quae tum Amplissimo Dodingtono, tum mihi, de uberrima tua in conatus nostros philosophicos voluntate, nec non de tralaticiis Tarantularum morsibus et eorum effectibus perscripsisti. Intellexit eadem, quam egregia multa tum de rei totius phalangia illa spectantis veritate, tum de argumentis aliis, sagaci tuo ingenio exploratis, deinceps communicare ipsi statuisti. Impense profecto gaudet, in oris etiam vestris, a tanto imprimis viro, institutum suum probari, uberemque adeo affectum elucescere, rem philosophicam fidis observantibus et experimentis provehendi. Perquam igitur volupe ipsi futurum est, juge per literas commercium philosophicum Tecum colere, ejusque beneficio tum quae in regione vestra occurrunt, a Te accersere, tum quae apud nos geruntur, Tibi communicare. Avide exspectamus, quae ad confutandos de Tarantulis historiolas, toto orbe receptas, observasti, quaeque in Puteolano agro, Cumano et Bajano littore, Vesuvio monte, et locis aliis pervestigasti. Dabimus operam, ut quae hinc vicissim praestolaris, commoda occasione Tibi transmittantur.

Jamjam praelo exiit Willisius noster de Brutorum Anima, deque Morbis caput humanum infestantibus.[1] Brevi sequetur Nobilis Boylii de Gemmarum Origine et Viribus Dissertatio.[2] Librum utrumque quamprimum fieri poterit, ad Te curabimus, tuam de iis sententiam exploraturi; quaeque de argumentis talibus ipse forsan es meditatus exquisituri. Vale, Vir Clarissime, et me Tibi addictissimum crede. Dabam Londini d. 24. April. 1672.

TRANSLATION

Henry Oldenburg greets the very famous Mr. Tommaso Cornelio, philosopher and physician of Naples

The Royal Society has seen what you wrote both to the worthy Dodington and to myself about your warm support for our philosophical endeavors and also concerning the commonplace bites of tarantulas and their effects. The Society understood that you had resolved henceforward to communicate to itself many remarkable occurrences concerning both the truth of the whole story about that phalangid and other topics examined by your sagacious intellect. It rejoices greatly that its design should be approved in your part of the world too, by so eminent a person as yourself particularly, and that so strong an intention to advance philosophy by faithful observations and experiments should be manifest. Accordingly it will be very glad to develop our continuing philosophical correspondence with you and by this means to seek from you an account of what happens in your part of the world, while communicating to you what is done in ours. We eagerly await those observations you have made refuting the stories about tarantulas that are given world-wide credence, and the investigations you have carried out in the countryside at Pozzuoli, on the shore at Cumae and Baiae, on Mount Vesuvius and elsewhere. And we will ensure that what you expect from us in return shall be sent you at a convenient opportunity.

Our Dr. Willis's book *De anima brutorum*, touching also on diseases affecting the head, has already issued from the press.[1] It will shortly be followed by Boyle's *Essay about the Origine and Virtues of Gems*.[2] We will take care to despatch both books to you as soon as may be in order to have your opinion of them, and to extract from you, perhaps, your own reflections on these topics. Farewell, famous Sir, and believe me most devoted to you. London, 24 April 1672.

NOTES

Reply to Letters 1911 and 1911a (Vol. VIII), both read to the Royal Society on 24 April.

1 A copy was presented to the Royal Society on 1 May.
2 Oldenburg presented the Society with a copy of this book as a gift from the author on 26 June.

1968
Boulliaud to Oldenburg
24 April 1672

From the original in B.M. MS. 4443, ff. 5–6

Paris le 4 May 1672 [N.S.]

Monsieur

Je croy que Mr Hevelius vous aura adverti, que par une lettre qu'il m'escrivit l'annee passee il me pria de vous envoyer quelque nombre d'exemplaires de ses livres, qu'il avoit envoyez a un de nos Libraires, qui est mort, & que sa vefve m'a rendus ne les voulant pas payer.[1] Pour satisfaire a ce que Mr Hevelius a desiré je prens l'occasion de vous les envoyer par le retour de Mr Smith,[2] qui est cognu de vous qui m'a promis de vous les rendre en main propre, pour en disposer suivant que Mr Hevelius vous en aura prié. Il y a 7. exemplaires du Prodromus Cometicus, & 23 du Mantissa Prodromi.[3] Je vous supplie d'en donner un exemplaire de chacun a Mr Smith pour le soign qu'il prend avec tant d'affection de vous les porter, Je suis asseuré que M. Hevelius ne vous desadvouera pas & l'on ne peut en faire present a un plus honneste que luy, avec lequel j'ay conversé tres agreablement, qui m'a aussi faict l'honneur de me promettre son amitié, comme il scait que je suis son treshumble servi[teu]r. Je vous envoye aussi un autre pacquet, que je vous supplie d'envoyer a Mr Hevelius, dans lequel sont les livres dont voyci les titres

Valerius de centro gravitatis[4] 4.º
Bibliotheca Bibliothecarium Labbe[5] 8º
Enchiridion Physicae restitutae[6] 24.º
Histoire des Indes Occidentales[7] 4.º
L'Egypte de Muttadi[8] 12.º
Voyages de Monconis 4.º Vol. III[9]
Voyage de l'Evesque de Beryte[10] 8.º
Damian. Heliodor. cap. Opticorum[11] 4.º
Je ne vous aurois pas donné la peine de luy envoyer ce pacquet, sans l'interruption du commerce, que la guerre entre S.M. et les Provinces Unies a causee, vous aurez la voye de Hambourg & de Lubeck pour les faire tenir a Danzigk.

Je ne vous donne point de nouvelles de ce qui se passe dans la Republique des lettres, Mr Smith vous en dira plus que je ne scaurois faire, & mesmes il vous dira que je m'appreste de mettre au net, ce que j'ay faict ad Arithmeticam Infinitorum.[12] Je vous supplie d'asseurer de mes respects Mrs de la Societé Royale, & de croire que je suis tres veritablement Monsieur

Vostre tres humble & tresobeissant serviteur
Boulliaud

ADDRESS

A Monsieur
Monsieur Oldenbourg Secre de la Societé
Royale
A Londres

TRANSLATION

Paris, 4 May 1672 [N.S.[

Sir,

I think that Mr. Hevelius must have told you that in a letter he wrote to me last year he requested me to send you a number of copies of his books which he had sent to one of our booksellers, now dead, whose widow, not wishing to pay for them, handed them over to me.[1] To satisfy the request of Mr. Hevelius I take this occasion to send them to you on the return of Mr. Smith[2] who is known to you, and who has promised to deliver them to you with his own hands, for you to dispose of as Mr. Hevelius has requested you to do. There are seven copies of *Prodromus cometicus* and twenty-three of the *Mantissa prodromi*.[3] I beg you to give a copy of each to Mr. Smith for the friendly care he has taken to transport them to you. I am sure that Mr. Hevelius will not disallow it, and a present could not be made to anyone more worthy than he, with whom I have talked very pleasantly, and who has also done me the honor of promising me his friendship, knowing that I am his very humble servant. I am also sending you another parcel which I beg you to send to Mr. Hevelius; in it are the books whose titles are given below:

Valerius, *de centro gravitatis.*[4] 4o
Labbe, *Bibliotheca bibliothecarum.*[5] 8o
Enchiridion physicae restitutae.[6] 24 mo
Histoire des Indes Occidentales.[7] 4o
L'Egypte de Murtadi.[8] 12mo
Monconys, *Voyages*, Vol. III.[9] 4o
Voyage of the Bishop of Beirut.[10] 8o
Damianus and Heliodus, *Cap. opticorum.*[11] 4o

I should not have given you the trouble of sending him this parcel, were it not for the interruption of communication caused by this war between His Majesty and the United Provinces; you have the route by Hamburg and Lubeck to get them sent on to Danzig.

I do not send you news of what is happening in the world of learning; Mr. Smith will tell you more than I could, and will at the same time tell you that I am preparing to make a fair copy of what I have written towards an *Arithmetica infinitorum*.[12] I beg you to assure the Fellows of the Royal Society of my respects and to believe that I am truly, Sir,

Your very humble and obedient servant
Boulliaud

ADDRESS

To Mr. Oldenburg
Secretary of the Royal Society
London

NOTES

1 In fact Hevelius had not mentioned this fact; see Letter 1978, below.
2 Probably Thomas Smith (1638–1710), well known to Justel; a nonjuring divine and scholar, he was a Fellow of Magdalen College, Oxford, and was returning from three years in Constantinople. He was later friendly with John Wallis.
3 Both published at Danzig in 1666.
4 Luca Valerio, *De centro gravitatis solidorum libri tres* (Rome, 1604; Bologna, 1661).
5 Philippe Labbe, S.J., *Bibliotheca bibliothecarum curis secundis auctior* (Paris, 1664; Rouen, 1672).
6 This work was published anonymously at Paris in 1623, and often thereafter; it is attributed to Jean d'Espagnet, who was perhaps a member of the Parlement of Toulouse.
7 It is probable that one (or both) of two books by Jean Baptiste du Tertre is meant: *Histoire Générale des isles de S. Christophe, de la Guadaloupe, de la Martinique* . . . (Paris, 1654); *Histoire Générale des Antilles habités par les Français* (Paris, 1667–71).
8 *L'Egypte de Murtadi* . . . *de la traduction de Pierre Vattier* . . . *sur un manuscrit arabe* (Paris, 1666); an English version by J. D. Davies was published at London in 1672.
9 Balthazar de Monconys, *Journal des Voyages*, III (Lyons, 1666).
10 Jacques de Bourges, *Relation du voyage de l'Evesque de Beryte au Royaume de Siam* (Paris, 1666).
11 *Damiani philosophi Heliodori larissaei de opticis libri II nunc primum editi et animadversionibus illustrati ab Erasmis Bartholino* (Paris, 1657).
12 Ultimately published as *Opus novum ad arithmeticam infinitorum* (Paris, 1682).

1969
Oldenburg to Malpighi

26 April 1672

From the original in Bologna MS. 2085, VII, ff. 21–22

Clarissimo Viro,
Domino Marcello Malpighio, Philosopho et Medico Bononiensi,
H. Oldenburg Salutem

En tibi, Vir Clarissime, fidem, quam dederam, liberatam.[1] Invenies, spero, Interpretem quendam Anglicum Bononiae; et comperies insimul, Te alia methodo hoc argumentum dignissimum pertractasse, nec non Observationes tuas longius provexisse. Quae causa est, quod Nostrates omnibus votis expetunt, ut Iconismes, quibus Dissertationem tuam egregiam, antehac nobis transmissam, et inter cimelia nostra repositam, elucidasti; quantocyus huc transmittas, siquidem consentire velis, ut eam typis nostris nitidissimis in orbem literatum et Philosophicum emittamus.[2]

Si visum tibi esset, Diagrammata istac ad tuam Plantarum Anatomen spectantia, prima quaque occasione commoda et tuta ad nos curare, fieri sane posset, ut utrumque scriptum tuum, de Plantis et Ovo, in unum librum sive volumen compingantur.[3] In mandatis quippe jam habent Typographi nostri, ut illus de Ovo quam primum fieri possit, imprimant.[4] Tuam de re tota sententiam edoceri maturrime percupio. Vale. Dab. Londini d. 26 April 1672.

TRANSLATION

H. Oldenburg greets the famous Mr. Marcello Malpighi, philosopher and physician of Bologna

Here you see, famous Sir, the fulfilment of the promise I made you.[1] You will find some English translator at Bologna, I hope, and may at the same time assure yourself that you have developed this investigation most worthily by another method and also extended your observations further. That is the reason why our Fellows unanimously desire that you should send here as soon as possible the drawings with which you will elucidate your extraordinary essay, previously sent to us and resting in our archives, if you will indeed agree that we may publish it in a very well-finished printed version for the benefit of literary and scientific circles.[2]

If it should seem proper to you to entrust these sketches relating to your anatomy of plants to us by the first safe and convenient opportunity, we could doubtless arrange to combine both your papers, that on plants and that on the egg, in one single book or volume.[3] Our printers have already been ordered to print that on the egg as soon as possible.[4] I much desire to be informed of your view of the whole matter quickly. Farewell. London, 26 April 1672.

NOTES

This letter did not, as its wording would suggest, accompany the copy of Grew's *Anatomy of Vegetables Begun* presumably sent on the same day; Malpighi received this letter in June, but the book had not reached him by August.

1 In Letter 1842 (Vol. VIII); to send Grew's book.
2 This was *Anatomes plantarum idea* (Vol. VIII, Letter 1805, note 2).
3 This notion was not pursued, and *De formatione pulli in ovo* appeared separately from Martyn's London press in 1673. The *Idea* only came out in 1675.
4 Strictly, it was only on 12 June 1672 that the Council ordered the printing of *De formatione pulli* by Martyn, and that the wording of its *imprimatur* was agreed; however, this formal act may imply that the impression was completed in fact.

1970
Oldenburg to Dodington

30 April 1672

From the original in Royal Society MS. O 2, no. 85

London April 30. 72.

Sir,

I can only tell you in the haste I am in, that I herewith send you a pacquet, made up of parcels, put up at two different times, Whereof the bound book is for Sigr Malpighi,[1] and the Transactions for yourself or yr friends. Besides wch, I must not omit to thank you for yr accompt concerning the Earth-quake (of wch we hope you'l let us know the remainder, as it shall come to yr hands,) as also for the two letters from Dr Cornelio,[2] wch were very acceptable to us, and ye reading of wch at the R. Society was follow'd by an order to return you their hearty thanks, to wch I cannot but adde those of Sir

yr faithful servt
Oldenburg

ADDRESS

A Monsieur
    Monsr Dodington
Resident desa Majté dela
Grande Bretagne á Venise
        Venise³

NOTES

Reply to Letter 1953.
1 Grew's *Anatomy of Vegetables begun,* promised in Letter 1842 (Vol. VIII); compare Letter 1969.
2 Presumably Letters 1911 and 1911a (Vol. VIII).
3 "To Mr. Dodington, Resident of His Britannic Majesty at Venice, Venice."

1971

Oldenburg to Newton

2 May 1672

Printed in Newton, *Correspondence,* I, 150–51, from the original in CUL MS. Add. 3976, no. 6

In this reply to Letter 1957, Oldenburg reports sending Letter 1957a to Pardies (presumably with Letter 1960). He suggests that when Newton's answers to Hooke and Pardies are printed, their names (if they so wish) be omitted "since those of the R. Society ought to aime at nothing, but the discovery of truth, and ye improvement of knowledge, and not at the prostitution of persons for their mis-apprehensions or mistakes." He also promises to deliver Newton's quarterly payment as a Fellow to the Treasurer.

The bulk of the letter is a quotation in French from the account of the reflecting telescope designed by an otherwise unknown M. Cassegrain, printed in Denis, *Mémoires,* no. 8, of 15 April 1672, N.S., and communicated to Denis by a M. de Bercé of Chartres; Oldenburg was to translate and print the whole account in *Phil. Trans.,* no. 83 (20 May 1672), 4056–57.

The Cassegrainian form of reflecting telescope is similar to the Gregorian, in that light reflected from the primary speculum is returned to the eye, placed on the optical axis of the instrument, by a secondary mirror through a hole in the primary mirror. However, in Cassegrain's telescope the secondary mirror is convex, whereas in the Gregorian it is concave; it is accordingly placed nearer to the primary speculum. Less light is obstructed by the secondary, but the image is inverted. Despite Newton's strictures upon these two forms of reflector (Letter 1973) the Gregorian type was much used in the eighteenth century and the Cassegrainian type has found favor in modern observatories—for example, it is one usable form of the 200 inch Hale telescope on Mount Palomar.

Gregory defended his form of reflector against Newton's strictures in a letter to Collins of 23 September 1672 (Turnbull, *Gregory*, 241–43); for Huygens' adverse reaction to Cassegrain's proposal, see Letter 2004.

1972
Oldenburg to Dodington
3 May 1672

Dodington's Letter 1953 is endorsed as having been received on 29 April 1672 and answered on 3 May. It must be assumed that this answer was in addition to Letter 1970.

1973
Newton to Oldenburg
4 May 1672

Printed in Newton, *Correspondence* I, 153–55, from the original in CUL MS. Add. 3976, no. 7

In reply to Letter 1971 Newton discusses the suggestions of Cassegrain for the improvement of telescopes, indicating that he is already familiar with Gregory's design. He suggests that it will have poor light-gathering ability, that the mirror will need to be hyperbolic to avoid aberration, that the distance from mirror to eyepiece is large enough to cause errors, and that the magnifying ability will contribute to increase these errors. He concludes: "You see therefore that ye advantages of this designe are none, but ye disadvantages so great and unavoydable that I feare it will never be put in practise with good effect."

He also agrees to Oldenburg's suggestions that in his printed reply the names of Pardies and Hooke may be omitted, although he rightly points out that Hooke will be readily identified by all.

The main part of the letter was printed in *Phil. Trans.*, no. 83 (20 May 1672), 4057–59 and summarized in French in the *Journal des Sçavans* for 13 June 1672 [N.S.].

1974
Oldenburg to Huygens

6 May 1672

From *Œuvres Complètes*, VII, 173–75
Original in the Huygens Collection at Leiden

A londres le 6 May 1672.

Monsieur

Voicy un autre journal Anglois, oú vous trouverez la suite de ce que Monsieur Newton a fait pour advancer sa nouvelle lunette.[1] Je trouve que dans le 8me memoire de Monsieur Denys on a descrit un telescope qui y est estimé plus spirituel, come parle l'autheur, que celuy de nostre Anglois.[2] Cependant, si ie ne me trompe fort on trouve la mesme façon donnée par Monsieur Gregory, l'Escossois, dans son *Optica Promota* p. 92. 93. 94. qui fut imprimée à Londres l'an 1663, que vous prendrez la peine, s'il vous plait, de considerer.

De plus, le mesme M. Denys a fait imprimer dans son 9me memoire les proportions de la trompette de Monsieur Moreland;[3] dont ie seray bien aise d'entendre vos pensees.

Vous trouverez, parmy les livres de ces Transactions, quelque chose faite par Monsieur Pell.[4] Si vous m'ordonnez de vous envoyer le livre mesme, ie vous obeiray come Monsieur

Vostre treshumble et tresobeissant serviteur
Oldenburg

Ce que vous m'avez escrit touchant vostre abregement de la construction du probleme d'Alhazen i'ay envoyé à Monsieur Sluse, dont i'attends une lettre tous les iours.[5] Touchant Kinkhuysen, son introduction est traduite en latin, et sera eslargie par les notes de Monsieur Newton, pour servir come une introduction à sa methode generale des quadratures analytiques;[6] et quand celles-cy viendront à Londres pour y estre imprimées la dite introduction de Kinkhuysen sera aussi imprimee.

De plus, le dernier livre dudit Kinkhuysen, des problemes geometriques, a esté traduit aussi en latin; la quelle traduction est astheur entre les mains de Monsieur Bernard professeur de l'Astronomie à Oxford, qui l'adjustera pour la presse.[7]

ADDRESS

A Monsieur
Monsieur Christian Hugens de Zulechem,
dans la bibliotheque du Roy à
Paris

TRANSLATION

London, 6 May 1672

Sir,

Here is another English journal, in which you will find the continuation of what Mr. Newton has written to promote his telescope.[1] I find that in the eighth of Mr. Denis's *Mémoires* a telescope is described which is there considered more ingenious, as its author says, than our English one.[2] However, if I am not much mistaken the same method is given by Mr. Gregory, the Scotchman, in his *Optica promota*, pages 92, 93, 94; this was printed at London in 1663, and you will please take the trouble to consider it.

Further, Mr. Denis has in his ninth *Mémoire* printed the proportions of Sir Samuel Morland's trumpet;[3] I should be very glad to have your thoughts on it.

Among the books in this *Transactions* you will find something written by Mr. Pell.[4] If you command me to send you the said book, I will obey as, Sir,

Your very humble and obedient servant
Oldenburg

I have sent what you wrote to me about your abridgement of the construction of Alhazen's problem to Mr. Sluse, from whom I expect a letter any day now.[5] As for Kinckhuysen, his introduction has been translated into Latin and will be enlarged with Mr. Newton's notes, to serve as an introduction to his general method of analytic quadratures.[6] When this arrives in London to be printed the aforesaid introduction of Kinckhuysen will also be printed.

Moreover, the last book by the said Kinckhuysen, on geometrical problems, has also been translated into Latin; this translation is at the moment in the hands of Mr. Bernard, Professor of Astronomy at Oxford, who is editing it for the press.[7]

ADDRESS

To Mr. Christiaan Huygens of Zulichem,
The King's Library,
Paris

NOTES

1 *Phil. Trans.*, no. 82 (22 April 1672), 4032–35, contains Newton's Letters 1937 and 1941 (Vol. VIII).
2 See Letter 1971.
3 The ninth *Mémoire* (dated 2 May 1672 [N.S.]) is entirely given over to Morland's speaking tube; the discussion of the best scale of proportions is by Cassegrain.
4 In *Phil. Trans.*, no. 82 (22 April 1672), 4050–52, is a review of Pell's *Tabula numerorum quadratorum decies millium* (London, 1672).
5 See Letter 1944 (Vol. VIII), which was sent to Sluse in Letter 1952.
6 See Vol. V, p. xxv, and Vol. VII, p. 160, note 4, for the fate of the translation of Gerard Kinckhuysen, *Algebra ofte stel-konst* (Haarlem, 1661).
7 Kinckhuysen's *Geometria ofte meet-konst* (Haarlem, 1663) was never published in Latin translation, and nothing is known of this projected edition.

1975
Magalotti to Oldenburg

10 May 1672

From Birch, *History*, III, 52

. . . .

June 12 . . . Mr. Oldenburg read a letter from Signor Magalotti, dated at Florence, 20th May, 1672, N.S., giving an account, accompanied with a scheme, of a Venetian project of a perpetual lamp made up in a crystal vial with spirit of wine and a wick of gold, so contrived, that supposing the spirit of wine converted from a liquor into smoke, and from smoke into vapour, will turn again into an inflammable liquor, there may be a perpetual circulation, and consequently a perpetual Lamp.

. . . .

NOTE

This letter, written in English, is now lost, as is its enclosure which was, according to Birch, a "relation" by G. B. Gornia (see Vol. VI, p. 89, note) about the pathological ulcer of "an antient man living in the mountains of Italy."

When Magalotti's letter was read several Fellows "declared, that spirit of wine being once destroyed by the fire will not turn into spirit of wine again."

1976
Pardies to Oldenburg

11 May 1672

From the original in Royal Society MS. P 1, no. 77

Paris 21. Mai. 1672. [N.S.]

J'estois malade quand M. Vernon partit d'ici,[1] ainsi je ne puis me servir de cette occasion pour vous ecrire comme je l'eusse souhaitté. Je le fais presentement pour vous témoigner combien je me suis obligé à M. Newton de la peine qu'il a bien voulu prendre de respondre à mes difficultez qui peut-estre n'en valoient pas la peine.[2] Je vous envoye quelques remarques que je fais sur sa response dont je suis tres-satisfait, et peut-estre qu'il le sera aussi de la mienne puisque j'acquiesce entierement à ce qu'il a repondu.[3] Je ne croy pas que ceci merite de trouver place dans vos scavantes Transactions: mais si vous jugez que cela puisse de rien servir je m'en remets à vous, à condition que personne n'y puisse trouver rien qui luy déplaise. et s'il ya quelque mot qui puisse chocquer tant soit peu M. Newton je vous prie de l'oster et de le changer. Je ne voudrois pas pour rien du monde déplaire à qui que ce soit et beaucoup moins à une personne pour qui j'ay toute sorte de respect.

Vous aurez sans doute dans les Memoires de M. Denis la lettre escritte de Chartres touchant la figure harmonique de la trompette de M. Morland.[4] Je m'estonne que ny l'autheur de la lettre ny celuy des Memoires n'ait remarqué que cette figure est parfaitement Hyperbolique. en sorte que la trompette dans son sens n'est qu'une portion de la surface engendrée par la revolution d'une hyperbole qui se mouvroit autour d'une de ses asymptotes immobile. J'avois deja remarqué il ya longtemps que l'hyperbole a un raport merveilleux avec la progression harmonique. en sorte que si l'on tire des paralleles à une des asymptotes qui devisent en parties egales l'autre asymptote, toutes ces paralleles (interceptées entre l'asymptote et l'hyperbole) seront en progression harmonique. Aussi je prens trois lignes qui determinent toutes les trois progressions, estant comparées avec une ligne droite. car dans l'angle rectiligne *ahA* on a la progression arithmetique en tirant les paralleles *aA*, *bB*, &c qui prennent des portions egales sur la ligne *ah*. Ainsi estant données deux lignes *aA*, *gG*, on peut trouver tant de moyennes que l'on voudra continuellement proportionelles arith-

metiquement. car on n'a qu'à appliquer parallelement ces deux lignes *aA*,
gG, à l'angle, et diviser la droite interceptée *ag*, en autant de parties egales
qu'il faut trouver de moyennes et une de plus: par exemple en six s'il
faut trouver cinq moyennes, et les paralleles tirées par ces divisions, scavoir
bB, *cC*, *dD*, &c. seront les moyennes cherchées.

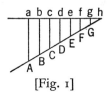

[Fig. 1]

De mesme si l'on prend l'hyperbole *AG*, dont les asymptotes sont *hg*,
hH. on pourra y trouver tout autant de moyennes que l'on voudra entre
deux données, en raison harmonique.   car soit les données *aA*, *gG*,
appliquées à l'espace hyperbolique, parallelement à l'asymptote *hH*. entre
lesquelles il faille trouver cinq moyennes continuelles en raison harmoni-

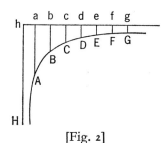

[Fig. 2]

que: soit l'interceptée *ag* divisée en six parties egales, et par les divisions
soient tirées les paralleles *aA*, *bB*, *cC* &c. Je dise que l'on aura 7 lignes continuellement proportionelles en raison harmonique.

que si on met cette ligne que j'ay décrite au livre 8e de ma geometrie[5] on
aura aussi le mesme moyen de trouver tout autant de moyennes que l'on
voudra en raison geometrique entre deux données. Car aprés avoir appli-
qué les extremes données *aA*, *gG*, à la figure entre la droite et la courbe, on

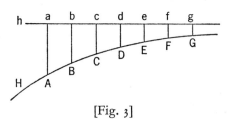

[Fig. 3]

n'a qu'á diviser l'interceptée *ag* en *b*. parties egales, et les paralleles tirées par ces divisions seront les moyennes requises.

Où l'on faut remarquer comme quoy la progression arithmetique peut croitre à l'infini, mais non pas diminuer à cause de l'angle *h*, où se terminent les lignes. l'harmonique au contraire diminue à l'infini, mais ne croit pas à cause de l'asymptote *hH* qui termine tout: Mais la geometrique croit et decroit à l'infini, cette ligne *Ag* estant asymptote avec la droit *ag* s'approche continuellement d'elle vers *i* et s'en esloigne aussi à l'infini de l'autre part vers *h* sans trouver aucun terme.

Quoyque la figure hyperbolique ait si grand rapport avec l'harmonie, je ne voudrois pas soutenir neanmoins que ce fust là la figure la plus propre de la trompette, je ne voudrois pas aussi le nier, mais je n'ay pas assez examiné cela pour le decider. cela depend dela maniere dont le son est determiné dans les flutes et dans les cornets dequoy on n'a pas à mon avis encore bien traitté. Et quoyque le son des cordes ait esté assés bien expliqué,[6] je ne croy pas qu'on ait dit encore rien de satisfaisant sur le son des instrumens à vent. J'espere que si je donne toute ma mechanique[7] on y trouvera quelque chose de nouveau touchant cette matiere et alors je pourray aussi parler de cette trompette et de sa figure. Je suis Tout à Vous.

Je suis en peine de scavoir des nouvelles de M. Butler[8] qui vous porta l'an passè de mes lettres. Je ne scay de quoy il est devenu car il ne m'a point escrit ny fait scavoir de ses nouvelles

ADDRESS
   A Monsieur
   Monsieur Grubendol
      A Londres

TRANSLATION

Paris, 21 May 1672 [N.S.]

I was ill when Mr. Vernon departed from here,[1] so I could not utilize that opportunity to write to you as I should have wished. I do so now to evince how much I am obliged to Mr. Newton for the trouble he has willingly taken to reply to my difficulties, which perhaps were not worth the trouble.[2] I send you some remarks made on his reply with which I am very well satisfied, and perhaps he will also be so with mine, since I entirely acquiesce in what he has replied.[3] I do not think that this merits finding a place in your learned *Transactions*; but if you judge that it can be of any use, I hand it over to you, provided that nobody can find anything displeasing to him in it. And if there are any words which might offend Mr. Newton even a little please remove and change them. I should not wish for any reason in the world to displease anyone, and much less so a person for whom I have every kind of respect.

You have doubtless [seen] in the *Mémoires* of Mr. Denis the letter written from Chartres about the harmonic figure of Mr. Moreland's trumpet[4]. I am surprised that neither the author of the letter nor the [editor] of the *Mémoires* has noticed that this figure is perfectly hyperbolic. So that the trumpet in this sense is only a portion of the surface generated by the revolution of a hyperbola which turns about one of its asymptotes which is at rest. I noticed long ago that the hyperbola has a marvelous relation with the harmonic progression, in such a way that, if one draws parallels to one of the asymptotes which divide the other asymptote into equal parts, all these parallels (intercepted between the asymptote and the hyperbola) will be in a harmonic progression. Thus I take three lines which determine all three progressions, when compared with a straight line. For in the rectilinear angle ahA one obtains the arithmetic progression by drawing the parallels aA, bB, etc., which cut off equal parts of the line ah [*see Fig. 1, p. 58*]. Thus being given two lines, aA, gG, one can find as many means as desired continually proportional arithmetically. For it is only necessary to apply these two lines aA, gG, as parallels to the angle, and divide the intercepted straight line ag in as many equal parts as the number of means sought plus one: for example in six if five means are sought, and the parallels drawn by these divisions, that is bB, cC, dD, etc. will be the sought-for means.

In the same way if one takes the hyperbola AG, whose asymptotes are hg, hH, it will be possible to find as many means as desired between two given lines in harmonic proportion [*see Fig. 2, p. 58*]. For let the given lines by aA, gG applied to the hyperbolic space and parallel to the asymptote hH; between these must be found five continual means in harmonic proportion: let the intercepted [line] ag be divided into six equal parts, and through these divisions be drawn the parallels aA, bB, cC, etc. I say that there will be seven lines continually proportional in harmonic proportion.

And if one takes the line which I described in Book 8 of my *Geometry*,[5] then one has the same method for finding as many means between the two given lines, in geometric proportion, as may be desired. For after applying the given extremes aA, gG, to the figure between the straight line and the curve, it only remains to divide the intercepted [line] ag in b equal parts, and the parallels drawn through these divisions will be the required means [*see Fig. 3, p. 58*].

Here it must be remarked that although the arithmetic progression can increase to infinity it cannot so diminish because of the angle h in which the lines terminate. The harmonic [progression] on the contrary diminishes to infinity, but does not so increase on account of the asymptote hH which terminates everything. But the geometric [progression] increases and decreases to infinity, that line Ag, being asymptotic with the straight line *ag*, continually approaches it towards *i* and also departs infinitely from the other part towards *h* without finding any limit.

Although the hyperbolic figure has so close a connection with harmony nevertheless I should not willingly maintain that it was the shape most suitable for the trumpet; nor should I wish to deny it; for I have not examined that enough to decide. It depends upon the way in which sound is determined in flutes and horns which, in my opinion, has not yet been thoroughly discussed. And although the sound of strings has been pretty well explained[6] I do not think that anything satisfactory has yet been said about the sound of wind instruments. I hope that if I complete my *Mechanics*,[7] something new on this point will be found there, and then I shall also be able to speak of this trumpet and its shape. I am yours sincerely.

I am troubled to learn news of Mr. Butler,[8] who brought you some of my letters last year. I do not know what has become of him for he has never written to me nor let me hear news of him.

ADDRESS

    Mr. Grubendol,
      London

NOTES

1 We have not discovered the exact date on which Vernon left Paris, probably in early May.
2 See Letter 1957a.
3 See Letter 1976a.
4 See Letter 1974, note 3.
5 *Elemens de Geometrie* (Paris, 1671), Bk. VIII, § 25; the line is a logarithmic where $gG = 1$, and *ag*, *bg*, *cg*, etc. are logarithms of the abscissae *aA*, *bB*, *cC*, etc. Hence the property stated by Pardies follows.
6 Notably by Marin Mersenne in *L'Harmonie universelle* (Paris, 1636).
7 See Letter 1859 and its note 3.
8 This traveler, unknown to us, was mentioned in Letter 1744 (Vol. VIII).

1976a
Pardies's Commentary on Newton's Letter 1957a

Enclosure with Letter 1976
The original is Royal Society MS. P 1, no. 79
Printed in *Phil. Trans.*, no. 85 (15 July 1672), 5012–13
and in Newton, *Correspondence*, I, 156–59

TRANSLATION

Your letter was delivered to me together with the comments of the famous and very ingenious Newton, in which he replied to my difficulties. I read these with much pleasure. And firstly as regards his experiment on the greater breadth of the colors than is required by the common theory of refractions, I confess that I supposed the refractions at opposite faces of the prism to be unequal, nor did I at all perceive in the letter quoted in the *Transactions*[1] that Newton had observed that greater breadth in the case where the refractions were made reciprocally equal, in the manner stated in these comments. But at that time I could not refer to those *Transactions* as I was unable to lay hands on them again. Accordingly as I now understand that in that case also the greater breadth of the colors was observed, certainly no further difficulty remains for me on that account. I say "on that account," for it seems that another reason for that phenomenon may be given without recourse to that various refrangibility of the rays. For in that hypothesis which our colleague Grimaldi has described at length,[2] by which light is supposed to be some very swiftly moving substance, there may arise some diffusion of the light after its passage through the aperture and the crossing-over of the rays.

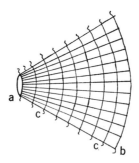

Further, in that hypothesis according to which light is held to travel as waves in a subtle medium, as the very subtle Hooke has explained it,[3] the colors can be explained as a certain diffusion and expansion of the waves occurring at the sides of the rays beyond the aperture through the actual contact and continuity of the [subtle] matter. Certainly I adopt such a hypothesis in the essay "On Wave-motion" which is the sixth part of my *Mechanics*,[4] so that I suppose those apparent colors to be uniquely caused by that communication of motion occasioned at the sides of waves traveling straight forwards. So that if rays entering by the aperture *a* should travel towards *b*, the waves should come to a halt along the straight line *ab*, obeying the natural and rectilinear motion [of light]; nevertheless, because of the continuity of the [subtle] matter there is some communication of the disturbance along the sides, *c*, *c*, where a certain vibration or undulatory tremor is excited; and so if it is supposed that colors consist of this lateral vibration I think that all the phenomena of colors can be explained, as I have set it out at greater length in the dissertation I spoke of. And on the same assumptions it appears why the divergence of the colors is greater than it should be, for the breadth of the colors must expand. It is enough, in fact, to have noted so much here.

As for his comment on the error which may, by calculation, arise through the quasi-aperture (as I called it) in the back face of the prism, that this error (I say) can give occasion for no perceptible variation—this is very well put; nor did I reckon that the breadth of the colors was much increased on this account, but wished only to indicate an accurate form of the calculation. Accordingly I too judge that it may be neglected in practise.

Concerning the *experimentum crucis*, I have no doubt at all that in his experiment he so disposed the apparatus that the incidence of the rays was at a constant angle, since he expressly asserts that he did so. But I could not guess this from what I read in the *Transactions* where two narrow and very distant apertures are described, and a single prism near the first aperture (which is in the window-shutter), through which prism the colored rays burst forth to strike the second, distant aperture.[5] He went on to say, however, that to make all the rays successively fall on the second aperture he rotated the first prism about its axis. But in this arrangement the inclination of the rays falling on the second aperture must necessarily be altered; and I pointed out in my letter that for this reason things should be so arranged that either, keeping the first prism fixed, the second aperture should be so raised or depressed that it can receive successively all the rays of the spectrum, or, keeping that second aperture fixed, the first prism should be rotated so that the spectrum should shift its position and each part of it fall successively on the [second] aperture. But no doubt the very skilful Newton employed other precautions.

I conclude that my objections about the colors have been quite resolved. When I called that theory an hypothesis I did so of no set purpose, but used the first term that came to mind. For this reason I wish him to think that such a word was not employed out of contempt. I have always made much of notable discoveries, and I particularly look up to and esteem the famous Newton.

NOTES

1 Letter 1891 (Vol. VIII).
2 See Francesco Maria Grimaldi, *Physico-mathesis de lumine* (Bologna, 1665), already
   noticed in *Phil. Trans.*, no. 79 (22 January 1671/2), 3068–70. Newton presumably
   read this notice (though not the book). Like Pardies, Oldenburg did not stress the
   fact that Grimaldi considered light to be a wave motion—an idea not at all clearly
   worked out in his book.
3 In *Micrographia* (London, 1665) pp. 47–67.
4 This was never published; see Letter 1859, note 3.
5 It may seem surprising that Pardies had misunderstood—and still had no exact conception of—Newton's precedure in this famous experiment. But it should be remembered that Newton's letter was in English, and the account of this experiment
   was not illustrated by a figure. When Newton spoke of putting his first pierced
   board (diaphragm) "behind" the first prism, it might be supposed that he meant
   between the shutter and that prism. Such a reading of Newton's words destroys the
   sense of the experiment.

1977
Oldenburg to Lister
11 May 1672

From the original in Bodleian Library MS. Lister 34, f. 59

Both yr letters, concerning the Excision of ye stone from under the
tongue, and the generation of Heir-Worms, have been produced, and
wth great satisfaction read to ye R. Society.[1] The former was from the
Arch Bp of Canterbury sent by a good hand to ym at their publick meeting,
to whom, it seems the Arch Bp of york had communicated it. We find, yt ye
subject, on whom yt excision was made, is yrself; wch makes us give
entire credit to ye relation. Several of the company told, on this occasion,
of the like cases they had met wth; and one of ym, besides ye case, related
by him, altogether like yrs, added another of a stone, found on the upper
side of ye arteria venosa,[2] and having there made such a compression,
whereby the motion of ye blood being hinder'd, the patient was killed.

As to ye Heir-worms, the Bp of Chester affirmed to have met wth the
like to yours. And having spoken wth Mr Willoughby, he saith, yt he
hath met wth such worms almost in all sorts of fishes and birds, and some
quadrupeds, yt he hath had occasion to open. I think both these observations worth communicating to ye publick in the Transactions.

I doe not acknowledge to Mr Brook himself the favour of his last letter,[3] because he intimated therein, yt he intended to come up to London during this terme; wch when he doth, I doubt not but I shall have the happiness to see him, yt I may give him an account of ye particulars, wch he desired to be informed off. I am apt to think, yt he is already in towne, but does not let us know of it.

Pray, Sir, give me leave to aske you, what is done about you for Nurseries, Orchards, Gardens, Groves. I hear, that these advance exceedingly on both sides of the Seaverne, and about Oxford. And some of the friends of our Society, yt live in Somersetshire, and would have Georgicks improved, wish very much, yt since ye maine improvement of yt kind should be in ye Champian Countries, all those yt have an interest in such places, might be desired to employ it accordingly.[4]

I suppose, you have seen, what hath been lately published in the prosecution of Mr Newtons reflecting Telescope; as also of De Graafs book de organis mulierum generationi in Servientibus.[5] Of wch therefore I shall say nothing more; but conclude wth assuring you of my constancy in being Sir

Yr faithfull servt

H. O.

London. May 11th, 72 .

Mr Sturdy hat been wth me once;[6] He then said, yt he intended to come and lodge nearer us; but I have not seen him since. He seems to be a knowing and sober person, whom I shall gladly serve, wherein I can.

ADDRESS
To his honored friend
Dr. Martyn Lister, at his
house in Stone-gate barr
at
York

NOTES

Reply to Letter 1929.
1 At the Society's meeting on 1 May 1672 Oldenburg read a letter from Lister to the Archbishop of York, communicated by Sir Robert Moray, which is printed in *Phil. Trans.*, no. 83 (20 May 1672), 4062–64, and also a letter from Lister to John Brooke (see Vol. VIII, Letter 1800, note 6), which is printed in the same number, pp. 4064–66. This second letter was again discussed at the meeting on 8 May when Willughby was present.

2 "vein-like artery," the pulmonary vein.

3 No letters of Brooke to Oldenburg in this period now survive.

4 The friend was, of course, John Beale. "Georgics" = agriculture (after the title of Virgil's poem on this subject). "Champian" (= champaign, Fr. *champagne*) was used to denote the unenclosed, common fields as distinct from the "closes," surrounded by walls or hedges and worked by individual farmers.

5 See Letter 1966, note 2.

6 This was just possibly John Sturdy (b. 1632) of Halifax, M.A. Christ's College, Cambridge, 1656, probably headmaster of Bradford Grammar School, *c.* 1658–71. But he did not settle in London, and Sturdy is not an uncommon Yorkshire name.

1978
Oldenburg to Boulliaud
20 May 1672

From the original in BN MS. Fr. 13034, f. 92

A Londres le 20. May 72.

Monsieur,

Quoyque Monsr Hevelius ne m'ait pas encor adverti de ce que vous me mandez par la vostre du 4me present [N.S.], ie ne laisseray pourtant pas de prendre soin de tout ce qui le puisse concerner, et particulierement de luy envoier les Exemplaires des livres, dont vous parlez, par la premiere commodité seure, qui se rencontrera, apres que ie les auray receus de Monsr Vernon, qui n'est pas encor arrivé.[1]

Je ne manqueray pas aussi d'en donner un exemplaire á Monsr Smith, qui se loue fort des graces et civilitez, que vous luy avez tesmoignées durant sa demeure á Paris.

Je suis bien aise d'entendre, que vous vous estez si bien employé, que de rendre l'Arithmetique des Infinis Geometrique.

Je ne doubte pas, Monsieur, que vous n'ayez vû le *Prodromus Astronomiae restitutae Francisci Levera Romani*, imprimé á Rome.[2] Je serois tresaise d'en scavoir vos pensees, à vostre commodité.

Je trouve, que Monsieur Cassini fait des belles observations Astronomiques. Je m'impatiente du temps de pouvoir scavoir, si cete petite estoille, qu'il apperceut l'année passee aupres de Saturne, est une nouvelle planete, ou un autre Satellite de Saturne; quoy qu'il y ait assez d'apparence desia, par les particularitéz que ce grand Observateur nous en a donnees, que c'est une planete nouvelle.[3]

J'entends, que Monsr Hevelius travaille avec grand soin à nous donner sa Machine celeste imprimée; et que Signr Montanari produira aussi quelque chose de surprenant dans la mesme science. Il ne se peut faire autrement dans une telle conjonction de bons esprits et de grande industrie par tout, que les sciences ne soient cultivées et advancées plus que d'ordinaire.

Je seray ravy, Monsieur, d'entendre quelquesfois de vos nouvelles, que ie tascheray de reconoistre autant qu'il me sera possible, en qualité de Monsieur

Vostre treshumble et tresobeissant serviteur
Oldenburg

Si vous me faitez l'honneur de m'escrire, vous m'obligerez de donner vos lettres à M. Justel, qui scait l'addresse, qu'il faut pour me les faire tenir seurement.

TRANSLATION

London, 20 May 1672
Sir,

Although Mr. Hevelius has not yet given me notice of what you report to me in yours of the 4th of this month [N.S.], I shall nevertheless not fail to take care of everything that can concern him, and especially to send him the copies of the books you speak of by the first sure means that presents itself, after I have received them from Mr. Vernon, who has not yet arrived.[1]

I shall not fail either to give a copy to Mr. Smith, who praises highly the favor and courtesy you showed to him during his stay in Paris.

I am very glad to hear that you are so well employed as to render geometric the arithmetic of infinitesimals.

I do not doubt, Sir, but that you have seen *Prodromus universae astronomiae restitutae* of Francisco Levera, printed at Rome.[2] I should be very glad to know your thoughts about it, at your convenience.

I find, that Mr. Cassini makes very fine astronomical observations. I fret at the time necessary until we can know if that little star which he perceived last year near Saturn is a new planet or another satellite of Saturn, although there is already the likelihood from the details this great observer has given us that it is a new planet.[3]

I hear that Mr. Hevelius is working with great care to produce his *Machina Coelestis* in print, and that Signor Montanari will also produce something notable in the same science. It cannot fail to happen that the sciences will be cultivated and advanced more than commonly with such a conjunction of clever wits and great industry everywhere.

I shall be delighted, Sir, to hear news of you sometimes, which I shall endeavor to acknowledge as well as I can, as, Sir,

Your very humble and obedient servant,
Oldenburg

If you do me the honor of writing to me, you will oblige me by giving your letters to Mr. Justel who knows the address necessary for them to reach me safely.

NOTES

Reply to Letter 1968. The date has been altered.
1 Boulliaud wrote of giving them to Smith. He did not say that the books were to be returned to Hevelius.
2 Published in 1663.
3 See Letter 1854a.

1979
Newton to Oldenburg

21 May 1672

Printed in Newton, *Correspondence*, I, 159–60, from the
original in CUL MS. Add. 3976, no. 8

Newton summarizes the end of Letter 1973 (to which he had not yet received a reply), and says that Oldenburg's arguments about anonymity have caused him to defer sending some experiments which he had planned to accompany his reply to Hooke. He promises to send this latter when he has received Oldenburg's next letter.

1980
Oldenburg to Newton

23 May 1672

Oldenburg's endorsement on Letter 1979 indicates that it was received on the twenty-second and answered on the twenty-third.

1981
Le Bourgeois to Oldenburg

26 May 1672

From the original in Royal Society MS. B 2, no. 13
Partly printed in Brown, p. 227

De Caen le 6e de Juin 1672 [N.S.]

Monsieur

Jay ordre de vous faire des Civilitéz de la part de nos Messieurs de LAcademie de Caen. Ils témoignent vous estre fort obliges de vôtre bienveillance, é lorsquils auront quelque chose qui meritera de vous en faire part, Ils le feront avec bien de la Joye; é ensemble vous marqueront leur ressentiments, é une partie de lestime quils ont pour votre Auguste societé, é pour vôtre personne en particulier.

Il ya quelque temps que ces Messieurs n'ont fait d'experience, parce que notre Intendant,[1] qui donne ordre aux frais é a la dépense, a eu des affaires pour cette guerre outre ses ordinaires.

Nous avons un Gentilhomme qui a trouvé le secret d'une horloge qui marchera une espece de temps prodigieuse, quelques uns disent Jusques a pres de Cent ans. Il est a Paris pour le Communiquer s'il reussit Cela sera beau é cette Invention est de Consequence.[2]

Nos Messieurs d'Icy n'ont point esté avertis d'une Comete qui a paru depuis le mois de février Jusqu'au mois d'Avril, Ce qui est facheux, Car nous en avons quelques uns dasses bons Astronomes. On ne l'a mesme sceû a Paris que vers la fin de Mars, que les Jesuites de la fleche, en écrivant a Ceux de Paris. Le Pere Pardies l'observa, é puis fit soutenir une these a l'occasion de la Comete, dont Il etablit le mouvement regulier é la nature durable. Il marqua le tour qu'elle devet faire suivant les Regles d'un livre Imprime a bordeaux sur la Comete de 1664 é 65.[3] sans doute que vous aurez veu un petit traitté du pere Pardies touchant la Conessance des bestes,[4] ce pere dans la premiere moitié de son livre met les sentiments de Descartes dans le plus beau Jour du monde, é d'une maniere a faire voir qu'il donne dans Ce sentiment; é dans l'autre moitié, ou Il parle de refuter, Vous disiez qu'il n'a dessein que de badiner. enfin vous verrez bien que cest le pere Pardies qui parle dans le Commencement é dans la fin le Jesuite.

Un Professeur en philosophie dans nôtre ville appellé Mr Cally[5] se dispose a nous donner des theses, ou Il prouve le doctrine de Descartes par l'autorité de l'Ecriture des Peres é Aristote: Ce qu'il fit a la fin du Cours precedent par la seule raison. Jestime asses ces theses la pour vous en envoyer a la premiere occasion.

Il faut que Je vous parle d'autre chose é que Je Vous die qu'en revenant de Paris Je restay quelques Jours chez nous a la Campagne, ou Je vis une fille, a qui le Chirurgien du lieu avoit fait recroistre toute la Chair du gras de la Jambe quune gangrane luy avet fait tomber. le Chirurgien m'asseura que toute la Chair avet été entierement emportee, é qu'on voyoit l'os tout a descouvert. Cette homme pour faire revenir la Chair bassina é etuva la partie d'une eau tiree dArum de grande serpentaire[6] é autres plantes qu'il avet leu avoir la qualité de faire revenir les Chairs. peu de Jours apres la Chair Crut en telle abondance qu'il se vit obligé affin de reffaire la Jambe de grosseur de se servir du Couteau dont Il retrancha quantité de Chair sans faire la moindre douleur a la fille presentement la Jambe malade est a peu pres de mesme grosseur que lautre, la peau la Couvre desja par tout, hors en un endroit ou en Coupant Il blessa une artere é des veines qui Jettant beaucoup de sang l'obligerent de mettre le feu. Ce qu'il fait encor de temps en temps é sans aucune douleur. Cette Chair est belle en apparence mais dure é trop ferme. Ce secret est supprenant é a quelque chose de bon mais Il est dangereux é Il ne sen faut servir quavec bien de la precaution.

Vous scavez les nouvelles aussy bien é aussy vitte que nous Cest pourquoy Je ne vous en parleray point.

Quelques Jours devant que de partir de Paris Mr Denis me promist de vous faire tenir une lettre de ma Part ce que Jespere qu'il aura fait.[7]

Je finiray Monsieur en vous asseurant de mes tres humbles respects é en vous Conjurant de faire quelque chose en ma faveur pour peu que l'occasion vaille é soit avantageuse, soit pour demeurer en Angleterre ou pour sortir.[8] J'eus tous les regrets du monde de partir sans saluer Mr le Conte d'Alisbury[9] Jespere quelque chose de luy si vous voules bien prendre la peine de luy parler quelque fois de moy Je vous ay desja asseuré que Je ne feray aucune difficulté de repasser leau lorsque vous me l'ordonnerez é que vous pouves promettre tout de moy. Au nom de Dieu Monsieur souvenez vous d'une personne qui vous honorera toute sa vie Cest Vôtre aquis serviteur

Esaie Bourgeois

Je vous écris par un marchand de nostre ville que je prie de ne point quitter londre sans prendre une lettre ches vous pour moy faveur que J'espere que vous aves la bonté de macorder si vous m'écriverez par quelquun qui vient a paris vous nauriez que mettre sur ma lettre a bourgeois Medicin le Jeune a Caen é luy dira de la faire mettre dans le bureau de la poste pour normandie.

ADDRESS
    A Monsieur
    Monsieur Oldenburg
        a Londres

TRANSLATION

From Caen, 6 June 1672 [N.S.]

Sir,

I am commanded to send you courteous greetings from our gentlemen of the Academy of Caen. They testify to being much obliged to you for your benevolence, and as soon as they have something which deserves being revealed to you they will do so gladly; and they record their feelings and a part of the esteem which they feel for your august Society, and for you in particular.

For some time these gentlemen have not made any experiments, because our *Intendant*[1] who supervises expenses and outlays has been busied with this war besides his usual concerns.

We have a gentleman who has discovered the secret of a clock which will run for a prodigious length of time, some say nearly a hundred years. He is in Paris to communicate it; if he succeeds that will be a fine thing and this invention is an important one.[2]

Our members here were not informed of a comet that was visible from February until April, which is annoying because we have some pretty good astronomers among them. It was not even known in Paris until towards the end of March, by the Jesuits of La Flèche writing to those at Paris. Father Pardies observed it and then had a thesis presented about the comet, whose regular motion and durable nature he established. He noted the circuit which it ought to make following the rules of a book printed at Bordeaux on the comet of 1664 and 1665.[3] You have without doubt seen a little book by Father Pardies on the consciousness of animals.[4] In the first half of his book this Father puts Descartes's opinions in the best light in the world, and in such a way as to show that he accepts this opinion; and in the other half, where he speaks to refute it, you would say he only intends to jest. In the end you perceive that Father Pardies is speaking at the beginning and the Jesuit at the end.

A teacher of philosophy in our town, called Mr. Cally,[5] is preparing to present us with some theses in which he proves Cartesian doctrine by the authority of Scripture, the Church Fathers, and Aristotle, as he did at the end of the last course of lectures, by reason alone. I think well enough of these theses to send them to you at the first opportunity.

I must speak of other things, and tell you that in returning from Paris I stayed for some days at our house in the country, where I saw a girl for whom the local surgeon had caused the flesh of the thick part of the leg, lost by a gangrene, to grow again. The surgeon assured me that all the flesh had been entirely carried away and that the bone could be seen all uncovered. To make the flesh return this man had bathed and warmed the part with a water drawn from Arum, from *Serpentaria major*, and other plants which, as he had read, had the property of regenerating flesh.[6] A few days after the flesh grew so plentifully that he found himself obliged, in order to reform the leg to size, to make use of a knife with which he cut back the flesh without causing the least pain to the girl. Now the sick leg is about the same size as the other, the skin already covers it completely except in one spot where in cutting he wounded an artery and the veins which spouting much blood obliged him to apply cautery. Which he still does from time to time without any pain. This flesh is fine in appearance, but hard and too firm. This secret is surprising and something good; but dangerous, and to be utilized only with great precaution.

You hear the news as well and as quickly as we do, and that is why I shall say nothing to you about it.

A few days before I left Paris Mr. Denis promised to have you sent a letter from me, which I hope he has done.[7]

I shall conclude, Sir, by assuring you of my very humble respects and by entreating you to take some step on my behalf, however trifling and unpromising the opportunity may be, whether it means living in England or going abroad.[8] I was most infinitely sorry to leave without paying my respects to the Earl of Ailesbury.[9] I have hopes of something through him, if you will take the trouble to speak to him of me sometimes. I have already assured you that I shall make no difficulty about recrossing the water if you command it of me, and that you can promise anything concerning me. In God's name, Sir, remember a person who will honor you all his life. That is

Your entire servant
Esaie Le Bourgeois

I write to you by a merchant of our town whom I begged not to leave London without taking a letter to your house for the sake of the interest which I hope you will have the goodness to accord to me. If you write to me by anyone coming to Paris you only need to write on my letter "A Bourgeois Medicin le Jeune à Caen" and tell him to have it put in the post office for Normandy.

ADDRESS
  Mr. Oldenburg,
    London

NOTES

For this young physician of Caen, see Letter 1810 (Vol. VIII), to which Oldenburg had replied on 11 November 1671, in a letter now lost.

1 The Intendant of the Généralité de Caen (1666–75) was Guy de Chamillard (b. 1624) who, according to Huet, unwittingly brought about the decline of the Académie de Physique at Caen by seeking to emulate the Académie Royale des Sciences. He obtained in 1667 Colbert's approval for the provision of pensions for its members from royal funds; henceforward their disinterested attachment to "curiosity" vanished (see Harcourt Brown, "L'Académie de Physique de Caen (1666–1675)," *Mém. de l'Acad. des Sciences Arts et Belles-Lettres de Caen, Nouv. Série,* IX, 1938, 131).

2 This clock is not mentioned by Huygens, who was much concerned for his country which was suffering the Anglo-French onslaught at this time.

3 This was Pardies's own work, *Dissertatio de motu et natura cometarum* (with an appendix, *De novo cometa*), (Bordeaux, 1665).

4 Compare Letter 1946.

5 Pierre Cally (1630–1709) studied philosophy at Caen and theology at Paris. He was principal of the College of Arts there from 1675, and curé of St. Martin from 1684. Because his strong Cartesian views permeated his theological writings (mostly polemical) he was exiled to Moulins in 1687. Probably the theses mentioned here were incorporated in his *Institutio philosophicae* (Caen, 1674).

6 *Arum maculatum* (wake-robin, cuckoopint, etc.) was traditionally credited with the virtue of healing ulcerated wounds; it is not clear what the other plant is, but it is possibly "pellitory of Spain," *Anacydus pyrethrum,* which is superficially like the wild arum and also has a pungent root.

7 This letter, presumably written earlier in 1672, is now lost.

8 The circumstances remain unknown, but it is likely that Le Bourgeois wished to enter the personal service of some important person.

9 Robert Bruce, first Earl of Ailesbury (d. 1685), an Original Fellow of the Royal Society besides having a minor public career, was credited with an interest in learning and certainly collected manuscripts.

1982
Oldenburg to Cassini

27 May 1672

From the copy in the Royal Society Letter Book V, 251

Celeberrimo Viro
Domino Johanni Domenico Cassino Christianissimi Regis Astronomo,
Henricus Oldenburg Regiae Societatis Sec.
Felicitatem

Cum literae tuae novissimae, Vir Illustris, nec non ornatissimi Vernonis nostri epistola, tuis sociata,[1] singularem tuam in Regiae Societatis nostrae institutum et studia voluntatem uberrimem fuerint contestatae; Tuque omnibus conscijs doctis, Rem literariam et nobilissimam imprimis Uraniam colere et ornare pro virili satagas: Dicta utique societas, eximiae virtutis ac doctrinae tuae amantissima, vigesimo secundo Maij nuperrimo, omnium conspirantibus Suffragijs, in sodalium suorum Album Te cooptavit, mihique ut protinus id Tibi significarem (quod laetabundus nunc facio) in mandatis dedit, confisa penitus, Te socij Regij mensuram, quam geminam pro merito tuo nunc sustines, cordate adimpleturum. Vale, Vir Clarissime, et de Iugi societatis Regiae benevolentia, deque flagranti officiorum meorum erga Te promptitudine securus esto. Dabam Londini d. 27. Maij 1672.

TRANSLATION

Henry Oldenburg, Secretary of the Royal Society, wishes happiness to the celebrated Giovanni Domenico Cassini, Astronomer of the Most Christian King

Whereas your very latest letter, illustrious Sir, and that of the excellent Mr. Vernon linked with yours,[1] testified very amply to your singular support for the designs and concerns of our Royal Society; and whereas you are known by all learned persons to devote yourself wholly to the development and perfection of learning and the most noble science of Astronomy in particular; the aforesaid Society being most cordially inclined towards your outstanding merits and knowledge did on the twenty-second day of May last past by an unanimous vote elect you into the company of its Fellowship and ordered me to inform you of the same forthwith, which now I most gladly do; being assured you will worthily sustain the rôle of a Fellow of the Royal Society, parallel to that which you now deservedly fill. Farewell, famous Sir, and be assured of the Royal Society's perpetual goodwill as well as of my own eager readiness in serving your wishes. London, 27 May 1672.

NOTES

Reply to Letter 1956. Cassini and Vernon were both proposed for election by Oldenburg on 24 April, and again on 1 May; both were elected on 22 May. This letter is a formal document; hence the reference to Louis XIV as the "Most Christian King."
1 Letter 1955, which enclosed Letter 1956.

1983
Malpighi to Oldenburg

28 May 1672

From the original in Royal Society Malpighi Letters, no. 15
Printed in *Opera Omnia*, II, 17 (sig. F).

Praeclarissimo et Eruditissimo Viro
Domino Henrico Oldenburg Regiae Societatis Anglicanae Secretario
Marcellus Malpighius S.P.

Sero ad nostras apellet oras Clarissimi Graef novissimum, quod innuis, de ovis, et utero opus, ob bellicos tumultus, quibus premitur Occasus: admodum tamen probabilem puto tanti Viri positionem; etenim certum est in foemineis testibus ova reperiri, etiam in nuper natis brutorum infantibus, et uteri tubas eandem omnino conformationem habere, quam superior ovarij portio possidet, unde eadem via, et ovorum introitus succedit. Memini, me in nobili Muliere ovum in tuba exiguum observasse, quod tunc temporis polypum putabam, et nuper prae manibus habui muliebris molae incoamentum, quod ovum erat, et exterius mirabili contextura pollebat. Transacto vere post solitas febriculas, et cordis palpitationes me ruri receperam, ut observationum tentamina subirem, sed in cassum; singulo namque die bis in Urbem remeare cogor invisendi gratia Virum nobilem aegrotantem, ita ut summo cum animi, et corporis maerore ad medicae praxis servitutem me damnatum experiar.

Bellorum impetus navium expeditionem in Italiam impedient, unde in longum libri de plantarum Anatome Doctissimi vestri Medici transmissio procrastinabitur. Interim, si liceret, te rogatum vellem, ut praecipuarum propositionum actuariolum mihi transmitteres; tam egregijs enim laboribus perfrui exopto. Diu vivas, et sociorum erga me benevolentiam perpetuam reddire ne desinas. Dabam Bononiae Die 7 Junij 1672 [N.S.]

ADDRESS
> Praeclarissimo et Eruditissimo Viro Domino Henrico
> Oldenburg Regiae Societatis Anglicanae Secretario
> Londini

TRANSLATION

Marcello Malpighi sends many greetings to the very famous and learned Mr. Henry Oldenburg, Secretary of the English Royal Society

Because of the disturbance caused by the warfare which troubles the West the recent study of eggs and the uterus by the famous De Graaf that you mention may well be late in reaching our part of the world, but I think the position taken by that notable person a very probable one; for it is certainly the case that eggs are found in the female testes, even in the newborn young of animals, and that the uterine tubes have exactly the same structure as the upper part of the ovary [in birds], whence too the introduction of the eggs follows by the same route. I remember that I observed a minute egg in the [Fallopian] tube of a noblewoman, which at that time I took to be a polypus, and I recently had in my hands the beginning of a woman's false conception, which was an egg, and its exterior had an extraordinary structure. After spring was over, following the usual touches of fever and palpitations of the heart, I went back into the country in order to make some attempt at observations, but to no purpose, for twice on particular days I was forced back home into town to visit a sick nobleman, so that with the greatest affliction of mind and body I find myself condemned to the servitude of medical practice.

The violence of war prevents the movement of ships to Italy, and so the transmission of the book on the anatomy of plants by your learned physician will be long deferred. Meanwhile, if you can, I ask you to send me a note of its chief propositions, as I am very eager to enjoy the results of such extraordinary efforts. May you live long, and never cease to continue perpetually the goodwill of the Fellows towards me. Bologna, 7 June 1672 [N.S.]

ADDRESS

To the very famous and learned Mr. Henry Oldenburg,
Secretary of the English Royal Society,
London.

NOTE

Reply to Letters 1966 and 1969.

1984
Sluse to Oldenburg

29 May 1672

From the original in Royal Society MS. S 1, no. 69
Partly printed in *Phil. Trans.*, no. 98 (17 November 1673), 6141
Printed in Boncompagni, pp. 659–60

Nobilissimo et Clarissimo Viro
D. Henrico Oldenburg Regiae Societatis Secretario
Renatus Franciscus Slusius S.P.D.

Miraberis fortasse, Vir Nobilissime, meque negligentiae nomine accu-
sabis quod binis tuis humanissimis tamdiu responsum debeam. Sed
mirari desines, meque, ut spero, absolves, posteaquam huius morae causam
intellexeris. Cum circa Kal: Apr: priores tuas accepissem, in Hollandiam
scripsi atque etiam in Italiam, ut de libris quos indicavas, fierem certior.
Dum responsum expecto, supervenit Gallicorum exercituum transitus, qui
nos mirum in modum exercuit, ne dicam afflixit.[1] Secutae sunt Hollan-
dorum minae, a quibus nondum etiam respirare licet. Puduit tamen diutius
differre gratiarum actionem quam tibi debeo: facit enim humanitas tua
singularis ut ab hac mihi semper incipiendum sit. Et sane nihil mihi literis
tuis iucundius accidere in hac περιστάσει, nihil quod a molestis illis cogitationibus animum magis avocare posset. Quod vero ad libros attinet,
scribitur ad me ex Italia illic ignorari Mengoli de Musica volumina.[2]
P. autem Gottignies aliquot opuscula prodiisse, quorum, ut existimo, iam
notitiam habes.[3] Expectabam ex Hollandia, tum magni Wallisii opus
ultimum de motu, tum Clarissimi Bartholini dioristicon, tuo atque huma-

nissimi D. Collini beneficio; sed expectationem meam elusit Elzevirius, negans se quidquam accepisse quod ante triennium ad me non misisset. Cumque Navarchae nomen quod adscripseras, ipsi indicari iussissem, negavit rursus quidquam sibi redditum esse. Itaque spe mea excidi, nec eo tamen minus obligatum me profiteor tuae ac Clarissimi Collinii humanitati, per quam non stetit quominus illius compos fierem.

Quae ad Alhazeni Problema meditatus fui hactenus, rudia licet et impolita, tui iuris sunt. De iis igitur dispone prout lubet. Simplicissima est et maxime ingeniosa Nobilissimi Hugenii constructio. Vidit quippe Vir acutissimus qua ratione ad omnes casus extendi posset hyperbola aequalium laterum, quam in casu anguli reguli recti, sese statim afferre praecedentibus meis insinuaveram. Posset quoque ex infinitis Ellipsibus quae adhiberi possunt, una seligi non difficilis constructionis, sed piget tamdiu in eodem Problemate haerere. Superest tamen aliquid quod contemplationem habet non iniucundam: Nimirum, cum sectiones, quae cum circulo dato ad solutionem Problematis adhibentur, illum in quatuor punctis secent, quorum duo tantum reflexioni serviunt, quaeri posset quodnam Problema solvant duo reliqua, et quanam verborum forma concipienda sit propositio ut quatuor illos casus complectatur. Deinde an non etiam iidem quatuor casus occurrant, cum puncta dato aequaliter distant a centro. Hoc ut Clarissimo Collinio proponas, eumque meo nomine plurimum salvere iubeas, enixe rogo.

De caeteris quae ad me scripsisti agam prima occasione prolixius. Vale itaque Vir Clarissime, meque perpetuo nexu tibi obligatum semper amare perge. Dabam Leodii VIII Junii 1672 [N.S.]

TRANSLATION

René François de Sluse sends many greetings to the very noble and famous Mr. Henry Oldenburg, Secretary of the Royal Society

You will perhaps have been surprised, most noble Sir, and charge me with negligence because I have owed you a reply to two of your kind letters for so long. But your surprise will cease and you will forgive me, I hope, when you have learned the cause of this delay. When I received your earlier letter about the first of April I wrote to Holland and also to Italy for information about the books you noted. While I was awaiting a reply the passage of the French armies took place, which caused us much harrassment, not to say damage;[1] after that came threats from the Dutch, which have not yet given us time to catch our breath. Yet it would have been shameful to defer longer the return of thanks I owe you;

your exceptional kindness causes me always to be setting about this task. And truly nothing could be more agreeable to me in these critical days than your letters and nothing serves better to relieve my mind from those unhappy reflections. As for the books, they write to me from Italy that Mengoli's volume on music is unknown there;[2] however, a few little tracts by Father Gottignies have appeared of which you already have an account, I think.[3] I was expecting from Holland both the latest study of motion by the great Wallis and the *Dioristice* of the famous Bartholin, thanks to yourself and kind Mr. Collins; but Elzevir disappointed my expectation by denying that he had received anything that he had not sent me three years ago. And when I gave instructions for the name of the seaman which you had written me to be conveyed to him, he again denied that anything at all had been delivered to him. And so I have given up hope, though professing myself no less obliged on that account to the kindness of yourself and Mr. Collins, which is independent of my possession of the books.

My past reflections on the problem of Alhazen, rough and unpolished as they are, are at your disposal. Do with them as you please, therefore. The construction of the very noble Huygens is very simple and exceedingly ingenious. For that most acute person saw how the equal-sided hyperbola, which as I had hinted in my previous letter presents itself at once in the case of the right-angled rays, can be extended to all cases. From the infinite number of ellipses that can be made use of, too, one can be chosen of an easy construction, but it vexes me to dwell so long on a single problem. There is, however, something else which it is not unpleasing to consider, and that is: as there are four intersections of the conic sections which (with the given circle) yield the solution to the problem with that circle itself, two of which only serve [to define the points of] reflection, one may inquire what problem is resolved by the other two intersections, and in what form of words the proposition may be couched so as to embrace all those four cases. And again: whether or not those same four cases arise, when the two given points [in Alhazen's Problem] are equidistant from the center [of the reflecting circle]. I warmly entreat you to propose this to the famous Collins, and to wish him good health in my name.

At the first opportunity I will deal at greater length with the other matters you wrote to me about. And so farewell, famous Sir, and continue always to love me, who am perpetually bound by obligation to you. Liège, 8 June 1672 [N.S.]

NOTES

Reply to Letters 1916 (Vol. VIII) and 1952.

1 On 27 March Louis XIV had declared war on the United Provinces; one French army from Charleroi and another from Sedan advanced through the principality of Liège towards Maastricht, where there was a strong Dutch garrison.
2 Pietro Mengoli, *Speculazioni di musica* (Bologna, 1670), often mentioned before, and described by Oldenburg in *Phil. Trans.*, no. 100 (9 February 1673/4), 6194–7000, where he says it had only recently become available to him.

3 Besides *Elementa geometriae planae* (Rome, 1669)—several times mentioned previously—Gottignies published some small astronomical pieces, including *Lettere intorno
alle macchie nuovamente scoperte nel pianeta di Giove* (Rome, 1666) and *De figuris cometarum qui annis 1664, 1665 et 1668 apparuerunt* (Rome, 1668).

1985
Sluse to Oldenburg

31 May 1672

From the original in Royal Society MS. S 1, no. 70
Partly printed in *Phil. Trans.*, no. 98 (17 November 1673), 6141
Printed in Boncompagni, pp. 660–61

Nobilissimo et Clarissimo Viro
D. Henrico Oldenburg Regiae Societatis Secretario
Renatus Franciscus Slusius S.P.D.

Ecce me iterum, Vir Nobilissime, sed ut ἀβλεψίαν duntaxat indicem,
quae in postremas meas irrepsit.[1] Cum enim Nobilissimi Hugenii constructionem quam ad me miseras,[2] animo variis curis distracto, ad calculos
revocassem, levi calami lapsu (sumto scilicet signo $+$ pro $-$) in aequationem
incidi, quae mihi persuasit, Virum acutissimum, diversam omnino a mea
Analysim instituisse. Facile autem falsa illa aequatio mutari poterat in
aliam ad parabolam; quod, absque ulteriori examine, occasionem mihi
praebuit ut ad te scriberem, parabolam dari ex illius Analysi, quae casibus
Problematis omnibus satisfaceret.[3] Dele igitur, si me amas, hoc postremum
ex mea Epistola, nam omnino falsum est. Cum enim eadem ipsa vespera,
qua ad te scripseram, in calculos meos forte incidissem, eosque attentius
relegerem, lapsum meum animadverti; ac tandem agnovi Clarissimum
Hugenium non alia usum Analysi quam mea, quae parabolam uno tantum
casu admittit. Quod ut evidentius tibi constet, aequationem quam construxit, hic adscribam. Repete memoria, si placet, quae secundis curis ad te
scripsi et invenies, me duas aequationes problemati per hyperbolam circa
asymptotos idoneas, assignasse,[4] has nimirum

$$2zbaa - 2znae - qqba + qqne = bzqq - zqqe,$$

et

$$bzqq - 2znae - qqba + qqne = 2zbee - zqqe,$$

ac subiecisse, levi mutatione (substituendo Ex.G. pro qq eius valorem $aa+ee$) inveniri posse infinitas hyperbolas et ellipses, quae cum circulo dato Problema solverent. Nunc in priore ex his aequationibus pro $b\chi qq$ ponatur eius valor, fiet

$$\chi baa - 2\chi nae - qqba + qqne = b\chi ee - \chi qqe$$

sive
$$aa - \frac{qqa}{\chi} = ee - \frac{qqe}{b} + \frac{2nae}{b} - \frac{qqne}{\chi b}{}^{5}$$

Atque haec est aequatio, quam magno ingenii acumine ac pari facilitate construxit Vir Doctissimus. Quod ut tibi pluribus probem, opus non est, quando labore non multo rem ad calculos revocando id agnoscere poteris. Vale itaque Vir praestantissime, et ἀβλεψίαν quae me importunum reddidit, benigne, ut soles, excusa.
Dabam Leodii X Junii 1672 [N.S.]

TRANSLATION

René François de Sluse sends many greetings to the very noble and famous Mr. Henry Oldenburg, Secretary of the Royal Society

Here I am again, most noble Sir, but only in order to point out an oversight that crept into my last.[1] For when I submitted the construction of the very noble Huygens that you sent me[2] to calculation my mind was distracted by a variety of responsibilities and by a trivial slip of the pen (putting a plus sign for a minus) in the equation I arrived at I convinced myself that that very acute person had effected an analysis totally different from my own. However, that false equation can easily be modified into another, to a parabola, which, without any further investigation, gave me occasion to write to you that a parabola resulted from his analysis, which would satisfy every case of the Problem.[3] If you love me, therefore, delete this last [statement] from my letter, as it is altogether false. For the very same evening that I wrote to you, happening by chance to look over my calculations again and reading them more attentively, I noticed my slip; and finally perceived that the famous Huygens used an analysis in no way different from my own, which will admit the parabola in only one single case. So that this will become the clearer to you, I am writing out here the equation he formed. Please recollect what I wrote to you on second thoughts and you will find that I assigned two equations to the problem employing a hyperbola [drawn] upon proper asymptotes,[4] namely

$$2\chi a^2 b - 2\chi aen - q^2 ab + q^2 en = b\chi q^2 - \chi q^2 e,$$

and
$$\chi bq^2 - 2\chi aen - q^2 ab + q^2 en = 2\chi be^2 - \chi q^2 e,$$

and I added that by a trivial modification (for example, substituting for q^2 its value, a^2+e^2) it is possible to discover an infinite number of hyperbolas and ellipses which together with the given circle solve the problem. Now if in the first of these equations you substitute for bzq^2 its value, it becomes

$$za^2b - 2zaen - q^2ab + q^2en = zbe^2 - zq^2e$$

or,

$$a^2 - \frac{q^2a}{z} = e^2 - \frac{q^2e}{b} + 2\frac{aen}{b} - \frac{q^2ne}{bz} \text{ }^5$$

And this is the equation for which that very learned person has given a construction, with great acuity of wit and no less facility. It is needless for me to go into more details for you, since by very little effort you can see this, by submitting the whole to calculation. And so farewell, most excellent Sir, and in your usual kind way forgive this slip, which makes me importune you again. Liège, 10 June 1672 [N.S.]

NOTES

1 Letter 1984.
2 In Letter 1952, quoting Letter 1944 (Vol. VIII).
3 As may be seen, Sluse seems to have misremembered the tenor of Letter 1984 (whatever his private calculations) as no such statement is made there.
4 See Letter 1843 (Vol. VIII, p. 408).
5 The "z" in the denominator of the final fraction has been (correctly) added in red ink; it is already missing from the copy of the final portion of the letter—from the reference to Huygens onwards—sent by Collins to Newton (C.U.L. MS. Add. 3971.1, 6r).

1986
Hevelius to Oldenburg

31 May 1672

From the original in Royal Society MS. H 2, no. 30

Viro
Illustri atque Eximio
Domino Henrico Oldenburgio
Regiae Societatis Secretario
J. Hevelius Salutem

Nullus dubito, quin literas meas die 9 Martij ad Te datas,[1] quibus significaveram brevibus, Cometam novum hic Dantisci apud nos observatum esse, recte acceperis; nunc fusiorem aliquam descriptionem, nec non accuratam istius Criniti sideris Delineationem, cum ipsis nostris Observationibus Tibi transmitto. Sed, cum hisce simul literis, ob nimis grande fasciculum fieri haud potuerit, navi quadam cura Dn. Kürbei (qui Te humanissime salutare iussit) Hafniam aliquot exemplaria transferri curavi, ut sic possent suo tempore Navi vestra Anglica, quae modo in Hellesponto Danico commoratur, nisi alia detur occasio, recte Tibi perferri, amicisque distribui.[2] Hocce recens phaenomenum inter reliqua gravissima negotia, inprimis in caussa hucusque fuit, quod tardius, quam debeam ad Tuas mihi longe gratissimas die 9 Novembris anni elapsi respondeam, tum quod responsum ad meas, die 7 Octobris St. n. ad Te datas hucusque,[3] ut ut frustra, exspectaverim. Gratias Tibi debeo permagnas, pro transmissis et illo Microscopio, et libris quibusdam; quae licet admodum tarde, optime tamen tandem obtinui; optarem, ut aliquo officiorum genere Tibi rursus gratificari, animumque meum ergo Te sincerum, vel aliquo saltem modo detegere possum, nihil unquam mihi accederet exoptatius. Ab amico quodam nuper percepi, novam omnino rationem Telescopia construendi, in Anglia inventam esse. An res ita se se habeat, ac quomodo succedat, avidissime exspecto. Lentes illas, pro longissimo Tubo 140 pedum tandem ab Illust. domino Burattino obtinui; singulari sane artificio sunt elaboratae, ac mirum in modum expolitae. Num vero expectationi Nostrae circa observationes Siderum satisfaciant, tempus docebit: quamprimum tantillum otij tantummodo obtinuero, vires earum explorabo. de phasibus Saturni opusculum illud Parisijs editum nondum videre obtigit.[4] Parisienses enim vix unquam mihi vel quiquam communicant; nec ad literas meas bene longas Illust. dominus Cassinus et Picardus die 7 Octobris anni praeteriti, responderunt: ad quas tamen ob quaestiunculam quandam, de rotunda Saturni facie a me motam merito mihi respondere debuissent. Laudo vero egregrium vestrum erga me affectum, quod adeo pronus estis in quibusvis ad rem literariam promovendam spectantibus, mihi morem gerere. Proinde multis nominibus Vobis sum obstrictus, imo longe maxime ero, si ea porro, quae ad contemplationes nostras Coelestes conducere videbantur, una cum Ephemeridibus Eruditorum a numero 68, nuper editis, mihi prima quaque occasione navi quadam si fieri potuerit, transmiseritis:[5] Sumptus non solum summa gratiarum actione restituam, sed rursus contendam omnibus modis, ut paribus gratissimis officijs promptitudinem Vestrum demereri non nequeam. Si Mars tantummodo non obstiterit, mari quoque transmittam frustrum illud succini, quod olim cessit sigillo:[6] quod si vero Tibi non videatur hoc periculosissimo tempore consultum, differendum erit id ipsum in tutiorem occasionem. Nollem enim succinum illud adeo rarum pericula exponere: quippe simile vix unquam a me obtinendum erit. Denique rogetur Cl. Johannes Flamsteadius, ut rei literariae bono singulis annis haud grave continuare appulsus observabiles Lunae ad Fixas, Planetasque: quo eo magis observatores incitentur ad phaenomena eiusmodi rarissima ac utilissima animadvertenda. Nam ex hujus generis observationibus, longe accuratius, meo quali quali judicio, differentiae Meridianorum obtinentur, quam per immersiones Iovialium in Umbram: si quicquam hac in parte iam prodierit, optarem ut illius quamprimum mihi detur copia. Denique Te etiam atque etiam rogatum volo, ut prima data occasione, quando exemplaria illa de Cometa nupero acceperis, ut fasciculum Cl. Domino Bullialdo destinatum Parisios transmittas. Volui namque amicis illis etiam aliquot exemplaria communicare: cum hoc tempore non videam quomodo aliter ea perferri debeam. Si quos sumptos feceris, lubentissime restituam. Non solum mihi; sed et amicis communibus facies rem pergratam. Vale et saluta quam officiosissime Totam Nostram Ill. Regiam Societatem. Dabam Gedani Anno 1672, die 10 Junij [N.S.]

TRANSLATION

J. Hevelius greets the illustrious and distinguished Mr. Henry Oldenburg, Secretary of the Royal Society

I have no doubt that you have safely received my letter addressed to you on 9 March [N.S.][1] in which I briefly informed you that the new comet had been observed by us at Danzig; now I send you a fuller description and an accurate depiction of the coma of that star together with our actual observations. But as this would make too big a packet to send with our letter I have taken steps to convey a few copies to Copenhagen by some ship of Mr. Kirkby's (who wishes me to greet you very kindly) so that they may be safely brought to you in due course by an English ship now waiting in the Danish sound (if some other opportunity does not present itself), and so distributed to friends.[2] This recent phenomenon has hitherto been the particular reason (among other pressing affairs) why I reply later than I ought to your letter of 9 November last year, which was most welcome indeed, especially as I had so long awaited, in vain, a reply to mine of 7 October N.S.[3] I owe you profound thanks for the conveyance both of the microscope and of some books which I have at length obtained, though very tardily. I wish that I could please you by some sort of service in return, and nothing at all could delight me more than to be able to demonstrate my sincere intentions towards you. I lately heard from a certain friend that a wholly new way of making telescopes had been discovered in England. I very eagerly anticipate learning whether it is really so and how it has succeeded. I have at last obtained those lenses for a very long telescope of 140 feet from the illustrious Mr. Burattini; they are truly worked with singular skill and wonderfully well polished. Time will tell whether they will come up to our expectations when we observe the fixed stars, and as soon as I can secure a little leisure I shall look into their power. I have not yet been able to get a glimpse of that little study of Saturn's phases published at Paris.[4] For the Parisians hardly keep in touch with me at all, nor have Messrs. Cassini and Picard made any reply to my very long letter of 7 October last year, to which, however, they justly owed me a reply because of a certain slight question I raised in it about the round aspect of Saturn. I do value your own remarkable goodwill towards me, because you are so ready to gratify me in any matters relating to the advancement of learning. Hence I am obliged to you on many accounts and shall indeed long be so, if you will continue to convey to me anything that seems to conduce to my observation of the heavens, and (if you can, at the first opportunity by some ship or other) the *Journal of the Learned* lately printed from number 68 onwards.[5] I will not only repay the expense with many thanks but will in return seek by every means proper to be deserving of your ready zeal by similar services welcome to you. If only Mars does not stand in the way I will also send by sea that piece of amber, which once took the impression of a seal;

or this shall be deferred to some safer time if it does not seem wise to you at this most dangerous period.[6] For I am reluctant to place so rare a piece of amber in jeopardy, since I shall hardly ever obtain another like it. Lastly, please ask Mr. John Flamsteed to continue each year, for the good of the learned world, his [list of] the observable appulses of the moon to the planets and fixed stars, so that observers may be the better encouraged to pay heed to such rare and useful phenomena. For in my judgment (such as it is) differences in longitude may be derived far more accurately by this method than by observing the immersion of Jupiter's satellites in the shadow; if anything of this sort has already been done, I wish that an account of it may be given me as soon as possible. Lastly, I wish to beg you over and over that at the first opportunity after you have received that copy of [the letter concerning] the recent comet, you will send to Paris the package intended for Mr. Boulliaud. For I meant to give some copies to those [French] friends also, and at this time I do not see how else I should convey them. If any expense is involved I will gladly reimburse you. You will do something very welcome not only to me but to those friends too. Farewell, and give my most dutiful greetings to all our illustrious Royal Society. Danzig, 10 June 1672 [N.S.].

NOTES

Reply to Letter 1817 (Vol. VIII). Birch, *History*, III, 55, notes that the present letter was accompanied by a "printed scheme, representing the motion of the . . . comet," but we have not discovered this, or what it was. It may have been (by analogy with other occasions) the printed cut showing the "Cursus cometae" in the sky, extracted from the work mentioned in note 2 below.

1 Letter 1915 (Vol. VIII).
2 Hevelius refers to his *Epistola de cometa anno 1672, mense Martio, et Aprili, Gedani observata. Ad illustrem & celeberrimum virum, Dn. Henricum Oldenburgium, Reg. Societ. Secretarium, Amicum honorandum* (Danzig, 1672); for its transmission, see Letters 1986 bis and 1999.
3 See Letters 1792 and 1792a (Vol. VIII).
4 See Letter 1807, note 1 (Vol. VIII).
5 That is, the *Philosophical Transactions*; no. 68 was dated 20 February 1670/1.
6 See Vol. VII, p. 49.

1986 bis
Hevelius to Oldenburg

31 May 1672

From the draft in Observatoire MS. XI, f. 43

Viro Illustri atque Eximio
Domino Henrico Oldenburgio
Regiae Societatis Secretario
J. Hevelius S.

Literas meas per tabellarium ordinarium die 10 Junii datas spero Te accepisse nunc quoque promissa exemplaria Historiolae de Cometa Tibi mitto, ut possis unum aut alterum exemplum Tibi reservare atque amicis et Fautoribus meo nomine distribuere; reliqua ac residua Bibliopolis concredere, nimirum 7 exempli pro uno Imperial; si plerum imposterum voluerint, mittam quantocyus. Fasciculum autem alterum examplarium rogo, data occasione Domino Bullialdo transmittis Parisiae, magis magisque me Tibi devincies. Vale et salute amicos omnes. Dabam Gedani Anno 1672, die 10 Junii [N.S.].

TRANSLATION

J. Hevelius greets the illustrious and distinguished Mr. Henry Oldenburg, Secretary of the Royal Society

I hope you have received my letter of 10 June sent by the ordinary post. I now send you also the promised copies of the brief account of the comet so that you may keep one or two for yourself and distribute some to my friends and well-wishers; the rest remaining over you may consign to the booksellers at the rate of seven copies for one Imperial ducat. If they wish for more I will send them as soon as possible. However, I beg you that when an opportunity presents itself you will send the other package of copies to Mr. Boulliaud at Paris, and so put me under ever increasing obligations to yourself. Farewell, and greet all my friends. Danzig, 10 June 1672 [N.S.].

NOTE

This appears to be the draft of Hevelius' note accompanying the first package mentioned in Letters 1986 and 1999, written on the same day as Letter 1986 (though Hevelius does not explicitly say so).

1987
Oldenburg to Newton

1 June 1672

From the memorandum in CUL MS. Add. 3976, no. 8
Printed in Newton, *Correspondence*, I, 160, note 3

Rec. May 22. 72
Answ. May 23.
Wrote again june 1 and pressed His Answ to Hook putting him in mind of his promise and desiring to acknowledge Pardies Candid return.[1]

NOTES

Second reply to Letter 1979.
1 Letters 1976 and 1976a.

1988
Pardies to Oldenburg

8 June 1672

From the original in Royal Society MS. P 1, no. 80

Paris 18. Juin 1672 [N.S.]

Monsieur

Je vous escris ce mot pour vous demander une grace aprés tant d'autres que vous m'avez faites. c'est d'avoir la bonté de nous envoyer toutes les semaines la Gazette francoise de Londres, avec les extraordinaires qui le feront en françois.[1] J'espere que vous me ferez cette grace ou que du moins si cela vous importune trop vous donnerez cette commission à quelqu'un de vos gens. J'esperois bien que M. Vernon me gairoit cette amitié, et je luy escrirois si je scavois son adresse, car c'est une personne pour qui j'ay toute la consideration possible. Il faudra s'il vous plaist envelopper ces gazettes et les adresser à M. le Duc de Bethune gouverneur de Calais à Calais, qui nous les fera rendre ici.[2] et je vous prie aussi que dorenavant quand vous me ferez l'honneur de m'escrire, de le faire par cette voye. joignant vos lettres à ces gazettes et les adressant dans l'enve- lope à M. le Duc de Bethune. Vous m'obligerez aussi sensiblement si vous y ajoutez vos Transactions à mesure que vous les ferez, et je ne manqueray pas de satisfaire à l'imprimeur pour tout ce qu'il me fournira. Je n'ay point pour le present autre chose à vous mander. M. Huygens fait imprimer enfin son ouvrage du mouvement. Je ne scay ce qui vous aura semblé *de la lettre d'un philosophe à un Cartesien*, elle paroitra icy la semaine prochaine, et nous verrons ce que diront ces messieurs qui sont ici en grand nombre. une autre fois je vous entretiendray d'un petit ouvrage latin que je vay faire imprimer intitulé Horologium Thaumanticum[3] à cause d'un Iris artificiel qui marque les heures.

J'ay entre les mains quelques ouvrages du feu P. Lalouvere.[4] Il ya 4. livres Problematum illustrium. Il ne l'est rien fait ce me semble de plus beau en geometrie. Il ya deux livres de questions Physico mathematiques sur Descartes et Gassendus. un livre intitulé Elucidatio verum Geo- metricarum, il est fort scavant et fort curieux, et outre cela un receuil de lettres. Tout cela feroit un bon tome in 4°. que ie voudrois faire imprimer ici. Vous m'obligeriez bien si vous pouviez me scavoir dire si vos libraires voudroient en prendre des exemplaires et en quel nombre. cela nous en faciliteroit ici l'impression où nos libraires sont fort difficiles sur ces matieres. Je suis tout à vous.

Pardies

ADDRESS
> A Monsieur
> > Monsieur Grubendol
> > > A Londres

TRANSLATION

Paris, 18 June 1672 [N.S.]

Sir,

I write this line to ask you a favor, after so many others which you have done me. It is to be so kind as to send us every week the French Gazette of London, with the supplements which they make to it in French.[1] I hope that you will do me this favor or if it is too troublesome that you will give this commission to one of your assistants. I should hope that Mr. Vernon would carry out this favor and I would write to him if I knew his address, for he is a person for whom I have the greatest possible respect. Please wrap these Gazettes and address them to "M. le Duc de Béthune gouverneur de Calais à Calais"; he will have them delivered here.[2]

And I also request you henceforth when you do me the honor of writing to me to do it by this route, putting your letters with the Gazettes and addressing them on the wrapping to the Duc de Béthune. You will also distinctly oblige me if you add to these your *Transactions* as you publish them and I shall not fail to pay the printer for all he supplies me with. At present I have nothing else to ask of you.

Mr. Huygens is finally having his work on motion printed. I don't know how the *Lettre d'un philosophe à un Cartesien* seemed to you; it will appear here next week and we shall see what these gentlemen, so numerous here, will say. Another time I shall tell you about a little Latin work which I am having printed, entitled *Horologium Thaumanticum*[3] on account of the spectrum which marks the hours.

I have in my possession some works of the late Father de la Loubère.[4] There are four books of famous problems. It seems to me that nothing finer in geometry has been written. There are two books of physico-mathematical questions on Descartes and Gassendi. One book with the title *Elucidatio verum Geometricarum* is very learned and interesting, and besides that there is a collection of letters. All this would make a good quarto volume and I should like to have it printed here. You will very much oblige me if you can let me know if your booksellers would be willing to take copies of it, and in what quantity. That would assist us in the printing here, where our booksellers are very difficult in these matters. I am altogether yours.

Pardies

ADDRESS
> Mr. Grubendol,
> London

NOTES

1 It seems that under the title *Gazette de Londres* a French edition of the official *London Gazette* (compare Vol. II, pp. 610, 625) was regularly printed—at any rate, the British Museum Library possesses a broken set extending from no. 288 (16 August 1669) to no. 391 (11 August 1670). Presumably Pardies was correct in supposing that the *Gazette de Londres* was still regularly issued in 1672.

2 We could not positively identify him; he was possibly a younger son of the famous Sully, bearing this (strictly incorrect) title.

3 See Letter 1859, note 2 (Vol. VIII). His latest biographer believes this work never to have been published; see August Ziggelaar, *Le physicien Ignace Gaston Pardies S. J. (1636–1673)* (Odense, 1971), p. 226.

4 These were apparently all in manuscript and never printed. We have had occasion previously to refer to the published works of Fr. La Loubère, all printed at an earlier period and including none of these titles.

1989
Oldenburg to Malpighi

8 June 1672

From the original in Bologna MS. 2085, VII, ff. 23–25

Clarissimo Viro
Domino Marcello Malpighi, Philosopho et Medico Bononiensi
H. Oldenburg Salutem

Quod jam tibi nunciatum eo, Vir Celeberrime, id ipsum paucos ante septimanas, cum fasciculum pro Te compergerem, per Residentem Venetum ad Te curandum, significavi.[1] Spero, fasciculum illum, qui continebat Doctoris Grewi libellum Anglicum, de Plantarum Anatome, Tibi rite traditum fuisse. Commemorabam eodem tempore, spem me fovere, te Interpretem quendam Anglicum Bononiae inventurum, qui libelli diciti medullam Tibi exponere valeat; Addebam in super, Te comperturum omnino, Argumentum hoc alia methodo a Te fuisse pertractatu, et observationibus egregiis longius certe provectum: Quam causam esse innuebam, quod omnibus votis Nostrates expetant, ut Iconismos, quibus tuam illam Exercitationem, antehac nobis generose adeo transmissam, et inter Cimelia nostra repositam, elucidasti, quantocius huc cures, siquidem consentire velis, ut eam Typis nostris nitidissimis in orbem literatum emittamus.

Si itaque visum Tibi esset, Diagrammata illa, ad tuam Plantarum Anatomen spectantia, prima quaque occasione tuta ad nos transmittere, fieri sane posset, ut doctissimum illud Scriptum tuum ante proximam hyemem typis extaret. Si in tempore huc appulisset, potuisset illud una cum Dissertatione de Ovo simul imprimi. At noluimus diu nimis rempublicam Philosophicam praecellentibus istis observationibus de pullo destituere. Quare eam praelo jam commisimus; unde brevi exituram speramus. Valeas, Vir Clarissime, et de salute tua, deque consilio super hac re tuo maturrime nos edocere digneris. Dabam Londini d. 8. juni 1672.

ADDRESS
   Al Illustrissimo Signore
   il Signore Marcello Malpighi
      mio Signore Colendissimo
         in
            Bononia

TRANSLATION

Henry Oldenburg greets the famous Mr. Marcello Malpighi, philosopher and physician of Bologna

I informed you of what I am about to relate now a few weeks ago, when I directed the package to you which the Venetian Resident is to take charge of on your behalf.[1] I hope that that package, which contained Dr. Grew's little English work on the anatomy of plants, has been safely delivered to you. On that occasion I remarked, that I hoped you would find some translator of the English at Bologna, who would be able to explain that book to you; I added further that you would surely discover that you had yourself treated this subject by quite a different method, and had certainly advanced it further by some outstanding observations. This, I suggested, was the reason why our Fellows are of one mind in desiring that you should entrust to us here, as soon as possible, the illustrations with which you have elucidated that essay of yours, now reposing in our archive, that you formerly so generously sent to us; that is, if you mean to consent to our setting it before the learned world in the most elegant print we have.

And so, if it seems good to you to send us those diagrams relating to your *Anatomy of Plants* at the first safe opportunity, it can surely be so arranged that that very learned paper of yours will be in print before next winter. If they should arrive here in time it could be printed at the same time as your dissertation on the egg. But we are reluctant to deprive philosophers of those first class observations on the chick for too long a period. On this account we have handed them to the printer already, and we hope they will come out soon. Farewell, famous Sir, and be so good as to inform us speedily of your state of health, and of your decision upon this point. London, 8 June 1672.

ADDRESS

    To the very illustrious Mr. Marcello Malpighi,
    My very good lord,
    in Bologna

NOTE

1 See Letters 1969 and 1970.

1990
Oldenburg to Huygens

10 June 1672

From *Œuvres Complètes*, VII, 177–79
Original in the Huygens Collection at Leiden

A Londres ce 10 juin 1672

Monsieur,

Venant de recevoir une lettre de Monsieur Sluse,[1] dans laquelle vous estez interessé, ie n'ay pas voulu vous envoier l'annexe de mon journal du mois de Mars,[2] sans vous faire part de ce que cet excellent homme m'a communiqué: ce qui ie feray dans ses propres paroles;

"Leodii, 10. Junii, 1672. [N.S.] Ecce me iterum; sed ut ἀβλεψίαν duntaxat indicem, quae in postremas meas irrepsit . . .

Atquae haec est aequatio, quam magno ingenii acumine ac pari facilitate construxit Vir doctissimus, quod ut Tibi pluribus probem, opus non est, quando labore non multo rem ad calculos revocando id agnoscere poteris."

C'est le contenu de sa lettre du 10 juin, mais puis qu'elle regarde une autre sienne, qu'il m'a escrite seulement deux iours devant ascavoir le 8. juin sans laquelle l'autre ne se peut pas entendre, ie me trouve obligé de vous en extraire ce qui touche cet argument; qui est:

"Quae ad Alhazeni Problema meditatus fui hactenus, rudia licet et impolita, tui juris sunt . . .

Deinde, annon etiam iidem 4tuor casus occurrant, cum puncta data aequaliter distant a centro."

Voicy, Monsieur, les particularitez, que ie croiois vous devoir communiquer; que vous pourrez conferer avec ce que ie vous envoiay, il y a quelque temps, de la mesme personne, extrait de sa lettre du 6. cal. januar. 1672 [N.S.].[3] que vous m'avez assuré d'avoir receue par la vostre du 9. Avril 1672.[4] Je seray bien aise d'entendre, que celle-cy vous ait esté rendue, come aussi les autres, que ie vous ay escrits depuis vostre derniere. J'espere que vostre Traité des Pendules est soubs la presse; et il me tarde d'entendre le succes, que vos Essays ont eu touchant le nouveau Telescope de Monsieur Newton. Au reste, ie suis Monsieur

Vostre treshumble et tresobeissant serviteur

Oldenburg

ADDRESS

     A Monsieur
     Monsieur Christian Hugens de Zulichem
     dans la Bibliotheque du Roy à
         Paris

TRANSLATION

London, 10 June 1672

Sir,

Having just received a letter from Mr. Sluse[1] in which you were concerned I did not wish to send you (annexed) my journal for March[2] without sharing with you what this excellent man has communicated to me; which I do in his own words:

"Liège, 10 June 1672 [N.S.] . . ." [*The next two paragraphs are taken from Sluse's Letter 1985, above, pp. 81–82, where the English may be found.*]

This is the contents of his letter of 10 June, but since it concerns another of his which he wrote to me only two days before, that is on 8 June, without which the other cannot be understood, I find myself obliged to extract from it for you what bears on this argument, which is:

[*The next four paragraphs are taken from Sluse's Letter 1984, above, pp. 78–79, where the English may be found.*]

Here, Sir, are the particulars which I thought I ought to communicate to you, and which you can compare with what I sent to you some time ago from the same person, extracted from his letter of 27 December 1672 [N.S.];[3] you assured me by your letter of 9 April 1672 [N.S.] that you had received it.[4] I should be very glad to learn that this one has been delivered to you, and the others as well which I wrote since your last. I hope that your treatise on pendulums is in the press; I am anxious to hear the success which your trials of Mr. Newton's new telescope have had. For the rest I am, Sir,

Your very humble and obedient servant

Oldenburg

ADDRESS

     Mr. Christiaan Huygens of Zulichem,
       At the King's Library,
         Paris

NOTES

1 Letter 1985.
2 Read: May.
3 See Letter 1899, enclosing a copy of Letter 1843 (Vol. VIII).
4 Letter 1944 (Vol. VIII).

1991
Newton to Oldenburg

11 June 1672

Printed in Newton, *Correspondence*, I, 193, from the original in Royal Society MS. N 1,
no. 39

Writing by the post to Oldenburg's address in Pall Mall Newton informs him that he has sent his answers to Pardies (Letter 1992) and to Hooke (Letter 1993). He believes he has written nothing to which offence can be taken and declares his wish to give none. Probably the two "answers," being bulky, were sent together either by the Cambridge carrier or the hand of a friend. They bear no address. Oldenburg produced the answer to Hooke at the Royal Society's meeting on 12 June.

1992
Newton to Oldenburg for Pardies

10 or 11 June 1672

Printed in Newton, *Correspondence*, I, 163–71, from the original in Royal Society MS. N 1,
no. 40

The paper is dated both 10 and 11 June; for consistency's sake Oldenburg altered the opening date to read 11 June. Headed "Isaac Newton's reply to the letter of the reverend Father Ignatius Pardies," it addresses Oldenburg in the second person. Newton reiterates at some length his belief that he has discovered a new property of light (that is, dispersion, in modern terms) which is independent of hypotheses about the nature of light. He repeats the description of the *experimentum crucis* in detail, with a sketch.

1993
Newton to Oldenburg

11 June 1672

Printed in Newton, *Correspondence*, I, 171–88, from the original in CUL MS. Add. 3976, no. 10

The original was misdated by Oldenburg 11 July. It is not known why, or when, it returned into Newton's possession. In this rejoinder to Hooke's criticisms of his original statement of his discoveries in optics (Letter 1891 in Vol. VIII) Newton states again his position that the experimental facts he discovered are independent of any hypothesis about the nature of light and are indeed compatible with any mechanical hypothesis of light. But such a hypothesis must be false if it presupposes any physical modification of light by refraction, or if it supposes that sunlight can be composed only of two primitive colors (for natural white requires the complete spectrum range), and these views are confirmed by the *experimentum crucis* and other experiments. This letter was printed in *Phil. Trans.*, no. 88 (18 November 1672), 5084–5103.

1994
Sluse to Oldenburg

12 June 1672

From the original in Royal Society MS. S 1, no. 71
Printed in *Phil. Trans.*, no. 98 (17 November 1673), 6141–43, and in Boncompagni, pp. 661–63

Nobilissimo et Clarissimo Viro
D. Henrico Oldenburgo Regiae Societatis Secretario
Renatus Franciscus Slusius Salutem

Problematis Alhazeniani memoriam iamdudum abieceram, Vir Nobilissime, pigebat enim tamdiu eadem in quaestione haerere; sed literis tuis admonitus temperare mihi non potui, quin faciliorem eiusdem constructionem quaererem. Incidi autem nuper in sequentem, qua breviorem cum dari posse vix credam, committere nolui, quin eam iudicio ac censurae tuae submitterem. Sint igitur puncta data *EB*, circulus cuius centrum *A*: iunctis *EA*, *BA*, secantibus circulum in *F* et *C*, fiant tres proportionales *EA*, *FA*, *VA*, et tres iterum *BA*, *CA*, *XA*: tum iuncta *VX* ac producta utcumque, vertice *X*, latere transverso *VX*, ac recto ipso aequali, des-

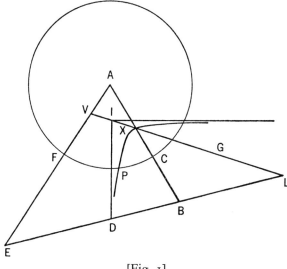

[Fig. 1]

cribatur hyperbola *XP*, cuius applicatae ad diametrum *VXG*, parallelae sint rectae *AB*: illa enim satisfaciet proposito in casu speculi convexi, ut eius opposita, in casu concavi. Si asymptotos desideres, facile reperiri possunt, producta *VX*, donec cum *EB* pariter producta concurrat in *L*, deinde bisecta *VX* in *I*, ac sumpta *LD*, aequali *LI*: iuncta enim *DI* erit asymptoton una, in quam alia normaliter incidit ad punctum *I*.

Sed fortasse tibi non erit ingratum intelligere, qua via ad hanc constructionem pervenerim: scias itaque, me ex priore mea Analysi deduxisse hoc modo.[1] Datis ijsdem quae prius, cadat in *EB* normalis *AO*, sitque punctum quaesitum *P*, ex quo in *AO* cadat normalis *PR*. Si *AO* sit *b*, *EO*, z, *OB*, *d*, *AP*, *q*, *PR*, *e*, *AR*, *a*, facile colligitur haec aequatio[2]

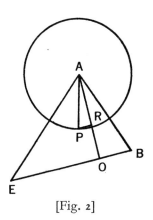

[Fig. 2]

$$\begin{array}{l} 2\zeta dae \\ +2bbae \\ -2bqqe \\ \hline \zeta b-bd \end{array} \quad + \quad ee \quad = \quad aa \quad - \quad \frac{qqa}{b},$$

quae mutari potest in has[3]

$$\begin{array}{l} \zeta dae \\ +bbae \\ -bqqe \\ \hline \zeta b-bd \end{array} \quad = \quad aa \quad - \quad \tfrac{1}{2}qq \qquad \frac{\tfrac{1}{2}qqa}{b}.$$

et

$$\begin{array}{l} \zeta dae \\ +bbae \\ -bqqe \\ \hline \zeta b-bd \end{array} \quad + \quad ee \quad = \quad \tfrac{1}{2}qq \quad - \quad \frac{\tfrac{1}{2}qqa}{b}$$

Huius ultimae constructionem olim ad te misi,[4] alterius vero Clarissimus Hugenius.[5] Primam autem, licet se statim in conspectum dedisset, ferme neglexeram, quod difficilioris constructionis esse praesumerem: Sed me vano timore delusum agnovi, cum in hanc, quam ad te mitto, constructionem desinere nuper sum expertus. Sit enim brevioris calculi causa, $\zeta-d = k$, $\zeta d+bb = bm$. fiet

$$ee - \frac{2qqe - 2mae}{k} = aa - \frac{qqa}{b}.$$

et additis utriumque

$$\frac{q^4 + mmaa - 2qqma}{kk}, \text{ erit}$$

$$ee - \frac{2qqe - 2mae}{k} + \frac{q^4 + mmaa - 2qqma}{kk},$$

hoc est, quadratum ex

$$e - \frac{qq - ma}{k},$$

aequale $aa - \dfrac{qqa}{b} + \dfrac{q^4 + mmaa - 2qqma}{kk}$. fiet igitur ἀναλογισμὸς

$$kk : kk + mm : aa - \frac{kkqqa}{bkk + bmm} + \frac{2qqma + q^4}{kk + mm} \text{ et quadratum } e - \frac{qq - ma}{k}.$$

qui ad aequationem faciliorem reduci potest, si posito $kk+mm = pp$ fiat $\dfrac{ky}{p} = a$; fit enim tandem, quadratum ex $e - \dfrac{qq}{k} + \dfrac{my}{p}$ aequale

$yy - \dfrac{qqky}{bp} - \dfrac{2qqmy}{kp} + \dfrac{q^4}{kk}$; quam aequationem constructioni superiori respondere animadvertes, si calculos applicueris;[6] ac simul observabis, ad quamcumque linearum *EA*, *AB*, *BE*, referatur Analyseos summa, easdem semper haberi posse sectiones, quamvis longiore circuitu et aequationibus valde diversis.

Ex hac constructione, κατὰ ἀναλογίαν deducere licet alterius Problematis effectionem, cum scilicet quaeritur punctum, a quo radius reflexus parallelus sit cuilibet lineae datae. Ut si dato puncto luminoso *B*, circulo ex centro *A*, quaereretur radius reflexus parallelus rectae *AE*. Idem

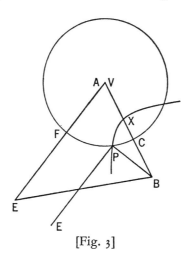

[Fig. 3]

enim est, ac si, in alio Problemate, distantia punctorum *A* et *E* supponeretur infinita; quo casu tertia proportionalis ipsarum *EA*, *FA*, abiret in nihilum, et puncta *A* et *V* coinciderent. itaque *VX* esset aequalis *AX*, et *AE* parallela *PE*. Applica igitur superiorem constructionem et Problema absolves: descripta scilicet (vertice *X*, latere transverso *VX*, vel *AX*, et recto ipsi aequali,) hyperbola *XP*, cuius applicatae ad diametrum *AX*, parallelae sint rectae *AE*: ἀλλὰ τούτων ἅλις. Vereor enim, ne ut olim silentium meum, ita nunc φλυαρίαν ac scribendi intemperiem incuses. Vale itaque Vir Nobilissime meque ut soles, tui observantissimum amare perge. Dabam Leodij XXII Junij MDCLXXII.

TRANSLATION

René François de Sluse greets the very famous and noble Mr. Henry Oldenburg, Secretary of the Royal Society

I had long put the memory of Alhazen's Problem behind me, most noble Sir, for it bored me to spend so long on the same topic; but stimulated by your letter I could not restrain myself from seeking a simpler construction of it. I have lately come across the following than which, I believe, none more direct can be found but I was unwilling to send it except in order to submit it to your judgment and criticism. Accordingly, let there be given points E, B, and a circle whose center is A; join AE, AB cutting the circle in F and C, construct three lines AE, AF, and AV in proportion, and again three more AB, AC, and AX [*see Fig. 1, p. 97*]. Then, having joined VX and extended it arbitrarily, with vertex X and transverse axis VX and latus rectum equal to it describe the hyperbola PX whose ordinates to the diameter VXG shall be parallel to AB. This will solve the problem in the case of the convex mirror, and its opposite branch in the case of the concave mirror. If you wish to know the asymptotes they can easily be found: produce VX until it meets EB likewise produced at L, then bisect VX at I and take [in EB] LD equal to LI. When joined DI will be one of the asymptotes which the other meets normally at I.

But perhaps it will not be unwelcome to you to learn how I attained this construction; so you may know that I derived it thus from my former analysis.[1] With the same things given as before, let the normal AO fall on EB and let P be the point sought for, from which let the normal PR fall on AO [*see Fig. 2, p. 97*]. If $AO = b$, $EO = z$, $OB = d$, $AP = q$, $PR = e$, $AR = a$ the following equation is easily formed:[2]

$$\frac{2adez + 2ab^2e - 2beq^2}{bz - bd} + e^2 = a^2 - \frac{aq^2}{b}$$

which may be changed into the following:[3]

$$\frac{adez + ab^2e - beq^2}{bz - bd} = a^2 - \tfrac{1}{2}q^2 - \frac{\tfrac{1}{2}aq^2}{b}; \text{ and}$$

$$\frac{adez + ab^2e - beq^2}{bz - bd} + e^2 = \tfrac{1}{2}q^2 + \frac{\tfrac{1}{2}aq^2}{b}.$$

I sent you the construction of this last equation some time ago,[4] and the famous Huygens [has given that] of the second.[5] Although the first equation had at once offered itself for examination I had quite neglected it because I presumed it to be more difficult to construct. But I have recognized that I was misled by my baseless timidity as I have learned recently, ending up with this construction that I send you. For the sake of brevity in calculation let $z - d = k$, and $dz + b^2 = bm$. There will then come to be

$$e^2 - \frac{2eq^2 - 2aem}{k} = a^2 - \frac{aq^2}{b}$$

By adding $\dfrac{q^4 + a^2m^2 - 2amq^2}{k^2}$ to each side, we make

$$e^2 - \frac{2eq^2 - 2aem}{k} + \frac{q^4 + a^2m^2 - 2amq^2}{k^2}, \text{ that is, } \left(e - \frac{q^2 - ma}{k}\right)^2,$$

equal to $a^2 - \dfrac{aq^2}{b} + \dfrac{q^4 + a^2m^2 - 2amq^2}{k^2}$. Expressed as a proportion, therefore,

$$k^2 : (k^2 + m^2) = \left(\frac{a^2 - ak^2q^2}{bk^2 + bm^2} + \frac{[-]2amq^2 + q^4}{k^2 + m^2}\right) : \left(e - \frac{q^2 - ma}{k}\right)^2.$$

This equation may be reduced to a simpler form if it is postulated that

$k^2 + m^2 = p^2$, and $\dfrac{ky}{p} = a$; for it then becomes

$$\left(e - \frac{q^2}{k} + \frac{my}{p}\right)^2 = y^2 - \frac{kq^2y}{bp} - \frac{2mq^2y}{kp} + \frac{q^4}{k^2}.$$ You will observe that this equation
agrees with the above construction by adducing [appropriate] calculation,[6] and you will simultaneously notice that the same [conic] sections may always be obtained, no matter which of the lines AE, AB, BE the pertinent analysis is referred to, although by a longer process and very different equations.

From this construction the solution of the other problem—that is, to find the point from which the ray is reflected parallel to any given line—may be deduced. For example, if the given source of light were B, the circle about center A, and the reflected ray parallel to the line AE be sought; this is the same as if, in the other problem, the distance of the points A and E were supposed infinite. In this case the third proportional to AE and AF would vanish into nothing and the points A and V coincide [*see Fig. 3, p. 99*]. Therefore VX will be equal to AX, and AE parallel to PE. Accordingly, apply the above construction and the problem is solved; that is to say, describe the hyperbola PX (with vertex X, transverse diameter VX or AX, and latus rectum equal to it), having its ordinates to the diameter AX perpendicular to AE. But this is fruitless. I fear that just as formerly you might blame my silence, now you may blame my folly and lack of proportion in writing. So farewell, most noble Sir, and as is your wont continue to love your most devoted. Liège, 22 June 1672 [N.S.].

NOTES

Third reply to Letter 1952.
1 See Letter 1843 (Vol. VIII).
2 From the condition that EP and BP make equal angles with AP.
3 By substituting $e^2 = q^2 - a^2$ and halving.
4 Though the allusion is hardly unambiguous, Sluse probably refers to Vol. VIII, Letter 1843. Compare also Vol. VII, Letters 1643 (first mention of "second thoughts,"

p. 483) and 1548. There are slight changes of notation between this present letter and Letter 1843.

5 See Vol. VIII, Letter 1944.
6 "The construction which results from this last hyperbolic equation, elaborated by Sluse in his following Letter 2100, is not in fact that described by him above. This was to cause Huygens much difficulty; in fact, in Letter 2066 he will query if there was not perhaps some error in the (faithful) transcript of the present passage passed on to him by Oldenburg as an enclosure to his Letter 2019. Sluse's preceding construction (evidently exactly equivalent to that which Huygens is about to communicate independently to Oldenburg in Letter 2004a) follows from his undoctored first equation by rewriting it in the form

$$\left(a + \frac{m+p}{k}e - \frac{q^2}{2b}\left(\frac{m+p}{p}\right) - \frac{q^2}{p}\right)\left(a + \frac{m-p}{k}e + \frac{q^2}{b}\left(\frac{m-p}{p}\right) + \frac{q^2}{p}\right)$$
$$= \left(\frac{q^2}{2b}\left(\frac{m+p}{p}\right) + \frac{q^2}{p}\right)^2 + \left(\frac{q^2}{2b}\left(\frac{m-p}{p}\right) + \frac{q^2}{p}\right)^2$$

which is the equation of a rectangular hyperbola $P(a, e)$ referred to origin $A(O, O)$, through which it passes, and having perpendicular asymptotes

$$\left(a + \frac{m}{k}e - \frac{q^2}{2b}\right) \pm \left(\frac{p}{k}e - \frac{mq^2}{2bp} - \frac{q^2}{p}\right) = O$$

meeting in the centre $I(a, e)$ where

$$a = \frac{(k^2 + 2bm)q^2}{2bp^2} = \frac{1}{2}\left(\frac{bq^2}{b^2 + d^2} + \frac{bq^2}{b^2 + z^2}\right)$$

and $e = \dfrac{(2b^2 - bm)kq^2}{2b^2p^2} = \dfrac{1}{2}\left(\dfrac{dq^2}{b^2 + d^2} - \dfrac{zq^2}{b^2 + z^2}\right).$

Evidently I is the mid-point of

$$V\left(\frac{bq^2}{b^2 + d^2}, \frac{dq^2}{b^2 + d^2}\right) \text{ and } X\left(\frac{bq^2}{b^2 + z^2}, \frac{-zq^2}{b^2 + z^2}\right),$$

while, since

$$2 \tan^{-1}\frac{p \pm m}{k} = \mp \tan^{-1}\frac{k}{m}$$

the asymptotes $a + \dfrac{m+p}{k}e - \dfrac{q^2}{2b}\left(\dfrac{\pm m+p}{p} \mp \dfrac{q^2}{p}\right) = O$

are equally inclined to

$$VX\left(a + \frac{m}{k}e - \frac{q^2}{2b} = O\right) \text{ and } EB\,(a = b).$$

That V and X lie in the hyperbola may be shown, somewhat cumbrously, by direct substitution of their coordinates in its equation. No wonder that Huygens, even "having reduced it to a very simple case," could not find "a good way out of the calculation" (Letter 2066)!" (D.T.W.)

1995
Cassini to Oldenburg

12 June 1672

From the original in Royal Society MS. C 1, no. 55

Clarissimo Viro
D. Henrico Oldemburg regiae societatis a secretis
Jo. Domenicus Cassinus S.

Regiae societati immortales gratias ago, quod me in Sodalium suorum album cooptavit, tantoque munere suam in me voluntatem volueris testari.

Omnibus enitar viribus, ut me tam illustri caetu dignum exhibeam, eiusque instituto rem literariam coniunctis studijs promovendi deserviam. Qua in re spero fore ut eius consilijs monitisque proficiam. Cum autem tu saepius, Vir Clarissime, me illius nomine hortatus fueris ut Ephemerides Jovialium Comitum continuarem, quid in hunc finem praestiterim adiunctis hic folijs reponam.[1] Videre hic erit in quas me angustias studium meas observationes cum Gallilei observationibus conciliandi coniecerit, quidque illius auctoritati, quid pactae ex me evidentiae tribuere mihi visum sit.[2] Qua in re modum ne videar servasse, libenter ex vobis intelligerem. Te etiam atque etiam oro, ut quae mihi ceu in Socios relato facienda erunt indigites, atque ut interim meo nomine Illustrissimo Praesidi Consiliarijs socijsque omnibus nobillissimis gratias agas, meumque in omnes et singulos studium obsequiumque testeris. Vale.
Parisijs die 22. Junij 1672 [N.S.]

TRANSLATION

Gio. Domenico Cassini greets the very famous Mr. Henry Oldenburg, Secretary of the Royal Society

I offer everlasting thanks to the Royal Society for electing me into its Fellowship, and because you have sought to manifest its cordial feeling towards me by so great an honor.

I shall strive with all my might to prove myself worthy of so illustrious a company and to devote myself to its object of advancing learning by joint researches.

Accordingly I hope to advance its plans and instructions. However, as you have quite often exhorted me in its name, famous Sir, to press on with the ephemerides of Jupiter's satellites, I make some recompense on the annexed pages with what I have accomplished to this end.[1] Here the Society will see into what perplexities my investigations have driven me for the sake of reconciling my observations with those of Galileo, and where it has seemed proper to me to rely upon his authority and where to rely on the evidence accumulated by myself.[2] I would willingly learn from you where I have failed to maintain a due standard of proportion in this matter. I beg you again and again both to let me know what it is proper for me to do as one elected into the Fellowship, and meanwhile to return thanks on my behalf to the very illustrious President, Councillors, and all the most noble Fellows, as also to assure them of my zeal and humble service towards one and all. Farewell.

Paris, 22 June 1672 [N.S.]

NOTES

Reply to Letter 1982.

1 On 26 June, when this letter was read, the accompanying "written paper of two sheets in folio, giving an account of his endeavour for settling an hypothesis of the motion of Jupiter and his satellites" was given to Hooke for consideration; on 10 July Hooke reported very favorably on it (Birch, *History*, III, 56, 57). We have not found this paper, which was later communicated to both Richard Towneley and Flamsteed; see below.

2 This sentence is by no means easy to understand.

1996
Oldenburg to Swammerdam

13 June 1672

From the draft in Royal Society MS. O 2, no. 86

Clarissimo Expertissimoque Anatomico et Medico
Domino Johanni Swammerdam
H. Oldenburg Salutem

Insigne munus tuum, Vir Clarissime, Societati Regiae, caetum publicum celebranti; lubentissime exhibui.[1] Eo magis Illa te aestimat amatque, quod difficillimo hoc tempore quo Mars gravis utrique Genti incubat,

atque Anglorum inter et Belgarum animos divortium internecinum moli-
tur, Tu cordate adeo commercium tueri philosophicum, quinimo gratissimo nos munere locupletare non dubitas. Id equidem viros candidos et
vere philosophos decet, dum scilicet Mundi Principes de Meo et Tuo
digladiantur, in Naturae adytis pacate scrutandis, veritatisque ac scientiarum finibus summo studio proferendis perdurare.

Dum Genti nostrae gloriam illam tribuis, quod, uti Christianus Orbis
non parva Religionis suae incrementa ipsi debet, ita novissimis his temporibus inita apud eam sit ratio, missis inanibus Scholasticorum disputationi-
bus utiles scientias et artes in solido locandi,[2] id sane facis, quod calcar
urgentissimum currentibus addit, institutum suum animose consectandi,
ita quidem ut intelligat aliquando eruditus Orbis, Societatem hanc, ab
Augustissimo Rege nostro conditam, non incassum plane laborasse, vel
conceptam de se Philosophorum spem elusisse.

Tu interim, Vir Doctissime, studia tua Anatomica eo quo caepisti pede
prosequi ne desinas, nec de propensissima Regiae Societatis nostrae erga
Te voluntate ullatenus dubites. Commisit illa libellum tuum Medicis
quibusdam e Caetu suo praestantissimis, qui eum evolvant et expendant,
suamque de eo sententiam Ipsi exponant: quod factum cum fuerit, officii
mei duxero, de re tota Claritatem tuam quantocius edocere. Vale, et me
Tibi addictissimum crede. Dabam Londini d. 13 junii 1672.

TRANSLATION

H. Oldenburg greets the very famous and skilful anatomist and physician,
Mr. Jan Swammerdam

I very willingly presented your handsome gift, famous Sir, to the Royal Society
at its ordinary meeting.[1] It thinks the more highly and warmly of you because
you so eagerly maintain a scientific correspondence and indeed do not hesitate to
furnish us with a very welcome present, in this very difficult period when the
weight of war lies heavy on both our peoples and tends to bring about a baleful
separation between the minds of Englishmen and Dutchmen. It is indeed proper
that honest and true philosophers should, while the princes of the world contend
fiercely over questions of *mine* and *thine*, persist in the peaceful search into nature's
secrets and in advancing with utmost zeal the limits of truth and knowledge.

When you say that our nation is distinguished not only because Christendom
owes to it no slight advancement of its religion, but because in recent times there
was begun among its people the method of setting aside the empty disputations
of the Schoolmen and placing the useful arts and sciences on a solid basis,[2] you

utter words that indeed give a further sharp spur to our eager course in pursuing our purpose with determination, so that at some time the learned world may surely learn that this Society, founded by our august King, has not labored quite in vain or been mistaken in the ideal of philosophers that it had cherished.

Do not you meanwhile, most learned Sir, fail in developing those studies in anatomy that you have begun, nor doubt in any manner of the very great goodwill towards you of our Royal Society. It has entrusted your little volume to some of the most outstanding physicians of its number who are studying and weighing it, and will express their judgment of it to the Society. When that has been done I shall make it my business to inform your excellency of the whole as soon as possible. Farewell, and believe me most devoted to yourself. London, 13 June 1672.

NOTES

This is Oldenburg's reply to Swammerdam's letter of 14 June [N.S.] to the Royal Society accompanying his presentation copy of *Miraculum naturae, sive uteri muliebris fabrica* (Leiden, 1672)—compare Letter 1938, note 2 (Vol. VIII).

1 Oldenburg had presented the book to the Royal Society on the previous day, 12 June.
2 In his review of Swammerdam's book in *Phil. Trans.*, no. 84 (17 June 1672), 4098–5001 Oldenburg quotes the relevant passage from Swammerdam's letter (translating from the Latin): "I am not unaware how fate has brought it about that, just as Christendom owes no slight advancement of its religion to the English people, so in these recent very difficult times there was discovered among it the method of setting aside the empty disputations of the Schoolmen and placing the useful arts and sciences on a solid basis: And as this is not the least part of Britain's glory, so it is the reason why no one dares, or ought to dare, to resort in matters of natural philosophy to any other tribunal than the Royal Society."

1997
Oldenburg to Magalotti
13 June 1672
From the draft in Royal Society MS. O 2, no. 87

Nobilissimo et doctissimo Viro
Domino Laurentio Magalotti
H. Oldenburg Salutem

Mirabuntur Amici tui Angli, Vir Nobilissime, dum Te lingua sua concinne adeo sermocinantem intelligerent. Inferebant inde, Te, tanta licet locorum intercapedine a nobis sejunctum, mentem tamen, quam coram testabaris nostri studiosissimam, eandem plane et invariatam gerere. Rem omnino gratam nobis praestas, quod quae curiosa per sagacissimam Italiam vestram occurrunt, per occasionem nobis impertiri dignaris. Exemplum, monticolae vestro cornigero geminum, nobis praebuit nobis nostra Cestria, ubi, a simili qualem Clarissimus vester Gornia exposuit causa, in vetulae cuiusdam occipite cornu excrevit, resectumque aliquoties repullulavit. Lampadem Venetiis excogitatam vix comprobabit usus; cum (ut alia ejus incommoda sileam) verisimile plane non sit, spiritum vini, in fumum et halitus vi flammae conversum, in liquorem inflammabilem post-liminio unquam reversurum. Et hoc ipso tempore, quo haec scribo, illustris Boylius noster ab Experimentis certum se esse mihi affirmat reciprocam illam conversionem praestari a se nequaquam potuisse.

Venetiis acceperamus, nuperum illum in Italia Terrae motum, quae luctuosam adeo stragem Arimini et circa universam maris Adriatici oram edidit, Florentiam quoque vestram concussisse.[1] Magnopere gaudemus, et hic (ut ferme semper) majorem vere famam esse, cum sine dubio non celassent nos literae tuae, si ad terras etiam vestras malum pervasisset. Si forte integra hujus rei historia ex virorum solertium observatis concinnata apud vos prodeat, ut eam nobis communicare non graveris, enixe rogamus. Quanquam pectus adeo generosum Te gerere testaris ut redhostimentum pro novis curiosis, a Te mihi transmissis, non exspectes, volenti tamen nolenti Nonnulla eorum quae inter nos geruntur, obtrudam.

Exhibuit non ita pridem Societati Regiae Dominus Newtonus Mathematum in Academia Cantabrigiensi Professor, et societatis dictae sodalis, novam suam de Lumine et Coloribus Theoriam, qua docet, Lumen esse crama Heterogeneum ex radiis diversimode refrangibilibus constans; vel componi illud ex infinitorum propemodum radiorum aggregatione, qui suapte natura, citra ullum ad eorum incidentiae differentiam respectum, suum quisque colorem referant et retineant. adeoque apti nati sint certa quadam et peculiari ratione, plus alii, alii minus refringi: Radios ejusmodi, dum promiscui in aperto lumine confunduntur, nullatenus discerni, sed candorem potius prae se ferre; in Refractione vero singulos unius coloris ab aliis alterius coloris secerni, atque hac ratione secretos sub proprio et nativo colore apparere: Ea corpora sub aliquo colore, v.g. rubro, spectari, quae apta sint reflectere aut transmittere radios solummodo rubros, alia sub colore viridi, quae virides, &c.

Haec doctrina una cum Experimentis, quibus nititur, Transactionibus Philosophicis No. 80, inserta est, quas, ni fasciculi timenda esset crassities, lubentissime ad Te transmitterem. Ingenium suum in eam exercuit Dominus

Gaston Pardies, Mathematum in Collegio Claremontano Parisiensi Professor; cujus Objectionibus ita videtur respondisse Newtonus, ut jam acquiescat Objector, suamque ἀβλεψίαν insigni candore agnoscat.

Nobilissimus Boylius, Diatribam nuperrime edidit, de Gemmarum Origine et Viribus egregie, pro more suo, philosophantem.[2] Paratam quoque habet Experimentalem de Corporum Effluviis, aliamque de Aeris et Flammae cognatione Dissertationem.[3] Porro, paucis ab hinc retro septimanis, hic prodiere Domini Willisii De Brutorum Anima Exercitationes duae; quarum prior Physiologica, Ipsius naturam, partes, potentias et affectiones tradit; altera Pathologica, morbos, ipsam, et sedem ejus primariam, cerebrum nempe et nervosum genus, afficientes, explicat, eorumque Therapeias instituit. Opus hoc Iconismis illustratur elegantissimis rarissimisque, Cerebrum, Ostreas, Astacos, et Lumbricos spectantibus. Nec praeterire mihi fas fuerit Domini Grewi de Plantarum Anatome Tractatum, nuper quoque in lucem emissum, ubi multa nova et egregia circa id argumentum panduntur, a quibus insignis Vester Malpighius non abludit.

Sed vereor, Amice Illustrissime, ne prolixitate mea Te obtundam, vel negotia tua graviora diu nimis sufflaminem. Alia occasione, dante Deo, plura. Hoc duntaxat adjiciam, aegerrime me ferre, aditum ad Te mihi non patere, quoties libet aut fert occasio. Si fieri commode posset, ut Oratoris Florentini, Magni Ducis nomine Lutetiae Parisiorum agentis, beneficio, literae et res nostrae philosophicae tuto possent citroque tuto commeare, frequentius equidem commercium hoc litterarium celebrarem. Tu, Vir Praestantissime, si quid hac in re vales (valere autem Te plurimum, putem) mihi indicare proximis tuis meminicris. Intcrim Vale, et me Tuum ex asse crede. Dabam Londini d. 13. junii 1672.

TRANSLATION

H. Oldenburg greets the very noble and learned Mr. Lorenzo Magalotti

Your English friends are astonished, most noble Sir, to find you discoursing so elegantly in their language. They gather from this that, though separated from us by the distance of geography, you still maintain quite unchanged that same spirit which when here among us you showed to be most cordial to us. You do something most welcome to us when you are so good as to impart to us, from time to time, those matters of interest that occur among you wise Italians.

Our city of Chester furnished us with a case exactly similar to that of your horn-bearing mountain-dweller; there, from a cause like that explained by your famous Dr. Gornia, a horn grew on the head of a little old woman, and when cut

away several times it has grown again. Practice will hardly approve the lamp
invented in Venice, since (to say nothing of other defects in it) it is not at all
probable that alcohol when converted into smoke and vapor by the flame will ever
revert to its former state of being an inflammable fluid. And at this very moment
as I am writing to you our illustrious Mr. Boyle assures me that he is certain upon
the basis of experiments that he himself could never effect such a reciprocal con-
version.

We have heard from Venice that the recent earthquake in Italy which caused
such dreadful loss of life at Rimini and on the neighboring Adriatic coast also
shook your city of Florence.[1] We shall be very glad if in this instance rumor
outruns truth, as it nearly always does, as surely your letter would not have kept
the truth from us, if the disaster had struck your region. If perchance the whole
history of this incident put together from the observations of careful witnesses
should be circulated among you, we earnestly beg you to communicate it to us.
Although you display so generous an intention as to seek no recompense for the
fresh curiosities you sent me, still willy-nilly I must thrust in some account of our
doings.

Not long ago Mr. Newton, Professor of Mathematics at the University of
Cambridge and a Fellow of the Royal Society, laid before the Society his new
theory of light and colors, in which he maintains that light is a heterogeneous
mixture consisting of variously refrangible rays, or composed of an aggregation
of an almost infinite number of rays, each of them according to its nature carrying
and retaining its own color without any respect to the difference in their incidence.
And so some are fitted to be refracted more, others less, in a fixed and individual
ratio. Rays of this sort, when randomly mingled in daylight, are quite impercept-
ible, but rather show themselves as white; but in refraction those of one color are
separated from those of another and in this way the hidden rays appear in their
own natural colors. Those bodies appear of some certain color, for example red,
which are suited to reflect or transmit only the red rays; other bodies appear green
which [reflect or transmit] the green rays, etc.

This theory is inserted in the *Philosophical Transactions*, no. 80, along with the
experiments with which it is adorned; I would gladly send this issue to you, did I
not fear the size of the package. Mr. Gaston Pardies, Professor of Mathematics in
the College of Claremont at Paris, has engaged his ingenious mind upon this
theory; to his objections Newton, it seems, has replied in such a way that the
objector now yields, and with unusual straightforwardness admits his mistake.

The very noble Boyle has very recently published an essay philosophizing in
his usual excellent style on the origin and virtues of gems.[2] He has also made ready
an experimental discourse on the effluvia of bodies and another on the relation
between air and flame.[3] Moreover Dr. Willis's two essays *De anima brutorum*
appeared here a few weeks ago, the first of which, being physiological, discusses
its nature, parts, powers, and attributes; the other, being pathological, explains

the diseases affecting [the psyche] and its principal seat, that is, the brain and nervous system, and sets up a therapy for them. This work is illustrated with beautiful and very extraordinary figures of the brain, oysters, maggots, and worms. Nor would it be right for me to pass over Mr. Grew's treatise on the anatomy of plants, which has also come out recently, which contains many new and interesting things on this topic, which your outstanding fellow-countryman Malpighi does not dissent from.

But I fear you may be stunned by my prolixity, most illustrious friend, or that I interrupt your more serious business for too long. God willing I will write more another time. Only this I will add, that I am very sorry that I cannot have access to you as often as I wish or opportunity offers. If it could conveniently be arranged for our letters and other philosophical concerns to pass to and fro safely and quickly by the agency of the Florentine Ambassador serving the Grand Duke at Paris, I should conduct this correspondence with greater frequency. If you, excellent Sir, can accomplish anything in this regard (for you are capable of many things, I think) remember to let me know in your next letter. Meanwhile farewell, and believe me wholly yours. London, 13 June 1672.

NOTES

Reply to Letter 1975; Oldenburg has noted on the draft: "The letter to which this is a reply is missing."
1 Compare Letter 1953 where, however, Dodington does not mention Florence as suffering from the earthquake.
2 See Letter 1963, note 5.
3 Robert Boyle, *Essays of . . . Effluviums* (London, 1673); *Tracts . . . containing new experiments, touching the relation betwixt Flame and Air* (London and Oxford, 1672).

1998
Flamsteed to Oldenburg
30 May/15 June 1672
From the original in Royal Society MS. F 1, no. 86

Derby May 30 : 1672 :

Mr Oldenburge
Sr

Tis now almost 3 moneths since I have reaceaved any thing from yu.[1] your last required an account of what I had wrote to yu in a letter yt miscarried:[2] which I gave yu soone after, & in it yu promised some communications, which tho mine may not have merited, yet I expected of yr goodnesse & hope if yu have leasure you will not long deteine from mee. In one of my last to Mr Collins[3] I gave him my thoughts of Mr Newtons new theorie of light & Colours with a request to let yu know them. hee informes mee ye like objections have beene made by Mr. Hooke & ye Pere Pardiez, & answered by Mr Newton which induced mee to forbeare prosecuteing my designed objections till I had seene theres which hee intimated I might expect in ye transactions but our booksellers Chapman has faild him of them since Februarys so that I have yet seene nothing of Mr Newtons answers which I much desire to heare of.[4] I have this moneth observed ye distance of Mars from a fixed star in Aquarius, & Jupiters returne to ye star in Virginis 9° 58′: of which I want leasure to give you an account for I made in my last observations of him but on Moonday & tuesday nights. and now am busied in transcribeing ye Numbers I have made for Mr Horrox his lunar theory which will much better satisfie those diameters of ye moone which I have observed then any other can doe.[5] these I promised Mr Collins should be ready to print with his workes. & shall send them him either this next week or ye following. afterwards, if I may heare from yu betwixt, yu shall have my late observations of Jupiter & Mars[6] in ye first of which I find ye error of our tables not lesse then I intimated in my last to yu.[7] Hugenius his Systema[8] I returne yu by ye bearer, & thankes for ye use of it, desireing yu would please at yr leasure wth ye promised communications to satisfie ye curiosity of Sr

Yr much obliged servant
John Flamsteed

this letter was deteined till now because I could not then send the booke.[9] this night I intend to observe ye transit of Mars by two fixed stars but I feare ye heavens will scarce permit the day is so cloudy. however if I may understand yt my observations can pleasure yu I shall send them in my next. Yrs

J F

Junij 15. 1672.

ADDRESS

For Henry Oldenburg
Esqr at his house in the
middle of ye Pell mell
in Westminster these
        present

NOTES

1 Oldenburg's last letter to Flamsteed known to us was dated 16 February (Letter 1901, Vol. VIII).

2 See Letters 1945 and 1918, note 1 (Vol. VIII).

3 Written on 17 April; see Rigaud, II, 133–37. Flamsteed did not find Newton's paper convincing. It seems possible that the frequency of Flamsteed's correspondence with Collins was the reason why Oldenburg had rather let him drop.

4 See Letters 1992 and 1993.

5 See Letter 1906, note 3 (Vol. VIII). There is much evidence of Flamsteed's lively interest in the editing of Horrox's *Opera posthuma* in his letters to Collins from the end of 1670 onwards; he settled down to work seriously on Horrox's lunar theory—determining parameters and calculating tables from his own lunar observations—in April 1672 (Rigaud, II, 133). It was Wallis who was most eager to secure Flamsteed's participation. Equally, Flamsteed was delighted to discover that Horrox's theory could give results according closely with his observations: "which convinced me that Bullialdus's, Wing's, and Street's theories were erroneous, and Horrox's near the truth." (Autobiography: Baily, p. 31). Flamsteed completed work on lunar tables to be published with Horrox's papers on 12 June (Rigaud, II, 148; it should be noted that the correspondence in Rigaud is at this point misdated and out of true order).

6 See Letter 2025 of 15 July.

7 See Letter 1945.

8 *Systema Saturnium*, lent by Oldenburg to Flamsteed early in March.

9 The carrier was delayed, and Flamsteed's activities suspended by the death of his uncle; he sent a message to Oldenburg about the delay through Collins on 12 June (Rigaud, II, 151).

1999
Kirkby to Oldenburg

15 June 1672

From the original in Royal Society MS. K, no. 10

Dantzigk 25th June 72

Honored Sr

After a tedious passage by sea yours [of] 18th March is at Last come to hand since the writeing whereof I hope you have received mine [of] 23th Aprill[1] giveing Covert to 100 Experiments of Doctor Conradts about colde: Monsieur Hevelius hath desired mee of Late to send you two small packets (of his printed Letters to you about the Late Comett)[2] The first packett was Sent by The Elephant of Dantzigk Edwardt Brandt Schipper; and I gave mr Lee espetiall order to take care it was conveyed to your hand; god sending the ship arrive well; which Monsieur Hevelius feareing another packett is sent by the St John of Dantzigk Peter Marquart Schipper; both are addressed to yrselfe by a Latine Inscription; & Mr Hevelius desires if the first packett miscarry yt some of the second may bee sent for france, as I suppose hee will himself have written; hee hath received the glasses from Monsr Boretini for a Telescope, of above 100 foote Long but hath not yett had an oppertunity to try it: The to be Desired Method of contracting them you have communicated to him;[3] hee would gladly have illustrated by a moddel and further Direction's where & at what Distance the Speculum's must bee placed in stead of which glasses ground after the same manner might in the Middle bee placed; & this his request proceeds from his want of time to make many tryalls himselfe; which hee judges hee must doe without this helpe. According to your Description of Sr Samuell MoreLand's Loude Speakeing Trumpett in ye Phil. transactions;[4] hee must have writt a treatise about it which I could wish for with a Diagram of The Trumpett it selfe;[5] I am resolved to adventure a tryall here; I am sorry you could procure mee Noe glass plates that I might encourage the poore man here, if [it] can bee yet effected pray Lett [it] bee done Mr Lee will againe pay what you May disburse for them; I perceive by the Phil Tran: that Bechers phisica subterranea & his supplementum are come to your hands:[6] I wish the promised Experiments might follow; Some considerable ones hinted at by this his first part have beene tryed here Not without Success & that chapter about fermentation is not despicable; The colde season wee have had thus Long hath hindered that I have not yett beene to gett some of that poisonous water I have formerly mentioned to you;[7] but god willing I intend thither as soone as wee have had any Hott & drij weather: Sr I Beg yr pardon for troubleing with Long Letters & entreate you present my humble service to Mr Boyle and to accept of the like from

your affectionate friend at Comand
Chri Kirkby

This I inclosed pray give address.

ADDRESS

A Monsieur
Monsieur Grubendol
presentement
a
Londres

Franco Anvers[8]

NOTES

1 Letter 1954.
2 Compare Letter 1986.
3 That is, Newton's invention of the reflecting telescope.
4 In *Phil. Trans.*, no. 79 (22 January 1671/2), 3056–58.
5 This is, of course, Samuel Morland, *Tuba stentoro-phonica* (London, 1671).
6 The allusion here is to the review of J. J. Becher, *Experimentum chymicum novum* (Frankfurt, 1671), the "supplement" to his *Physica subterranea* (Frankfurt, 1669) in *Phil. Trans.*, no. 74 (14 August 1671), 2232–35.
7 See Letter 1838 (Vol. VIII).
8 "To Mr. Grubendol, promptly, at London. Franked to Antwerp."

2000
Oldenburg to Pardies

17 June 1672

From the memorandum in Royal Society MS. P 1, no. 80

Rec. le 15 juin 1672.
 Resp. le 17 juin.

If they will take considerable books, as Wallis and Barrow late Books, Barrows Conicks going to be printed, and Horroxes Astronom. he needs not to doubt of taking of a competent number.[1] We doubt not, but we shall take off a matter of 30. in ready mony, if we have them a little before the stationers receive ym. We doubt not but an hundred more in barter.

We want a honest one, for ye bartering of books; you will doe yrself and us a kindness, to find out an Agent for bartering of books, we will find out one here; wch would much befriend us both.

NOTES

Reply to Letter 1988.
1 This answers Pardies's suggestion that English booksellers should undertake to buy a number of copies (in sheets, obviously) of the proposed posthumous edition of La Loubère's geometrical writings. The books of Wallis and Barrow have been many times mentioned before; as yet unpublished were Barrow's "Conicks" (see Vol. VIII, Letter 1906, note 4) and Horrox's *Opera posthuma*.

2001
Newton to Oldenburg

19 June 1672

Printed in Newton, *Correspondence* I, 194, from the original in private possession

Writing from his family home at Woolsthorpe, Lincolnshire, Newton thanks Oldenburg for sending him (possibly with Letter 1987) copies of *Phil. Trans.*, no 83 (20 May 1672) containing his replies to various suggestions and criticisms concerning his optical discoveries. Newton notes a couple of errors in the printing, and desires that "you would not yet print any thing more concerning the Theory of light before it hath been more fully weighed."

2002

Oldenburg to Newton

20 June 1672

Mentioned in Oldenburg's Letter 2012.

2003

Oldenburg to Thomas Henshaw

20 June 1672

Mentioned in Henshaw's reply, Letter 2015, as having arrived on 5 July.

Thomas Henshaw (1618–1700), an Original Fellow of the Royal Society like his younger brother Nathaniel, was educated in law. He took the Royalist side in the Civil Wars and went into exile early, travelling extensively and entering into the French King's service. He returned to England in 1654 and was rewarded at the Restoration by court appointments which included that of French undersecretary, a post he held later under James II and William III. In 1672 he went to Denmark as secretary to the English Embassy and assistant to the Ambassador, the Duke of Richmond; upon the Ambassador's death at the end of the year Henshaw was appointed envoy extraordinary.

2004

Huygens to Oldenburg

21 June 1672

From the original in Royal Society MS. H 1, no. 73
Printed in *Œuvres Complètes*, VII, 185–87

A Paris ce 1er Juillet 1672 [N.S.]

Monsieur

Je vous rends graces treshumbles de la continuation de l'envoi de vos Transactions dont les dernieres sont celles du mois de May. J'avois priè Mr. Vernon de me procurer tout le volume, et encor quelques autres livres, mais je n'ay pas encore eu de ses nouvelles. J'ay vu avec plaisir ce

que vous avez pris la peine de me communiquer des dernieres lettres de
Mr. Sluse sçavoir son approbation et ses doctes remarques touchant la
construction du probleme d'Alhazen, sur le quel il me semble que nous
rafinons de mesme que les deux peintres Grecs sur la division de la ligne.[1]
Vous verrez ici[2] mon dernier calcul, different de celuy de ce scavant geo-
metre, et qui mene naturellement a la bonne construction que je vous ay
envoyée cydevant. Il est vray, et mesme admirable, qu'elle se trouve aussi
par le calcul qu'il en a fait apres le changement de qq en $aa+ee$, mais cela
semble casuel, et la simplicitè de la construction n'y paroit pas, qu'apres
qu'on s'est donnè la peine de la faire.

Vous aurez vu dans le dernier Journal des Scavants, mon sentiment
touchant la lunette du Sr. Cassegrain[3] car c'est moy qui ay donnè les
remarques que vous y voiez, mais elles estoient plus succinctes. Mr. Newton le traite plus doucement qu'il ne merite a mon avis,[4] parce qu'outre
que ce n'est pas son invention, c'est une temeritè de vouloir encherir sur
les inventions d'autruy qui sont eprouvees par d'autres que ne le sont point.
Au reste pour ce qui est des lunettes de Mr. Newton il devroit, ce me semble, luy mesme tascher de les perfectionner et d'en faire de plus grand volume que celles de 7 ou 8 pouces. Je vous ay mandè des le commencement[5]
que j'en esperois de grands effects pourvu qu'on trouvast de la matiere qui
fut capable d'un beau poli comme celuy du verre, et que l'on pust donner ce
poli sans alterer la figure des miroirs. J'ay encore peur que ce ne soit la le
grand obstacle, parce que dans les essais que j'ay fait dernierement, j'ay
trouvè cette matiere de fonte incomparablement plus molle que celle du
verre. ce qui paroit en ce que le dernier poli des miroirs concaves, que je
n'ay sçeu donner qu'en me servant de quelque chose de mol, comme sont le
linge ou le cuir, a gastè visiblement la perfection de la figure spherique, qui
faisoit desia auparavant une reflexion tres reguliere, mais obscure. J'avois
donnè la figure et le douci en frottant deux miroirs de mesme matiere l'un
sur l'autre, et puis j'y appliquay du linge entre deux avec de la pottee
d'estain, et cependant je trouvay que cette maniere de polir gastoit de plus
en plus la parfaite sphericitè. Vous m'obligerez de me mander ou en est
Mr. Newton luy mesme ou d'autres qui ont entrepris ce travail. Mon
miroir estoit de 12 pieds de foier, mais seulement de 4 pouces de diametre.

Pour ce qui est de sa nouvelle hypothese des couleurs dont vous sou-
haittez scavoir mon sentiment, j'avoue que jusqu'icy elle me paroit tres
vraisemblable, et l'experimentum crucis (si je l'entens bien, car il est ecrit
un peu obscurement) la confirme beaucoup. Mais sur ce qu'il dit de l'abberration des rayons a travers des verres convexes je ne suis pas de son

avis. Car je trouvay en lisant son escrit que cette aberration suivant son principe devroit estre double de ce qu'il la fait scavoir $\frac{1}{25}$ de l'ouverture du verre, a quoy pourtant l'expérience semble repugner. de sorte que peut estre cette aberration n'est pas tousjours proportionelle aux angles d'inclinaison des rayons.[6]

Si vous avez dessein de publier quelque chose de ce que je vous ay envoiè sur le Probleme de cy dessus illa tui juris facio, de mesme que Mr. Sluse, et en finissant icy je demeure, Monsieur

Vostre treshumble et tresobeissant serviteur

Hugens de Zulichem

ADDRESS

    A Monsieur

    Monsieur Grubendol

        A

            Londres

TRANSLATION

Paris, 1 July 1672 [N.S.]

    Sir,

I send you very humble thanks for continuing to send me your *Transactions*, the latest of which are those for May. I have asked Mr. Vernon to obtain the whole volume for me and some other books besides, but I have not as yet had any news from him. I have read with pleasure what you have taken the trouble to communicate to me of the latest letters of Mr. Sluse, that is his approval and his learned remarks about the construction of Alhazen's problem, on which subject it seems to me that we are discussing refinements just like the two Greek painters over the division of a line.[1] You will see here[2] my latest calculation, different from that of the learned geometer, which leads on naturally to the better construction which I sent formerly. It is true, and even wonderful, that it can be found as well by the calculation which he made after changing qq into $aa+ee$, but that seems accidental and the simplicity of the construction does not appear until one has taken the trouble to carry it out.

You must have seen my opinion of Mr. Cassegrain's telescope in the last *Journal des Sçavans*,[3] for it was I who made the remarks you see there, but they were more succinct. Mr. Newton treats him more gently than he deserves in my opinion,[4] because aside from the fact that it is not his invention, it is rash to seek to outdo the proven inventions of others with ones which are not proven. For the rest, touching Mr. Newton's telescopes, he ought, it seems to me, to try to perfect them himself and to make them bigger in size than those of seven or eight inches.

I told you from the beginning[5] that I had hopes of great results provided that a material could be found which would be capable of [taking] a good polish like that of glass, and that this polish could be given without altering the figure of the mirrors. I still fear that this may be the great hindrance because in the trials I have made lately I have found this cast bronze material incomparably softer than glass. Which shows in the fact that the final polish of the concave mirrors, which I did not know how to give except by using something soft like linen or leather, visibly spoiled the perfection of the spherical figure which just before had given a very regular although dark reflection. I had obtained the figure and smoothed it by rubbing together two mirrors of the same material, and then I applied linen between the two with some tin putty and nevertheless found that this method of polishing spoiled the perfect sphericity more and more. You will oblige me by telling me where Mr. Newton himself stands, or others who have undertaken this work. My mirror had a focal length of twelve feet but was only four inches in diameter.

As for his new hypothesis of colors of which you wanted to know my opinion, I confess that up to now it has seemed very probable to me, and the *experimentum crucis* (if I understand it aright, for he has written a little obscurely) confirms it very well. But I do not agree with what he says about the aberration of the rays through convex lenses. For I found in reading what he wrote that this aberration according to his principle ought to be twice what he makes it, that is to say one twenty-fifth of the aperture of the lens, which however seems contrary to experiment. So that perhaps this aberration is not always proportional to the angles of inclination of the rays.[6]

If you plan to publish something of what I have sent you on the Problem [of Alhazen] above, I give you the right just as Mr. Sluse does, and in concluding here I remain, Sir,

Your very humble and obedient servant
Huygens of Zulichem

ADDRESS
Mr. Grubendol
London

NOTES

Reply to Letter 1990.

1 Apelles and Protogenes (both fourth century B.C.) had a contest (according to Pliny, *Nat. Hist.*, XXXV, xiii) as to who could draw the finest line in paint.

2 In Letter 2004a.

3 Huygens' *Reflexions sur la description d'une Lunette publiée sous le nom de M. Cassegrain* appeared in the *Journal des Sçavans* for 13 June [N.S.] (*Œuvres Complètes*, VII, 189–91); in it he asserted James Gregory's priority in describing this type of reflector, and defended Newton's form against Cassegrain's criticisms of it. Compare Letter 1971.

4 See Letter 1973.
5 See Letter 1886 (Vol. VIII).
6 For Newton's reply, see Letter 2019.

2004a

Alhazen's Problem

Enclosure with Letter 2004
From the copy in Royal Society MS. H 1, no. 73
Printed in *Phil. Trans.*, no. 98 (17 November 1673), 6143–44
and in *Œuvres Complètes*, VII, 187–88

Problema Alhazeni

Dato circulo, cujus centrum *A* radius *AD* et punctis duobus *B*, *C*; invenire punctum *H* in circumferentia circuli dati unde ductae *HB HC* faciant ad circumferentiam angulos aequales.

Ponatur inventum, ductaque *AM* recta, quae bifariam secet angulum *BAC*, ducatur ei perpendicularis *HF*, itemque *BM CL*. Jungatur porro *AH* cui perpendicularis sit *HE* rectaeque *BH HC* occurrant *AM* in punctis *K. G.*

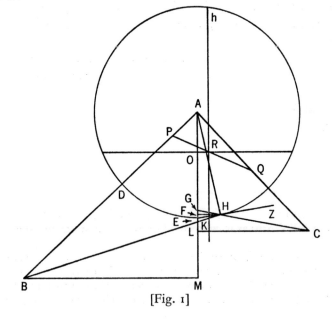

[Fig. 1]

Sit jam $AM = a$

$MB = b$

$AL = c$

$LC = n$

rad. $AD = d$

$AF = x$

$FH = y$

Quia ergo aequales anguli KHE et CHZ sive EHG: estque EHA angulus rectus, erit ut KE ad EG ita KA ad AG. Quia vero BM ad MK ut HF ad FK erit ut $BM+HF$, ad HF ita MF ad FK

$$b + y : y : a - x : \frac{ay - xy}{b + y}$$

add. $FA\,[=]\,x$, fit $KA\,\dfrac{ay + bx}{b + y}$

Rursus quia CL ad LG ut HF ad FG erit permutenda et dividendo $CL - HF$ ad HF ut LF ad FG

$$n - y : y : c - x : \frac{cy - xy}{n - y},$$ qua ablata ab $AF = x$ sit

$GA = \dfrac{nx - cy}{n - y}$. Est autem $EA = \dfrac{dd}{x}$, quia proportionales FA, AH, AE.

Ergo $EA - GA$, hoc est EG, $= \dfrac{dd}{x} - \dfrac{nx + cy^{\mathrm{I}}}{n - y}$. Et $KA - EA$, hoc est,

KE, $= \dfrac{ay + bx}{b + y} - \dfrac{dd}{x}$.

Sed diximus quod KE ad EG ut KA ad AG.

$$\text{Ergo } \frac{ay + bx}{b + y} - \frac{dd}{x} : \frac{dd}{x} - \frac{nx + cy}{n - y} : \frac{ay + bx}{b + y} : \frac{nx - cy}{n - y}$$

Unde invenitur

$$\begin{aligned}
&2anxxy + 2bnx^3 - ddbnx - ddnxy \\
&- 2acxyy - 2bcxxy + ddbcy + ddcyy
\end{aligned} = \begin{aligned}
&naddy + nbddx \\
&- addyy - bddxy
\end{aligned}$$

Et quia $n = \dfrac{bc}{a}$, fit

$$\frac{2bbc}{a}x^3 - \frac{2bbddcx}{a} - \frac{ddbcxy}{a} - 2acxyy + ddcyy = - addyy - bddxy.$$

Est autem

$$\frac{2bbc}{a}x^3 = \frac{2bbcddx}{a} - \frac{2bbcyyx}{a}, \text{ quia } xx = dd - yy$$

Ergo

$$-\frac{2bbcxyy}{a} - \frac{ddbcxy}{a} - 2acxyy + ddcyy = - addyy - bddxy.$$

Et divisis omnibus per *y* et ductis in *a*

$$-2bbcxy - ddbcx - 2aacxy + ddcay = -aaddy - bddax$$
$$abddx - cbddx + acddy + aaddy = 2aacxy + 2bbcxy$$
$$\frac{abddx - cbddx + acddy + aaddy}{2aac + 2bbc} = xy$$

quae aequatio est ad hyperbolam.

Vel quia $bc = na$, $\dfrac{abddx - anddx + acddy + aaddy}{2aac + 2bbc} = xy$

Sit $\dfrac{add}{aa + bb} = p$, ergo $\dfrac{pbx - pnx + pcy + pay}{2c} = xy$.

Unde porro non difficulter invenitur sequens constructio.

Jungatur *BA AC* et applicato seorsim ad utramque quadrato radii *AD*, fiant inde *AP*, *AQ*,[2] et juncta *PQ*, dividatur ipsa bifariam in *R*, et per punctum *R* ducantur *RD*,[3] *RN* sese ad rectos angulos secantes quarumque *RD*[3] sit parallela *AD* quae dividit bifariam angulum *BAC*. Erunt jam *RD*[3] *RN* asymptoti oppositarum hyperbolarum quarum altera per centrum *A* transire debet, quaeque secabunt circumferentiam in punctis *H* quaesitis. Transibunt autem hyperbolae per puncta *P,Q*.

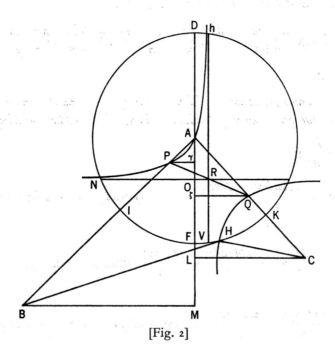

[Fig. 2]

Ratio constructionis apparet ductis $P\gamma$ et $Q\zeta$ perpendicularibus in AM.

fit enim $A\gamma = \dfrac{add}{aa+bb}$ sive p. et $A\zeta = \dfrac{ap}{c}$. Item $P\gamma = \dfrac{pn}{c}$, et $Q\zeta = \dfrac{pb}{c}$.

Quare $AO = \dfrac{pc+pa}{2c}$, et $OR = \dfrac{pb-pn}{2c}$.[4] Unde caetera facilia.[5]

TRANSLATION

Alhazen's Problem

To find the point H on the circumference of a given circle whose center is A, and radius AD whence two lines HB, HC, drawn to two given points B and C, make equal angles with the circumference [*see Fig. 1, p. 120*].

Suppose this point to be found, and the straight line AM drawn besecting the angle BAC, and to it drawn the perpendicular HF, as also BM and CL. Further, let AH be joined and HE be drawn perpendicular to it, and the straight lines BH, CH, meeting AM at the points K and G.

Now let $AM = a$, $MB = b$, $AL = c$, $LC = n$, radius $AD = d$, $AF = x$, $FH = y$.

Because the angles KHE and CHZ (or EHG) are equal and $\angle EHA$ is a right angle, $KE : EG = KA : AG$. And because $BM : MK = HF : FK$, $(BM+HF) : HF = MF : FK$; or,

$$(b+y) : y = (a-x) : \frac{ay-xy}{b+y}.$$

Adding $AF = x$, AK becomes $\dfrac{ay+bx}{b+y}$.

Again, because $CL : LG = HF : FG$, *permutendo* and *dividendo*
$$(CL-HF) : HF = LF : FG; \text{ or,}$$
$$(n-y) : y = (c-x) : \frac{cy-xy}{n-y}.$$

Subtracting FG from $AF = x$, $AG = \dfrac{nx-cy}{n-y}$. But $AE = \dfrac{d^2}{x}$ because AF, AH, and AE are proportional. Accordingly $AE - AG$, that is

$EG, = \dfrac{d^2}{x} - \left(\dfrac{nx-cy}{n-y}\right)$.[1] And $AK - AE$, that is EK, $= \left(\dfrac{ay+bx}{b+y}\right) - \dfrac{d^2}{x}$.

But we have said that $EK : EG = AK : AG$; or,

$$\left(\frac{ay+bx}{b+y} \quad \frac{d^2}{x}\right) : \left(\frac{d^2}{x} - \frac{nx-cy}{n-y}\right) = \left(\frac{ay+bx}{b+y}\right) : \left(\frac{nx-cy}{n-y}\right).$$

Whence it is found that $(2anx^2y + 2bnx^3 - d^2bnx - d^2nxy - 2acxy^2 - 2bcx^2y + d^2bcy + d^2cy^2)$ is equal to $(nad^2y + nbd^2x - ad^2y^2 - bd^2xy)$.

And because $n = \dfrac{bc}{a}$,

$$\frac{2b^2cx^3}{a} - \frac{2b^2d^2cx}{a} - \frac{d^2bcxy}{a} - 2acxy^2 + d^2cy^2 = -ad^2y^2 - bd^2xy.$$

But $\dfrac{2b^2cx^3}{a} = \dfrac{2b^2cd^2x}{a} - \dfrac{2b^2cxy^2}{a}$ because $x^2 = d^2 - y^2$; therefore,

$$-\frac{2b^2cxy^2}{a} - \frac{bcd^2xy}{a} - 2acxy^2 + cd^2y^2 = -ad^2y^2 - bd^2xy.$$

And dividing all the terms by y and multiplying them by a,

$$-2b^2cxy - bcd^2x - 2a^2cxy + acd^2y = -a^2d^2y - abd^2x.$$
$$abd^2x - bcd^2x + acd^2y + a^2d^2y = 2a^2cxy + 2b^2cxy$$
$$\frac{abd^2x - bcd^2x + acd^2y + a^2d^2y}{2a^2c + 2b^2c} = xy$$

which is the equation to an hyperbola.

Or because $bc = an$, $\dfrac{abd^2x + and^2x + acd^2y + a^2d^2y}{2a^2c + 2b^2c} = xy.$

And if $p = \dfrac{ad^2}{a^2 + b^2}$, $\dfrac{pbx - pnx + pcy + pay}{2c} = xy.$

Whence, further, the following construction is found without difficulty.

Join AB and AC, and dividing both into the square of the radius AD form AP and AQ;[2] join PQ and bisect it at R [*see Fig. 2, p. 122*]. Through the point R draw Rh and RN at right angles, Rh being parallel to AD which line bisects the angle BAC. Now Rh and RN will be the asymptotes to opposite branches of an hyperbola one of which passes through the center A, and which cut the circumference at the sought-for points H. The hyperbolas will pass through the points P and Q.

The reason for this construction is made apparent by drawing $P\gamma$ and $Q\zeta$ perpendicular to AM. For $A\gamma = \dfrac{ad^2}{a^2 + b^2} = p$. And $A\zeta = \dfrac{ap}{c}.$

Also $P\gamma = \dfrac{pn}{c}$ and $Q\zeta = \dfrac{pb}{c}.$

Hence $AO = \dfrac{pc + pa}{2c}$ and $OR = \dfrac{pb - pn}{2c}$.[4] Whence the rest is easy.[5]

NOTES

Huygens' final thoughts on Alhazen's Problem—never published, to his own chagrin —may be found in *Œuvres Complètes*, XX, 330–33. They date from September 1673.

1 Although Huygens' change of sign here (in the Latin text) appears to be arbitrary, the complicated expression he arrives at below is in fact correct; clearly, what he means is $+\dfrac{-nx+cy}{n-y}$.

2 That is, $AP = \dfrac{AD^2}{AB}$, $AQ = \dfrac{AD^2}{AC}$.

3 Read: Rb (as in the translation).

4 Note that OR is normal to AD.

5 "For at once $xy = OR \cdot x + AO \cdot y$, or $(x-AO)(y-OR) = AO \cdot OR$, a hyperbola of origin $A(o, o)$, of centre R and asymptotes parallel to AO, OR." (D.T.W.)

2005

Heinrich Vollgnad and Johannes Jaenisch
to Oldenburg

21 June 1672

From the original in Royal Society MS. V, no. 29

PERILLUSTRI ATQUE INCOMPARABILI VIRO
DOMINO HENRICO OLDENBURG,
EMINENTISSIMAE SOCIETATIS REGIAE LONDINENSIS
SECRETARIO
PATRONO SUMMO DEVENERANDO
SALUTEM FELICITATEMQUE
ATQUE OBSERVANTIAM
PERPETUAM!

Non absque causa, TUA, VIR PER-ILLUSTRIS, negotia ac medita-tiones magis arduas interpellare turbareve hactenus quoddammodo veriti sumus, donec sanctior NOMINIS Tui veneratio nec subinde velli-caret, illas quas 22. Decembris praeteriti Anni[1] ad Dn. J. Sachs a Lewen-haimb, Fautorem Collegam et Amicum nostrum, non ante, quam haec nos vita destituet, absque honore nobis memorandum, dederas, sed nec ab Ipso visas,[2] omnino responsione, etiam qualicunque mactandas esse. Ipse etenim Vir modo laudatissimus, cum propria manu candidissimi et officiosissimi sui non minus, quam eruditi characteres animi chartis imprimere tunc, quando litterae afferebantur, amplius non posset, nobis, suis velut interpretibus, Venia inprimis TUA, umbras saltim quasdum illius delineatas concessit.

Maximas proinde, quas concipere possumus, Tibi, VIR PERILLUS-TRIS, referimus gratias, pro communicatis, stupendis sane, tam inventae Tubae vocalissimae, quam observatae, ast ante hac inauditae Excretionis ossium, quam Parisiensis ille patitur; Miraculi utriusque pleniorem et notitiam et eventum cognoscendi plurima exspectatione desiderantes. Quod itaque Dejectiones tot ossium bene conformatorum spectat, fatemur nobis quidem esse judicium hebetius, quam ut rem, quam acutissima ingenia penetrare hac ante non potuerunt, declarare debeamus conari: quod si tamen non invitae, aures etiam futili conjecturae praeberentur, existimaremus (modo Affectus is est mere ac vere naturalis, nec ullae subsint praestigiae) credi posse, Virum indigitatum esse hominem geminum seu duplicem i.e. hominem aliud hominis individuum, ex prima conformatione sibi congenitum, gerentem. Conjectura haec quod non penitus absurda videtur, facit Obs. 37. Anni 1. Ephemerid. Germ. Med. Phys.[3] ubi p. 122 inter varia alia foetuum foetorum exempla refertur foemella recens nata utero suo aliam foemellam perfactam gestasse. at Viros etiam geminos dari posse, exemplo illius, cujus Bartholinus Hist. 66. Cent. 1. meminet,[4] quemque nostram etiam Vratislaviam spectasse meminimus, conjectari possemus; nisi hunc ipsum quis inter Bicorpores referre malit. Sed ne Luci facem praeferre nos velle videamur hoc filam rumpimus, optantes solum, ut vir ille diligenti custodia observari queat, quo tanto certius olim demortui Cadaver cultro Anatomico subjiciatur, reique certitudo sic luci exponatur.

Sed modo ad Virum Clarissimum cujus paulo ante mentionem faciebamus, Sachsium inquam, Academiae Nostrae merito suo Decus, si narrationem rursum deflectere licet, non dubium est, quin dudum de Eo fama retulerit, quam acerbo is funere naturae debitum persolvere coactus sit; proinde verbo nunc saltim indicabimus Ipsum post diuturnum fastidium fere omnium alimentorum, ex lenta prostratione virium, quam frequentes haemorrhagiae admodum serosae, et quidem nocturnae, e nare sinistro comitabantur, occubuisse. Evisceratum Corpusculum praecipue exhibebat oculis lustrandum, 1 ventriculi qua substantiam qua contenta vitium; 2. Sanguinis tantam penuriam, ut etiam majora quaedam vasa vix guttatim residuum stagma funderent; 3. Renis dextri prae sinistro insignem amplitudinem, quippe duos in suo Infundibulo recondebat Calculos, quorum minor ℈ iiss, major vero ℥ ij. exacte pendebat, hos inter et renis parenchyma plurima pinguedo interjecta erat, quo minus hospes tam validus, hospitium suum gravare posset. Reliqua referet Historia Vitae et Mortis, quae Anno III Miscellaneorum Curiosorum inseri curabitur.[5] Quoad etenim per nos fieri licebit, DEO inprimis annuente, atque quicquid est vitae virium ac valetudinis conservante, non patiemur ut opus tanto labore inceptum in suis quasi incunabilis una cum Parente suo vim fati expertam esse dicatur. Verum, hoc dum molimur, opus omnino Magnorum inter Eruditissimos Virorum Patrocinio atque Favore, nobis esse sentimus.

Itaque et TUAM, VIR PERILLUSTRIS, Prothymiam, quam hactenus D. Sachsio, Totique Academiae Nostrae, toties tantisque testimoniis declarasti, in nos quoque derivare contendimus, non per merita nostra, sed in gratiam Academiae Nostrae, immo vero per Amorem Philosophiae Naturalis, quam Totam Totus non solum diligis, sed intima consuetudine familiariter cognovisti: Per Philosophiae inquam, Amorem perquam observanter TE, VIR PERILLUSTRIS, rogatum venimus TUAE Gentis conatibus porro favere, hoc est, eosdem vel solo adnutu adjuvare ac excitare non dedignari velis.

Pro tanto beneficio non nostra TIBI aetas, debitam venerationem persolvet, sed et Posterorum posteritas perpetuam TUI memoriam dignissima gratitudine recolet. VALE, VIR PER ILLUSTRIS, ut ex voto Faveas INCOMPARABILIS TUI NOMINIS

Dab. Vratislaviae	Observantissimis Cultoribus
d. 21 Jun. Ao. 1672.	*Henrico Vollgnad* et
	Johanni Jaenisio, Medd. Dd.
	ac S.R.I. Academ. Nat. Curios.
	Collegis

ADDRESS
    PERILLUSTRI ATQUE INCOMPARABILI
           VIRO,
    DOMINO HENRICO OLDENBURG
    REGIAE SOCIETATIS LONDINENSIS
          SECRETATIO
  Domino ac Patrono summe devenerando
        London

TRANSLATION

Greetings, happiness, and eternal respect to the very illustrious and incomparable Henry Oldenburg, secretary of the most eminent Royal Society
of London, most esteemed patron!

Not without cause have we feared to interrupt and disturb in some way your
more arduous concerns and thoughts, most illustrious Sir, until knowing that
respect for your esteemed name had not immediately elicited a reply to that
[letter] which you addressed on 22 December last year[1] to Mr. J. Sachs von Lewen-
heimb (our patron, colleague, and friend who, while we still breathe, is not to be
recalled by us without honor), and which was not seen by him,[2] we felt that it
must be honored by some sort of reply.

That most meritorious person himself could no longer with his own hand
then impress on paper the honest and dutiful as well as learned qualities of his
mind at the time when the letter was delivered, and so he gave to us as his spokes-
men certain shadowy sketches of his, for which we beg your indulgence.

And so, most illustrious Sir, we return you the best thanks we can offer for the
truly marvelous communications, both of the invention of the speaking trumpet
and of the observation of the hitherto unheard of excretion of bones suffered by
the Parisian. We anticipate most eagerly a fuller account of both miracles, and
knowledge of the outcome. As for the excretion of well formed bones, we confess
indeed that to us it seems that judgment should be given only slowly, so as to
resolve a matter that the acutest wits have not hitherto been able to penetrate.
However, if it will not be unpleasing to you to listen to possibly futile conjecture,
we think it possible to suppose (if only that occurrence is an ordinary and truly
natural one, without sleight of hand) that the man in the published [description]
is a twin or double, that is, that he is a man bearing another individual man,
congenital to him from his first conception. That this conjecture is not wholly
absurd is shown by Observation 37 of the first year of *Miscellanea Curiosa*,[3] where
on p. 122 the instance is mentioned among other examples of morbid fetuses of a
newly born female bearing another perfect female in the uterus. But that there may
be twinned men we may conjecture from that example recorded by Bartholin in
the sixty-sixth *History* of his first century,[4] and which we recall having also seen at
Breslau, unless one should rather classify this among Siamese twins. But we shall
leave the subject lest we should seem to be putting ourselves forward in offering
enlightenment, only desiring that an eye may be kept on that man, so that he may
certainly be dissected after his death and the truth of the matter exposed.

But now let us return the discourse to the distinguished person whom we
mentioned before, that is Sachs who was, by his merit, the ornament of our
Academy: no doubt rumor long ago reached you that he was forced to pay his
debt to nature by bitter death. Briefly we may now indicate that he died after a

prolonged distaste for almost all food and consequent weakening of his strength, accompanied by frequent, very serous and even nocturnal hemorrhages from his left nostril. At a post mortem the chief features observable in his body were, (1) the ventricle diseased as to substance and content; (2) so great a shortage of blood that scarcely any stagnant residue issued drop by drop from even some of the larger vessels; (3) the right kidney notably greater in size than the left, and hiding in its infundibulum two stones, of which the lesser weighted two and a half scruples, the greater exactly two ounces. Between these and the substance of the kidney was interposed much fatty matter, so that so terrible a guest might the less injure its host. For the rest you may refer to the history of his life and death to be inserted in Vol. III of the *Miscellanea Curiosa.*[5] So far and so long as we can, with God's will, keep our health and strength, we shall not permit it to be said that a work begun with so much labor succumbed to the blows of fate in its infancy at the same time as its progenitor. In truth, as long as we strive to this end we wholly feel the patronage and support of the great men in the learned world.

So we exert ourselves to obtain your good will, most illustrious Sir, which formerly you declared many times with such notable manifestations to Mr. Sachs and to all our Academy, not on account of our own merits but as a favor to our Academy and, indeed, out of love to natural philosophy which you not only esteem as all in all, but have known with intimate familiarity. Out of love of philosophy, we say, we very respectfully beg you, very illustrious Sir, to continue to befriend us by [communicating] the endeavors of your nation, that is, to be so good as to aid and stimulate the same even if only by a kind word.

For such kindness not only our age will pay you due respect, but posterity will eternally recall your memory with due gratitude. Farewell, most illustrious Sir, and, according to our desires, look favorably upon

> The most respectful devotees of your
> incomparable fame
> *Henricus Vollgnad* and
> *Johannes Jaenisius*, M.D.'s
> and Fellows of the Academia
> Naturac Curiosorum

Breslau, 21 June 1672

ADDRESS

To the very illustrious and incomparable
man,
Mr. Henry Oldenburg
Secretary of the Royal Society of London,
Most esteemed patron,
London

NOTES

Heinrich Vollgnad (*c.* 1635–82), a physician of Breslau, wrote much on medical and related topics. Johannes Jaenisch (1636–1714), also of Breslau, practised medicine in that city having taken his M.D. at Leiden in 1663 after study at Wittenberg and Jena. He was physician to the pesthouse and physician-in-ordinary to the city of Breslau. Both were (as the letter shows) active members of the Academia Curiosorum and contributors to its *Miscellanea*.

1 Letter 1845 (Vol. VIII).
2 Sachs died on 3 January 1672.
3 This is in a contribution by Thomas Bartholin on "Herba ossifraga."
4 See Thomas Bartholin, *Historiarum anatomicarum rariorum centuria I* (Copenhagen, 1654).
5 The *Memoria Sachsiana* by Johann Daniel Major is actually to be found (with a portrait of Sachs) in the *Miscellanea Curiosa*, fourth and fifth years (i.e., 1673 and 1674; Leipzig, 1675)—seventy-six pages, separately paginated.

2006

Oldenburg to Pardies

Late June 1672

From the memorandum in Royal Society MS. P 1, no. 80

Escrit la seconde fois, et envoyé No. 84.[1]

TRANSLATION

Wrote a second time, and sent no. 84.[1]

NOTES

Second reply to Letter 1988.
1 *Phil. Trans.*, no. 84 (17 June 1672), contained Pardies's commentary on Newton.

2007

Oldenburg to Newton

25 June 1672

Memorandum printed in Newton, *Correspondence*, I, 194, note 1, and extract, *ibid.*, p. 205
(quoted in Letter 2018), both from the originals in private possession

Rec. jun. 24.72. Answ. jun. 25. repeating what I had said june 20.[1] and adding yt P. Pard[ies's] obj[ections] and his Answers were already in ye presse[2] and would please, espec[ially] if the sequel of ye same P[ardies] wth his answer should follow. That to Mr Hook to be differrd till further order.

.   .   .   .

... Whether a physicall point in a Glasse may not by the diversity of the pores & angles in it cause in the rays falling thereon such really different though seemingly equall refractions, that thence may proceed those severall distinct colours wch in [your] Doctrine are esteemed to proceed from the aggregate of the rays of light?

.   .   .   .

NOTES

Reply to Letter 2001, on the back of which the memorandum which makes up the first paragraph is written.

1 Letter 2002, now missing, had been sent to Cambridge, whereas the present letter was addressed to Newton at Woolsthorpe.

2 *Phil. Trans.*, no. 84 (17 June 1672), 4087–93, contains Pardies's Letter 1942 (Vol. VIII) and Newton's reply, Letter 1957a.

2008

Swammerdam to Oldenburg

25 June 1672

This is mentioned by Birch (*History*, III, 56) as having been read before the Society on 3 July 1672; it announced that Swammerdam was presenting the Society with some specimens of human anatomy.

2009
Pardies to Oldenburg
29 June 1672

From the original in Royal Society MS. P 1, no. 81

Paris 9. Juil. 1672 [N.S.]

Monsieur

Tout ce que vous m'avez fait la grace de m'envoyer m'a esté fidellement rendu. Je ne scay comment j'ay oublié dans mes lettres de vous remercier de vostre Transaction et beaucoup plus de l'honneur que vous m'avez fait d'y mettre le livre dela connoissance des Bestes.[1] J'ay recu depuis le pacquet par la voye de Calais, et depuis encore deux gazettes, de quoy je vous suis extremement obligé.[2] Mais il ne sera plus besoin que vous vous donniez cette peine. nous avons ici un pere Anglois qui recevra toutes ces Gazettes, de sorte que le P. Deschampsneuf qui est tout de la maison de Bethune et qui m'avoit donné cette adresse pour avoir les gazettes, n'a plus besoin de nostre entremise. ainsi je vous prie de ne m'escrire plus par cette voye à moins que je vous le demande. Vous me ferez encore plaisir de vous servir de la voye d'ami quand il s'en trouvera et non pas de la poste, comme je suis ici d'une communauté religieuse, je ne puis pas faire tout ce que je voudrois, et il est raisonnable de s'accommoder au sentimens de ceux qui nous gouvernent. J'espere pourtant que je n'y perdray rien de vostre part, et que l'occasion de quelque ami se presentant vous me ferez la grace de m'envoyer ce que vous m'auriez envoyé par d'autres voyes.

Je suis tres-satisfait de la derniere réponse que M. Newton a bien voulu faire à mes instance.[3] le dernier scrupule qui me restoit touchant *l'experience de la croix*, a esté parfaitement levé. Et je concois tres-bien par sa figure ce que je n'avois pas compris auparavant. L'experience ayant esté faite de cette façon je n'ay rien à dire. Vous me ferez un grand plaisir de luy temoigner que j'ay pour luy toute l'estime imaginable, que je me sens tres-obligé de la bonté qu'il a eu de m'instruire et de vouloir bien examiner mes remarques et y répondre. Outre l'estime que j'avois deja de sa capacité, cette maniere obligente m'a deplus gagné et m'attache a luy d'affection. Son invention des Lunettes me paroit admirable. je l'ay defendue en diverses rencontres où je voyois quelques personnes peu intelligentes qui ne l'approuvoient pas autant qu'il falloit. J'espere qui'il ne s'arrestera pas là et qu'il nous donnera encore des fruits de son esprit fecond.

Le mesme pere pour qui je vous avois prié de faire venir les Gazettes me parle d'aller passer quelque mois à Calais avec M. le duc de Bethune. Je vous assure que l'unique vue qui me porteroit à consentir à ce voyage, c'est la facilité que j'aurois à passer un peu plus avant et à vous aller voir. Je vous avoue que j'aurois bien dela satisfaction si j'avois le bien de vous voir et tant d'illustres personnes qui composent vostre Royalle Societé.4

Vous aurez sceu sans doute que M. l'Abbé Picard a porté de Dannemark les Originaux de Tycho, on fera tout imprimer de l'impression du Louvre, tant pour reparer les fautes qu'ils disent estre dans l'historia coelestis qu'a fait imprimer le P. Curtius, que pour supplier à ce qu'il manque dans cette *histoire*.5 Le P. Curtius n'avoit que des copies, encore luy manquoit-il une année qu'il a suppléé par *Observationes Hafnianae*.6 cette année c'estoit agarée, et M. Picard l'a de la mesme copie des autres qu'avoit le P. Curtius.7 Il y a encore les Observations que Tycho a fait en allemagne à l'age de 15 ans comme il le rapporte luy mesme dans La Mechanique celeste.8 et tout cela se trouve conforme avec ce qui est marqué dans cette mechanique qu'il avoit observé. Tout cela à mon avis est plus curieux qu'utile à la reserve des fautes qui pourroient estre dans Curtius, et dont je voudrois qu'on fist une liste avec la correction. Il a encore porté une piece de la pierre fondamentale d'Uraniburg, posée par un Ambassadeur de france avec une partie de l'inscription Ferdinand . . .

Carolus Danzaeus9

Ils enchasseront cette piece dans quelque bel endroit de l'Observatoire. Il a aussi du crystal d'Islande qui fait deux refractions.

On devoit hyer faire un essay celebre des trompettes mais je ne scay si le mauvais temps le permit.

Vostre tres-humble serviteur
Pardies

Je voudrois bien scavoir ce qu'il vous a semblé de la proprieté que j'ay marquée de l'hyperbole pour la progression harmonique, semblable en cela au triangle rectiligne et à cette ligne des Logarithmes pour les progressions Arithmetique et Geometrique.10

ADDRESS
  A Monsieur
    Monsieur Grubendol
      A Londres

TRANSLATION

Paris, 9 July 1672 [N.S.]

Sir,

All that was sent me by your kindness has been faithfully delivered to me. How I can have forgotten to thank you in my letters for your *Transactions*, and much more for the honor you have done me in inserting there a mention of the book the *Connoissance des Bestes*,[1] I do not know. I have since received the packet sent by the Calais route, and still more recently two gazettes, for which I am extremely obliged to you.[2] But it will be needless in the future for you to take this trouble. We have an English father here who is to receive all these gazettes, so that Fr. Deschampsneuf (who is entirely occupied as [a member of] the household [of the Duc de] Béthune and who had given me that address so that he could have the gazettes) no longer requires our mediation. So I ask you not to write to me by that route any longer unless I ask you to do so. You would also please me by using the means of a friend when one is to be found rather than the post; as I am here a member of a religious community I cannot do everything I should wish and it is reasonable to respect the opinions of those who rule over us. Nevertheless I hope that I shall lose nothing from you and that when the opportunity of a friend serves you will do me the kindness to send me what you would have sent by other routes.

I am very well satisfied with the last reply Mr. Newton willingly made at my entreaty.[3] The last scruple which I still retained on the subject of the crucial experiment has been quite removed. And I perceive quite well with the aid of his figure what I had formerly not understood. The experiment having been made in this way I have nothing to say. You will give me great pleasure by bearing witness to him that I have all possible esteem towards him, that I feel very much obliged for his goodness in instructing me and for being willing to examine my remarks carefully and replying to them. Besides the esteem I already had for his ability this obliging manner has gained my affection and attached me to him. His telescopic invention seems to me admirable. I have defended him in various encounters when I saw certain people of little intelligence who did not approve of him as much as they ought. I hope that he will not stop there but will give us more of the fruits of his fertile mind.

The same priest for whom I had requested you to send the gazettes speaks to me of [my] going to pass some months at Calais with the Duc de Béthune. I assure you that the sole consideration which might lead me to consent to this journey is the advantage I might have of going a little farther and coming to see you. I confess to you that I should take great satisfaction in having the benefit of seeing you and so many of the famous people who make up your Royal Society.[4]

You have already learned no doubt that the Abbé Picard has brought back from Denmark the original [manuscripts] of Tycho; they will all be printed with the Louvre imprint, as much to correct the errors which are said to exist in the

Historia Coelestis published by Father Curtz as to supply what is missing from that history.[5] Father Curtz had only copies and besides he lacked one year which he supplied from the *Observationes Hafnianae*.[6] This year was lost and Mr. Picard has it from the same copy as the other years which Father Curtz had.[7] There are besides the observations which Tycho made in Germany at the age of fifteen, as he recounts himself in his *Celestial Mechanics*.[8] And all this is found to agree with what he marked in that mechanics as what he had observed. All this in my opinion is more curious than useful except for the errors there may be in Curtz, and of which I should like to have a list made, with the corrections. There is besides a piece of the foundation stone of Uraniburg placed by a French ambassador with a part of the inscription Ferdinand . . .

Carolus Danzaeus[9]

This piece will be set up in some suitable place in the Observatory. There is also an Iceland crystal which gives a double refraction.

Yesterday there should have been made a famous trial of the trumpets, but I do not know whether the bad weather allowed it.

Your very humble servant,
Pardies

I should very much like to know what you thought of the property I noted of the hyperbola in regard to harmonic progression, similar to that with a rectilinear triangle and to that line of logarithms for arithmetic and geometric progressions.[10]

ADDRESS
> Mr. Grubendol,
> London

NOTES

Reply to Letter 2000.
1 This was reviewed in *Phil. Trans.*, no. 82 (22 April 1672), 4054.
2 See Letter 1988, note 1.
3 Letter 1992.
4 Pardies did not visit London.
5 [Albert Curtz, ed.], *Historia coelestis complectens observationes astronomicas varias . . . Tychonis Brahe* (Augsburg, 1666); for criticisms of this work by John Wallis, see Vol. V, especially p. 236; J. L. E. Dreyer judged it "not far from being an Augean stable" (*Tycho Brahe*, London, 1890; repr. 1963, p. 373). We briefly related the history of Tycho Brahe's manuscripts in Vol. IV, p. 575, note 6. The originals were taken to Paris by Ole Rømer—whom Picard had persuaded to accompany him thither to work in the Observatory—and returned to Copenhagen, where they remain, in 1707. The Louvre impression proceeded to about 68 pages before work was stopped by the financial pressures of Louis XIV's wars.
6 The classified copy, made under Tycho's direction, of his observations had remained in Austria when Johannes Kepler took the originals with him to Germany. The

observations for 1593 were missing from it; instead, Curtz printed others made at Cassel by Christoffel Rothmann (d. 1599) and at Wittenberg for this year, which he presumably obtained from Willebrord Snel, *Coeli et siderum in eo errantium observationes Hassiacae . . . Principis Wilhelm . . . institutae* (Leiden, 1618). Pardies has corrupted "Hesse" to "Copenhagen."

7 This remark is wrong, and indeed obviously self-contradictory. Picard did not copy any of the observations himself. Those made by Tycho during 1593 were, however, later copied from the original manuscripts while they were at Paris by Philippe de la Hire and printed in the eighteenth century by Lalande.

8 *Astronomiae instauratae mechanicae* (Wandsbeck, 1598); see H. Raeder, E. Strömgren, and B. Strömgren, *Tycho Brahe's Description of his Instruments and Scientific Work* (Copenhagen, 1946), pp. 106 ff.

9 Charles Dancey, French ambassador at the Danish Court, was a close friend of Tycho's who laid the foundation stone of the observatory at Hven. The first name should perhaps be "Frederick," as Frederick II (1534–88) was the King of Denmark who installed Tycho Brahe at Hven.

10 See Letter 1976.

2010

Oldenburg to Flamsteed

2 July 1672

From the memorandum in Royal Society MS. F 1, no. 86

Rec. jun. 20.
Answ. july 2. 72
See my book of ye min[utes] of Letters.[1]

NOTE

Reply to Letter 1998.
1 In spite of this assertion, no trace of the draft now survives.

2011

De Graaf to Oldenburg

2 July 1672

From the original in Royal Society MS. G 1, no. 10

Clarissimo et Doctissimo Viro
D. Henrico Oldenburgio Reg. Soc. secretario
R De Graaf Salutem

Epistolam vestram 24 Aprilis una cum Transactionibus vestris ad me missam non per amicum quendam sed per tabellarium rite accepi: respondissem citius nisi totius Patriae nostrae calamitas omne scribendi desiderium abtulisset: ut tamen desiderio vestro quodammodo satisfaciam mitto vobis per D Kolderman vesiculas seminarias meo modo praeparatas, ut videatis semen quod per vasa deferentia in illas excernitur non necesse habere ut extremum vesicularum subeat; nam repletis vesiculis, quod per vasa deferentia affluit, aeque bene, imo facilius (quia in procinctu est) in urethram erumpere potest, quam illud semen quod in vesiculis seminariis asservatur. Cum tractatum meum De succo panc[reatico] ad te missum non acceperis[1] alterum exemplas hac opportunitate data ad te mitto. Quae Malpigius et Grew de pulli generatione ediderunt avide expecto[2] ut et ea quae dominatio vestra in transactionibus suis de tractatu meo publici iuris fecerite.[3] Quandoquidem a D Denis toto hoc belli tempore nihil litterarum viderim simul me certiorem facias rogo quid ipse de tractatu meo in transactionibus suis dixerit[4] vale et uti cepisti amare pergas

Tuum
R De Graaf

ignoscas tumultuanti ac conturbato calamo Delphis
12 Iulii 1672

ADDRESS
A Monsieur
Monsieur Oldenburg
A Londres

TRANSLATION

R. De Graaf greets the very famous and learned Mr. Henry Oldenburg, Secretary of the Royal Society

I received safely your letter of 24 April together with your *Transactions*, not by the hand of some friend of yours but by the post. I should have replied sooner had not the disaster falling upon the whole of my country stifled all desire for correspondence. However, in order to satisfy your desires to some extent I am sending to you by the hand of Mr. Kolderman the seminal vesicles prepared in my way, so that you may all see how needless it is to suppose that the semen filtered into them through the *vasa deferentia* must reach the upper limit of the vesicles; for when the vesicles are full because the flow through the *vasa deferentia* is copious it can just as well, indeed more readily (because it is near at hand), burst out into the urethra, as that semen can which has been stored in the seminal vesicles.

As you did not receive my treatise *De succo pancreatico* that I sent you, I take this opportunity to send you another copy.[1] I eagerly await Malpighi's and Grew's writings on the embryology of the chick,[2] as also [reading] what your excellency has published in your *Transactions* concerning my treatise.[3] Since I have seen no scrap of letter from Mr. Denis throughout this time of warfare I likewise beg you to inform me of what he said of my treatise in his transactions.[4] Farewell, and just as you have begun continue to love

Your
R. De Graaf

Forgive my disordered and hurried handwriting. Delft, 12 July 1672.

ADDRESS
To Mr. Oldenburg,
London.

NOTES

Reply to Letter 1964.
1 For this work and De Graaf's sending it to London, see Letter 1729 (Vol. VIII).
2 As regards Grew De Graaf is, obviously, confused.
3 Oldenburg's notice of *De mulierum organis generationi inservientibus* . . . was published in *Phil. Trans.*, no. 82 (22 April 1672), 4052–54.
4 This appeared in Denis's twelfth *Mémoire* of 11 June 1672 [N.S.].

2012
Oldenburg to Newton
2 July 1672

Printed in Newton, *Correspondence*, I, 206–208, from the original in CUL MS. Add. 3976, no. 9

In this second reply to Letter 2001, Oldenburg sends Newton the relevant passages from Huygens' Letter 2004 (above, p. 117) and asks for Newton's comments. He adds in a postscript "If Mr Hook make any return to your answer (as he is like to doe) I doubt not but I shall have the liberty of imparting it to you."

2013
Oldenburg to Hevelius
5 July 1672

From the original in BN MS. N.a.L. 1641, ff. 20r–21v. An extract is printed in Olhoff, pp. 135–36

Per-illustri Viro
Domino Johanni Hevelio
Gedanensium Consuli et Astronomo celeberrimo
Henr. Oldenburg Salutem

Cum patescat ex binis tuis, 9 Martij [N.S.] et 10 Junij [N.S.] ad me datis literis, Vir Amplissime, Te indefesso affectu et studio Observationibus Caelestibus jugiter incumbere, nec quicquam eorum, quae in isthoc argumento diligentiae tuae occurrerint, Soc. Regiam celare, non possum non, Ipsa sic jubente, summam ejus erga Te benevolentiam identidem tibi contestari atque hac ratione ad gnavam studii illius Astronomici consectationem Te sollicitare.[1] Tua nuperrimi Cometae Observata non adeo a Parisiensibus, quorum hic Exemplar jungo, videnter abludere.[2] Iam nactum te esse ex Germania putem, quae inibi de eodem Phaenomeno, Argentorati imprimis, a doctissimo Reichelio, Mathematum ibidem professore, inde a 12/22 ad 18/28 Martij animadversa, mihique a Consultissimo Domino Erico Mauritio, Imperialis Camerae Assessore, communicata fuere.[3] Miror sane, Clarissimum Cassinim Observationes suas tum de hoc

Cometa, tum de insignis illius in Jove maculae permanentis Revolutione
periodica, 9 horarum et 56 scrupulorum spatio celebrari solita, nuperoque
mense Martio Parisiis evulgata, nil quicquam significasse.⁴ Legisti sine
dubio, quae Anno superiori Academia Regia Parisiensi tum de maculis
Solaribus, tum de Saturni phasibus in lucem emisit.⁵ Domini Hugenij sub
idem tempus ad nos scriptae literae memorabant, se globosae Saturni
figurae sub illius Anni finem reditum praenuntiasse, adeoque die 6.
Novembris [N.S.] Planetae istius brachia vix ac ne vix quidem videre
potuisse.⁶ Domini Cassini vero literae die 9 januarii 1672 [N.S.] ad nos
datae perhibent, Saturnum qui Anno 1671. inde ab ortu Heliaco ad d. 11.
Augusti [N.S.] visus fuerat rotundus, et a d. 14 ejusdem mensis deinceps
cum brachiis conspectus, figuram hanc posteriorem ad diem 8. Decembris
[N.S.] retinuisse, a die autem 13. Decembris [N.S.] et deinceps plane ro-
tundam habuisse.⁷ Adjicit idem, se rotunditatem priorem nimiae radiorum
visualium supra annuli Saturni planum obliquitati tribuere, cum is motu
apparente directo ferme ad 20 gr. ♓ pervenisset, quam causam cessasse ait,
quando motu retrogradu ad gr. 18. ejusdem signi restitutus fuit, cum adhuc
a Sole videretur in gr. 16.

Posterioris vero rotunditatis causam magis tribuit nimiae obliquitati
radiorum Solis supra idem planum Annuli, cum a Sole videretur Saturnus
excedere 19. gr. ♓, licet a Terra in ejusdem signi gr. 14° conspiceretur.
Hos terminos, quos pro Telescopiorum longitudine et praestantia variari
necesse esse dicit, 17. pedum Telescopio, a Campano artifice elaborato,
definitos esse, idem affirmat.

Hugenius censet, Observationes dictas Hypothesin suam de Annulo
plane confirmare, annique istius phases ansam insignem praebere, figurae
globosae reditum multo praecisius, quam hactenus factum, praenuntiandi.⁶

Accepimus, Clarissimum Picardum egregiis in Dania variarum Observationum laboribus defunctum ad suos rediisse, quarum disertam enarra-
tionem avide indies exspectamus.⁸

Significavit mihi Celeberrimus Erasmus Bartholinus, Tychonis Brahei
Observationum Impressionem ex sua recensione Parisiis se moliri: cui
consilio successum felicissimum comprecamur.⁹

Clarissimus Montanarius, qui Observator eluet diligentissimus, Bononiae Mathematum professor, tum ex Altitudinis Arcturi, tum ex Horologio
collegit, Eclipseos Lunaris, die 8/18 Septembris 1671. celebratae, tempus, a
totali immersione ad initium emersionis, minutorum duntaxat 46. fuisse;
notata hac in re ingenti tam Tabularum quam aliorum Observantium ab hac
Observatione differentia.¹⁰

Doctissimus Bullialdus mihi scribit, se aliquot librorum, antehac a Te ad bibliopolam quendam Parisiensem missorum, Exemplaria navi, ad me vehenda curasse, Tibi restituenda; iisque libros quosdam alios in usum tuum adjunxisse.[11] Quamprimam appulerint; commoda occasione ea omnia, una cum Tractatulis quibusdam philosophicis, hic non ita pridem editis, ad Te transmittam.

Caeterum dum haec scribo, tabellarius mihi fasciculum tuum, qui editam a Te de nupero Cometa Epistolam continet, perquam opportune tradit.[12] Exhibeo eam Societatis Regiae, caetum publicum proximo die Mercurii celebraturae; quae solemnes sine dubio gratias pro tuo Tibi merito decernet.[13] Quod vero mihi, Sociorum minimo, Historiam illam inscribere dignatus es, amicissime habeo, et pro amplissimo illo honore et affectu summas gratias ago, operam omnino daturus, ut, cum paria non possim, saltem quae possum, in doctrinae et virtutis tuae decus et augmentum impendam. Vale, Vir Illustrissime, meque animitus Tibi divinctum crede. Dabam Londini die 5. julij 1672.

ADDRESS
    Illustrissimo Viro
  Johanni Hevelio, Gedanensium
    Consuli dignissimo, etc.
        Dantzick

TRANSLATION

Henry Oldenburg greets the very illustrious Mr. Johannes Hevelius, most celebrated Senator and astronomer of Danzig

As it is obvious from your two letters addressed to me on 9 March [N.S.] and 10 June [N.S.], excellent Sir, that you continue to devote yourself to astronomical observations with tireless zeal and goodwill, and conceal from the Royal Society nothing that your diligence encounters in this pursuit I cannot but, upon its instructions, assure you of its great kindliness towards you and entreat you to the earnest continuation of astronomical research of this sort.[1] Your observations of the most recent comet do not seemingly differ much from the Parisian ones, of which I here attach a copy;[2] I think you will have already obtained from Germany [an account of] what was noted there, particularly at Strasbourg by the learned Reichelt, who is Professor of Mathematics in that city, between 12/22 and 18/28 March. These were communicated to me by the sagacious Mr. Erich Mauritius, Assessor of the Imperial Chamber.[3]

I am really very much surprised that the famous Cassini has imparted no word to you of his observations alike of this comet and of the period of revolution of that notable and permanent spot on Jupiter, which is completed in nine hours and fifty-six minutes; these were recently, in March, published at Paris.[4] You will doubtless have read what the Parisian Académie Royale [des Sciences] has made public last year concerning both sunspots and the phases of Saturn.[5] At about the same time a letter from Mr. Huygens to me recorded that he had predicted the return of the round shape of Saturn towards the end of that year [1671], and accordingly on 6 November [N.S.] he could scarcely or not at all discern the "arms" [ring] of that planet.[6] In a letter of 9 January 1672 [N.S.] Mr. Cassini told me that Saturn, which in the year 1671 from the time of its heliacal rising until 11 August [N.S.] was seen as round, and from the fourteenth of that month onwards was seen with arms, retained this latter appearance until 8 December [N.S.], but from 13 December onwards had a perfectly round shape.[7] He added that he himself attributed the former [phase of the] round shape to the extreme obliquity of the visual rays falling upon the plane of Saturn's ring as the planet was carried in its direct apparent motion right up to 20° of Pisces; this cause ceased to be operative, he says, when the planet returned to 18° of the same sign in its retrograde motion, for by then it would be seen from the sun [as if] in 16°.

But he rather assigns the cause of the second round phase to the excessive obliquity of the solar rays upon this same plane of the ring, as Saturn would be seen from the Sun as exceeding 19° in Pisces although from the Earth it was observed in 14° of the same sign. These limits, which he says will vary according to the length and quality of the telescope one uses, he states were defined with the aid of a 17-foot telescope made by Campani's skilful hands.

Huygens is of the opinion that the above observations fully confirm his hypothesis of the ring, and furnish very useful means for predicting its annual phases and the return of the round appearance much more exactly than has been done before.[6]

We have heard that the famous Picard, having gone through extraordinary efforts in making a variety of observations in Denmark, has returned home; we are in eager expectation from day to day of a formal account of his observations.[8]

The very celebrated Erasmus Bartholin has informed me that he is trying to get the observations of Tycho Brahe, edited by himself, printed at Paris. We wish a happy outcome to this plan.[9]

The famous Montanari, Professor of Mathematics at Bologna, who reveals himself as a very diligent observer, has inferred both from the altitudes of Arcturus and from his clock that the period of the lunar eclipse that took place on 8/18 September 1671, from total immersion to the commencement of emersion, was only 46 minutes; in this case there is a noteworthy discrepancy both from the tables and the observations of other observers.[10]

The very learned Boulliaud writes to me that he has sent on shipboard to be brought to me a few books that you formerly dispatched to some Paris bookseller, for return to yourself.[11] To these he has added certain other books for your own use. As soon as they have arrived I will send the lot on to you at the first convenient opportunity, together with some little scientific treatises printed here recently.

Furthermore, while I am writing these lines the postman has very opportunely brought me the package containing your recently published *Epistola de cometa*.[12] I shall present it to the Royal Society, whose meeting will take place next Wednesday, which will no doubt resolve on returning you such solemn thanks as you deserve.[13] I take it as a most cordial action on your part that you should have been so good as to address that letter to me, the least of the Fellows, and for this very generous honor and act of goodwill I offer you my best thanks. I shall make every effort, not to do likewise, for that is beyond my abilities, but at least to exert myself to their limit in promoting esteem and respect for your learning and merits. Farewell, most illustrious Sir, and believe me to be one bound by the warmest sense of obligation to yourself. London, 5 July 1672.

ADDRESS

To the very illustrious Johannes Hevelius,
Most worthy Senator of Danzig, etc.,
Danzig.

NOTES

Reply to Letters 1915, 1986, and 1986 bis.
1 Letter 1986 was read to the Royal Society on 19 June.
2 See Letter 1956, note 1.
3 See Letters 1927 and 1927a (Vol. VIII).
4 See Letter 1956, note 1. Cassini's observation of the period of revolution of Jupiter from the rotation of the great red spot was first made (with the same result) long before; see Vol. III, pp. 25, 27.
5 See Letter 1807, note 1 (Vol. VIII).
6 See Letter 1807 (Vol. VIII).
7 See Letter 1848, dated 1 January, which Oldenburg has confused with Letter 1854a.
8 See Letter 1962.
9 See Letters 1962 and 2009 (note 5).
10 See Letter 1956.
11 See Letter 1968.
12 See Letter 1968, note 2.
13 For some unknown reason Oldenburg did not present the *Epistola* at the meeting of 10 July, which was the last before the summer recess; he did so on 30 October, at the first meeting of the new session.

2014

Oldenburg to Kirkby

5 July 1672

Kirkby's Letter 1999 is endorsed as having been received on 4 July and answered the next day.

2015

Henshaw to Oldenburg

6 July 1672

From the original in Royal Society MS. H 3, no. 12

Copenhaguen: July 6.–72.

Sr

Yours of June 20th, came to mee but yesterday. ye D of Richmond[1] doth give me constantly so much imployment or else takes me abroad wth him, that though I sent yr letter to Dr Eras: Bartholinus[2] as soon as ever I came to this towne, as also ye booke Mr Collins sent him, and a copie of Sigr Cassini's letter concerning the new spot in Jupiter,[3] yet I have not been able to this day to comply so much wth ye respects I owe yu, and the Ambition I have for his Acquaintance as once to give him a visit, so that I was forced instead of going myself to send Triboulet to him, as also to the ships riding in this haven to inquire about ye bookes in quires sent yu by Mr Hevelius,[4] there are no ships yet come from Dantzick, but some expected every day, I will bee sure to use all diligence possible to find them when they come, and to send ye papers to yu by ye first convenience. I had no Instructions from ye Society, when I came away; but since yu desire some information from Iseland, pray bee pleased to send me by yr next ye antient Quaeries,[5] wch I remember were drawne up in Latine, though I am afraid ye season for this yeare is passed, for about a month since they sent to me for passes to secure theyr fleet from Scotch Capers[6] and 6 weeks hence they expect theyr ships home. if theyr bee any Curiositys to bee found in them I will make inquiry for them for ye use of

ye R.S. I have ye honour to bee very well received and known by ye great
Admiral heere, and to young Monsr Gabelli,[7] the one being Govr. of
Izeland and ye other proprietour of ye Island of Fero,[8] what questions they
are not provided to answer I must referre to ye solution of another yeare,
for ships goe from hence thither but once a yeare; I have met since I came
hither wth a discourse in print of Olaus Wormius de Mure Norvagico, wch
I had never seen before, with a designe (if they have it not) to put it into ye
library of ye Royall Soc:[9] I bought it; ye Narrative is curious, they being
sayd to bee brought into ye Country by winds or Clouds as Locusts in
southerne parts, wch gave me the Curiosity to inquire of Monsr Guldenlew
ye viceroy,[10] and Monsr Cruys Tolmaster[11] in that Country who both
affirmed to me by a voluntary Oath, that some of them have some time
fallen upon theyr hats as they have been riding abroad, how great a plague
they are to that Country some years, and ye pretty odde pyed Coulours
they are beautified wth, theyr genius and inclination, and how short lived
they are I have not time to inlarge on now, but must referre to ye printed
relation, wch I will send yu by ye first convenience, they are called Le-
mings or Lemmers in ye Norwagian toung, I had met with some accounts
of them long agoe in Olaus Magnus and Heylin,[12] but gave little Credit to
it, but here it is a thing so well testified that Nobody doubts of it. In our
tedious voyage hither I had ye pleasure to bee some houres on that uncouth sand of Norway wch lookes like ye backside of ye world, where after
ye fabrick was compleated ye Rubbish was layd on heaps, yet ye being but
on ye skirts of ye Country, ye honest and happy ignorance of ye people, and
my want of language hindred me from gaining any advantage by my
curiosity. Sr I pray excuse my hast (wch these lines will too much discover)
the post being this day forced to stay for our pacquets. I pray present my
most humble service to My Ld Bronker, to Sr Robert Morray; and tell
him I have every where inquired for that Digestum of theyr laws in Latine
he desired here, but they know nothing like it, so much as in danish.[13]
it is here ye worst and ye dearest place in ye whole world for books unlesse
at an Auction, wch I purpose to try my fortune at if I can have time hereafter. my most humble service to ye Noble Mr Boyle and to all other
friends of ye society that aske for me, if you could find an opportunity to
send me his book de Gemmis (a coppie or two) it would bee very acceptable here to some of ye Grandees who are learned and curious some few of
them. Sr I am withall my respects due to yr worth

Yr most affectionate humble servant
Tho Henshaw

There is one Mr Hanning last week sent from hence by ye D of Richmond and Expresse for Whitehall, if yu please to inquire for him at ye Dukes Lodgings at Court he will bring any papers yu have for this place.

ADDRESS

For
Henry Oldenburg Esq
at his house in the ould
Pell Mell
London

Franc a Amsterdam

POSTMARK IV 29

NOTES

1 See Letter 1907, note 1 (Vol. VIII).
2 Letter 1907 (Vol. VIII).
3 See Letter 1956, note 1, and Bartholin's Letter 2044.
4 See Letters 1986 bis and 1999.
5 See Vol. VII, pp. 506–9. Replies to a list of such questions were received much later via Erasmus Bartholin and reported to the Royal Society by Oldenburg on 24 February 1675/6.
6 Privateers.
7 Presumably Valdemar Gabel (1650–1725), son of Kristoffer Gabel (1617–73), former chief minister of King Frederick III (who had died in 1670) and chief engineer of the absolutist revolution in Denmark (1660).
8 The Faeroe Isles.
9 Olaus Worm, *Historia animalis quod in Norvagia quandoque e nubibus decidit, et sata ac gramina, magno incolarum detrimento, celerrime depascitur* (Copenhagen, 1653); there is still a copy in the Royal Society's library, which was presented on 23 April 1673. This marvelous "Norwegian mouse" is, of course, the lemming, *Myodes lemmus*.
10 Ulrik Frederick Gyldenløve (1638–1704), an important Danish statesman, Statholder in Norway. He was the natural son of King Frederick III of Denmark.
11 Possibly Philipp Cruse (1597–1676), Statholder at Tallinn (Esthonia).
12 Olaus Magnus, *Historia de gentibus septentrionalibus* (Rome, 1555); Peter Heylyn, *Cosmographie* (London, 1652).
13 The only collection of Danish Laws published at this time appears to be *Corpus juris danicum eller den fuldkomme danske Low-Bog ... colligeret aff Christian Cassuben* (Copenhagen, *c.* 1670), which is in Danish.

2016
Oldenburg to Willughby
6 July 1672

From *Philosophical Letters*, pp. 109–11, and the copy in Royal Society MS. O 2, no. 90

[To Mr Willughby]

London July 6. 1672.

Sir,

After my long Silence, I must now put you in mind of some Particulars, which were recommended to you and Mr. Ray, when you were with us here.[1] One was, to communicate what you had observed concerning the *Vermis Setaceus*,[2] or Heire-worm; of which Mr. Lister had made so rational a Narrative already.[3] Another, to experiment, to what Degree of Magnitude a Maggot may be advanced, by continuing to give it new Flesh every 2 or 3 Days, upon the occasion of Sir Sam. Tuke's Relation of a Maggot, which, within 2 Months, by that way, [was said to have] increased to the Bigness of a Man's Thigh.[4] A third, to try whether Insects will be bred in a Beef's Bladder so closed that no Passage be left for any Fly-blows? And because Flies may be said to have blown on the outside of the Bladder, and the Fly-blows to have eaten through the Bladder, it will be proper to include such a Bladder in a Case, to defend it from Fly-blows outwardly as well as inwardly. A fourth, to try, if Occasion serveth, the Virtue of *Lichen cinereus terrestris*,[5] which was [by one of our Fellows] said to be exceedingly efficacious in curing Dogs bitten by Mad Dogs. A Fifth, to enquire of Mr. Fisher whether he be Master of the Experiment of dissolving Glass, and reducing it into a white Calx; and after the Glass is well moisten'd with the Menstruum, whether it be capable to be shaved with a Knife, almost like Horn?[6] And farther, whether the Menstruum employ'd for that Purpose, performs upon all Sorts of Glass?

I intreat you, Sir, to present Mr. Ray with my hearty Service; and, he being concern'd in some of these Particulars, to give him the reading of this Paper.

Dr. Grew is now amongst us at Arundel-House,[7] making now and then[8] very good Observations upon Plants, and having shew'd to the Company, among divers Particulars, the Tracheae mention'd by Malpighi in his Discourse of Vegetables that you have seen.[9]

He hath been desired to endeavour, whether he can discover any such thing as a Peristaltick Motion in Plants when growing? For which Purpose he hath been directed to chuse some of the bigger Sort, wherein that Motion, if there be any such, is like to be more discernible.

[We hope, Sir, that you and your Friend will join in making also Research of so considerable a particular.]

I presume you know, that Mr. Boyle's Essay of the Origine and Virtues of Gems is now abroad. And I believe, that Seignior Malpighi's Discourse *de formatione pulli in ova foecundo, tam non incubato quam incubato,* will be printed in a short time. I desire very much to know that these Lines are come to hand [from Sir

Your faithfull servant
H. Oldenburg]

NOTES

It is probable that Derham had access to the original of this letter and we have followed his text, adding in brackets additional words found only in the copy retained by Oldenburg. Willughby had died before the writing of this letter, on 3 July.

1 Willughby was certainly and Ray possibly in London during May 1672; see Letter 1977, note 1.
2 "hair-like worm."
3 See Letter 1977.
4 For Sir Samuel Tuke, see Vol. III, p. 332, note. This absurd tale (related in a letter from one Francis Finch) was brought up at the meeting of 23 November 1671, when Ray and Willughby were present, and were asked to investigate it.
5 "ash-colored ground lichen." This plant was said by Sir Robert Moray (on 16 November 1671) to have this property.
6 This experiment was reported by John Ray on 23 November 1673, quoting a letter to himself from "Mr. Fisher"—possibly Samuel Fisher; see Vol. VII, p. 387, note 2.
7 John Wilkins proposed at a meeting of Council on 10 April 1672 that Nehemiah Grew be employed as curator to the Society for the anatomy of plants during one year, at a salary of fifty pounds to be subscribed by the Fellows. This proposal was approved by the Council and by the Society on 18 April; Grew began his demonstrations at once.
8 "from time to time" in the copy.
9 This was on 12 June.

2017

Newton to Oldenburg

6 July 1672

Printed in Newton, *Correspondence*, I, 208–11, from the original
in private possession, and in *Phil. Trans.*, no. 85
(15 July 1672), 5004–5

In this reply to Letters 2002, 2007, and 2012 Newton disposes firmly of Oldenburg's
suggestion that irregularities in the prism might occasion the dispersion of light associated with normal refraction. He goes on to declare that one cannot reach scientific truth by
examining possible causes for phenomena. "You know the proper Method for inquiring
after the properties of things is to deduce them from Experiments. And I told you that
the Theory wch I propounded was evinced to me, *not by inferring tis thus because not otherwise* . . . but *by deriving it from Experiments concluding positively & directly.*"

Newton then formulates a series of questions which he wishes to be determined by
experiment, in order to decide whether his theory be correct or not, wishing that all
objections against it springing from hypotheses should be suspended, and discussion limited either to any insufficiency in his own experiments to support the conclusions he drew
from them, or to the introduction of new experiments incompatible with his theory. He
notes a possible confusion in his reply to Hooke, and admits his obligation to Huygens
for his comments. He asks Oldenburg to delay the printing of Pardies's second letter.

2018

Newton to Oldenburg

8 July 1672

Printed in Newton, *Correspondence*, I, 212–13, from the original in private possession

In this further reply to Letter 2012 Newton expresses satisfaction at Huygens' attempt at a larger reflecting telescope, though without success, and inquires after Cock's
endeavors. He admits that concision and lack of figures made his initial expositon of this
optical work obscure, and then produces a geometrical argument to show why, if the
dispersion of the rays of light is about one twenty-fifth of the refraction, the diameter of
the circle of chromatic aberration produced will be about one-fiftieth of the diameter of
the lens.

2019

Oldenburg to Huygens

8 July 1672

From *Œuvres Complètes*, VII, 195–96
Original in the Huygens Collection at Leiden

A Londres le 8 Juillet 1672

Monsieur,

A la vostre du 1 juillet [N.S.], que ie receus le 27 juin (st. vet.) ie me trouve obligé de vous dire d'abord, que le iour auparavant, asscav. le 26 juin du mesme style, ie receus une lettre de Monsieur Sluse, datée le 22 juin [N.S.], qui renferma l'original de la copie, que voicy.[1] Come ie vous envoye ses meditations, ainsi ie prends la liberté de luy envoyer les vostres,[2] à fin que la subtilité de vos esprits puisse perfectionner la solution du probleme, dont il s'agit, iusques au dernier point. Je suis persuadé, Monsieur, que de vostre part vous ne manquerez nullement de nous mander encor vostre sentiment sur cete piece come ie m'assure, que Monsieur Sluse fera le pareil sur la vostre.

J'ay mandé a Monsieur Newton ce que vous pensez du plus propre sujet pour perfectionner ses lunettes; come aussi de ec qu'il dit de l'abberration des rayons à travers des verres convexes.[3] Quand i'auray sa responce la dessus,[4] ie ne manqueray pas de vous en faire part. Le livre de Monsieur Boyle touchant l'origine et les vertus des pierres precieuses est astheur public. J'en ay empacqueté un Exemplaire avec d'autres livres pour Monsieur Justel qui ne fera point de difficulté de vous le faire voir, lors qu'il sera arrivé a Paris. Le discours, ce me semble, est bien philosophique et fort instructif.

Vous trouverez dans ces Transactions[5] deux lettres latines touchant la theorie de Monsieur Newton sur la Lumiere et les Couleurs J'en ay deux autres, qui suivront, ie croy, dans le Journal prochain.[6] Cependant vous m'obligerez de me communiquer vos pensees sur ce que vous verrez à present dans l'annexe, que vous accepterez de la part de Monsieur

Vostre tres humble & tresobeissant Serviteur
Oldenburg

ADDRESS
A Monsieur
Monsieur Christian Hugens de Zulichem
dans la Bibliotheque du Roy à
Paris

TRANSLATION

London, 8 July 1672

Sir,

To yours of 1 July [N.S.] which I received on 27 June (Old Style) I find myself obliged to say first, that the day before, that is to say 26 June of the same style, I received a letter from Mr. Sluse, dated 22 June [N.S.] which contained the original of the copy, which is here.¹ As I send you his reflections, so I take the liberty of sending him yours,² so that the subtlety of your minds may perfect the solution of the problem which is the subject of discussion, to the last point. I am persuaded, Sir, that you for your part will not fail to let us know again your opinion of this paper, as I assure myself that Mr. Sluse will do the same with yours.

I have let Mr. Newton know what you think is the best method for perfecting his telescopes, as well as what [you] say of the aberration of the rays in passing through convex lenses.³ When I have his reply thereon,⁴ I shall not fail to share it with you. Mr. Boyle's book on the origin and virtues of precious stones is now published. I have put a copy in the parcel with the other books for Mr. Justel, who will make no difficulty in letting you see it when it arrives in Paris. It seems to me that the discussion is very philosophical and very instructive.

You will find in these *Transactions*⁵ two Latin letters on Mr. Newton's theory of light and colors. I have two others which, I think, will follow in the next journal.⁶ However you will oblige me by sending me your thoughts on what you now see in the enclosure which you will accept from, Sir,

Your very humble, obedient servant
Oldenburg

ADDRESS
To Mr. Christiaan Huygens of Zulichem
in the King's Library
Paris

NOTES

Reply to Letter 2004.
1 Letter 1994; the copy sent by Oldenburg is printed in *Œuvres Complètes*, VII, 197–99.
2 See Letter 2004a.
3 See Letter 2012.

4 See Letter 2018.
5 *Phil. Trans.*, no. 84 (17 June 1672), printing Letters 1946a and 1957a.
6 *Phil. Trans.*, no. 85 (15 July 1672), printing Letters 1976a and 1992.

2020

Oldenburg to Newton

9 July 1672

Printed in Newton, *Correspondence*, I, 211, note 7, from
the memorandum in private possession

Answ. july 9. acquiesce in his answer to H[ooke].[1] intend to print his set of Inquiries, and to recommend ym at ye R.S.[2] Desired to take off the suspension of printing the 2 let[ter] of Pard[ies][3] and to send me his answer to Huygens.

NOTES

Reply to Letter 2017.
1 Oldenburg evidently took Newton's meaning to have been that he wished the printing of Letter 1993 (the answer to Hooke's objections) to be delayed until he had checked the numbering of the sections; and in fact it was to be printed only in the November issue of the *Philosophical Transactions*.
2 This Oldenburg did at the meeting of 10 July.
3 Letter 1976a.

2021
Oldenburg to John Wilkins
10 July 1672

From the draft in Royal Society MS. O 2, no. 91

London July 10. 72.

My Lord

This very day at the meeting of ye R. Society hearing from Dr Pell ye very sad news of Mr Willughby's death[1] I was commanded to desire yt you, who are so well acquainted wth all the philosophical concerns and collections of yt worthy gentleman, would be pleased to take good care, yt such writings and curiosities of his as are sutable to ye purpose of our society, may be truely secured, and hereafter transferred unto their archives and repository: wch we hope, will be the more easily effected by yr lordship because of ye interest you have in Mr Ray, ye fidus Achates[2] of ye deceased.

The Society adjourned this day, appointing a Committee to meet in Gresham Colledge once a weeke during their recess.[3] Dr Grew hath produced divers considerable Observations among us, and been hitherto punctual enough in describing ym for our Register.[4]

Our forrain Correspondents continue very vigorous and respectfull to us. Among ye rest Signor Cassini hath been upon his desire elected into our body, and upon notice given him thereof returned not only verbal, but reall thanks by sending to ye Society a considerable Astronomical paper, about ye motion of Jupiter and his satellites, improving and mending Galilaei upon yt subject;[5] as yr Lordship will more fully understand, when your occasions shall permit you to visit London and Arundel-house, where your presence will be very welcome to all, in ye persuasion of My Lord

Yr Lordships very humble and faithfull servant,

NOTES

It seems obvious that this letter was intended for John Wilkins, Bishop of Chester, who had linked himself particularly closely with the work of Ray and Willughby, and entertained them in his palace.

1 See Letter 2016, note.

2 "Faithful companion." Ray completed Willughby's *Ornithologia* (London, 1676) and
  Historia piscium (Oxford, 1686).
3 On Friday afternoons, at Gresham College.
4 See Letter 2016, note 7.
5 See Letter 1995.

2022

Oldenburg to Sluse

11 July 1672

From the draft in Royal Society MS. O 2, no. 88

Illustri et Reverendo admodum
Domino Renato Francisco Slusio, Canonico Leodensi,
H. Oldenburg Salutem

Vix acceperam tuas novissimas, felices Alhazeniani problematis com-
pendifactrices, quin Cl. Hugenii de eodem argumento tractantem hanc
chartam tabellarius afferret;[1] Tacita sum usus venia tua impertiendi Hugenio
meditationem tuam;[2] nec minori jam utor libertate, cogitata ipsius vicissim
Tibi communicandi, uti sequitur;

"Vous verrez icy mon dernier calcul, different de celuy etc."

Vide Hugenii literas d. 1. julii 1672 [N.S.].
Spero non obfuturum Martem, quo minus a Te intelligam, literulas has
rite Tibi traditas fuisse. Vale, Vir Illustrissime, meque Totum tuum crede.
Dabam Londini d. 11. Julii 1672.

TRANSLATION

H. Oldenburg greets the illustrious and very reverend Mr. René François de
Sluse, Canon of Liège

I had barely received your recent very successful abbreviation of the [solution to]
the Problem of Alhazen when the postman brought this paper of the famous
Huygens discussing the same question;[1] I have taken your permission for granted
in imparting your considerations to Huygens[2] and *vice-versa* in communicating his
to you, as follows:

"You will see here my latest calculation, different from that . . .," etc.

See Huygens' letter of 1 July 1672 [N.S.].

I hope Mars will not obstruct my hearing from you that this trifling letter has been safely delivered to you. Farewell, most illustrious Sir, and believe me wholly yours. London, 11 July 1672.

NOTES

Reply to Letter 1994, received on 26 June; Huygens' Letter 2004 arrived on the following day.

1 Letter 2004.
2 See Letter 2019.

2023
Dodington to Oldenburg
12 July 1672
From the original in Royal Society MS. D 1, no. 29

Venice July 22. 1672 [N.S.]

Sr

I send you the Extract of part of a leter, Padre Athanas[ius] Kercher wrote to my sonn the last month.

"Habbiamo poj preso con noj una Tromba, gia avanti, 24. Anni qui pratticata, la quale fece maravigliosi effetti, poj che con essa habbiamo parlati alli Castelli Vicini 3 et 4 miglia lontani, e di piu anche, invitandoli alla nostra festa, che ha caggionata tanta ammiratione appresso tutti quej popoli circomvicini, che ogni giorno, da lontano somo venuti a vedere questo prodigioso instrumento, che fu fatto con singolar industria Che il Sigre Cardinale Pio a posta se conferi a S. Gregorio a poter sentir l'effetto, tanto raro; e da S. Gregorio sin a Guadagnuolo habbiamo parlati assieme:[1] poj che nostra Tromba, non solo parla di lontano, ma anche riceve la Risposta delli Corrispondenti, lequale non si e saputa d'altri.

"Et adesso faro fare un altra por L'Imperatore mio Signore[2] che arrivera facilmente a 20 miglia, a congregar un esseccito, con sono di cosi fatta

Tromba: Et e un secreto solamente riservato al Cesare, et con tempo, sapra anche lej il secreto essendo che sempre.³ son desideroso d'aver meco il mio amantissimo Giovanni & & &"

I have transcribed it verbatim. Two or three things I observe viz. That Father Kercher had this Invention 24 years since, Secondly That he hath made it capable of receiving Answeres. Thirdly That it is Intelligible 20 miles. I should be loath to detract from ye Honor of Sr Sam. Moreland, yet Amica veritas praeter Socratem et Platonem.⁴ I am preparing by his Majesties order to come hence towards England⁵ But whereever I am I shall endeavour to merit ye esteeme of Being Hond sr

> yr most humble servant
> *John dodington*

ADDRESS
   Monsieur
   Monsieur Oldenburg Secretaire
     de la Societe Royalle
        A
         Londres

POSTMARK IV 30

TRANSLATION

. . . .

"We have, then, a trumpet near at hand which was made twenty-four years ago, and which does remarkable things, so that we have spoken through it to the neighboring castle, three or four miles distant, and even further, inviting them to our festival; which has aroused so much wonder in the surrounding populace that they come from long distances every day to see this marvelous instrument which was made with exceptional skill. That Cardinal Pio purposely took himself to S. Gregorio in order to experience its effects, and from there even to Guadagnuolo we have spoken together;¹ further that our trumpet does not only speak over great distances but also receives the reply from one's interlocutor, which is not known to be done by others.

And at present I am having another made for my lord the Emperor,² which will easily come up to twenty miles in order to assemble an army, with the sound of a trumpet fashioned in this way. And this is a secret reserved for the Emperor alone, and in time you too shall know the secret, being always [etc.].³ I am eager to have my very loving John with me."

. . . .

NOTES

1 As Guadagnolo is a hill (alt. 1218 metres) in the foothills of the Apennines not far from Palestrina, about 38 km. east of Rome, it is likely that the other place is S. Gregorio da Sassola, less than 5 km. distant, towards Rome.
2 Athanasius Kircher was born in Hesse, Germany.
3 Or possibly: "he too shall know the secret, it remaining such always."
4 "Truth is a friend dearer than Socrates and Plato"; another version of an oft-quoted and ancient tag.
5 Dodington's appointment as Resident at Venice was revoked by Charles II on 30 April 1672, but he took leave of the Venetian Senate (who treated him cordially) only on 8 November, beginning his journey on the twentieth. He reached London about the end of January, 1673. Dodington died of a carouse at the Bear in Leadenhall Street in early December 1673. He left a wife and six children.

2024

Newton to Oldenburg

13 July 1672

Printed in Newton, *Correspondence*, I, 217–18, from the original in private possession

In this reply to Letter 2020, Newton gives Oldenburg permission to print Letters 1976a, 1992 and 1993. He inquires about the four-foot telescope which Christopher Cock has in hand, especially about the "steely matter" of which it is made and of which he asks for a sample. He asks Oldenburg to ascertain whether Cock or some one else will 'prepare the Metalls, Glasse, Tube & Frame" of such a telescope, leaving the polishing to him.

2025

Flamsteed to Oldenburg

15 July 1672

From the original in Royal Society MS. F 1, no. 87

Derby July. 25. 1672

Mr Oldenburg

Sr

By yours of July 2d: yu excuse yr former silence, of which I had not compleined but that the transactions unusually failed mee. I know that yr affaires allow yu not time for a frequent intercourse of letters: which therefore I expect not; but I hope too yu will now & then comand so much time from them, as to let mee know how ye papers I communicate are accepted, & when it is no great trouble how ye ingenious world imployes itselfe. before I reaceaved yr letter our bookseller delivered mee the Transactions I wanted, In one of which yu are pleased to insert my observations of Joves transits by ye fixed stars[1] I thanke yu for yr paines in correcteing the language of that paper; in ye impression of which a materiall error or two have happened which I give yu notice of, yt yu may print them amongst ye errata of some moneth: Nom 28[2] pag 4036 lin 27: in ye observations of Feb: 17 for *distitit* 50″ shoulde 21′ 50″ & in ye following pag. 4037, in ye observations of Martij 19. for *Alto* ♃ 49°. 35′ should be *alto* ♃ 29°. 35′ these I suppose yu would not have to passe: pray remember them to be corrected.[3]

The places yu have noted in my paper of ye moons appulse[4] are faulty, I thanke yu heartily for markeing them, & could wish you had done as much by some of my former papers, which I am confident were not better pend. but really Sr, you doe ill to depreciate your owne ingenuity, that yu may seeme to excuse my ignorance in ye latine tongue; of which I have got that little knowledg I have, by readeing onely; my frequent businesses, & distempers, not haveing permitted mee time for such exercises, as are requisite to acquire a tollerable skill in it: I shall not hereafter write with that hast I have beene forced hitherto, but intend to be more carefull both how I write, & pointe; but since I know, I can not but I shall fall into some sore errors of language, I must beg, & I know you will not denie it, yr pen to rub out ye errors of mine.

I have sent yu ye observations yu desire:[5] in which pray alter my language as yu think fit it will be an obligation to me which I shall not stick to
acknowledge. Since this, of Mars I have observed his transit by 2 fixed
stars in ♓ 11°–44′ & 12°. 12′ on ye 17 & 18th of June last in ye morneing:
of which I give yu no account reserveing it till his returne, which will be
observable in ye 10 last days of September, & first of October, when by
measureing his distance & position from ye same fixed star & 2 several
times ye same night I hope to find his parallax & by consequence ye Suns:[6]
for hee then will be but little past ye Acronicall phasis, in Perihelio; & I
find yt being very carefull my instruments will show 5 seconds, so yt I no
longer doubt to determine his parallax if God permit mee health & a cleare
sky I have given Mr Townely notice of these phainomena who will not
faile to observe them, I am confident, if my letter but come to his hands.[7]
If I thought there were any with you would endeavour to observe them
accurately, I would send yu a figure of ye planets transit by ye 3 stars & an
Ephemeris for Mars at that time, which I intend this weeke to compose.[8]
if yu desire it, pray let mee know yr mind, & I will send it. The same June
18 that I last observed Mars I allso saw Saturn his anses were now very
conspicuous, but glareing & not so well defined as last October, either
because I used a wider aperture on ye object glasse, or that ye lightnesse of
ye morneing & hazinesse of ye aire caused it. since then, I have neither
observed him, nor Mars.

I perceive by yr postscript that Hevelius hath seene my appulses or
heard of them by you: which hee wishes continued & I, that I had time
to doe them for now I have severall instruments to fit up for my owne use,
which I dare not trust to any workeman; & my fathers affaires, which lie
most upon my shoulders, are double to what they have beene; so yt I
cannot gaine time to make such accurate calculations as formerly, but something I shall doe that ye Phamomena may not be unforeknowne; tho I cannot spend so much time as formerly to calculate them accurately I find that
ye cloudes have deprived mee of many opportunitys, & therefore instead of
makeing calculations, I shall rather have to waite for observations, which
will be of no lesse use & more pleasant to ye ingenious nor need I sorrow
the losse of an appearance when ye heavens are clouded if I have beene at
no great paines to find it. I had something to adde but my freind stays & I
have onely time at present to subscribe Sr

> Your very affectionate servant
> *John Flamsteed*

ADDRESS

For Henry Oldenburge Esqr
at his house in ye middle of ye
    Pell mell these

NOTES

Reply to Letter 2010.

1 See *Phil. Trans.*, no 82 (22 April 1672), 4036–38.
2 Read: 82.
3 Oldenburg inserted these corrections at the end of *Phil. Trans.*, no. 85 (15 July 1672), 5026.
4 See Letter 1824, note 1 (Vol. VIII)—Flamsteed seems to allude to Oldenburg's criticism of his Latin style, not employing the word "place" in its astronomical sense.
5 See Royal Society MS. F 1, no. 88: "Lunae ad Pleiades Appulsus Anno 1672 Feb: 23 st. v. observatus Derbiae" [An appulse of the Moon to the Pleiades, observed at Derby on 23 February 1672], which was to be printed in *Phil. Trans.*, no. 86 (19 August 1672), 5034–36. This account was enclosed with this letter.
6 Knowing the precise position of Mars in opposition when close to the earth at two distinct times, and the planet's own motion in that interval, Flamsteed will determine its parallax at this point in the orbit; this being known, and the relative size of the orbits of Mars and the Earth being known also, the smaller solar parallax is indirectly established. As will appear later, Flamsteed found the parallax of Mars to be always less than 25″, and so the solar parallax less than 10″ (*Phil. Trans.*, no. 96 (21 July 1673), 6000).
7 Flamsteed was in fact to be away from home on his father's business at the time when this second observation was to be made; however, he was able to make it in conjunction with Richard Towneley in Lancashire (Baily, p. 32).
8 See Letter 2036.

2026

Oldenburg to Newton

16 July 1672

Printed in Newton, *Correspondence*, I, 219, from the partial copy in Royal Society MS. O 2, no. 92

In this reply to Letter 2024, which in fact did not reach Newton, Oldenburg reported from a conversation with Cock that the four-foot telescope had a bronze principal mirror, six inches in diameter, giving a dark image. This telescope Cock was willing to sell for £5. Oldenburg proposed sending a piece of the speculum metal, which Newton in due course received and returned. The steely speculum, three inches in diameter, was made from pure Venice steel; this also Cock was willing to lend.

2027
Beale to Oldenburg
16 July 1672

From the original in Royal Society MS. B 1, no. 56

Deare bror,

After my thankfull acknowledgements of yr oblieging pacquet[1] wch hath many remarkables. I must say, yt I am not sorry to find yu full of businesses, especially such as may affoord yu some avaylable encouragements, because I am assured yt they are for ye public, & ye concernments of posterity. Yu aske my sentiment of Mr. Listers—of stones—hayreworms. I remarke yt, He hath pointed out ye cause or manner, Howe stones may be generated in any part of humane body, not excepting ye very hearte. And perhaps all bodyes, solid, concrete, or liquid, may be petryfyed, not excepting Gold, & glasse, though esteemed incorruptible. And ye generation of chrystall by coagulation of dewe by nitrous steames, was luckily annexed in ye same Tract.[2] For Hayre-wormes, I do not suspect Mr. L. but I wish it farther enquired, Whether from ye Manes & Tayles of horses, ye hayre by abideing in pits of rayne-water be not sometimes in Spring animated. Tis about 44 yeares, since I tryed it often in vaine. But then Mr. Dunscomb[3] (one far more industrious than my selfe) assurd me yt he obtained ye effect. And he was perfectly honest and candid. Soe I grant, yt sometimes, & frequently, spiders do spit out the aereall threds, and yet perhaps ye Sun doth spin, or concreate many, of ye dewy air. I sawe in a wide common, many bushes covered with dewy cobwebs. Examining ye cause, I found under ye cobwebs innumerable magots, or very small aurelias,[4] & every [one] of them could spin their threads. There may be many differing causes of like things. I doubt not at all of ye distemper attributed to ye Tarantula; & ye cure by Music; yet for Cornelios direction it may be enquired more thoroughly, whether ye biteing of a spider be constantly the cause of ye distemper:[5] Or may it not be ye original cause, & yet ye distemper become infectious. As ye late comedians infected Abderites.[6] We heare little of ye mischief done by spiders of Bermudas; Nor have you yet given us their description, or more then their strong webs. John Lederer tells, Howe a spider bitt him in Carollina, wch had beene his present death, if an Indian had not usd his best in sucking out ye poysone, If in this hasty scrible I am not mistaken.[7] In hot countreyes, Insects, Serpents, &c are all more dangerous. In some places huge. As I walkt in ye Piazzos of Geneva, I saw such a large spider fall from ye lofty roofe yt ye fall made me startle. And Bats are there bigger than ours. Trusty Greaves sawe in ye Pyramides Bats above a foote long viz bigger then our owles.[8] And in some parts Cats are winged. I wish Mr. Doddington would enquire whether the fountaine of Aponum holds up ye fame of healing, as in ye days of Claudian and as Moderne Men of Note do reporte.[9]

Just as I am scribling this I receive ye inclosed from Mr. Strode,[10] by wch yu will find, yt I have furnished him wth some bookes, wch have opened his eyes & fitted him to do us good service. In another letter, he sayth, he is nowe ashamed of wt I sent yu, because he finds it done by our Lord Bp. Sarum to Bullialdus.[11] I answere, yt his way being his owne Invention, & done by Algebra, will be no lesse oblieging & acceptable. I pray yu dispose of these, yt he may not be discouraged. I have a thousand things more to say to yu, but not a minute of time more than to subscribe Sr.

Yr. most affectionate servant
Beale.

Munday by carrier. Jul. 16. 72.[12]

I pray yu accept of my poore mite sent by Carrier 10s. only to buy a Sugarloafe for yr. Infantry.[13] God blesse yu all.

The eloquence of Demosthenes & Cicero compared is ye best of yt kind yt ever appeared, deepe, learned, iudicious, acute.[14] Done undoubtedly by ye same hand wch gave us The Eloquence of these times, but more faultlesse.[15]

Tis doublesse an Englishman, who pretends Translation yt he may be Incognito. Or if ye compar[ison] be transl[ated] The other is his owne.[16] You take notice of Panorganon by Leybourne.[17] The Catalogue n.9. He is worthy to be encouraged.

Marriage is excellently defended by a young sparkle.[13]

NOTES

1 Evidently *Phil. Trans.*, no. 83 (20 May 1672) which contains (pp. 4062–66) Lister's "Account of a Stone cut out from under the tongue of a Man" and his letter "concerning animated Horse-hairs" (in which he shows that these are in fact worms generated in the normal way).

2 "Reflections made by P. Francisco Lana S.J. upon an Observation . . . of some mines

in Italy, concerning the formation of Crystals: English'd out of the XI. Venetian *Giornale de Letterati*," pp. 4068–69.

3 He is not identifiable.

4 "chrysalids."

5 Compare Letter 1911a (Vol. VIII), printed on pp. 4066–67 of the same issue of the *Philosophical Transactions*.

6 We cannot explain what Beale meant; the inhabitants of Abdera were traditionally reputed to be stupid.

7 The book alluded to is [John Lederer], *The discoveries of J. L., in three several marches from Virginia to the West of Carolina . . . collected and translated out of Latine . . . by Sir W. Talbot, Baronet* (London, 1672).

8 John Greaves, *Pyramidographia* (London, 1646).

9 Compare Letter 1919 (Vol. VIII), printed again in the same issue of the *Philosophical Transactions*, pp. 4067–68.

10 Letter 2027a.

11 See Letter 2027a, notes 2 and 3. The earlier letter with enclosure from Strode has not survived.

12 July 16 was a Tuesday.

13 This is presumably a reference to Oldenburg's eldest child, Rupert (d. 1724), of whose birth the exact date is unrecorded.

14 [René Rapin], *A Comparison between the Eloquence of Demosthenes and Cicero* (Oxford, 1672); this work appeared in French at Paris in 1671.

15 [René Rapin], *Reflections upon the Eloquence of these Times* (London, 1672), the French book having appeared at Paris in the previous year.

16 As is obvious, Beale was mistaken; but the name of the translator is not known.

17 William Leybourne, *Panorganon: or a Universall Instrument performing all such conclusions as are usually wrought by the Globes, Spheres, Sectors, Quadrants etc.* (London, 1672). The instrument was devised by Walter Hayes. Leybourne, now in middle life, was a prolific writer on applied mathematics, but none of his books was ever reviewed in the *Philosophical Transactions*. Beale probably means that this book was listed in a catalogue of his books for sale annexed by John Martin to *Phil. Trans.*, no. 80 (the end of the sixth volume). But there is no such catalogue in the copies we have examined.

2027a
Thomas Strode to Beale
14 June 1672

Enclosure with Letter 2027
From the original in Royal Society MS. S 1, no. 115

Maperton June 14. 1672.

Reverend Sr

I have perused the inclosed tracts and have returned them all except one; if you sent for these for mee, it is nothing but reason but I should have them, and will rather then it shall bee in the least preiudiciall unto you, I doe take notice that give an account of excellent bookes, I would desire you when an opportunitye offers it selfe to inquire the prize of Fergusus Labarinthus Algebra[1]

There were 2 causes that moved to acquaint you with what I fancied that I had discovered, the usefulnesse and the newnesse;[2] my Lord Bishop of Salisburye inquisition &c. doe fully shew the usefulnesse, and without doubt all the tables that were calculated according to Bulialdus method were false;[3] and of the newnesse of it you may perceive that it was new to mee by the papers herewith sent,[4] and the method new, but I now see there are more wayes to [cut] wood then one. and truly had not my promise made it yours, I should not have communicated it unto you

I have sent you my method with examples and their demonstration and being their demonstration doe depend on a proposition not common in the conicks I have likewise cleered that; and given a rule for finding the semi-diameter in the epicycle according to Bulialdus method which is like the correcting of an old Almanache, but if I had not done it I could not so easilye have discovered Mr Wings mistakes[5] I had almost forgot my cheifest businesse, that is to send you 11s. viz 10s. 4d. for the former bookes and 8d. for this now kept by mee; by your letter I perceive that the bookes are not deffective Sr

I am your most humble servant
Tho Strode

NOTES

Thomas Strode of Somerset had entered University College, Oxford, in 1642, after which he traveled for some time in France during the Civil Wars, returning to settle at Maperton near Wincanton. He began a direct correspondence with Collins in a letter dated 11 July 1672 (Rigaud, II, 438–43) which gives some account of the development of the matters touched on in this and later letters. He also had correspondence with Newton in 1676. Strode published a treatise on permutations and combinations (London, 1678) and another on dialing (London, 1688).

1 Johan Jacob Ferguson, *Labyrinthus algebrae* (The Hague, 1667).

2 In reading Ismael Boulliaud's *Astronomia Philolaica* (Paris, 1645) Strode found reason to disagree with his treatment of the theory of a planet's motion in an elliptic orbit (which was based on the supposition of its uniform angular motion about the empty focus). Strode communicated his mathematical discussion of this problem to Beale in May, from whom it reached Collins, who in turn reported it to Flamsteed in a letter of unknown date. For on 6 June 1672 (probably; the letter is misdated in Rigaud, II, 137) Flamsteed wrote his thoughts on Strode's method to Collins, pointing out that the same criticism of Boulliaud had been made and corrected by Seth Ward nineteen years earlier. Writing again to Collins on 10 July (Rigaud, II, 151–53) Flamsteed complains that although he has now heard from Oldenburg at last (Letter 2010), Oldenburg has not sent him Collins' "solution of Mr. Strode's problem, which yours had caused me to expect."

3 See Seth Ward, *In Ismaelis Bullialdi "Astronomiae Philolaicae" fundamenta, inquisitio brevis* (Oxford, 1653); the theme is continued in Ward's later writings.

4 There is nothing more with this letter; they were presumably sent to Collins.

5 The work mentioned in Letter 1945, note 2.

2028

Oldenburg to Huygens

18 July 1672

From *Œuvres Complètes* VII, 207–8
Original in the Huygens Collection at Leiden

A Londres le 18 juillet 1672.

Monsieur

Vous ayant escrit le 8me juillet et envoyé la copie de la lettre, de Monsieur Sluse[1] ie ne vous eusse pas si tost importuné de nouveau, si quelques lignes de Monsieur Newton, qui regardent une partie de la lettre, que vous me fistes l'honneur de m'escrire le 1. juillet,[2] ne m'y eussent obligé. Je vous les donneray dans la mesme langue, que ie les ay receu. Il dit donc,[3]

"I am glad to find by ye abstract of Monsieur Hugenius his letter, which you transmitted to me, that he who hath done so much in Dioptricks hath been pleased to undertake the improvement of Telescopes by Reflexions also; though without ye desired success. I hope, ye event of his next essay, if he shall think fit to attempt any thing further, will prove more happy by a litle altering ye manner of his proceding. As for me, I know not, whether I shall make any further tryals myself, being obliged to prosecute some other subjects.

As to ye Theory of Light and Colors, I am apt to believe, that some of the Experiments may seem obscure by reason of ye brevity, where with I writ ym, which should have been described more largely, and explained with schemes, if they had been intended for the publick. But I see not, why the Aberration of a Telescope should be more than about $\frac{1}{50}$ of ye Glasess aperture. For, suppose DF be ye Lens, CD and EF two lines parallel to

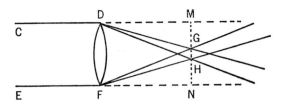

its Axis, in which or indefinitely near to which, all variety of difforme rays are successively incident on two opposite parts of its Perimeter: And of those rays let DH and FG be the most refracted, and DG and FH ye least refracted, intersecting ye former in G and H. Draw GH, and produce it both ways, till at M and N it occur with CD and EF, also produced. Now, since by my Principles ye difference of Refraction of ye most difforme rayes is about ye 24th or 25th part of their whole refraction, ye Angle GDH will be about a 25th part of ye Angle MDH, and consequently the subtense GH (which is ye diameter of ye least space, in to which ye refracted rays converge) will be about a 25th part of ye subtense MH, and therefore a 49th part of ye whole line MN, ye diameter of ye Lens; or, in round numbers, about a fiftieth part, as I asserted."

Apres avoir transcrit cecy, ie n'y ay rien à adjouster, si non que ie fais imprimer a present dans mon journal la plus propre methode descrite de Monsieur Newton pour establir sa doctrine de la Lumiere et des Couleurs.[4]

Quand il sera achevé d'imprimer, ie vous l'envoieray des aussi tost, come
Monsieur

> Vostre tres humble et tresobeissant serviteur
> *Oldenburg*

ADDRESS

A Monsieur
Christian Hugens de Zulechem,
  a la bibliotheque du Roy à
             Paris

TRANSLATION

London, 18 July 1672

Sir,

Having written to you on 8 July and sent a copy of Mr. Sluse's letter,[1] I would not have intruded upon you so soon again if some lines from Mr. Newton which concern part of the letter you honored me with on July first[2] had not compelled me to do so. I shall give them to you in the very language in which I received them. He says then,[3]

. . . .

Having transcribed this I have nothing more to add except that I am now having printed in my journal Mr. Newton's best method for establishing his doctrine of light and colors.[4] When it is finished printing, I shall send it to you immediately, as, Sir,

> Your very humble and obedient servant
> *Oldenburg*

ADDRESS

Mr. Christiaan Huygens of Zulichem,
  The King's Library,
      Paris

NOTES

1 Letter 2019 with its transcript of Letter 1994.
2 Letter 2004.
3 The following quotation is the whole of Letter 2018.
4 Letter 2017.

2029
Oldenburg to Swammerdam
20 July 1672
From the memorandum in Royal Society MS. O 2, no. 82

Scripsi denuo d. 20. julij. 72. per Dominum Scroter,[1] et misi No. 84.[2]

TRANSLATION

Wrote again 20 July 1672 by Mr. Schröter[1] and sent no. 84.[2]

NOTES

This was written at the end of Letter 1965, Oldenburg's first reply to Letter 1938 (Vol. VIII). Oldenburg had meanwhile written Letter 1996.

1 The exact identity of this traveler is difficult to ascertain. He is probably to be identified with the William Schroter who was an Original Fellow of the Royal Society (elected 17 September 1662). He was interested in both medical and optical problems as demonstrated by his appearance at the meeting of the Society on 11 December 1672. Hooke knew him as "Scroter," and mentions his alchemical and optical activities. He was to help Oldenburg to transmit parcels to Leibniz in later years.

2 *Phil. Trans.*, no. 84 (17 June 1672); see Letter 1996.

2030
Oldenburg to De Graaf
20 July 1672
From the memorandum in Royal Society MS. G 1, no. 10

Acc. d. 18. julij 72. resp. d. 20. julij per Dominum Scröter: misi N. 82 Transact[ionum].

TRANSLATION

Received 18 July 1672. Replied 20 July by Mr. Schröter; sent no. 82 of the *Transactions*.

NOTE

This memorandum of a reply to Letter 2011 is written on that letter. *Phil. Trans.*, no. 82 (22 April 1672) contained the review of De Graaf's *De mulierum organis generationi inservientibus*.

2031

Oldenburg to Vollgnad and Jaenisch

22 July 1672

From the draft in Royal Society MS. O 2, no. 93
Partly printed in J. D. Major, *Memoria Sachsiana* (Leipzig, 1675), p. 44

Excellentissimis Doctissimisque Viris
D. D. Henrico Vollgnadio et Johanni Janisio
Medicinae Doctoribus, et S.R.S. Academiae Naturae
Curiosorum Collegis ornatissimis
Henr. Oldenburg Salutem

Lugubrem Epistolam vestram, Viri Illustres, tristissimam Nobilis Sachsii obitus nunciam, lacrimis sane perfundissem, ni sanctior me philosophia, praeparato in quamvis sortem pectore sui cultores instruens, cohibuisset. Evasit ille (quod ipsi invidere nefas fuerit) ad Naturae, quam hic scrutabatur cum molestia, Authorem Sapientissimum, ab eoque quae hic penetrare non dabatur summa cum facilitate juxta ac jucunditate nunc edocetur. Eo et nos mentes nostras sublevemus jugiter, Naturaeque contemplationi eo imprimis fine incumbamus, ut ipsa ceu scala commodissima ad exoptatam Caelorum Arcem consurgamus.

Verum hoc misso, ad vos potius me converto, Viri Prae-clarissimi, et generosum pectoris vestri Candorem, egregiamque vestram in tuendo commercio philosophico voluntatem exosculor. Quaecunque a me pusillo proficisci officia possunt, quae vel ambobus vobis seorsim vel Inclytae vestrae junctim, gratae fuerint, ea ut audacter imperetis, magnopere a vobis Contendo.

Hamburgensis Schultzius inter vestrarum secundi anni Ephemeridum Exemplaria, quae Bibliopolae nostrati Martino vendidit et mihi unum transmisit, ex quo facile liquet, anni illius segetem multo esse priori locupletiorem. Multa ibi occurrunt memoratu digna, quae certe accuratum magis Typothetam, qui et rerum et literarum mendas diligentius emaculasset, omnino merebantur. Quae inibi de Bohemiae et Hungariae fodinis enarrantur, ampliorem profecto investigationem exposcunt.[1] Quibus et ea, quae de Cracoviensibus,[2] omnibusque Germaniae nostrae fossilibus resciri possunt, jungatur, operae omnino precium iudicamus.

De caetero, id nobis omnibus cordi quam maxime fuerit, ne quid falsi fucative penui nostro philosophico ingeratur; sed omnia, quantumpote, summa fide et cura [literarum][3] monumentis illata ad posteritatem transmittenda.

Ea inter, quae nunc apud nos geruntur, eminet nova lucis et Colorum theoria, ab Isaaco Newtono, Cantabrigiensi Mathematum Professore, Regiaeque Societatis Collega, non ita dudum excogitata in hanc sententiam.[4]

Lumen scilicet constare ex aggregatione infinitorum quasi radiorum, qui suapte indole suum quisque colorem referent retineantque, atque adeo apti nati sint certa quadam ratione, plus alij, alij minus refringi, radios ejusmodi, dum promiscui in aperto lumine confunduntur, nullatenus discerni, sed candorem potius referri, in refractione vero singulos unius coloris ab alijs alterius coloris secerni, et hoc modo secretos, sub proprio et nativo colore apparere, ea corpora sub aliquo colore, v.g. *rubro*, videri, quae apta sint reflectere aut transmittere radios solummodo rubros &c.

Integra haec doctrina Num. 8omo Transactionum Philosophicarum fuit inserta, quaeque dehinc ea in rem disceptata fuere, inque uberriorem Theoriae illius disquisitionem ab ipso Authore suggesta, Numeri 83. 84. 85 contenta reperientur. Cum autem verear, ne tarde nimis ad vos quaesita perveniant, quae idem ille in totius rei stabilimentum proposuit, et Philosophorum quorumvis ingenio et industriae discutienda commisit, hic subjicere non gravabor; in eorum gratiam, qui tanti momenti argumento elucidando occupari voluerint

Vid Transact. philosoph. no. 85[5]

Si qui sint inter Academiae vestrae Collegas, quos haec studia inviant, praeter rem haud fore putem, ipsis scripti huius mei apographum communicare, eosque ad totius rei disquisitionem exhortari. Taedium sine dubio surrexit ex tanta prolixitate; pellam illud, postquam solummodo monuero,

Nobilissimum Boylium nuper edidisse tractatum suum de Gemmarum origine et viribus, sermone quidem Anglico, sed jam in Latinum verso, inque hac lingua typis ante aliquot septimanas commisso. Brevissimo temporis spatio in publicum prodibit; tumque numerosa Exemplaria Hamburgum, ni fallor, transmittentur. Valete, Viri Eximij, et Oldenburgium Vestrum amare pergite. Dabam Londini d. 22. Julij 1672.

TRANSLATION

Henry Oldenburg greets the very excellent and learned Messrs. Heinrich Vollgnad and Johannes Jaenisch, Doctors of Medicine and most worthy members of the Imperial Academia Naturae Curiosorum

I should surely have shed many tears over your melancholy letter announcing the sad death of the noble Sachs, illustrious Sirs, if I had not been restrained by a more holy philosophy, preparing the minds of those who cultivate it with a resolution to withstand any blows of fate. He has gone to the most wise Creator of Nature (which here he investigated with so much labor), and it would be wrong to envy him that; from Him now he may discover, with great ease and joy, what we may not learn here below. We too should continually raise our thoughts to Him, and indulge in the contemplation of Nature particularly in order to ascend through that means as a stairway to the longed-for heavenly citadel.

And now having written this, I turn rather to you, excellent Sirs, greatly rejoicing in the generosity of your spirits and in your outstanding goodwill towards the maintenance of a philosophical correspondence. I earnestly beseech you boldly to require of me whatever services my humble self may render which will be welcome either to yourselves singly or to your distinguished Academy collectively.

[The bookseller] Schulz of Hamburg has sent me a copy of the second year of your *Miscellanea* among those which he sold to our bookseller Martin, from which it is readily seen that its harvest is far richer than that of the first volume. Much that is noteworthy is there to be found, which was surely deserving of a more accurate printer who would have carefully remedied the faults both literal and affecting the content. What is there related of the mines of Bohemia and Hungary certainly calls for fuller investigation.[1] We judge it would be well worthwhile to add to [the results of] that whatever may be learned concerning the minerals of Cracow,[2] and of all our Germany.

Moreover, we are above all anxious that nothing untrue or feigned should be introduced into our philosophical treasury, but that so far as may be everything should be inserted with the greatest trustworthiness and care into the [literary][3] repositories which are to be handed down to posterity.

Among other matters to which we are now giving our attention there stands out the new theory of light and colors devised not long ago by Isaac Newton, Professor of Mathematics at Cambridge and a Fellow of the Royal Society in this formulation:[4]

That light consists of an aggregation of an almost infinite number of rays each of which carries and retains a color according to its nature, and so is made fit to be refracted to a certain definite extent, some more, some less. When rays of this kind are mingled together confusedly in open daylight they cannot by any means be detected but are rather called pure white light, whereas in refraction individual rays of one color are separated from others of another and in this way what was hidden appears in its own natural hue. Those bodies appear of a certain color, for example red, which are suited to reflect or transmit only the red rays.

The whole of this theory was inserted in No. 80 of our *Philosophical Transactions*, and the later discussion of the subject and the author's suggestions for the better examination of that theory may be found in Nos. 83, 84, and 85. However, as I fear that longed-for things may come to you but too tardily, I make it no burden to annex below what he has put forward towards the determination of the whole question, and committed for discussion to the industry and intelligence of all philosophers, for the satisfaction of those who delight to occupy themselves in enlightening questions of so great moment:

See *Philosophical Transactions*, no. 85.[5]

If there are any members of your Academy who pursue these studies it will be no bad thing to communicate a copy of this letter of mine to them, and urge them to an examination of the whole business. No doubt a feeling of boredom has been created by so great prolixity; I will dispel it, after merely advising you that the very noble Boyle has recently published his tract on the origin and virtues of gems, which is in English but already translated into Latin, and was entrusted to the printer in this language a few weeks ago. In a very short space of time it will be published and then, if I mistake not, plenty of copies will be sent to Hamburg. Farewell, excellent Sirs, and continue to love your Oldenburg. London, 22 July 1672.

NOTES

Reply to Letter 2005.

1 Observation 78 of the second volume of *Miscellanea Curiosa* is by Johann Georg Greisel: "Metallifodinarum Regni Bohemiae consideratio"; there is also (Obs. 28 by Johann Paterson): "Morbi Hungariae Endemii. Mineralia quaedam Hungariae."

2 Near Cracow there are not only metalliferous mines but the celebrated saltmines of Wieliczka.

3 This word has been inserted by Oldenburg only in the copy entered in Royal Society Letter Book, V, 300.

4 This précis has appeared before: compare Letters 1946a and 1952.

5 Oldenburg means to include here his own Latin version of an extract from Letter

2017 printed in *Phil. Trans.*, no. 85 (15 July 1672), 5006–7; this is the section including Newton's own *Quaeries* about his theory. Oldenburg attached so much importance to this extract that he not only gave Newton's English form first place in the issue but followed it immediately with his Latin translation for the benefit of readers abroad.

2032

Oldenburg to Pardies

22 July 1672

From the memorandum in Royal Society MS. P 1, no. 81

Rec. le 10. juillet 72.
resp. le 22. juill. sent him M. Boyls Experiment of sound.[1]

TRANSLATION

Received 10 July 1672.
Replied 22 July . . .

NOTES

Reply to Letter 2009.
[1] It is not obvious what this was, except Boyle's air-pump experiment of long before showing that sound is not transmitted through a (near) vacuum.

2033

Oldenburg to Flamsteed

22 July 1672

From the memorandum in Royal Society MS. F 1, no. 87

Rec. july 20. 72. answ. july 22. and sent Collins Answer to Strode.[1]

NOTES

Reply to Letter 2025. Oldenburg also asked for the diagram showing the transit of Mars past the three stars in Pisces.

1 See Letter 2027a, note 2. This answer has not, apparently, survived; the letter in which Strode acknowledged it was dated 11 July (Rigaud, II, 438–43).

2034
Malpighi to Oldenburg
23 July 1672

From the original in Royal Society Malpighi Letters, no. 16
Printed in *Opera Omnia*, II, *De formatione pulli in ovo*, p. 18

Praeclarissimo et Eruditissimo Viro
Domino Henrico Oldenburg Regiae Societatis Anglicanae Secretario,
Marcellus Malpighius S.P.

Sero Mantuanus Tabellarius gratissimas tuas epistolas sexto Idus Junij exaratas mihi reddidit Vir praeclarissime. Libri fasciculus, quem Regio Mandatario vestro apud Venetos transmissum innuis, non adhuc ad manus meas devenit; interim tamen quales quales possum innumeras tibi gratias ago. Pulli exercitatiunculae editionem, quam profusa Societatis Regiae humanitas iam paravit, remorari non audeo: licet enim rudem admodum hanc observationum delineationem primo prompserim, quoniam tamen incomparabili vestrae humanitatis affectu eam ita fovistis, et adoptastis, ut vestri iuris feceritis, ideo paterna in eandem etiam auctoritate gaudere vos aequum est. Ob graviores curas, incubatorum ovorum perquisitionem in hoc usque tempus protractam, iam prae manibus habeo, et quae alias innui, pro ut instrumentorum, meaeque mentis rudis acies attingit, confirmata video; singula tamen iconibus, minus forte rudibus, pro virium modulo iterum delineare contendo.[1] Te interim, et reliquos sapientissimos socios monitos velim, folliculum illum in meis, praecipue primis, figuris delineatum,[2] quo carinam[3] contineri putabam, vesiculam esse repletam aere vel saltem perlevi diaphanoque humore, unde licet supra pulli carinam cubet, ipsam tamen non omnino velat: haec inclinata etiam cicatrice[4] perpetuo summitatem tenere tentat, et quarta die abdomini haerens valde manifestatur, ex indeque obliteratur. Plexum, omenti instar, de quo dubitabam, Allantoidem⁵ esse insuper deprehendi; completa observatione, si quae occurrent digna scitu, ea tibi communicabo.

Plantarum iconismi tam cito in promptu esse nequeunt, tali etenim peritia non polleo, ut singula rite, et opportune mea manu delineem, nec artifex seu minister presto est, quem laboris socium efficiam, cum similis artis peritos Micrologiae taedeat: His accedat Plantarum anatomen ita late dispersam esse, tamque in abditis iacere, ut improbum laborem, longamque exigat patientiam. Reliquum igitur vitae in hac pertractanda insumam, et quo citius potero, expediam. Regiae interea Societati aeternas debeo gratias ob egregia officia, quibus me meaque studia fovere non desinit. Diu vivas. Dabam Bononiae, die secunda Augusti, 1672.

ADDRESS

    Praeclarissimo et Eruditissimo Viro Domino Henrico Oldenburg Regiae Societatis Anglicanae Secretario
          Londini

TRANSLATION

Marcello Malpighi presents many greetings to the very famous and learned Mr. Henry Oldenburg, Secretary of the English Royal Society

The Mantuan post delivered me your very welcome letter dated 8 June tardily, famous Sir. The book package which you mention as being sent to the King's Resident at Venice has not yet come to my hands; in the interval I send you such countless thanks as I can offer. I do not venture to hold back the publication of the little essay on the chick which the ample kindness of the Royal Society has already prepared [to print]; for although it was I who first produced a very crude rendering of the observations, since nevertheless with your incomparable kindly goodwill you have adopted and cherished it so as to make it your own it is but fair that you should enjoy a parental authority over it. The investigation of the incubated egg has been postponed up to the present time because of more serious business; I still have it in hand and as I have hinted elsewhere so far as my instruments and my poor wits go, I find it confirmed and I am striving according to the measure of my abilities to delineate each [observation] again in far less crude drawings.¹ Meanwhile I wish to advise you and the rest of your very well-instructed Fellows that the follicle which is depicted in my drawings,² especially the first ones, which I thought contained the *carina*³ is a vesicle filled with air or at any rate a very tenuous and transparent humor, whence although it may lie above the chick's *carina* it does not envelop it at all. Even when the cicatricula[4] is slanted at an angle this vesicle constantly seeks to keep above it and on the fourth day is very obvious as adhering to the abdomen and from then onwards is obliterated. The plexus resembling the omentum about which I was doubtful I have, moreover, discovered to be the allantois;[5] when the observations are completed if something worth knowing is met with I shall communicate it to you.

The drawings of plants cannot be so quickly prepared for I do not possess sufficient skill to draw each observation correctly and at the proper time with my own hand, and there is no artist or assistant available to me whom I may employ as a collaborator, since those who have such artistic skill find microscopy tedious. To this I may add that the anatomy of plants is so diffuse a subject and so recondite that it demands enormous labor and great patience. I might therefore spend the rest of my life in pursuing it and I shall extricate myself as quickly as I can. Meanwhile I owe the Royal Society eternal thanks for the outstanding services which it continues to devote to myself and my researches. May you have long life. Bologna, 2 August 1672.

ADDRESS

To the very famous and learned Mr. Henry Oldenburg, Secretary of the English Royal Society,
    London

NOTES

Reply to Letter 1989.
1 Malpighi was already engaged in preparing his second embryological essay, *De ovo incubato observationes* (see Vol. VIII, Letter 1936, note 2).
2 This has long been identified with the *nucleus cicatriculae* of Pander (1817); it is not a follicle or saccule but is described by Adelmann as a "conical plug of white yoke" adjacent to the nucleus of the egg, to whose development it probably contributes nourishment. (See Adelmann, pp. 835–6, 1016 ff.)
3 The Greek word *tropis* ("keel"; Latin *carina*) was introduced by Galen to describe the spine of vertebrates; not only is it the foundation of the animal but the ribs spring from it as in a ship. Malpighi, like his predecessors Harvey and Fabricius, applies *carina* to the embryonic spinal column, but also (like them) sometimes extends its meaning to include the head, spinal cord, and even the thorax as these are first seen to constitute the "foundation" of the embryo. (See Adelmann, pp. 1087 ff.)
4 The blastoderm (a term introduced by Pander, 1817) of modern embryology, a disk of cells formed in the early stages of development.
5 For Malpighi's pioneer recognition of this fetal membrane in the embryology of the chick, see Adelmann, pp. 1550 ff.

2035

Newton to Oldenburg

Late July 1672

Mentioned in Letter 2041, which repeats its contents, as having been written "last week."

2036

Flamsteed to Oldenburg

27 July 1672

From the original in Royal Society MS. F 1, no. 89
Partly printed in Latin translation in *Phil. Trans.*, no. 86 (19 August 1672), 5040–42

Derby July, 27 1672

Mr Oldenburge
Sr

Included I send yu a scheme of ye transit of Mars by ye 3 Stars in ♓ of which I gave yu an intimation in my last,[1] & yr answer demanded. I have made what hast I could with it that those to whom yu shall impart the prediction of this opportunity may have leasure to provide for such accurate observations, as the appearance requires. The places of Mars in ye Ephemeris underwritten are calculated from Streets tables to 8h oo′ p.m. at Derby. & ye equall time: those transcribed from Hecker are brought to it by reduction. I have calculated ye planets place accurately from Streets tables, yt so his diurnall motion may be found exactly, for compareing it with ye observed motions in a given space of time, & findeing ye parallaxes; tho I really beleive, & thinke I have good cause for it, that Heckers Ephemerides doe shew ye true places of Mars far more truely then Streets numbers.

1672 Derbiae 8h.00'.00" p.m.	Martis locus in ♓	latitudo M.A.	dist. martis a Terra qual. ☉ 100,000	Heckeri Ephem Mars in ♓	Lat MA	Martis Parallaxes Street	Kepler	Wing
	° ′ ″	° ′ ″		° ′	° ′	′ ″	′ ″	′ ″
Sept 15	13 11 13	4 50 11	41318	12 54	4 46	0 36	2 55	5 41
stv. 16	13 01 26	4 45 26		12 45	4 42			
17	12 52 25	4 40 43		12 36	4 37			
18	12 44 10	4 36 0	42296	12 28	4 33	0 35	2 22	5 33
19	12 36 41	4 31 10		12 22	4 28			
20	12 29 58	4 26 21		12 14	4 24			
21	12 24 00	4 21 34	43385	12 08	4 19	0 34	2 18	5 25
22	12 18 48	4 16 44		12 04	4 14			
23	12 14 24	4 11 52		12 00	4 09			
24	12 10 46	4 07 00	44589	11 56	4 04	0. 33	2 14	5 16
25	12 07 56	4 02 09		11 53	4 00			
26	12 05 03	3 57 18		11 51	3 55			
27	12 04 38	3 52 27	45895	11 50	3 50	0 32	2 11	5 07
28	12 04 12	3 47 38		11 50	3 45			
29	12 04 34	3 42 50		11 50	3 40			
30	12 05 43	3 38 03	47302	11 51	3 36	0 32	2 07	4 58
Octob 1	12 07 42	3 33 16		11 53	3 31			
2	12 10 29	3 28 30		11 56	3 26			
3	12 14 04	3 23 46	48804	12 00	3 21	0 31	2 03	4 49

The Suns horizontall parallax is to Street. 0′ 15″ Kepler. 1–00 Wing. 2–21. from which & the distances of Mars a terra I have found his parallax as in the table which, being sufficiently large & sensible quantity in my instruments I doubt not but if God afford mee health & opportunity I shall easily find whether the heavens will admit of them.[2] I expect them lesse then Keplers, larger then Streets but findeing how much I have failed in my conjectures formerly I am resolved to let my observations lead mee, not with others to wrest them, I desire yu will please to engage whomsoever yu impart this paper to, to give mee theire naked observations, with the times of them well taken, & if this be not enough, my observations shall be throwne in to recompense theires if ye heavens permit us any.

I hope yu will endeavour to have ye Moons passages by ye Pleiades, & ye Suns & Moons Eclipses next moneth observed at London. I shall doe my best wth no bad instruments at Derby. Tho the French are beforehand wth us in encouragements, & an observatory, yet I despaire not altogeather of doeing somethings as great as they, tho not so many Quidquid in arte mea possum promittere curae non deerit[3] if God grant mee health & time. this wthout further complement is from yrs

John Flamsteed

(5042)

Martis, *prope Fixas in* ♒
transeuntis, loci depicti:
ad hor. 8. *p. m.*
    Derbiæ
    1672.

3. ☉   ☉ 3 Octobris

2. ☉

Octob. 1. ☉

30. ☉   ☉. 30

29. ☉

28. ☉

27. ☉   ☉. 27

26. ☉   ✳
                 ♒

25. ☉   ☉. 24 26

24. ☉   ✳
        27

23. ☉   ☉. 21

22. ☉

21. ☉

20. ☉   ☉. 18

18. 19. ☉

A Tabulis Carolinis
16. 17. 18. ☉
Sept. 15. ☉   ♂ ☉. 15   *Ab Ephemeride Heckeri.*
  ♂ ☉   ✳
                  28

	Streetio			Keplero			Lat.		
	°	′	″	°	′	″	°	′	″
♒. 26	11 — 40 — 22			11 — 44 . 0			3 — 58 — 0		
✳. 27	12 — 8 — 22			12 — 12 — 0			4 — 10 — 30 *Auſt.*		
28	12 — 11 — 52			12 — 15 — 30			4 — 44 — 0		
	✳			✳					

An

ADDRESS
    For Henry Oldenburg Esq
    at his house in ye middle
    of ye Pell mell neare
    St James's Westminster
        these present

POSTMARK AU 2

TRANSLATION

. . . .

1672 at Derby at 8 P.M., September, October, O.S.
The place of Mars in Pisces. Latitude at meridian altitude. Distance of Mars from the Earth, of which the sun's distance is 100,000 parts. From Hecker's *Ephemerides*: place of Mars in Pisces; latitude at meridian altitude. Parallaxes of Mars [according to] Streete, Kepler, and Wing.

[*For the Table, see page 178*]

. . . .

A depiction of the places of Mars passing by the fixed stars in Aquarius at 8 P.M. at Derby 1672.

[*For the figure, see page 179*]

NOTES

    Reply to Letter 2033. The date on the original has been altered from 27 July to (possibly) 31 July; the former date is given in the Letter Book copy; the latter in the printed version.
    1 See Letter 2025. The original diagram is not now to be found but was printed in the *Philosophical Transactions*, whence we reproduce it here. The plot of Mars' position on successive evenings is computed both from Streete's *Astronomia Carolina* (on the left, columns two and three of the long table) and from Hecker's *Ephemerides* (on the right, columns five and six of the table). The little table below the figure gives the latitude and longitude of the three fixed stars numbered by Flamsteed 26, 27, 28, according to both Streete and Kepler. Note that although these stars are members of the constellation Aquarius, their ecliptic coordinates (owing to the precession of the equinoxes) refer them to the zodiacal sign Pisces; Mars, of course, is moving through the same sign. These three stars, with longitude about 342° (in Flamsteed's day; about 346° at the present time owing to precessional motion) and south latitude about 4°, are the three denoted by Bayer as ψ 1, 2, and 3 in Aquarius. Flamsteed seems not to have known of Bayer's *Uranometria* at this time.
    2 In this sentence Flamsteed proceeds inversely—starting from the solar parallaxes

postulated by Streete, Kepler, and Wing he computes the anticipated parallaxes (hence, "distances of Mars from the earth") to be expected at Mars' late-September positions. Contrary to his expectations, he will find the observed parallax of Mars (and hence that of the sun) to be even less than the least postulated value, that of Streete.

3 "Whatever [I can accomplish] in my science, I can promise it shall not be lacking in care."

2037

Thomas Platt to Oldenburg

27 July 1672

From the original in Royal Society MS. P 1, no. 82
Largely printed in *Phil. Trans.*, no. 87 (14 October 1672), 5060–66

Florence Aug: 6: 1672 [N.S.]

Sr

The quiet & delicious way of liveing heare hath had so great an influence on my nature, that you must not wonder, if you have hitherto found in me the effects of that lazy tranquillity wch hath thus long induced me to neglect (for want of publick intelligence) the occasions of payeing my humble respects to you: But though I partly attribute my silence to the scarcity of news, yet I would not have you thinck, that that barrenness proceeds from any other cause, then that wch redounds much to this Countreys praise & happiness, & that is its being free from Warres & all publick calamityes, for otherwise haveing had so much experience of the excellency of the Italian Witts, I know, as I'm sure you cannot also but be well inform'd of it, that noe countrey affords more ingenious novelty, nor more curious observations then Italy does, wittness the many famous workes & experiments sett forth within few yeares by this citty, or to speake more properly by this Court, since all or most of the Authours have bin beholding for their subject & meanes to the genius & generosity of these most serene Princes. I shall now give you an account of what I lately did see, wch though it be noe new thing, is yet of some consequence: I had that happiness in Sigr Lorenzo Magalotti's house, who willingly abstain'd from communicateing it to you himselfe not to deprive me of so faire an opportunity of kissing your hands, & of improveing by this meanes the honor of yr freindship.

To turne back a little I must begin to tell you, that in conversation last winter, where I had the good fortune to make one of ye number, the discourse was of an opinion of Monsr. de la Chambre,[1] who to prove that the Spiritts are animated, alledges amongst many other arguments, their aptness to discerne; by wch: he supposes that, in their heat of anger, those spiritts gather the poison from the severall parts of the blood, & doe carry them to the teeth of ye. irritated animal, from which they are afterwards transfused into ye. wound by biting. This concejpt was by some of ye. company receaved with much applause, because they knew, how difficult a thing it would have bin to ym: to come to an explanation of that poison wch: Mr. de la Chambre makes mention mention [*sic*] off so in general, that the spiritts proceed from the blood of the irritated animal; so they agreed *paucis mutatis*[2] to frame upon this modell a new Hipothesis, sayeing, that such poison is nothing else but a new & malignant activity of the same spirrits while they are irritated & bent towards revenge; upholding ye. truth of such ideal effects with divers examples, as that of the Toade, the Weezle, the mad Dog, the Spider of Puglia,[3] & such like, wch: were all found very weake & insubsistent: Wherefore most of the Gentlemen did incline to applaude Mr. de la Chambre's first fundamental opinion, since at least that supposes, that those animals wch: poison by their biting, have already a real poison within themselves, & that anger workes noe other effect, but to gather all the venomous parts together in one particular place, whence they may easily be instill'd in the wounds caused by the teeth. for all this, as it most commonly happens in such discourses, every one remain'd in his own oppinion, & a motion haveing bin made of Sigr: Francesco Redi's opinion, held in his booke of Vipers,[4] which for severall yeares passes almost in this countrey as an article of faith, that the vipers poison, does consist in something incompatable with this new alloy of Mr. dela Chambre's opinion, by them reduced to the irritated spiritts, but not from that of his wch is taken purely from its first grounds.

This gave occasion to a new dispute concerning the validity of Sigr: Redi's maxime so generally receav'd at *Florence*; some sayeing that it would doe well to examine the grounds of it, it being but a thing believ'd by many without knoweing *wherefore*; & that it could not be said by all people that they had seen the experiment of it. Upon this those of the other party undertook to come to a Trial, that all might be satisfyed, as soone as ye. Spring would give leave to Vipers to appeare abroad.

Now Sr., you must know, that being at Mr. Magalotti's one[5] the 2d. of June last in the afternoone, there came Dr. Francini (who is the same person, that Mr. Magalotti writt to you about 3 years since, that had thoughts of goeing for England to improve himselfe there in ye. study of Physick, in wch: if one may iudge of his succes by his ingenuity & application, I can confidently say that he will shortly become a very famous man in it:)[6] This same Doctor had formerly bin one of the most obstinate Assertors of this opinion of Mr. Redi's concerning the Vipers poison, & being come, sent to his lodging for a box, in wch: there was a great many Vipers heads, lately come from Naples, that had bin cut off that morning: he immediately desired to have some animalls to begin his experiments but there being at that time noe other company with Mr. Magalotti but his brother[7] & I, it was thought fitt to delay that business till next morning, that those gentlemen, that ware at the dispute last winter, might be present, as it fell out then. I, that had not so much patience, desir'd the Dr. to make at least one experiment: wch: being granted, wee gott Sigr: Magalotti to send to the publick market for a couple of Pigeons, to be sure of haveing some, that might not have bin prevented by some antidote. The Pigeons being come, the first was wounded with the teeth of a Vipers head, that had bin cutt off about 7 or 8 a clock ye. same morning. the way of makeing ye. wound was by thrusting twice the Master-teeth in the fleshy part of the Pigeons breast, till such time as pressing the upper part of the Jawe, the too litle bladders or Blisters that serve as gummes to the teeth, did empty out upon the wound some of that yellow liquor, wch: heare is supposed to be ye. true & only poison of the Viper. This Pigeon being bitt in this manner, & being sett upon ye: ground, began to stagger immediately & dyed in less then 3 or 4 minutes. The second Pigeon was hurt in the same manner, but at the first wound there only enter'd one of the teeth, wch: brought forth a great deale of blood, the second time they both enter'd & this had ye. same fate, with this difference only, that he languish't halfe a quarter of an houre.

The next morning there met at Sigr: Magalotti's chambers, besides his brother, Dr. francini & I, Sigr: Carlo Dati, Sigr: Vincenzo Viviani, Sigr: Paolo dell'Ara, Dr. Savona, Dr. Neri, Dr Fabrini & some others;[8] whereupon six Pigeons & a Cock haveing bin brought, the first thing that Dr. francini did was, to thrust several thornes of Roses into ye. breast of one of those Pigeons, to manifest, that such accidents, as might arrive to those that should be wounded by the teeth of the dead Vipers, ware not caused purely by ye. wound: and by reason that one of the company began to make some nice reflections, & to take some of the heads to measure the iust proportions of their teeth to see what difference there might be 'twixt them & the thornes, this made the Dr. loose patiance; therefore calling for a pinn, wch: prov'd to be none of the least, [and seizing] the first Pigeon that he could lay hands on, [he] gave him a very deep wound in the breast, who noe sooner was gott free but began to leap & frisk about the roome, as if he had not bin concern'd in the least.

After this first triall, the sport began to be in earnest: for takeing another Pigeon, he was bitt in the breast by both the Master-teeth of a Vipers head that had bin cutt off the morning before. the way of this execution was exactly like unto that of the former day, so that I shall not need to repeat it to you, only shall tell you that the effect was that the Pigeon had the same shakeing fitts, after wch: falling upon his belly he dyed, giveing many signs, a litle before of a painfull agony by his often gapeing; his end was not only very sensible to him, but also tedious in comparison of that of the other day; for this lived 5 or 6 minutes after his wound. Another haveing bin serv'd after the same manner with another head, had likewise ye. same accidents & dyed within a quarter of an houre, this observation was made on him, that his wound lett out a great deale of blood, whereas not so much as one drop was seen to come out of any of the others.

All this appearing as yet to the Doctor but litle to exclude ye. doctrine of the spiritts, wch: now did begin to loose ground after so many experiments of dead Vipers heads; he took three stalks out of a broom, & haveing made them smooth, & then sharp at the ends after the manner of a launcett, drew from the gummes of severall heads enough of that yellow juice to daub two of those stalks; wch being thus wetted with that liquor, ware both put into ye. breasts of two Pigeons, & there left, the same thing haveing bin done to another with a stalk not covered with that Juice, wch: was at least one third part bigger & longer then the other two; in a word, the two first dy'd within 4 or 5 minutes, & this last continues to this very day, in Mr. Magalotti's Pigeon-house, as briske and as fatt as ever; his wound in his breast, instead of haveing caused an Inflammation, is now allmost perfectly heal'd, & he is not to be distinguish't from the next there, but by a marke made in his wings, & when one takes him in ye. hand by the scarre made by ye. stalke, wch. is still to be felt in his breast.

Whilest these experiments were makeing, it came into the heads of some to try another, upon the report that Signor Paolo dell'Ara (lately come from Paris) had given; that some had asserted there as a thing infallible, that, to swallow a Vipers head, was a most certain preservative & remedy against ye biting of a Viper. The Doctor smil'd at that phancy; & to give full satisfaction concerning that supposition, made two experiments; the first was, by makeing the Cock swallow a Vipers head, & by causing him to be well bitten in both ye. thighs by a live one: But the Cock continueing some time before he gave any signs of death or sickness not to loose time he came to ye. second, & thrust the teeth of a dead head into another pigeon, haveing first gott downe one of those heads into his body: the conclusion was, that both dyed, the Cock within a quarter of an houre, & the Pigeon in less than four minutes.

The news of these experiments made many persons envious to see them perform'd once more; so that some few days since a rendezvous was made in Signor Magalotti's garden, where there mett, besides the forenamed Gentlemen, Mr. Thomas Frederick[9] & Mr. John Godscall (two English Gentlemen) Abbot Strozzi, his most Christian Majestyes Publick Minister in this Court, Signor Paolo Falconieri, first Gentleman of the bed-chamber to the Great Duke, Signor Luigi del Riccio, Monsieur Pelletier, Monsieur Morelle, the one Physitian, & the other Chirugeon to the Great Duchess, Dr Gornia Physitian in ordinary to his Highness,[10] Dr. Bellini Professor of Anatomy in the University of Pisa,[11] Signor Lorenzo Lorenzini a Mathematitian,[12] & Signor Pietro Salvetti. But, by the by, give me leave to tell you, that this Signor Pietro salvetti who is one of the Great Dukes Musicians, & plays on all Bow-Instruments, Invented about 4 yeares agoe a new tuneing of the ancient Lira Viol with the usual 13 strings; by meanes of wch: tuneing it is rendred wholly perfect, so that one may express upon it all concords, discords, & also the imperfect concords as seavenths, sixths &c; aswell as upon any Virginall that has ye. quarters of Notes upon itt: 'tis true, 'tis only for melancholy & passionate things, and not for division,[13] as is the proper nature of the Lira; I shall only say, that with the above sd. tuneing he ascends in alte as high G, Sol, re, Ut, & descends as low as double C, Sol, fa, ut, and can make every where the same concords as above.

This same person haveing apply'd himselfe to the study of the Mathematicks, & particularly about the proportions of Harmony relating to his profession of Musick, began to delight himselfe of Opticks & of its other parts; & not being content with the Theory, took upon him to putt it in practice by makeing Telescopes of all sizes, as also Microscopes in imitation of those of Campani & Divini. I can tell you that he lately shew'd one of his Microscopes to the Great Duke, wch: was Judged by all much better then any of the best his Highness hath; & I was an Eye-Witness to this, that as for magnifying, termination, & clearness, it was found most excellent. The same day he likewise shew'd his Highness a litle Prospective Glass, wch: he made according to Mr. Newton's new Invention, though he had received but a confused relation of it; & yet notwithstanding, that this was the first, & was not above halfe a foot long, it had the same effect as one of two. He is now makeing another of a bigger size after the conceit of that of Monsieur Cassegrain, whom Monsieur Denis speakes of in his 8th Memoire: As for now, the opinion of Signor Salvetti is, that those Prospective glasses, haveing a due termination & clearness, cannot be brought to magnifye so much as that of Mr. Newton's does, as it is writt out of England; but that the proportion is as from one to eight, that is, that the Magnifying, termination, & clearness of this new Prospective Glass, is the same as that of an ordinary Telescope eight times as long. He does not aggree neither with that opinion of Monsr: Cassegrain to make that little Glass convexe into wch: one looks into by meanes of the Ocular glass; & believes the french Authour only thought upon that, to disguise as much as is possible his pretended new invention, wch: he endeavours to make appeare anteriour to Mr. Newton's most noble one. As for the rest, he holds that he hath found a way to make objects seeme right with one only glass

But now to returne againe, after a digression wch: I believe hath not bin unpleasing to you to our first discourse, you must know that the Assembly at Mr. Magalotti's haveing first bin inform'd by Dr. Francini of the grounds of this dispute & of the former observations, he began the same experiments by causing two Pigeons to be bitt by a Vipers head that had bin dead above ten houres, in such a manner as yt. by pressing the gums some of that yellow liquor might drop into the wound. they both dyed, one in 6 minutes, & the other in eight, & not being content with this, with another Vipers head poison'd a Chicken, who had the like misfortune only had two minutes longer to prepare himselfe for his Journey. There afterwards appeared another Pigeon that had bin wounded many houres before by a dead vipers head, but it had bin dead so long a while, that the Liquor being quite dry'd up in ye. gums was become so hard & consistent that for all ye. squeesing of it nothing could arrive to the teeth; from hence it hapned, that that Pigeon was very chearfull & healthy without any other signs of being ill, but those small scarres left in the breast by the biteing: Notwithstanding this that every one might be an eye-witness Dr. Francini made ye. same Pigeon be bitt againe by ye. same dry'd head, who after a litle fluttering of his wings, whilst the paine of being bitt lasted, had noe other harme.

A Live Viper being then taken, four Chickens ware bitt by it one after another; the two first either because the liquor did not penetrate into the wound, or that the blood did expell it had not the least beginning of any distemper; the fourth look't as if he would have dy'd presently; for he noe sooner had bin bitt but imediatly gave signs of being ill, but a litle while after, haveing pickt up his crummes againe, he gott cleare off for that time; & the third, who seemd at first to be very brisk & lively dyed within an houre & a halfe.

They haveing afterwards brought a yong Bitch of a pretty bigg size, she was bitt twice by a live viper in the middle of the hanging part of ye. eare; where upon she began very soone to give mortall signs, by staggering, Vomitting, & convulsive fitts; afterwhich haveing a litle recovered her selfe, the same accidents came upon her againe, wch: still growing greater & greater reduced her into such a lamentable condition, that 4 houres after she was bitt she could not stirre herselfe any more, & seem'd iust as if she had bin dead, holding her toungue out, & looking very gashly without any other sign of life, but that of sighing, or rather of a painfull breathing; to wch: sometimes she addcd a faint barking & a languishing howling. In this very same condition was she found next morning, but only yt. her respiration was yet weaker, & as if her life had bin iust then at an end. Observation was made that noe part of her body was swell'd nor had any spotts upon itt: she had voided backward some matter of a very black colour, of wch her hind parts were becomes so fowle that there was a swarme of knatts & waspes that did devoure her, whilst yet she was living: this moved ye. compassion of one of ye. servants of ye. house, out of an untimely charity, to ridd her from these torments by strikeing her on ye. head with a stick.

As for the other experiments, two Capons & a Poullet were bitt by a fresh Viper moved to anger apurpose, &, by reason they gave not then any signs of being ill, were sent back to their coopes, & there continueing well till the evening, were afterwards surprised at night of a distemper, wch: according to all likelyhood proceeded from the poison; for next morning one of the capons & the poullet were found dead. I had allmost forgott to tell you, that ye. last thing that was done, was, to send to the Pigeon-house, for that Pigeon that had in his breast the stalk that had not bin poison'd by ye yellow liquor; where he had bin kept during all that interval of time that had bin from the first to these last experiments, & was found by all not only very chearfull, but also in a thriveing condition; the place of his wound haveing bin search't, the stalk was easily felt, & before the eyes of all the company with a litle pair of Pinchers was drawn out.

This is, Sr., what I can confidently affirme haveing bin an eye wittness to it, & because tis not my buisness to make Philosophicall reflections upon the occasions of these accidents, but only to relate the matter of fact, I'le leave it to you to draw the consequences, wch: will be most convenient for the decideing of the dispute of the last winter. I know I have not said any thing but what will be most exactly found in Dr. Redi's first & 2d. book;[14] but that, wch: urged me to make this repetition, was the thought that it might be acceptable to you, to see his assertions corroborated by the testimonye of so many persons, who are the more able to be Judges of ym: because their understandings are such, that tis not possible to pass any iugling tricks upon them.

If I shall be so happy as to receave sometimes from you an account of the curious Transactions of ye famous Royal Society, I shall make use of that favour of yours, to animate these Virtuosi heare to doe something that may not be unworthy of yr: knowledge: But before you afford me this honour I must first beseech you to impose yr: commands on me, by the execution of wch: you shall then plainly see, with how much reality I am sr

> your most humble servant
> *Thomas Platt*

NOTES

The original is endorsed by Oldenburg: "Letter of Mr Plat to Mr Oldenb." It was enclosed by Magalotti with Letter 2038. It is obvious that the writer had some previous acquaintance with Oldenburg, but the only positive biographical data relating to him are contained in a letter of 28 July 1673 from Thomas Derham (see Letter 2038, note 7) to Sir Joseph Williamson recommending "Mr. Platt" for appointment as his secretary. Derham claims that Platt is a master of Italian, Spanish, French, and Dutch and that "the Grand Duke [of Tuscany] would not have placed him where he now is, if he had seen he did not well deserve it" (*C.S.P.D.*, 1673, 465).

1 Marin Cureau de la Chambre (1594–1669) became Conseiller du Roi, a royal physician, and a founder-member of the Académie Française. He wrote much on philosophy and psychology as well as physiology, in a delightful and fluent French style; his works brought him an enormous reputation though he was an old-fashioned naturalist and given to credulity. His point of view was psychosomatic; the state of the body is determined by the spirits, whose movements are governed by the soul. Thus the passion of anger causes bile and other evil matters in the veins to be separated out as offensive weapons for use against the enemy: "D'où vient que les morsures de toutes sortes d'animaux sont en quelque façon venimeuses quand ils sont en

colère, & plus ils sont irritez plus elles sont dangereuses & difficiles à guerir" ("Whence it happens that bites of all kinds of animals are in some sort venemous when they are angry, and the more enraged they are the more dangerous the wounds and the more difficult to heal."—*Les Caractères des Passions*, Vol. II, "De la Colère," Ch. III; 2nd. ed., Paris 1660, pp. 374–75). Boyle at one time held a similar opinion, which he perhaps derived from De la Chambre; see Vol. I, p. 133, and p. 135, note 3.

2 "with a few modifications."

3 Apulia; that is, the tarantula.

4 *Osservazioni intorno alle Vipere* (Florence, 1664).

5 *Sic*; read "on."

6 See Letter 1526 (Vol. VII).

7 Probably this was his elder brother Alessandro (1622–87), a priest, who was to become Abbot of San Benedetto di Savignano at Naples; however, there were two other brothers, Carlantonio and Vincenzo (as well as a number of sisters all shut up in a convent).

8 Mr. dell'Ara was twice mentioned by Magalotti in Vol. IV, apparently as residing in Paris in the Florentine service. Dati and Viviani are well known, the others we have not identified.

9 Probably this was the Thomas Frederick of St. Olave's, London, whose son went up to Cambridge in 1695, aged 18; he may also have been a son of Sir John Frederick, the great London merchant.

10 See Vol. VI, p. 89, note.

11 Lorenzo Bellini (1643–1704), having been educated at the University of Pisa, began his academic career by teaching philosophy there, until on the instructions of the Grand Duke Leopold he transferred to anatomy, which he taught for twenty years before moving to Florence, where he was first physician to Cosimo III. He wrote much on anatomy and physiology mostly in support of iatromechanical principles. He was a close friend of Malpighi.

12 Lorenzo Lorenzini (1652–1721) impressed his teacher Viviani by his youthful talent for mathematics. He entered the household of the Grand Duke Ferdinand de' Medici. For what the duke's successor, Cosimo III, considered an offense Lorenzini was for twenty years imprisoned at Volterra, where he worked at Apollonian conic sections in a way which, unfortunately, the advance of mathematics had rendered pointless by the time he regained his freedom.

13 The execution of a rapid melodic passage.

14 The title of the second book is given in Letter 2038, note 4.

2038

Magalotti to Oldenburg

28 July 1672

From the original in Royal Society MS. M 1, no. 51

florence Aug: 7th: 1672

Sr

I hope you will believe me if I shall tell you that your obligeing letter of ye 13th June made me blush in so much that I was almost repented of ye boldness I had in writing to you about those trifles of ours, not onely because they were so empty, and weake, but because it could appeare that my chiefest aime was to undertake a commerce wth you in wch I might be onely passive. I would in deed fain contribute something from my part that might free me from my title of a meer receiver so much ye more after you have bin pleased out of your naturall goodness to reward me in so noble a way by communicating to me so many worthy productions of your virtuosi wch ought to encourage us to follow such an example and wake us so far as to make us blush of that drowsiness, and idlness, in wch wee are burried since so many yeares. But I doe'nt know whether I must attribute to some secret quality of your letter an effect wch being very extraordinary it needs must be adduced to an extraordinary cause. I herewith send you some experiments wch were made in my house about ye poison of Vipers as you will see by ye enclosed letter of Mr Platt[1] who having bin one of ye number desired me not [to] envy him so faire an opportunity to present you his service and give you a new assurance of his respects to you. Tis true ye most part of them were made before your letter came to my hands, but it happened (may be) as when ye rising Sun pulling on ye aire may be perceived by a cheerfull gale as a forrunner of its coming to us, though it has yet but approached ye East. But setting a side such philosophicall considerations wch could easily make me slip in some scholasticall phancy, as ye *Actio in distans,*[2] or such like, I shall presently come to ye buisness by telling you, that all these experiments were onely made to cleare Dr Redi's book[3] of one exception, wch put into Mr Charas his hands ye best weapon to destroy, or at least to render suspect ye truth of his experiments.[4] That is that Dr Redi did never boast in any book of his of haveing made his experiments as ye Mountebancks doe in ye presence of

many people being content of some friends of his, wch he thought fitt
to assure him by theyr approbation, that noe particular affection towards
his own conceits had made him oversee. I suppose you have seene what
Mr Charas hath writt againe against his new addition all wch being not
able to perswade ye Dr to change his first opinion, nor call in question ye
faithfulness of his experiments, he did not vouchsafe so much as to take
any paines about it. Notwithstanding that some of his friends, and chiefly
Dr francini would not lett Dr Redis opinion want that advantage of being
confirmed by so many eye witnesses, as his Antagonist braggs of haveing
to his, so much ye more that a dispute that was made ye last winter about
some opinion of Mr de la Chambre[5] furnished a good opportunity to kill
(as ye sayeing is) two birds with one stone. I desire you to oblige me so
much as to gett Mr Platt's letter printed, and to have it inserted, (if you doe
not think it inconvenient) in one of yr monthly philosophicall transactions,
that so Dr Redi's credit may be ye better established in ye world, and what
is of a great deal more importance in England, nay (what is yet more) in
Arundell house.[6] I hope you will not be offended at this boldness of mine
since after so many proofs of ye affection and partiality you have for this
countrey I had a just occasion to beleive that you would willingly embrace
an opportunity to make it appeare once more. As for ye money I desire this
very evening Mr Thomas Derham[7] MyLord Arlington['s] gentleman of ye
horse to reimburse you, and afterwards I shall begg ye favour of you that
you will send me some of ye prints. Ye way to send ym as also yr letters,
and all what may concerne our philosophicall commerce may be ye very
same you have appointed in yr last, that is directing ym to Abbot Gondy
ye G. Dukes Resident at Paris, with this superscription A Monsieur
Monsieur L'Abbé Bassetti Secretaire de Monsieur le G. Duc de Toscane a
Florence. I beseech you not to make me appeare in anything concerning
ye print, nor to publish that I have had a hand in this business nor of ye
particulars of Mr Platt's chief aime in his letter. All what I have said to you
is to endeavour to approve by it my sincerity wth wch I am and will ever be

Sr

Concerning the title of ye printed letter I referr it to you, but I think it
would not be a miss to have it in this manner

Some experiments concerning ye poison of Vipers in a letter to Henry
Oldenbourg Esqr Secretary to ye Royall Society.

I must also tell you that that letter will be translated in French, and Italian
and printed at Lyons, and at Rome;[8] by this meanes 'tis thought the

Author's credit will be enough assured without any entring upon new engagements, and if notwithstanding Mr Platt's circumspection and niceness in not sayeing any thing that might be offensive, any thing should have happened beyond his intention, t'is wholly left to you to alter any part as you shall think most convenient for ye best. When I desired you to keep secret my medling in this buisness I did never intend to include Mr Boyle in my number, for whom I have so great a respect that were it a secret concerning ye security of my life I would willingly participart it to him, and pray lett him know how much I am his humble Servant. As for Mr Boyle's new book de Gemmis, I gave order to have it sent to me when I told ye G. Duke of it, his High: ask'd me; well (sayes he) doe you think Mr Boyle remembers yet ye desire I have of seeing once something about ye Amber's generation writt by him? I drew up my shoulders. Pray let him know so much, and beleive me Sir

your most humble and obediant servant
Lor: Magalotti

NOTES

Reply to Letter 1997.

1 See Letter 2037.
2 "action at a distance."
3 See Letter 2037, note 4.
4 See Letters 1940 and 1943 (Vol. VIII). Redi had confirmed his views in *Lettera . . . sopra alcune opposizione fatte alle sue osservazione intorno alle vipere . . .* (Florence, 1670).
5 See Letter 2037, note 1.
6 As already noted, this was done. The Royal Society was still meeting at Arundel House; it did not resume meetings at Gresham College until November 1674, having been invited to do so by representatives of the College and the City of London in April 1673.
7 One of this name proceeded B.A. from Clare College, Cambridge, in 1649. For his friendship with Thomas Platt, see Letter 2037, note. On returning to England Derham was appointed (25 July 1673) Clerk of the Court of Chancery and Patents in Jamaica, an office he naturally exercised by deputy.
8 The only other printing of Platt's letter we encountered was in the *Giornale de' Letterati* (30 December 1673), 167–72, from the *Philosophical Transactions*.

2039
Oldenburg to Huygens

29 July 1672

From *Œuvres Complètes*, VII, 215
Original in the Huygens Collection at Leiden

A Londres le 29 juillet 1672

Monsieur,

Vous ayant escrit assez amplement le 8 et 18 de ce mois,[1] et envoyé par la 1re de ces deux lettres la copie de celle de Monsieur Sluse du 22 juin[2] et par l'autre, la copie de celle de Monsieur Newton du 8 courant;[3] ie ne vous importuneray de rien à present, si non que ie voudrais bien vous prier de vouloir bien examiner ce que Monsieur Newton a proposé et recommendé dans ce journal 85me, touchant sa doctrine de la lumiere,[4] et d'en communiquer vos pensees a Monsieur

Vostre tres humble et tres obeissant serviteur
Oldenburg

Vous verrez par les lettres passées entre Monsieur Newton et le P. Pardies[5] que ladite theorie de la lumiere commence à gagner pied.

On nous dit, que vous faites imprimer quelque Traité;[6] vous m'obligerez de m'en dire le sujet.

ADDRESS
A Monsieur
Monsieur Christian Hugens de Zulechem
dans la Bibliotheque du Roy à
Paris

TRANSLATION

London, 29 July 1672

Sir,

Having written to you pretty fully on the eighth and eighteenth of this month,[1] sending by the first of these letters the copy of that by Mr. Sluse dated the twenty-second of June,[2] and by the other the copy of that by Mr. Newton of the eighth instant,[3] I shall not trouble you further at present except that I very much wish to beg you to be willing to examine carefully what Mr. Newton has proposed and recommended in this 85th journal concerning his doctrine of light,[4] and to communicate your thoughts to, Sir,

Your very humble, obedient servant
Oldenburg

You will see by the letters exchanged between Mr. Newton and Father Pardies[5] that the said theory of light begins to gain a footing.

We have been told that you are having some treatise printed;[6] you will oblige me if you tell me the subject of it.

ADDRESS

To Mr. Christiaan Huygens of Zulichem,

In the Kings' Library,

Paris

NOTES

1 Letters 2019 and 2028.
2 Letter 1994.
3 Letter 2018.
4 Letter 2017.
5 Letters 1976a and 1992.
6 This was of course *Horologium oscillatorium.*

2040

Nicolaus ab Hoboken to Oldenburg

29 July 1672

From the original in Royal Society MS. H 3, no. 19

Spectatissimo et doctissimo Viro,
Domino Henrico Oldenburgio, Regiae Societati Londinensi a Secretis
P.P.

Spectatissime et doctissime Vir,

Quod praesens munusculum (*Anatomiae* puta *Secundinae humanae*, a me *repetitae* exemplum) transmittam nunc, suadet, beneficio Clarissimi Viri mei amici e primis, D. Swammerdami suppeditata, occasio.[1] Cum alioquin Martis (cui adeo nihil cum Musis nostris commercij, ut cuncta susque deque habeat, modo dominari contingat; ruere, interimere, perdere ac delere solitus) furoribus invia via deterruisset, uti deterruit hactenus.[2] Et quod Regiae vestrae Societati mittam donemque, vult apud me fixa, semperque acceptissima sententia, quam expressi saepius: videlicet Apollinis et Musarum sacro caetui illi nunquam non honorem deberi ac reverentiam. Et non optatiore hoc posse fieri modo, quam si suis quisque laboribus conferendis, eique offerendis gratificari conetur. Maxime dum persuasissimum habere licet, hoc illustribus illis Antistibus optatissimum opus, huncque illorum laborem esse, qui bonis Artibus ac Scientijs, et ijs, queis eaedem cordi sunt, promovendis vacent. Ut mihi negligenti esse minime licuerit, uti nec insuper licebit: imo quaecunque curta mea supellex conferre potuerit symbola, nunc et nunc sum collaturus. Quemadmodum huic succedaneam promittere mihi, et vobis proxime expectare datur Uteri ovini, atque Secundinae agninae, quousque tulit institutum, Anatomiam, jammodo prelo paratam; nisi per injuriosissimorum temporum rationem impedimentum, quod vereor, obnascatur.[3] Hacque, quae Ovium genitalibus, atque Secundinis agninis cum alijs communia sunt, quaeque peculiaria, particulatim atque clare ex observatis descripta, et per Figuras necessarias monstrata videbitis. Prae caeteris Cotyledoniferorum a glanduliferis, et Placentiferis differentia, quam recte asserit ingeniosissimus vester Needhamus, Lib. de form. faetu, c.4. p.32. 33. 214. 215. nov. edit. juste vindicatur.[4]

Et te quidem compello, cupioque pararium, cujus humanitatem, cum caeteris ingenua mente dignis virtutibus, probe intelligo. Itaque, vir spectatissime, optime feceris, si honoratissimo Domino Praesidi reddideris, mihique accepti rationem quamprimum concesseris. Sed has abrumpere nequeo, quin Verbo voti nonnullius mei sensum exprimam. Actorum inquam vestrorum partem vidi, a Johannae Sterpino Latinitate donatam: nescio autem an reliquae partes, quas magnum adhuc numerum hodieque constituere puto, similiter vertendae fuerint? Desiderant certe nostrates (utpote Linguae Anglicanae rudes) impensissimeque cupiunt continuatam omnium ac singulorum versionem: qua insimul bene fateor fiet orbi literario universo. Interea equidem percuperem mihi per te posse fieri unius exempli vestro idiomate editorum Actorum omnium copiam: quippe qui etiam nunc aliunde frustra speravi, et hic illicve apud amicos nonnisi imperfecta quaedam et mutila videam. Obstrinxeris, si compotem hujus voti dederis, tibi tuisque optime volentem

N. Hobokenum

Raptim dabam quod me p[ro] t[empore] habet, Amstelodami d. viii Augusti MDCLXXII [N.S.]

Si ad Clarissimum Dominum Swammerdamum responsum tuum dirigatur, recte curabitur, mihi reddendum. Propterea autem quid necdum distrahantur Exemplaria, hoc unicum impraesentia tantum mitto. Vale.

TRANSLATION

Greetings to the highly respected and learned Mr. Henry Oldenburg, Secretary of the Royal Society of London

Highly respected and learned Sir,

The opportunity furnished by the kindness of my particular friend the famous Mr. Swammerdam induces me to send you at this time the present trifling gift, that is, a copy of *Anatomia secundinae humanae repetitae* by myself.[1] Since otherwise the route now made impassable by the furies of Mars (who now happens to hold sway, paying no heed to our commerce with the Muses which he holds indeed to be of no consequence, accustomed as he is to ruin, slaughter, and destruction) would have deterred me as it has in fact done hitherto.[2] And my giving and sending [this gift] to your Royal Society signifies my very favorable opinion [of it]; indeed, nothing but honor and respect are owing to that assembly, devoted to

Apollo and the Muses. And there is no better way for honor and respect to be paid to it than for each individual to endeavor to please it by bringing forward his labors and offering them to it. One may, then, most confidently be assured that such an action is most suitable for these illustrious experts and that this is the [proper] labor for those at leisure to promote sound arts and sciences and such things as are dear to them. And as I ought not ever to have been neglectful in any way, so I should not be so any longer; therefore I do now indeed bring forward what small contribution my meager abilities allow. In the same way, I promise myself a continuation of this [work], and you may shortly expect the anatomy of the uterus of a sheep and the afterbirth of a lamb, now already prepared for the press so far has my plan developed—unless some obstruction arises from the most damaging character of the times, as I fear it may.[3] In this way you will see what the reproductive organs of a sheep and the afterbirth of a lamb have in common with others and also what is peculiar to them, all described clearly and in detail according to observation and illustrated by the requisite figures. Among other things, the differences of the cotyledonifera from the glandulifera and the placentifera, correctly affirmed by your very ingenious Needham in his book *De formato foetu*, chap. IV, pp. 32, 33, 214, [and] 215 in the new edition, are justly vindicated.[4]

And I wish for and ask for a fair exchange from you, whose kindness together with other virtues worthy of a candid spirit I fairly appreciate. Thus, worthy Sir, you will do me a kindness by delivering [this] to the honorable Lord President and by allowing me [to know] as soon as possible the manner of its acceptance. But I cannot break off without expressing in a word a pretty strong desire I feel. I mean, that I have seen a part of your *Transactions*, produced in Latin by John Sterpin, but I do not know whether the remaining parts, which I think must today amount to a considerable number, have been similarly translated? Our people (being clumsy in the English language) certainly very much desire and long for a continued translation of each and every part, and in this way I confess he would do a real service to the whole world of learning. Meanwhile I should be very pleased if I could, through you, possess a single copy of all the published *Transactions* in your language; this is in fact something I have vainly hoped for from some other source up to the present, for here and there among my friends I see only imperfect and defective copies. If you were to grant this wish you would place under a great obligation a warm wellwisher to yourself and your concerns,

N. Hoboken

Written in haste, for so it stands with me at present.
Amsterdam, 8 August 1672 [N.S.]

If you will direct your reply to the famous Mr. Swammerdam it will be safely taken care of and delivered to me. Moreover I send you only this single copy as the others are not yet distributed at present.

NOTES

Nicolaus ab Hoboken, M.D. (1632–78), of Utrecht, became Extraordinary Professor of Medicine and Mathematics there in 1663; in 1669 he moved to fill a similar post at the University of Harderwijck, where he died. He was a prolific author.

1 "The anatomy of the human afterbirth done a second time"; this work was published at Utrecht in 1672, his *Anatomia secundinae humanae* having been issued there three years before. There is no account of either book in the *Philosophical Transactions*.

2 Because of the Anglo-Dutch War this letter and the book only reached Oldenburg on 30 July 1673. They were presented to the Royal Society on 30 October 1673.

3 Hoboken's work on the ewe seems not to have been published; however, *Anatomia secundinae vitulinae* appeared at Utrecht in 1675.

4 Walter Needham, *Disquisitio anatomica de formato foetu. Editio altera priori emendatior* (Amsterdam, 1668). The reference is actually to Chapter II, "De placentis & glandulis." The distinction between the placenta of other mammals and the cotyledonous placenta of most ruminants had been known since Aristotle, was illustrated by Fabricius, and is preserved in modern embryology. Needham, however, declared that the "glandules" of most ruminants were wrongly called cotyledons, and accordingly wished to denote these mammals as "glanduliferous." He wished to restrict the term "cotyledoniferous" to sheep and goats only (these species also being ruminant, of course) thereby establishing a threefold classification.

2041

Newton to Oldenburg

30 July 1672

Printed in Newton, *Correspondence*, I, 221, from the original in Royal Society MS. N 1, no. 41

Newton briefly repeated what he had apparently written in Letter 2035 (which miscarried) that the piece of speculum metal sent to him by Oldenburg "was well for closenesse & hardnesse but yet of a colour not very brisque & inclining to red." He asked Oldenburg to repeat the contents of Letter 2026, which he had not received; he does not say how he knew of its existence. He sends thirteen shillings for his quarterly subscription as a Fellow of the Royal Society.

2042
Oldenburg to Henshaw
31 July 1672
From the memorandum in Royal Society MS. H 3, no. 12

Rec. july 30. 72.

Answ. july 31. and sent him Lat. Quaeres for Iseland, and 2 copies of Boyles books de Gemmis for ye Courtiers there; and news of ye French Academies diligence, and ye Duke of Sav[oy] making a way through ye Mountains,[1] and Kirchers Tromba for hearing.[2]

Desired him to frame Quaeres for Fero.

NOTES

Reply to Letter 2015.

1 According to a letter dated 16 July 1672 in C.S.P.D. (1672, p. 347) Charles Emmanuel II (1634–75), Duke of Savoy, wished to convey a statue he had bought in Rome to Turin, and asked permission of the Republic of Genoa to enlarge the "way to get it home" from that port, at his own expense. At the same time he raised an army reputedly to serve the French; then, claiming that the Genoese had damaged his precious statue, he advanced upon them until within seven miles of the city.

2 See Letter 2023.

2043
Oldenburg to Newton
31 July 1672
Printed in Newton, *Correspondence*, I, 221, note 2, from the memorandum in Royal Society MS. N 1, no. 41

Rec. July 31. 72. Answ. eodem[1] and repeated ye contents of my letter of July 16.[2]

NOTES

Reply to Letter 2041.

1 "The same [day]."

2 Letter 2026.

2044

E. Bartholin to Oldenburg

4 August 1672

From the original in Royal Society MS. B 2, no. 17

Vir Clarissime Celeberrime

Habeo gratias de ista tam liberali tamque erga me prolixa voluntate, quam per binas nuper literas mihi significasti.[1] Abeunti Domino Picarto literas dedi per Dominum Fogelium tibi mittendas,[2] quibus de Tychonis nostri observationibus certiores vos facere volui: Eas demum salvas Parisios delatas esse, narrant ultimae literae mihi a Domino Picart redditae.[3] Hic, ut omittam illa quae vobis jam spectata sunt, ingenium, judicium, doctrinam, quantus quantus est totus labor, totus industria est; in Turri vero nostra Astronomica,[4] nec non in insula Huenna, strenue observationibus per totum tempus quo hic vixit, vixit autem mecum per octo menses, varia atque egregia annotavit quae ad Astronomicas observationes, praesertim Tychonis Brahe, vel confirmandas, vel corrigendas facere possunt, inprimis in rationem inveniendae differentia longitudinis inter Huenam et Parisiense observatorium, per immersiones atque emersiones circumjovialium, totus incubuit. Hanc, collatis observationibus eodem tempore a Domino Cassino in novo observatorio Parisiensi, eodemque instrumentorum apparatu habitis, publico haud dubie ipse communicabit, ut ipsi et, omnibus inservire poterit in calculo ex Observationibus Tychonis Brahe.[5] Observavit praeterea his Maculae Solaris transitum Ao. 1671 a die 3 Sept. ad 16. Stilo Novo, nec non Cometam Ao. 1672 a die 22 Mart. ad 27 Mart. et quod excurrit Stil. Nov. Quas observationes, cum epistola non capiat, inserere volui in Actis nostris Academicis a fratre Domino Thoma Bartholino mox edendis.[6] Sex pedam Parisienses cujus archetypum secum detulerat, cognovimus exacte ad tres ulnas Hafnienses, esse ut 720 ad 701, cum animadverterimus Snellij rationem non constare sibi.[7] De lineae Meridianae mutatione a tempore Tychonis non levis nobis orta est dubitatio, quam ut eximat posteritas confecimus, constitutis exacte angulis positionum.[8] Egregium et lectu dignissimum est ejus opus, cui titulus est La Mesure dela Terre, in quo exprimere conatur quot miliaribus terrestribus definiatur gradus unius quantitas, exactissimis adhibitis organis, quorum adjungit descriptionem; suntque eadem quae secum ad

nos pro observationibus heic instituendis detulerat, ex solido metallo, diop-
tris, tubo Optico ad accuratissime collimandum instructis; perpendiculo,
centro, fulcro, aliisque tanta industria adornatis, ut nihil excogitari possit
exactius. Et supposito pede Parisiensi partium 1440, invenit pedem Rhin-
landicum Leidensem partium 1390, Londinensem 1350: Gradum Vero
Maximi Circuli Terrae continere miliaria Gallica 25 seu 2282 hexapedes
fere,[9] miliaria vero Navigantibus usitata 20 seu 2853 hexapedas, atque
miliaria Anglica $73\frac{7}{200}$, quorum quodlibet valet 5000 pedes. Porro ex
mensura temporis, longitudineque penduli definire constituit pedis
archetypum, ne varijs injurijs obnoxia esset ejus longitudo. Meas quod
attinet curas, quarum certiores fieri desideratis Tu et Dominus Collins,
sciatis urgeri me tot negotijs publicis, ut raro ad studia experimentorum
vel sublimiora Mathematica transire liceat. Meo nomine rogo plurimam
salutem dicas Clarissimo Domino Collins, cujus recepi gratissimus
gratissimum munus transmissum per Amplissimum Dominum Henshau,
praelectiones opticas Domini Barrow,[10] et cognovi ipsius erga me singulare, atque erga studia Mathematica perpetuum studium, quo valde sum
laetatus. Tractatum, quem desiderat Domini De Beaune de Angulo Solido,[11]
reddidi Domino Picart in Gallias revehendum, cum spes omnis eum apud
nos, vel Batavos imprimendi, jam decollasset. Quod si possem eniti atque
consequi, ut ex istis curis atque occupationibus quibus oneror, emergam,
pertexeram quidem opus promissum Matheseos Universalis,[12] sin minus
reliquorum eruditionis, vestrorumque praesertim studij in promovendis
scientijs admirator ero et praeco. De planta subterranea meam observationem missam Domino Sachs, Ephemeridibus Germanicis curiosorum
insertam videbis in secunda parte edita.[13] Avide desidero tractatus Illustris
Domini Boyle nondum publico usui traditos, vel latine translatos de gemmis; de origine formarum nondum vidit haec regio tractatum. Morisonem
de plantis umbelliferis, Henricumque More de incorporeis misit Illustris
Dominus Bertij.[14] Reliquos a te nominatos avide exspectamus Mechanico-
rum Wallisij partem tertiam Willisij de Brutorum Anima morbisque Capitis.
Bohuni Historiae Ventorum: utinam opportunitas non invideret nobis,
ea aliaque praeclara ingenij vestrorum monumenta. Dominum Stenonem
nostrum ex Italia reducem,[15] scias, nunc apud nos ingenium scientiamque
ad studiorum utilitatem conferre. Prolixitati quaeso ignoscas, et ames
voluntatem summamque in te meam benevolentiam qua tuam humanitatem
imitari studiose constitui. Vale.

Hauniae die 4 Augusti 1672.   *T.*

Erasmius Bartholin

TRANSLATION

Most famous and celebrated Sir,

I thank you for your generous and copious goodwill towards me, of which you informed me in two recent letters.[1] As Mr. Picard was leaving I gave him a letter to be sent to you by Mr. Vogel,[2] in which I sought to give you information about the observations of my countryman Tycho; that these have been at length borne safely as far as Paris the latest letter delivered to me from Mr. Picard tells me.[3] Here I need not dwell on what you already know, his intelligence, good judgment and learning; how he is devoted to hard work and diligence; here in our Astronomical Tower[4] and also on the island of Hven he gave himself whole-heartedly to making observations throughout the whole period of his stay here, and he lived with me eight months, in various and unusual ways taking note of everything that can be done for verifying or correcting astronomical observations, especially those of Tycho Brahe, and what is necessary for discovering the differ-ence in longitude between the observatories of Hven and Paris by the immersions and emersions of Jupiter's satellites. This [difference in longitude] he will no doubt himself communicate to the public when the observations made by Mr. Cassini with an identical set of instruments at the new Paris observatory have been col-lated, as it can be of service to himself and everyone else in making calculations from the observations of Tycho Brahe.[5] Moreover he observed here the passage of the sunspot from 3 to 16 September 1671, N.S., and the comet [seen] from 22 to 27 March, N.S., in the present year 1672. As a letter cannot contain these observa-tions I mean to insert them in our *Academic Transactions* soon to be published by my brother Thomas Bartholin.[6] We found out that six Paris feet (whose standard measure he had brought with him) are to three ells of Copenhagen exactly as 720 to 701, whence we observed that Snel's ratio is not consistent with itself.[7] No slight doubt was provoked in us concerning a change in the meridian line since the time of Tycho; we have made preparations so that posterity may decide this issue by laying down the angles of position precisely.[8] His work entitled *Mesure de la Terre* is a remarkable one and well worth reading; in this he has endeav-ored to express the number of terrestrial miles contained in a single degree, meas-ured with very precise instruments of which he has annexed a description. These are the same instruments that he brought with him to this place for making the observations to be carried out here; they are made of solid metal and fitted with sights in the telescope tube that are most exquisitely collimated. They are perfectly fitted as regards the perpendicular, the center, the fulcrum, and in every respect so that anything more precise is unimaginable. And postulating the Paris foot to contain 1440 parts he found the Rhineland foot of Leiden to contain 1390 parts and the London foot 1350; that the degree of a great circle of the earth contains 25 French miles [leagues] roughly, or 2282 fathoms,[9] and 20 customary sea-miles, or 2853 fathoms, roughly, and $73\frac{7}{200}$ English miles each of 5000 feet. Furthermore, by making time-measurements and the length of the pendulum he has managed to define the standard foot, in case its length should be exposed to a variety of damages. As for my own concerns of which you and Mr. Collins desired to be informed, you know that I am pressed by so much public business that I can rarely transfer to experimental researches or the higher mathematics. Please give many greetings from me to the famous Mr. Collins from whom I have most gratefully received the most welcome gift brought by the worthy Mr. Henshaw, Mr. Barrow's *Lectiones opticae*,[10] and I have recognized his singular zeal towards myself as well as his constant devotion to mathematical studies, in which I greatly rejoice. I handed to Mr. Picard when he was about to return to France the treatise by Mr. de Beaune *De angulo solido*[11] that he longed for, as every hope that it might be printed here by ourselves or else in Holland had already expired. If I could have successfully worked my way through the duties and business by which I am oppressed so as to free myself from them, I would certainly have put together that promised work, *Matheseos universalis*;[12] if I cannot do this I shall nevertheless admire and proclaim the learning of others, and in particular the enthusiasm of your countrymen for the advancement of science. You will see my observation of the subterranean plant, sent to Mr. Sachs, inserted in the second published part of the *Miscellanea curiosa*.[13] I greedily long for the as yet unpublished (or untranslated into Latin) treatises on gems of the illustrious Mr. Boyle; this part of the world has not yet seen his treatise *On the Origine of Forms*. The illustrious Mr. Bertet sent Morison on the umbellifera and Henry More on incorporeal things.[14] The remaining books named by yourself we eagerly await—the third part of Wallis's *Mechanics*, Willis's *De anima brutorum* and Bohun's *History of Winds*; would that [lack of] opportunity might not defraud us of these and other distinguished monuments to the intelligence of your countrymen. You may know that our fellow-Dane Mr. Steno has returned from Italy,[15] thus bringing among us now an intelligence and a knowledge of science valuable to the studious. Please forgive my prolixity and look kindly upon my great goodwill and good feeling for you, by which I have resolved zealously to imitate your own kindness. Farewell.

Copenhagen, 4 August 1672.

Yours,
Erasmus Bartholin

NOTES

1 Presumably Letters 1552 (Vol. VII) and 1907 (Vol. VIII), unless indeed Oldenburg sent an unrecorded letter to Bartholin with Letter 2003.
2 Letter 1962.
3 See Letter 2009, note 5.
4 Usually known as the Round Tower, it was built as an observatory for the astronomer Christian Longomontanus (1562–1647) by Christian IV of Denmark. Rømer was

to work there after his return from Paris. It was destroyed in the fire that ravaged Copenhagen in 1728.

5 The publication of these results was delayed for several years—see Jean Picard, *Voyage d'Uranibourg, ou observations astronomiques faites en Dannemark* (Paris, 1686 [-82?]). We give the B.M. Catalogue date; the official date is 1680 but this is clearly false as the work contains cartographical observations of 1681!

6 Compare Letter 1962, note 2, the sunspot observations being in no. 128 (p. 222) and the cometary ones in no. 129 on the same page. Both are very laconic.

7 Willebrod Snel in *Eratosthenes Batavus* (Leiden, 1617) through some mistake gave the ratio of the ell of Copenhagen to the Rhineland foot as 934 : 1000. In fact the ell was about twice as big, for Picard and Bartholin found (as the comparison here suggests) that the Copenhagen ell equaled almost exactly two Rhineland feet (see no. 123, p. 215, in the *Acta medica*).

8 See no. 127, p. 220, in the *Acta medica*.

9 What Bartholin means is that each French mile contains 2282 *toises*, and each sea mile 2853 *toises*; all these figures were given by Vernon in Letter 1854 (Vol. VIII, p. 436).

10 Compare the beginning of Letter 2015.

11 Florimond de Beaune (1601–52); compare Vol. IV, p. 344, note 3. It is known that Bartholin had access to De Beaune's manuscripts since he edited one in Van Schooten's edition of Descartes's *Geometrie* (Amsterdam, 1659) and he presumably kept copies at least. The MS. mentioned here was not printed and its fate is unknown. The desirability of printing it is mentioned in a letter from Collins to Gregory of 14 March 1671/2 (Turnbull, *Gregory*, p. 224).

12 In fact Bartholin did publish no more on mathematics.

13 *Miscellanea curiosa*, Vol. II (for 1671; Jena, 1671), no. 170.

14 The name of Bertet, now in Paris (see Vol. VII, p. 380, note 14), is a guess, but no other suggests itself; for Morison's book, see Letter 1701, note 4 (Vol. VIII); for Henry More's, see Letter 1907, note 3 (Vol. VIII).

15 Steno had been in Florence since 1665, where he became a convert to Roman Catholicism; he returned there in 1674.

2045

Oldenburg to Flamsteed

5 August 1672

From the memorandum in Royal Society MS. F 1, no. 89

Rec. Aug. 2. 72.
Answ. Aug. 5. by a friend M. Cook[1] intimated, yt Cass[ini's] paper[2] is to be sent him by M. Townley, and yt I will print ye contents of this.[3] Desired a Catal[ogue] of aged persons.[4]

NOTES

Reply to Letter 2036.

1 This cannot be Miles Cook (see Letter 1940, note 2 in Vol. VIII), and no other Cook is mentioned by Flamsteed at this time.

2 See Letter 1995, note 1.

3 That is, Letter 2036.

4 Oldenburg had been interested in this subject for at least two years; see Vol. VII, Index, s.v. "Longevity." On 13 August in a letter to Collins Flamsteed wrote "Present my services to Mr. Oldenburg, and tell him I shall be careful to make inquiries of the old people, and how they have lived, as he desired, but, having no great acquaintance, I fear I cannot procure any long list" (Rigaud, II, 159).

2046
Oldenburg to Henshaw

5 August 1672

From the memorandum in Royal Society MS. H 3, no. 12

Aug. 5. 72. I wrote another letter, giving him notice of ye Danish book in Sr R. M.s hands,[1] and desiring him to get a Danish Dictionary.

NOTES

Second reply to Letter 2015.

1 It was a book on Danish law, in Danish, perhaps that mentioned in Letter 2015, note 13.

2047
Flamsteed to Oldenburg

12 August 1672

From the original in Royal Society MS. F 1, no. 90

Derby August 12. 1672

Mr Oldenburge

Yrs of ye 5th instant came to my hands last Saturday by Mr Cooke, & yr former by my neighbor I reaceaved safe from him, if my last[1] intimated not so much twas my forgetfulnesse onely, I am sorry my last paper was not so faire writ as to be legible. the Number yu note out of ye 7 line, & 5th columne of Numbers ought to be 12°–08′, for so I find it in a copy of that little Ephemeris I keepe by mee.[2] Yours seemes to intimate that yu intend to print that praediction in the Transactions; As I have committed it into yr hands, so I permitte yu to dispose of it as yu please, but in my opinion yu may doe well to communicate it onely to your freinds in private that will take care to observe it diligently, that so our countrimen may have the honor of haveing first truely found ye parallaxe of Mars, which if the Ephemeris & prediction be made publick, the French may deprive us of, & perhaps render our better observations suspected, by the contradiction of such as they have not, I thinke, the conveniencies for makeing so accurately, nor will be so exact as ours, if God permitte us those opportunitys. I have measured the distances of those stars, by which Mars makes his transit, & I find them otherwise then upon my protraction from the Tychonick data, for August 8 vesperim[3] a cleare Aire I measured

betwixt ye 26 & 27 stars 5435 = 32′–20″
betwixt ye 27 & 28 stars 5010 = 29′–48″
Tychonice sunt[4] 30′–40″, 33′–35″

$*$ 26
$*$ 27

$*$ 28   ≈≈≈ ij

But of the places of those stars & how they ought to be corrected when have occasion to write what wee shall observe of that appulse, I may let yu fully know. I am now prepareing & ordering my instruments to observe the Eclipse this afternoone, but it raines so frequently & the heavens yeeld so many clouds from ye west that I almost despaire of observeing any thinge, tho I am resolved wth some assistants to attend it.[5] I have not yet seene the Transactions yu mention,[6] but expect them at this weekes end. tho P. Pardies have altered his opinion, yet I find no reasons to alter mine; but rather many to confirme it. of which hereafter I may write at large to yu. at present I must bid yu farewell, & rest

Your obliged & affectionate servant
John Flamsteed

Pray tell Mr Collins when yu see him I have reaceaved the boxe & glasse.[7]

J F

ADDRESS

    For Henry Oldenburg Esq
    at his house in the middle
    of ye Pell mell in St
    James'es Westminster
        these

NOTES

    Reply to Letter 2045.
1 Letter 2036.
2 They are so in the manuscript we have printed.
3 "in the evening."
4 "they are according to Tycho."
5 A little group of the Royal Society met in the afternoon of the same day in Hooke's rooms at Gresham College but were unable to observe the eclipse of the sun.
6 *Phil. Trans.*, no. 85 (15 July 1672), containing Letters 1976a, 1992, and 2009, from which it appeared that Pardies was entirely satisfied by Newton's answers to his objections touching the theory of light and colors.
7 On 23 July Flamsteed had written Collins requesting him to send to Derby an object-glass for a three foot tube, which was to form the telescopic sight on Flamsteed's brass quadrant of the same radius.

2048
Vogel to Oldenburg
13 August 1672
From the original in Royal Society MS. F 1, no. 37

Viro Nobilissimo & Doctissimo HENRICO OLDENBURG S.P.D.
Martinus Fogelius

ad eas, quas 15 Aprilis ad te dedi,[1] literas nihil hactenus responsi accepi, sive illae perierint, sive occupationibus tuis istud dilatum fuerit. Siferus suas etiam meis adjecerat.[2] neque huic responsum missum est. Expectavi pridem cum Vita Galilaei Morisoniam Umbelliferarum Plantarum Historiam,[3] quae commode cum libris, quos Joan. Martinus Schulzio nostro mittit, conjungi poterunt. Ego in vicem Loeneisium[4] mittam & alia. Interea tibi significandum duxi, me civi nostro, Edingio, tradidisse Epistolam egregiam Langelotti,[5] Medici Principis Holsatiae, quam a D. Bristero, medicam artem apud vos faciente, repetes.[6]

Accepi nuper ab eodem Chirurgo, qui Groenlandicum iter descripsit,[7] aliquot Piscium Hispanorum figuras, ad vivum depictas, quarum paucissimas in Rondeletio reperio.[8] Schulzio velim hortatus sis, ut Groenlandicum iter curet imprimi. Valde enim curiosum est. ille causatur figurarum multitudinem non comitatam prolixia Historia. quid enim opus est inutili vectorum copis, & aliunde congesta Narrationum mole? Volui ipsum nihil scribere, nisi quod ipse certo comperisset.

Quia Lynceorum Historia hac aestate non potuit praelo subjici, Commentariolum meum de Turcarum Maslaga fere perfeci.[9] Sunt vobiscum plures viri Turcicae, Arabicae, Persicae lingua periti, quidam etiam ex his diu apud Turcas vixerunt. Quod si igitur, Vir Clarissime, tibi molestum non est, fac, quaeso, ut prima occasione sciam, quid Vir doctissimus Pocockius, tuus amicus, quid Ricautius[10] de hoc medicamento cognoverit, quid item alii Viri docti apud Turcas versati, mihi non noti, de eodem compererint. Multa non vulgaria jam de eo congessi. vellem tamen libellum meum vestratium testimoniis augere. Singulis qui me aliquid docebunt, laudem debitam tribuam. Quae ex Lexico Heptaglotto[11] Or[ientalem] peti possunt, nil attinet repetere mei causa. Eadem occasione scisciteris velim ex iisdem quae in Scheda adjecta consignavi. Quia vero Clar. Semannum[12] Turcicae linguae inprimis gnarum esse scio, volui hunc seorsum compellare.¹³ Quod tanto excusatius facio, te, Vir Nobilissime, pararío. Tu etiam operam dabis, ut quamprimum mihi respondeat.

Heri observavimus hic caelo inconstanti post primum h. 7 vespert. quadrantem, discum Solis obscuratum. aucta fuit obscuratio ad 2 circiter digitos circa hora 7, deinceps non amplius coelum favit. Foglii Calendariographi¹⁴ calculum a vero longissime aberasse deprehendimus, initium ad h. 3 53′ collocantis.

Vale Vir Nobilissime & me amare perge. Scribam Hamburgi d. 13. Aug. 1672.

Inter eas plantas, quarum forma nondum novimus, etiam sunt Baccae Piscatoriae, *Cocolo di Levante*.¹⁵ quod si de his Experimenta quidam habes, velim mihi omnes [non] invideas, neque obliviscatis Mercatores Anglos qui Alexandriae versantur, monere, ut Folia, & Flores nobis mittant cum caeteris adhuc nobis incognitis plantis, de quibus alias tibi scripsi. An Auctorem libelli de Statu hodierno Russiae,¹⁶ 1671 Londini impressi non inquirere potes, si non no[v . . . *paper torn*]. Iterum Vale.

ADDRESS
        A Monsr
        Monsr Grubendol
                Londres

TRANSLATION

Martin Vogel sends many greetings to the very noble and learned Henry Oldenburg

I have received no reply at all as yet to the letter which I wrote you on 15 April,¹ either because it was lost or because your reply was postponed by your own concerns. Sivers added his letter to mine,² and no answer has been sent to him either. I had expected [to receive] soon along with the life of Galileo Morison's account of the umbelliferae³ which could conveniently have been added to the books which John Martin sent to our Schulz. In exchange I will send Lonicer⁴ and others. Moreover I should let you know that I have delivered the very interesting letter of Langelott,⁵ physician to the Prince of Holstein, to my fellow citizen Eding, which you may recover from Mr. Brister who practises medicine in your country.⁶

I recently received from the same surgeon who described the voyage to Greenland⁷ a few drawings of Spanish fishes, drawn from the life, of which I find very

few in Rondelet.[8] I wish you to urge Schulz to take charge of the printing of the
Greenland voyage. For it is extremely curious. He makes excuses about the multitude of illustrations not being proportionate to a short narrative. But what is the
use of a great deal of padding and another massive narrative from yet another
place? I meant him [the author] to write nothing that he had not most certainly
discovered for himself.

Since the history of the Lincei could not be sent to the press this summer, I
have almost perfected my little commentary on the Turkish *maslac*.[9] In your
country there are many who are familiar with the Turkish, Arabic, and Persian
languages, some of whom have lived long among the Turks. If it is no trouble to
you then, famous Sir, let me be informed at the first opportunity, please, of what
your friend the very learned Pocock and [Paul] Rycaut[10] know of this medicament,
and also what other learned men who have dwelt among the Turks, whose names
I do not know, have discovered about it. I have already assembled much out of
the way material concerning it, but I wish to swell my little book with the evidence
of your countrymen. I shall make due acknowledgment to those who shall instruct me on some point. There is no need to repeat for my sake what can be
gleaned from the oriental *Lexicon heptaglotton*.[11] At the same time I wish that you
should make inquiries from the same persons concerning the points I have set
down on the attached sheet. Because the famous Seaman[12] is, I know, particularly
learned in the Turkish language I wish this to be addressed to him individually.[13]
To render so much trouble the more excusable I will do the like for you, most
noble Sir. You will also make it your business to have him reply as soon as possible.

In a troubled sky we yesterday observed here an obscuration of the sun's disk
after a quarter past six in the evening. The obscuration was increased to about two
digits by about seven o'clock but after that the heavens favored us no more. We
gathered that the calculation in the ephemerides[14] was very far from the truth for
it timed the beginning [of the eclipse] for 3.53'.

Farewell, most noble Sir, and continue your affection for me. Hamburg, 13
August 1672.

Among those plants whose morphology is not yet known to us is the fisher-
man's berry or *coccole di Levante*.[15] If you have any experience of this plant please do
[not] grudge it to me, and do not forget to advise the English merchants who trade
with Alexandria to send us the leaves and flowers, along with the other plants still
unknown to us of which I wrote to you elsewhere. Can you not inquire of the
author of the book on the present state of Russia, printed at London in 1671,[16]
whether he does not [know . . . *paper torn*]. Farewell again.

ADDRESS
    To Mr Grubendol,
    London.

NOTES

1 Letter 1959; we have no record of a reply.
2 As already noted, this letter is missing.
3 See Letter 1701, note 4 (Vol. VIII).
4 See Letter 1885, note 5 (Vol. VIII).
5 Joel Langelott, *Epistola ad praecellentissimos Naturae Curiosis. De quibusdam in chymia praetermissis* . . . (Hamburg, 1672). A German version appeared in the same year from Nuremberg and Oldenburg gave a partial English translation in *Phil. Trans.*, no. 87 (14 October 1672), 5052–59. Langelott (1617–80) had been physician to Frederick IV of Holstein-Gottorp since 1647.
6 We have identified neither of the two last-named.
7 See Letter 1885, *ad fin.* (Vol. VIII).
8 Guillaume Rondelet, *De piscibus marinis* (Lyons, 1554–55).
9 Parkinson, p. 363, gives a short account of the European botanists' notions about this Turkish opiate; Clusius thought it was derived from some sort of henbane (*Hyoscyamus* spp.). Bauhin that it was rather obtained from a kind of thorn apple (*Datura stramonium*); both belong to the modern family Solanaceae, which is very rich in narcotics. But *maslac* (the word is variously spelled) seems to have caused difficulties even among oriental scholars of the later seventeenth century, being defined either as a preparation of opium or of cannabis; the latter seems the more likely on the authority of F. Mesgnien von Meninski, in *Thesaurus linguarum orientalium* (Vienna, 1680) s.v. "esrar" (in Arabic script). The derivation is uncertain, as Seaman indicates in his letter of 9 September 1672 to Vogel in reply to this query (there is a copy in Royal Society MS. S 1, no. 125); the popular derivation from the words "Mashallah" ("what God hath willed") often stamped on cakes or lozenges of various narcotic preparations is suspect. For an English nineteenth-century view see A. T. Thomson, *London Dispensary* (London, 1822), p. 421 note. (Dr. V. L. Ménage and Dr. M. P. Earles).
10 See Vol. III, p. 344, note.
11 Edmund Castell, *Lexicon heptaglotton* (London, 1669). Compare Vol. II, p. 250, note 13.
12 William Seaman (1606–80), author of *Grammatica lingua Turcicae* (Oxford, 1670). Compare Vol. II, p. 214, note 6.
13 There is no longer any attached sheet with the letter. For Oldenburg's action, see Letter 2061.
14 These two words are puzzling. *Foglii* is not a Latin form. However, as it is impossible to attribute a specific meaning to them we have rendered them in a general sense.
15 The singular is properly *coccola*, plural *coccole*: "Levantine berries." These are the fruits of *Anamirta paniculata* (or *A. cocculus* according to others) called "cocculus Indicus" when dried for commerce. The plant is a large climbing shrub native to India and Malaya but also growing in the southern United States. The fruits contain a poisonous alkaloid, picrotoxin, and were used by fishermen in the Far East to stupefy fish.
16 Samuel Collins, *The Present State of Russia in a Letter written to a Friend at London* (London, 1671). The author, who had been the Czar's physician for eight years, had returned to London in 1659.

2049
Towneley to Oldenburg
15 August 1672
From the original in Royal Society MS. T, no. 23

Towneley Aug: 15 1672

Sr

The hopes I had yt ye heavens would have beene more favorable unto me, were ye cause I differd one post ye thanks due for your kindnesse, of Cassinies paper[1] but as they have beene for some considerable time before so they were on Munday last[2] quite overcast, so yt nothing could be seene, howsoever in some measure I was obliged unto them, for in hopes of observeing ye Eclipse I came sooner home yn otherwise I should have done. It may be Mr. Flamsteed was more fortunate and then no matter,[3] howsoever I shall take care to have ye paper safelie conveyed unto him, and from thence againe unto you, but in case of failer, ye Copie I shall keepe will enable me to send send [*sic*] it unto you. I doubt not but he will make admirable use of it. I shall see how it agres with my observations, of wch of late I have made but verie few, but what can be done in this case, I think you may without anie more adoe, expect from Mr. Flamsteed who shall not want anie assistance I shall be able to afford him, particularlie of ye observations I have made

I have not yett ye Julie's Transactions but expect them next weeke, and Long much for ye 3 bookes you mention, but particularlie for a perfect account of ye Quicksilver phenomenon yours mentions, and ye thoughts of Monsr. Hugens about ye solution of it.[4]

I have of late beene so much from home yt I could not attend ye successe of my water bellows, wch yett prooves not according to expectation, not for anie fault I find in ye machine it selfe but for ye ill condition of ye water (if so I may call it) in wch they were to play, for it brings with it such a cancard matter yt in lesse yn a weeks time it eates them to pieces so yt for ye present I am forced to make use of other engines.

As for my Thermometer[5] it was taken out of ye coale pit before I was acquainted of it howsoever it stoode so long both in ye couldest weather, and in ye hottest of this yeare without ye least alteration, yt I have no reason to doubt but that the temper of ye aire in ye place where it stoode continues still ye same. If you think a particular account of ye depthe of ye pit ye situation of ye place where it stoode, or anie other circumstances more, may be of anie use, I shall obey your commands in sending them.

I onelie once mett with ye Dr. who promised me ye account of aged persons you desir'd,[6] for he hath beene latelie much from home, and then he tould me yt about 2 winters agoe neare halfe of ye aged persons in these parts died, I shall howsoever as soone as his convenience will permit, be urgeing his promisse in this businesse, for I shall not rest satisfied till I find some occasion of makeing return to your kindnesses wch must ever be acknowleded [*sic*] by Sr

Your most humble & obliged servant
Rich. Towneley

ADDRESS

These
For Mr Henry Ouldenbourg at
his house in ye Pelmaill
London

POSTMARK AU 19

NOTES

1 See Letter 2045 and its note 1. The letter which Oldenburg wrote to Towneley when enclosing Cassini's paper on Jupiter's satellites has not survived. Compare Letter 2055.
2 August 12.
3 Flamsteed also missed the eclipse owing to the bad weather (Rigaud, II, 159).
4 Probably Oldenburg had described the contents of the *Journal des Sçavans* for 25 July 1672 [N.S.] where he certainly found Huygens' letter on the anomalous suspension of mercury (see Letter 2058 and its note 1). If so, then the three books were (1) I. G. Pardies, *Discours de la Connoissance des Bêtes*; (2) J. C. Gallet, *Tabula revolutionum et motuum solis* (Avignon, 1672); (3) Moses Maimonides, *Tractatus de consecratione calendarum et de ratione intercalandi*, translated into French by Louis de Compiègne (Paris, 1672).
5 See Letter 1958.
6 Compare Letter 2045.

2050
Oldenburg to Hevelius
16 August 1672
From the original in BN MS. N.a.L. 1641, f. 22r and v

Illustrissimo Viro
Domino Johanni Hevelio, Gedanensium Consuli dignissimo
Henr. Oldenburg Salutem

Accepi tandem, Vir Clarissime, Exemplaria de Cometa nupero omnia, quae binis navibus ad me transmittere dignatus es.[1] Morem geram mandatis tuis, quibus ea partim amicis tuis hic distribuenda, partim bibliopolis nostra[2] vendenda jussisti.

Redditae mihi etiam sunt litterae tuae, quibus significas, captas a nostratibus esse aliquot naves, quae magnam fortunarum tuarum partem vehant.[3] Summo certe dolore angimur, quod furens Mars in innoxios etiam philosophiae cultores saeviat; nec velimus quenquam periculosissimo hoc tempore facultates suas navibus marique committere. Exhibui Nobilissimo Brounckero litteras tuas,[4] qui omnem Tibi operam spondet in dictarum navium liberatione procuranda. Intelligimus, navim huc in Angliam avectam pristinae jam esse libertati restitutam: Et quanquam duas illas naves, in Scotia detentas, jam condemnatas esse dicant, protestatione tamen et inhibitione in contrarium injecta, operam dabimus, ut jubentibus literis Regiis dimittantur.

Transmisit mihi nuper Dominus Bullialdus fascem satis crassem librorum, rogavitque, ut prima quaque occasione navi Anglica Dantiscum velificatura ad Te curarem.[5] Tradidi libros illos mercatori Lee, Domino Kirckbeo notissimo. qui eorum curam suscepit, eosque brevi ad te transmittendos curabit. Vestrum erit inquirere apud primam navim, quae ex Anglia Dantisci appellet: cujus nomen hactenus edoceri non potui. Vale et Tibi addictissimum Oldenburgium porro ama. Dabam raptim d. 16. Augusti 1672.

TRANSLATION

Henry Oldenburg greets the very illustrious Mr. Johannes Hevelius, very worthy Senator of Danzig

I have at last received all the copies of [the letter] concerning the recent comet, famous Sir, that you were good enough to send me aboard two vessels.[1] I have obeyed your instructions to distribute some of them among your friends here and to sell some to our booksellers.

That letter of yours has also been delivered to me in which you inform me of the capture by our forces of a few ships conveying a great part of your fortune.[3] We are truly tormented by utmost distress that the mad rage of war should violate even harmless lovers of philosophy, nor by our choice would anyone at this most perilous moment have to entrust his goods to ships and the sea. I showed your letter to the very noble Brouncker,[4] who promises you his every exertion in obtaining the liberation of the said vessels. We understand that a vessel carried off hither to England has already been restored to its former freedom; and although it is reported that those two vessels detained in Scotland have already been condemned [as prizes] we shall see to it that an opposing protest and injunction is interjected so that they may be discharged upon the order of a Royal Letter.

Mr. Boulliaud recently sent me a pretty stout package of books and asked me to see to sending it to you by the first opportunity of an English vessel sailing for Danzig.[5] I have handed those books over to the merchant Lee, well known to Mr. Kirkby, who has undertaken responsibility for them and will soon have them sent on to you. It will be your task to inquire of the first ship calling at Danzig from England, whose name I could not yet learn. Farewell, and continue your affection for your most devoted Oldenburg. Written in haste, 16 August 1672.

NOTES

1 See Letters 1986, 1986 bis, and 1999.
2 Read: "nostris."
3 Hevelius' letter has not been traced, having been doubtless sent to Brouncker or some other official person. Nor have we come across any other record of the incident. Since Hevelius had a large brewing business at Danzig it is possible that the ships taken by the privateers were freighted with beer. Danzig, of course, was neutral in the war; however, north German shipping was often confused with Dutch.
4 Brouncker was one of the Commissioners of the Navy.
5 See Letters 1968 and 1978.

2051

Denis to Oldenburg

August 1672

From the original in Royal Society MS. D 1, no. 7

Aoust 1672

Monsieur

Jay receu vostre derniere avec La Transaction que vous avez eu la bonté de m'envoye touchant lhypothese de Monsr. Newton sur les couleurs.[1] Jay esté fort aise de la lire parce qu'il y avoit bien autant de Latin que d'Anglois. iay conceu par la ce que mon traducteur n'avoit [pu] me faire comprendre dans les precedentes. Je vous envoye Lonzieme memoire[2] que je vous ay desja envoyé cydevant, s'il vous manque quelque autre chose en quoy ie vous puisse rendre service, ie vous prie de ne m'epargne pas. Je vous envoye aussy la troisieme de mes conferences,[3] où comme vous verrez je traite des matieres fort eloignées de celles dont jay parlé dans la premiere, mais J'y suis obligé, on ayme icy la diversité, on ne veut pas des pieces de Longue haleine, et on ne veut pas estre entretenu deux fois de suite d'une mesme matiere. Si dieu me conserve de la santé je ne Laisseray pas de donner une physique entiere qui sera dispersée en plusieures conferences, et que l'on pourra facilement rassembler. Vostre derniere Transaction m'a fait souhaiter que toutes les autres fussent aussi toutes en latin. et je crois que si vous les faisiez imprimer en latin aussi bien qu'en Anglois et en mesme temps dans ces deux langues il s'en debiteroit baucoup en france, en Allemagne, en Italie et autres payis eloignez. Je suis Monsieur

Vostre tres humble serviteur
Denis

ADDRESS
Monsieur
Monsieur Grubendol
Londres

TRANSLATION

August 1672

Sir,

I have received your last with the *Transactions* you kindly sent me concerning Mr. Newton's hypothesis of colors.[1] I was very happy reading it because there was as much Latin as English. I grasped by that what my translator had not made me understand in the preceding ones. I send you the eleventh *Mémoire*[2] which I had already sent you before; if you lack anything else in which I can serve you please do not spare me. I also send you the third of my *Conferences*,[3] wherein, as you will see, I treat matters very far removed from those of which I spoke in my first. But I was obliged to do so: here people love variety, they don't like long-winded essays nor do they wish to be entertained by a subject twice in a row. If God preserves my health I shall not fail to give a complete natural history which will be dispersed in several *Conferences* but which can be easily reassembled. Your last *Transaction* made me wish that all the others had also been entirely in Latin. And I think that if you were to have them printed in Latin as well as in English, and at the same time in the two languages, they would sell largely in France, Germany, Italy, and other distant countries. I am, Sir,

Your very humble servant
Denis

ADDRESS

Mr. Grubendol,
London

NOTES

1 Oldenburg's letter has not survived. *Phil. Trans.*, no. 85 (15 July 1672) contains Pardies's and Newton's Latin interchange.
2 Dated 1 June 1672 [N.S.], on botany.
3 Dated 15 August 1672 [N.S.], on the spleen.

2052

Oldenburg to Flamsteed

20 August 1672

From the memorandum in Royal Society MS. F 1, no. 90

Rec: Answ. Aug. 20. 1672. desired to know in ye name of Mr Hook, whether ye Eclipse of Cor ♌ by ye Moon Oct. 6. next, in ye morning will not be visible, and, in case it be, whether he, Flamsteed, will observe it. To send a speedy answer.

NOTES

Reply to Letter 2047. There is a note in Hooke's *Diary* for 19 August 1672: "Gave Oldenburg paper for Flamsteed." See also Letter 2055.

2053

Sluse to Oldenburg

21 August 1672

From the original in Royal Society MS. S 1, no. 72
Printed in *Phil. Trans.*, no. 98 (17 November 1673), 6145–46, and in Boncompagni, pp. 663–65

Nobilissimo et Clarissimo Viro
D. Henrico Oldenburg Regiae Societatis Secretario
Renatus Franciscus Slusius
χείρειν

Mirari desine, Vir Clarissime, eandem in Alhazeniano Problemate constructionem ex diversis aequationibus deduci, quandoquidem illa omnes, quibus hactenus usi sumus, in una eademque generali Analysi contineantur. Quod ut ostendam, datus sit circulus, cuius centrum A, puncta H et I; sitque punctum quaesitum K, ad quod ex punctis I et H ducantur rectae HK, IK, et tangens KD. Tum ex A ducatur quaelibet AG, occurrens HK in E, IK in B, tangenti KD in D, (ijs nimirum pro-

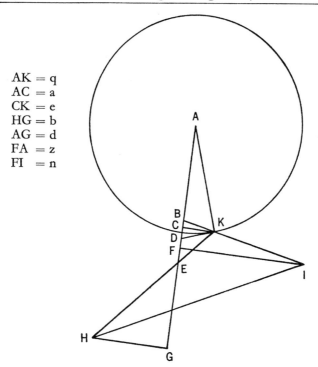

AK = q
AC = a
CK = e
HG = b
AG = d
FA = z
FI = n

ductis, quas produci opus est). His positis, evidens est, ob angulos *EKD*, *DKB*, aequales, et angulum *AKD* rectum, tres *AE, BE, DE* fore semper harmonice proportionales. Itaque ductis ad *AE* normalibus *KC, IF, HG*, ac denominatis partibus, ut in laterculo; habebitur, methodo, quam in secunda huius Problematis Analysi olim adhibuj,[1] haec generalis aequatio

$$ndaa - bzaa - nqqa + bqqa = ndee - zbee + 2bnae + 2zdae - dqqe - zqqe$$

Finge nunc *AG* esse perpendicularem ad *HI*, nihil varietatis erit in aequatione, nisi quod *AF* et *AG*, hoc est *d* et *z*, erunt aequales.

posito itaque *d* pro *z* fiet

$$ndaa - bdaa - nqqa + bqqa = ndee - dbee + 2bnae + 2ddae - 2dqqe$$

sive applicatis omnibus ad *nd−db*

$$aa - \frac{qqa}{d} = ee + \frac{2bnae + 2ddae - 2dqqe}{nd - db}.$$

eadem nempe, quam ex prima mea Analysi,[2] licet alia via, deduxeram, et quam nuper modo facili constructam ad te misi.[3]

Pone deinde *AG* coincidere cum *AH*: abibit igitur *HG* sive *b*, in nihilum. expunctis itaque ab aequatione partibus, in quibus *b* reperitur, remanebit.

$$ndaa - nqaa = ndee + 2zdae - dqqe - qqze.[4]$$

Hanc autem, si meministi, curis secundis inveni,[5] et aliam huic similem in casu quo recta *AG* transire intelligitur per *I*.

Supponamus demum rectam *AG* secare bifariam angulum *HAI*. Erit ob similitudinem triangulorum *HAG IAF*, ut *HG* ad *GA* ita *IF* ad *FA* sive ut *b* ad *d* ita *n* ad *z*, et *nd* = *bz*. Ablatis igitur aequalibus, fit:

$$bqqa - nqqa = 2bnae + 2zdae - dqqe - qqze.$$

Illa ipsa, quam, ut ex literis tuis nuper intellexi, Clarissimus Hugenius construxit.[6] Intelligatur tandem eadem recta *HG*, secare bifariam rectam *HI*. Erunt igitur aequales *HG IG*, hoc est *b* = *n*. etque ablatis aequalibus

$$bdaa - bzaa = bdee - bzee + 2bbae + 2zdae - dqqe - qqze.$$

quam, licet non admodum difficilem nemo nostrum hactenus construxit. Hae autem ut et ipsa generalis aequatio in duas alias dividi possunt, posito, ut nosti, pro *aa* vel *ee* eius valore *qq* − *ee* vel *qq* − *aa*.

Vides igitur, Vir Clarissime, quidquid hactenus praestitum est, in eandem Analysim resolvi, quae et infinitas alias constructiones per circulum datum et hyperbolam complectatur. Sed eas investigare non est tanti cum in hoc Problemate, ut olim fortassis inopia, sic nunc copia laboremus. Addam tantum constructionem per parabolam, idque via duplici: quae licet alijs per Hyperbolam operosior videatur, Lineae tamen simplicitate, qua parabola inter reliquas sectiones commendatur, operam compensat.

Ijsdem igitur datis iungatur *AI* et producatur in *S*, donec *AS* fiat aequalis *AH*, iunctaque *HS*, et bisecta *IS*, in *M*, ducatur per *M* recta *RMQ* normalis ad *HS*, in quam cadat ex *A* normalis *AQ*, et cui parallelus ducatur radius *AC*. Tum factis tribus proportionalibus *IA*, *AC*, *AE*, fit ut *SA* ad *AE*, ita *MQ* ad *AD*, et *RS* ad *AP*, (in recta *AQ* versus *Q*.) et in eadem ab alia parte sumatur *DO* aequalis *DC*. Demum, bisecta *PD* in *X*, inclinetur per *X* angulo semirecto ad *AX*, recta *VXL*, occurrens normali in *D* erectae in puncto *V*, et in quam ex *O* cadat normalis *OB*. Aio si fiat ut *VX* ad *XB*, ita *XB* ad *BL*, punctum *L* esse verticem, *LV* axem, *XV* latus rectum parabolae, quae Problemati satisfacit omni casu; secans nimirum circulum datum in punctis *K*, quorum supremum et infimum ad Problema Alhazenianum pertinent, reliqua ad aliud, de quo nuper ad te scripsi.

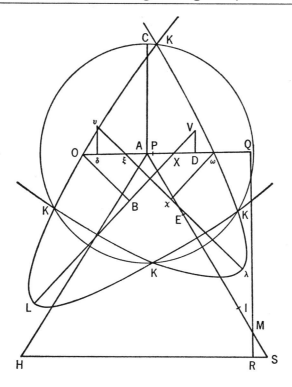

Datur, ut supra indicavi alia quoque parabola, quae cum hac paria facit et cuius descriptio ex hac adeo facile deducitur, ut nova non sit opus. Sumatur enim $A\delta$ in directum DA et ipsi aequalis, et in directum OA ipsi quoque aequalis $A\omega$. Tum bisecta $P\delta$ in ξ, ducatur per ξ recta $\upsilon\xi\chi$ normalis ad XB, concurrens cum $\delta\upsilon$, normali ad OA, in υ, et in quam cadat normalis $\omega\chi$. Ac fiat ut $\upsilon\xi$ ad $\xi\chi$, ita haec ad $\chi\lambda$: Erit λ vertex, $\lambda\xi$ axis, $\upsilon\xi$ latus rectum parabolae, quae in ijsdem cum priore punctis circulum datum secabit. Sed de Problemate Alhazenj iam plusquam satis.[7]

Venit nuper ad hanc civitatem Serenissimus Cardinalis Bulloniensis,[8] primam (ut loqui solemus) residentiam incepturus in Ecclesia nostra, cuius est Canonicus. Est autem in eius comitatu R.P. Johannes Bertet S.J.[9] cum quo multa mihi mentio de studijs et εὑρήμασίν Regiae Societatis quae iuxta mecum admiratur et commendat Vir doctissimus. Is iussit ut plurimum tibi suo nomine salutem dicerem. Vale et a me quoque, Vir nobilissime, et quo soles affectu, tui semper observantissimum porro proseque perge. Dabam Leodij prid. Kal. Septembr. MDCLXXII [N.S.]

TRANSLATION

René François de Sluse sends greetings to the very noble and famous Mr. Henry Oldenburg, Secretary of the Royal Society

You may cease to be surprised, famous Sir, that the same construction in the case of Alhazen's Problem may be deduced from different equations, in so much as all of those [equations] we have used hitherto may be embraced within one and the same general analysis. In order that I may show this, let there be given a circle whose center is A, and the points H and I; and let the required point [of reflection] be K, to which from the points H and I the lines HK, IK are drawn and the tangent KD [*see the figure, p. 219*]. Then from A let any line AG be drawn meeting HK at E, IK at B, and the tangent KD at D (or these lines produced if necessary). When this has been set out it is obvious (because the angles EKD and BKD are equal, and the angle AKD is a right angle) that the three lines AE, BE and DE will always be in harmonic proportion. And so having drawn the normals CK, FI and HG to AE, and denoting the various lines as in the inset [figure], one obtains, by the method that I formerly applied in my second analysis of this problem,[1] this general equation:

$$nda^2 - b\zeta a^2 - nq^2a + bq^2a = nde^2 - \zeta be^2 + 2bnae + 2\zeta dae - dq^2e - \zeta q^2e.$$

Imagine now that AG is perpendicular to HI; there will be no change in the equation except that AF and AG, that is to say d and ζ, will be equal. Therefore substituting d for ζ we have

$$nda^2 - bda^2 - nq^2a + bq^2a = nde^2 - dbe^2 + 2bnae + 2d^2ae - 2dq^2e.$$

Or by dividing all the terms by $d\,(n-b)$,

$$a^2 - \frac{aq^2}{d} = e^2 + \frac{2bnae + 2d^2ae - 2dq^2e}{d(n-b)}$$

which is the same as that which I had deduced in my first analysis,[2] though by a different approach, and of which I recently sent you the construction done in an easy way.[3]

Next suppose AG to coincide with AH; then HG (or b) will vanish to zero. So striking out from the equation those terms in which b appears, there will remain

$$nda^2 - nq^2a = nde^2 + 2\zeta dae - dq^2e - \zeta q^2e.[4]$$

This equation, you will recall, I found as a result of my second thoughts[5] and another one similar to this in the case where the straight line AG is understood to pass through I.

Lastly, let us suppose that the line AG bisects the angle HAI. Because of the similarity between the triangles HAG, IAF, $HG:AG = FI:AF$, or $b:d = n:\chi$ and $nd = b\chi$. Removing equal terms therefore

$$bq^2a - nq^2a = 2bnae + 2\chi dae - dq^2e - q^2\chi e.$$

And that is the equation which as I learned from your recent letter the famous Huygens has constructed.[6] Finally, let it be understood that the same line HG bisects the line HI. Then HG and IG will be equal, or $b = n$. And removing the equal terms

$$bda^2 - b\chi a^2 = bde^2 - b\chi e^2 + 2b^2ae + 2\chi dae - dq^2e - q^2\chi e.$$

This equation no one of us has constructed as yet, though it is not very difficult. However, this like the general equation itself may be divided into two others by substituting for a^2 or e^2, as you know, its value $(q^2 - e^2)$ or $(q^2 - a^2)$.

And so you see, famous Sir, that I have resolved in the same analytical process whatever had so far been arrived at; and this also includes an infinity of other constructions employing the given circle and an hyperbola. But it is of no importance to investigate them since in relation to this problem we now have to cope with a superfluity where there was once, perhaps, a scarcity. I shall add only a construction by means of a parabola, and that in two ways, which though it may seem more laborious than others employing the hyperbola still the simplicity of that curve (which commends the parabola above the other [conic] sections) may compensate for the effort inolved.

Accordingly with everything remaining as before let AI be joined and produced to S so that AS equals AH, let HS be joined and IS be bisected at M. [*see the figure, p. 221*]. Through M draw the straight line RMQ normal to HS upon which drop the normal AQ from A, and parallel to which draw the radius AC. Then having drawn the three proportional lines AI, AC and AE, make $MQ:AD$ and $RS:AP = AS:AE$; P being on the line AQ towards Q, and on the other side along the same line mark off $DO = DC$. Lastly, having bisected PD at X, incline through X at an angle of forty-five degrees to AX the straight line VXL meeting at V the normal erected through D, to which (from O) let fall the normal OB. I say that if $VX:BX = BX:BL$, the point L is the vertex, LV is the axis, and VX the latus rectum of a parabola which satisfies every case of the problem, for it cuts the given circle in points K of which the highest and lowest are relevant to Alhazen's Problem and the other points that other [problem] about which I recently wrote to you.

As I have indicated above there is another parabola which makes a pair with the present one, and whose description is so easily deduced from this that a fresh description is unnecessary. For taking $A\delta$ on the straight line DA and equal to it, and $A\omega$ on the straight line OA and also equal to it; then bisecting $P\delta$ at ξ, and drawing the straight line $\upsilon\xi\chi$ through ξ normal to BX, meeting $\delta\upsilon$ normal to OA at υ, and letting fall upon this the normal $\omega\chi$ such that $\upsilon\xi:\xi\chi = \xi\chi:\chi\lambda$, λ will be the vertex, $\lambda\xi$ the axis, and $\upsilon\xi$ the latus rectum of a parabola which will cut the given circle at the same points as the former parabola. But this is now more than enough on Alhazen's Problem.[7]

There lately came to this city the Most Serene Cardinal de Bouillon the first (as we say) Resident to be inducted in our church,[8] of which he is a canon. In his retinue, however, is the reverend father Jean Bertet S.J.[9] between whom and myself much has been said concerning the researches and discoveries of the Royal Society, which like myself that very learned man very much admires and praises. He requested me to give you a grand salute on his behalf. Farewell, [with many salutations] from myself also, most noble Sir, and continue always to bestow your customary affection upon your most dutiful [servant]. Liège, 31 August 1672 [N.S.].

NOTES

Reply to Letter 2022. The present letter was not transcribed by Collins for Newton's benefit, perhaps because of its speedy publication.

1 In Letter 1843 (Vol. VIII).
2 Letter 1548 (Vol. VII) seems to be intended, but lacks any analysis. This equation first appears in Letter 1994 (in slightly different notation).
3 In Letter 1994.
4 The second term of the equation was first inadvertently entered as "*nqaa*" and has been justly corrected in red to "*nqqa*."
5 In Letter 1843 (Vol. VIII), near the beginning, but the notation is different.
6 In Letter 2004a; Huygens' notation was again different and he explored the geometrical equivalent of his expression further but his solutions are structurally the same.
7 Dr. Whiteside has kindly furnished the following analysis of Alhazen's Problem as discussed in the foregoing pages: "Given the figure on p. 219 and the lines denoted by the same letters as Sluse there uses, it follows that

$$AD = \frac{q^2}{a}; \quad AB = z\,\frac{-n}{n-e}(z-a) = \frac{-na+ze}{e-n}; \quad AE = a+\frac{e}{e+b}(d-a) = \frac{ba+de}{e+b}.$$

Also $BD : DE = AB : AE$, or $AB \cdot DE = AE \cdot BD$. Whence,

$$\frac{-na+ze}{e-n}\left(\frac{ba+de}{e+b}-\frac{q^2}{a}\right) = \frac{ba+de}{e+b}\left(\frac{na-ze}{e-n}+\frac{q^2}{a}\right), \text{ or}$$

$$2a(bna^2 + (dn-bz)ae - dze^2) + q^2((b-n)ae + (d+z)e^2 - 2bna + (bz-dn)e) = 0.$$

Also $a^2 + e^2 = q^2$, whence (if $e \neq 0$)

$$(dn-bz)(a^2-e^2) - 2(bn+dz)ae + q^2(b-n)a + (d+z)e = 0.$$

This is Sluse's "general equation" on p. 222.

Case 1. Let AG be normal to HI, so that G coincides with F and $d = z$. Then the general equation assumes the form given on p. 222, line 21 of the text. This case has also been treated by Sluse in Letter 1994.

Case 2. Suppose the point G to coincide with the point H, whence $b = 0$ and the general equation assumes the form given on p. 222, line 28 of the text.

Case 3. Suppose AG to bisect the angle HAI. Then $AG : GH = AF : FI$, or

$z = \dfrac{dn}{b}$. This is the case solved by Huygens (Letter 2004a) using the rectangular hyperbola $2ae = 4Aa + 4Ee$ $\left(\text{where } 4A = \dfrac{q^2}{n} \cdot \dfrac{b(b-n)}{b^2+d^2} \text{ and } 4E = \dfrac{q^2}{n} \cdot \dfrac{d(b+n)}{b^2+d^2}\right)$, which expression is easily transformed into that given by Sluse on p. 223, line 3.

Case 4. Suppose that $HG = GI$, that is $b = n$; by removing n from the general equation Sluse's expression on p. 223, line 8 is obtained.

The general conic $a^2 + e^2 - q^2 + \lambda(2ae - 4Aa - 4Ee) = 0$ is through the meet of the hyperbola of Case 3 with the circle $a^2 + e^2 = q^2$; when $\lambda = \pm 1$, the equations to two parabolas are formed,

$$(a \pm e)^2 = \pm(4Aa + 4Ee) + q^2.$$

These meet AO (or $a = 0$) such that $e^2 = \pm 4Ee + q^2$ and thus $e = \mp(-2E \pm \sqrt{4E^2 - q^2})$. Their *latera recta* are $\pm\sqrt{2}(A \pm E)$ and their axes $a \pm e = \pm(A+E)$ and so the parabolas have vertices L, $\lambda \equiv (\acute{a}, \acute{e})$ determined by

$$\acute{a} \pm \acute{e} = \pm(A \pm E), \text{ or } \pm 2(A \mp E)(\acute{a} \pm \acute{e}) = 2(A^2 - E^2);$$

and $$\pm 2(A \mp E)(\acute{a} \mp \acute{e}) = -(A \pm E)^2 - q^2; \text{ whence}$$

$$\acute{a} = \frac{1}{\pm 4(A \mp E)}(-(A \mp E)^2 + 4E^2 + q^2), \text{ which may be re-written as}$$

$$[\tfrac{1}{2}(A \mp E - \sqrt{4E^2 + q^2})]^2 = \mp(A \mp E)(\acute{a} \mp \tfrac{1}{2}[A \mp E - \sqrt{4E^2 + q^2}]).$$

Sluse's construction, p. 223.

Take E to be the inverse with respect to the circle of $I\left(\dfrac{dn}{b}, n\right)$ whence

$E \equiv \left(\dfrac{(dn/b)q^2}{(dn/b)^2 + n^2}, \dfrac{nq^2}{(dn/b)^2 + n^2}\right)$, and so $AE = \dfrac{q^2}{n} \times \dfrac{b}{\sqrt{b^2+d^2}}$. Where $S \equiv (d,b)$ is a mirror-image of H in AG, Sluse constructs $M \equiv \left(\dfrac{d(b+n)}{2b}, \dfrac{b+n}{2}\right)$ as the midpoint of IS, whence $RS = \tfrac{1}{2}(b-n)$, $MQ = \dfrac{d(b+n)}{2b}$ and $\dfrac{AE}{AS} = \dfrac{bq^2}{n(b^2+d^2)}$.

Then AD (or $-A\delta$) $= 2E = \tfrac{1}{2}\dfrac{q^2}{n} \times \dfrac{d(b+n)}{b^2+d^2}$; and

$$AP = 2A = \tfrac{1}{2}\dfrac{q^2}{n} \times \dfrac{b(b-n)}{b^2+d^2}. \text{ Further,}$$

$\tfrac{1}{2}PD$ (or $-\tfrac{1}{2}P\delta$) $= XD$ (or $-\xi\delta$) $= \mp(A \mp E)$, and so XV, $\xi\upsilon$ are the *latera recta*.

Sluse constructs also OA (or $-\omega A$) $= \pm(\sqrt{4E^2 + q^2} \mp 2E)$, hence OX (or $-\omega\xi$) $= A \mp E - \sqrt{4E^2 + q^2}$, and

BX (or $-\beta\xi$) $= \dfrac{1}{\sqrt{2}}(A \mp E - \sqrt{4E^2 + q^2})$. Finally,

LX (or $-\lambda\xi$) $= \acute{a}\sqrt{2}$ and so LB (or $-\lambda\beta$) $= \sqrt{2}(\acute{a} \mp \tfrac{1}{2}(A \mp E - \sqrt{4E^2 + q^2}))$.
Whence $BX^2 = XV \cdot LB$, or $-\beta\xi^2 = \xi\upsilon \cdot \lambda\beta$, and so VX, XB, BL (or $\upsilon\xi$, $\xi\beta$, $\beta\lambda$) are in continued proportion."

8 See Vol. V, p. 88, note 2. The bishopric of Liège, a territory of the Archbishop of Cologne who was friendly towards Louis XIV, was now occupied by the French forces.

9 See Vol. VII, p. 380, note 14.

2054

Oldenburg to Edward Pocock

Late August 1672

This is mentioned in Oldenburg's Letter 2057, dated 3 September 1672, as having been written "last week." It contained inquiries about some Turkish words, and was prompted by Letter 2048.

For Edward Pocock (1604–91), at this time Professor of Hebrew at Oxford, and often mentioned in the correspondence, see Vol. I, p. 292, note 3.

2055

Flamsteed to Oldenburg

28 August 1672

From the original in Royal Society MS. F 1, no. 91

Derby: August 28: 1672:

Mr Oldenburge.
Sr

The day after I reaceaved yr last, I reaceaved the Copy of Cassini's paper from Mr Towneley[1] which haveing transcribed, I remit to yu: if you expect my opinion of it, I must crave your pardon for I have made but a few observations of ye Satellits & those onely within these last ten moneths, nor have I ever considered them further then to deduce a Radix[2] or 2, wth ye elongations of ye Remotest Satellit from Jove, so that it would be a vast peece of Indiscretion in mee to judge where I have no experience. further then, that this Theory being conceded for true the deductions are very Ingenuous. Mr Towneley & others who have made some yeares observations on ye Satellits are likely to afford yu the best sentiments of it. & I doubt not but that they will give them willingly:

You enquire whether ye occultation of Cor ♌s is on October 7 Mane,[3] next, will be visible. assuredly I thinke not to us, for ye moon riseing is truely in the same longitude with ye star, at 1h. 05′ mane, according to Heckers Ephemerides at London; but her parallax of longitude will promote her above 40′ from ye star, so yt no occulation of ye star will be seene. but I designe with my instruments, which take in 80 minutes, to measure her distance from it after her riseing; & I hope Mr. Hook will be carefull to make ye like observations at London:4

I have of late beene forth of towne almost every day, so yt I have not had time to make enquiries after aged persons as yu desire; but now I hope to be almost constantly at home, & so to have leasure both to enquire my selfe, & engage my freinds in the like search; but I feare it will be some space of time ere I can give you any good account. I am in hast Sr

Yr affectionate & obliged servant
John Flamsteed

ADDRESS

For Henry Oldenburge Esq
at his house in ye middle of
ye Pell mell in St James's
Westminster these
present

NOTES

Reply to Letter 2052.
1 See Letter 2049.
2 Parameter.
3 "in the morning."
4 It does not seem that either did so.

2056
Oldenburg to Malpighi
31 August 1672

From the draft in Royal Society MS. O 2, no. 95, and the copy in O 2, no. 94
Printed in *Opera omnia*, II, *De formatione pulli in ovo*, pp. 19–20

Celeberrimo Viro
Domino Marcello Malpighio, Philosopho et Medico Bononiensi
Henr. Oldenburg
Salutem

Male profecto me habet, quod Doctoris Grewi libellus, quem Oratori
Veneto, apud Aulam nostram agenti, Tibi transmittendum commen-
daveram, necdum ad manus tuas, cum novissimam ad me Epistolam, 2º
Augusti datam, ad me scriberes, pervenerat. Vix tamen ullum mihi dubium,
quin ex eo tempore Bononiam appulerit, cum asseveraverit apud me Vir
memoratus, se fasciculum illum summa qua potuerit cura amicis suis tum
Lutetiae tum Lugduni Galliarum concredidisse.

Caeterum, etiamsi caetus suos publicos hoc tempore non celebret Regia
Societas (mensibus quippe Julij, Augusti, et Septembris feriari quotannis
consuevit) neutiquam tamen officio meo deesse volui, quin Epistolae tuae
summa capita primariis quibusdam Illius Sociis communicarem, eorumque
de egregiis illis argumentis, inibi a Te delibatis, sensa exquirerem.

Vehementer sane collaudant eximium tuum in Nostrates affectum,
atque indefessam in augenda cognitione physica industriam; imprimis,
quod tanta mentis pertinacia (maximo genii vere philosophici decore) Ovi
scrutiniam urgere, nec non abditam juxta ac late patentem Plantarum
Anatomen pertractare decrevisti. Facis certe, quod in sempiternum nominis tui, quin imo totius Italiae vestrae, ipsiusque Societatis Regiae,
cujus partem tam insignem facis, decus, cedere omnino oportet?

Insero hic Iconismorum specimen, quae ad perdoctam tuam de Incubatis
Ovis Dissertationem pertinent, ut videas, non perfunctorie ea apud nos
tractari quae Tu de Naturae Arcanis in lucem profers et nobiscum com-
municas. Secundam eorum Tabulam, aeri quoque jam incisam, nunc
jungerem, ni literarum molem, tabellario committendam, vererer. Brevi
rem totam, dante Deo, praelum conficiet, nec tum deerit, sic spes est,
occasio, aliquot Tibi totius Diatribae Exemplaria navigio transmittendi.

Quibus accedet Illustrissimi Boylii nostri de Gemmarum Origine et Viribus Exercitatio, sermone Latino propediem edenda.[1] Mediatur idem nonnulla emittere Experiementa, Aeris et Flammae Cognationem indicantia; quibus Tractatum succenturiabit, quo Effluviorum naturam, amplissimamque eorum in rebus Physicis provinciam explicatam dabit.[2]

Disceptatur jam apud nos, quid veri subsit Novae et Ingeniosae Clarissimi Newtoni nostri de Luce et Coloribus doctrinae, quam objectionibus suis inter alios agitavit Ignatus Gaston Pardies S.J. in Collegio Claremontano Parisiensi Mathematum Professor doctissimus; at eas ab Authore habuit responsiones, quibus hactenus lubens (is est Viri candor) acquievit.

Vellem sane occasiones dari frequentiores ac tutiores, quam hactenus factum, ista et similia, quae apud nos depromuntur, Physiologiae argumenta ad Te transmittendi. Facerem illud summa cum lubentia, atque hac ratione tuam erga nos liberalitatem quadantenus redhostire conarer. Vale, Vir clarissime, et affectum tuum Tui studiosissimo conserva. Dabam Londini pridie Calend. Septemb. 1672.

TRANSLATION

Henry Oldenburg greets the very celebrated Mr. Marcello Malpighi, philosopher and physician of Bologna

I take it very ill that the copy of Dr. Grew's little book which I had entrusted to the Venetian ambassador to our Court for transmission to yourself has not yet come to your hands, as you write to me in your most recent letter of 2 August [N.S.]. Yet I can hardly doubt that it must have reached Bologna by this time as the person above mentioned has assured me that he consigned the parcel with all the care he could to his friends both in Paris and in Lyons.

Moreover, although the Royal Society does not hold its open meetings at this time of year, for it is accustomed to take a vacation during the months of July, August, and September in each year, yet I was reluctant to be wanting in my duty to communicate the heads of your letter to certain of the principal Fellows of it and seek their views of the notable points you have discussed in it.

They warmly praise your remarkable goodwill towards us and your tireless industry in increasing knowledge of natural history, especially because with so great continuity of purpose (the greatest distinction of a truly philosophical mind) you persist in your research upon the egg and have also resolved to occupy yourself with the recondite and wide-open [subject of] the anatomy of plants. Certainly what you are about must surely bring eternal renown to your own name, to Italy your country, and to the Royal Society itself of which you are so distinguished a member.

I attach to this letter a specimen of the [printed] figures belonging to your very learned essay on incubated eggs so that you may see that what you put in our hands and offer to the public concerning the secrets of nature is handled by us in no perfunctory fashion. I would now annex the second sheet of figures [also], which are already engraved on copper too, did I not fear to swell excessively the bulk of a letter which is to be entrusted to the post. In a little while, God willing, the printing will be completed and it is our hope that then an opportunity will not be lacking to send some copies of the whole treatise to you by ship. To these will be added our very illustrious Boyle's essay on the origin and virtue of gems, which is to be published in Latin any day now.[1] The same person is thinking of publishing some experiments indicative of the relation between air and flame, which will be accompanied by a treatise explaining the nature of effluvia and their wide-ranging significance in matters of natural history.[2]

We are now discussing among ourselves the extent to which the new and most ingenious theory of light and colors of our famous countryman Newton is true, which question has been raised by the objections (among others) of Ignace Gaston Pardies, S.J., a very learned professor of mathematics at the Clermont College in Paris; but these have received answers from the author [of the theory], with which he (such is the openness of the man) has so far declared himself quite satisfied.

I could wish for more frequent and safer opportunities than we have so far had for imparting to you these and other matters concerning natural science which have arisen amongst us. I should do so with much pleasure and endeavor in this way to make some return for your liberality towards us. Farewell, famous Sir, and continue your kindly feeling towards your most zealous [Oldenburg]. London, 31 August 1672.

NOTES

Reply to Letter 2034. The name of the Venetian ambassador mentioned below was Piero Mocenigo.

1 *Exercitatio de origine et viribus gemmarum* (London, 1673); there was also a Hamburg Latin edition with a different title.

2 See Letter 1997, note 3. These became separate publications, not (as Oldenburg seems to mean) companion pieces in the same volume.

2057

Oldenburg to Bernard

3 September 1672

From the original in Bodleian Library MS. Smith 45, f. 73

London Sept. 3. 72.

Sir,

I lately received a letter out of Holstein from an ingenious professor of the University of *Kiel* , called Dr Morhofius,[1] who making a very generous offer concerning some books, wch he hears are reprinting here in England, I thought good to acquaint you therewth, wch I shall doe in his owne words:

"Audio, apud vos Geoponicorum Editionem novam et accuratam parari;[2] quam cum cupiam esse omnium perfectissimam, significare tibi volui, esse apud nos, qui diligentissimam eorum collationem cum antiquo codice instituerit, et non paucas lacunas ex illo suppleverit; Ne quid dicam de variis Lectionibus, quas magno numero collegit notavitque. Est is Marquardus Gudius, Principis nostri Consiliarius, maximae doctrinae et acerrimi judicii Vir, cujus apud Italos, Gallos, Belgas, acerrimum nomen est;[3] quod vel e Menagii Animadversionibus in Laertium[4] observes, qui insignes locorum emendationes Viro illi debet. Facile ejus copiam parabo Editori a Viro mihi amicissimo."

But then, for others books, he saith further;

"Sed majores latent apud illum thesauri Scriptorum, Mathematicorum, Medicorum, Physicorum, qui vel hactenus inediti, vel mutilati et vitiosissime editi sunt; e quibus nunc succurrunt Heronis multa[5] et Ptolomaei,[6] hactenus inedita. Eorum Catalogum data [?] occasione transmittam. Caeterorum scriptorum ac justorum Codicum et collatorum tanta seges est, ut seculi labor illis producendis vix sufficiat. Ex ejusdem bibliotheca Aeginetae nova Editio parabitur e Codice accurato, quem Scaliger manu sua emendavit."[7]

Not finding, yt those Geoponick Authors are reprinting here in London, I concluded, yt they might be so either in yr university, or at Cambridge; and therefore make it my request, you would inform me, wehther any thing be doing or resolved to be done of yt nature wth you. To wch you may please to add, what encouragement I may give to those generous persons in reference to the other Manuscripts, they speak of.

Last week I wrote to Dr Pocock about the Explication of some Turkish words, desired by a Curious person at Hamburg,[8] yt is publishing some uncommon things: I pray, favour me to inquire, whether yt Letter came to hand;[9] and give yrself this further trouble, to inform me, if you can,

"An Badroddini liber de Voluptate animi extet uspiam in Anglia MS, an editus sit?"[10]

Monsr Hugens in now in earnest, I heare, to publish his Dioptricks, and Pendulum-watches. Frenicle, something extraordinary in Numbers;[11] and Picard his Measure of ye Earth in a smal volume, for common use.[12] This in hast from Sir

Yr very afft and humble servt
Oldenburg

Pray tell Dr Wallis I received his late pacquet and intend to write to him [about]? the contents very shortly[13]

ADDRESS
>   For his worthy friend
>   Mr Edward Bernard
>   At the house of Dr Wallis
>   in Oxford

TRANSLATION

.   .   .   .

"I hear that a new and accurate edition of the writers on agriculture is in preparation among you;[2] as I am anxious that it should be of the utmost perfection I wished to let you know that there is a person here who has undertaken a very careful collation of them with the ancient codex and supplied not a few omissions from it to say nothing of variant readings which he has collected and noted to a great number. He is Marquard Gude, Councilor to our Prince, a man of great learning and most acute judgment whose reputation is high in Italy, France, and the Low Countries;[3] as you may observe from the commentary of [Gilles] Ménage on [Diogenes] Laertius,[4] who owes many notable corrections of places [in the text] to that man. I can easily make ready plenty of material for the editor from this great friend of mine."

.   .   .   .

"But there lie in his hands great treasures of the writers on mathematics, medicine, and natural history which are either still unpublished, or published in a mutilated and very imperfect form. Among these there now come to my mind many things by Hero[5] and Ptolemy[6] not yet in print. I will send a list of them when opportunity serves. He has garnered so great a harvest of other writers and accurate manuscripts and collations that the efforts of a whole century would scarcely suffice to bring them out. A new edition of Aegineta will appear from his library [taken] from an accurate codex which Scaliger corrected with his own hand."[7]

.   .   .   .

"Is the book of Badr al-Din on the pleasures of the mind extant anywhere in England in manuscript, or has it been published?"[10]

.   .   .   .

NOTES

1 See Vol. VII, p. 234, note. We have no other knowledge of Morhof's letter. Oldenburg replied to it in Letter 2068.
2 See Letter 1811, note 10 (Vol. VIII).
3 See Letter 1811, note 11 (Vol. VIII) and Oldenburg's letter to Gude of 28 April 1673.
4 [Gilles Ménage], *Laertii Diogenis de vita dogmatis et apophthegmatis ... libri X. Cum uberrimis Aegidii Menagii observationes* (London, 1664). This seems to be, curiously, the first edition. Gilles Ménage (1613–92) was well known as poet, philologist, and scholar as well as for the *mercuriales* (Thursday assemblies) that took place at his house in Paris from 1656 until his death.
5 Although several works of Hero of Alexandria had already appeared in Latin and Italian, the first Greek editions of the *Pneumatics, Automata,* and *Belopoiica* were printed by Melchisédec Thevenot in *Veterum mathematicorum opera graece et latine edita* (Paris, 1693). More fragments were published in the nineteenth century, including some only extant in Arabic translation.
6 Many works by Ptolemy were already available in Greek as well as Latin, notably the *Mathematical syntaxis* (Basel, 1538), the *Geography* (Basel, 1533), and the *Tetrabiblon* (Nuremberg, 1535). John Wallis was to edit his *Harmonica* in Greek and Latin in 1682. The other main work of Ptolemy's still unpublished was his *Optics,* of which there is no known Greek original.
7 The encyclopaedic *Seven books on medicine* of Paulos Aegineta (seventh century A. D.) was printed in Greek by Aldus at Venice in 1528. There was no late-seventeenth century publication. Julius Caesar Scaliger (1484–1558), who was a physician and edited both Aristotle and Theophrastos, is probably meant rather than his son Joseph Justus.
8 See Letter 2048.
9 No copy of this letter has been found, but we have recorded it as Letter 2054.
10 Numerous writers in Arabic bear the name Badr al-Din but it has not proved possible to connect any of them with a work bearing this title.
11 Bernard Frénicle de Bessy died in 1675; his *Traité des triangles rectangles en nombres* was published posthumously at Paris in 1676.

12 This was a false rumor; republications of the *Mesure de la Terre* were only to appear long after Oldenburg's death.
13 Any such letter appears to be lost.

2058
Oldenburg to Huygens
5 September 1672

From *Œuvres Complètes*, VII, 220–23
Original in the Huygens Collection at Leiden

A Londres le 5 Sept. 1672.

Monsieur,

Vous verrez dans l'annexe, que i'ay pris la liberté d'y inserer en Anglois vostre solution de cet estrange phenomene de la suspension du Mercure bien purgé de l'air a la hauteur de 75 pouces etc.[1] Nos curieux y voyent autant de difficulté que vous, et ne laisseront pas d'y resver iusques a ce qu'ils en soient mieux esclaircis.

Je viens de recevoir une assez longue lettre de Monsieur Sluse,[2] et me trouve obligé de vous en faire part, elle traitant encore du probleme d'Alhazen, qui a esté tant raffiné entre vous deux. Voicy donc ce qu'il en dit pour cete fois.

"Mirari desine, eandem in Alhazeniano problemate constructionem ex diversis aequationibus deduci, quandoquidem illae omnes, quibus hactenus usi sumus, in una eademque generali Analysi contineantur ... Sed de problemate Alhazeni jam plus quam satis." [*Here Oldenburg quoted all except the last paragraph of Letter 2053.*]

Estant quasi lassé, ie n'y adjousteray rien si non que nous serions bien aises d'entendre, que vostre Pendule[3] et vos dioptriques soient dans la presse. Nostre Societé ne s'assemblera qu'apres la St. Michel. Cependant les particuliers ne laissent pas de travailler, et entre autres Monsieur Boyle fait astheur imprimer des Experiences touchant l'affinité qu'il y a entre l'Air et la Flamme, avec quelques autres qui touchent l'hydrostatique:

lesquelles seront bien tost suivies des Experiences de natura et efficacia Effluviorum etc.⁴ Vous pardonnerez cette prolixité à Monsieur

Vostre treshumble et tresobeissant serviteur
Oldenburg

ADDRESS

A Monsieur
Monsieur Christian Hugens de Zulichem
dans la Bibliotheque du Roy
à
Paris

TRANSLATION

London, 5 September 1672

Sir,

You will see by the enclosed that I have taken the liberty of inserting there in English your solution of that strange phenomenon of the suspension of mercury carefully freed from air at the height of 75 inches, etc.¹ Our scientists see as much difficulty as you do in it, and will not cease from pondering over it until they are better enlightened about it.

I have just received a pretty long letter from Mr. Sluse² and find myself obliged to share it with you, since it deals again with Alhazen's problem, which has been so highly refined by you two. Here is what he says this time:

[*Here follows all the text of Letter 2053 except the last paragraph; for a translation, see pp. 222–24 above.*]

Being almost exhausted I shall add nothing except that we should be very glad to hear that your pendulum³ and your dioptrics were in the press. Our Society will not meet until after Michaelmas. However the individual members do not cease to work, and among others Mr. Boyle is now printing some experiments concerning the affinity which there is between air and flame, with some others which concern hydrostatics, and these will soon be followed by some experiments on the nature and efficacy of effluvia, etc.⁴ You will forgive this prolixity to, Sir,

Your very humble and obedient servant
Oldenburg

ADDRESS

Mr. Christiaan Huygens of Zulichem
The King's Library
Paris

NOTES

1 See *Phil. Trans.*, no. 86 (19 August 1672), 5027–30, for "An Extract of a Letter of M. Hugens to the Author of the *Journal des Sçavans* of July 25. 1672. attempting to render the Cause of that odd Phaenomenon of the Quicksilvers remaining suspended far above the usual height in the Torricellian Experiment." For Huygens' original discovery of the anomalous suspension of mercury, see Vol. II, pp. 123–27. In this paper he attributes the effect to an aether pressure which is perhaps also responsible for the cohesion of solid bodies.

2 Letter 2053.

3 *Horologium oscillatorium.*

4 See Letter 1997, note 3. To the first volume is annexed "An Hydrostatical Discourse" and "An Hydrostatical Letter."

2059

Oldenburg to Flamsteed

5 September 1672

From the memorandum in Royal Society MS. F 1, no. 91

Rec. Sept. 3. 72.
Answ. Sept. 5. and sent No. 86.[1]
Sent Mr Hook the answer to his Quaere.[2]

NOTES

Reply to Letter 2055.

1 That is, *Phil. Trans.*, no. 86 (19 August 1672), containing astronomical observations and predictions by Flamsteed.

2 See Letters 2052 and 2055.

2060

Hevelius to Oldenburg

6 September 1672

In Letter 2083 Hevelius notes that a letter of this date from himself was brought to England by the envoy Nixdorf, but only the enclosed account of the solar eclipse (Letter 2060a) has survived.

Johann Nixdorf (1625–97), born like Hevelius at Danzig and educated at Rostock, was from 1662 secretary to the King of Poland. In the summer of 1672 he was sent to Scotland to clear up the matter of the ships that had been captured and detained there (Letter 2050 and its note 3). In 1675 Nixdorf passed into the service of the city of Danzig.

2060a

The Solar Eclipse of 12 August 1672

Enclosure with Letter 2060
From the original in Royal Society MS. H 2, no. 31

Eclipsis Solaris observata GEDANI
Anno 1672, die 22 Augusti st. n. vesperi.

Juxta horl. amb. vesperi	Observatio Eclipsis Solis	Altitudine	Tempore correcto	Notanda
Hor. ' "		° ' "	Hor ' "	
5 2 10	Altitudo Solis	17 18 0	5 5 39	Sol coepit obscurari a parte inferiori 30 grad. a puncto sc. Nadir occasum versus
6 35 30	Verum Initium Eclipsis		6 39 0	
6 39 0	½ dig. obscuratus erat		6 42 15	
	Posthac nubes intervenere, ut nihil amplius observare licuerit.			
9 1 10	Alt Lucidae Coronae[1]	40 50 0	9 4 28	
9 4 5	Eadem altit.	40 23 0	9 7 39	

Secundum Calculum Rudolphinum initium incidit hor. 6 36′ 33″; Sic ut Tabulae Rudolphinae, in hac Eclipsi satis exacte Caelo respondeant. Quid Vos hac de re observastis, data occasione exspecto. Vale memor nostri et porro Ill. Regiae Nostrae Societati optime modis (quam decenter salvere cupio) res nostras commenda.

Tuus ex animo
J. Hevelius

Dabam Gedani Anno 1672, die 16 Septembris st. n.

TRANSLATION

The solar eclipse observed at Danzig on 22 August
1672 N.S. in the evening

Clock-time P.M.	Observation of the solar eclipse	Altitude	Corrected time	Notes
Hrs min secs			Hrs min secs	
5 2 10	Sun's altitude	17° 18' 0"	5 5 39	The sun began to be obscured in its lower part 30° west of its lowest point
6 35 30	True beginning of the eclipse		6 39 0	
6 39 0	Half a digit was obscured		6 42 15	
Afterwards clouds came across so that nothing more could be observed				
9 1 10	Altitude of the bright star in Corona[1]	40° 50' 0"	9 4 28	
9 4 5	Alt. of the same	40° 23' 0"	9 7 39	

According to the Rudolphine calculation the beginning of the eclipse occurred at 6h. 36' 33". Thus the Rudolphine Tables corresponded pretty closely with the heavens in this eclipse. I await when opportunity serves what you have observed of this. Farewell and be mindful of me, and continue to commend my affairs in the highest terms to our illustrious Royal Society, whom I wish to greet courteously.

Wholeheartedly yours,
J. Hevelius

Danzig, 16 September 1672 N.S.

NOTE

1 Probably α Coronae Borealis.

2061

Oldenburg to Vogel

10 September 1672

From the memorandum in Royal Society MS. F 1, no. 36
and the extract in Royal Society MS. F 1, no. 41

Rec. Apr. 28. 72
Resp. Sept. 10. 72

.   .   .   .

. . . addit (Pocokius) quamvis olim ipse fuerit inter eos in Turcia, qui frequenter utuntur Opio, Berch[1] & Benge, eorumque nomina recordetur, res tamen ipsas memoria sua excidisse post lapsum tot annorum.

.   .   .   .

TRANSLATION

.   .   .   .

. . . he (Pococke) adds that although he frequently mingled in Turkey with those who use opium, "leaf,"[1] and marijuana and recollects their names, any recollection of the things themselves has gone from his memory after the passage of so many years.

.   .   .   .

NOTES

Reply to Letters 1959, 2048. The single sentence of this letter survives as quoted by Vogel in Letter 2268 (Vol. X) on 4 July 1673.

1 We assume this is the modern Turkish "berk."

2062

Johannnes Hecker to Oldenburg

12 September 1672

From the copy in Royal Society Letter Book V, 340–41

Illustri et Celeberrimo Viro
Domino Henrico Oldenburgio Regiae Societatis Secretario
Johannes Hecker S.P.D.

Cum generosam Societatis Vestrae audaciam omnis fere orbis admiretur, qua in intima Naturae mysteria eam irruere aspicit, indeque ea nobis proferre, quae occulta diu mortalium oculis jacuere; non possum mihi temperare, quin et vestrae huic felicitati gratuler, et animi mei gaudium Communi omnium laetitiae adjungam, nihil magis in votis habens, nisi ut tanti successus majora indies sumant incrementa: Simul vobis offerens scriptum aliquod levidense, admonitionis instar emissum ad Astronomos de Marcurij in solem incursu observando.[1] Quod licet Magnitudini vestrae longe impar sit; tamen judicio illud vestro sistere atque subjicere non vereor: Spe fretus, Vos temeritati huic meae veniam daturos esse, qui laudatissimas pariter atque magnanimas occupationes vestras sollicitaque studia interpellare non extimescam. Si gratiam labor hic meus mereri videbitur, habebo unde mihi gratuler; quippe qui placuerim jis, quibus placere omnes, qui literarum nomen fatentur, student: Allaboraturus inposterum, ut tenuis hic meus agellus benigno humanitatis vestrae rore superfusus plures ac novos subinde proventus vobis afferat. Quod si vero displicuero, non excandescam, sed curabo potius atque viribus omnibus eniter, ut me emendem; Vos, tantos judices, vestrumque judicium, quod justum universus literarum orbis agnoscit, atque uno ore fatetur, aeternum devota mente deveneraturus. Vale. Dab. Gedani, Anno aerae Christianae 1672 die X Calendar. Octob.

TRANSLATION

Johannes Hecker sends many greetings to the illustrious and celebrated Mr. Henry Oldenburg, Secretary of the Royal Society

Since almost the whole world admires the generous boldness of your Society, seeing it plunge into Nature's deepest secrets on this account and thence bring back to us things that have so long lay hid from mortal eyes, I could not restrain myself from congratulating you on this success and adding [an expression of] my own intellectual pleasure and the common delight of all, having no wish more dear to me than that this great success should wax still greater from day to day, and at the same time offering to you a certain trivial paper of my own circulated as a piece of advice to astronomers about observing the transit of Mercury across the sun.[1] For although it is very ill-matched to your excellence yet I was not afraid to present and submit it to your judgment, borne up by the hope that you will pardon me for this rashness in not fearing to interrrupt your praiseworthy and magnanimous affairs and your anxious studies. If this labor of mine seems to deserve thanks I shall have a cause for self-congratulation since, forsooth, I shall have given satisfaction to those who make it their business to satisfy all who call themselves learned. I shall strive in the future to cause this little vineyard of mine, nourished by the gentle rain of your goodness, to yield up to you a new and plentiful harvest of fruits. But if I give no satisfaction to you I shall not become enraged but shall rather direct myself to strive with all my might to improve myself; pledging in humility of mind an eternal devotion to you as such powerful judges, whose decisions all the learned world acknowledges and with one voice acclaims as just. Farewell. Danzig, 22 September in the year of our Lord 1672 [N.S.].

NOTES

Johannes Hecker (d. 1675), whose *Ephemerides motuum coelestium* (Danzig, 1662; Paris, 1666) have often been mentioned, was a cousin of Hevelius. He came of a patrician family in Danzig, becoming a Member (1654) and a Senior (1664) of the Magistrates College in the City.

1 Johannes Hecker, *Mercurius in sole seu Admonitio ad astronomos, geographos, . . . de incursu Mercurii in discum solis observando A. C. 1674 d. 6 Maji st. n.* (Danzig, 1672). According to Halley (*Phil. Trans.*, XVII, 1691–93, no. 193, pp. 511–22) this transit occurred at 12h. 29m. on 26 April 1674 (as predicted by Hecker) but was invisible in northern Europe. No observations of it were reported.

2063

Bernard to Oldenburg

14 September 1672

From the copy in B.M. Birch MS. 4277, f. 22

Sept. 14. 1672

Honored Sir,

I received yesterday the 2 Copyes, the guift of Monsr Thevenote[1] & desire you to acquaint me with your Opportunity of Returning to him, that I may enclose my thanks also & Mr Hydes;[2] who desires his humble service to you.

The proposalls of the freind of the learned Gudius are very valuable: & a Catalog of the Authors collated or expounded by him will make our freinds here more affected with his offer, than what other meanes may. The want of an Observatory damps Astronomique studies here, For without the proofe of our owne eyes & Instruments, the whole businesse is too precatory,[3] & the lines that have been drawen upon trust to the certainty of former Observations too too many: Whereas taking up with the Copernicane hypothesis & adjoining some nights & dayes Attendance, the matter is of no hard Comprehension, as farre as is likely here on earth these great & glorious bodyes can be discovered & treated of. I see no great matter in the proposition of Alhazen as it is delivered in a paper, which was lately here shewen mee; but shall take occasion to draw the proposition pointed at into a shorter Compass; though the prolixity of the booke proceeds from the ignorance of the Interpreter rather than Inelegance of the Arabe.[4] There is in Cambridge a Manuscript of Alhazen in one of the Colledges; Dr. Jame's Catalogue of Mssts long since printed tells the place:[5] & Mr Gale the Mr of St Pauls schoole[6] is very likely to have knowledge of the booke.

I am your very affectionate Servt
E. Bernard

I have been quicker than I at first thought & now trouble you with the Enclosed against the time of your first conveyance

ADDRESS

These
For his worthy freind Mr Henry Oldenburgh
at the Pellmell neare St James's
London

NOTES

Reply to Letter 2057.

1 Presumably copies of the fourth and final part of Thevenot's *Relations de divers voyages curieux*, published at Paris in 1672. There is an account of it in *Phil. Trans.*, no. 89 (16 December 1672), 5128–30.

2 Thomas Hyde (1636–1703); see Vol. II, p. 165, note 2.

3 Bernard seems to mean "precarious" (a word not yet wholly established in the ordinary current sense at this date) although the normal sense of "precatory" is "supplicatory."

4 All this passage is difficult to comprehend. It is possible that Wallis had shown something of the Huygens-Sluse interchanges to Bernard. But we do not know what the "book" is.

5 Thomas James, *Ecloga Oxonio-Cantabrigiensis* (London, 1600), p. 112, lists only two manuscript works of Alhazen, both at Peterhouse, Cambridge: *Perspectiva* and *Liber de ascensionibus nubium*. Both are fourteenth-century Latin transcripts (see M. R. James, *Descriptive Catalogue of the Manuscripts in the Library of Peterhouse*, Cambridge, 1899, p. 251).

6 Thomas Gale (1635?–1702), Professor of Greek at Cambridge since 1666, had only recently been appointed High Master of St. Paul's School. He was a notable classical and historical scholar. He was elected F.R.S. in 1677 and twice served as Secretary to the Royal Society.

2064
Oldenburg to Towneley
14 September 1672

Towneley's Letter 2049 is endorsed as answered on 14 September 1672; but although Oldenburg has written "see copy" nothing was ever entered in the Royal Society's Letter Book.

2065

Sylvius to Oldenburg

17 September 1672

From the original in Royal Society MS. S 1, no. 101

Amplissimo, Doctissimoque Viro
D. Henrico Oldenburgio
Illustrissimae Regiae Anglicanae
Societati a Secretis, &c.
S.P. Franciscus De Le Boe, Sylvius

An literas meas 15/25 Augusti anno superiore ad Te datas,[1] quibus ad Tuas 5° Julij ad me scriptas, et 12/22 Augusti demum redditas respondebam, acceperis valde dubito, quia circa Hyemis initium hac transiens Germanus tuo nomine me salutans nullam earum fecit mentionem: unde animus erat denuo ad Te scribere, ac simul Praxeos meae Librum primum iterato praelo subjectum ad Te mittere.[2] Verum imminentis nostris cervicibus belli rumor ab his laboribus gratioribus animum avocavit ad studia magis solicita, unde segnius processit editio, et siluerunt pene hic Musae. Nunc autem animus paulatim excitatur denuo Viris probis et pacem diligentibus;[3] qua propter ad Vos reditum parante Juvene modesto, D. Guilielmo Jonstonio,[4] Auditore meo sedulo, rogavi eum, ut nuperrime ad finem deducti Opusculi exemplaria duo, prae festinatione discedentis haud compacta secum sumeret, eadem Tibi obtaturus; nil autem huic editioni pene additum, praeter alteram Praefationem, qua Medicos Veritati addictos, ac mea legentes hortor, ut meam manum operi admoveant, et, quod in primis a Vestra Regia Societate, opto, expetoque, si alicubi me errasse putaverint, amice moneant, &c.

Idem expectavi hactenus a laudatae Vestrae Societatis Medicis; qua de causa etiam minus festinavi ad Te scribere, atque tua negotia saepius interturbare. Si proinde, a quo Libellum meum habuerunt, aliquid apud aegros suos notarint, quod possit me aut in cogitationibus meis confirmare, aut amplius erudire, aut erroris convincere, gratissimam rem fecerint, eadem mihi communicando, sicut Ipsos Te interprete nunc quoque rogo et obtestor.

Coepi nuper Secundum Praxeos meae librum corrupte tum in Germania, tum in Gallijs cum Tertio editum amplificare, atque dum privatis meis

Auditoribus eum explicabo, Typis mandare; quo sic quoque omnibus tester, cordi esse mihi, Bonorum expectationi pro virili respondere.

Tu interim, quemadmodum hactenus sponte fecisti, me favore tuo amplius prosequere. Rogo insuper, ut, si res sinat officia mea Illustrissimae ac Regiae Societati Vestrae et, qua par est, mei erga Ipsam reverentia, offeras. Vale, Vir Amplissime, atque publicum bonum alacritate solita feliciter promove. Dabam Lugd. Bat. 17/27 7bris 1672

ADDRESS
Amplissimo, Doctissimoque Viro,
D. Henrico Oldenburgio,
Illustrissimae Societati Regiae
Anglicanae a Secretis
        Londinum
amica manu

TRANSLATION

Franciscus de le Boë Sylvius sends many greetings to the very worthy and learned Mr. Henry Oldenburg, Secretary to the Most Illustrious English Royal Society, etc.

I very much doubt whether you have received my letter to you of 15/25 August last year[1] in which I replied to yours of 5 July which was finally delivered to me on 12/22 August, because a German passing through here about the beginning of winter who came to greet me on your behalf made no allusion to it; whence I had it in mind to write to you anew and at the same time send you the first book of my *Medical Practice* which has gone into a second impression.[2] When the rumor of imminent war reached our ears it drew our attention from these pleasing labors to more distressful concerns, for which reason the printing has proceeded rather tardily: the Muses have been absolutely mute here. Now however our spirits have been somewhat revived again by honest men who are eager for peace;[3] on which account as a modest young individual, Mr. William Johnston,[4] a diligent auditor at my lectures, is making ready to return home to Britain, I have asked him to take two copies of the recently completed edition of my little work, not properly bound because of the haste of his departure, for conveyance to yourself. However, there are hardly any additions to this edition except a second preface in which I exhort my readers who are medical men seeking the truth to give me a helping hand in the work, and particularly I ask and desire of the Royal Society that if they think me in error anywhere, they will give me friendly notice of the fact.

I have previously sought the same thing from the medical men of your meritorious Royal Society for which reason I have been the less hasty about writing to you and the more frequently interrupting your business. Accordingly if, after they have received my book, they shall observe anything in their patients which may either confirm me in my ideas or give me better information or convince me of my mistakes, they will do a welcome service by communicating it to me, as I now ask and beseech them also by your intercession [to do].

I have lately begun to amplify the second book of my *Medical Practice*, imperfectly published both in Germany and in France along with the third, and while I shall be explaining it to my private auditors, [I shall be] sending it to the press; by which also I shall testify to all that it is my intention to respond as much as I can to the expectation of good men.

Meanwhile, just as you have hitherto freely done, you will continue to bestow your good will upon me. Additionally I beg you, if circumstances permit, to assure your most illustrious and Royal Society of my services and, as is fitting, of my respect for it. Farewell, excellent Sir, and continue your successful advancement of the public good with your customary zeal. Leiden, 17/27 September 1672.

ADDRESS
    To the very worthy and learned
    Mr. Henry Oldenburg
    Secretary to the most Illustrious
    English Royal Society
        London

By a friendly hand

NOTES

1 Letter 1774 (Vol. VIII).
2 There appears to have been only one complete edition of Sylvius' *Praxeos medicae idea nova*, five parts of which were issued in four volumes by Justus Schrader of Leiden between 1671 and 1674; to this edition Sylvius refers here. Perhaps he reckoned the Frankfurt, 1671 impression of Part I of this work as a first edition.
3 Presumably the reference is to the recent overthrow and murder of the De Witts and the election of William of Orange as Stadtholder; but the expression is curious.
4 Unless a date has been misread, this man is not included by R. W. Innes Smith in *English-Speaking Students of Medicine at the University of Leyden* (Edinburgh, 1932).

2066
Huygens to Oldenburg

17 September 1672

From the original in Royal Society MS. H 1, no. 74
Printed in *Œuvres Complètes* VII, 228–29

A Paris ce 27 Sept. 1672 [N.S.]

Monsieur,

Je crois devoir response a trois de vos lettres, du 8e et 18e Juilet la dernier du 5 Sept. Ce sont en partie d'autres occupations, en partie mon indisposition, qui dans cette saison me vient donner d'ordinaire quelque attaque, qui m'ont obligè de differer si longtemps a satisfaire a ce devoir. Dans la premiere de ces lettres vous avez eu la bontè de m'envoier la derniere construction de Mr. Sluse du probleme d'Alhazen, avec le calcul dont il dit l'avoir tirée.[1] Mais cela auroit estè bien difficile a ce qui me semble sans l'aide de ma construction;[2] qui est peu differente comme vous voiez, puis qu'elle donne la mesme hyperbole, determinee par les asymptotes, au lieu que M. Sluse la construit par les ordonnees du diametre. Je voudrois au reste qu'il eust monstrè comment sa construction suit de l'aequation qu'il donne, car cela m'a donnè de la peine, et l'ayant reduite a un cas fort simple, je n'ay pas trouvè une bonne issue au calcul, ce qui me fait douter s'il n'y a pas quelque faute a la copie.[3] Mais il y a longtemps que je ne songe plus a ce probleme et j'ay estè estonnè de voir par vostre derniere que Mr. Sluse y avoit encor travaillè de nouveau, quoyqu'en effect il n'a point perdu sa peine en cela, car son aequation universelle est tresbelle et scavante, et sa construction par la parabole fort bien trouvee, quoyqu'un peu longue. Je ne scay si vous avez encore dessein de faire imprimer quelque chose de ce que nous vous avons communiquè sur ce sujet. Si vous prenez cette peine je vous prie de mettre la suite de nos speculations et decouvertes dans l'ordre qu'elles sont venues a vos mains.

Ce que vous avez mis de Mr. Newton dans un de vos derniers Journaux confirme encore beaucoup sa doctrine des Couleurs. Toutefois la chose pouroit bien estre autrement, et il me semble qu'il se doibt contenter que ce qu'il a avancè passe pour une hypothese fort vraisemblable. De plus quand il seroit vray que les rayons de lumiere, des leur origine, fussent les uns rouges les autres bleus, &c. il resteroit encore la grande difficultè d'expliquer par la physique mechanique en quoy consiste cette diversitè de couleurs. Ce que j'avois dit de l'aberration des verres objectifs, estoit asseurement mal entendu,[4] et c'estoit en lisant les Transactions que j'avois fait cette note a la marge, que je devrois avoir examinee avant que de vous l'envoier. Pour ce qui est des regles de Mr. Wallis pour les Tangentes,[5] dont vous avez voulu scavoir mon opinion, je trouve que la premiere ne differe point de celle de M. de Fermat qui est expliquée dans Herigone.[6] Elle y est de la mesme façon comme la conçoit Mr. Wallis, mais a mon avis ni l'un ni l'autre n'en monstrent le vray fondament, que j'ay trouvè toute autre. La seconde methode ne m'estoit pas inconnue non plus, de la quelle M. de Roberval se vant d'estre le premier inventeur il y a longues annes, et je me souviens qu'il nous l'a expliquee cy devant dans nostre Assemblee.[7] Mais il y a une autre Methode meilleure et beaucoup plus compendieuse que tout cela pour les Tangentes, que j'ay expliquée a la mesme assemblee,[8] et qui est connue de Mr. Sluse et de Mr. Hudde il y a longtemps.[9] A celle la il ne faut que voir seulement l'aequation qui exprime la nature de la ligne, et de cette aequation l'on en tire d'abord, et sans aucune peine, une autre, qui donne la construction de la Tangente.

J'ay receu par la faveur de M. Vernon le recueil entier de vos Transactions et les oeuvres de Mr. Boile qui me manquoient. Vous m'obligerez de me mander de temps en temps ce qu'il produit de nouveau, comme vous venez de faire, afin que j'en fasse venir des exemplaires. Mon traite des Pendules va estre imprimè bientost et j'en ay desia vu la premiere feuille. Je suis Monsieur

Vostre treshumble et tresobeissant serviteur
Hugens de Zulichem

Je prens la libertè de vous recommander l'inclose à M. Vernon.

ADDRESS
> A Monsieur
> > Monsieur Grubendol
> > > à Londres.

TRANSLATION

Paris, 27 September 1672 [N.S.]

Sir,

I think I owe a reply to three of your letters, of the eighth and eighteenth of July and the last of 5 September. It is partly other affairs, partly my ill health, which ordinarily at this season brings on an attack, which have obliged me to defer for so long the fulfillment of this duty. In the first of these letters you were so good as to send me Mr. Sluse's latest construction of Alhazen's Problem, with the calculation from which he said he had drawn it.[1] But that would have been very difficult as it seems to me without the help of my construction[2] which, as you see, is little different, since it gives the same hyperbola determined by the asymptotes, while Mr. Sluse constructs it by the ordinates of the diameter. For the rest I should have liked him to have demonstrated how his construction follows from the equation which he gives, for that gave me some trouble; and having reduced it to a very simple case I did not find a good way out of the calculation, which makes me wonder whether there is not some mistake in the copy.[3] But for a long time I have thought no more about this problem, and I was astonished to see by your last that Mr. Sluse had worked at it afresh, even though he has really not wasted his efforts since his universal equation is very elegant and learned and his parabolic construction very well displayed, although a little long. I don't know whether you still have a plan to print something of what we have communicated to you on this topic. If you take the trouble to do that I do beg you to put the series of our speculations and discoveries in the order in which they came to hand.

What you have put in your last Journals from Mr. Newton confirms still further his doctrine of colors. Nevertheless the thing could very well be otherwise, and it seems to me that he ought to content himself if what he has advanced is accepted as a very likely hypothesis. The more so since even if it were true that the rays of light were, by their origin, some red, others blue, etc. there would still remain the great difficulty of explaining by the mechanical philosophy what this diversity of colors consists of. What I said about the aberration of objective lenses was certainly badly conceived;[4] it was while reading the *Transactions* that I made that note in the margin and I ought to have checked it before sending it to you. As for Mr. Wallis's rules for tangents,[5] about which you wanted my opinion, I find that the first does not differ at all from Mr. Fermat's which is explained in Hérigone.[6] It is after the same method as that conceived by Mr. Wallis, but in my opinion neither the one nor the other demonstrates the true basis, which I found to be quite otherwise. The second method was not unknown to me either; of this Mr. de Roberval boasted of being the first inventor long years ago, and I remember that he explained it formerly in our meetings.[7] But there is another method, better and much more compendious than all those for tangents, which I explained to the same meeting[8] and which has been known to Mr. Sluse and Mr. Hudde for a long time.[9] In that, it is only necessary to see the equation which expresses the nature of the line, and from this equation to extract at first and without any trouble another one, which gives the construction of the tangent.

By the kindness of Mr. Vernon I have received the entire run of your *Transactions* and Mr. Boyle's works which were lacking to me. You will oblige me by informing me from to time about whatever new books he produces as you have been doing, so that I can have copies sent to me. My treatise on pendulums will soon be printed; I have already seen the first sheet. I am, Sir,

> Your very humble and obedient servant
> *Huygens of Zulichem*

I am taking the liberty of addressing the enclosed to you for Mr. Vernon.

ADDRESS
>   Mr. Grubendol
>   London

NOTES

Reply to Letters 2019, 2028, and 2058.
1 Letter 1994.
2 Letter 1944 (Vol. VIII).
3 We do not find any discrepancy in the copy as printed in the *Œuvres Complètes*. Perhaps Huygens was a little unperceptive, but see Letter 1994, note 6.
4 In Letter 2004.
5 See Letter 1949 and its note 4 and Letter 2078; it should be noted that in this paper Wallis insisted that the two methods for finding tangents compendiously described in it had been more fully explained by himself in earlier writings. He did not claim that they were novel methods.
6 The allusion is to Pierre Hérigone, *Cursus mathematicus, nova, brevi et clara methodo demonstratus*, where in a "Supplementum Algebrae" (tome 6; Paris, 1644) Hérigone introduced Prop. 26 (pp. 59–69) "On maxima and minima." (The whole work is written in both Latin and French.) This outlines Fermat's method, taken from his *Methodus ad disquirendam maximam et minimam*, written in 1638; this manuscript was to be printed only in 1679. Meanwhile, the correspondence between Fermat and Descartes concerning maxima and minima had already been printed by Clerselier in 1667. In an annotation upon his "Regula ad inveniendas tangentes linearum curvarum" (see note 8) Huygens wrote (our translation): "The same Fermat sought for tangents to curved lines by a rule of his own, of which Descartes suspected he did not himself understand the basis, as appears by the letters of Descartes on this subject. It is true that in the posthumous works of Fermat the application of the rule is not very well set out and a demonstration is totally lacking. Now, I find that in the letters mentioned above Descartes shows that he has more or less understood the reason for this rule, but that nevertheless he does not explain it as clearly as is done in what we shall propose here; besides we have here a piece composed long before the letters of Descartes were published.

"At that time it was important to me to abridge Fermat's rule. Having made it as succinct as I could, I found that it became identical with the elegant rules of Hudde and Sluse, which these gentlemen had made known to me almost simultaneously. I still do not know if they arrived at their results in the same way that I did, or by another route."

7 Gilles Personne de Roberval also compiled his *Observations sur la composition des Mouvemens, et sur le moyen de trouver les Touchantes des lignes courbes* about 1638; this work was read to the Académie Royale des Sciences in 1668 (Duhamel, 5 1–5 2), first printed in *Mémoires de l'Académie Royale des Sciences* in 1693, and reprinted in *Mémoires de l'Académie royale des sciences Depuis 1666 jusqu'à 1699*, VI (Paris, 1730), 1–89.

8 Huygens read his paper "Regula ad inveniendas tangentes linearum curvarum" to the Académie on 13 April 1667 and it was first printed in *Divers ouvrages de Mathématique et de Physique. Par Messieurs de l'Académie Royale des Sciences* (Paris, 1693); it is included in the *Œuvres Complètes*, XX, 1940, 243–5 5. This paper had been drafted some years earlier.

9 For Sluse's tangent rule (known to him before 1660), see his letters to Oldenburg in Vol. VII, especially pp. 116–19, 251, and 255; he describes it in a future letter to Oldenburg of 7 January 1672/3 (see below, Letter 2124). "Johann Hudde's equivalent rule was communicated to Franz van Schooten on 21 November 1659 and was widely known also, although it remained unprinted till the time of Leibniz's fluxion priority squabble with Newton (when it appeared in the *Journal Literaire* for July/August 1713). Hudde later told Leibniz (Gerhardt, p. 228) that this method of tangents was more complete than that of Sluse since he allowed a multiplication of the curve's Cartesian equation by any arithmetical sequence of numbers: 'Hinc possint constructiones reddi simplices, dum pro arbitrio tollentur termini.'" (D.T.W.). The correspondence of Huygens and Sluse on the subject of tangents began on 8 August 1662, when the latter wrote (*Œuvres Complètes*, IV, 1891, 207) that he had recently taken to its limit of facility the method of tangents which he had discovered many years before.

2067
Oldenburg to Newton
17 September 1672

Printed in Newton, *Correspondence*, I, 218, note 1, from the memorandum in private possession

July 15.72. Ans. July 16. See Copy. Written again Sept. 17, 72. to inqre, whr he received my last of July 16,[1] and of Boyle,[2] and Glisson.[3]

NOTES

Second reply to letter 2024.
1 Letter 2026.

2 Probably this refers to one or both of the essays noted in Letter 1997, note 3.

3 No doubt describing Francis Glisson, *Tractatus de natura substantiae energetica, sive de vita naturae* (London, 1672), of which there is an account in *Phil. Trans.*, no. 87 (14 October 1672), 5076–77.

2068
Oldenburg to Morhof
20 September 1672

From the copy in the Kgl. Bibliotek, Copenhagen, Boll. Brevs. U⁴, no. 733

Nobilissimo & Consultissimo Viro
Domino Danieli Georgio Morhofio J.V. Doctori
Henricus Oldenburg Salutem

Haud levi me gaudio affecerunt literae tuae, Vir Consultissime, quas post aliquot annorum lapsum nuper ad me dare voluisti.¹ Agnosco in iis eximiam tuam in me humanitatem, qua caeptae inter nos amicitiae nodum, candissimae Illustris Langeloti Epistolae² dono, simul & scriptorum Wasmuthianorum³ promisso exsolvendo, adstringere dignatus es. Quam liberalitatem quam maxime accumulas, dum Celeberrimi Gudii doctas in Authores Geoponicas Notas, aliorumque ipsius M[anuscrip]torum Medicorum, Physicorum & Mathematicorum Catalogum transmissurum Te spondes.⁴ Significavi hoc Viris, tum Londini, tum in Academiis nostris, scientiarum & artium augmenta enixe spirantibus. Praedicant ad unum omnes, tum tuam, tum laudatissimi Gudii in provehenda & ornanda re philosophica voluntatem, mihique in mandatis dedere, ut gratias quas possem maximas utrique vestrum rescriberem, oblatamque a vobis generositatem amplexarer. Quamprimum itaque libuerit, Vir Amplissime, perdoctam Dn. Gudium officiossime nostro nomine salutabis, utque notas suas Geoponicas, una cum dicto Catalogo occasione commoda ad me transmittat, amicissime invitabis, eumque certum omnino facies, nihil plane in eorum, quae ab ipso proficiscentur impressione omissum iri, quae honori ipsi debito litare posse censebuntur. Sub praelo nunc, tam Graeco quam Latino, apud nos versatur Iamblichus de Mysteriis AEgyptiorum, nec non Pythagorae Vita, perquam mendose hactenus edita:⁵ Lucianus insuper, Graece itidem & Latine brevi hic imprimendus.⁶ Scire avemus, ullaene Domino Gudio suppetant Notae, quae ad horum Scriptorum vel emendationem vel elucidationem spectent. Adhaec, si quicquam vobis de Bosii edendi Josephi consilio, vel de conditionibus, quibus suas circa ipsum Collationes aliis concedere cupit, innotuerit, id quoque ut nobis significes, obnixe rogamus.⁷ Hisce ita expeditis, duo mihi tecum agenda supersunt. Prius est, ut Clarissimum Dominum Langelottum de Cultu & officiis meis certiorem reddas, ipsique indices, se totum Orbem Philosophicum sibi devinxisse, dum operationes illas Chymicas, Epistola sua ad Naturae Curiosos exarata, tanto candore publici juris fecit; multoque eundum sibi devincturum arctius, si, ex promisso suo, Laboratorii Gottorpiensis Acta pari candore, quamprimum poterit, in genuinae Chymiae decus & tutamen, quin imo in Almae Germaniae nostrae, suamque adeo ipsius, gloriam, luci publicae exponat. Alterum est, me cum Jacobsiis Mercatoribus de illo debito, quod mihi commendasti, locutum, deprehendere, ipso nil quicquam argenti impetrare hactenus potuisse; nec etiamnum posse, quamdiu Fisci Regii clausura, omnibus nota, duret.⁸ Necesse erat, flagrante hoc difficili bello, thesauros Regios in nullum nisi publicum usum impendere, proindeque privati aeris solutionem in pacata tempora protelare. Quamprimum illa redierint, si quid Ego vel scorsim, vel junctim, praestare ea in re potero, nequaquam detrectabo. De hoc securum Te esse velim. Vale interea & me Tui studiosissimum crede. Dabam Londini d. 20. Sept. 1672.

ADDRESS
>Nobilissimo & Consultissimo Viro
>Domino Danieli Georgio Morhofio
>>J.V. Doctori & in Academia Kilonensi Professori,
>>>Amico suo plur. colendo
>>>>Kiel

TRANSLATION

Henry Oldenburg greets the very noble and wise Mr. Daniel George Morhof, LL.D.

The letter which you recently decided to write to me after the lapse of some years brought me no little pleasure, most wise Sir.¹ I recognize in it your exceptional kindness towards me, in wishing to strengthen the bond of friendship between us by making the gift of the very honest letter written by the illustrious

Langelott[2] and by promising at the same time the writings of Wasmuth.[3] You add greatly to this generosity when you promise to send over the learned notes of the famous Gude upon the writers on agriculture and a catalogue of his other manuscripts on medicine, natural history, and mathematics.[4] I have imparted this information to those men both in London and in our universities who are earnestly striving for the advancement of the arts and sciences; one and all commend alike your own intention and that of the worthy Gude to advance and perfect philosophy and instructed me to write back our best thanks to both of you and to accept your proffered generosity. As soon as you can, therefore, excellent Sir, greet the learned Mr. Gude very dutifully in our name and invite him most cordially to send me by the first convenient opportunity his notes on the agricultural authors together with the above-mentioned catalogue, and make him absolutely confident that nothing shall be omitted in the printing of those matters that have originated with him which can be thought of as redounding to his credit. We have now in press with both Greek and Latin texts Iamblichos *On the Egyptian Mysteries* and the *Life of Pythagoras*,[5] which has hitherto been very falsely printed. Moreover Lucian is to be printed here soon, likewise in both Greek and Latin.[6] We are eager to know whether Mr. Gude has any annotations relating to either the emendation or the elucidation of these texts. Further, if anyone among you is acquainted with Bose's intention to edit Josephus or of the conditions under which he might be willing to impart to others the collations he has made concerning him, we earnestly beg you to let us know of these things also.[7] With these things out of the way there are two matters remaining for me to discuss with you. The first is that you should assure the famous Mr. Langelott of my regard and willing services and tell him that he has placed the whole learned world in his debt by so honestly making public those chemical operations [treated] in his letter addressed to the investigators of Nature; and he will greatly increase this obligation if, as he promises, he will as soon as he is able and with equal plain honesty publish the proceedings of the chemical laboratory at Gottorp, for the credit and safety of the genuine chemical art, not to say the renown of our dear Germany and his own personal fame. The other is that I have spoken to the Jacobs, the merchants, about that debt of which you gave me notice and have learned from them that they could as yet obtain no money in settlement of it, and cannot do so, so long as the Stop of the Exchequer of which everyone is aware lasts.[8] It is necessary that for the duration of this tiresome war the royal treasury pay out no sums but those devoted to public purposes and consequently the settlement of private debts is deferred until times of peace return. As soon as they do, I shall not be failing in anything I can accomplish in that business, either singly or jointly [with others]. Please be confident of this. Meanwhile, farewell, and believe me most zealously yours. London, 20 September 1672.

ADDRESS

To the very noble and wise
  Mr. Daniel George Morhof, LL.D. and
  Professor at the University of Kiel
  His most respected friend
          Kiel

NOTES

1 Compare Letter 2057. For Morhof, see Vol. VII, p. 234, note. Although Oldenburg had received news of Morhof from Vogel there had been no direct correspondence between them since Morhof's departure from England.
2 See Letter 2048 and its note 5.
3 Matthias Wasmuth (1625–1688) studied in many universities before becoming Professor of Logic at Rostock in 1657, whence he moved to a chair of Oriental Languages at the new University of Kiel in 1665, so becoming Morhof's colleague. He wrote on the establishment of ancient chronology by the use of astronomical data.
4 Compare Letter 2057, where the relevant extract from Morhof's letter is quoted.
5 The publication of the former edition was deferred for several years; see [*Greek title*] *De mysteriis liber . . . T. Gale . . . Graece nunc primum edidit, Latine vertit, et notas adjecit* (Oxford, 1678). Thomas Gale (see Letter 2063, note 6) left a manuscript version of Iamblichos, *De vita Pythagorae* unpublished when he died.
6 There were numerous renaissance editions of the writings of the Greek satirist Lucian (*c.* 125–190 A. D.), but none printed in England in the seventeenth century.
7 Johann Andreas Bose (1626–74) had been Professor of History at Jena since 1656. He was a prolific author. His intention of several years' standing to publish an edition of the *Jewish History* of Josephus (A.D. 38–100) was frustrated by death.
8 The Stop of the Exchequer had been imposed in January 1672, the government ceasing to pay interest on its debts.

2069

Newton to Oldenburg

21 September 1672

Printed in Newton, *Correspondence* I, 237–38, from the original in private possession

In this reply to Letter 2067, Newton thanks Oldenburg warmly for his "elegant translation" of Letter 1992 and for Oldenburg's activities on Newton's behalf. He apologizes for his delay both in answering Oldenburg's letter, and in drawing up a list of experiments in support of his "Theory of colours." He suggests that Letter 1993 will serve this purpose, and authorizes Oldenburg to publish it: "To wch end I desire you to mitigate any expressions that seem harsh." He offers to discuss his theory further for private communication, but not for publication.

2070

Oldenburg to Newton

24 September 1672

Printed in Newton, *Correspondence*, I, 242–43, from the original in CUL MS. Add. 3976, no. 11

Although this is a reply to Letter 2069, it is almost entirely concerned with news from abroad, especially with the optical references in Platt's Letter 2037, and the remarks on Newton's theory of colors by Huygens in Letter 2066. He also asks whether there might be a job in Cambridge for a chemical assistant of Boyle's, named Thomas Huyck (known to Hooke as "Tom Hewk").

2071

Winthrop to Oldenburg

25 September 1672

From the original in Royal Society MS. W 3, no. 27

Salem in Massachuset Colony
in New England Sept: 25: 1673[1]

Sr

By yours of the 18 of March 1671: wch I received in June I understand you had mine of Nov: 28: 1671: from Hartford wch was but the substance of a former[2] wherwth were also other letters, but its like were not received when you wrote having not mentioned them in your letter: neither is there intimation of an other pacquet sent by way of New Yorke. I came lately hither from N. Plymouth, where I was upon the occasion of a meeting of the commissioners from the severall colonies, & am to returne shortly to Hartford: and although there is yet no certainty of any ships to saile from Boston to London, yet these are intended, to be at Boston for oportunity of a passage: How it came to passe that the Indian Dialogue,[3] & the other sheets, where eyther not sent, or not delivered I cannot learne, I left them at Boston, and ordered them to be sent, & having inquired since I am told they were delivered to one to be conveied, but it is forgotten to whom it was, but there are now more of the same sort wch lye ready at

Boston, and had there beene oportunity of any ship ready I should have seene them delivered on board my selfe, but it is my great disadvantage in reference to conveiance into England, that I am so farre from ye port, whence the ships returne. I have now severall things at Boston, for the repository of the Royall Society, wch I must leave for the helpe of some freind till a probable way of safe conveiance, it being so hazardous this warr tyme, and would not willingly have them lost, it being very doubtfull to escape the capers:4 I thanke you very much for those Transactions, wch I received wth your letter, and that excellent treatise by the Honble mr Boyle about the rarefaction & condensation, & spring of ye aire: as also yt information from Dantzick of ye comet seene there by monsr Hevelius: I have inquired much heere whether a comett were seene by any in these parts, and am informed that it was reported that there was one seene in some place not farr from Boston in Feb: last in the morning a little before day, towards ye Northeast, but cannot yet heare by whom it was seene: but was told by one Richard Smith, a plaine country farmer, that he saw a comett or blazing star (as he calleth it) severall evenings the beginning of March last: I shall make yet more inquiry concerning it, & if I find any more certainty concerning that thing It shalbe further intimated from

> your affectionate servant
> *J Winthrop*

I spake wth that Richard Smith before I came from Hartford (he liveth about 5 miles from yt place), he is an understanding man,& very observing: I blamed him much yt he did not give me notice of it but he thought many others might have seene it, being (he saith very plainly to be seene, and saith he saw it every cleere evening for about 3 weekes together from the begining of March (old stile) & saith that his family all saw it, & some neighbour (wth whom I hope to speake also when I returne) and saith it was much northerly when he first saw it, & afterward appeared much more westerly.

ADDRESS

>   For Mr Henry
>   Oldenburg Secretary
>   of the Royal Society
>   at Pell Mell
>   In
>   London

NOTES

Reply to Letter 1925 (Vol. VIII).

1 Inherent probability suggests that this date is a slip of the pen; Winthrop did visit Plymouth for the reason described in September 1672, as also Salem; whereas in 1673 he was totally preoccupied with the Dutch invasion of Long Island Sound.

2 Letter 1834 (Vol. VIII) possibly repeated the contents of Letter 1789; it has not survived.

3 By John Eliot; see Letter 1925, note 2.

4 Privateers.

2072

Wallis to Oldenburg

26 September 1672

From the original in Royal Society MS. W 1, no. 140

Oxford Sep. 26. 1672

Sir

I am very glad to find in your Transactions for ye last Month,[1] that Monsr Hugens doth endeavour an account of that Odde Phaenomenon in the Torricellian Experiment, which hath for many years been observed here amongst us, & of which I give an account in my Treatise *De Motu Cap. 14. prop. 13.* that Quick-silver, thoroughly cleansed from Air, hath been found to stand in ye Torricellian Experiment at ye hight, above ye stagnant Quick-silver, of 40, 50, 60, Inches or more; (I did not then remember ye praecise hight of 75 inches, which had been then observed; & therefore so spake as to be sure to keep within compass.)

Two reasons I did there hint (though I was not perfectly satisfied in either:) The one of my own, concerning the Spring of ye Air necessary to put heavy bodies in motion, not impelled by any other force. The other, of my Lo. Brounker, that there might yet be in the Air a greater weight or pressure than is necessary for ye hight of 29 inches, in case there be nothing but ye bare weight of Quick-silver to be supported. I find Monsr Hugens to fall in with that reason of My Lo. Brounker, save that what wee comprehend under ye name of Air, he calls a "more subtile Matter:" which alters not ye case at all, but onely ye name. By Air, I find Mr Hobs (at least

PLATE I. Thomas Hobbes
A portrait attributed to J. B. Caspars
Presented to the Royal Society by John Aubrey in 1670
By courtesy of the Royal Society

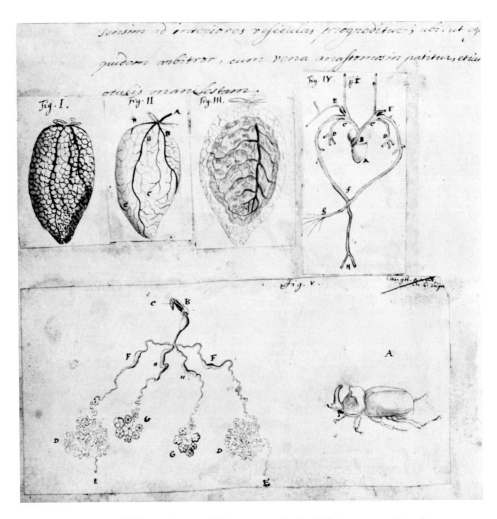

PLATE II. Dissections of Lungs and the Rhinoceros Beetle
By Swammerdam with Letter 2173

sometimes, as in his *Dialogus Physicus*, pag. 4.) would have us understand, a "pure Æther," or (as he speakes) "Aerem ab omni Terrae Aquaeque effluvijs purum, quales putatur esse Æther;"[2] to which I suppose answers ye "Materia Subtilis" of Descartes; & Monsr Hugens his "more subtile Matter:" On ye other hand, Mr Hugens here, by "Air", seemes to understand onely that feculent matter arising from those ye "Earths & Waters Effluvia," which are intermingled with this "Subtile Matter": Wee mean by "Air," ye "Aggregate of both those," or whatsoever else makes up that "Heterogeneous Fluid" wherein we breath, commonly called Air. The purer part of which, is Mr *Hobs's* "Air": & ye feculent part of it is Monsr *Hugens's* "Air". And therefore where I speak of "Vacuity" caused by ye Torricellian Experiment, or such other ways, I do expressly caution (*de Motu cap. 14.* & *Hobb. Heaut.* p. 152.[3] & elsewhere) not to be understood as affirming absolute Vacuity (which whether or no there be, or can be, in nature, I list not to dispute,) but at lest an absence of "that Heterogeneous Misture which we call Air, such as that is wherein we breath;" without dissenting against Mr *Hobs's,* "purus Æther"; or the "materia Subtilis" of *Des-Cartes* or of Mr *Hugens*; as not necessary to ye inquiries then in hand. The pressure of this Defecated Matter (clensed from ye grosser part of ye Air) is yt to which My Lo. *Brounker* & Mr *Hugens* do ascribe ye suspension of ye Quicksilver to so great a hight. And My Lo. *Br.* in particular, while that piece of mine was under ye Presse, had a design (as he then signified to me,) of prosecuting ye Experiment (as Monsr Hugens doth now advise) to see if he could bring it to some fixed Hypothesis; of which I might there have given an account, if it could have been dispatched time enough. But his leisure not then serving him to pursue it so fully as he would; I onely gave yt brief account of his Notion, as it is there inserted: & whether hee have since had leisure (amidst a great presse of other busynesse) to pursue it; I am not certain. That ye suspension of the lower of two contiguous *Marbles*, in Mr *Boile's* Engine,[4] longer than is well accountable for, from ye common pressure of Air, (which Mr *Boile*, hath long since found by his own experience;) & that of a *Siphon* so running, in ye exhausted Engine: are doubtless to be referred to ye same cause with that of ye Quicksilver so suspended. But I must confesse, as I was not satisfied with yt reason when first alleged by my Lo. *Brounker*; so neither am I yet (under ye favour of those two great persons) as repeated by Monsr *Hugens*; But (though I would not wholly exclude this if such be found to be,) I think, there must be somewhat more in it, then that of this Subtile Matter, to solve ye Phaenomenon. For if this matter be so subtile as to presse downwards through ye Top of ye Glass upon ye Quick-silver, as well as upwards at ye bottome; (& consequently through ye upper of ye two Marbles upon ye neather of them suspended;) as is acknowledged; (& without which it is no more able to praecipitate ye Quick-silver while impure, & when it is in part subsided, than when it is pure, & ye tube perfectly full:) I do not see, why it should not balance it selfe (above & below) in ye same manner as common Air would do if ye Tube were pervious to it at both ends. And ye Answere; yt though ye glass be penetrable by it, yet not in so copious a manner as below where no glass is: doth not, to me, salve ye difficulty; because the same obstacle doth just in ye same manner remain, when ye tube is in part emptied, & when the quick-silver is unpurged; the pores of ye glasse not being, by either of these, made more open or more pervious. And if wee suppose ye subtile matter by percolation to be strained through, with some difficulty, (as air or water would be through a cloth,) this might possibly make the quicksilver gradually to sink, but not (as wee see it) suddenly to fall, to the hight 29 inches.

The connexion or cohesion of the parts of the Quicksilver, which he supposeth to require for their separation a greater force than is in these percolated particles till they have room made for them to combine; seemes to me ye lesse considerable, because it is not so necessary to separate them from each other, since yt they may unseparated slide down by ye sides of ye glass; to which, it is well known, & visible to the eye, the quicksilver is not at all apt to stick, but doth rather decline that contact; in like manner as wee find water not apt to join with Oyle or Grease; though Water to Glass, & Quick-silver to Gold, do very readyly apply themselves. So yt there needs no such force, to disjoin ye Quicksilver from ye glass, whatsoever there may be for disjoining its parts one from another.

I know not whether it have been yet tryed, (if not, I should advise yt it may yet be;) whether, when a Tube thus filled with well cleansed Quicksilver, (so as to stand higher than ye ordinary standard,) if part of it be, by concussion, made to run out, & then a stop put to ye rest, this remainder might not be reduced so to hang as the whole did, notwithstanding the voyd room at ye Top above the hight of 29 Inches. For if so; then this reason is quite insignificant. I have no opportunity here, of making ye Experiment, & therefore must refer it to those with you who have.

I might adde allso, that ye want of room for ye percolated particles to recollect themselves; would be of like force, when ye Quicksilver is not well clensed of other air, as when it is; if the Spring of yt Air so remaining did not operate.

I adde further; that, if the want of room to recollect, be ye reason why the percolated particles do not act on ye purged Quick-silver, while ye Tube is full; the same reason would hold in this case following; viz. Suppose the Tube (filled with such Quick-silver) at first immersed so deep as yt the Top be lesse than 29 Inches (suppose 20 Inches) above ye stagnant Quick-silver; the Tube being gently lifted up, the Quick-silver will rise with it (as is well known) till it be 29 Inches high, (being thrust up by ye pressure of ye ordinary Air on ye stagnant Quick-silver;) the Tube thus long remaining full: But, if ye assigned reason be good, it must allso (which it hath not yet, that I know of, been found to do,) continue still to rise (with the raised Tube) even to ye hight at least of 75 Inches; this Subtile matter pressing upward at ye bottom with its full force; but not downwards at the Top (to balance it) for want of roome to recollect or gather itself into a Body of competent force & bignesse.

I will not be confident, but that this Experiment may succeed, (for yt of a Siphon continuing to run, as is sayd, in the Exhausted Receiver, seemes to favour it;) I onely say (though it well deserve to be curiously examined) I do not know yt it hath yet been found so to do.

I am apt therefore, as heretofore, to ascribe the cause of this Phaenomenon to ye Spring which is in the remaining Air. For, that in Air there is a Spring, is now undoubted: But in Water, cleansed of Air, (though many experiments have been attempted to that purpose;) it hath not yet been found yt there is any: And I am apt to think ye like of Quick-silver; though I do not know that this hath been yet so rigorously examined. Now supposing, yt Matter, being at Rest, will so continue til it be putt in Motion by some force: this force may be either that of *Percussion* from some body before in Motion, (which is the case when ye Quicksilver falls by shaking or striking ye Tube,) or of *Pulsion* from a contiguous Body beginning to move, as by ye Expansion of some adjacent Spring, (which is ye case, when ye Springy parts of ye Air expanding themselves thrust away ye Quicksilver, if not first purged of this Air;) Or else by a *Conatus* or Endeavour of its own, such as is that of a Spring (from whatsoever cause it be, which I do not here inquire;) but hath place onely in Springy bodies: & therefore if Water & Quicksilver be not such, they will not on this account putt themselves in motion. Gravity or Heavynesse is I know (if wee knew what it were) reputed to be such a *Conatus*, or Pronity to move downwards, & to put itself in Motion; & the Wonder at present is, why it doth not so here. But if this, which we call Gravity, should chance to be, not a positive Quality or *Conatus*, Originally of itself, but onely the effect of some Pulsion or Percussion from without, (which possibly may be the case, & principally, from ye Spring of ye Air about us;) then, while this Pulsion & Percussion is wanting (however obviated) the Bodies, accounted Heavy, will not of themselves begin to fall. Which seems to be the present case.

And this is ye more considerable, because wee cannot (at lest not as yet) find, what is the utmost hight at which, the Quicksilver thus accumulated may be found to stand without falling: there having been (for ought I know) no hight yet attempted at which it will not stand; and that of 75 Inches, considering the Weight of Quicksilver, is a very great one; being more then 80 foot of Water.

These are, at present, my thoughts of this matter, (the same with what I have expressed formerly:) not out of a desire to contradict these persons whom I so much esteem: But (none of us being yet so well satisfied as not to think a further search needfull) to suggest matter of further inquiry, for ye perfect discovery of what I esteem a thing so very considerable in the search of the true nature of Gravity. I am Sr

Your very humble servant
John Wallis

For Mr Henry Oldenburg, Secretary to
    the Royal Society, at
        London

NOTES

This document is in large part duplicated (in Royal Society MS. W 1, no. 141) by a longer paper, also in Wallis's hand, with a heading suitable for the *Philosophical Transactions*; this begins as a letter but contains no signature. Neither document has an envelope. The longer version was published in *Phil. Trans.*, no 91 (24 February 1672/3), 5160–70.

1 See Letter 2058, note 1.
2 "An air purified from all effluvia of earth and water, such as may be considered an aether." The *Dialogus physicus* was published at London in 1661.
3 John Wallis, *Hobbius Heauton-timorumenos*, (Oxford, 1662).
4 His air pump.

2073
Malpighi to Oldenburg

28 September 1672

From the original in Royal Society Malpighi Letters, no. 17
Printed in *Opera Omnia*, I, Appendix, p. 16

Praeclarissimo et Eruditissimo Viro
Domino Henrico Oldenburg Regiae Societatis Anglicanae Secretario
Marcellus Malpighius S.P.

Pullorum generationem in incubatis ovis iterum elapsa aestate observatam, et in actuariolum redactam, ad te transmittere placuit, ut studiorum meorum, qualiacunque sint, normam habeas. Rude igitur hoc compendium inter otium percurres, quod, si non indignum Regia Societate
tuo iudicio censebitur, meo nomine ipsi exhibebis.[1] Scio perpetuis, et
gravioribus quidem curis Socios adeo detineri, ut in evolvendis annuarum
observationum inconditis hisce studiis omnino tempus non vacet.

Jam accuratissimam Plantarum Anatomen Praeclarissimi Viri Domini
Grewe transmissam reccepi, et pro tanto munere debitas tibi gratias ago:[2]
Doctissimum opus, amici ope in latinum versum, prae manibus habeo, et
licet plaeraque, ob interpretis non exactam peritiam, mentem meam fugi-
ant, praecipua tamen Auctoris inventa tenere puto. Gaudeo interim, me
cum Accuratissimo Viro in quamplurimis convenire observationibus et
placitis; reliqua autem in quibus intercedere aliquid diversitatis videtur,
ulteriori instituta indagine solertius examinabo, ne, quae tanti Viri aciem
effugere, illusione quadam languidae meae imponant phantasiae. Vidi in
laudato opere varias Auctorum circa flores, spinas & folia, indicari sententias; libenter scirerem, an hujusmodi iam typis editae sint. Valeas interim
diu foelix. Dabam Bononiae die 8. Octobris 1672 [N.S.].

TRANSLATION

Marcello Malpighi sends many greetings to the very famous and learned Mr.
Henry Oldenburg, Secretary of the English Royal Society

I have decided to send you the generation of chicks in incubated eggs as it was
observed by me a second time last summer and reduced to a brief record, so
that you may have a strict measure of my studies, such as they are. This unpolished

summary you may, then, look through at leisure, and if your judgement finds it not unworthy of the Royal Society you will present it to them on my behalf.[1] I know that the Fellows are so engrossed in continual and more serious tasks that they are quite without time to examine these uncouth studies of yearly observations.

I have now received the very accurate anatomy of plants by the very famous Mr. Grew [that you] sent [me], and return you due thanks for so rich a gift.[2] I have this very learned work in my possession, translated into Latin by the aid of a friend, and although many points escape my understanding because of the translator's less than perfect skill, I think I have grasped the author's chief discoveries. Meanwhile I rejoice that in very many observations and opinions I find myself in agreement with such an accurate writer; as for the rest, where some difference seems to arise between us, I will examine them more carefully in a future investigation lest my feeble fancy should impose [as true], through some illusion, what escapes such a keen observer. I have noted in this praiseworthy book hints of the author's various views concerning flowers, thorns, and leaves; I would be glad to know whether anything of this sort has been published already. Meanwhile farewell, and may you long be happy. Bologna, 8 October 1672 [N.S.]

NOTES

1　Oldenburg presented this letter to the Royal Society together with the manuscript of *De ovo incubato observationes* (as this second study was to be called) on 22 January 1672/3.

2　For the sending of Grew's *Anatomy of Vegetables Begun* to Malpighi, see Letter 1912 (Vol. VIII) and Letter 1969.

2074
Oldenburg to Wallis
28 September 1672

Mentioned in Wallis's reply, Letter 2078, as containing an extract of Huygens' Letter 2066.

2075

Oldenburg to Lister

30 September 1672

From the original in Bodleian Library MS. Lister 34, f. 65

London. Sept. 30. 72.

Sir,

By this good opportunity of ye return of Mr Sturdy[1] and Mr Wilkinson I must take the liberty of acquainting you, yt I saw the other day yr Letter written to our Worthy friend Mr Brook,[2] lamenting ye death of yt eminent virtuoso Mr Willughby,[3] and expressing a kind of presage for our slower correspondence hereafter. We all have cause to Joyne wth you in ye lamentation, as of a losse hardly reparable; but that losse, me thinks, should make the survivors ye more vigorous in prosecuting such designs and purposes, as yt friend of ours was upon, wth the greater resolution, to ye end yt by our industry and care some part, at least, may be repaired of yt whole.

I can but offer my readinesse, and the franc communication of what coms to my hands; leaving it to my philosophical correspondents, what use or improvement they shall think fit to make of it, and what return they shall please to remit in exchange.

At the present I shall intimate unto you, that I shew'd to these two Ingenious persons, yt bring this letter to you, a printed Epistle of one Dr Langelot, of Holstein, *De quibusdam in Chymia praetermissis, quorum occasione Secreta haud exigui momenti, proque non-entibus hactenus habita, candide deteguntur et demonstrantur.*

The Import is, in short, that by *Digestion, Fermentation,* and *Triture* or Grinding, much more may be perform'd in Chymistry, than hitherto hath been. Wch the Author undertaketh to make out by some very considerable and un-common Experiments, wch he saith he made himself wth very good success; reciting two Tryals for each of those three Operation; as 1. the Preparation of ye Volatil Salt of Tartar, and of a Tincture of Corall, by *Digestion*: 2. A true Volatilization of Salt of Tartar, and the making of an excellent Opiat, by *Fermentation*: 3. The preparation of a True Aurum potabile, and the Extraction of a current Mercury out of Antimony, by *Triture*; wch is perform'd by an Engin, described and delineated by this

Author, and call'd *Mola philosophica*. All wch I intend, God permitting, to impart to the Curious more fully in the Transactions of October, since I know of no other copy of yt Epistle, than mine, to be as yet in England.

I am confident, Sir, you are not unmindfull of what you intimated, a while since, of yr intention to prosecute the Anatomy of plants, and particularly ye Inquiry about the Veines of Plants, concerning wch you then affirm'd, yt there are no other vessels, (yt may properly be so call'd) besides those milky-veines and yt these veines hold the only vital Juices of Plants;[4] wch you undertook to confirme by divers reasons and Experiments: adding wthall, yt you would say more of this, when you did acquit yrself of ye commands of ye R. Society. Having put you in mind of this, I shall conclude wth assuring yrself of my being constantly Sir

yr faithfull servt
H. Oldenburg

ADDRESS

To his honored friend
Dr Martyn Lister, at his house
in
York

NOTES

There had been a long pause in this correspondence: Oldenburg last wrote to Lister on 11 May (Letter 1977) but there is no record of a reply from him.

1 See Letter 1977, postcript; we know nothing of Mr. Wilkinson.
2 See Letter 1800, note 6 (Vol. VIII).
3 See Letter 2016, note.
4 See Letter 1863 (Vol. VIII).

2076
Towneley to Oldenburg
30 September 1672
From the original in Royal Society MS. T, no. 24

Towneley Sep. 30. 1672

Sr

This last weeke a troublesome sute brought Mr. Flamsted into our parts,[1] and during his stay he was so kind as to afford me his companie, twas iust about ye time he expected to find Mars amongst ye 3 starrs[2] but ye heavens were allmost all ye time overcast (our weather haveing for 5 or 6 weeks beene so verie bad yt much of our corne, is yett out of doors, though 2 or 3 faire days long since would have gott it all in) onelie once he had a little oportunitie of makeing an observation, and found yt Mars did not follow ye course astronomers expected, he saw him neare ye star marked in ye Transactions 27.[3] and thinks yt if he could have seene him 5 or 6 howers after, he would have coverd it. since he left us wee have made some other observations wch I intend to send to him, and since I know he will acquaint you with all particulars I shall not now further trouble you with them, but in ye mean time as he desired me present his humble service unto you, as I am obliged to doe my cordiall thanks for ye ye philosophicall intelligence in your last. I had done it sooner but yt I could not before now accompanie it with ye particulars of ye pit where my Thermometer stoode wch I onelie learnt from ye collier this day, and so now I pray accept of it.[4]

Twas but Fryday last I received ye Transactions you mentioned and doubt not but yr odd mercuriall experiment will sett manie heades at worke.[5] I never saw ye experiment for I never yett could fill a tube so as to free it totalie from aire, and if there be anie particular way of doeing it you will oblige me in letting me know it, as allso whether ye experiment will succeed except ye tube be of a small boore, and what it must be.

I am not a little ashamed yt I have not yett made anie experiments with ye barometer Mr. Boile was pleasd to send me, but ye truth is ye servant I us'd to employ about such things,[6] hath for above this 12 monethes beene troubled with a ague and yett unfit to stir abroad and to trouble him without some information, I esteem'd a greater fault, howsoever Sr. I hope you will in part beg my pardon and present my most humble service unto him.

I have had manie promises of an account of aged persons butt yet no more: I shall howsoever endeavour to quicken them, I heare of one not farr from us yt died about a monethe agoe of above 120. years ould.[7]

The papers you mention Mr. Moore[8] inform'd you of I have wch though then they containd manie novelties yett now I think they would not be much estemd [*illegible*][9] Mr. Flamsted had ye perusall of them and hath taken notes out of them howsoever if you shall think otherwise you may command ye perusall of them likewise. If you think ye enclosed paper containes anie thing worth takeing notice of I shall beg it may be showne to Mr. Boile.

I have not latelie heard from Mr Colins so feare some of mine to him may have miscarried, so I pray present my service unto him.[10] I feare allso ye like fate hath attended either some of mine to Monsr. de Sluse or his answers wherfore lett me beg to know, your usuall superscripts and way of sending your letters unto him.[11]

Rather then differ writeing anie longer I venterd to send onelie this scribled paper and hope you will for so during[12] pardon Sr

Your humble servant
Rich: Towneley

ADDRESS
These
For Mr. Henry Ouldenbourg
at his house in the pailmail
Westminster

POSTMARK OC 4

NOTES

Reply to Letter 2064.
1 "My father's affairs caused me to take a journey into Lancashire, the very day I had designed to begin my observations: but God's Providence so ordered it that they gave me an opportunity to visit Towneley, where I was kindly received and entertained by Mr. [Richard] Towneley, with whose instruments I saw Mars near the middlemost of the three adjacent fixed stars" (Baily, p. 32, from Flamsteed's autobiography). The astronomer assisted his father in his malting business.
2 See Letter 2047 and *Phil. Trans.*, no. 86 (19 August 1672), 5042.
3 On the figure printed in *Phil. Trans.*, no. 86 (note 2 above).
4 See Letter 2076a.
5 See Letter 2058, note 1.
6 His name, possibly, was George Kemp and he had assisted the Towneleys in their scientific experiments over a number of years.
7 Compare Letter 2045.

8 Jonas Moore. Earlier in 1672 Flamsteed had copied some papers of William Gascoigne's on dioptrics which he greatly admired (Baily, p. 32); if not these, then probably
papers by Jeremiah Horrox or William Crabtree—which Flamsteed had also seen on
a previous visit—are intended here.

9 The word looks like "above," which makes no sense.

10 Three letters from Towneley to Collins written earlier in 1672 are printed in Rigaud,
Vol. I. Their acquaintance was of long standing.

11 Compare Towneley's similar remark in a letter to Collins; Rigaud, I, 191. Sluse says
the same in a letter to Oldenburg of 17 June 1675. Towneley was Sluse's first English correspondent (at least since 1662, if the reference in *Œuvres Complètes*, IV, 207
is correctly interpreted) but none of the correspondence between them seems to have
survived.

12 Read: "doing."

2076a
Towneley's Experiment

Enclosure with Letter 2076
From the original in Royal Society MS. T, no. 23a

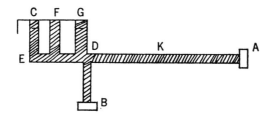

A one pit upon ye heade of ye Sough or audit[1] about 80 yards long
B an other pit, either 27 yards deepe

The darkned spaces represent ye places out of wch coales had been gott
when ye thermometer was first sett in ye pitt. of these

AD 120 yards long & 1½ broade beeing made to convey away ye water:
C, F, G. ye heades where coales had beene gott about 30 yards long, their
greatest breadths about 2 yards. *DB.* 19 yards long.

C ye place where ye Thermometer stoode constantlie at ye same haight
viz 4$\frac{4}{10}$ from De: 26 till March ye 3d onelie from Feb: 12 to ye 26 it was sett
at *K*, and then it stoode about 1. higher yn yt in ye house, placed in a N.E.
window in a room without a fire but next to one yt had one constantlie in
it, and onlie parted with wainscote.

May ye 9th it was againe sett at *C* and continued there till ye beginning of August and constantlie kept its ould station for hight.

During ye first time of ye Ther: being lett in ye pit ye weather was verie could especiallie about ye Latterend of Jan: & beginning of Feb: when ye Ther: in ye house stoode at 1.9 under o, yt is 5.3 lower then that in ye pit

And after it had beene lett downe into ye pit ye 2d time wee had extreame hott weather, by ye Ther: 11.4 May 28 yt is 7. higher yn yt in ye pitt stoode.² So yt yt above ground varied 13.3 whereas yt in ye pit, alterd not perceptibly.

Note yt everie primairie division in my Thermometers whereof one was graduated by Mr. Shortgrave containes about 1½ inche, and those againe divided decimalie.

Your last Sir seemd to desire ye Situation of ye coal pit and therfore I shall add yt ye scale³ comes out neare a little plaine ground lieing betwixt ye hill where ye coales are and one other verie craggie. ye plaine is a spongie piece of ground and verie boggie out of wch there springs water whereof ye one halfe runs into ye East ye other into ye West Sea makeing ye heads of 2 brookes ye one called East ye other West Calder but I think this small valley if I may so call it is ye highest of our parts.⁴

NOTES

This document is an amplification and extension of the account of the experiment already described by Towneley in Letter 1958. The matters touched on here have been sufficiently elucidated in the notes upon that letter.

1 adit.

2 The high temperature is about 27.4° C—indeed warm for the time of year in the north of England—as compared with 10.6° C in the pit.

3 Ladder (leading down into the mine).

4 That is, on the watershed east of Burnley, Lancashire, whence the two rivers Calder flow through Lancashire and Yorkshire respectively.

2077
Salomon Reisel to Oldenburg

1 October 1672

From the original in Royal Society MS. R 1, no. 37

Nobilissime atque Clarissime Vir

Dici non potest, quanto gaudio suffussus fuerim, cum Nobilissimus Dominus Schroderus hic transierit,[1] pars Regiae vestrae Societatis mihi innotesceret, a quo tam raros & felices in Philosophia progressus discerem; majori, cum quaereret qui mitteret literas vestras ad Curiosos Naturae, easque mihi crederet.[2] Accepi igitur proxime mittendas, qui postridie demum ad Illos scripseram, de tertio Ephermeridum anno hic excudendo, simul etiam quid alii de Collegio ipsorum, & Arte nostra perficienda sentirent. Verum rerum novarum desiderium moram illam post menses demum aliquot audiendi, quae intus laterent, rupit, simul et literas, annuente tamen & spondente Domino Schrodero nihil aliud contineri, quam quod ad Collegium pertineret, Vidique et legi Vestrum tam officiosum animum, Doctrinae subtilissimae de Luce et coloribus communicationem, et spem Originis Gemmarum ab Illustrissimo Boyle. Ignoscent scio Curiosi suo bono hanc proterviam. Ignosces, spero et Tu, Vir Clarissime propter publicum bonum, cui tam generosi studes. Studere vero Te Germanae patriae et Curiosorum adhuc aedificando Collegio, indicavit saepe laudatus Dominus Schöderus neque deero brevi ipsis mentem utriusque vestrum Germanam significare de corrigendis quibusdam legibus et Institutis, quam ambabus manibus gratoque animo accipient, ut qui prudentiorum judicia, juvamina, remedia quaerunt, Patronos poscunt, Fautores ubique ambiunt. Inter quos de tuo favore sibi merito gratulantur. Perge patriae ulterius favere, et favete quoque mihi per amorem patriae. Adferet secum Dominus Schroderus Historiam literarum in medio fagi trunco lectarum Illustrissimae Societati proponendam & excutiendam, quae humillima oblatio si grata fuerit, et aliud quod rari occurrerint, pura mente ad aram Veritatis et Sapientiae offeram.[3] Et ne hac vice symbolo vacus veniam, ecce Observationem meditatione, ut mihi videtur dignam a Francofurtensi Physicoordinario, Jos. Ludovico Witzelio D. mihi missam, quae antevertet editionem publicam Ephemeridum, cui inserta est, sed sero ad Vos veniet.[4] Cujus causam si fortasse ab aliis exemplis, aut Vestro-

rum examine didiceris, docueris, magno erit mihi pretio. Vale, vive et
fave qui te veneratur Vir Clarissime

Salomo Reisel D.
Archiater Hanoicus

Hanoviae Kal. Octobr. 1672

"Generosissimus Dominus Comes Guilielmus a Greiffenstein arcem in
rupe inhabitat, e cujus altitudine antehac Herbornam⁵ neque se, neque
ullum e praesidiariis videre potuisse, sancte affirmabat, nunc in pede
montis, et ad introitum, ad quem annosa tilia, et turrium et maeniorum
partem ipsemet clare videre potui; retuli hoc Serennissimo Principi
Adolpho Nassovico, qui me certiorem fecit Schaumburgi ad Lanum, quae
ejus est habitatio, se nunc videre posse pagum ditionis suae, de quo ante
aliquot annos ne tantillum quidem cernere potuerit. Praeterita septimana
cum essem apud Nobilissimum et Strenuum Dominum Hundium a Saulheim, Fortalitii Königsteinensis Praefectum,⁶ exspatiatus in hortum intra
muros, dissitum longe Rhenum ad Wormatiam et Oppenhemium conspexi-
mus, interroganti mihi quaenam arx illa (ne dimidii quidem milliaris
spatium distans) Eppsteinium⁷ respondit, de quo qui ante 30 annos hic
commorati, nil prorsus videre potuerunt, ante 14 annos cum advenirem,
turres ego vidi, nunc tu totam arcem vides. Quaeremusne causam in
fermentatione locorum in quibus tanta moles? ergo in subsidentia montium
qui siti ante illa loca olim visum arcere potuerunt."

Ita ille XVI. Augusti 1671. ubi simul historiam Corvorum alborum
addit, quae cum tertio quoque anno Ephemeridum lucem videbit.⁸

Tale quid novum oculis objici circa Kanstad oppidum Wirtenbergeuse,
dixit nuper amicus.⁹

ADDRESS
 Viro
 Clarissimo et Consultissimo
  Domino Oldenburgio
 Regiae Societatis Secretario dignissimo
   Fautori optimo
    Londini

TRANSLATION

Most noble and famous Sir,

I cannot tell you with how much joy I was filled when the very noble Mr. Schröter passed through here [and] made the nature of your Royal Society known to me,[1] from whom I learned of such rare and successful progress in philosophy; all the more so, when he asked who should send your letter to the Investigators of Nature and entrusted it to me.[2] I accordingly agreed to send it very soon and wrote to them on the next day following about having the third year of their journal printed here and at the same time also about what others think of their College and the perfecting of our [medical] art. In truth the desire of hearing of the novelties that lay within would brook no delay after the last few months, and as Mr. Schröter approved and promised that the letter contained nothing but what concerned the College, I saw and read your very obliging intentions, your communication of the very subtle theory of light and colors, and expectation of [a book on] the origin of gems by the most illustrious Boyle. The Investigators will, I know, forgive this impudence out of their goodness. I hope that you too, famous Sir, will forgive it by reason of the public good for which you strive so generously. The praiseworthy Mr. Schröter has often indicated that you take great pains on behalf of our fatherland, Germany, and the still-to-be constructed College of the Investigators; and I shall not fail in a little while to signify to them the Germanic ideas of both of you concerning the amendment of certain rules and schemes, which they will embrace with both hands and a grateful spirit being men who seek the judgments of the wise, [with their] assistance and remedies; who demand patrons and look everywhere for supporters. Among whom they will congratulate themselves on deserving your favor. Continue to cherish your native land still further, and cherish me because of your love for your country. Mr. Schröter will take away with him the account of the letters read in the middle of the trunk of a beech tree for communication to and discussion by the most illustrious Society, which if it will be welcome (together with other things of rare occurrence) I shall offer with a pure mind as a most humble oblation to the altar of truth and wisdom.[3] And so that I do not come to you empty-handed this time, here is an observation that was sent to me, the work (and a worthy one as it seems to me) of the Frankfurt Ordinary Physician, Josef Ludwig Witzel, anticipating its publication in the journal, where it is inserted, but which may come tardily to you.[4] It will be of great value to me to instruct me as to its cause, if you have happened perchance to learn it from other instances or the study of your group. Farewell, live long and cherish him who venerates you, famous Sir,

Salomon Reisel
Chief Physician of Hanau

Hanau, 1 October 1672

"The very highborn lord Count Wilhelm von Griffenstein lives in a castle upon a rock, from which height neither he nor any of his garrison could formerly see Herborn,[5] as he most religiously affirmed; now from the foot of the mountain I myself could clearly see towards the entrance-gate where there are ancient lime trees and a part of the towers and walls. I related this to his Serene Highness Prince Adolf of Nassau who informed me that at Schaumburg-on-the-Lahn, which is his dwelling-place, he can now see the countryside of his dominion, of which a few years ago he could not discern the least trace. Last week when I was with the very noble and active Mr. Hundius von Saulheim, Governor of the fortress of Königstein,[6] wandering in the garden between the walls, we looked out at the far-distant Rhine about Worms and Oppenheim and when I asked what was that castle (not even half a mile distant) he replied that it was Eppstein,[7] of which those who lived here thirty years ago could see absolutely nothing; when I came fourteen years ago I saw the towers, and now you see the whole castle. We ask what is the reason for this disturbance of places in which the masses are so great? It must be in the subsidence of the mountains whose positions in front of those places formerly hid them from sight."

So far he on 16 August 1671. At the same time he adds a tale about white crows which will see the light in the third year of the journal.[8]

A friend lately told me that something new was to be seen about Cannstatt, a town in Wurttemburg.[9]

ADDRESS

To the very famous and wise
Henry Oldenburg,
Most worthy Secretary of the Royal Society,
    Best of patrons,
           London

NOTES

Salomon Reisel was chief physician to Frederick Casimir, Count of Hanau, later moving to Stuttgart where he served the Duke of Württemburg. He contributed to *Miscellanea Curiosa*.

1 See Letter 2029.
2 Letter 2031.
3 Reisel's letter to the Royal Society dated 30 September was read on 11 December, and entered in Letter Book V, 415–18. See further below, Letter 2131 and its note 1.
4 See *Miscellanea Curiosa*, Vol. III for 1672 (Leipzig and Frankfurt, 1681), Observation 58, p. 82.
5 Herborn is a village or small town in Hesse between Siegen and Wetzlar.
6 This place is about 18 km. northwest of Frankfurt-am-Main.

7 Eppstein is about 22 km. west of Frankfurt and (in fact) about 8 km. from König-stein.

8 See *Miscellanea Curiosa*, Vol. III for 1672 (Leipzig and Frankfurt, 1681), Observation 57, p. 81.

9 Cannstatt lies across the river Neckar from Stuttgart.

2078
Wallis to Oldenburg
2 October 1672

From the original in Royal Society MS. W 1, no. 142

Octob. 2. 1672. Oxford.

Sir,

What was intended you by last Thursday's Post,[1] had he not been to quick for mee; (about ye suspended Mercury) I did not keep till ye Post following, but sent it in ye interim by Bartlets flying Coach on Saturday, that you might have it time inough to show my Lo. Brounker on Munday, your usual day of attending him: which I hope came well to hand. Since wch I have yours of Sept. 28, and therein Monsr Hugens's note of my two Methodes.

That Monsr Fermat's methode, as it is in Herigone differs not much from ye first of mine, is very true, though when mine was first published in my Treatise of Conick Sections,[2] I had never seen yt of Fermat; & Mr Hugens may very well remember, (if at lest I do not mistake Hugens for Schooten,) yt, after that book had been a good while published, Mr Hugens in a letter of his to mee having occasionally mentioned Fermats methode de maximis et minimus; I wrote in my next to him, (having not before heard of it,) to inquire what it was, & he directed me to this in Herigon:[3] whereupon I replyed in my next, (having in ye mean time consulted Herigon. Supplement. Algebr. prop. 26.)[4] that if that were it; he might find I allready made use of a Methode aequivalent, in my Conick sections, (to find ye tangents of Parabola, Elipsis, Hyperbola &c.) though I knew it not by yt name. Nor is mine, so much the same with yt of Herigon or Fermat; but yt one of his own (not more unlike it than mine is,) was (after mine) published as a new one, in Schotens second Edition of Geom. Cartesiana, (which in ye first Edition was not) pag. 255.[5] that whole discourse from pag. 253. lin. 28. Verum enimvero &c. to pag. 264. lin. 18. Et sic de alijs being an insertion in yt Edition of 1659, which in the former of 1649. was not.[6] And to this I suppose Monsr Hugens would as well have referred, had not my Conick Sections of 1655, been ancienter than it. But though mine were purely my own; yet I will not deny but Monsr Fermat had one much like it (though otherwise deduced) before mee. 'Tis true allso, that in ye same place Schoten mentions a Method of Hudden's;[7] but what it is, though perhaps he may have told his friends, & Mr Hugens to ye Assembly, of Paris, yet none of them have yet told ye world. 'Tis likewise true, yt it hath been long since sayd yt Roberval hath a Method for Tangents by Concurse of Motion.[8] but what it is, he hath never published; and though perhaps he may of late have told it to ye Parisian Assembly, (& sooner possibly to some of his friends,) it doth not follow but what others invent may be their own; nor yet, because he had before, a Method by concurse which he kept to himself; therefore all Methods by concurse which others shal after invent, must be thought to be his. For 'tis not fair play, to keep all to himself, & then to lay claim to all that others (without his help) shal find out & publish. But I list not to contend with Monsr Hugens. What my way is, I have published; Roberval may publish his when he please; which if it be found to be ye same which I had published before him, I cannot help it. And if any, before me, have published mine, they have ye credit of having first published it, without my regret. If they find fault with me for not citing them; they have been before hand with me, for neither did they (in ye place cited; or any where else that I know of,) cite yt of my Conick Sections, though in print (& read by themselves) divers years before. And even that which Hugens now publisheth, as his account of ye High suspension of ye Mercury,(without taking any notice of me,) is but just ye same yt I had before published as my Lo. Brounkers account of it, De Motu, pag. 741.[9] So yt if this be a fault, Veniam dabimus, petimusque vicissim.[10] 'Tis not ye fashion in France to take notice of what hath been done before them by us in England, but to publish their own things as new; & we are as little obliged (though we do it oftener) allwayes to cite them. But these are not things to quarrel about. Schoten & Hugens (though I was before hand with them, & they knew it,) did no more cite mee, than I did Fermat, which I knew not of; & divers others have since made use of ye like, without citing either of us. But it will not be necessary to say any thing of this to Monsr Hugens, (with whom I have no quarel,) nor to ask his conceled Method, for I suppose we shall have it ere long, in Slusius, without asking. No more at present but that I am

Your friend to serve you,
John Wallis

ADDRESS

For Mr Henry Oldenburg
in the Palmal near
St James's
London

POSTMARK OC 4

NOTES

Reply to Letter 2074, which is lost, quoting extracts from Letter 2066.

1 Letter 2072, written Thursday, 26 September.

2 John Wallis, *De sectionibus conicis, nova methodo expositis, tractatus* (1656) is reprinted in his *Opera mathematica* (Oxford, 1695), I, 291–354.

3 In a letter of 9 June 1659, N.S. (*Œuvres Complètes*, II, 417) Huygens did indeed say (of Schooten's 1659 work): "You will see there too that method of Hudde's for the determination of maxima and minima, (for which, however, we are not chiefly indebted to him, but rather for its first discovery to Fermat)"; this was a comment unjust to Hudde, who had provided an effective algorithm in place of Fermat's general method. Not enough of the subsequent correspondence remains to substantiate the rest of Wallis's story. He certainly also discussed maxima and minima in his correspondence (now largely vanished) with Schooten, who had mentioned Hudde's method to him before February, 1659 (*Œuvres Complètes*, II, 359–60).

4 See Letter 2066, note 6.

5 See Letter 2066, note 9. We have not been able to see a copy of the 1649 edition of Schooten's work, but have no reason to doubt that the passage correctly delimited by Wallis was indeed an addition to the second edition of 1659. In this, on p. 255, Schooten wrote: "And this is the way that Huygens took, I am sure, as he told me that he had himself sought the tangents to curved lines otherwise than Fermat by this same method."

6 This important passage begins (our translation): "But in truth as this line *CP* may also be investigated by another method, thanks to the method of maxima and minima discovered by the famous Mr. Fermat . . . which Hérigone illustrated by a few examples in his supplement to his *Cursus mathematicus*, and in the same place shows how it may also be applied to the finding of tangents . . ."

7 Schooten wrote (p. 256): One may expect from Hudde other methods of finding tangents and secants, maxima and minima, and many other things "for he has discovered so many and splendid things concerning these topics that I think no peer to him in the study of them can be discovered."

8 See Letter 2066, note 7.

9 See Letter 2058, note 1, and Vol. VIII, page 467, note 5.

10 "We forgive it and ask a like forgiveness in return."

2079

Wallis to Oldenburg

5 October 1672

From the original in Royal Society MS. W 2, no. 1

Oxford Octob. 5. 1672

Sir,

Hearing nothing from you by ye two last posts concerning what I sent you about the high-suspended Mercury;[1] I thought fit to send you this Addition thereunto, to be inserted toward ye Close of it next before ye last paragraph.[2]

As to that *Subtile Matter*, therefore, of M. *Hugens* (as likewise yt of *Des Cartes*) supposed to penetrate the Glasse, Quicksilver, & other Bodies: I do neither affirm, nor deny it, but only suspend my Assent till it be proved; & if it be proved, I admitt it. But admitting (without affirming) such to be; and admitting it allso to be Heavy or presing downwards (for else it makes nothing to ye present busyness:) I am not satisfied yt this Matter having free admission (though perhaps not equally free) as well above as below, should make this difference; since, whatever power it have, should equally operate (for ought I see) whether ye Quicksilver be or be not cleansed of common Air. And therefore the chieff (if not ye onely) thing which doth determine whether it can or cannot be suspended at such a hight, being this, whether it be or be not cleansed of common Air: It seemes to me most likely, yt ye cause of difference should be in that Air, on whose absence or presence it doth depend, whether ye Quicksilver do stand or fall & what therein should make ye difference I see nothing more likely than the Spring of it.

As to that of My Lo. Brounker, the case is somewhat different. For though he doth allso attribute ye effect to somewhat in ye external Air, which may give a further pressure than what is commonly observed in ye Torricellian Experiment: yet I do not remember that he doth expressely say whether it do or do not penetrate ye Glass.[3] And I think we may more easily give an account of it (and perhaps more sutable to his sense) if we say, it do not. Which I should thus do.

Our common Air, being an Aggregate of very Heterogeneous parts; we may well suppose some of them to be springy, & others not to be so. The

Springy parts, we may conceive to be so many consistent bodies, like small haires or springy threads, wrapped up in different formes, & variously entangled; so as to form many vacuities, capable of admitting (what other parts of ye Air may be supposed to be) some fluid matter, which may insinuate into those vacuities (as Water in bundle of Bones,) without disturbing ye texture of those springy parts. and which may press, as a Weight; but not, as a Spring.

Now if we suppose, in the Torricellian Tube, a quantity of such springy matter, the Spring hereof will be of equal strength with that of ye external Air, because admitted with such a tensure, (as I demonstrate Cap. 14 de Motu, prop. 12.) and therefore able to balance it. And this, though its weight be so much lesse than that which it doth counter balance; (as is there shewed, prop. 13.)

But if there be onely an Un-springy fluide, which presseth by its weight onely without ye assistance of a spring; and this defended, by ye Glasse-Tube, from any other pressure save that of its own weight: This will still be too weak to force its own way, till its own single weight be equivalent to that with which it is to incounter; and that is, not onely the Springy part of ye Ayr, but allso yt Fluid Un-springy part; which though (because fluid) it would give way to a springy body pressing through it; yet not to this fluide, like itself, & destitute of such a spring; & is therefore able to keep it suspended at a much greater hight than it could do if it were uncleansed of Springy Air; so long at least, as till some springy body be admitted, or some concussion equivalent to it, to put it in motion. But being once in motion, there must then be a positive equivalent force to stop it.

This difference, between such bodies as presse by their Spring, & such as press by their Weight onely, (the former of which may in a smaller quantity be as strong as in a greater; but not so ye latter;) you have there intimated Schol. prop. 11. pag. 729, 730. and Schol. prop. 13. pag. 732, 733. and may be of use in ye present inquiry: the ordinary effects commonly observed in the Torricellian Experiment, belonging chiefly to the Springy Air; not its Un-springy part.

That this cause assigned, may as well be applied to ye supporting of ye lower of two polished Marbles in ye Exhausted Receiver, (so as to hang to ye upper without falling, for want of a springy Body between, to thrust them asunder,) is obvious. But as to that of a Syphon continuing to run in the Receiver so exhausted; there seemes to be need (beside this) of some assistance from that little which remains of Springy Ayr.

On ye same ground I am apt to think (though I do not know that it hath been tryed) that Quicksilver thus cleansed, may remain suspended in a Tube inverted, not onely when ye open end is immerged in cleansed Quicksilver; but even if at lest immerged in water so cleansed: though not perhaps if left open to ye Common Air, because ye Air by reason [of] its spring will be apt to insinuate itself & disturb its rest. But of this, Experiment will be ye best Judge. These are my present thoughts &c.

Yrs,
John Wallis

ADDRESS
These
For Mr Henry Oldenburg
in the Palmal neare St
James's
London

POSTMARK FE 12

NOTES

1 Letter 2072.
2 In fact the whole paper was (as already noted) re-written before publication.
3 In the published version, it is stated: "But his Lordship (if I mistake not) though he allow his (Springy) Subtile matter to penetrate Glass . . ." The alteration suggests that Brouncker was consulted about what was said of his opinions in Wallis's letter and that changes were made in consequence (see *Phil. Trans.*, no. 91, 24 February 1672/3, 5166).

2080

Oldenburg to Hill

9 October 1672

Mentioned in Hill's reply, Letter 2192.

2081
Lister to Oldenburg
10 October 1672

From the original in Royal Society MS. L 5, no. 47
Partly printed in *Phil. Trans.*, no. 87 (14 October 1672), 5059–60

Yorke. Oct. 10th. 1672.

Sir

I had yours dated Sept. 30. You must excuse my passion for a person I loved as well as admired.[1] I assure you I reckon ye Correspondance I have wth you, an honour to me, & a great pleasure. The truth is, this summer has been a sorrowfull time wth me & I have not had ye hart & leisure to acquit my selfe, as I fully purposed, but I am not wholly negligent of ye commands of ye R.S. in ye meane time you must be content wth one thing for an other, & if you have not my papers about ye veines in plants, we will find out something else to entertain you wth, 'till they be in a readinesse.

We must correct as well as inlarge out Notes concerning Kermes:[2] & yet there will be much difficulty in resolving ye question concerning ye original & efficient of Kermes. These things are certain.

1. yt we have this year seen, ye very gumm of ye Apricock & Cherry-laurel trees transudated, at least, standing in a chrystal drop upon some (though very rarely) of ye topps of these Kermes.

2. yt they change colour from a yellow to a darke browne: yt they seem to be distended & to wax greater, & from soft, to become britle.

3. yt they are filled wth a sort of Mites; as well yt small powder (wch I said to be excrement) is mites as yt liquamen or softer pulp, (wch I tooke to be Bees meat) concerning both wch particulars I am pretty well assured by my owne & alsoe by my ingenious friend Dr Johnson of Pomfrets[3] more accurate Microscopical Observations.

4. yt ye Bee-grubbs actually feed on mites, there being noe other food for ym.

5. yt there are other species of Bees or Wasps besides those by me described; wch are sometimes found to make these Mites their food. Dr Johnson having opened one Huske, wth one only larg maggot in it.

6. yt there are probably different sorts of mites in these Huskes, making

possibly different species of Kermes; for some I have found to hold carnation coloured Mites, enclosed in a fine white cotton, ye whole Huske starting from ye Twigg, sriveling up, & serving only for a cap or cover to yt company of Mites. Other Mites I have seen white (& wch is most usuall) ye Huskes continuing intire & not coming away from ye Twigg they adhaere to, & but little cotton at ye bottom. Those of ye first sort are ye white Cobwebbs on ye Vine described by Mr Hooke (Micrograph. obs. 56.)[4]

7. yt ye sriveled cap to be found upon ye Mites enclosed in Cotton, as also ye whole Huske it selfe, if taken early in April while soft, will, dryed in ye Sun, srinke into ye very figure of Cochineil: whence we guesse yt Cochineil may be a sort of Kermes, taken thus early & sun-dried.

Hitherto this Summers notes concerning Kermes. This advantage at least we have by ym, yt ye account taken from Varney by Dr Croon & published in one of yr Transactions,[5] is made more intelligible. The small scarlet powder there mentioned being to be understood of those Mites, & they to be distinguished from ye Bee-grubbs, wch are changed into ye Skipping Fly, yt is, ye Bee (for kind at least) by us described formerly.

Concerning ye Epistle of Langelot, of wch you was pleased to send me an account. I am glad yt Chimists begin to be lesse misterious & speake common sense. I hope ye Vanitie & name of *Adepti* will in time be layed aside. ye Bishop of Chester was pleased to aske my opinion this summer concerning ye Spaw waters of this County & I am willing to entertain you wth my thoughts upon yt subject; but desire nothing of this nature from me may be made publick by ye presse for quiet sake. We have likewise an account ready for you of a certain Milke-yeilding Mushrome, wch I found plentifully in our Northern Alpes & wch has hitherto escaped ye diligence of our Botanists. I am wth as much earnestnesse & heat as ever

Your most humble servant
Martin Lister

ADDRESS
    To my honoured friend
    Henry Oldenburg Esqr
    at his house in ye Palmal
        London

POSTMARK OC 11

NOTES

Reply to Letter 2075.
1 Francis Willughby.
2 Compare Vol. VII, p. 523, and Vol. VIII, Letter 1703, on the "English Kermes." Dr. K. Boratynski of the Department of Zoology, Imperial College of Science and Technology, London, has kindly supplied the following entomological commentary on the content of this letter:

"*1*. These are certainly Scale Insects (Homoptera, Coccoidea) more precisely "brown scales" belonging to the family Coccidae. *Kermes* (= *Coccus*) *ilicis* L., the Mexican cochineal and Polish cochineal insects (*Dactylopius coccus* Costa and *Porphyrophora polonica* (L.)) belong to the same group but to different families (Kermococcidae, Dactylopiidae, and Margarodidae respectively).

"*2*. The "husks" are adult females, which after oviposition die, become dark brown, brittle but hard, and shelter the eggs deposited under their bodies.

"The "small powder" is the powdery waxy secretion produced by the females at oviposition preventing adhesion of the rather sticky eggs into lumps.

"The "mites" are the first instar nymphs (crawlers) which eventually crawl out from under the body of the mother and settle separately on twigs.

"The small "Bee-grubbs" are, no doubt, the larvae of small parasitic wasps (Hymenoptera: Aphelinidae or Encyrtidae) which feed internally on tissues of the female coccid and some also on eggs.

"The single "larg maggot" appears to be a predacious larva of a fly (Diptera, possibly *Leucopis* sp., family Chamaemyiidae) which are known to feed on eggs of some of these coccids.

"The "Chrystal drop" is the "honey dew," that is, excess of water and sugar exuded in drops by the fast growing adult females from the dorsally situated anal opening (a delicacy for ants).

"*3*. From Lister's descriptions it appears that he was dealing with at least three species:

a. *Parthenolecanium corni* (Bouché)—common, or plum brown scale. The female of this species is permanently attached to the twig of the host along the entire margin of the body and the crawlers are pale-yellowish or white. The females are rarely parasitized by the wasps (in Britain anyway) but if so usually only immature females are attacked and only one small parasitic larva within the body of the individual coccid can be found.

b. *Eulecanium coryli* (L.)—hazel nut scale. Generally as the above species but of more globular shape and the crawlers are pale-pinkish. Usually parasitized and often several (a dozen or more) larvae of the parasitic wasp may be found in one female.

c. *Pulvinaria vitis* (L.)—cushion scale of vine. At maturity the posterior end of the body of the female is lifted up, partly covering the comparatively large ovisac composed of cottony felted waxy threads; the crawlers are reddish-pink. This species is often attacked by internal hymenopterous parasites, as well as by the predacious, egg-feeding larvae of some flies. The eggs and a crawler of this species are illustrated by Hooke in his *Micrographia* on Pl. 36, Fig. 3: A & B and X, respectively, as Lister remarks.

"*4*. All three species may occur on Apricot (*Prunus armeniaca*) and Cherry-laurel (*Cerasus pseudocerasus*) grown in the open."
3 Pontefract, Yorkshire. Dr. Nathaniel Johnston (the usual spelling: 1627–1705) was evidently of Scots origin since he matriculated at St. Andrew's, but proceeded M.D.

from Cambridge (1656). He practised at Pontefract until 1687 when he moved to London and wrote Tory pamphlets. In the same year he was admitted F.C.P. He was a keen student of antiquities and natural history.

4 See Robert Hooke, *Micrographia* (London, 1665), pp. 215–16, and Plate 36. Hooke thought these scale insects to be the young of woodlice.

5 See *Phil. Trans.*, no. 20 (17 December 1666), 362–63. "Monsieur Verny" is there identified only as "a French Apothecary at Montpellier."

2082

Oldenburg to Hecker

10 October 1672

From the draft in Royal Society MS. O 2, no. 96

Clarissimo Viro
Domino Johanni Heckero Astronomo Dantiscano
H. Oldenburg Salutem

Cum Caetus suos publicos, quos per tres quatuorve menses ob alia Sociorum complurium negotia, quotannis intermittere consuevit, necdum instauraverit Regia Societas, non licuit hactenus epistolam tuam, X Calend. Octob. ad me scriptam, tui erga Ipsam affectus et studii testem uberrimam, exhibere.[1] Quod factum cum fuerit, quantocius sine dubio in mandatis mihi dabit, ut gratis pro eximia tua in Ipsam voluntate Tibi rescriptis, de singulari sua in Te benevolentia certum Te reddam.

Caeterum, scriptum illud Tuum, Admonitionis instar emissum ad Astronomos de Mercurii in solem incursu observando, quod ais Te simul litteris tuis ad me datis Societati nostrae offerre, nusquam hactenus apparet,[2] quod sane anxios nos reddit, quid factum de eo fuerit, dubiosque, an per oblivionem forte epistolae non inserueris, an vero per mare ad mercatorem aliquem Londinensem transmiseris. Pervelim igitur prima occasione, dubium hoc nobis eximere ne graveris.

Accepi Parisii, Clarissimum Dominum Cassinim Nizzam profecturum, egregiis instrumentis Astronomicis instructum, ut liberioribus inibi observationibus indulgeat.[3] Idem suam de Jovis et jovialium Systemate Dissertationem pronuper nobis communicavit, ubi videre est, in quas angustias studium ipsius observationes suas cum Galilaei observationibus conciliandi eum conjecerit, quidque illius authoritati, quidque pactae sua cura evidentiae tribuerit.[4]

Putem, Diatribam hanc cum aliis Viri Docti observatis brevi proditura, Tychonianis Observationibus, ex Autographo Danico Lutetiae Parisiorum correcte edendis subjungendam.

Prodere nuper ex Typographia Londinensi jeremiae Horroccii Opera Posthuma, vid. Astronomia Kepleriana defensa et promota: Excerpta ex Epistolis ad Crabtraeum suum: Observationum Caelestium Catalogus: Lunae Theoria nova. Quibus accessere Guil. Crabtraei Observationes Caelestes; et Johannis Flamstedii de Temporis Aequatione Diatriba, atque ad Horroccianam Lunae Theoriam Numeri.[5]

Non dubito, quin Bibliopolae nostrae, quam primum tute poterunt, hujus libri Exemplaria Dantiscum, inter alia loca sint transmissuri. Vale, Vir Clarissime, et Tui studiosissimo Fave. Dabam Londini d. 10. Oct. 1672.

TRANSLATION

H. Oldenburg greets the very famous Mr. Johannes Hecker, Astronomer of Danzig

As the Royal Society has not yet resumed its ordinary meetings, which it usually interrupts each year for three or four months because of the other concerns of many of its Fellows, I have not yet been able to present to it your letter to me of 12 September as an eloquent witness to your goodwill and devotion towards the Society.[1] When I have done so no doubt I shall at once be instructed to reply to you with thanks for your extraordinary concern and with assurance of the Society's singular good feeling towards yourself.

Further, that paper of yours, published as a piece of advice to astronomers about observing the transit of Mercury across the Sun, which (you write) you are offering to our Society along with the letter addressed to myself, has turned up nowhere as yet;[2] which makes us anxious to know what has become of it and doubtful whether perhaps by forgetfulness it was not enclosed with the letter, or whether you have in fact sent it to some London merchant by sea. I urgently beg that you will at the first opportunity, therefore, be so good as to put an end to our doubts.

I have heard from Paris that the famous Mr. Cassini is to set out for Nice provided with excellent astronomical instruments in order to engage more freely in observations there.[3] He has recently imparted his essay on Jupiter and Jupiter's system to us, in which one may see into what perplexities his investigations have driven him, for the sake of reconciling his observations with those of Galileo, and where it has seemed proper to rely on Galileo's authority and where to rely on the evidence accumulated by himself.[4]

I think that this essay will soon be published along with other things observed by that learned man as an appendix to the observations of Tycho, which are to be issued at Paris correctly printed from the Danish autograph manuscript.

There lately came from the press here in London the *Opera posthuma* of Jeremiah Horrox, namely: the Keplerian astronomy defended and promoted; extracts from letters to his [friend] Crabtree; a catalogue of celestial observations; a new theory of the moon. To which are added the celestial observations of William Crabtree, and John Flamsteed's essay on the equation of time and [his] numbers [to fit] Horrox's theory of the moon.[5]

I have no doubt that as soon as they can with safety do so our booksellers will send copies of this book to Danzig, as well as to other places. Farewell, famous Sir, and cherish him who is most zealous for you. London, 10 October 1672.

NOTES

Reply to Letter 2062.
1 This was done on 13 November 1672 (the Society having resumed its meetings on 30 October).
2 It had not yet arrived on 13 November.
3 Although Cassini won fame as a professor of mathematics at Bologna, he was born near the city of Nice—then in the territory of the Dukes of Savoy. This rumor seems to be false.
4 Compare Letter 1195, whence this sentence was taken.
5 The preparation of this volume and Flamsteed's share in it have been mentioned many times before. Oldenburg gives here the full subtitle (in not quite identical words). The book was reviewed in *Phil. Trans.*, no. 87 (14 October 1672), 5078–79. Hence it was presumably put on sale in September.

2083
Hevelius to Oldenburg

19 October 1672

From the original in Royal Society MS. H 2, no. 32

Illustri Viro
Domino Henrico Oldenburgio
Illustrissimae Regiae Societatis Secretario
J. Hevelius Salutem

Quod commercium literarium consuetum hactenus aliquantisper segnius, quam decuit, Tecum exercuerim, partim, ut scis, molestissimis, gravissimisque quibusdam occupationibus, partim gravissimo morbo, quo hucusque charissima coniux conflictata est, adscribendum habes.[1] Quare non dubito, quin Tu pro eo, quo me nunquam non prosequeris affectu benevolo facile me hac in parte excusatum habeas. Ut autem nunc aliquanto plenius ad ternas Tuas mihi multo gratissimas literas, die videlicet 18 Martij, 5 Julij, et 16 Augusti datas respondeam; primo gratias iterum iterumque Tibi ago maximas, pro transmissis quibusdam libris, inprimis gratissimo munere Cl. Wallisij, quem meo nomine humanissime Salutes, Eique rursus officiola mea debite offeras rogo. Pro communicatis binis illis novis inventionibus Morelandi et Newtonij plurimum quoque Tibi debeo; inventa ista sane perplacuerunt: quanquam tantum otij hucusque nondum concessum fuerit, ut ipse illius rei fecerim experimenta. Ad posteriorem inventionem puto aliquid minimum contribuisse polemoscopium nostrum, ex binis Speculis totidemque lentibus anno 1673 constructum.[2] Nam iam eo tempore bene perspexi, Tubos ex speculis compositos notabiliter posse abbreviari: prout ex nostra Selenographia pag. 27 perspicies. De illis quae Parisienses de Saturni phasibus ut et de nupero Cometa in lucem emiserunt nihil quicquam mihi communicarunt, nec ad meas literas 7 Octobris anni praeteriti datas, tam Celeberrimus Cassinus, quam Praeclarissimus Picardus respondere dignati sunt. Ego illis necdum adstipulari possum, Saturnum omnino rotundum revera extitisse; concedo tamen illis ita apparuisse; sed Tubo breviori 17 vel 20 pedum, tum Saturno in crepusculo existente. Nuper die videlicet 19 Octobris, cum citius ob aeris summam iniuriam fieri nequiverit, eius faciem Tubo 55 ped. contemplatus sum, annulo fere adhuc tenuior apparuit quam anno praeterito, prout ex adiuncto Schemate videbitis [*see the figure, p. 289*]. Telescopium vero nostrum 140 pedum Coelo adhibere nondum licuit: ab aliquot enim mensibus continue fere aerem habuimus nubilosum, et frequentissimas pluvias. Cl. Picardus quid in Dania peregerit necdum rescivi; nisi quod observationes Tychonicas manuscriptas ex dania Parisios transtulerit: ea forte gratia, ut ibidem imprimentur: utinam Tychonis residua opera omnia cum Epistolis simul lucem adspiciant! Fasciculum illum librorum, quem mihi navi quadam transmissisti, nondum quidem accepi; brevi tamen illum me accepturum spero. Nuper Plenipotentiarium aliquem Nob. dominus Nixdorfium, Regis nostri Secretarium ad Vos misimus ratione illarum navium a Scotis detentarum, quem Tibi nunc denuo optimis modis commendo, ut et totum istud negotium; ne quicquam intermittas, vel promotione, intercessione, vel valida tua commendatione, quod eo spectare videbitur, vehementer rogo; ego rursus nunquam non contendam, ut paribus gratissimis officijs Tuam benevolentiam demereri nonnequeam. De reliquo in suscepto nostro Siderali negotio assidue et strenue pergo: Machina Coelestis, ut iam Vobis innotuit, sub praelo fervet, proximo anno Pars prior, nimirum Organographia deo annuente in lucem prodibit. Hactenus parum admodum, exceptis illis nostris consuetis Planetarum Fixarumque observationibus, in coelo a nobis observatum est, quod Vestrum scire magnopere intersit: nisi quod stella illa nova sub capite Cygni hoc anno haud affulserit; altera vero in Collo Cygni hac aestate ad finem usque Mensis Septembris clarissime apparuit.[3] De Eclipsi Solis quid obtinuerim, Spero Te ex literis meis posterioribus die 16 Septembris ac per Nob. dominum Nixdorfium translatis iam accepisse. Apud Vos vero sine dubio plura hactenus impetrata fuere, quae avidissime una cum Eruditorum Vestrorum Ephemeridibus, tum alijs quibusdam operibus, si quae prodierint, exspecto. Inprimis obnixe peto, ne obliviscetis instrumentulum illud Tubo inserendum, iam dudum promissum, pro distantijs minoribus capiendis transmittere;[4] maxime me iterum iterumque devincietis. Vale Vir honorande memor nostri; et saluta totam Illust. Regiam nostram Societatem, Cui, profiteor me esse cupidissime deditum. Dabam Gedani Anno 1672 die 29 Octobris st. n.

Saturnus observatus
Telescopio 55. pedum
Anno 1672, die 19 Octobris Gedani in
27° ♓ , et Maxima Latitudine Meridiana

TRANSLATION

J. Hevelius greets the illustrious Mr. Henry Oldenburg, Secretary of the most illustrious Royal Society

You must attribute the fact that I am somewhat later than would be fitting in conducting our customary correspondence partly to certain very troublesome and serious affairs that you know of, and partly to a very serious illness from which my very dear wife has been suffering up to the present time.[1] On which account I have no doubt you will easily forgive me as to this point, with the warm goodwill you have ever bestowed upon me. But now in order to reply rather more fully to your three letters, most welcome to me, namely those dated 18 March, 5 July, and 16 August: in the first place I return you repeated and warmest thanks for sending me some books and especially for the very welcome gift of the famous Wallis, whom I beg you to greet most courteously on my behalf and to offer him in exchange my little services. I am also much indebted to you for the communication of those two new inventions made by Morland and Newton; those inventions are indeed most satisfactory though I have not yet enjoyed sufficient leisure to make any experiments upon them myself. I think that my polemoscope, likewise constructed with two mirrors in 1637,[2] has contributed some small trifle to the latter invention. For I perceived very plainly at that time that [telescope] tubes containing mirrors could be shortened to a notable extent, as you may see from my *Selenographia*, p. 27. The Parisians have communicated nothing at all to me of what they have published regarding Saturn's phases and the recent comet, nor have either the celebrated Cassini or the most famous Picard seen fit to reply to my letter of 7 October last year. I cannot yet agree with them that Saturn is really quite round; I admit that he appeared so to them, but [only] with a rather short telescope of seventeen or twenty feet, Saturn being then in the twilight. Lately, namely on 19 October, for I could not do it before because of the extremely harmful condition of the air, I studied his appearance through a tube of 55 feet, and his ring appeared even thinner than last year as you will see from the annexed figure [*see the figure, p. 289*]. Indeed I have not yet been able to direct my telescope of 140 feet to the sky, for we have had an almost continually cloudy atmosphere during the last few months, and very frequent showers. I have not yet learned what the famous Picard achieved in Denmark, except that he has conveyed the manuscript observations of Tycho from Denmark to Paris, perhaps so that they may be printed there. Would that the remainder of Tycho's works and his correspondence might all see the light at the same time! I have still not yet received that package of books which you sent me by sea; yet I hope I shall receive it soon. We recently sent to you as a plenipotentiary a certain person, the noble Mr. Nixdorf, secretary to our King, on account of those ships detained by the Scots, whom I commend to you again in the highest terms, as I do that whole affair; I most urgently beseech you to spare no effort by way of assistance, intercession, or your powerful support as far as he seems to be concerned. In return I shall never fail to strive not to be undeserving of your kindness by performing similar welcome services. For the rest, I continue unceasingly and vigorously with the astronomical pursuits that I have undertaken; as you know already, *Machina coelestis* is in press and with God's grace Part I, that is the description of the instruments, will appear next year. Hitherto we have observed very little in the heavens that is of much interest to you apart from our routine observations of the planets and the fixed stars, except that that new star under the head of Cygnus hardly shone at all this year; the other one, in the neck of Cygnus, appeared very clearly this summer up to the end of September.[3] What I could collect from the eclipse of the sun you will, I hope, already have received in my last letter of 16 September brought to you by the noble Mr. Nixdorf. No doubt many things have been accomplished so far among yourselves, which I eagerly look forward to, together with the *Transactions* of your learned men and some other publications, if any have appeared. And especially I ask you earnestly not to forget to send that little instrument to be inserted into a [telescope] tube, for measuring small distances, that was promised long ago;[4] again and again you will increase my great obligations to you. Farewell, honored Sir, be mindful of me and greet the whole of our Royal Society, to whom I acknowledge myself most passionately devoted. Danzig, 29 October 1672, N.S.

Saturn observed on 19 October 1672 [N.S.] at
Danzig, with a telescope of 55 feet, when in
27° of Pisces and maximum south latitude

[*For the figure, see page 289*]

NOTES

Second reply to Letters 1924 (Vol. VIII), 2013, and 2050.

1 Hevelius' second and young wife, Catherina Elizabetha Koopman, whom he had married in 1663, was a learned woman. She became his assistant both in observation and in computation and is twice depicted in *Machina coelestis* observing with her hus-

band. The letter probably refers to an attack of smallpox that she is known to have suffered.

2 See Vol. II, p. 189, note 11.

3 See Vol. VIII, p. 570, and Vol. VII, *passim*.

4 Hevelius first requested this micrometer in 1668 (see Vol. V, p. 187); it had been mentioned at intervals by both Oldenburg and Hevelius ever since. See Vols. VII and VIII index s.v. Instruments, micrometer.

2084
Lister to Oldenburg
23 October 1672
From the original in Royal Society MS. L 5, no. 48

Sir

To acquit my selfe & to take away all suspition of a sloe & lingering Correspondance, I have enclosed yis Paper[1] wch is, indeed, a Table cutt in two parts & wch I had noe thoughts of parting wth, untill ye whole had been finished: but to show you, yt you may have any thing from me & yt I am a sure druge for Philosophy, I send you this; wch subsists well enough of it selfe, & yet it had been better, if what is promised in ye Title, had been there too; but for ye reasons alledged it cannot be; only it may incite others to assist & be fellow labourers wth us.

I had sent you ye other Papers promised in my last,[2] but yt ye one concerning ye Mushrome is sent to Mr Ray for his perusal;[3] wch when it shall be returned me I will not fail to communicate to you. I am Sir

Your most humble servant
Martin Lister

Yorke Oct: 23d 1672

I shall take care to returne speedily my annual Contribution.[4]

ADDRESS
     These
For his ever honoured friend
Henry Oldenburgh
Esq at his house in
ye Palmal
          London

                         POSTMARK OC 25

NOTES

1 See Letter 2085.
2 Letter 2081.
3 Lister's letter to Ray on mushrooms, dated 12 October 1672, is printed in *Philosophical Letters*, pp. 111–13; it is virtually identical with what Lister sent Oldenburg in Letter 2096.
4 I.e., his subscription as F.R.S.

2085
Lister to Oldenburg
23 October 1672

From the copy in Royal Society Letter Book V, 351–53
Partially printed in *Phil. Trans.*, no. 105 (20 July 1674), 97–99

York Octob. 23. 1672

     Sr

I send you the first part of these Tables and the Queries belonging to them; reserving the sea-shells & shell-stones for an other time; the parts you have at present being at a stand with me, & the other encreasing upon my hands dayly; which though that be not a signe of perfection (for there is undoubtedly work for many ages) yet is it of good advancement & progresse; this other, of the copiousnesse of the subject. Again, in that part of the tables, you have from me at present, authors are but very little concerned, in the other of sea-shells and stone-like-shells there are many authowrs, which are to be consulted and taken in, if possibly wee can understand them treating of the same species. Lastly, the 2 lesse compleat draughts, being the remaining parts of these Tables, are much a kin, at least in most mens thoughts, & therefore ought to be most neerly examined and things largely & throughly handled, that the dispute may not always be depending; whether the rocks have not their own proper Animal-like-brood, different from the Sea.

Some generall Queries concerning Land & Fresh-water snailes.

1. whether there be other shell-snailes at land, than Turbinate?[1]

2. whether this kind of insect are truly androgyna and equally participate of both sexes, as Mr. Ray first observed;[2] and whether both of them two, which shall be found in the act of Venery, doe accordingly spawn or lay those perfectly round and clear eggs, soe frequently to be mett with in the surface of the earth, and the circumstances of those eggs hatching?

3. whether the way of fatting snailes, in use amongst ye Romans, that is, to make little paved places incompassed with a circle of water, be not alsoe very expedient in order to the tru noting ye manner of their Generation?

4. what light the Anatomy of this kind of insect may give to the rest, and for that purpose, which are the most convenient for size and plenty?

5. whether the black spotts observable in the hornes of some snailes are eyes, as some authors affirme; and not rather parts meerly equivalent to the *Antennae* of other insects; as the flat and exceeding thin shape of the hornes of other species of snailes seem to confirme.[3]

6. Whether the coccinea sanies,[4] some of our Water-snailes yeild, be not an excrement, rather than an extravasated blood (the vessel containing it being compared to the Heart (by Rondeletius, and the purple juice to blood),[5] that is, whether these Animals part not with and voluntarily (at least upon light provocation) ejaculate this liquor in their owne defence, as the Cuttle-fish doth its inke, & whether the feeding upon any peculiar herbe cause not a different coloured, as well as other ways qualified, *saliva* in any of them.

7. In what sort of snailes are the *stones*, mentioned by the Ancients, to be found; and whether they are not to be found (in such as yeild them) at all times of the yeare; and whether they are a cure for a Quartan, or have other reall vertue.

8. Whether stones found in snailes, their artificiall covers and shells will dissolve in Vinegar & with what circumstances.

9. what medicinall vertues snailes may have, as restorative to Hectik persons, highly venereall, at least the necks of them, if wee credit the Romans; & particularly C. Celsus commends them to be boni succi stomacho aptas &c.[6] Also enquire concerning the mechanicall uses of the saliva of these Animals, as in dying, in the whitening of wax, Haire &c.

Tabulae Cochlearum Angliae tum terrestrium, fluviatiliumque, tum marinarum, quibus accedunt lapides ad Cochlearum similitudinem atque alias vel suo modo figurati[7]

Cochleae Terrestres testis intectae

  Turbinatae

    breviore figura. Numero V.

      1. Cochlea cinerea maxima edulis, cujus os operculo gypseo per hyemem tegitur, agri Hardfordiensis.[8]

      2. Cochlea cinerea striata, operculo testaceo Cochleato donata.

      3. Cochlea et colore et fascijs multa varietate ludens.[9]

      4. Cochlea altera subflava, maculata atque unica fascia castanei coloris per medium voluminis insignita.

      5. Cochlea vulgaris major, hortensis, maculata et fasciata.[10]

    longiore figura

    ad sinistram convoluta. N.IV.

      6. Buccinum[11] exiguum, retusum, in musco degens.[12]

      7. Buccinum alterum parvum, acutum, ibidem vivens.

      8. Buccinum rupium, in minimis numerandum circiter senis orbibus protractum.[13]

      9. Buccinum sive Trochilus sylvaticus agri Lincolniensis.[14]

    ad dextram. N. II.

      10. Buccinum pullum ore compresso, circiter denis spiris fastigiatum.

      11. Buccinum alterum pellucidum, subflavum, intra senos fere orbes mucronatum.

    depressae. N. II.

      12. Cochlea cinerea fasciata, Ericetorum.

      13. Cochlea altera pulla Sylvestris, Voluminibus in aciem depressis.[15]

Cochleae Terrestris nudae, limaces dictae.

      14. Limax maximus striatus et maculatus, lapillo sive ossiculo insigni donatus.[16]

      15. Limax parvus cinereus, pratensis.[17]

      16. Limax ater.[18]

Cochleae Fluviatiles Turbinatae

  Cochleae N.I.

      17. Cochlea fasciata. ore ad amussimum rotundo, fluvij Cam.[19]

Buccina N.V.[20]

    18. Buccinum subflavum, pellucidum, intra tres spiras terminatum.

    19. Buccinum alterum pellucidum majus, 4 spirarum.

    20. Buccinum 5 spirarum plenarum, mucrone obtuso.

    21. Buccinum alterum 5 spirarum atque operculo testaceo cochleato.

    22. Buccinum longum 6 spirarum, in tenue acumen ex amplissima basi productum.[21]

depressa testa, Coccum fundentes. N. III.

    23. Cochlea ex utraque parte Cava, plenis voluminibus.

    24. Cochlea altera parte plana, et limbo donata, 4 circumvolutionum.[22]

    25. Cochlea altera parte plana, sine limbo, 5 circumvolutionum.

Cochleae Fluviatiles Bivalvae. N. II.

    26. Musculus fluviatilis, maximus.[23]

    27. Musculus alter parvus, sive concha rotunda lacustris.[24]

Cochleae Marinae &c.

TRANSLATION

.   .   .   .

Tables of the land, freshwater, and marine snails of England, to which are added the stones formed in the likeness of snails and other things or in their own way.[7]

Land snails covered with shells

  of spiral form

    of shorter length, five kinds:

      1. The largest edible grey snail, whose mouth is coated over with a calcareous cover in winter; in the fields of Hertfordshire.[8]

      2. The striped grey snail having a spiral shell cover.

      3. The snail displaying great variety of color and banding.[9]

      4. Another yellowish snail, spotted, and marked with a single chestnut-colored band round its middle.

      5. The common large garden snail, spotted and banded.[10]

  of greater length

    convoluted to the left, four kinds:

      6. The slender, blunt *buccinum*[11] living in moss.[12]

      7. The small, sharp *buccinum* living in the same habitat.

8. The *buccinum* of rocks, to be reckoned among the smallest, extended into about six whorls.[13]

9. The *buccinum* or woodland trochlear snail from the fields of Lincolnshire.[14]

convoluted to the right, two kinds:

10. The dark-grey *buccinum* with a narrow mouth, banded with about ten whorls.

11. Another clear yellowish *buccinum*, [being] pointed among about six whorls.

depressed [*or*, compressed], two kinds:

12. The banded grey snail of heathlands.

13. Another dark-grey woodland snail, with rings squeezed into sharp edges.[15]

Land snails without shells, called slugs

14. The largest striped and spotted slug, having a remarkable little stone, or bone.[16]

15. The small grey slug of meadows.[17]

16. The black slug.[18]

Spiral river snails

snails, one kind:

17. The banded snail, having a perfectly round mouth. River Cam.[19]

buccina, five kinds:[20]

18. The clear, yellowish *buccinum*, terminated in three whorls.

19. Another larger, clear *buccinum*, having four whorls.

20. The *buccinum* of five full whorls, having a blunt apex.

21. Another *buccinum* of five whorls, with a spiral cover of shell.

22. The long *buccinum* of six whorls, extending from a wide base to a fine apex.[21]

with depressed shells bearing a protuberance, three kinds:

23. The snail hollow on either side, with full rings.

24. The snail flat on one side, of four turns, and having a border to it.[22]

25. The snail flat on one side without a border, of five turns.

Bivalve river shellfish, two kinds:

26. The largest freshwater mussel.[23]

27. The other little mussel, or round pond shell.[24]

Marine shellfish, etc.

NOTES

The queries and table were finally published as having been sent with his letter of 12 March 1673/4 (Vol. X); the printed version has various slight emendations, especially in the Tables. This is the first appearance of the work that was to prove Lister's major contribution to science: "By general acclaim Lister is the originator of British conchology" (F. J. Cole, *History of Comparative Anatomy*, London, 1949, p. 231). In 1694 Lister published a large work on the subject, *Exercitatio anatomica, in qua maxima agitur de buccinis fluviatilibus et marinis*, whose production cost him £2000.

1 *Turbinate* may describe either a conical or a spiral form, or a combination of the two. Lister presumably means: are there any snails whose shells are not convoluted? It is noteworthy that he correctly links the slugs with the shelled snails, while excluding other creatures provided with shells or carapaces but not of the same morphological character.

2 Hermaphroditism in snails and slugs was first remarked on by Ray in his notes on *Atropa belladonna* (*Catalogus plantarum circa Cantabrigiam nascentium*, Cambridge, 1660, 156–58; see Raven, *Ray*, 101).

3 Lister was, of course, mistaken in entertaining this doubt; gastropods have well-developed eyes.

4 "scarlet serum." It is difficult to know exactly what is meant here; but see the next note.

5 Guillaume Rondelet, in *Universae aquatilium pars altera* (Lyons, 1555), p. 71, in describing what he calls *Purpura* (not *Murex*), refers to the pigment contained in an organ which, he thinks, corresponds to the heart though, as he says, these creatures do not have the organs proper to mammals. Rondelet does *not* say that the purple juice is blood.

6 See *De re medica*, Book II, Chapters XX, XXIV.

7 Lister enumerates here only a few of the large number of British snails and slugs, either because he had not as yet collected or examined many or because he did not yet wish to draw fine distinctions. It is not possible to identify all Lister's types precisely, since some of his descriptions are vague and others possibly refer to variant forms of the same species. However, Lister has observed examples of the principal British groups.

8 *Helix pomatia* L., the Roman snail.

9 This and the next are *Cepaea* spp., one of them presumably being *C. nemoralis* L.

10 *H. aspersa* Mull.

11 Literally, "whelk," and so any snail of an elongated, whelklike form. The British Clausilacea are typically sinistrous, though most other snails are dextrous.

12 This may well be *Clausilia rolphii* Leach and the next *C. rugosa* (Drap.).

13 Probably *Balea perversa* (L.)

14 Possibly *Marpessa laminata* (Mont.)

15 Probably *Helicigona lapicida* (L.)

16 *Limax maximus* L. It is noteworthy that Lister has observed the reduced shell in this creature, only discoverable by dissection.

17 *Arion* spp.

18 *Arion ater* (L.)

19 *Viviparus* spp.

20 All these are species of Lymnacea.

21 Probably *Lymnaea stagnalis* (L.)

22 This is pretty clearly *Planorbis carinatus* Mull. and probably these are all members of this genus; the next may be *P. planorbis* (L.).

23 *Anodonta cygnaea* (L.)

24 *Sphaericum* or *Pisiduum*

2086

Wittie to Oldenburg

23 October 1672

From the original in B.M. MS. Add. 4432, no. 18

Hon'd Sir

Being lately in discourse with some Learned Gentlemen about the Usefulnes of Naturall & Medicinall Observations, I had Occasion to produce some of my own, & among others of a Country woman in this County of York that brought forth an Hermaphrodite, & after that another strange Birth, the draught whereof has laid by me 12 or 13 years; The Circumstances whereof appeared to them so full of Curiosity, that they prevailed with me for a promisse to communicate it to you, which if you deem it worthy of your Knowledge & acceptance, I have my reward.[1]

But perhaps you might rather have expected from me an Answere to a Book lately printed entituled (a new years gift for Dr. W.)[2] wch was dedicated to the Royal Society.—Sir, though I designe no formall Answere,[3] yet I judge it necessary to say something for your Satisfaction, & who else you thinke fit, in reference to that Book, which some wise men think was rather made at the Midsummer Moon. The Dedication is that wherin at this day the pretended Authour therof most prides himself, as having thereby got some advantage.—I was certainly before him in my Appeal to those Noble Patriots about the same Subject, to wit, Scarbrough Spaw, when I presented them with the Extracts & Spirits which I had drawn from that Water, which you were pleased to mention with my Letter in N. 60 of your Phil. Trans.[4] And those alone reviewed may serve (I think) as a sufficient Confutation of what is pretended to by this Authour about the Principles of the Spring, while he denies Iron & its Vitriol.

It is indeed against my Promisse & Declared Resolution to trouble my self or the world with any peculiar Tract in reference to that Authour, which gave Occasion to him to take more Liberty then a Sober & good man ought to have done. Such also are the Circumstances of that Piece, that my Answere must have been very short, if not also too tart, even as that of the Preacher that in a word confuted Bellarmine.[5] For

1. He is not the right Authour that sets his name to it, as I am most credibly informed by severall Observant Persons. The Different Stile of the two Books[6] may also convince any man of this truth.

2. He answeres not my Arguments save only in denying my Conclusions without regard had to the Premisses only Magisterially asserting what before he had said to which I had made a reply, which in the Judgment of unbiassed Readers may very well suffice for the latter Book.

3. I am not skilled in the Billingsgate Dialect in which that Book is writ, wch all Generous Spirits disrelish as both unreasonable & unchristian, while he had not the least Provacation from me, allowing me a liberty to dispute with him in defence of truth.

4. That Book is a Narrative of matters of fact that are not so proper for an Argumentative debate, as to be examined by Experiment, & Testimony of such as are concerned, He affirmes in point of Experiment that Alome Stone gives a black Tincture to spring water with Gall; & thence inferres that the black Tincture which Scarb[rough] Water takes with Gall, is from Alome, & therefore it has no Vitriol or Iron.[7] This is the Basis of all his discourse in both those Books, against my declared Principles of that Spring.—

Sir, I shall wave his Consequence at this time, & do refer the Tryall of the Experiment to your own Eye, having sent you herewith[8] some of that wherein we are all agreed, That it is the Alome stone, which I took from the Cliffe neer the Well, of which there are 100 Loads which lyes like flags intermixt with the Earth. If you please to bruise some of it, & lye it in water to be infused more or lesse time, or use it any other way, you will not find that the water takes a black Tincture with Gall. And the same I assert concerning all that body of Alome stone that is in that Bank, excepting only where it lyes in one or 2 places in a Vitrioline bed, which yet I can cover with my hands, where the vitrioline salt breaks out of the Earth of the Colour of Ochre. If you please calcine it also, & then try whether the Gall will strike a black Colour in the water wherin you infuse it, wch has sometimes been disputed among us, & I was alwayes in the negative.

In his Enumeration of particular Persons who had drunk of that Water, he tells of severall that fell into fits of the stone, either while they drank of the water or soon after, & voyded stones, while they never had felt any Symptome of the stone before. Quaere whether that was a fault in the water or no? He traversed the Country to enquire if any man had any sort of ill fit after he had drunk of that water, & if he heard of any, he reports it with advantage, & thereupon will perswade that is a dangerous water.— Truly it works no miracles, though excellent cures are done by it, & men may be ill again after the drinking of it, as well as after any other Processe in Physick. Nor yet does it sute every Case, or Constitution. But might not

a man at the same rate condemne all sorts of Medicines & Meats too, because some stomachs disgust them, or ill fits have ensued after them?

I am certaine he has mentioned those stories without the Consent of
the Persons, yea & with the abhorancy of most of them, as such of them
whome I know have said such to me & others, & some whome I know not
have sent me word. And I think it were no hard task for me to make it out
concerning all of them that are Persons of Quality, or any Reputation.

As for those 2. Stories which I was forced to relate concerning the Ld
E. & that of consulting me about his wife &c. the former wherof he denies
Verbo Medici;⁹ & the latter he shuffles off unthankfully enough—I do
humbly appeale to God, & then to his own Conscience concerning the
truth of what I assert in my Book: though for the latter I have also an
Honest & Learned Gentleman to witnes with me, vid. Mr James Duncan-
son a Scots Minister, who abhors a false report.

This being the Case, I suppose no man can expect that I should concern
my self with that pretended Authour or his Book, but Leave it to Divine
Providence & wise men Reason to judge betwixt us. I now proceed to
what I first propounded.

York. Wednesday Oct. 23.

Mulier quaedam Rustica de Wetwang in Comitatu Eboracensi annorum
35, per Quadriennium Maniaca, et ex quorundam Opinione Daemonica,
gravida facta Animalcula quinque monstrosa tandem enixa est, Catulorum
formam aliquantulum ferentia: Capita autem habebant paulo latiora
magisque depressa, crura breviora, cutes lanugine fusca hic et illic colore
luteo maculata obtectas, cum Caudis tanquam in Pisces desinentibus. Visa
erant a Ministro ejusdem Villae (mihi satis noto) viro probo ac fide digno,
ab Obstrice alijsque mulieribus veritatem Historiae praedicantibus, a
quibus accepi. Non sine Sanguine et dolore monstrosos hos foetus peperit
infelix Mater, per Triduum ob dolorem uterinum ejulans, quos tamen in
partu strangulavit, et Lintea lochijs defoedata e fenestra praetereuntibus
insaniens exposuit publice. Unde vero conceperat dubitatur; an ex intem-
pestivo congressu cum Marito; vel impura alicujus Bestiae mixtura; vel
Damnati Spiritus conjunctione, quem ut fertur se compressisse asseruit
Maniaca sub humana Specie, quocum ait saepe se pictus lusisse chartis; vel
ex justo dei judicio (quod magis credo) cum Voluntatem divinam impa-
tienter tulisset, sceleste murmurando et blasphemando quod partum alijs
dissimilem non ita pridem enixa esset.—Nam ista ante sex Annos Her-
maphroditem pepererat, jam domi suae superstitem, inter femellas habitum,

in Cujus imo ventre conspicitur rima pudendi muliebris speciem perfecte ferens primo intuitu, quae tamen a penitiori investigatione imperforata deprehenditur, vaginam uteri non habens: Ex cujus rimae superiori parte prominet Penis, ad longitudinem extremae pollicis juncturae, et ad medij mej digiti crassitudinem, attamen sine scroto et testiculis. Praeputium habet perbrevi, extremitatem glandis vix attingens. Meatus Urinae excretionj dicatus in loco freni collocatur, non in fine glandis [Qualis apud veteres Graecos Hypospadiaeus vocatur] adeo ut parte pendula retro semper mingat, sicut ipsa Mater (remedijs a me ei adhibitis ad se jam redacta) explanabat, dum Filiolum mihi in praesentia Obstetricis ut observarem denudabat. Hoc non satis animadvertentes Mulierculae nativitati Ejus adstantes, in dijudicatione Sexus erravere, et Infans Elizabethae Nomine baptizabatur, atque etiamnum pro femella habetur, Rusticorum more adblandientium Bessa vocatur.

Sed Bessus Votum solvit, quod Bessa vovebat.

Praeterea quod visu rarum est in Puerulo sex Annorum, Natura quasi Erroris sui Paenitens has partes abscondit Pilis, eisque nigris ad triam granorum Nordej longitudinem delictum plorat.

This from Sir,

Your most humble servant
Rob. Wittie

ADDRESS
For the much Honoured
Henry Oldenburgh Esq
these   with a parcell of
London   Alome stones

SUMMARY

.   .   .   .

A certain countrywoman of Wetwang in Yorkshire, aged thirty-five, who had been insane for four years and in the opinion of some was possessed by the Devil, became pregnant and at length brought forth five monstrous creatures bearing some resemblance to puppies. They were seen by the minister of this same village, a man well known to myself, honest and trustworthy, by the midwife, and other women swearing to the truth of the tale, from whom I had it. The unhappy mother suffered much in the birth, and strangled the monsters. Whence they were conceived is doubtful, whether from some untimely union with her husband, or act of bestiality, or union with some damned spirit which the madwoman claimed had often lain with her in human form and with which (she says) she has often played cards, or else (as I prefer to believe) from the just judgment of God, since she was impatient with the divine will, complaining vilely and blaspheming because she had not long before given birth to an abnormal child. For she bore an hermaphrodite six years ago, still living in her house and treated as a female, possessing imperfect sexual organs of both male and female, as I saw for myself when I examined the little boy in the presence of the midwives. Because the goodwives who attended the birth of this infant did not pay enough attention to its male characteristics they erred in the judgment of its sex and baptized it Elizabeth; and it is still treated as female and called "Bess," as is the way of chattering country folk.

But what promised to be a *Bess*, had proved to be a *Bill*.

.   .   .   .

NOTES

1 The account is discreetly given in Latin at the close of the letter.
2 George Tonstall's attack was reviewed in *Phil. Trans.*, no. 85 (15 July 1672), 5019–21, where the date of publication is given as 1671; however the B.M. catalogue gives it as 1672.
3 In spite of this, Wittie published *Scarbroughs Spagyrical Anatomizer Dissected* at London in this same year.
4 Wittie's Letter 1440 (Vol. VI) was printed in *Phil. Trans.*, no. 60 (20 June 1670), 1074–82. Oldenburg mentioned "Mineral Waters, and Extracts made out of them" in the heading to the letter as printed.
5 Roberto Francesco Romolo Bellarmino (1542–1621) gained fame as a controversialist; his *Disputationes de controversiis christianae fidei adversus huius temporis haereticos* published between 1581 and 1593 produced a great many replies by Protestants, but we cannot identify Wittie's reference.
6 Tonstall also published *Scarbrough Spaw Spagyrically Anatomized* (London, 1670), which Oldenburg had reviewed at the same time as *A New-Year's-Gift for Dr Wittie*.
7 For Wittie's earlier concern with alum as an ingredient in this mineral water, see Letter 1440 (Vol. VI, esp. p. 611) and Letter 1478 (Vol. VII, p. 52).
8 This is possibly the material described by Grew; see *Musaeum*, p. 353.
9 "As the word of a doctor."

2087

Sivers to Oldenburg

25 October 1672

From the original in Royal Society MS. S 1, no. 121

Nobilissimo Doctissimo atque Clarissimo Viro
Domino HENRICO OLDENBURG, Societatis Regiae Anglicanae
membro primario
Henricus Syvers Salutem & Officium

Non est, Nobilissime Domine, cur ullam responsi tamdiu protelati excusationem offeras; cum satis superque notum esse possit, quantis animus tuus & quam multis occupationibus distineatur atque urgeatur. Quin mecum potius fuerit, taedium illud, quod, ut facile conjicio, responso meo experimentis nullis praegnanti sed sterili admodum affero, deprecari. Dabis sine dubio sterilitati huic veniam ob causas primis meis literis[1] expositas, quibus inter alias plures & haec accedit, quod totus in eo sum, ut Deo favente, (cujus gratiam opemque super hoc labore diu desiderato digne imploro,) opusculum illud Phoranomicum Jungij nostri ex scedulis ejus subinde auctum perficiam, illustratumque diagrammatis convenientibus publici tandem juris faciam.

Mense quidem Augusto proxime praeterlapso Eclipsin illam Solarem 12mi diei observaturi eramus; sed nubium iniquitas accuratam observationem prohibebat.[2] Animadvertimus tamen errorem Calendariographorum nostrorum non exiguum; cum initium ejus Eclipseos, quod asscripserant horae circiter 4tae, hora demum 6ta appareret. Tribus tantum civibus solem obscuratum, (qui imminente sexta omnino liber adhuc erat) inspicere licuit, et primum quidem uno quadrante post 6tam: deinde paulo post sesquiquadrantem; et postremum ad mediam 7mam, uti ex diagrammate, quod, si placet, addo, videre est [*see the figure, p. 304*].

Perjucundum sane mihi est illud Nobilissimi Domini Judicium de Logica nostra Jungij.[3] Cui proinde gratulor, quod, cum hic ob plerorumque inscitiam nonnullorum etiam invidiam, conculcata quasi jaciat, alibi saniores mentes reperiat, quae illam erigere et debita dignitate ornare non dubitant. Quid? Si clarissimus Fogelius commentariolum, dudum promissum, de praestantia hujus Logicae prae reliquis, edat? Tractatum illum, cui titulus *L'Art de penser*, perlegi.[4] Non adeo displicet, cum ejus Auctor

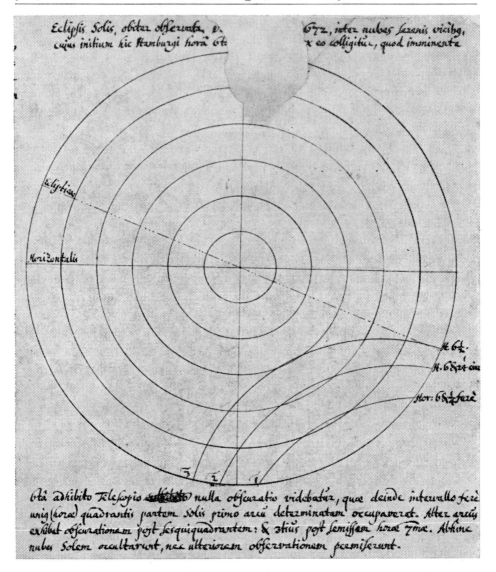

verae philosophiae studiosus a vulgaris littore non parum recedere ausus
sit. Alterum a Domini du Hamel videre nondum contigit.[5] Copiam ejus
desidero, & quamprimum illum Bibliopolae nostri obtinuerint, comparabo
eundem mihi, ut et hujus laudata sententia atque sapientia nobis hic loci
innotescat.

Transactiones vestras philosophicas apud Dominum Fogelium intueri
quidem licuit; sed cum plane ignarus sim linguae Anglicae, mentem
Clarissimi Newtoni circa lucem & colores penetrare haud potui, utut

Dominus Fogelius nonnihil interpretatus sit. Operam igitur dabo, ut aliquam ejus Theoriae (ut et Domini Flamstedij observationum) translationem obtineam, quo magis penetralia ejus intrare queam. Interim, cum et meum qualem qualem laborem in maculis solaribus anni praedecentis 1672 mense Augusto obiter observatis vestrae industriae intersertum reperierim, non possum, quin maximas agam gratias, quod illum tanto honore dignari voluistis.⁶ Sunt quidem etiam nonnulla mihi observata de stellae mirae in ceto varia apparitione, tum ratione temporis, tum ratione magnitudinis, quae quondam celeberrimo Domino Hevelio transmissa sunt; sed cum dubium nullum sit, quin accuratius haec ipsa (stella) tum apud vos tum alibi observata fuerit, praestare puto illa retinere, quam noctuas Athenas ferre.⁷ Vale igitur Nobilissime Vir, fautor plurimum observande, meque, utut indignum, Tui tamen studiosissimum, diligere perge.

Dabam Hamburgi die 25to Octobris Anno 1672.

ADDRESS

   Nobilissimo atque Doctissimo Viro
   Domino HENRICO OLDENBURG:
   Societatis Regiae Anglicanae membro primario:
   Musarum Patrono, & Fautori meo
   summe venerando &c.
               Londini

TRANSLATION

Heinrich Sivers presents his greetings and services to the very noble, learned, and famous Mr. Henry Oldenburg, chief member of the English Royal Society

There is no reason why you, most noble Sir, should offer any apology for a reply so long delayed; for it must be more than obvious that your mind is distracted and oppressed by affairs both great and numerous. It is rather for me to excuse that tedium which (as I can readily guess) I induce by my reply, sterile as it is and devoid of experiments. You will no doubt forgive this sterility for the reasons explained in my first letter:¹ among many others this one, that I am wholly intent on completing, with God's aid—whose grace and assistance I duly beseech for this long desired work—that little work *Phoranomica* of our Jungius from his manuscripts, to which he made repeated additions, so that I may at last give it to the public with convenient figures.

We were to have observed the eclipse of the sun on 12 August last past, but the vileness of the clouds forbade accurate observation.[2] Yet we noticed no mean error in our calendar makers, since the commencement of the eclipse, which they ascribed to about four o'clock, only appeared at last at six. We were only able to see the eclipsed sun three times, which was quite clear at nearly six o'clock: the first time was at a quarter past six, the second at a little after a quarter to seven, and the last time at half past seven, as you may see from the figure which I add.

The judgment of that very noble person upon the *Logic* of our Jungius is most pleasing to me.[3] And so I rejoice for him, because, having lain here as if it were contemptible on account of the ignorance of the many and the envy of not a few, it has elsewhere found wiser heads who do not hesitate to set it out and adorn it with due dignity. What if the famous Vogel does publish that long-promised little commentary, praising the excellence of this *Logic* beyond others? I have perused that treatise called *The Art of Thinking*.[4] It is not displeasing because, like a student of the true philosophy, the author had dared to wander off the beaten track. I have not yet happened to see the other treatise by Mr. Duhamel.[5] I long for a copy of it, and as soon as our booksellers have obtained the book I will buy one for myself so that its praiseworthy opinions and wisdom may be known to us here.

I have indeed examined your *Philosophical Transactions* at Mr. Vogel's, but as I am quite ignorant of the English language I could hardly have made out the famous Newton's views concerning light and colors, if Mr. Vogel had not interpreted a good deal for me. Accordingly I will make it my business to procure some translation of his theory (and of Mr. Flamsteed's observations), so that I can enter more deeply into their secrets. Meanwhile as I have discovered, also inserted by your industry, my efforts (such as they were) towards casual observations of the sunspots made during August of the previous year 1671, I could not but return you very many thanks for thinking them worthy of such an honor.[6] Now there are also several observations of mine upon that wonderful star in Cetus, variable in appearance both as to magnitude and period, which were formerly sent to the celebrated Mr. Hevelius; but as no doubt this very star has been observed more accurately by yourselves and others elsewhere, I think it better to keep my observations to myself rather than become a laughing-stock.[7] So farewell, noble Sir, most attentive benefactor, and continue to favor me, being, though all unworthy, yet most devoted towards yourself. Hamburg, 25 October 1672.

An eclipse of the sun casually observed on [12 August] 1672 in the clear intervals between clouds, whose commencement here at Hamburg at six o'clock may be deduced from the fact that, employing a telescope, no obscuration was to be seen just before six. Almost a quarter of an hour later the obscuration covered a definite portion of the sun in the first arc. The second arc was covered after three eights of an hour and the third after half past six [i.e. German reckoning]. After this clouds hid the sun and allowed no further observation.

[For the figure, see page 304]

ADDRESS

To the very noble and most learned
Mr. Henry Oldenburg, chief member
of the English Royal Society, patron
of the Muses and my highly esteemed benefactor
London

NOTES

Reply to Letter 1935 (Vol. VIII), of which only a memorandum survives.

1 This has not survived, nor do we know when it was written; see Letter 1959, note 10.
2 For details of this eclipse, see Letter 2060a, where Hevelius's observations are given.
3 This presumably refers to Jungius's *Logica Hamburgensis* (Hamburg, 1638); "that very noble person" is possibly Boyle, who had been interested in seeing the book in 1667 (see Vol. IV, p. 59).
4 Antoine Arnauld and Pierre Nicole, *La Logique ou l'Art de Penser* (Paris, 1662) went through many editions.
5 Probably *De mente humana libri quatuor* (Paris, 1672), which is reviewed in *Phil. Trans.*, no. 87 (14 October 1672), 5081–82.
6 See Letter 1811a (Vol. VIII, pp. 335–36).
7 The "new star" in Cetus (the Whale), Mira (ο Ceti), has often been mentioned in the correspondence, and had been observed periodically by Hevelius and many others at least since 1666. See further, Vol. III, p. 327.

2088

Wallis to Oldenburg

25 October 1672

From the original in Royal Society MS. W 2, no. 2

Oxford. Octob. 25. 1672

Sir,

Having heard nothing from you since my last;[1] I am apt to think the experiments concerning the Mercury mentioned in my former letters are not yet dispatched, so as to determine matter of fact. I have no copyes by me of my 3 last letters on that subject:[2] But the experiments suggested therein I think will furnish us with matter to determine ye Hypothesis. I could wish the experiments were all carefully made; wch I know not where to have done but either with my Lo. Brounker or Mr Boyle. And I wish

I could be by at the experiments being made, but since I cannot, I hope for an account of them from you. Those I would desire to be made are these.

1. That suggested by my Lo. Brounker; whether a large low Tube of lesse hight than ye standard of 29 Inches will not stand top full of cleansed mercury, though a small hole be left open in the top: At lest, under water.

2. Whether a Tube of more length than 29 Inches but so immerged as to be not so much above ye levell, filled with cleansed mercury may not be gently lifted up so as yt ye contained mercury may rise with it, somewhat higher than the standard.

3. Whether if such a Tube so filled be at first sloped so as its perpendicular hight be not 29 Inches, [it] may not be leisurebly & gently erected till it come to be more than 29 Inches of Perpendicular hight. Which is, in effect, much ye same with ye former; but more easyly administered.

4. Whether a Tube, higher than ye standard, first so filled as to stand top-full of mercury; & then, jogging it so as to let out some smal part of it & stopping ye rest from falling, ye remainder may not be made to stand higher than the ordinary level, notwithstanding the voyd room at ye top.

5. Whether in an Exhausted Receiver, a Siphon may be made to run (at the lower orifice) with Mercury or Water at a greater hight than the Airs pressure will account for. This Mr Hugens affirms upon his experience; & it is worth repeating for fuller satisfaction.

6. Whether a Siphon filled with Mercury (well cleansed of Air, wch I allways suppose in these Experiments) will not run in ye open Air, at ye lower leg, though higher than 29 Inches.

7. If not in ye open Air (because of the Spring) whether will it not run if ye lower legge open into well-clensed water.

8. Whether an Inverted Tube (at lest a short one, with a small cavity,) will stand full of Mercury; though ye orifice be not immerged in Mercury; but either in ye open air, or at lest in water. And, if so, then

9. Whether it will so do, if a little being forced out, there be left some room at ye top.

I am apt to think that divers of these experiments may succeed: &, if so, it will give a good light to the present inquiry.

I do not mention that of two polished marbles remaining suspended in an exhausted Receiver: because I think Mr Boyle, in his printed experiments, mentioned it from his experience.[3]

The chief thing inquirable, seems to me, to be this: Whether it can or cannot be made to stand (above ye common standard of 29 Inches) while it is not top-full. If it may; wee may not then admit that the Springy Air doth penetrate ye glass. If it cannot; wee may admit it, & say yt though it may so passe (unravelled, all at length, as soldiers when they file away through a narrow passage) yet cannot act as a spring, till they have room to recollect, & rally or be wound up, into bowed positions; wch they have not till some room be made. But, both ways, the motion doth take rise from ye expansion of such a springy body: which, like fired gun-powder, doth impresse a motion on ye mercury or like heavy body; wch, though suddenly impressed, flyes (like a bullet out of a gun, or arrow out of a bow) much farther than the Impellent can follow it. Nor need the Experiment be made in very long Tubes; if but 34 or 35 Inches it sufficeth to this experiment; so yt the hight of ye suspended Mercury above ye stagnant be clearly more than 29 or 30 Inches; according as ye present weight of ye Atmosphere shall require. I adde no more but that I am

Your humble servant
John Wallis

ADDRESS
　　These
　For Mr Henry Oldenburg
　in the Palmal near
　　　St James's
　　　　London

POSTMARK OC 27

NOTES

1 Letter 2079.
2 Letters 2072, 2079, and the paper referred to in Letter 2072, note.
3 In *New Experiments Physico-Mechanicall, Touching the Spring of the Air, and its Effects* (Oxford, 1660), Experiment 31, Boyle described how he had tried the experiment of placing two flat, polished pieces of marble, which had been made to adhere by wetting, in his receiver, and then pumping out the air. The two marbles did not separate; he explained this in *A Defence of the Doctrine touching the Spring and Weight of the Air* (London, 1662), under the same Experiment 31, by assuming that there was still a fair quantity of air remaining in the receiver. This he confirmed in Experiment 50 of *A Continuation of New Experiments Physico-Mechanical, Touching the Spring and Weight of the Air, and their Effects* (Oxford, 1669), by repeating the experiment in a better air pump, when he was able to remove enough of the air to cause the marbles to separate.

2089
Oldenburg to Lister
31 October 1672
From the original in Bodleian Library MS. Lister 34, ff. 67–8

London Oct. 31. 1672.

Sir,

I have differr'd till now ye acknowledging of your two late pregnant letters, concerning *kermes* and *Snailes*, because I would first exhibit ym to the R. Society (wch I could not do sooner than yesterday, when they began their publick Assemblies again, after three months recess,) who heard ym read and received ye contents of ym wth great satisfaction, wch they commanded me to let you know, and to Joyne to it their hearty thanks for your continuance of imparting to ym such considerable matters for their design and purpose. Besides, they presuming yt you had already enabled yrself by yr diligent observations to resolve those queries yrself, wch you propose about Snailes, they expressed their desires to see those resolutions; as they also will be very glad to receive in due time, what you have reserv'd, as to Sea-shells and Shellstones.[1]

Sir, whatever matters you shall please to communicate unto me, I shall manage, as to their publishing or keeping privat, as you shall direct. Whatever you shall intimate you would not have made publick, I shall faithfully keep privat; but what you forbid not, I shall presume you will not deny ye knowledge of to ye philosophical and curious world. And taking this measure, I have caused to be printed ye substance of yr letter containing yr alterations and enlargements of yr former Notes about *kermes*,[2] especially since it seemed necessary, yt those, who had read these former Notes of yrs, might be more fully and more exactly instructed by these latter concerning that subject. And I further suppose, you will not contradict my publishing yr letter about Snailes,[3] wch I intend, God willing, to doe the next month, if I be not stopped. But as to your thoughts concerning ye Spaw-waters, you may rest assured, I shall spread them no further than you will allow of; I mean, I shall not print ym, though I may shew ym to our Society, who will be glad to receive ye sentiments of so judicious and sincere a person upon that subject. I hope, Mr Ray will not keep too long yr paper concerning ye Milk-yielding Mushrome, yt we also may have the perusal of it, together wth ye lately-mentioned account about ye Spaw-waters.

Malpighi de ovo[4] is now public; and so will be, in 2 or 3 days, Langelot about ye use of Digestion, Fermentation, and Triture;[5] and soon after yt, Mr Boyles Tracts, touching ye relation betwixt Flame and Air, and yt betwixt Air and ye Flamma Vitalis of Animals, together wth New Experiments about Explosions: as also, his Tract of ye Positive or Relative Levity of Bodies under water; and another, about the Pressure of ye Air's Spring on Bodies under Water; and a third, about ye different Pressure of Heavy Solids and Fluids; to wch three last Tracts is premis'd an Hydrostatical Discourse, refuting ye Objections of Dr More in his Enchir. Metaphysicum against some Explications of Experiments made by Mr Boyle.[6] And not long after yt, we shall have finisht by ye Presse Mr Willoughbies and Mr Rays Voyages;[7] of wch I have already seen divers sheets printed off.

Dr Grew shew'd us yesterday very curious and new representations of ye structure of ye roots of several plants, much also applauded by ye Company at Arundel-house; wch is not wanting, on all occasions to encourage all those Ingenious men, yt by their industrious researches of nature endeavor to augment their philosophical store-house. I am Sir

Yr faithfull servt
Oldenburg

ADDRESS

To my honor'd friend
Dr Martyn Lister at his
house in Stone-gate at
Yorke

NOTES

Reply to Letters 2081, 2084, and 2085.

1 The minutes record only the reading of the letters, not the comments mentioned by Oldenburg.
2 Letter 2081 and its note 2.
3 Letter 2085, which was eventually published in July 1674.
4 "on the egg."
5 See Letter 2048, note 5.
6 All these essays were published in *Tracts . . . Containing New Experiments, touching the Relation betwixt Flame and Air . . . .*
7 John Ray, *Observations Topographical, Moral, & Physiological; Made in a Journey through part of the Low Countries, Germany, Italy, and France* (London, 1673). To this was annexed *A brief Account of Francis Willughby Esq; his Voyage through a great part of Spain.* The book was reviewed in *Phil. Trans.*, no. 91 (24 February 1672/3), 5170–72.

2090

Oldenburg to Wallis

2 November 1672

This reply to Letters 2078, 2079, and 2088 is mentioned in Wallis's reply, Letter 2095. In it Oldenburg reported the discussion at the Society's meeting on 30 October 1672 of Huygens' work on the anomalous suspension of mercury, when Hooke promised to bring in some "trials" of the experiments proposed earlier by Brouncker and Wallis. He also asked Wallis's permission to make his letters public.

2091

Oldenburg to Wallis

7 November 1672

This was a letter of introduction to Wallis carried, together with Letter 2090, by its subject, John Bagger (1646–93). He was a Danish university graduate who traveled in Germany and England, returning to become first Professor of Oriental Languages at Lund, and then successively a Lutheran minister and bishop at Copenhagen.

2092

Hecker to Oldenburg

8 November 1672

From the original in Royal Society MS. H 3, no. 21

Illustri Viro
Domino Henrico Oldenburgio Secretario Regiae Societatis
Ioannes Hecker Salutem

Literas tuas die 10 Octobris exaratas accepi, ex quibus Mercurium meum in Sole[1] tibi non redditum doleo. Calamitas bellorum, vias terra marique, ultro citroque iter facientibus occludit, navemque etiam nostram in freto Danico, praesidiarias expectantem detinet: quae si (quod Deus clementer avertere velit) vim hostilem experta fuerit, damnum leve erit, ac facili negotio resarciendum, daturo operam ut alia exemplaria in ejus locum substitura propediem sequantur.

Clarissimi Hevelii consobrini mei, Machinae coelestis pars prior, seu Organographia, exhibens apparatum variorum Instrumentorum Astronomicorum eorumque usum, ut ut pars posterior, rerum Uranicarum observationes exactissimas continens, brevi lucem videbit,[2] sed adhuc sub praelo sudat, occasionem, nobis, corrigendi tabulas Astronomicas, quae a Caelo valde aberrant, datura.

Declinationem Magnetis Londini, communicare mecum ne graveris, hanc enim cum loco non esse perennem multoties observavi. Sed hoc non novum: jam pridem enim Angli Mathematici, Borussus, Gouterus, Gillebrandus hoc deprehenderunt.[3] Anno praeterito 1671 Sole in principio Cancri existente, Gedani reperi ejus declinationem 7° 30' a Septentrionali versus Occidentem quam tamen Petrus Crugerus Mathematicus nostrae Civitatis Vir doctrina clarus, qui Anno 1639 obiit, annotavit fuisse 8° 30' a Septentrionali versus orientem.[4] Quaenam variationis causa, an a globo terreno, vel caelesti? difficile est statuere: Ego vero hoc accidere per naturam ejus ipsi caelitus innatam existimem.[5] Vale Vir Illustris et me ulterius tuo amore prosequi dignare.

Gedani d. 18 Novemb. A. 1672

ADDRESS

A Monsieur Grubendol

à

Londres

TRANSLATION

Johannes Hecker greets the illustrious Mr. Henry Oldenburg, Secretary of the Royal Society

I have received your letter written on 10 October, from which I learn with regret of the nondelivery to you of my *Mercurius in sole*.[1] The misery of war closes the sea and land routes to those who would travel hither and yon, and even detains our vessel in the Danish Sound, awaiting a convoy; if this vessel shall have suffered some hostile act (which Heaven mercifully forfend), it will be a slight loss and one to be easily repaired [for] I will make it my business that other copies shall follow soon to take its place.

There will soon appear the *Machina coelestis pars prior*, or description of instruments, by my cousin the famous Hevelius, displaying his outfit of different astronomical instruments and their uses, as also *Pars posterior* containing the most exact astronomical observations;[2] but it is still in press giving us opportunity to correct the [current] astronomical tables which show remarkable discrepancies from the heavens.

Please impart to me the magnetic declination at London, for I have many times observed that this does not remain perpetually stable at one place. But this is no news: for long ago the English mathematicians Borough, Gunter, and Gellibrand understood this fact.[3] Last year (1671), when the sun was at the first of Cancer, I found that the declination at Danzig was 7° 30′ west of north, which Peter Cruger (a mathematician of our city, and a man of firm theoretical understanding), who died in 1639, had recorded as 8° 30′ east of north.[4] Does the cause of this variation [of the declination] lie in the terrestrial or the celestial globe? It is difficult to decide. I myself consider that it is brought about by its nature [being] inherent in its heavenly self.[5] Farewell, illustrious Sir, and continue to honor me further with your affection.

Danzig, 18 November 1672

ADDRESS

    To Mr Grubendol
    at London

NOTES

Reply to Letter 2082.
1 See Letter 2062, note 1.
2 The first part appeared at Danzig in 1673, and the second in 1679.
3 See Vol. VII, p. 49 and p. 50, notes 7–9.
4 See Vol. VII, p. 48.
5 The exact meaning is far from clear.

2093

Oldenburg to Sluse

11 November 1672

From the draft in Royal Society MS. O 2, no. 98

Reverendo admodum et Per-Illustri Viro
Domino Renato Francisco Slusio Canonico Leodiensi etc.
Henr. Oldenburg Salutem

Utut ferat Bellona inter Terrarum dominos non tamen ideo necessum, Musarum cultores penitus silere. Distuli aliquantisper, Vir Illustrissime, respondere tuis, pridie Cal. Septembris ad me datis ut copia mihi fieret priusquam rescriberem, Hugeniana ad novissimas illas tuas sensa, quae exquirere libebat Tibi communicandi.[1] Ea sermone Gallico, quo Author passim utitur, ita se habent;

"Vous avez eu la bonté de m'envoier la derniere construction de Monsieur Sluse du probleme d'Alhazen, avec le calcul dont il dit l'avoir tirée. Mais, à ce qui me semble, cela auroit esté bien difficile sans l'aide de ma construction, qui est peu differente, comme vous voiez, puisqu'elle donne la mesme hyperbole, determinée par les asymptotes, au lieu que M. Sluse la construit par les ordonnees au diametre. Je voudrois au reste, qu'il eut montré, comment sa construction suit de l'aequation qu'il donne; car cela m'a donné de la peine, et l'ayant reduite à un cas fort simple, ie n'ay pas trouvé une bonne issue au calcul ce qui me fait douter s'il n'y a pas quelque faute à la copie. Cependant son aequation universelle est tres-belle et scavante, et sa construction par la parabole fort bien trouvée, quoyqu'un peu longue."

Haec ille. Persuasissimum mihi, Vir Optime, Te mentem gerere adeo generosam, ut loquendi modis etiam asperioribus non facile offendaris; proindeque haud sinistre Te accepturum, quae ille in priore hujus sui scripti paragrapho notat, Apographum imprimis mendoso forte transmisso; quod tamen cavere alias sollicite consuevi.

Aperte Tecum agere mihi libuit nec quicquam celare verborum, quibus uti communis Amicus voluit, nullus dubitans, quin valeas in omnibus doctissimo Observatori satisfacere.

Caeterum scire Te putem eundem Hugenium non ita dudum edidisse

suam de causa illa sententiam quae in Experimento Torricelliano Hydrar-
gyrum, ab Aere probe depurgatum, longe ultra altitudinem solitam, etiam
ad usque 75. uncias, suspensum tenet.[2] In causa illa assignanda ex parte
cum Nobilissimo Societatis nostrae Praeside Domino Vice-Comite Brounckero, (et Wallisius noster annotavit parte 3a de Motu prop. 13. sub finem
p. 741). qui suspicetur inesse Aeri particulas quasdam adeo exiles, ut
penetrent vitrum, alias crassiores, ut penetrare nequeant.[3]

Eas quae non penetrant, contraponderare 29. vel 30 unciis, caeteras vero
multo esse ponderosiores. In eo autem forte ipsi disconvenit cum Hugenio,
quod hujus materia subtilis non statuitur elastica, cum illius (Vicecomitis
inquam) materia aerea elastere praedita supponatur.

Num Tu, Vir Illustrissime, Experimentum hoc insigne unquam pera-
geris aut ab aliis peractum videris, quidque de assignata phaenomeni causa
Tibi videatur, scire perquam avemus.

Si etiamnum in urbe vestra commoratur R.P. Bertetus, officiocissime
eum ex me salutes, proque uberrimo eximiae suae ergo me humanitatis
testimonio gratias quam maximas agas, enixe rogo.

Sub praelis Londinensibus nunc calet tum Algebrae Anglica Systema, a
Doctissimo Domino Kersejo, Anglo, compositum,[4] tum Clarissimi Barrovii quatuor priorum Apollonii de Sectionibus Conicis librorum, prout a
Commandino sunt editi, Compendium, directas per omnia demonstrationes
continens. Cui Bernhardus Oxoniensis tres subjunget libros posteriores, ex
manuscriptis binis Oxoniensibus, Bene Musae scilicet et Abdelmelechi,
quorum alterutrum vitiato illi, quod Ecclesius et Borellus publicarunt,
longe praestat; eorum altero ipsismet Eutocii notis locupletato.[6] Accedent
illis dicti Barrovii Archimedes, et Theodosius, una cum 30. circiter
Lectionibus, Mathematicas scientias in genere spectantibus.[7] Vale, et Tui
Observantissimo jugiter fave. Dabam Londini d. 11 Novemb. 1672.

TRANSLATION

Henry Oldenburg greets the very reverend and illustrious Mr. René François
de Sluse, Canon of Liège, etc.

Although Mars rages among the lords of the earth yet it is unnecessary for the
lovers of the Muses to desist altogether. I have deferred for a little, most
illustrious Sir, my answer to your letter to me of 31 August [N.S.] so that, before
I wrote in reply, I might have the Huygenian opinion of your latest letter and
freedom to communicate that opinion to you.[1] This is as follows, in French, a
language that author employs now and then:

[*For the translation, see Letter 2066, p. 249*]

So far he. I am quite certain, excellent Sir, that your mind is of so generous a stamp that you will not easily take offense even at somewhat harsh expressions; and hence you will not take in a bad sense his remark in the first paragraph of this letter, that perhaps the copy sent [him] was particularly bad; which I have nevertheless on other occasions been accustomed to be scrupulously careful to avoid.

It was proper for me to be open with you and to suppress none of the words which our common friend chose to employ, not doubting that you are capable of satisfying this learned commentator on every point.

Moreover, I wish to inform you that the same Huygens published not long ago his opinion, why it is that in the Torricellian experiment when the mercury is quite purged of air it will remain suspended to a height far above the normal, even to that of 75 inches.[2] In assigning the cause [of this phenomenon he agrees] in part with the very noble President of our Society, the Viscount Brouncker (and our Mr. Wallis has recorded this in Part III of his *Mechanica*, Proposition 13, at the foot of p. 741), who guessed that there are in air some particles so slender that they can penetrate glass and other coarser ones that cannot.[3] Those which cannot penetrate counterpoise 29 or 30 inches whereas the rest are much heavier. However, he perhaps disagrees with Huygens on this point, because his subtle matter is not supposed to be elastic, whereas the former's aerial matter (I mean that of the Viscount) is supposed to be endowed with elasticity.

We are very anxious to know whether you, most illustrious Sir, have ever performed this experiment yourself, or seen it performed by others, and what you think of the cause assigned to the phenomenon.

If Father Bertet is still resident in your city, I earnestly beg you to greet him most dutifully in my name, and to offer him my warmest thanks for his copious testimony of kindness towards me.

There is at the printer's in London now both an English system of algebra composed by the learned Mr. Kersey,[4] an Englishman, and[5] "A Compendium of ye 4 first books of Apollonius, as publisht by Commandinus, but by direct demonstrations whereas his lead ad absurdum. To wch Mr Bernard of Oxford will subjoyn ye 3. [latter] books, out of two Copies, they have in their libraries, one of Bene-Musa, ye other of Abdel-melech's, either of ym better yn yt corrupt one publisht by Eccles and Borellus; one of ym having ye very notes of Eutocius;[6] to wch Dr Barrow will subjoyn his Archimedes, his Theodosius, and about 30 Lectures concerning ye Mathematical sciences in general."[7] Farewell, and always cherish your most devoted [servant]. London, 11 November 1672.

NOTES

Reply to Letter 2053.
1 See Letter 2066, from which Oldenburg proceeds to quote.
2 See Letter 2058, note 1.
3 Compare Wallis in Letter 2072.
4 There is a notice of John Kersey, *The Elements of that Mathematical Art Commonly called*

Algebra (London, 1673), in *Phil. Trans.*, no. 90 (20 January 1672/3), 5152–54, and a review in *Phil. Trans.*, no. 95 (23 June 1673), 6073–74.

5 The following English version (indicated by quotation marks) is found in Oldenburg's holograph on the verso of this Latin draft.

6 For Barrow's edition and the manuscripts mentioned here, see Vol. VIII, p. 547, notes 4 and 5. Borelli's edition of Books V, VI, and VII of the *Conics* of Apollonius was published at Florence in 1661; the translation from the Arabic was by Abraham Ecchellensis (d. 1664), a Syrian Maronite Christian who was Professor of Arabic at Rome.

7 Barrow's editions of Archimedes' works and Theodosius' *Sphaerica* were prefixed to his edition of Apollonius. His mathematical lectures were published posthumously as *Lectiones mathematicae XXIII* (London, 1683).

2094
Oldenburg to Huygens
11 November 1672

From *Œuvres Complètes*, VII, 231–33
Original in the Huygens Collection at Leiden

A Londres le 11 novembre 1672

Monsieur,

Lorsque la vostre du 27 septembre estoit sur le chemin de Paris à Londres, Monsieur Vernon estoit sur le chemin de Londres à Paris, de sorte que ie ne pouvois pas luy bailler la lettre, que vous aviez mise sous mon couvert pour luy. J'en feray ce que vous m'ordonnerez, ou en la gardant iusques à son retour en Angleterre, ou en vous la renvoiant à Paris.

J'ay pris la liberté de communiquer à Monsieur Sluse les lignes de vostre lettre qui le touchent;[1] le croiant estre si genereux, qu'il ne prendra pas en mauvaise part la franchise philosophique de ses amis, entre les quels ie vous crois estre au premier rang.

Quant à ce que vous ditez des regles de Monsieur Wallis pour les Tangentes ie le conois si bien, que ie suis persuadé, que bien que Monsieur Fermat eut une de ces methodes lá devant luy, qui soit semblable à la premiere des siennes, Monsieur Wallis pourtant se ne l'adtribueroit pas, si elle n'estoit purement de luy mesme et autrement deduite. Et quoyque

Messieurs Sluse, Hudden et Roberval, et vous, ayez des methodes pour le mesme sujet, que vous ayez expliqueez à vos amis en particulier, elles ne sont pourtant pas encor conues au monde. Vous n'ignorez pas, Monsieur, que par fois les bons Esprits, qui scavent et prennent le vray chemin pour descouvrir des veritez, s'y rencontrent heureusement ensemble, ce qui ne doit prejudicier à personne des Inventeurs.

Monsieur Newton s'est encor plus amplement expliqué sur sa theorie des couleurs, à l'occasion de quelques objections, qu'un scavant Anglois y avoit fait contre.[2] Peut estre, que cete explication sera imprimer dans peu de temps, pour donner occasion a d'autres encor de la considerer davantage.

Je vous envoye un pacquet bien gros y ayant les Transactions de deux mois ensemble;[3] oú vous trouverez, entre autres choses, des Experiences sur la vipere repetées à Florence en faveur de Signor Redi;[4] comme aussi la responce de Monsieur Wallis au livre de Monsieur Hobbes, qui porte le titre, *Lux Mathematica*, etc.[5] Monsieur Kersey fait imprimer icy un Systeme d'Algebre en Anglois.[6] Monsieur Barrow fait imprimer les 4 premiers livres d'Apollonius, avec ses demonstrations directes: Auxquelles Monsieur Bernhard d'Oxford adjoustera les 3 posterieurs, tirez des deux manuscripts de cete université, asscavoir de Ben musa et d'Abdelmelech, bien meilleurs que l'Edition d'Eciles et Borelli, un de ces manuscripts estant mesme enrichi des notes d'Eutocius.[7] A tout cela fera joint l'Archimede du mesme Barrow, avec une trentaine de ses lecons mathematiques qui regardent ces sciences en general.[8]

Monsieur Boyle nous donnera bientost plusieurs petits Traitéz; de la Flamme et de l'Air; de la Positive ou Relative legereté des corps soubs l'Eau; de la Pression du ressort le l'Air sur des corps soubs l'Eau; avec un Discours Hydrostatique contre quelques objections du Docteur More dans son Enchirid. Metaphysicum.[9]

Nous sommes tres aises d'entendre, que vostre Traité des Pendules est enfin sous la Presse; esperants que vous ne manquerez pas de mettre aussi au public vos autres meditations, touchant la Dioptrique, le mouvement etc.

Permettez moy de vous demander, si vous avez vû le traité de Signor Redi *de Figuris Salium* que nous n'avons pas encor icy.[10] Comme aussi, si le Discours de Monsieur Picard, de la mesure de la Terre sera bien tost achevé d'imprimer en petit, puis qu'il n'y a pas moien de l'avoir en grand.

Je vous envoye la phase de Saturne, come Monsieur Hevelius dit l'avoir veu le 19. octobre 1672. où il adjouste ces paroles;[11]

"Ego Astronomis Parisiensibus necdum adstipulari possum, Saturnum omnino rotundum revera extitisse; concedo tamen, illis ita apparuisse, sed tubo breviori, 17 vel 20 pedum; tum Saturno in crepusculo existente. Nuper d. 19. Octobris, cum utique ob aeris summam injuriam fieri nequiverit, faciem Ejus Tubo 55 ped. sum contemplatus; annulus fere adhuc tenuior apparuit quam anno praeterito, prout ex adjuncto schemate videbitis."

Je seray bien aise d'entendre vostre sentiment dessus cete remarque, qui suis Monsieur

Vostre tres-humble et tres-obeissant serviteur
H. Oldenburg

ADDRESS

A Monsieur
Monsieur Christian Hugens de Zulichem
dans la Bibliotheque du Roy à
Paris

TRANSLATION

London, 11 November 1672

Sir,

While yours of 27 September [N.S.] was on its way from Paris to London, Mr. Vernon was on his way from London to Paris, so that I could not give him the letter which you had put in my envelope. I will do whatever you ask me to do with it, either keeping it until his return to England or returning it to you in Paris.

I have taken the liberty of communicating to Mr. Sluse those lines in your letter which concern him,[1] believing him to be sufficiently generous not to take in bad part the philosophical candor of his friends, among whom I believe you to be one of the chief.

As for what you say about Mr. Wallis's rules for tangents, I know him so well that I am certain that even though Mr. Fermat had one of these methods earlier than he did (a method which seems similar to the first of his), Mr. Wallis nevertheless would not ascribe it to himself if it were not genuinely his alone, and deduced in another way. And although Messrs Sluse, Hudde, and Roberval, and you also, have methods for the same matter, which you have explained to your friends in private, they are nevertheless not yet known to the world at large. You are not unaware, Sir, that sometimes keen minds, who know and take the true road to the discovery of truths, happily meet together there, which should not be prejudicial to any of the discoverers.

Mr. Newton has expatiated further on his theory of colors on the occasion of some objections made against it by an English scientist.[2] Perhaps this explanation will give occasion to yet others to consider it further.

I am sending you a pretty big packet containing the *Transactions* for two months combined:[3] here you will find, among other things, some experiments made on vipers at Florence in favor of Signor Redi,[4] as also the reply of Mr. Wallis to Mr. Hobbes's book with the title *Lux Mathematica*, etc.[5] Mr. Kersey is having a *System of Algebra* printed here in English.[6] Mr. Barrow is having printed the first four books of Apollonius with his own direct demonstrations; to this Mr. Bernard of Oxford will add the last three [books] taken from two manuscripts in that University, that is to say of Beni Musa and Abdelmelech, much better than the edition of Ecchellensis and Borelli, one of these manuscripts being even enriched with notes by Eutocius.[7] To all this will be added the Archimedes of the same Barrow, with thirty of his mathematical lectures on the sciences in general.[8]

Mr. Boyle will soon give us several small tracts: on flame and the air, on the positive or relative lightness of bodies under water, on the pressure or spring of the air on bodies under water, with a hydrostatical discourse against certain objections of Dr. More in his *Enchiridion Metaphysicum*.[9]

We are very pleased to hear that your treatise on pendulums is finally in the press, and hope that you will not fail to make public your other thoughts on dioptrics, motion, etc.

Permit me to ask if you have seen the treatise of Signor Redi *De figuris salium* which we have not yet had here.[10] As also whether Mr. Picard's discourse *Mesure de la Terre* will be printed in a small format, since there is no way to get it in the large one.

I send you [a sketch of] the phase of Saturn as Mr. Hevelius says he saw it on 19 October 1672 [N.S.] to which he adds these words:

[*Here follows two sentences from Letter 2083; for the translation, see p. 289*].

I should be very glad to hear your opinion on this remark, and remain, Sir,

Your very humble and obedient servant
H. Oldenburg

ADDRESS

> To
> Mr. Christiaan Huygens of Zulichem
> At the King's Library
> Paris

NOTES

Reply to Letter 2066.
1 In Letter 2093.
2 For Newton's reply to Hooke, see Letter 1993.

3 *Phil. Trans.*, no. 87 (14 October 1672) was "for the monthes of September and October."

4 Letter 2037.

5 Hobbes's *Lux mathematica, collisionibus Johannis Wallisii S. Th. D. & Thomae Hobbesii Malmesburiensis, excussa* (London, 1672), was dedicated to the Royal Society and formally presented to it on 30 October 1672; Oldenburg had briefly reviewed it, forecasting a reply by Wallis, in *Phil. Trans.*, no. 86 (19 August 1672), 5047–48. Wallis's reply, dated 31 August 1672, was published with an annexed mathematical paper in *Phil. Trans.*, no. 87 (14 Ocotber 1672), 5067–73; no manuscript survives.

6 See Letter 2093, note 4.

7 See Letter 2093, note 6. The name we have reprinted here as "Eciles" should probably be read as "Eccles."

8 See Letter 2093, note 7.

9 See Letter 2089, note 6.

10 Oldenburg had been looking for this work, which remained unfinished, since 1668; see Vol. V, p. 36, note 3.

11 For Hevelius's original drawing and the translation, see Letter 2083; Oldenburg's version is reproduced in *Œuvres Complètes*, VII, 233.

2095
Wallis to Oldenburg
14 November 1672
From the original in Royal Society MS. W 2, no. 3

Oxford Nov. 14. 1672

Sir,

I thank you for your two letters of Nov. 2. & Nov. 7. with the Transactions inclosed. The Gentleman M. Bagger who brought them, I have indeavoured with all civility, & have brought him into ye favour & acquaintance of those other three persons whom you mentioned to his good content. I am glad the Experiments, you mention, are in hand;[1] for examining the cause of the Mercury standing above its common standard, as I suggested. For since the first discovery of ye Phaenomenon was in our own Society, I would willingly that ye true Cause should be there determined allso; and not that we should be therein prevented from abroad. As to your shewing my letter which concerns ye particulars alleged in yt of Mr Hugens; you may use yr discretion, to shew it to whom you think fit,

& to those to whom you shew his. Onely I would not have it occasion any difference or contest, because ye businesse is not worth it; & I have a kindness for Monsr Hugens, which makes me not desirous of any contest with him.

I thank you for your pains in that wherein I am concerned in these last Transactions;[2] I am sorry it gives you so much trouble; & find you have taken a great deal of care in it. Notwithstanding which, I find there be yet some few mistakes; but I am not confident but yt some of them may be in my own copy. Those wch I have noted, as disturbing the sense (for others are not worth noting) are to be thus amended.[3]

pag. 5067. *l.* 32. Hobbii Dialogo *l. pen.* Tractatu. *pag.* 5068. *l.* 43. demonstratas. *p.* 5069. *l.* 10. non in Ax. *p.* 5070. *l.* 23. defensionem. *lin. 35. for* 2*PQL*, put − 2*PQL*. *Ibid. lin. 29. Marg.* Vide Tab. II. fig. III. *p.* 5071 *l.* 16. est media. *lin. 31. for* 1L $\sqrt{c\frac{1}{2}}$. *put* 1 − $\sqrt{c\frac{1}{2}}$. *p.* 5072. *l.* 35, *for* $\frac{4}{100,000}$, *put*

$\frac{4}{10,000}$. *p.* 5073, *l.* 18. *for* quid, *put* quin. *p.* 5074. *l.* 23, 27, *&c* for *σT*, *put* 6*T*. *lin.* 23. *for* ∫² *put* S². *lin.* 31. *for* $\frac{TD^3}{3L}$, *put* $\frac{L}{6T}D^3$. *p.* 5075. *l.* 2. *for* $\frac{1}{4}LD^3$, *put* $\frac{1}{4}LD^2$. *lin. 39.* Hyperbola sit sca—

Yours of Nov. 2. mentions an account to be brought in ye Wednesday following, yt is, Nov. 6. but yours of Nov. 7. giving no particulars of it, makes [me] conclude it was not perfected; but perhaps by this time it may [be].[4] I am, Sir

Your humble servant
John Wallis

ADDRESS
These
For Mr Henry Oldenburg,
in the Palmal near
St James's
London

NOTES

1 See Letter 2090.
2 See Letter 2094, note 5.
3 These errata are printed at the end of *Phil. Trans.*, no. 88 (18 November 1672), 5106.
4 When Wallis's Letter 2088 was read at the meeting of 6 November 1672 it "was delivered to Mr. Hooke," who finally made his report on November thirteenth.

2096
Lister to Oldenburg
15 November 1672

From the original in Royal Society MS. L 5, no. 49
Partly printed in *Phil. Trans.*, no. 89 (16 December 1672), 5116–17

Yorke Novemb. 15. 72

Sir

I had your obliging letter of ye 31st of October: for wch I give you my hearty thanks. As to ye resolving of ye Quaeries, I made concerning Snailes, it is tru, yt they are not rashly proposed; yet I willingly reserve ye Observations & Experiements, wheron they are grounded, for ye particular Histories to wch they belong. I am not backward to part wth any thing in my power & shall be ready at any time to give answer to any Querie I have advanced: but, I hope, ye longer I keep these things by me, ye more correct & enlarged they may be.

I understand, yt my Letter sent to Mr *Wray*[1] did not find him in Warwick-shire & therefore possibly may either miscarry or be long before it come at him. The same person informed me, yt Mr Wray would be at London this Terme, and therfore you may please there to have his sense of ye notes about this Plant, when you shall see him. I shall transcribe ym for you, as I entred ym in my *Adversaria*.

The 18th of August I passed through *Marton* woodes under *Pinne-moore* in *Craven*: in these woods I than found an infinite Number of Mushroomes, some witherd & others new sprung & fluourishing.[2] They were of a large size, something bigger than ye *ordnary red-gilled eatable Mushroome or Champignon* & very much of their shape: yt is, wth a perfectly round Cap or *stool* (as we vulgarly call it) thick in flesh & wth open Gills underneath; a thick, fleshy, not-hollow, & round Foot-stalke, of about 6 fingers breadth high above ground & ordnarily as thick as my Thumb. The foot-stalke, gills & Cap all of a pure white colour. if you cutt any part of this Mushroome, it will bleed exceeding freely a milke-white juice, concerning wch note. 1. yt ye this milky juices tasts much hotter upon ye Tongue than Pepper. 2. yt it is not clammy to ye touch. 3. yt ye aire does not much discolour it or ye blade of a knife, as is usual wth most vegetable juices. 4. yt it became in ye *glass-viol* I drew it into suddainly concreet &

stiff, & did in some dayes dry into a firme Cake. 5. yt it than alsoe, when well dryed retaine its fierce biting tast & white colour.

Further I observed these Mushromes full of juice & not to be endured upon ye tongue to abound wth Fly-Maggotts: Alsoe ye yongest & tendrest of ym, yt is such as are most juicy, to have been very much eaten by ye *grey meadow naked-Snail* & lodging ym selves within ye sides of ye Plant. Concerning this *kind* of biting Mushrome, I find in a certain late peice of ye state of Russia, these words[3]

"*Groozshidys* fungorum maximi, palmam lati, instar Omasi bubuli sunt crassi et candidi: dum crudi sunt succo (lactio puta) abundant; eos sicut Tithymallum muria corrigunt Rutheni; aliter fauces et gutter inflamabunt. Ipse semel nimis inconsiderate assatos comedere tentabam, non sine suffocationis periculo."

The reference to ye Cutts or figures is here confused & ye description too concise, to say, yt ours agrees in any thing wth theirs, save ye great acrimony of ye juice they both yield.

I may some time acquaint you wth ye medicinall uses, I have caused to be made of this *white Resin*: in ye meane time I shall only mind you of ye great affinitie it hath wth *Euphorbium*.

The Season is almost over, soe yt ye account we can give of ye Veines in Plants, must rest as it is, untill further opportunity. My sense of these Veines (according to ye experience I have yet of ym) you may command: but what I cheifly aimed at, I have found exceeding difficult to effect, yt is, an *ocular demonstration* of ym; yet in some measure I have attained to yt alsoe. I am Sir

Your most humble servant
Martin Lister

ADDRESS
    For my honoured friend
    Henry Oldenburg
       Esquire
  at his house in ye Palmal
      London

POSTMARK NO 18

NOTES

Reply to Letter 2089.
1 See Letter 2084, note 3.
2 Marton-in-Craven is still used as the designation of a district in Western Ribblesdale,

Yorkshire, but "Pinne-moor" seems to have vanished. The fungus is most probably *Lactarius piperatus* (Mrs. Sheila Francis).

3 See Samuel Collins, *The Present State of Russia*, p. 137; Lister has added two words in parentheses. Collins' own English version (p. 140) runs: "*Groozhdys*, the greatest of Mushrooms, an hand breadth [across], like a Cow-tripe thick and white, whilst raw very juycy [or rather, milky—Lister]; the Russians correct it (as they do Sea-lettice) with brine, else they will inflame the chops and throat, once I rashly adventur'd to eat them roasted, not without danger of choaking."

2097
Flamsteed to Oldenburg
16 November 1672

From the original in Royal Society MS. F 1, no. 92
Partly printed in *Phil. Trans.*, no. 89 (16 December 1672), 5118–19

Derby 16 No: 1672

Mr Oldenburge

I suppose wth this you expect the list of aged persons which I promised yu:[1] I am sorry that I cannot at this time answer yr expectation. I moved this businesse by my friends abroad whom I could not persuade to take any paines: As for my selfe I have found that in our Towne of Derby wee have twenty men aged 80 yeares or within a yeare of 80. I am well informed of the customes of theire lives & habits, of which I shall give yu an account when ever yu desire. but as for old women tho I beleive they be as many yet I have not enquired after them for it is generally observed & voiced by the common people that if a woman outlive the dangers of child bearth & leave beareing, she lives often to a very old age.

In the roome of them I send yu an annuall taske but slightly done as yu will find by a view of it.[2] Indeed my frequent Journeys abroad & the businesse of my fathers trade at home have kept mee so employed I have not had time to make such calculations as I intended. Further I find that the most of those I have made are but lost labor for I have not had faire weather to observe 1 appearance of 5 I calculated; I have therefore onely noted the time of the moones true Conjunction wth the fixed stars, from Heckers Ephemerides, wth the point then ascendeing at London; wth a conjecture therefrom when the visible occultations shall happen from which the intelligent observer may be sufficiently informed when to waite for any appearance, & what will be observable.

I have of late observed some appulses of the other planets to fixed stars. & haveing collected all next yeare observable wth my 7 foot tube I have added them to the lunar appulses. both are very slendor labors but may be very usefull: yu may print them in the transactions if yu judge such sleight things worthy.³ if not yet you may present them to Mr. Hook. who by them will see when hee may expect opportunitys for observations. and, if hee observe how much the heavens differ from the Rudolphine Numbers. Last September I was at Towneley the first weeke that I intended to have observed Mars.⁴ there wth Mr. Towneley I twice observed him, but could not make 2 observations as I intended in one night. the first night after that of my returne I had the good hap to measure his distances twice from 2 stars the same night whereby I find yt his parallax was very small certeinely not 30 seconds. So yt I beleive the Suns is not more then 10″. Of this observation I intend to write a small tract when I shall gaine leasure in which I shall demonstrate both the diameter & distances of all the planets by observations.⁵ for which I am now pretty well fitted: Haveing observed the distances & positions of the 3 stars by which Mars made his transit I find that Tycho erres 5 minute at least both in the places & latitudes of them compared one wth another. and certeinely hee erres as much in many other So yt the labor of Mons Hevelius to rerectifie theire places is very needfull. I find not fault wth Tycho it is a wonder considering how difficult it is to set plaine sights to a small star that ever hee performed so much and so well. but if Monsr. Hevelius use not glasses in theire roome which I am informed hee does not it will be difficult to judge whether wee ought to make use of Tychoes Catalogues or his when they come forth: I could wish some one wth us who is furnished would undertake this taske for wthout this restitution wee cannot expect any thinge certeine much lesse accurate in Astronomy: I would gladly know whether the French designe this for one of the labors of theire observatory. what they there engage themselves in or what wee may expect from them: I desire likewise to heare from yu on the receipt of those papers & rest Sr

Yr affectionate & obliged servant
John Flamsteed   Derb.

I have wrote to Mr Collins to procure mee a thermometer who writes mee word hee will move the Society. if that need I know yu will assist him. of whom I would have scarce desired such a kindnesse that would put him to so much trouble had I knowne it before hand. for I am alwaies putting him to trouble. and I know not whether hee may take it kindly:

J F

ADDRESS

For Henry Oldenburge Esq
at his house in the Middle of the
Pell mell neare St Jamese's
  Westminster   these

NOTES

Reply to Letter 2059.
1 Oldenburg had requested this in Letter 2045, and Flamsteed promised a reply in Letter 2055.
2 This (Royal Society MS. F. 1, no 93) was Flamsteed's usual calculation of the moon's appulses for the next year; it was printed *in extenso* in *Phil. Trans.*, no. 89 (16 December 1672), 5120–24.
3 They are printed after the lunar appulses.
4 See Letter 2076 and its note 1.
5 See Letters 2036, 2047, 2076, and Baily, pp. 32–33. The results were announced in "Johannis Flamstedii . . . ad Clarissimum Cassinum Epistola," *Phil. Trans.*, no. 96 (21 July 1673), pp. 6099–6000 [*sic*].

2098
Hill to Oldenburg
20 November 1672

This is mentioned in Hill's Letter 2192 of 31 March 1673 as having enclosed a letter from Father Valentin Estansen. It never reached Oldenburg. It was presumably in reply to Letters 1780 and 1780a.

Padre Valentin Estancel, or Stancel (Stansel), was a Jesuit mathematician and astronomer, who taught mathematics at Elvas and subsequently at the College of Santo Antão in Lisbon. He went to Brazil in 1663, where he continued his astronomical work. He is said to have published in 1658 *Orbe Affonsino*, or *Horoscopo Universal*, and, in 1705, *Tiphys Lusitano*, or *Regimento Náutico novo*, but we have found no more about these works. The BN lists *Uranophilus caelestis peregrinus, sive mentis uranicae per mundum sidereum peregrinantis extases, authore Valentino Estancel* (Ghent, 1685).

2099
Hobbes to Oldenburg

26 November 1672

From the original in Royal Society MS. H 3, no. 201
Printed in *The English Works of Thomas Hobbes*, ed. Sir Wm. Molesworth (London, 1845), VII,
465–66

Worthy Sr

In the last Transactions for September and October I find a letter address-ed to you from Dr Wallis, in answer to my Lux Mathematica.[1] I pray you tell me that are my old acquaintance,[2] whether it be (his words and characters supposed to be interpreted) intelligible. I know very well you understand sense both in Latine, Greeke, and many other Languages. He shows you no ill consequence of any of my arguments. Whereas I say there is no proportion of Infinite to Finite. He answers he means Indefinite; but derives not his conclusion from any other notion then simply Infinite. I said the Root of a Square number cannot be the length of the side of a Square figure, because a Root is part of a Square number, but Length is no part of a Square Figure. To wch he answers nothing. In like manner he shuffles of all my other objections, though he know well enough, that whatsoever he has written in Geometry (except what he has taken from me and others) dependeth on the truth of my objections. I perceave by many of his former writings that I have reformed him somewhat, as to the Principles of Geometry, though he thanke me not. He shuffles and struggles in vaine, he has the hooke in his guills, I will give him line enough, for (which I pray you tell him) I will no more teach him by replying to any thing he shall hereafter write, whatsoever they shall say that are confident of his Geometry. Qui volunt decipi decipiuntur.[3] He tells you that I bring but "crambe saepe cocta."[4] For which I have a just excuse, and all men do the same; they repeat the same words often when they talke with them that cannot heare.

I desire also this reasonable favour from you, That if hereafter I shall send you any paper tending to the advancement of Physiques or Mathe-matiques, and not too long, you will cause it to be printed by him that is

Printer to the Society, as you have done often for Dr Wallis, It will save me some charges. I am Sr

Your affectionate frend and humble servant
Thomas Hobbes

November the 26th. 1672

ADDRESS

> For my worthy and much honoured frend
>> Mr. Henry Oldenburgh Secretary
>> to the Royall Society

NOTES

1 See Letter 2094, note 5.
2 See Letter 32 and notes (Vol. I, pp. 74–76).
3 "Those who wish to deceive will be deceived."
4 "oft cooked cabbage."

2100

Sluse to Oldenburg

26 November 1672

From the original in Royal Society MS. S 1, no. 73
Printed in Boncompagni, pp. 665–68

Nobilissimo ac Clarissimo Viro
D. Henrico Oldenburg Societatis Regiae Secretario
Renatus Franciscus Slusius Salutem

Miror solertiam tuam, Vir Nobilissime, qua me loquendi modis etiam asperioribus offensum non iri praevidisti. Agnosco enim meam hac in parte ἀναισθησίαν non virtuti, sed naturali potius inertiae adscribendam. Hinc etiam fortasse est, quod minus ducar illis, ut Tacitus vocat, felicium hominum affectibus:[1] nec tanti mihi fuerit unquam, vel sint etiamnum Geometriae studia (cuius subtilitates quod tibi in aurem dictum sit, quotidie minoris facio) ut eapropter cum quoquam contentionis funem

ducere velim; nedum cum Viro Docto et Amico: cuius ingenium et eruditionem qualibet occasione commendare soleo. Itaque nihil ad tuas 11a
Novembris datas, quod quidem ad Problema Alhazenianum attinet,
reponerem, nisi vereres[2] ne silentium meum, secus ac vellem, interpretare-
ris. Accipe igitur constructionem, quam a me desideras, ex schedis meis
excerptam:[3] Sed ne actum agam relege, si placet, quae scripsi 22 Junij, cum
aequationem in quam omnium primam incidi,[4] nempe

$$\frac{2\zeta dae + 2bbae - 2bbqe}{\zeta b - bd} + ee = aa - \frac{qqa}{b}$$

in hanc verti debere indicavi:[5]

$$\text{quadratum } e - \frac{qq}{k} + \frac{my}{p} = yy - \frac{qqky}{bp} - \frac{2qqmy}{kp} + \frac{q^4}{kk}$$

Sint itaque data puncta E, B, circulus cuius centrum A. Ductis EA,
AB, EB, eat per tria puncta A, E, B, circulus alius, et cadat in EB
normalis AO, producta ad eundem circulum in T, ductaque diametro AS,
iungatur ST. punctum quaesitum sit P ex quo in AO cadat normalis PR.

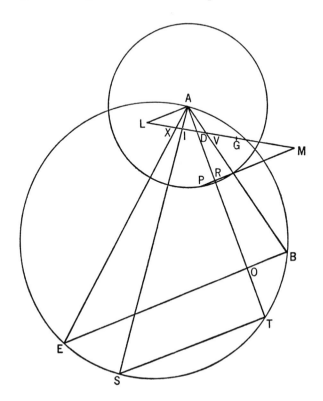

Nunc in terminis Analyticis, erit $AR = a$, $PR = e$, $AO = b$, $AT = m$, $EO = z$ $OB = d$, $ST = z - d = k$, $SA = \sqrt{mm + kk} = p$ et radius circuli dati $= q$.

fiat ut ST^6 ad radium, ita hic ad $AI = \frac{qq}{p}$. Eodem modo ut $TA = m$

ad q, ita hic ad $AD = \frac{qq}{m}$. Producatur ID utrimque donec occurrat rectis AE, AB, PR productae in punctis X, V, M, et rectae AL parallelae PM in L. Erit q pariter media inter EA AX et BA AV, et quoniam est ut TS ad SA, sive k ad p, ita RD ad DM, vel $RA = a$ ad ML; erit

$ML \frac{pa}{k} = y$. Eadem ratione ut ST ad TA, sive k ad m, ita $DR = a - \frac{qq}{m}$

ad $RM = \frac{ma - qq}{k}$, sive (posito pro a eius valore $\frac{ky}{p}$) erit $RM = \frac{my}{p} - \frac{qq}{k}$

et tota PM $e + \frac{my}{p} - \frac{qq}{k}$. Habes eodem modo $AL = \frac{qq}{k}$ cum sit ST ad TA, ita DA ad AL. Et cum angulus AVL, aequalis sit angulo AEB (ob proportionales) et angulus ad L communis triangulis ALX, AVL, erit ut VL ad LA, ita LA ad LX, et rectangulum VLX, aequale quadrato

$LA = \frac{q^4}{kk}$. Sumta itaque VG aequali XL erit rectangulum $GVL = \frac{q^4}{kk}$.

Nunc est ut ST ad TA, ita AI ad $IL = \frac{qqm}{kp}$, et ut AO ad OE, ita AI ad

$IV = \frac{qqz}{bp}$. Igitur tota $LV = \frac{qqm}{kp} + \frac{qqz}{bp}$. Est autem ut AO ad OB, ita AI

ad $IX = \frac{qqd}{bp}$. Igitur LI minus IX, erit $\frac{qqm}{kp} - \frac{qqd}{bp} = LX$ vel VG. Et tota

$LG = \frac{2qqm}{kp} + \frac{qqz - qqd}{bp}$ hoc est (quoniam $z - d = k$) $\frac{2qqm}{kp} + \frac{qqk}{bp}$. Itaque

MG erit $y - \frac{2qqm}{kp} - \frac{qqk}{bp}$ et rectangulum $LMG = yy - \frac{2qqmy}{kp} - \frac{qqky}{bp}$, quod

cum rectangulo $LVG = \frac{q^4}{kk}$ aequatur rectangulo XMV (ob aequales scilicet LX, VG). Est itaque rectangulum

$XMV = yy - \frac{2qqmy}{kp} - \frac{qqky}{bp} + \frac{q^4}{kk}$.   Ostendimus   autem PM esse

$e + \frac{my}{p} - \frac{qq}{k}$, inventa igitur est hyperbola aequalium laterum quam aequatio indicabat, cuius latus transversum XV, vertex V, una applicatarum PM, et quae proposito satisfacit, ut patet regrediendo per vestigia Analyseos.

Caeterum quamvis lineae omnes quas duximus, ad constructionem ex Analysi deducendam necessariae sint, ad hyperbolam tamen, cum innotuit, describendam, evidens est ea sufficere quae in alia Epistola indicavi[7].

Atque haec quidem hactenus eo tantum fine ut tibi morem gererem, Vir Clarissime, nam Clarissimo Hugenio communicari fortasse non expedit, ne, quod nollem, aliquid adhuc sit quod ipsi displiceat. Universalis mea Analysis iisdem principiis nititur, quibus summam aequationis ad AE vel AB, olim retuleram: inventione nimirum tirum harmonice proportionalium, quarum usum in huismodi Problematibus iamdudum ostendi. Poterit autem, qui calculi prolixitatem non aversabitur, aliam quoque similem prorsus instituere, ducta qualibet linea non modo per A, sed etiam per E et B. Verum, ut existimo res non est tanti. Sed de Alhazeni Problemate, ohe iam satis est.

Mirabile illud experimentum quo Mercurius ad 75 unciarum altitudinem attollitur, iam a multis annis didici ex Illustrissimi Boylii Epistola ad te data.[8] Et sane ingeniosa est hypothesis, qua vir acutissimus nuper illud explicare conatus est; sed ut verum fatear, si eam recte capio, non adeo difficultates omnes solvere videtur, ut in illa omnino quiescere possit animus. Cum enim materia illa aere subtilior premat Mercurium, non a latere tantum sed etiam perpendiculariter per tubi poros, cur aliquatenus saltem non deprimit? quandoquidem minima aeris ipsa levioris, bulla sufficiat, ut ab altitudine unciarum 75 ad consuetam 28 vel 30, ferme in momento deprimatur. Accedit quod, si materia illa subtilis aere gravior sit, mirum videatur cur in ea non perpetuo ascendat aer, quemadmodum ignis in aere. Inciderat mihi olim rem explicari posse si supponeremus omnem pressionem ac gravitatem a vi elastica aeris, etiam corporibus inclusi, pendere: unde sequebatur liquorem aere spoliatum et non nisi a parte inferiori pressum, hac aeris externi pressione, in qualibet altitudine sustineri posse. Sed commenti vanitatem vidi cum Mercurium ab aere liberum ac suspensum ad altitudinem etiam unciarum 75, unica aeris in tubum immissi bulla praecipitari ad consuetam 30 unciarum agnovi. Debuisset enim, si veritati niteretur hypothesis, vel supra vel infra eandem altitudinem, pro varia aeris in tubum recepti ratione, Mercurius subsistere. Itaque ἐπέχω et expectandum censeo longioris aevi diligentiam quae id quod nunc latet, aperiat. Helmontius sane tum in operibus praelo datis, tum in MS de fontibus quod legi, ait aquam sub terra extra aeris pressionem, legibus hydraulicis non subiacere:⁹ sed penes ipsum erit fides, donec eam nobis vel ratione vel experimentis fecerit.

Scripsi ad te iam saepius de Regula ducendarum tangentium ad curvas quaslibet geometricas absque omni calculo, quam publico dare decreveram;¹⁰ sed absolvere, quae animo conceperam, hactenus non licuit. Eius enim usum, tum in determinatione Problematum, tum in pluribus alijs ostendere volebam, quorum aliqua, ni fallor, tibi antehac indicavi. Verum cum nec mihi otium sit, decrevi, si ita videatur, Regulam absque demonstratione et corollariis (ne moles nimia sit) ad Te mittere, Transactionibus Philosophicis inserendam, quo virorum doctorum censuram subire possit. Fac igitur me certiorem quid ea de re censeas: Ego enim iudicio tuo parebo lubens, eamque, cum tibi placere indicaveris, statim transmittam. Vale interim Vir Nobilissime ab eo qui ex asse tuus est, atque humanitati tuae plurimum semper debere se profitetur. Dabam Leodii VI Decembris Gregor: MDCLXXII.

P. Bertitus iam a duobus mensibus hinc discessit, amicam tamen salutationem tuam ad eum scribam cum primum sese offeret occasio. Iterum Vale.

TRANSLATION

René François de Sluse greets the very noble and famous Mr. Henry Oldenburg, Secretary of the Royal Society

I marvel at your shrewdness, most noble Sir, in foreseeing that even addressing me in rather harsh terms would not move me to anger. For I confess that my insensitivity is to be attributed not to virtue but rather to a natural sluggishness. Hence perhaps it is that I am the less drawn (in Tacitus' phrase) by the concerns of happy men;¹ and none of these were ever so important in my eyes, even geometrical studies (the subtleties of which, let me whisper it in your ear, appeal to me less day by day) that on their account I should wish to be dragged into contention with anyone; and least of all with a learned friend whose intelligence and knowledge I am accustomed to praise at every turn. Accordingly I would make no reply to what concerns the Problem of Alhazen in your letter of 11 November, did I not fear² that you might interpret my silence otherwise than as I wish. So, accept the construction you sought from me, extracted from my papers;³ but in order to do nothing vain, I beg you to read again, please, what I wrote on 22 June when I indicated that the equation I came across first of all,⁴ namely

$$\frac{2zdae + 2bbae - 2bbqe}{zb - bd} + ee = aa - \frac{qqa}{b}$$

should be transformed into this one[5]

$$\left(e - \frac{q^2}{k} + \frac{my}{p}\right)^2 = y^2 - \frac{kq^2y}{bp} - \frac{2mq^2y}{kp} + \frac{q^4}{k^2}.$$

Therefore let the given points be E, B, and A the center of the circle [*see the figure, p. 331*]. Having drawn EA, AB, and EB let another circle be drawn through the three points A, B, and E. Let the normal AO fall upon EB and be produced to the same circle at T. Draw the diameter AS and join ST. Let P be the point sought for, from which the normal PR falls on AO. Now in analytical terms $AR = a$, $PR = e$, $AO = b$, $AT = m$, $EO = z$, $OB = d$, $ST = z - d = k$, $SA = \sqrt{m^2 + k^2} = p$ and the radius of the given circle $= q$.

Make AI [in AS] to the radius, as the radius is to ST,[6] that is, $AI = \frac{q^2}{p}$.

In the same way, make AD [in AO] to q as q is to $AT = m$, that is, $AD = \frac{q^2}{m}$.

Let ID be produced either way until it meets the straight lines AE, AB, PR produced in the points X, V, and M, and the straight line AL parallel to PM in L. q will be likewise a mean between AE and AX, and between AB and AV, and since $\frac{ST}{AS}$ or $\frac{k}{p} = \frac{RD}{DM}$ or $\frac{a}{ML}$, $\frac{MLpa}{k} = y$. In the same way,

$$\frac{ST}{AT} = \frac{k}{m} = \frac{DR}{RM} = \frac{\left(a - \frac{q^2}{m}\right)}{\left(\frac{ma - q^2}{k}\right)}, \text{ or } \left(\text{writing for } a \text{ its value } \frac{ky}{p}\right), RM = \frac{my}{p} - \frac{q^2}{k},$$

and the whole $PM = e + \frac{my}{p} - \frac{q^2}{k}$. In the same way you have $AL = \frac{q^2}{k}$, since

$\frac{ST}{AT} = \frac{AD}{AL}$. And as the angle AVL is equal to the angle AEB (because of the proportional lines) and the angle at L is common to the triangles, ALX, AVL, $\frac{VL}{AL} = \frac{AL}{LX}$ and the rectangle VLX is equal to the square of AL, that is, to $\frac{q^4}{k^2}$.

Therefore taking VG equal to XL, the rectangle $GVL = \frac{q^4}{k^2}$. Now $\frac{ST}{AS} = \frac{AI}{IL}$

$= \frac{q^2m}{kp}$, and $\frac{AO}{EO} = \frac{AI}{IV} = \frac{q^2z}{bp}$. Therefore the whole $LV = \frac{q^2m}{kp} + \frac{q^2z}{bp}$. But

$\frac{AO}{BO} = \frac{AI}{IX} = \frac{q^2d}{bp}$. Therefore IL minus $IX = \frac{q^2m}{kp} - \frac{q^2d}{bp} = LX = VG$. And the

whole $LG = \frac{2q^2m}{kp} + \frac{q^2z - q^2d}{bp}$, that is (since $z - d = k$), $\frac{2q^2m}{kp} + \frac{q^2k}{bp}$. And so

$MG = y - \frac{2q^2m}{kp} - \frac{q^2k}{bp}$ and the rectangle $LMG = y^2 - \frac{2q^2my}{kp} - \frac{q^2ky}{bp}$, which together with the rectangle $LVG = \frac{q^4}{k^2}$ is equal to the rectangle XMV (because

$LX = VG$). And so the rectangle $XMV = y^2 - \frac{2q^2my}{kp} - \frac{q^2ky}{bp} + \frac{q^4}{k^2}$. But we

we have shown that $PM = e + \frac{my}{p} - \frac{q^2}{k}$, and therefore an equilateral hyperbola

is found which was indicated by the equation, whose transverse side is XV, whose vertex is V, one of whose ordinates is PM, and which satisfies the proposition, as is made clear by retracing the track of the analysis.

Moreover, although all the lines we have drawn are necessary in order to deduce the construction from the analysis, it is evident that for drawing the hyperbola those are sufficient which we indicated in the other letter.[7]

And what I have done so far is only to gratify you, famous Sir, for perhaps it will not be expedient to communicate this to the famous Huygens, lest there should still be something he dislikes, which I should regret. The whole of my analysis rests upon the same principles by which I formerly established the summary equation of AE to AB, that is, the discovery of three harmonic proportionals, whose utility in this kind of problem I showed long ago. However, anyone not averse to length of calculation may also pursue another quite similar [method], by drawing any line not only through A, but also through E and B. But truly I think this business not worth the trouble. But ho! this is quite enough of Alhazen's Problem.

That remarkable experiment in which mercury is brought to a height of 75 inches I learned of many years ago, from a letter of the very illustrious Boyle to yourself.[8] And truly that is an ingenious hypothesis by which the very acute man has recently tried to explain it; but to admit the truth, if I understand it rightly it does not seem to dispose of all difficulties so that one's intellect can quite peacefully confide in it. For when that matter more subtle than air presses on the mercury, not only sideways but perpendicularly through the pores of the tube, why should it not depress it a little bit at least? Since the least bubble of that lighter air suffices to depress it completely, in a moment, from the height of 75 inches to its normal 29 or 30. It may be added that if that subtle matter is heavier than air, it seems extraordinary that the air does not continually ascend through it, just as fire does in air. It occurred to me once that one might explain the effect if one should suppose all pressure and weight to depend upon the elastic force of the air, even when enclosed within bodies; whence it would follow that a fluid deprived of air, and only pressed upon at its lower part by this external pressure of the air, could be maintained at any height whatever. But I perceived the futility of this hypothesis when I recognized that mercury freed of air and suspended at the height of 75 inches even falls to the usual 30 inches when a single bubble of air is admitted to the tube. For if the hypothesis were founded on truth the mercury ought to stand either above or below the same height, according to the different proportions of air received into the tube. And so I pause, believing that the diligence of a remote age must be awaited, by which what is now concealed will be revealed. Helmont, indeed, says both in his printed works and in a manuscript on springs that I have read, that the waters under the earth away from the pressure of the air do not observe the laws of hydraulics;[9] but this will rest upon his word alone, until he shall have proved it to us by reason or experiment.

I have already written to you often enough about the Rule for drawing tangents to any geometrical curves whatever without calculation of any kind, which I have decided to make public;[10] but hitherto I could not effect my purpose. For I meant to show its usefulness both in solving problems and in many other ways, some of which, if I am not mistaken, I have indicated to you formerly. In fact I have decided, as I lack leisure, if it shall seem fit, to send you the Rule without demonstration and corollaries (lest the bulk should be excessive) for insertion in the *Philosophical Transactions*, where it may undergo the criticism of the learned. Tell me, therefore, what your opinion is, for I willingly submit myself to your judgment, and will send it to you just as soon as you have indicated your approval. Meanwhile farewell, most noble Sir, from him who is wholeheartedly yours, and who acknowledges himself always your debtor in many ways. Liège, 6 December 1672, N.S.

It is already two months since Father Bertet left here, yet I will write your friendly greeting to him as soon as opportunity serves. Farewell again.

NOTES

Reply to Letter 2093. Oldenburg sent a copy of the mathematical portion relating to Alhazen's Problem to Huygens in Letter 2129; this copy is printed in *Œuvres Complètes*, VII, 248–50.

1 We have not been able to locate this phrase in the works of Tacitus.
2 For "vereres" read, presumably, "vererer."
3 The construction proper was, of course, given in Letter 1994; what follows is not strictly a justification of the construction.
4 See above, p. 100. The last quantity in the numerator should be $2bqqe$.
5 See above, p. 101.
6 Read: SA.
7 Letter 1994.
8 See Letter 298 (Vol. II, pp. 123–26); Sluse's knowledge of this letter is explained by the note on p. 126.
9 Helmont's printed discussion of the origin and behavior of springs and fountains is to be found in "A Treatise of Disease," Ch. 95 ("Of the Fountains of the Spaw; the First Paradox"), pp. 688–90 of *Oriatrike* (London, 1662), where he is not so explicit as Sluse here makes him.
10 Rules for drawing tangents to curves had been often discussed in previous years; see the indexes to, especially, Vols. VI, VII, and VIII, s.v. "Mathematics." Sluse's method is described in Letter 2124. This passage was certainly communicated by Collins to Newton, and was in fact copied by Collins on the last page of Newton's letter to him dated 10 December 1672. Compare Letter 2136.

2101

Oldenburg to Finch

28 November 1672

From the draft in Royal Society MS. Classified Papers, XIX, no. 79
The original is summarized in Historical Manuscripts Commission *Report on the Manuscripts of the late Allan George Finch Esq. of Burley-on-the-Hill, Rutland,* II (1922), 6–8

Philosophical Matters and Inquiries
Recommended to the favor and care
of His Excellency Sir John Finch Knight, for
ye use of ye R. Society

I. To take notice of ye Directions and Inquiries, relating both to Land and Sea, publisht in ye Phil. Transactions No. XI and XXIV; of each of wch a Copy accompanies these.[1]

2. To excite the English Consuls, Vice-consuls, and Factors, yt reside in the Turkish Dominions in the Levant and in Egypt, to impart all the Observables of Nature and Art, yt have already occurr'd or may henceforth occurr to their Observation.

3. To endeavor to procure out of Egypt a particular Answer to ye ensuing Quaere's, formerly proposed by Sr R. Moray to Monsr. de Monceaux a late curious traveller in those parts,[2] the resolution of wch was prevented by yt Gentlemans death.

They are;

Whether a Mapp may not be obtain'd, to represent the Scituation and Figure of yt place of ye Red Sea, where the Israelites did passe; its extent towards ye Mediterranean Sea, and ye scituation of those Old Towns, Rameses, Succoth, Etham, Pihahiroth, Migdol and Baal-Zephou;[3] together wth ye true figure of ye shores of yesd Red Sea, as also a line drawne to shew the lowest Water-Mark: All wth a Scale of distances upon ye foot of France, Rome, or England.

What is ye perpendicular hight of ye highest water at ye place where the Hebrews did passe?

At what houre ye Tide is highest there, when the Moon is full? At what place 'tis believed ye Israelites did passe ye Red Sea? Whether it be commonly passd there at this day?

What kind of Earth is there found, when the Sea is fallen away; and whether there be different kinds of Earth; and of what nature they are, how scituate and of what extent?

Whether there be places of quick sand and whether men sink into it when tis cover'd wth water, as well as when ye water is retired? And whether it be thesame, when the Water falls away from it, leaving it bare, as when it floweth and advanceth?

How farr distant the place, where ye Waters are bitter, is from that shore of ye sea where the Israelites pass'd.

Whether ye way, wch the Israelites went, was easy to passe, or whether it was Mountanous and craggy between Rameses and ye Sea?

By what marks one may know the place of ye Red Sea, where the Israelites entred into it? And whether about yt place there be Hills on both sides?

So far these Quaere's.

4. To inquire, in what part of Turky ye Rusma[4] is found and in what quantity? Whether the Turks employ it to any other Uses besides yt of taking away hair wth it? To procure some of it, and to send it over?

5. To learn, whether in ye Mines of Hungary, especially those of Cremnitz and Schemnitz, (Wch are Gold and Silvermines,) and in the rest of ye Hungarian Mines, as those of Copper, Iron, Lead, there is found every where Quicksilver and Sulphur: And to transmit some of ye best Hungarian Vitriol, Cinnabaris Nativa, Antimony etc. especially some of all kinds of Antimony occurring in those Mines, etc.

6. Whether the Turks doe not only take opium ymselves for strength and courage, and curing ye megrim; but give it also to their Horses, Camels and Dromedaries when they find ym faint in travelling? And what is ye greatest dose, yt any man or woman are known to have taken of it?

7. Whether those Mummies, yt are found in ye Deserts of Arabia, being ye dryed flesh of men buried in those Sands in travelling, have the like vertue wth ye Embalm'd ones?

8. Whether the Earth-quakes in Zante and Cephalonia be so frequent, as now and then to fall out 9 or 10 times in a month? And whether those Isles be not very cavernous?

9. To procure a good description of ye Hills in Turky, and of the Observables about ym, and particularly of Mount Caucasus and of mt Libanus? As also a good accompt of ye Trees or Shrubbs of *Thus* and *Myrrha*; likewise of what *Bdellium* is, some esteeming it to be a Gum, others a Gem, others a kind of Pearle?[5]

10. Whether there be such a Tree about Damascus, yt is call'd *Mouslae*,

wch every year in September is cutt down close by ye root, and in five months time so shoots up again, as to bring forth not only leaves, but also flowers and fruit, though bearing but one apple a year?

11. Whether about Reame in the most Southern part of Arabia faelix,[6] there grow grapes wthout any grains at all in them?

12. Whether in some parts of Arabia faelix many people live to ye age of 120. years, in good health?

13. Whether all fruits, herbs, earths, fountains, are naturally saltish in the Island of Cyprus? And whether those parts of yesame Island, yt abound in Cypres-trees, are more healthfull than others? What store of Amianthus[7] there is in Cyprus; and how the people work it?

14. What is ye Art of tempering steel at Damascus? And whether the Cimeters made thereof will cutt very thick Iron-nailes in pieces; and no Helm or Shield is proof against them?

15. To procure a particular description of ye remainder of ye Castle and Temple of Balbec, said by Monsr Monceaux, (a great Traveller and very skilfull Architect,) to be the best piece of Architecture, he ever saw; not far distant from Damascus in a fair plaine.

16. To observe and describe the structure and dimensions of ye Aqueducts, caused to be made by Solyman the Magnificent in several places about Constantinople; and any other Edifices, yt have any thing considerable in ym.

17. To get a particular Account of ye whole way of breeding and ordering the Angra-goats.

18. To observe and describe ye particular dexterities and suplenesses of ye bodies of Turks, and any other thing, they excell in.

Henry Oldenburg S.R.S.

London Nov. 28. 1672.

More Quaeries

1. An vox *Maslag* apud Turcas unicum medicamentum notet an plura? Et quaenam notet, et qua forma illa sumantur, an pulveris, an electuaris, et an simplex tantum sit medicamentum, an compositum?[8]

2. Quid sit *Heiranluc* Turcarum? Quid *Bergs*? quid *Doam-Samec*? quid *Bangue*? quid *Asseral*?[9]

NB. To inquire after Succus Cyrenaicus, made of Laserpitium, ye gum Laser.[10]

NOTES

Sir John Finch had left Florence in the summer of 1670. He was appointed English Ambassador to the Sublime Porte in November 1672, which was evidently the occasion for Oldenburg's presenting him with these queries. He did not in fact leave England until May 1673, arriving in Paris on 16 June 1673. He stopped in Italy on the way, to negotiate successfully with the Tuscan court over the capture of an English ship carrying the Pasha of Tunis by a Livornese corsair. He went next to Malta, thence to Smyrna, and finally overland to Constantinople, arriving there by the end of March 1674. Oldenburg's queries remained in his papers.

1 Boyle's "General Heads for a Natural History of a Countrey" were published in *Phil. Trans.*, no. 11 (2 April 1666), 186–89; *Phil. Trans.*, no. 24 (8 April 1667), 433–48 is entirely devoted to directions for observations to be made at sea.

2 See Vol. VII, p. 88, note.

3 Rameses, Succoth, and Etham are all supposedly places on the ancient canal connecting the Nile with the Red Sea, described by Herodotus, whose line is marked by the modern Wadi Tumilat; the first was possibly at Tell Rotab and the second at Tell el Maskhuta, being identical with or near to Pithom. The other places are further south, in the neighborhood of the Bitter Lake.

4 See Vol. III, pp. 371, 470, 603, and 607, note 3.

5 *Thus* is another name for frankincense; for bdellium, see Vol. VIII, p. 334, note 14.

6 *Arabia felix* was the ancient appellation of the highlands behind the southern coast —parts of the Yemen and Hadhramaut—where there is a moist, temperate climate, and whence the resins, etc., came. We have not found *Reame*.

7 Asbestos.

8 "Whether the word *Maslac* among the Turks designates a single medicament, or more than one? And what it signifies, and in what form it is taken, whether as a powder or an electuary, and whether it is a simple drug or a complex one?" For *Maslac*, see Letter 2048, note 9.

9 "What is the *Heiranluc* of the Turks? What is *Bergs*? What is *Doam-Semec*? What is *Bangue*? What is *Asseral*?" For "bergs" and "bangue," see Letter 2061.

10 A gum resin (known to Roman authors) obtained from umbelliferous plants of the genus *Laserpitium*.

2102

Oldenburg to Malpighi

28 November 1672

From the original in the Bibl. Archivio Arcivescovile, Bologna MS. A II, C. VI, 15; from a
microfilm copy lent by Cavaliere d'Aurizio
Printed in Adelman, I, 698, note 5

Illustri Viro
Domino Marcello Malpighio, Ph. et Med. Bononiae
Henr. Oldenburg S.P.

En Tibi, Vir Clarissime, Exemplaria aliquot accuratae Tuae Dissertationis de Formatione Pulli in Ovo, quae Regiae Societatis Iussu, una cum benevola Ipsius Salute, Tibi transmitto.[1] Perspicies inde, ni fallor, haud parvi nos ea pendere, quae depromuntur tua vestigatione, atque industria tua elaborantur. Persuasum omnino habemus, Te haud feriaturum, quin quae de eodem hoc Argumento, deque Plantis, inquirenda supersunt, in lucem pertraxeris, et Societatis nostrae monumentis inserueris.

Felicem auguramur navi velificationem, cui haec Exemplaria, (triginta numero) commisimus. Suscepit Excellentissimus Johannes Finch, Serenissimi Regis nostri ad Portam Ottomanicam Legatus, jam jam abiturus,[2] se Livorniae mercatori cuidam ea commendaturum, qui postmodum commoda occasione data Bononiam ea transmittat. Vale, nostri memor et a Tui studiosissimo plurimum salve. Dabam Londini 28 Nov. 1672.

ADDRESS

> Al Excellentissimo Signor
> Signor Marcello Malpighi
> Dottore Medico. Padrone
> mio Colendissimo in
> > Bononia

TRANSLATION

Henry Oldenburg presents many greetings to the illustrious Mr. Marcello Malpighi, Philosopher and Physician of Bologna

Here you may see, famous Sir, a few examples of your exquisite dissertation, *De formatione pulli in ovo*, which I send you by the Royal Society's order, together with its benevolent greetings.[1] Unless I am mistaken you may gather from this that we attach no light weight to the matters elucidated by your research and perfected by your industry. We are quite confident that you will not relax but will rather illuminate the points that still remain for inquiry in this subject, and in the study of plants, and will deposit [the results] in the archives of our Society.

We pray a good voyage for the vessel to which we have committed these copies, thirty in number. The very excellent John Finch, ambassador from our Royal Majesty to the Ottoman Porte, who will be setting out immediately,[2] has undertaken to entrust them to some merchant at Livorno, who will afterwards send them on to Bologna when a convenient opportunity arises. Farewell, be mindful of us; with many wishes for your good health from your most zealous [friend].

London, 28 November 1672.

ADDRESS

To the most excellent Mr. Marcello Malpighi, M.D.
My most revered lord,
Bologna

NOTES

1 The printing of this work, authorized by the Council of the Royal Society on 12 June (compare also Letter 2016), was completed by October 1672; on 30 October a copy was presented to the Society which (on 13 November) ordered that thirty copies be sent gratis to the author. Meanwhile, Hooke had purchased a copy for himself as early as 12 October. It seems certain that the present letter was enclosed with the package, for Malpighi's first knowledge of these events came from Oldenburg's later Letter 2155 of 18 February 1672/3, which he acknowledged on 10 May.

2 See Letter 2101. To anticipate later correspondence, Malpighi actually received the package in the early summer of 1674.

2103
Duhamel to Oldenburg
29 November 1672
From the original in Royal Society MS. H 1, no. 111

Monsieur

Jay receu il y a deja quelques temps la lettre qu'il vous á plû m'escrire.[1] Mais iay differé á vous faire response, iusqu'á mon retour á Paris, parce que ie craignois, que l'on n'eust pas besoin de porter ma lettre á la poste. Je suis arrivé depuis 5 ou 6. iours. Jay receu depuis ce temps la vos Transactions, ou vous parlez du livre de Mente humana, de la maniere la plus obligeante du monde, dont ie vous remercie tres humblement;[2] J'y ay leu encore de tres belles choses et tres utiles, particulierement lextrait de la lettre de Mr Langelot,[3] qui vaut bien seule un iuste volume.

Mr petit le fils qui est mon libraire et tres honnest ieune homme á envoyé 100 de mes livres á Mr Martin; Je crois qu'il l'en aura receue. Jay vu le memoire des livres latins que Mr Martin luy envoye; Mr petit luy escrit et le prie de luy en envoyer un certain nombre de chacun; je seray bien aise que ce commerce continue entre eux.

Je ne scache point de bons livres imprimés depuis peu. Vous aurez bientost un iournal, ou il aura quelque chose de curieux, de linvention de Mr Hugens;[4] ie crois que cest une nouvelle façon de barometre; on avance fort son livre des pendules; il pourra estre achevé au commencement du mois de mars; dans peu de iours on commencera á imprimer le livre des nombres de Monsr frenicle,[5] qui sera fort curieux; Nous attendons avec impatience les livres de Monsieur boyle. Jay receu celuy des pierres pretieuses, qui me paroist admirable: Mais il nous donne une plus grande envie de iouir ce quil á travaillé sur les mineraux, de effluviis, succo lapidifico &c[6] ce sera quand son loisir, et sa santé qui est pretieux à tous les gens de lettres, luy permettront.

Je ne scais si Mr de St hilaire est de retour en Angleterre; Mais sil n'y est pas, ie vous prie Monsieur, d'avoir la bonté, quand vous me ferez lhonneur de m'escrire, d'envoyer les lettres a Mr Joli,[7] chez Monsieur l'Ambassadeur, Je n'ay pû encore revoir Mr Justel.

ioubliois á vous dire que le p. pardies fait imprimer plusieurs traittez de Mathématique fort curieux.[8] pour moy i'espere mettre sous la presse ce qui

me reste, vers le caresme;⁹ si la paix se faisoit, les livres se debiteroient
mieux; car le grand commerce est du costé du Nord; Mais ce sera quand il
plaite á dieu. Faites moy tousiours lhonneur de m'aimez, et me faite la
grace de croire que Je suis avec sincerité, et de tout mon coeur Monsieur

> Vostre tres humble et
> tres obeissant serviteur
> *J. b. du hamel* p. de. St. l.

de paris ce 9em de decembre [N.S.]

ADDRESS
    A Monsieur
    Monsieur grubendol
        a Londres

TRANSLATION

Sir,

I received the letter you were pleased to write to me some time ago now.¹ But I
have put off replying until my return to Paris, because I feared to give the
trouble of conveying my letter to the post office. I arrived here five or six days
ago. I have during this time received your *Transactions*, where you speak of the
book *De mente humana* in the most obliging manner in the world, for which I very
humbly thank you.² I read there other very fine and useful matters, especially the
extract from Mr. Langelott's letter³ which alone would be very well worth a
whole volume.

Mr. Petit the younger, who is my bookseller and a very honest young men,
sent one hundred of my books to Mr. Martin; I hope that he has received them.
I have seen the list of Latin books which Mr. Martin sent him; Mr. Petit wrote to
him and asked him to send a certain number of them. I should be very pleased if
this trade continued between them.

I do not know of any good books printed lately. You will soon have a new
Journal [*des Sçavans*] in which there will be something of interest, invented by Mr.
Huygens.⁴ I think it is a new kind of barometer. They are getting on with his
book on pendulums; it could be finished by the beginning of March. In a few
days they will begin to print Mr. Frénicle's book on numbers,⁵ which will be of
very great interest. We await Mr. Boyle's books with great impatience. I have
received that on gems which seems to me admirable; but it makes us long even
more to enjoy what he has done on minerals, effluvia, the petrifying juice, etc.⁶—

but only when his leisure and his health (which is precious to all men of letters) will permit.

I don't know whether Mr. de St Hilaire has returned to England; but if he is not there, I request you, Sir, to be so good, when you do me the honor of writing to me, to send the letters to Mr. Jolly,[7] at the Ambassador's. I have not yet been able to see Mr. Justel again.

I was forgetting to tell you that Father Pardies is having printed several mathematical treatises of great interest.[8] As for me, I hope to get what I have by me to the press towards Lent.[9] If peace is made books will be worth more, for the largest trade is in the North; but this will be in God's good time.

Do me the honor to continue to love me and do me the favor of believing that I am sincerely and with all my heart, Sir,

Your very humble and
Very obedient servant
J. B. Duhamel, Prior of St. Lambert

Paris, 9 December [N.S.]

ADDRESS

> To Mr. Grubendol
> London

NOTES

The year is established both by internal evidence and from Oldenburg's endorsement, "resp. le 16 Dec. 1672."

1 This is the only surviving evidence that correspondence between Oldenburg and Duhamel had continued since their exchange in 1670 (for which see Vol. VII).

2 See Letter 2087, note 5.

3 See Letter 2048, note 5.

4 The *Journal des Sçavans* for 12 December 1672 [N.S.] contains "Extrait d'une . . . Lettre de M. Hugens touchant une nouvelle maniere de Barometre, qu'il a inventee." Huygens in fact suggests two methods of extending the scale to make it easier to detect small changes in pressure by superposing a short column of water upon the mercury column, the two fluids meeting in a wide bulb so that the displacement of the water is magnified. The second method, which he prefers, consists in making a U tube with a bulb near the top of one leg and near the bottom of the other; this is then filled with mercury in the ordinary way, after which a mixture of water and alcohol (to avoid freezing) is added. Of the two forms of two-liquid barometer described by Huygens, the first had been invented previously by Descartes (1650) and the second by Robert Hooke (1668). There is no reason to suppose that Huygens was aware of these anticipations. See W. E. K. Middleton, *History of the Barometer* (Baltimore, 1964), 87–89.

5 Frénicle's *Traité des triangles rectangles en nombres* was published posthumously at Paris in 1676.

6 Most of these books have been mentioned often before. Boyle published nothing on

the "petrifying juice" after 1665, when a brief discussion was published in *Phil. Trans.*, no. 6 (6 November 1665), 101–2.

7 This must be the man mentioned by Pardies; see Vol. VIII, p. 628.

8 In 1673 were published both *La Statique* and *Deux machines propres à faire les quadrans.*

9 This very likely refers to Duhamel's *De corpore animato libri quatuor* (Paris, 1673), which is reviewed in *Phil. Trans.*, no. 98 (17 November 1673), 6151–54.

2104

Lister to Oldenburg

30 November 1672

From the original in Bodleian Library MS. Lister 34, f. 71

Sir,

You was pleased to remind me of ye Commands of ye R.S. & yt something further was expected from me concerning ye Veines in Plants:[1] we therefore are not willing to delay ym any longer, at least this *Breviate* of our present thoughts.

We have formerly given you certain reasons for their existence; to wch we might add others of later notice; as yt ye *skin* of a plant may be cutt cleer off wth part of ye *spongy Parenchyma* & yet noe signe of *blood* follow, yt is noe incision made in a Vein. Again we have stript ye plant of its *skin* (by pulling it up by ye roots & exposing it to ye wett weather, untill it became flaccid as a wet-thong) without any injury to ye Veines, wch yet upon incision would freshly bleed.

It will be little satisfaction to tell you these & many other fruitlesse Attempts, wch we have made to praepare & facilitate an *Ocular demonstration* of these Veines; & yet without yt, ye discovery of ye more particular accidents belonging to ym, cannot reasonably be expected to be made wth accuratenesse & certainty. This I say is a worke of much labour & patience & yt wch renders matters very difficult is ye infinite Number, smallnesse & perplexitie of these Vessells.

It is tru ye *Transverse-Cutts* of Plants give us some good light to our purpos; but they leave us again in ye darke. We see as it were a certain Order & Number of ye bloody Orifices of dissected Veines: & yet they disappeare as soon as they have parted wth their juice, not unlike ye *lacteal Veines* in sanguineous Animals.

Assisted by a Microscope, we observe in a Leafe (wch we take to be ye simplest part of a plant)

1. That ye Veines keep company wth ye Fibres; and are distributed into all ye parts of ye Leafe, according to ye subdivisions of ye Fibres; these in all probabilitie adding strength & support (whatever else) to ym, as ye Oake does to ye Ivy.

2. That in a *Transverse-Cutt* of a Leafe, ye midle Fibre for example, seemes to yeild one bigg drop of juice, springing as it were from one Vein: yet ye Microscope plainly shews us, yt there are many Veines, wch contribute to ye making up of yt drop.

3. That if a Fibre be carfully taken out of ye leafe, ye Veines will appeare, like small pillars running up those great ones in ye bodies of our Minsters.

4. That those many Veines, for ought we have yet discovered to ye contrary, are all of an equall bignesse.

5. That though we seem to be more certain of ye ramifications of ye Fibres, we are not yet soe, yt these Veines are any wher Capillary or lessned; though very probabilie it may be soe: yt wch makes us doubt it, is ye exceeding smalnesse of these veines already, even those where they seem to be Trunck Veines & of ye largest size; & being there alsoe in very great Number, & running in direct lines along ye Fibre, we Guesse, yt one or more of ym may be distributed & fall off on either side ye leafe wth ye subdivided Fibre & not suffer any diminution in their bulke.

6. That we cannot discern any where throughout ye whole Plant larger & more Capacious Veines, than those we see adhering to ye Fibres of ye Leaves, wch alsoe does appear from Comparing ye bleeding Orifices.

An Herculean labour followes to trace & unravel ym, throughout ye whole body & root of ye Plant. our opinion is, yt these Veines doe still continue in company with their respective Fibres. And as all ye Fibres of ye leafe are joined in ye stalke of ye Leafe, & yt stalke again explicated in cloathing ye Twig or stem of ye Plant (wch is ye reason of ye various Order of ye breaking forth of leaves) soe are we to thinke of the veines their perpetual Companions. And indeed, a transverse-cutt of ye top-twig or of a plant, shewes us one single Circle of bleeding Orifices (I meane in respect of ye order of those dropps, not ye number of Veines; wch we have said are many even in ye simple Fibres of ye leaves) yt is, according to ye number of ye Fibres of ye leaves cloathing yt Twigg: ye succeeding branches shew a multitude of bleeding Orifices, ye Body & Root yet more numerous, according to ye number of Coates cloathing ym.

these few particulars we have, concerning ye Veines in ye Roots of plants. 1. if a single Coat of ye Root be separated, we shall find ye Veines therin variously decussate, reticular & implicate; not in ye same simple order, as in ye leaves: ye like we thinke of ye barke of ye bodies of Trees. 2. Again where ye juice of these Veines springs sloly & is hardly discernable, but by ye discolouring it receives from ye Aire; as in ye roots of *Cicuta*[2] etc. *Specks* or *drops* of divers magnitudes appeare upon a transversely-cut root; wch to me seemes, as though ye Coates of ye roots of Plants were but soe many setts of leaves, ye greater spotts being from ye more numerous veines adhaering to ye larger Fibres & ye lesser from ye fewer veines accompanying ye sudivisions of ye Fibres.

From what hath been said, it may well be doubted, whether there be any such thing as a gathering togather of Veines into one Common Trunk, as is ye manner of ye Veines in sanguineous Animals: but rather, yt there are a multitude of equally bigg Veines, each existing apart by it selfe, or at least such a number of ym & by Parcells. We, indeed, have found it very difficult soe to wound a plant by dissecting ye Veines only, as to kill it; although, I say, much vital juice be exhausted by a multitude of incisions. Many other Instances there are, wch seem to favour this Notion of ye parcelling & discontinuance of ye Veines in Plants & ye little relation & intercourse they have wth one another. As one branch of a Tree having large & well growne fruit, before ye other branches of ye same Tree & fruit spread their leaves & flowers, from ye different situation & other circumstances of Culture: any small part of a Tree growing: ye Cyon governing: ye indefinite & perpetual growth of Trees: ye artificial encrease of ye roots of naturally annual or sesqui-annual Plants to a vast bulke & ye continuance of this growth for many years: The juices of these Veines being of very different colours in divers parts of ye same plant; as of a brimstone colour in ye root of *Spondilium*[3] & white in ye stem; alsoe ye *Virginian Rhus*[4] struck at ye bottom of ye bowle of ye Tree, yeilds a much browner milke yn at ye topp.

Thus farr we have taken our information concerning these Veines by ye helpe of a Glasse. And yet we find great difficulties in discovring ye Accidentes belonging to these Vessells, as External figure, Coates, Capacitie etc—

Concerning ye Coates or Membranes we thinke ym to be exceeding thinn & transparent filmes; because they suddainly disappeare & subside— after their being exhausted of their juice: & wch is a plain evidence, in yt they shew us, quite through their Coates, ye yellow liquour they hold (in *Chelidonium majus*[5] for example) noe otherwise than a tincture of saffran in Chrystalline Pipes.

We have thought, yt ye several Accidents belonging to ym as Vessells, would have been made manifest to us, if it were possible to coagulate ye juice they hold without much srinking ye Plant; for to inject a coagulating & stiffning liquor we see noe probabilitie of doing it into such small Vessells. We were in great hopes freezing would have affected this:wch, (though it did not succeed as we promisd our selves in respect of ye manifestation of these Accidents); yet it gave us some further light into ye nature of ye juice of these Veines. In ye keenest frost wch hapned ye other Winter, we dissected ye frozen leaves of ye *Garden Spurge*. Here we observed yt all ye juice, besides yt wch these Veines hold, was indeed frozen into perfect hard Ice & to be expressed out in ye figure of ye containing pores; but ye *milkie-juice* was as liquid as ever, but not soe briske as in open weather.

This Experiment we take to be good proofe, yt ye liquor of these Veines is ye only *vital juice* of plants, yt is, wch hath a fermentative motion within it selfe, wch preserves it from ye injuries of ye Weather, & yt consequently these Vessells are ye only proper Veines in Plants. Thus we have seen Insects (as Hexapode Wormes etc) ly frozen upon ye Snow into very lumps of Ice; wch did not only cause ye Glasse to ring we struck ym against but did endanger ye breaking of it: And yet put under ye Glasse & exposed to ye warmth of ye fire, they quickly recovered their leggs & vigour to escape: wch we thinke could not be, unlesse ye Vital liquor of their Veines, as in Plants, had been untouched & little concerned in ye frost.

Further, we doe hence alsoe argue ye different *Use* of these juices: & wth some colour compare ye frozen Icicles wthin ye *Spongy parenchyma* of Plants or yt more *copious dilute* liquour to ye Aliment of Animals & call these Pores ye Intestines; as we doe ye other Vessells, holding ye not-frozen liquor, Veines. And possibly there are many more mouths in a Plant, than what are supposed to be in ye root only, ye every-where-open Pores of ye leaves & barke receiving into all parts of ye plant above ground ye moist particles in ye Aire, as ye root does those other in ye Earth.

Lastly since (according to ye knowledge we yet have of ye parts of Plants) there are noe Viscera analogous to ye hart of Anamals; noe common Trunck, where ye Veines are united; noe Pulsation; noe stop or swelling upon ye application of a Ligature more on ye one side, than on ye other; noe difference in Veines, we must thinke, yt these Veines *bleed*, because ye juice they hold is fermentative & not by reason of any exteriour impulse from ye mechanick of Vessells, as in Animals.

We might alledge many things in confirmation of ye intestine motion or fermentation of this juice. As ye motion of ye bleeding Veines & Fibres newly taken out of ye Plant, aemulating yt of wormes: Also ye breaking of this juice into whey & Curds. Again ye transparency of some Gumms, wch in bleeding are thick & troubled liquors, like ye barme of beare; & yet, I say in a few howres after drawing, fall & become quiet & chrystalline, as ye Gumme of ye *Virginian Rhus* etc. Further, we doe affirme (if we may be credited awhile, untill we publish ye Experiments, togather wth ye different Natures of ye juices of these Veines: of wch at present we shall only say Experimentally, yt more usefull preparations are to be made & a truer Analysis & Separation of ye parts of Vegetable Druggs is to be effected, whilst they are liquid & in bleeding from their respective Veines, than after they are once setled, become lumpish & have lost their natural ferment) we doe also affirme, I say, yt these juices will give a vivid & lasting ferment to ye most insensible of liquours & yt for some weekes, cold & exposed in open vessells to ye Aire; wch is beyond ye power of any known ferment. And this we take to be ye reason not only of Vegetation in general; but particularly of some Trees bleeding soe plentifully after a frost; ye vital juice of these Veines some way or other communicating its ferment to ye other more dilute & copious liquor of such Trees & making yt, wch was before & of it selfe torpid, briske & vigorous.

And thus much concerning ye Veines in Plants in general Terms, avoiding ye Circumstances of Experiment & Observation as much as could be for brevity sake, yt these lines might not be as tedious, as they are rude. I leave it to your discretion either to Excuse us & suppresse ym, or if you will venture ym, we doe submit ym to their great judgements, leaving you our Intercessour. We hope to worke herafter by their directions & guidance, being conscious to our selves of noe other Talent, but a willingnesse to labour; acknowledging ye little progresse & successe we have had in a matter where we are left to our selves. I am Sir

Your most humble servant
Martin Lister

Yorke Novemb: 30th
    1672

NOTES

As becomes obvious from subsequent correspondence, Lister asked for this letter back in view of various comments made upon it, and rewrote it as Letter 2125.

1 In Letter 2075.
2 Common hemlock, and related species.

3 Cow parsnip.
4 Sumach.
5 Greater celandine.

2105

Henshaw to Oldenburg

12 December 1672

From the original in Royal Society MS. H 3, no. 13

Decbr. 12th—72 Coppenhagen
Mr Oldenburg

Sr

The later end of last week some of ye Kgs fregats arriving in ye Categat brought wth them one Mr Flexny a servant of ye D of Richmonds who delivered me your two letters, one of July 31 and ye other of Aug: 5. as also two copies of Mr Boyles booke of Gemmes; and can never thanke yu enough for ye most pleasing divertissements I received in ye reading both yr letters and ye booke, wch in this tedious dull place where I at least can fasten uppon no ingenious conversation, did not a little refresh me by reviving in my thoughts ye many pleasant houres I have had in ye R Society. Yet I cannot but lament Mr Hannings imprudence that would not send me so much as one of these letters by ye post, but let them both languish for a tedious opportunity of conveying them to mee; especially since being now ready to bee shut up by the ice, there will bee no means of sending yr inquiries to Iseland or fero till may next; and though I feare oure confinement here will bee somewhat longer, yet if wee should bee called home before I will take all care possible to have them sent to ye best hands those Islands will afford, though I am not certaine whether there bee any inhabitants that abide the whole yeare about on Fero, and I much doubt that in Island there will not bee found any capable to give answers to those quaeries wch are very curious especially such as require any mathematicall practice for theyr solution, but if they doe theyr best it is all yu can expect. ye same quaeries I suppose will serve for Fero as being not farre off ye other. I cannot yet think of any other quaeries to adde except it bee about ye Eydder downe, wch is a most delicate soft warme light and springy downe wch in these northern Countrys they fill theyr winter coverlets wth, and indeed is ye only thing of delicacy I have met wth here, its sold for 10s ye pound but sixe pound of it is enough for ye biggest bed and ye coverlet is made like a sack or bagge for they say it will not endure quilting for that currupts it, all ye information I can gain of it is that it is taken out of certain birds nests in Island and Norway, and indeed it comes hither very foule and there is great loss in ye Cleansing of it wch makes it so deare, but what a vast number of nests must there bee to furnish every house in Denmarke and Sweden wth such great quantitys of it? scarse any bed being without it. if yrself or Mr Boyle or any other good freind think it may be usefull I shall readily provide any quantity yu desire the other is concerning ye Sea unicorne,[1] of wch there hath formerly been considerable quantities brought formerly to this town taken on ye Costs of Groenland Island and Norway, but they say now there hath none of them been seen there these 30 yeares they are now growun very scarse and of great value here since ye last Kg employed almost all were to be gotten in making of a large throne for ye Kgs of Denmarke to bee crowned in, wch I have often seen and handled and thinke it one of ye Magnificent things I ever beheld though I should exclude ye 3 lions of Silver as big as ye life that are placed about it wth other rich Ornaments of silver and Jewels. neverthelesse I made shift to buy two hornes of young unicornes the shortest of them is a yard long, ye finelyest taperd and ye most beautifull that ever I had seen but by misfortune I showd them ye D of Richmond who could never bee at rest till he had them, and he hath put gold heads and ferules to them to make walking staves of them, and though since the vice-Roy of Norway hath given him a very long and large one richly set in gold yet he values these beyond it; I have yet gotten but 4 ₃ of ye shavings of this horne and a pretty round piece cut through ye horne, wch is heare counted by ye physitians an excellent cordiall and sudorifick; but it shall goe very hard if I doe not get a faire one to present ye R Society at my returne.[2] Since yu have not seen Wormius de Mure Norvagico[3] I for hast sent yu one I had made use of, by ye returne of these fregats, it is gone wth some Eydder-downe to Sr John Clayton[4] who will take care to bring it yu and since it is scarse in England I will provide another for ye library of ye RS. perhaps yu will not bee displeased wth an attestation of ye truth that I have scribbled before ye booke. The Mouse that yu will see pictured in ye booke and ye Skeleton of another, I have severall times looked uppon in this Kgs Kunst chambers[4a] whose father bought ye Musaeum Wormianum,[5] and indeed that Kgs whole collection of raritys of Nature and art is much ye largest and finest that ever I saw. as for the Danish law book yu sent me ye title of, I doe assure yu booksellers here are such blockheads that ye very same man that uppon sight of ye title [did] immediately find it out and sold it me did more then once before deny to me he had any such booke; wch I have found not only usuall wth him but wth others of them also; because Sr Robert Murrey hath one of them already in Danish I did not send him this; Heer is one Mr Clarke one of my Ld Ds[6] secretarys who was formerly imployd by Sr Robert to procure him this booke we have both used our best endeavours to find one in Latin but it is not to bee had, nor any other book of ye Laws of Denmark either in Danish or latin that I can here of; there is a very ingenious and industrious frenchman Monsieur Sterpin[7] that hath lived long in England and hath now for some years served ye Ricks Chancellor here who is arrived to a great perfection in all these Northern tongues, hath Made a grammar of ye Danish language one of wch he presented me at my first comming, he is a great acquaintance of Mr Clarkes to whom I proposed whether he thought Monsr Sterpin might not bee prevailed wth to translate this book into Latine or french for 5 or 10 ll, for he has but a very ordinary service of it, who tould me he had formerly treated wth Sterpin about it and that he did refuse to doe it for mony, but if Sr Robert would promise to get him any tollerable employment in England where he had much rather spend his time he would immediately fall to ye translation of it but as to that I had no commission to say any thing. as for Danish or Island dictionaries there are not such things to bee had heer is [it] was ye first inquiry I made among ye booksellers at my comming; and because they could not bee had I have neglected this toungue and made a digression into ye High Dutch, wch is not onely ye Court language here, but is so vulgar that every servant Maide and boy in ye streets understands it. onely for curiosity sake I have bought Stephani Stephanij Nomenclaturam latin and Danish and Comenij Orbis Sensualium Pictus, wch came out neither but last yeare.[8] I have written to our Masters Envoyé in Sweden to send me a Swedish Dictionary if there bee any, as also for two Copies of Shefferus relation of Lapland, and that other relation of Moscovy if they bee yet publick as also of Loccenius his Swedish laws, that I might send yu one of each.[9] if they bee to bee had I know he will not faile me, he hath allready sent me 3 paires of Laps boots and as many paire of theyr gloves, all made of Rene deare slinkd[10] skins and finely embroydered after ye manner of that country, some Swedish guns and what ever I writ for. Shortly after my comming when after all ye inquiry I could make I could meet wth nothing addressed to yu from Monsr Hevelius, I sent to him by a Merchant of Dantzick, that if there were any thing he desired to send to yu he might rely on my care that I would send it forward, but I never since heard word from him, and suppose he hath found out some more easy conveyance. I have onely seen his account of ye late Comete dedicated to yu[11] but I found Monsr Otto Gericks new booke here to bee sold, and have read him over, wth extraordinary delight though there were not many things in it new to me, I confesse he prevailes much uppon my weake capacity but I long to know what they who are able to iudge wth yu thinke of him. Oh but ye Good Bishop Chesters death I most heartily Lament![12] for beside ye losse of a very worthy freind to my own particular, I feare ye R.S. may stagger by ye losse of such a proppe and incourager. as I was concluding this paper I had news of ye sad and deplorable death of ye Duke of Richmond who departed this life on ye 12 current in ye evening as he was comming in a boat from aboard ye Kgs fregate there riding in ye cold by a suddain fit of an apoplexy assisted by ye rigour of a bitter cold night, so that before he got half way to Elsineur he was stiffe and dead. I am sent for away in haste to Elsineur, wee are all in a sad confusion at this losse and doe not know what will become of us, but I foresee a greate deale of trouble wee are to undergoe, and I feare not without considerable losse to my self. therfore in great haste and much esteeme for yr person I remain Sr

Your most faithfull and humble servant
Tho: *Henshaw*

NOTES

Reply to Letters 2042 and 2046.
1 Narwhal.
2 Grew, *Musaeum* lists a piece of narwhal's horn.
3 See Letter 2015, note 9.
4 He was an Original Fellow, and a member of the Inner Temple, who had been knighted in 1664.
4a "King's cabinets of curiosities."
5 The famous collections of Olaus Wormius were described in *Museum Wormianum* (Leiden, 1655).
6 "my lord duke's."
7 See Letter 1638 (Vol. VII, pp. 468–69).
8 Stephan Stephanius, *Nomenclatoris latino-danici libri IV* (Copenhagen, 1634); A. Comenius, *Orbis sensualis pictus* (London, 1659) had many editions.
9 Johann Scheffer, *Lapponia* (Frankfurt, 1673), was translated into English as *The History of Lapland* (Oxford, 1674). Johannes Loccenius, *Sueciae regni leges civiles* (Stock-

holm, 1672), is more probably meant than his other book published in the same year, *Sueciae regni leges provinciales*.

10 Prematurely born reindeer.

11 See Letter 1986, note 2.

12 Wilkins died on 19 November 1672 in London.

2106

Oldenburg to Lister

12 December 1672

From the original in Bodleian Library MS. Lister 34, ff. 73–75

London Decemb. 12. 1672

Sir,

You shew yrself very generous in performing yr engagements and promises to ye R. Society, wch is very sensible of yr merit, and hath again commanded me to let you know so much, not doubting but you will still proceed in all yr curious philosophical Inquiries and Observations; and continue yr imparting ym upon occasion. After the reading of yr letter of Nov. 30th, thesd Society order'd, yt it should be communicated to Dr Grew, to peruse and consider it, and to give in his thoughts upon it:[1] Wch being done by him accordingly, we find, first, yt he agrees wth you in the main; as the existence of Veins in Plants; and yt they are reticular; yt there are a multitude of equally big veins, each existing apart; yt ye Milky Juyce is ye higher preparation of ye liquor in plants, though he acknowledge it not to be the only vital Juyce in ym; yt yesame Milky Juyce hath a fermentative motion wthin itselfe, wch he esteems to be there more vigorous and briske, than in ye limpid sap; though he judges this latter not to be altogether destitute of yt motion, for all its being subject to freezing; and yt particularly what you alledge in yr last paragraph, is as full of good matter, as 'tis large.

Secondly, ye remarques made by Dr Grew upon yr said letter, giving occasion to the following Quaere's, I had order also, to transmit ym to you; viz.

1. Whether it be a sufficient proof of ye existence of Veins in Plants, yt

ye skin of a Plant may be cutt sheer off wth part of ye spongy parenchyma, and yet no signe of blood follow, yt is, no incision made in a vein; And again, yt you have stript ye plant of its skin wthout any injury to ye veins, wch yet upon incision would freshly bleed?

2. Whether you ever observ'd yrself any true ramifications in any part of any vegetable, so as yt ye lesser tubes or fibres be successively derived of ye greater?

3. Whether there be any thing *essential* in any part of a Plant, yt is not in a Leaf?

4. Whether ye Veins of Plants, as they are *reticular*, (wch is granted,) are also any where *implicated*, or do any where *decussate*, or are any where inosculated; tho it be granted, yt ye Pithy, and Cortical, and several other Fibers of a vegetable are Joyn'd together by all yesd ways of contexture?

5. Whether ye Limpid sap in Plants be not also to be call'd *Vital*, it being acknowledged to be ye Aliment of ye Plant; though ye Milky Juice may be allow'd to be ye higher perfection of it?

6. Whether it be a Conclusive proof of ye want of any Vegetable Juices fermentative motion, because it may be frozen; since beer, wine etc. will be frozen, and yet are fermentative?

7. Whether ye advancement of ye Sap from ye bottom to ye top of ye Trunk can be effected otherwise than by ye structure or mechanisme of ye parts of a vegetable?

Sir, you see our philosophicall freedome, wch we are persuaded you will not only take in good part, but also make use of for further search and information; wch we shall be very glad to receive the successe of, at yr conveniency.

The note inclosed[2] shows my having discharged yr commission in making ye payment of yt money, you sent hither for ye use of ye Society to Sir

Yr very humble and faithf. servt
Oldenburg

Sir,
You will also remember yt part of yr letter of Nov. 15,[3] in wch you say, yt some time you will acquaint us wth ye medicinal uses, you have caused to be made of ye white resin of yt biting kind of Mushrom, you there describe.

ADDRESS
To his much honor'd friend
Dr Martyn Lister at his
house in Stone-gate
            in
                Yorke

NOTES

Reply to Letter 2104.
1 Grew's commentary is in Royal Society MS. G 1, no. 35, and was copied into Letter
  Book V, 405–7, under the heading "Some Remarques of Dr Grew upon the next
  forgoing letter." Grew was in London at this time, so there was no accompanying
  letter. His "remarques" are accurately summarized by Oldenburg.
2 Letter 2106a.
3 Letter 2096.

2106a

Receipt

Enclosure with Letter 2106
From the original in Bodleian Library MS. Lister 34, f. 74

Received this 4 December **1672.** of Martin Lister Esquire the summe of
two pounds twelve shillings by the hand of Henry Oldenburg Esquire and
is in full for his Quarterly payments to the Royal Society untill Christmas
1672. next coming: I say received for the use of the said Society———
2:12:0———

Dan: Colwall FRS

NOTE

Daniel Colwall (d. 1690) had been Treasurer since 1666, an office he was to retain
until 1679.

2107

Collins to Oldenburg

Mid-December 1672

From Royal Society Classified Papers XXIV, no. 15

To Slusius

To intimate that his method of Tangents and Determinates thereby will be very welcome and shall be printed in the Transactions from time to time though large, which need not hinder his publishing the same apart when he shall have leisure more fully to explaine himselfe

To desire his thoughts about Huddens Annexa Geometriae Cartesianae concerning the dividing of high Æquations into their Components and what he sayth p503[1]

Diversas adhuc alias regulas . . . [*for the remainder of this quotation, see p. 361*].

And of the Assertion of Dulaurens of taking away all the intermediate degrees of the unknowne quantity in high Æquations leaving only the highest and lowest power equall to an absolute or Homogeneum[2]

Some of them numerall rules promised by Hudden we beleive are explained according to the old Cossick mode[3] with great variety of Examples in the Dutch Algebra's of Brasser[4] and Ferguson[5] the former whereof hath at least 8 Examples of finding the rootes of such Cubick aequations that wanting the 2d tearme, are solvable by trisection of an angle,[5a] and that by the ayd of the Cube rootes of Binomialls in such cases where the Cube of $\frac{1}{3}$ part of the Coefficient of the rootes exceedes the Square of $\frac{1}{2}$ the Absolute or Homogeneum Comparationis

To which if he would vouchsafe to adde his considerations about shewing what Æquations are solved or constructed by any of the Conick Sections drawne or supposed to be drawne in any Position by chance,[5b] it would much elucidate some things as yet in obscurity

See Transaction No 71 and accquaint him that John Ott[6] promised the shortening of Tellescopes without hurting their perfection by excluding the laterall Rayes, crave his opinion thereof, and of an Instrument by him promised that will describe any Conick Section or Segment of a Circle,[7] crave the procurement of that small Booke, and of another de Auditione printed at the same time and place,[8] and as soone as we can find an opportunity we shall send him Dr Wallis 3d part of Mechanicks seeing the former miscarried, as also Horroxs Posthuma Astronomica,[9] in which he will find a new Excellent Theory of the Moone with Lunar Numbers thereto

For Mr Oldenburgh

NOTES

This is again a memorandum of unknown date, addressed to Oldenburg, which we have placed immediately before the letter which Oldenburg based, quite literally, upon it.

1 This refers to Johann Hudde's 1657 tract "De reductione aequationum" published in the second edition of Franz van Schooten's *Geometria, a Renato des Cartes anno 1637 Gallice edita* (Part I; Amsterdam, 1659).

2 See Vol. VII, pp. 180, 186, where much the same had formerly been said to Sluse by Collins, referring to François Dulaurens, *Specimina mathematica* (Paris, 1667). By "Homogeneum" Collins signifies N, the quantity to which the expression $f(x)$ is made equal.

3 That is, pre-Cartesian algebra; *coss* (Ital. *cosa*, "thing") is the unknown quantity.

4 Jacob R. Brasser, *Regula Cos, of Algebra* (Amsterdam, 1663).

5 See Letter 2027a, note 1.

5a Dr. Whiteside has pointed out already (Newton, *Mathematical Papers*, II, 419, note 101) that Collins did not have a clear understanding of the problems concerning the solution of cubic equations, for Newton was compelled to point out to him that only cubics with three real roots could be solved by the method of "trisection" described by Descartes, while simple cubic equations (such as could be solved by finding two mean proportionals) had only one real root.

5b That is, freehand. Collins had just studied Newton's "Problems for Construing Æquations" (*Mathematical Papers*, II, 450–516; note 2, p. 450).

6 See Johannes Ott, *Cogitationes physico-mechanicae de natura visionis* (Heidelburg, 1670), reviewed in *Phil. Trans.*, no. 71 (22 May 1671), 2163–65. Oldenburg's Letter 1867 to him (Vol. VIII) had apparently elicited no reply.

7 See Vol. VIII, pp. 25, 28 and notes.

8 See Vol. VIII, pp. 292, 296 and notes.

9 See Letter 1998, note 5. The printing of the *Opera Posthuma* had been completed in early October and a copy presented to the Royal Society on the thirtieth of that month.

2108

Oldenburg to Sluse

16 December 1672

From the draft in Royal Society MS. O 2, no. 100

Illustrissimo Viro
Domino Renato Francisco Slusio Canonico Leodiensi
Henr. Oldenburg Salutem

Dum ad Cl. Hugenium transmitto tuam,[1] Vir Illustrissime, de Problemate Alhazeniano Constructionem, quam ex Schedis tuis excerptam, mihi nuper per literas 6. Decemb. datas communicasti, liceat tantisper, de reliquis in eadem epistola contentis Tecum sermocinari, aliaque nonnulla ad Physicam et Mathesin spectantia explorare. Et quidem primo, quoad mirum illum Phaenomenon, quo Argentum vivum, omni Aere purgatum, ad 75. unciarum altitudinem suspensum haeret; in eo nunc sunt Nostrates, ut genuinam ejus, si pote, causam variis Experimentis indagent. Tantum abest ut Vir antehac commemoratus suam illius explicandi hypothesin certam judicet, ut varia ipse etiamnum Experimenta proponat, quibus vel veritas ejus exploretur, vel falsitas detegatur. Quem illa successum sortientur, alias, favente Deo, Tibi me perscripturum spero.

Interim, si placet, Tuam de Tangentibus et Limitibus Methodum nobis impertiri, summa animi lubentia eam quantumpote amplam, Transactionibus Philosophicis inseram. Rogat Dn. Collinius, qui plurimam Tibi salutem dicit, ut sententiam ipsi tuam de Huddenii ad Geometriam Cartesianam Annexis circa superiorum Aequationum in suas Componentes Divisionem, aperire ne graveris, nec non de iis, quae p. 503. habet,[2] viz.

"Diversas adhuc alias regulas paratas habeo, quas hic simul adjungerem, si non aliquid in futurum reservare animus esset: nimirum, inter caeteras una est, per quam omnes Irrationales radices tam numeralium quam literalium Aequationum invenio; una, per quam omnes aequationes numerales, quae ex duabus rationalibus produci possunt, ad easdem reduco, non cognitis divisionibus ultimi termini; idem alia, per quam saepe literales aequationes reduco, quaeque in eo consistit, quod unam aut alteram pono = o vel = alii alicui quantitati quam libuerit, et quod hanc aequationem inde resultantem prius reducere coner, et postea etiam propositam per hanc."

Idem porro sciscitatur, quid de Laurentij sentias Assertione; Tollendi scilicet omnes gradus intermedios quantitatis incognitae in Aequationibus superioribus, relicta duntaxat suprema et infima potestate, aequali Absoluto vel Homogeneo.[3]

Quasdam ex regulis illis Numeralibus, ab Huddenio promissis, explicatas credimus more illo antiquo Cossico, cum magna Exemplorum varietate, in Brasseri et Fergusonis Algebra; quorum prior octo (minimum) Exempla tradit inveniendi radices Cubicarum ejusmodi Aequationum, quae, deficiente termino secundo, solvi possunt Anguli trisectione, idque beneficio cubicarum radicum in Binomiis, eo quidem casu quo Cubus $\frac{1}{3}$ Coefficientis radicum excedit Quadratum $\frac{1}{2}$ Absoluti sive Homogenei Comparationis.

Cui si adjicere velles μελετήματα tua, quibus ostenditur, Quaenam Aequationes solvantur vel construantur beneficio ullarum ex Sectionibus Conicis quae ductae sunt casu, vel ita ductae supponuntur; id sane nonnulla hactenus obscura multum elucidaret.

Priusquam finio, ut Tibi significem patiaris, (id quod etiam *Transactionibus Philosophicis* No. 71 inserui) Doctissimum quendam Helvetium, johannem Ott, promississe in libro suo Heidelbergae Anno 1670 impresso, cui titulus *Cogitationes Physico-Mechanicae de natura visionis,* Telescopiorum absque effectus fraude contractionem, facta radiorum Lateralium curata seclusione. Scire pervelim, num Tibi sit notus Author; et si sit, quid ea de re sentias, deque Instrumento illo ab eodem promisso, quod quamvis Sectionem Conicam vel quodlibet Circuli Segmentum describere aptum sit. Libelli, quic haec tradit, copiam petimus (non enim hactenus in Anglia venalis prostat) nec non alterius, ab eodem Authore editi, de Auditione tractantis, eodemque tempore et loco impressi. Quamprimum feret occasio, aliud tertiae partis Operis Wallisiani Exemplar ad Te curabimus, quandoquidem prius interivisse rescivimus addituri Horroxii Astronomica Posthuma, ubi insignem de Luna Theoriam Novam, numeris Lunaribus auctam, reperies. Vale, Vir Eximie, et importunitati meae ignosce. Dabam Londini d. 16. Decemb. 1672.

TRANSLATION

Henry Oldenburg greets the very illustrious Mr. René François de Sluse, Canon of Liège

While I am sending to Mr. Huygens,[1] most illustrious Sir, your construction of the Problem of Alhazen extracted from your papers which you sent me recently in your letter of 6 December [N.S.], may I meanwhile discuss with you the other points raised in your letter and look into some other matters in physics and mathematics? And first, as for that astonishing phenomenon, in which mercury purged of all air remains suspended at a height of 75 inches, our Fellows are now seeking its cause, if they can, through a variety of experiments. So far is that person of whom I spoke before from considering that hypothesis of his own for explaining it to be reliable that he himself has proposed experiments by which its truth may be confirmed or its falsity exposed. What success they meet with I hope, God willing, to communicate in my future letters.

Meanwhile, if you please, I embrace [your offer of] imparting your method of tangents and limits to us with the greatest possible intellectual satisfaction; and will insert it in the *Philosophical Transactions*. Mr. Collins asks, while sending you many greetings, if you will be so good as to disclose to him your opinion of Hudde's appendix to the *Geométrie* of Descartes concerning the division of equations of higher degrees into their components, and of what he [Hudde] writes on p. 503;[2] namely:

"I have prepared still other rules, which I would at this same time annex here, if it were not my purpose to reserve something for the future; there is, actually, one among them by which I discover all the irrational roots of equations, both numerical and algebraic; another, by which I reduce all numerical equations which can be derived from two rational [numbers], to these same [rationals], without knowing the factors of the final term; and also another, by which I often reduce algebraic equations which consists in this [operation]: I make one or the other equal to zero, or equal to any quantity at pleasure, and then I try to reduce the equation formed in this way to the former, and afterwards [to reduce] the [originally] proposed equation by means of this one."

The same person further inquired what you think of Dulaurens' assertion that all the intermediate powers of the unknown quantity in higher equations may be removed, leaving only its lowest and highest powers equal to an absolute or homogeneous [quantity].[3]

[*The remainder of the letter is simply an adaptation in Latin of Collins' English in Letter 2107.*]

Farewell, excellent Sir, and forgive my importunity.

London, 16 December 1672.

NOTES

Reply to Letter 2100.
1 Oldenburg delayed doing so until 13 January 1672/3 (in Letter 2129).
2 See Letter 2107, note 1.
3 See Letter 2107, note 2.

2109

Oldenburg to Duhamal

16 December 1672

Duhamel's Letter 2103 is endorsed as having been answered on 16 December 1672.

2110

Lister to Oldenburg

17 December 1672

From the original in Royal Society MS. L 5, no. 50

Yorke. Decemb. 17. 72

Sir

I had yours of Decemb. 12: wherin you mention yt Dr Grew agrees to ye main of those particulars I sent you lately concerning ye Veines in Plants. his Assent is a great pleasure to me, since I have cause to believe, yt his owne diligence hath furnished him wth other arguments to confirme, what I there but obscurly deliver. In expectation yt he will at length gratify ye inquisitive wth ym, ye Quaeries are welcome to me. They have a double appeal; as they may assist me in future researches, I reserve ye successe untill occasion; & as they alsoe seem to invalidate my notions, be pleased to accept of these answers to ym: desiring you still to remember, yt I undertooke not ye explication of ye Oeconomie & use of all ye parts in

Plants, but only to look up & revise certain remarkes I had made, several yeares agoe, concerning ye Veines in plants analogous to human Veines. But to ye Quaeries.

1. Quaerie. whether it be a sufficient proof of ye existence of Veines etc.] Those Expts I tooke to be good proofe against such as did believe (& most men were latly of yt opinion) ye juice of plants to be one uniforme Sap extravasate & in noe vessel, but to be in ye parenchyma of Plants as water in a Sponge. And these kind of arguments (wch we call *ad hominem*) have ever been admitted, though they conclude nothing directly. After ye attainment to an *Ocular demonstration* (of wch there are many plain instances thoughout ye letter) of a matter of Fact, I stood in noe need of other arguments, yt being I conceive all-sufficient: but I would not omitt ye hinting some wayes I tooke to praepare a further Examination of ye Veines in Plants & alsoe to apply ym as they would beare it, against ye general opinion.

2 Quaerie] whether you ever observed any tru Ramifications etc. if ye question be limited concerning Veines, I answer as formerly yt I doubt it, from ye extreme smallnesse & great numbers of equally big veines.

3 Quaerie. whether ye Veines in Plants, as they are Reticular (wch is granted), are alsoe any where implicate etc] I understand by *reticular, implicate, decussate* one & ye same thing, yt is, yt what veines in a Leaf are in *direct lines*, seem to me to run in *cross* ones, to be confusd & perplext in ye several coats of ye Root. As for *inosculations*, since yt notion has puzzled & misled ye most industrious Anatomists in sanguineous Animals, I pretend not to know any thing of it in Plants, where ye veines are marvelously small.

4. Quaerie. whether there is any thing Essential in any part of a Plant, wch is not in a Leaf?] the Veines are our present Task & in reference to ym, we have noted an accidental difference at least, yt they are in ye leafes in a more simple & plain Order, than in ye root.

5 Quaerie. Whether ye limpid sap of Plants be not alsoe to be called vital etc] if ye Chyle, whilst an external fluid in ye Gutts & not yet received into ye Veines, be to be called vital, I shall not deny ye notion to agree alsoe to ye limpid juice of Plants; All I meane to contend for is, yt ye milky juice is ye only proper Vital juice.

6. Quaerie. whether it be a conclusive proof of ye want of any vegetable juices fermentative motion &c] in my opinion few liquors, if any at all, are wholly devoid of fermentative motion, much lesse would I be thought to deny yt to ye limpid sap of Plants in some small degree; but yt fermentation

being soe little discernable in respect of motion, & as quickly freezing, as fountain water, I had reason to exclude it yt sense, especially when compared to ye milkie juice, wch always moves briskly & never (yt I know of) freezes.

7 Quaerie. whether ye advancement of ye sap from ye bottome to ye top etc] I am very farr from setting aside ye frame of Parts in ye advancement of ye juice; but have great reason to thinke its motion in ye veines to be very differently performed from yt in Animals. But this & other matters, we shall use our best endeavours to search further into according to our leisure. And if wee misse of our purpos, we doubt not but ye happy Genious of Dr Grew will bring much to light. I am Sir

Your most humble servant
Martin Lister

if you thinke of inserting ye last Paper, about ye Veines of Plants, into ye Transactions, I desire I may first retouch it & make it less lyable to exceptions[1]

P.S.

Mr Wray returned me this Answer to my letter about ye biting Mushrome[2]

"At my return to Midleton I found a letter from you, containing ye description of a Mushrome by you discoverd in Marton Woods under Prinne-moore. I doubt not but it is yt described in Jo: Bauhinus. lib. 40. cap. 6. under ye Title of *Fungus piperatus albus, lacteo succo turgens*;[3] only he saith 1. yt it doth in bignesse exceed ye Champignon, wheras you writ yt there are few of ym much bigger, yn yt: but yet in saying soe, you alsoe grant ym to be bigger. 2. He saith for their bignesse, they are not soe thick as yt, you describe yours to be thick in flesh. in all other points your descriptions agree exactly for ye colour, yt it is *white* Gills & all: for ye *place*, yt it growes in woods: & for ye *tast*, yt it is hotter than Pepper. Several particulars mentioned by you, are not observed or not mentioned by him. I cannot say yt I have as yet met with this Mushrome".

Soe far Mr Ray.

Sir,

I beg your pardon for ye trouble of these Scribles but you have suffered me hitherto, I am like to goe on, unlesse you silence me.

ADDRESS
   For my much honoured friend
      Henry Oldenburg
   Esquire at his house
      in ye Palmal
            London

NOTES

   Reply to Letter 2106.
1 See Letter 2104, note.
2 See Letter 2096. Ray's contribution was published after Lister's in *Phil. Trans.*, no. 89 (16 December 1672), 5117–18.
3 "White peppery fungus, full of milky juice." See Johannis Bauhin, J. H. Cherlerus, D. Chabraeus, and F. L. a Graffenried, *Historiae plantarum universalis, tomus* III (Yverdon, 1651), 825.

2111

Oldenburg to Swammerdam

19 December 1672

From the copy in Royal Society MS. O 2, no. 101

Clarissimo Viro
Domino Johanni Swammerdam Med. Doctori
Henricus Oldenburg Salutem

Post varios casus, post mille periculae Maris, Vir Clarissime, tandem ad manus meas, nonnisi initio huius Decembris pervenit Elegantissimum juxta ac solertissimum tuum Uteri Muliebris aliarumque humani corporis partium munus, quo Societatem Regiam ejusque penum philosophicum locupletare voluisti. Mancum interim id mihi traditum fuisse scias, cum in uno Arculae latere ei scilicet cui uterus haerebat, obverso, locus esset vacuus, acicularum punctis notatus, cui affixum quid fuisse, sed ademptum, plane existimo. Caetera satis integra et incolumia deprehendi; Uterum nempe puerperae, Virginis pudendum cum Clitoride,[1] humani Lienis Arterias ac Venas, Arteriae Hepaticae ramos, Lienis vitulini Arterias, Intestini

Jejuni valvas conniventes,[2] Intestini Rajae cochleam,[3] Penis, Urethrae etc clitoridis portiunculas, una cum Arteria primi generis in piscibus, per quam sanguis ad Branchias amandatur,[4] nec non Arteria secundi generis, per quam sanguis e venis piscium branchialibus immediate per totum corpus distribuitur, denique Lymphaticum peculiare ex abdomine Gallinae omnia sane curiosissime et per quam affabre adornata.

Cum ea nonnisi tarde admodum acceperim, non potui ea citius quam hesterno die societati Regiae exhibere,[5] quae quidem omnia pronis oculis et serenissima fronte lustravit, Artem aeque ac Industriam tuam depraedicans, utque summas, ipsius nomine, gratias tibi reponerem, sollicite jubens.

Generosum Veri philosophi pectus te gerere persuasum omnino habemus; nulli dubitantes, quin, ex promisso, scientiam Anatomicam gnaviter porro sis provecturus, eaque inprimis, quae in Anatomicis sunt subtilisima, omnium oculis subjecturus.

Nostrates Anatomici, Willisius nempe, Lowerus, Needhamus, Croonius, alijque (omnes a Societate Regia) operas suas strenue, ni fallor, sociabunt, in eoque toti erunt, ne te tuique similes ullatenus paeniteat, vos diligentiae vestrae fructus nobis communicaste. Vale, Vir doctissime, meque Virtutis et Eruditionis tuae cultoribus accense. Dabam Londini d. 19. Decembris 1672.

TRANSLATION

Henry Oldenburg greets the famous Mr. Jan Swammerdam, M.D.

Your most elegant and skilfully prepared gift of a woman's uterus and other parts of the human body, with which you intended to enrich the Royal Society and its philosophical repository, has at length come to my hands, famous Sir, after a checkered career and countless perils of war, at the beginning of this month of December. But it was delivered to me incomplete, for on one side of the box (that to which the uterus was attached), facing it, there was an empty space marked out by pinholes, to which I think it is clear that something was fixed, which has been removed. I found the rest sufficiently whole and undamaged, that is to say the uterus of a woman in labor, the pudenda of a virgin with the clitoris,[1] the veins and arteries of the human spleen, the branches of the hepatic artery, the arteries of a calf's spleen, the sphincters of the intestine of a fasting subject,[2] the convoluted intestine of a ray,[3] sections of the penis, urethra, clitoris, etc., together with the artery of the first kind in fishes (by which blood is brought to the gills),[4] and also an artery of the second kind through which the blood [coming] from the gill vessels of the fish is directly distributed about the whole body, and lastly the peculiar lymphatic [vessel] from the abdomen of a cock—all things which are certainly very fascinating and prepared with exceeding ingenuity.

As I received these things only after a great delay, I could not present them to the Royal Society before yesterday;[5] the Society examined them most favorably and with great content, praising your art and industry, and ordered me earnestly to return you its best thanks on its behalf.

We are quite convinced that the heart of a true philosopher beats in your breast, harboring no doubt but that you will, as you promise, continue sedulously to pursue the science of anatomy and that in particular you will set before the eyes of all those points of anatomy which are the most delicate.

Our anatomist Fellows, namely Willis, Lower, Needham, Croone, and others (all of the Royal Society) will, if I mistake not, associate themselves eagerly with your labors and will do their best so that you and others like you shall have no reason whatever to repent the communication of the fruits of your diligence to us. Farewell, learned Sir, and count me among the number of the admirers of your distinction and learning. London, 19 December 1672.

NOTES

In his first extant letter to Oldenburg of 26 March 1672 (Vol. VIII, p. 617) Swammerdam had spoken of sending these preparations to the Royal Society; in April Oldenburg had regretted the difficulties of transport caused by the war (above, Letter 1965) and he had written twice more to Swammerdam since (Letters 1996 and 2029).

1   This is probably a slip, as the Journal Book (Birch, *History*, III, 71) says "with the hymen."
2   The Journal Book adds: "observed by Ruysch and sketched by Kerckring."
3   The Journal Book adds: "described by Steno."
4   The Journal Book adds the word "pulmonary."
5   That is, at the meeting of 18 December, as printed by Birch, *History*, III, 71. These preparations are also described from the repository by Grew, *Musaeum*, 7–8; from Grew's account it is learned—though not mentioned here—that the structures were not only carefully dissected and dried by Swammerdam, but were injected with wax to make the vessels and so forth more conspicuous.

2112

Oldenburg to Wallis

24 December 1672

This letter, acknowledged by Wallis in Letter 2114, evidently concerned his feud with Thomas Hobbes, and contained a copy of Letter 2099. An earlier copy had miscarried; we do not know the date on which that was sent, but as Letter 2114 makes plain, Oldenburg had written several times to Wallis since Letter 2091.

2113
Gornia to Oldenburg
25 December 1672
From the original in Royal Society MS. G, no. 29

Clarissime Vir,

Quo tempori mihi per litteras Equitis de Vaux[1] nunciatum est Fatis cessisse Propraesidem[2] Societatis Regiae: accepi itidem Messanae in Sicilia obiisse Carolum Fracassatum[3] Concivem, Amicum et per plures annos Pisis convictorem meum dum ea in Universitate Primariam Medicinae Cathedram decora abunde existimatione teneret,[4] quapropter utrinque mihi dolendum est dum Amicorum, atque Patronorum undique Facio jacturam. Malpighius noster, qui Fracassatum deperibat ut suum Pyladem alter Orestes contumaci Maerore conficitur, nec tanti mali par solamen admittit:[5] Eques de Vaux iussit meam me aperire sententiam de Egritudine et morte Propraesidis, quod ut morem ipsi gerem pro viribus sum executus, an autem quicquam rationi consentaneum adduxerim vereor, eaque propter tuam erga me benevolentiam oro, ut si forte ad tuas manus Scheda illa in Societate pervenerit, testatum cuique facias me eam tantummodo exarasse, ut amici mandatis obtemperarem, non vero ut aliquid Lucis afferrem ubi summum Litterarium iubar eruditis omnibus nitet, cum etenim mihi non constet an Medici vestri circa illius morbi cognitionem dissenserint,[6] huiusmodi Cautione quiescit animus, et se totum Amico concredere fidit. Italiam nostram sua usque adhuc pax beat faxitque Deus ut pro bella per hostes pacem Musis amicam, quamprimum consequi, eaque quamdiutissime et felicissime frui. Valeas itaque, et me ut humaniter caepisti pergas amare. Florentiae pridie Nonas januarii 1673
    Dominationis tuae Addictissimus et obvinctissimus servus

Jo. Baptista Gornia

ADDRESS
    Clarissimo ac Ornatissimo Viro
    Domino Henrico Oldenburg
    Regiae Societatis a Secretis
            Londinum

TRANSLATION

Famous Sir,

At the time when I received through a letter from Sir Theodore de Vaux[1] the news that the Vice-President[2] of the Royal Society had gone to his fathers, I heard also from Messina in Sicily of the death of Carlo Fracassati,[3] my fellow citizen, friend, and table companion through many years at Pisa while he occupied the chief professorship of medicine in the University, winning many good opinions;[4] for which reason I have cause to grieve on both accounts, while I feel the loss of friends and patrons everywhere. My countryman Malpighi, who doted on Fracassati as another Pylades to his Orestes, is made prostrate by inconsolable sorrow, finding no comfort equal to so great an ill.[5] Sir Theodore instructed me to disclose my opinion concerning the sickness and death of the Vice-President, which I have done in order to obey him as well as I could; but I doubt whether I have suggested anything agreeable to reason and so I beg your kindness towards me on that score. If that paper perchance shall have come to your hands in the Society, assure everyone that I only wrote it in order to comply with the behest of a friend—not indeed to bring in fresh illumination to a place whence shines upon all the learned the most brilliant light of science—for although it is not clear to me whether your physicians will have disagreed as to recognition of that disease,[6] the mind is calmed by such a stipulation and disposed to place all its trust in a friend. Hitherto peace blesses our Italy; may God ensure that peace, friendly to the Muses, will very soon follow in the place of war between the enemies, and that it will be long and profitably enjoyed. So farewell, and continue to love me as you have kindly begun to do. Florence, 4 January 1673 [N.S.].

> Your excellency's most devoted and obliged servant,
> *Jo. Baptista Gornia*

ADDRESS

To the famous and excellent Mr. Henry Oldenburg,
Secretary of the Royal Society,
London

NOTES

1 Sir Theodore de Vaux (1628–94), born in Guernsey (Channel Islands), was physician to both Charles II and (after his death) the dowager Queen Catherine. He had taken an M.D. at Padua (1655) and was elected F.R.S. in 1665. Gornia's letter in reply to him is Royal Society MS. G, no. 30.
2 John Wilkins; see Letter 2105, note 12.
3 Compare Vol. III, p. 534, note. Fracassati died at Messina on 12 October 1672.
4 While still holding a lectureship at Bologna, the city of his birth, Fracassati taught at Pisa from 1663 to 1668. He occupied the primary chair at Messina only from 1670.

5 Malpighi composed the inscription for a memorial tablet to his friend and collabora-
    tor (Adelmann, I, 375, note; the relations between Fracassati and Malpighi are fully
    recorded in Adelman's biography of the latter).
6 Wilkins died of the stone.

2114

Wallis to Oldenburg

26 December 1672

From the original in Royal Society MS. W 2, no. 4

Oxford. Dec. 26. 1672

Sr

Yours of Dec. 24. coming to hand but just now since I came from sermon, & the Post going by twelve a-clock, allows me no more time
than just to tell you that I have it, & yt I received one a little before concerning D. Baggerus[1] whom I acquainted with it, & he hath (by that meanes)
received what had here, unknown to him, lyen for him a month at ye
Carriers. As to ye letter from Hamburg, I am sorry it is lost,[2] but he hath
no reason to blame you, who sent it hither in pursuance of his directions,
since it was here to be answered. That of M[r]. H[obbes] I think, as to me
needes no answere. If others think mine intelligible, I am not troubled, yt
he understands it not. As to his Teachings: As I do not know what I have
yet learned from him, (unlesse, how little he is a Geometer,) so neither have
I any hopes of so doing. If he have learned from me: much good may it
do him. As to his last clause, of your publishing things for him. You are
therein to be guided by others, not by mee; & they will (I presume) do or
not do it, as they find ye papers to deserve. I am Sir

Your very humble servant
John Wallis

ADDRESS
        These
    For Mr Henry Oldenburg
    at the Palmal near
        St. James's
            London   POSTMARK DE 27

NOTES

1 Since this cannot refer to Letter 2091, a letter must be missing, besides that mentioned below as lost in the post.
2 This lost letter also contained a copy of Hobbes's Letter 2099; the letter from Hamburg was from Vogel, but its date and subject are unknown; however from Oldenburg's remarks in Letter 2185, below, it would appear to have contained a linguistic query.

2115
Oldenburg to Lister
28 December 1672

From the original in Bodleian Library MS. Lister 34, f. 78

London Decemb. 28. 1672

Sir,

Though I have not yet had an opportunity of declaring ye contents of yr last of Dec 17th. at our Society, wch is adjourned till jan. 8th; yet I thought myself obliged not only to acknowledge more timely ye receipt of yt letter, but also to Desire to know, whether you would have me send you back yr former letter about the Veins of Plants,[1] for yr retouching, before I insert it in the Transactions; or whether you intend to revise and alter, and send me yr second thoughts in a paper by itself, and leave it to me to insert ym.

I have very lately received from Monsr Hugens his contrivance of a New Barometer, yt maketh ye variations of ye weight and pressure of ye Air farr more discernable than the received ones; and will serve wthall for a measure of hights of difficult accesse.[2]

After it hath been examined by ye Curious here, I am likely to publish yt also in one of ye Monthly Tracts[3] of Sir

Yr very humble servant
Oldenburg

NOTES

Reply to Letter 2110.
1 Letter 2104.
2 See Letter 2103, note 4. But Huygens had not sent a copy of the *Journal des Sçavans* to Oldenburg, as he says in Letter 2122. A letter, however, may be missing, to which Oldenburg may have replied in a letter also now missing.
3 He never in fact did so.

2116
Oldenburg to Hobbes
30 December 1672
From the draft in Royal Society MS. W 2, no. 4

To Mr. Hobbes

Sir,

I could not read yr letter of Novemb. ye 26th, wch came to my hands no sooner than Decemb. 11th, before ye R. Society, (as by ye Bearer's intimation you seemd to desire me to doe) it being very improper, in my Judgement, to expose so worthy a member of yt Body, as Dr Wallis is, by reading publickly an Invective agst him. Yet I sent a Copy of it to him, who doubtless had return'd an Answer to it some dayes since if ye first Copy had not, I know not how, miscarried, and I been obliged to send him another.[1] To wch ye Doctor maketh return to this effect, That yt letter of yrs needs no other answer but this, yt, if the generality of men vers'd in Algebra think his letter intelligible, he is not troubled, yt a particular man, not so versed, understands it not. And as to yr expressions of having taught him, I have no mind to repeat his Answer, being far more inclined, if I were capable, to make you friends, than set you further asunder. Neither is ye R. Society willing to enter into ye decision of the disputes betwixt you, having regard to yr age, and esteeming yr parts, but doubting you doe mistake in these controversies. However, I am ready to comply wth your desires in yt particular, wch concerns ye publication of such papers, you shall send me tending to ye advancement of Physiques and

Mathematiques, as are not too long, nor interwoven wth personal reflexions; in a word, yt shall be licensed by ye Council of ye R.S. I am Sir

Your affectionate friend and humble servant

H. Oldenburg

Dec. 30. 1672.

NOTES

Reply to Letter 2099.
1 See Letter 2114.

2117

John Hoskins to Oldenburg

? 1672/3

From the original in Royal Society MS. H 1, no. 90

3 of the clocke

Sr

Before I can hope yu should vowchsafe my letter a reading I must beg
yr pardon for not having provided it as soone as I should have done:
and believing, upon ye experience of yr goodnesse, yt that pardon is as
soone granted as demanded Ile now venture to give the best description I
can remember, of ye place for keeping tender plants from ye cold wch was
an oblong pit of such depth and bignesse as ye plants to bee kept in it doe
require; this is to bee lined on ye sides, and the bottom covered, with
dung of 2 or 3 foot thicknesse. Then about a yard below the surface of ye
earth it is made wider by a foote at least on each side and at that place is a
frame, that compasses the pit about and has shutters of wood wch being
let downe cover it close; but the one side of the frame to which the hinges
are made fast is lower than the other that the moysture that comes upon the
shutters may run of to the side. The 3 foote space betweene these shuttes
or trapdoores and the surface of the earth is filled and heaped wth more
dung so that the heate of it being on all sides of the plants (wch grow and
continue in pots) preserves them from cold, and when the sun shines

cleare these shutters being uncovered and lift up let ye sun into ye plants for a litle time and keepe out ye wind, and besides I remember Mr Balam[1] (yt unparalleld botanist) told mee among other curious observations of this kind yt plants thus kept close must have ye fresh and open ayre sometimes else they would dye as if they to were in danger of being stifled for want of breath.

This I saw at Poycke neere Worcester at one Mr Higham his garden[2] who promotes many plants to as great a heighth of perfection as any I have seene & there the shutters opend to the South.

But now for Russia in a part of wch Sigismundo Baro de Herberstein[3] & others say that men are frozen in the winter and revive in the spring. the province hee calls Lucomoria.

Tis sayd likewise yt ye whole nation of the Samoeds[4] have one leg shorter than the other.

And this if yu thinke worth yr while yu may bee easily certifyed of if true.

And give mee leave Sr to borrow one doubt from the news booke though it has bin one wth mee ever since I read Mr de Beauplan.[5] And that is how the Tartars feed their horses when they make their inroads upon their neighbours while the earth is all covered wth snow frozen over that being the season they account most advantageous   And the countrey scarcely inhabited.

In yr french correspondence please yu to remember Mr de Marolles his Catalogue and whether hee goes on in his history of paynting &c.[6]

Sr if any of the subjects I have mentioned by yr command bee thought worth yr owne enquiry for any satisfaction yu desire for yr selfe; or to bestow, as yu still use to doe, upon those yu please to oblige I am glad if I have served you.

Otherwise, the writing about them is much a greater trouble then can any way bee deserved by

> Yr obliged servt.
> *JH*

ADDRESS
> For Mr Henry Oldenburg
> at the white balcone neere ye
> midle of The Pallmall
> 2 doores beyond ye Lady Ranelaghs

NOTES

This letter carries no indication of date, and was not entered in any Letter Book. It could have been written at any time between 1666 and 1676. We have somewhat arbitrarily placed it here, when the Royal Society's interest in plants was keen. It is endorsed by Oldenburg, "Mr. Hoskins of preserving tender plants in winter."

For John Hoskins (1634–1705), often mentioned in the correspondence, see Vol. II, p. 148, note 2. He was not knighted until 1676.

1 We cannot identify this man, unless he was a connection of Richard Balam, who was a pupil of William Oughtred.

2 Powyke Court is outside the village of Powick, which is three miles west of Worcester.

3 Sigismund von Herberstein (1486–1566) was twice Imperial envoy to Russia; his *Rerum Moscovitarum Commentarii* (Vienna, 1549) was often reprinted.

4 The Samoyeds, a Uralic people living in Siberia.

5 Guillaume Le Vasseur, Seigneur de Beauplan, published two books which Hoskins might have read: *Description des Contrees du Royaume de Pologne* (Rouen, 1650) and *Description d'Ukraine* (Rouen, 1660).

6 Michel de Marolles, *Catalogue de Livres d'Estampes et de figures en Taille Douce* (Paris, 1666, 1672). His *Le Livre des Peintres et Graveurs* was only published in 1855, but the first edition of his *Catalogue* (which describes a different collection from the second one) contains an outline of the projected work.

2118

Lister to Oldenburg

1 January 1672/3

From the original in Royal Society MS. L 5, no. 51

Sir

I desire to retouch ye former Paper,[1] having somethings in my mind to adde, others to explaine & alter: & for yt purpos doe pray you to remitt it to me again, not having any perfect coppy of it by me: you shall receive it back ye very next Post. To this purpos, you may likewise be pleased to suspend ye reading of my last[2] before ye R.S. untill you receive this back. And than you may dispose of it & all yt comes from me, as you thinks fitting. I am very much obliged to you for ye benefit & favour of your monthly Tracts. Your indefatigable Industrie having given us ye opportunity of a Register, wch if it had been on foot some yeares agoe, ye English had not lost ye Credit of soe many new discoveries, wch did more properly belong to ym, than ye first Publishers. For my owne part, I should be lesse forward in exposing my selfe in such darke & untroden subjects as those of Plants, but yt I have more desire of improving, at least hastning & setting an edge on others in ye designe of ye improvement of usefull Philosophy, than Covetous of a reputation I am sensible I can scarce say any thing this yeare but I may repent it ye next; & let us lay our observations & Experiments as prudently together as we can, a few dayes labour & perseverance starts something new & unexpected, wch is apt to ruin all again. This I say in reference to our notions; For, for matter of Fact, I should be sorry to advance any thing, yt was not precisely true & sincerely deliverd.

I thanke you for ye philosophical news of ye Barometer. I am Sir

Your most humble servant
Martin Lister

Yorke Jan. 1st. 1672

ADDRESS
        For
    his very honoured friend
        Henry Oldenburg
    Esq at his house in ye
    Palmal
                London

NOTES

Reply to Letter 2115.
1 Letter 2104.
2 Letter 2110.

2119
Oldenburg to Le Bourgeois
2 January 1672/3

Le Bourgeois's Letter 1981 is endorsed as answered the day after Oldenburg received it, which he did on 1 January 1672/3.

2120

Oldenburg to Sivers

2 January 1672/3

Oldenburg's endorsement to Letter 2087 indicates that he answered it on this day.

2121

Oldenburg to Vogel

2 January 1672/3

From the memorandum in Royal Society MS. S 1, no. 121

Resp. d. 2. jan. 1672/73.
Eodem tempore respondi Fogelio ad literas ejus in via ad Oxonium deperditas.

TRANSLATION

Answered 2 January 1672/3.
At the same time I replied to Vogel about his letter lost in transit to Oxford.

NOTE

This is written on the back of Letter 2087 to Sivers. The loss of Vogel's letter has already been mentioned in Letter 2114.

2122

Huygens to Oldenburg

4 January 1672/3

From the original in Royal Society MS. H 1, no. 75
Printed in *Œuvres Complètes*, VII, 242–44

A Paris ce 14 Jan. 1673 [N.S.]

Monsieur

Je vous aurois fait responce dans le temps que je devois a deux de vos lettres,[1] si des occupations un peu plus pressées qu'a l'ordinaire ne m'avoient emportè le temps ailleurs. Je vous rends graces de vos deux Journaux, et j'aurois eu soin de vous faire tenir le dernier de M. Galois,[2] si je ne croiois qu'on vous les envoie reglement, et qu'il ne faut pas vous charger deux fois du port d'un tel pacquet. Vous y aurez vu mes considerations sur Saturne, et la construction d'un nouveau barometre, dans la quelle il y a à corriger a la page 154, à la 4e ligne, ou il faut lire de 28 pouces et demi au lieu de 27½. Et a la mesme page ligne 4e d'embas il faut mettre *MN* au lieu de *BC*. car pour la faute qui est dans la figure ou il y avoit un *L* au lieu d'*M*, je crois que l'imprimeur l'aura fait corriger.[3] Dans la pratique de ce barometre, qui reussit tresbien, j'ay remarquè qu'il est necessaire, sur tout pour mesurer des hauteurs, d'adjouter un perpendicule a la planche qui porte le barometre, parce qu'il importe fort qu'il soit tousjours dressè de mesme. Ce perpendicule est attachè par en haut, et passe en bas par un petit trou de cette largeur $\bigcirc$, du quel on juge facilement quand il occupe le milieu. Pour ce qui est de l'huile que j'ay dit qu'on pourroit mettre sur l'eau, je ne le trouve pas necessaire jusqu'icy, ayant experimentè que l'eau contenue dans un tuyau si long et si estroit ne s'evapore aucunement, au moins pendant cette saison de l'année. J'ay veu comme Mr. Newton prend peine a soustenir sa nouvelle opinion touchant les couleurs.[4] Il me semble que la plus importante objection qu'on luy fait en forme de *Quaere* est celle, s'il y a plus de deux sortes de couleurs? Car pour moy je crois qu'une hypothese qui expliqueroit mechaniquement et par la nature du mouvement la couleur jaune et la bleue, suffiroit pour toutes les autres, parce que cellescy estant seulement plus chargees, (comme il paroit par les prismes de Mr. Hook) produisent le rouge et le bleu obscur,[5] et que de ces quatre tout le reste des couleurs se peut composer. Je ne vois pas aussi pourquoy Mr. Newton ne se contente pas des 2 couleurs, jaune, et bleu; car il sera bien plus aisé de trouver une hypothese par le mouvement qui expliquest ces deux differences, que non pas pour tant de diversitez qu'il y a d'autres couleurs. Et jusqu'a ce qu'il ait trouvè cette hypthese il ne nous aura pas appris en quoy consiste la nature et difference des couleurs, mais seulement cet accident (qui assurement est fort considerable) de leur differente refrangibilitè. Pour ce qui est de l'autre, à scavoir la composition du blanc de toutes les couleurs ensemble, il se pourroit faire que le jaune et le bleu seroient encore suffisans pour cela. ce qui vaut la peine d'estre essayè, et il se peut par l'experience que M. Newton propose, de recevoir contre la muraille d'une chambre obscure les couleurs du prisme, et d'esclairer par leur lumiere reflechie sur un papier blanc. Il faudroit empescher les couleurs des extremitez, scavoir le rouge et le pourpre de donner contre la muraille, et laisser seulement les couleurs d'entredeux, le jaune, verd, et bleu, pour voir si la lumiere de cellescy seules ne feroit pas paroistre blanc le papier, aussi bien que quand elles esclairent toutes. Je doute mesme si l'endroit le plus clair du jaune ne feroit pas tout seul cet effect, et je l'essaieray a la premiere commoditè, car cette pensee ne m'est venue qu'a cette heure. Vous voiez bien cependant, Monsieur, que si ces experiences succedent, l'on ne pourra plus dire que toutes les couleurs sont necessaires pour composer le blanc, et qu'il sera tresvraisemblable que toutes les autres ne sont que des degrez de jaune et bleu, plus ou moins renfoncez.

Au reste, pour ce qui est de l'effect des differentes refractions des rayons dans les verres de lunette, il est certain que l'experience ne s'accorde pas avec ce que trouve Mr. Newton; car a considerer seulement la peinture que fait un objectif de 12 pieds dans une chambre obscure, l'on voit qu'elle est trop distincte et trop bien terminée pour pouvoir estre produite par des rayons qui s'escarteroient de la 5ome partie de l'ouverture.[6] de sorte que, comme je vous crois avoir mandè desia cydevant, la difference de la refrangibilitè ne suit pas peut estre tousjours la mesme proportion dans les grandes et petites inclinations des rayons sur les surfaces du verre. En passant a ce costè du feuillet je commence a apprehender que je vous ennuie par de trop longs raisonnements. C'est pourquoy je n'adjousteray plus rien sinon pour vous assurer que je suis parfaitement Monsieur

Vostre treshumble et obeissant serviteur
Hugens de Zulichem

dans la disposition du barometre quand on y adjoute le perpendicule il y a encore cecy a remarquer, qu'il ne faut pas que les tuyaux montants soient tout a faits perpendiculaires, mais environ en sorte que les 2 boetes soient perpendiculairement l'une au dessus de l'autre; parce que dans cette situation l'eau montera le plus haut dans le tuyau. ce qui me surprit lors que je n'en scavois pas encore la raison.[7]

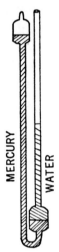

MERCURY   WATER

Mr. Leibnitz est parti d'icy pour Angleterre et vous le verrez bientost qui vous montrera une ebauche de sa machine pour les multiplications de nombres qui est fort ingenieuse.[8]

TRANSLATION, mainly from *Phil. Trans.*, no. 96 (21 July 1673), 6086–87

[Paris, 14 January 1673 [N.S.]

[Sir,

I would have replied to two of your letters[1] at the time when I ought to have done, if rather more pressing affairs than usual had not occupied my time otherwise. I thank you for your two *Transactions*, and I should have taken care to get you the last *Journal* of Mr. Gallois,[2] had I not thought that you were sent them regularly and that it was not necessary to make you pay twice over for such a package. You will have seen therein my thoughts on Saturn, and the construction of a new barometer, in which there are the following corrections: page 154, line 4, read $28\frac{1}{4}$ inches instead of $27\frac{1}{2}$; and on the same page, line 4 from the bottom, read *MN* in place of *BC*; as to the mistake in the figure where there was an *L* in place of *M*, I think the printer will have corrected that.[3] In the use of this barometer, which works very well, I have noticed that it is necessary, especially to measure heights, to add a plumb-line to the board which supports the barometer [tube], because it is very important to have it always set up the same way. This plumb-line is attached at the top, and passes downwards through a little hole so big:◯, from which one easily estimates when the line is in the middle. As for the oil which I have said should be put on the water, I have not so far found it necessary, having found by experiment that the water contained in such a long and narrow tube does not evaporate at all, at least at this season of the year.]

I have seen, how Mr. Newton endeavours to maintain his new Theory concerning *Colours*.[4] Me thinks, that the most important Objection, which is made against him by way of Quare, is that, Whether there be more than two sorts of Colours. For my part, I believe, that an *Hypothesis*, that should explain mechanically and by the nature of motion the Colors *Jellow* and *Blew*, would be sufficient for all the rest, in regard that those others, being only more deeply charged (as appears by the Prismes of Mr. Hook) do produce the dark or deep-Red and Blew;[5] and that of these four all the other colors may be compounded. Neither do I see, why Mr. Newton doth not content himself with the two Colors, Yellow and Blew; for it will be much more easy to find an *Hypothesis* by Motion, that may explicate these two differences, than for so many diversities as there are of others Colors. And till he hath found this *Hypothesis*, he hath not taught us, what it is wherein consists the nature and difference of Colours, but only this accident (which certainly is very considerable,) of their *different Refrangibility*.

As for the composition of *White* made by all the Colors together, it may possibly be, that *Yellow* and *Blew* might also be sufficient for that: Which is worth while to try; and it may be done by the Experiment, which Mr. Newton proposeth, by receiving against a wall of a darkn'd room the Colours of the Prisme, and to cast their reflected light upon white paper. Here you must hinder the Colors of the extremities, viz. the Red and Purple, from striking against the wall, and leave only the intermediate Colors, yellow, green and blew, to see, whether the light of these alone would not make the paper appear white, as well as when they all give light. I even doubt, whether the lightest place of the yellow color may not all alone produce that effect, and I mean to try it at the first conveniency; for this thought never came into my mind but just now. Mean time you may see, that if these Experiments do succeed, it can no more be said, that all the Colors are necessary to compound White, and that 'tis very probable, that all the rest are nothing but degrees of *Yellow* and *Blew*, more or less charged.

Lastly, touching the Effect of the different Refractions of the Rays in Telescopical Glasses, 'tis certain, that Experience agrees not with what Mr. Newton holds. For to consider only a picture, which is made by an object-glass of 12 feet in a dark room, we see, it is too distinct and too well defined to be produced by rayes, that should stray the 50th part of the Aperture.[6] So that, (as I believe I have told you heretofore) the difference of the Refrangibility doth not, it may be, alwayes follow the same proportion in the great and small inclinations of the Rayes upon the surface of the Glass.

[In turning over to this side of the sheet I begin to realize that I am wearying you with over-long arguments. This is why I shall add nothing more except to assure you that I am perfectly, Sir,

Your very humble and obedient servant,
Huygens of Zulichem

About the arrangement of the barometer when the plumb-line is added, there is this to add, that the rising tubes must not be quite perpendicular, but approximately so that the two bulbs are perpendicularly one above the other [*see the figure, p. 382*]; because in this position the water will rise higher in the tube. Which surprised me before I knew the reason.[7]

Mr. Leibniz has left here for England and you will soon see him; he will show you a version of his machine for the multiplication of numbers, which is very ingenious.[8]]

NOTES

Reply to Letter 2094.

1 Unless Huygens was confused, a letter is missing; see also Letter 2115.
2 The *Journal des Sçavans* for 12 December 1672 [N.S.]. Compare Letter 2103, note 4.
3 The printed figure is correct.
4 This is a commentary on Newton's Letter 1993 as printed in the *Philosophical Transactions*.
5 Properly "red and dark blue." Robert Hooke in *Micrographia* (London, 1665), pp. 73–75 had described an experiment in which he had filled two wedge-shaped glass vessels with, respectively, tincture of aloes and a dissolved copper salt. The former, according to the thickness of the fluid through which light passed, appeared to vary in tint from pale yellow to deep red; the second gave "all manner of blues." Hooke claimed that by combining two rays of light after passing each through one of these variable filters he could reproduce all tints.
6 Oldenburg's marginal note directs the reader to *Phil. Trans.*, no. 80 (19 February 1671/2), 3079, where Letter 1891 (Vol. VIII) is printed in full.
7 The figure alongside explains this remark, relating to the *second* barometer.
8 Leibniz had been invited to Paris early in 1672 by a letter from Simon Arnauld de Pomponne (1618–99), French Secretary of State, as a result of his various political writings, especially those in which he suggested that France should attack Holland by invading Egypt, which would interfere with Dutch trade with the East. He left Mainz in March 1671/2. He was present at a meeting of the Royal Society on 22 January 1672/3, where he did indeed show the Fellows "a new arithmetical instrument, contrived, as he said, by himself, to perform mechanically all the operations of arithmetic with certainty and expedition" (Birch, *History*, III, 73). He left again for Paris about 10 March 1672/3.

2123
Reed to Oldenburg
4 January 1672/3
From the original in Royal Society MS. R 1, no. 28

Worthy Sr

Yours I have received,[1] I will accordingly provide to observe your Commande betwixt this & Candlemas. The animadversions of my Cosen Dr Beale upon my letter you were formerly pleased to promise me[2] I have not yet seene, though I like wise desired ye same from him, for I am more desireous to learne then able to teach haveing beene rather industrious then Curious, & more a Clowne then a Philosopher in this poynt of husbandry of Orcharding. The certeyne knowledg whether ye sap does discend or not will be of constant & speciall use to me therein. I am confirmed more & more in that part of yt of planting late, rather then early.[3] The last yeare I transplanted many not much before St Mary day & some after, & ye spring fell out much to disadvantage, being very dry, yet I thinke not one miscarryed, though my Constant sicknesse all ye last yeare, wch yet abides upon me made me negligent in lookeing to them. This yeare if (please God I live) I intend to plant an Orchard and though this season being mild and moyst is most favourable, yet I reserve yt till the spring. I could wish I were able to serve your hoble. society in a greater matter, but wherein I am able you will please to accept from Sr

your very faithfull servant
Ric Reed

Jan. 4. 72.

ADDRESS
To his much honoured
Frend Henry Oldenburgh
Esqr at his house in ye
Pell-Mell these
Westminster

POSTMARK IA8

NOTES

We have assumed that Reed dated his letters in Old Style and therefore have assigned this and subsequent letters to 1672/3, rather than to 1671/2; there is unfortunately no internal evidence to substantiate either year. However Reed did send some grafts to the Society in February 1672/3.

1 We have found no trace of any correspondence between Oldenburg and Reed since Reed's Letter 1652 (Vol. VII) of March 1670/1.
2 This perhaps refers to Beale's Letter 1700 (Vol. VIII), although it was published in the *Philosophical Transactions*, or perhaps to some other "paper" by Beale.
3 See Vol. VII, pp. 513–14.

2124

Sluse to Oldenburg

7 January 1672/3

From the original in Royal Society MS. S 1, no. 75
Printed in Boncompagni, pp. 673–77, and in *Phil. Trans.*, no. 90 (20 January 1672/3), 5143–47

Nobilissimo et Clarissimo Viro
D. Henrico Oldenburg Regiae Societatis Secretario
Renatus Franciscus Slusius
S.P.D.

Methodum meam ducendarum ad curvas quaslibet Geometricas tangentium, mitto ad te, Vir Nobilissime, imo censurae tuae, ac per te virorum doctissimorum Societatis vestrae submitto. Brevis mihi visa est ac facilis, quippe quam puer ἀγεωμέτρητος doceri possit, et quae absque ullo calculi labore ad omnes omnino lineas extendatur: malo tamen alijs talem videri quam mihi, cum in rebus nostris caecutire plerumque soleamus. Data sit igitur quaelibet curva *DQ*, cuius puncta omnia referantur ad rectam quamlibet datam *EAB* per rectam *DA*: sive *EAB* sit diameter, seu alia quaelibet; sive etiam aliae simul lineae datae sint, quae vel quarum potestates aequationem ingrediantur: parum id refert. In aequatione Analytica, facilioris explicationis caussa, *DA* perpetuo dicatur *v*, *BA, y*. *EB* vero et aliae quantitates datae, consonantibus exprimantur. Tum supponatur ducta *DC*, tangens curvam in *D*, et occurens *EB*, productae, si opus sit,

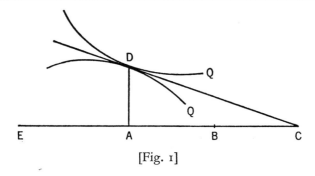

[Fig. 1]

in puncto C; et CA perpetuo quoque dicatur a.[1] Ad inveniendum AC vel a, haec erit Regula Generalis.

1 Reiectis ab aequatione partibus in quibus y vel v non invenitur; statuantur ab uno latere omnes in quibus est y, et ab altero illae in quibus habetur v, cum suis signis $+$ vel $-$. Hoc dextrum, illus sinistrum latus, facilitatis caussa, vocabimus.

2 In latere dextro, praefigatur singulis partibus, exponens potestatis quam in illis obtinet v. seu quod idem est in illum ducantur partes.

3 Fiat idem in latere sinistro, praeponendo scilicet unicuique illius parti exponentem potestatis quam in illa habet y. Sed et hoc amplius: unum y in singulis partibus vertatur in a.

Aio aequationem sic reformatam, modum ostendere ducendae tangentis ad punctum D datum. Cum enim eo dato, pariter datae sint y et v, et caeterae quantitates, quae consonantibus exprimuntur; a non poteri ingnorarj. Si quid forte sit obscuritatis in Regula aliquot exemplis illustrabitur. Data sit haec aequatio $by - yy = vv$: in qua EB sit b, BA, y, DA, v. et quaeratur a sive AC talis, ut juncta DC tangat curvam DQ in D. Ex Regula, nihil rejiciendum est ab hac aequatione, cum in singulis eius partibus reperiatur y vel v. Ita quoque disposita est, ut ab uno latere sint omnes illius partes in quibus y, ab altero omnes, in quibus v. Singulis itaque tantum praefigendus est exponens potestatis, quam in illis habet y vel v; et in latere sinistro unum y, vertendum in a, ut fiat $ba - 2ya = 2vv$. Aio nunc, hanc aequationem ostendere modum ducendae tangentis ad punctum D, sive

$$a = \frac{2vv}{b-2y} = AC.$$

Sic si data fuisset aequatio $qq + by - yy = vv$; eadem plane fierit cum priori aequatio pro tangente: abiecto sc. qq ut Regula praescribit. Sic ex

$$2byy - y^3 = v^3 \text{ fit } 4bya - 3yya = 3v^3 \text{ sive } a = \frac{3v^3}{4by - 3yy}. \text{ ex } bby + zyy + y^3 = qvv,$$

fit $bba + 2\zeta ya + 3yya = 2qvv$ et $a = \dfrac{2qvv}{bb + 2\zeta y + 3yy}$. Ex $b^4 + by^3 - y^4 = qqvv + \zeta v^3$,

fit $3byya - 4y^3a = 2qqvv + 3\zeta v^3$ et $a = \dfrac{2qqvv + 3\zeta v^3}{3byy - 4y^3}$. Verum in similibus aequationibus nullam arbitror accidere posse difficultatem. Aliqua fortasse in
illis occurret, quarum partes quaedam constant ex productis y in v. Ut yv,
yyv, y^3vv, &c. Sed haec quoque levis est, ut exemplis patebit. Detur enim
$y^3 = bvv - yvv$. Nihil ab illa rejiciendum erit, cum in singulis eius partibus
reperiatur y vel v. Sed ut ex Regulae prescripto disponatur, bis sumendum
erit yvv, et statuendum tam in latere dextro, in quo sunt partes quae habent
v, quam in sinistro, cujus partes habent y; quandoquidem yvv, tam y quam
v contineat; faciendum igitur erit

$$y^3 + vvy = bvv - yvv.$$

Tum mutata ut prius, hac aequatione in aliam $3yya + vva = 2bvv - 2yvv$,
dabitur $a = \dfrac{2bvv - 2yvv}{3yy + vv}$.

Ita enim intelligenda est Regula, ut nempe in latere sinistro non con-
sideretur potestas ipsius v, ideoque ipsi yvv exponens vv praefigi non debeat,
sed tantum ipsius y; sicut contra ab alio latere, in yvv considerari non debet
potestas ipsius y, sed v tantum, eique suus exponens praeponi. Sic si foret
$y^5 + by^4 = 2qqv^3 - yyv^3$, faciendum esset $y^5 + by^4 + v^3yy = 2qqv^3 - yyv^3$; et
haberetur aequatio pro tangente $5y^4a + 4by^3a + 2v^3ya = 6qqv^3 - 3yyv^3$ et
$a = \dfrac{6qqv^3 - 3yyv^3}{5y^4 + 4by^3 + 2v^3y}$. Atque his exemplis arbitror me omnem, quae dari

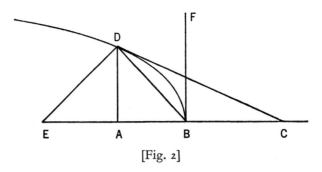

[Fig. 2]

possit, casuum varietatem complexum esse. Caeterum non erit fortasse
inutile si ea quae generatim exposui, ad lineam aliquam singularem
applicem. Dato sit igitur curva BD, cuius ea sit proprietas, ut sumto in illa

quolibet puncto D, si jungatur BD, et erigatur ad illam normalis DE, occurrens rectae BE in E, recta DE sit semper aequalis datae rectae BF. Ut habeatur aequatio in terminis analyticis, sit $DA = v$, $BA = y$, BF vel

$DE = q$. erit itaque $EA = \dfrac{vv}{y}$. et cum quadratum DE aequale sit duobus

DA, AE; erit aequatio $qq = \dfrac{v^4}{yy} + vv$. Sive $qq\,yy = v^4 + yyvv$.   quae pro

tangente, ex Regulae praescripto, sic reformanda erit

$$qq\,yy - vvyy = v^4 + yyvv$$
$$2qq\,ya - 2vvya = 4v^4 + 2yyvv$$
$$a = \frac{4v^4 + 2yyvv}{2qq\,y - 2vvy}$$

Quomodo autem aequationes hujusmodi ad faciliores terminos pro constructione reduci debeant, id sane solertem Geometram minime latebit. Ut ecce in hoc exemplo, quoniam rectangulum BAE supponitur aequale quadrato AD, & EA dicatur e, erit $vv = ye$, et $v^4 = yyee$, et $qq = ye + ee$. Itaque pro illis, posito in aequatione eorum valore, fit $a = \dfrac{4\,yyee + 2y^3e}{2eey + 2eyy - 2eyy}$,

sive $a = \dfrac{2ey + yy}{e}$, hoc est, $ae = 2ey + yy$, et addito ee utrimque

$ae + ee = ee + 2ey + yy$. erunt itaque tres $e : e + y : e + a$ sive EA, EB, EC, in continua analogia, et facillima evadet constructio.

Caeterum quoniam hactenus supposuisse videmur tangentem versus partes B ducendum esse, cum tamen ex datis accidere possit, ut vel parallela sit ipsi AB, vel etiam ducenda ad partes contrarias: definiendum nunc superest, quomodo haec casuum diversitas in aequationibus distinguatur. Facta igitur fractione pro a, ut in exemplis supra adductis, considerandae sunt partes tam numeratoris quam denominatoris, et earum signa.

1 Nam si in utroque, partes vel habeant omnes signum$+$, vel saltem affirmatae praevaleant negatis, ducenda erit tangens versus B.

2 Si affirmatae praevaleant negatis in numeratore, sed aequales sint in denominatore, recta per D ducta, parallela AB, tanget curvam in D; hoc enim casu, a est infinitae longitudinis.

3 Si tam in denominatore, quam numeratore partes affirmatae minores sint negatis; mutatis omnibus signis, ducenda erit rursus tangens versus B. hic enim casus cum primo in idem recidit.

4 Si in denominatore praevaleant, in numeratore minores sint, vel

contra; mutatis signis illius in quo sunt minores, ducenda erit tangens versus partes contrarias, hoc est, AC sumenda erit versus E.

5 Ac tandem si in numeratore partes affirmatae sint aequales negatis, quomodocumque se habeant in denominatore, a abibit in nihilum. Itaque

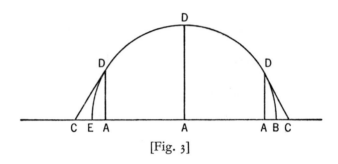

[Fig. 3]

vel ipsa AD erit tangens vel ipsa EA; aut ei parallela, quod ex datis facile dignoscitur. Horum autem casuum varietas explicari potest per aequationes ad circulum. Sit enim semicirculus, cujus diameter EB, et in eo punctum D datum, ex quo cadat normalis $DA = v$. Sit $BA = y$, $BE = b$. erit

aequatio $by - yy = vv$, et ducta tangente DG, erit AC sive $a = \dfrac{2vv}{b - 2y}$.

Nunc si b maior sit $2y$, ducenda est tangens versus B; si aequalis, fit parallela EB; sin autem minor, ducenda est versus E, ut 1, 2. et 4. diximus. Detur rursus alius semicirculus inversus, cujus puncta referri intelligantur

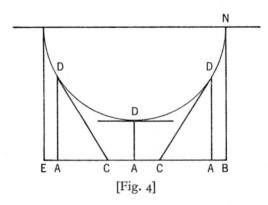

[Fig. 4]

ad rectam diametro parallelam, et eidem aequalem, ut in schemate. denominatis, ut prius, partibus et $NB = d$ fit aequatio $by - yy = dd + vv - 2dv$.

Igitur AC sive $a = \dfrac{2vv - 2dv}{b - 2y}$. Cum vero in exemplo supposuerimus v

semper esse minorem d; si b sit maior $2y$, ducenda erit tangens versus E; si aequalis erit parallela; sin minor, mutatis omnibus signis, ducenda erit versus b.[2] ut n. 4, 5 et 3. Nulla autem ducenda esset tangens, seu tangens foret ipsa EB, si supposuissemus NB aequalem semidiametro; sive

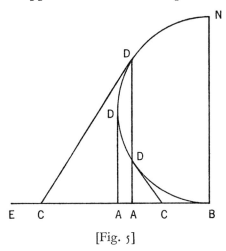

[Fig. 5]

$2d = b$, ut n. 5. Sit tandem alius semicirculus, cujus diameter NB normalis sit ad rectam BE, ad quam ejus puncta referri intelligantur. NB dicatur b, et aliae partes denominentur, ut supra; fiet aequatio $yy = bv - vv$. et

$$a = \frac{bv - 2vv}{2y}.$$ Jam si b sit maior $2v$, tangens ducenda erit versus B; si minor versus E; si autem aequalis, ipsa DA erit tangens ut n. 1º, 4º et 5to. et haec est, ni fallor, casuum omnium varietas quae ex aequationum consideratione deprehendi potest. Quomodo vero ex doctrina tangentium constituantur aequationum limites, non est quod pluribus exponam, cum evidens esse existimem, maximam vel minimam applicatarum vel utramque simul, determinari a tangente parallela: de quo et alias ad te scripsi et aliquid etiam attigi Miscellaneorum cap. [ ][3] ubi et qua ratione flexus contrarii curvarum ex tangentibus inveniantur, ostendi. Eadem ratione reperitur quoque μοναχὸς λόγος, ut vocat Pappus,[4] et multa alia, quae si explicare vellem, liber mihi scribendus esset. Nam et in Physico-mathematicis usus quoque hujus regulae opinione major est; licet enim falsum sit axioma, naturam agere per lineam brevissimam, verissimum tamen est, viam sequi determinatam, et ubi nullam invenit, agere αορίστως; de quo alias plura, si tanti tibi visum fuerit: jam enim epistolae modum excessi, ac vereor nedum obscuritatem vitare satago, in prolixitatem inciderim. Addo tantum me Regulae meae demonstrationem habere facilem, et quae solis constet

Lemmatibus passim notis; quod mirum tibi fortasse videbitur. Ad caetera quae in Epistola tua, 16ma mensis elapsi data continentur, ob temporis angustias (a triduo enim mihi reddita est) nihil nunc aliud reponere possum, nisi maximas me habere gratias humanitati tuae pro ijs quae me scire voluisti. Rogo tantum ut eadem humanitate certiorem me facias, te has accepisse, statim atque ad te pervenerint: et summopere obligabis eum, qui se constanti semper affectu tuum tuique observatissimum profitetur. Vale vir Nobilissime et meo nomine plurimam Clarissimo Domino Collinio salutem imperti. Dabam Leodii die 17a anni AE. C. MDCLXXIII. quem tibi faustum ac felicem apprecor ex animo.

TRANSLATION

René François de Sluse sends many greetings to the very noble and famous Mr. Henry Oldenburg, Secretary of the Royal Society

I send you, most noble Sir, my method of drawing tangents to any geometrical curves and, of course, I submit it to your own criticism and, through yourself, to that of the learned Fellows of your Society. It seems to me short and easy, indeed any boy ignorant of geometry could master it, and a method that can be extended to all curves without exception and without any labor of calculation. But I should prefer that it should seem so to others rather than to myself, since in matters concerning oneself one is commonly blind to many things.

Therefore let any curve DQ be given, every point of which is related to any given straight line EAB by the straight [ordinate] DA [*see Fig. 1, p. 387*]; whether EAB be the diameter or any other line whatever, or whether also other lines be simultaneously given which, or the powers of which, enter into the equation matters little. For ease of explanation DA will always be denoted as v in the analytical equation and BA as y. EB and other given quantities will be denoted by consonants. Then supposing DC, the tangent to the curve at D meeting EB produced if necessary) at C, to be drawn, CA will always be denoted as a. This will be the General Rule for finding AC, or a.[1]

1. Having rejected from the equation all those terms in which neither y nor v appears, all the terms in y are arranged on one side and all the terms in v on the other, with their positive and negative signs [observed]. For ease we shall call the former the left side and the latter the right side.

2. To each of the terms on the right side is to be prefixed the exponent of the power of v in them; or what is the same thing each is to be multiplied by its power of v.

3. Do the same thing also on the left side, that is place before each term of that side the exponent of the power of y in it. But there is this further to be done; one y in each of the terms is to be altered into a.

I say that the equation thus reformed shows the way to draw the tangent at the given point D. For, since that is given and likewise y and v and the other quantities which are expressed in consonants, a cannot be unknown. If there is perhaps some doubtful point in the Rule, a few examples will illustrate it. Let this equation be given, $by - y^2 = v^2$; in which $EB = b$, $BA = y$, $DA = v$, and $AC = a$ is sought such that, joining DC, it touches the curve DQ at D. According to the Rule nothing is to be rejected from this equation, for y or v is to be found in each of its terms. Also it is so arranged that all the y terms are on one side and all the v terms on the other. Therefore it is only necessary to prefix each term by the exponent of its power of y or v, and to transform one y [in each term] on the left-hand side into a, so that the equation becomes $ba - 2ya = 2v^2$. I now say that this equation tells us how to draw the tangent at D, or $a = \dfrac{2v^2}{b - 2y} = AC$. Thus if the equation $q^2 + by - y^2 = v^2$ had been given it would obviously be the same as the former equation as to the tangent; that is when q^2 has been rejected in accordance with the Rule. Thus $2by^2 - y^3 = v^3$ becomes $4bya - 3y^2a = 3v^3$, or $a = \dfrac{3v^3}{4by - 3y^2}$.

$b^2y + zy^2 + y^3 = qv^2$ becomes $b^2a + 2zya + 3y^2a = 2qv^2$, and $a = \dfrac{2qv^2}{b^2 + 2zy + 3y^2}$.

$b^4 + by^3 - y^4 = q^2v^2 + zv^3$ becomes $3by^2a - 4y^3a = 2q^2v^2 + 3zv^3$ and $a = \dfrac{2q^2v^2 + 3zv^3}{3by^2 - 4y^3}$. Indeed, I think that in similar equations no difficulty can arise. But some difficulty may be met with in those whose terms consist of some product of y and v, such as yv, y^2v, y^3v^2, etc. But this is trifling, as examples will show. For let it be given that $y^3 = bv^2 - yv^2$. Nothing is to be rejected from it, as y or v is to be found in each of its terms. But in order to arrange it according to the doctrine of the Rule, yv^2 is to be taken twice, and placed both on the right hand side (with the v terms) and on the left hand side (with the y terms), since yv^2 contains both y and v; therefore this will be formed:

$$y^3 + v^2y = bv^2 - yv^2.$$

Then having modified this equation as before into another one, $3y^2a + v^2a = 2bv^2 - 2yv^2$, it will give $a = \dfrac{2bv^2 - 2yv^2}{3y^2 + v^2}$.

For the Rule is to be so interpreted that the power of v is not taken into account on the left hand side, and so to the term yv^2 the exponent of v^2 should not be prefixed but only that of y; and by contrast on the other side the power of y should not be taken into account in yv^2 but only v, and its exponent placed before the term. Thus if $y^5 + by^4 = 2q^2v^3 - y^2v^3$, it would become $y^5 + by^4 + v^3y^2 = 2q^2v^3 - y^2v^3$; and the equation would be obtained for the tangent, $5y^4a + 4by^3a + 2v^3ya = 6q^2v^3 - 3y^2v^3$ and

$$a = \frac{6q^2v^3 - 3y^2v^3}{5y^4 + 4by^3 + 2v^3y}$$

And these examples include, I think, all the types of complexity that can occur. Further, it will perhaps be useful if I apply what I have explained in general terms to some particular [curved] line. Therefore let the curve BD be given, whose property it is that taking any point D and joining BD, if the normal DE be drawn to meet the straight line BE at E, the straight line DE will always be equal to a given straight line BF [*see Fig. 2, p. 388*]. To obtain the equation in analytical terms, let $DA = v$, $BA = y$, BF or $DE = q$. Therefore $EA = \dfrac{v^2}{y}$. And as

$DE^2 = DA^2 + AE^2$, the equation will be $q^2 = \dfrac{v^4}{y^2} + v^2$, or $q^2y^2 = v^4 + y^2v^2$. And this, for the tangent, is to be reformed as follows according to the Rule

$$q^2y^2 - v^2y^2 = v^4 + y^2v^2$$
$$2q^2ya - 2v^2ya = 4v^4 + 2y^2v^2.$$

[Therefore] $\qquad a = \dfrac{4\,v^4 + 2y^2v^2}{2q^2y - 2v^2y}.$

No skilful geometer will fail to see how equations of this kind may be reduced to easier terms for ease of construction. As may be seen in this example, since the rectangle $BA \cdot AE = DA^2$, and EA may be called e, $v^2 = ye$ and $v^4 = y^2e^2$, and $q^2 = ye + e^2$. Therefore substituting these values for the terms in the equation, $a = \dfrac{4y^2e^2 + 2y^3e}{2e^2y + 2ey^2 - 2ey^2}$ or $a = \dfrac{2ey + y^2}{e}$, that is, $ae = 2ey + y^2$ and, adding e^2 to either side $ae + e^2 = e^2 + 2ey + y^2$. Therefore the three quantities e, $e+y$, $e+a$ or EA, EB, EC will be continuously analogous, and the construction proves very easy.

Moreover, since we seem hitherto to have supposed the tangent to be drawn in the direction of B, yet from the data it may happen that the tangent is either parallel to AB or is even to be drawn in the opposite direction, it now remains to define the way of distinguishing this variety of cases in equations. Accordingly, having formed the fraction for a as in the examples adduced above, the terms both of the numerator and of the denominator are to be considered, and their signs.

1. For if the terms in both all have a positive sign, or if at any rate the positive are greater than the negative, the tangent is to be drawn towards B.

2. If the positive terms are greater in the numerator but equal in the denominator, a straight line drawn through D parallel to AB will touch the curve at D, for in this case a is of infinite length.

3. If the positive terms are less than the negative in both numerator and denominator then, after changing all the signs, the tangent is again to be drawn towards B. For this case reduces to identity with the first.

4. If the positive terms are greater in the denominator but less in the numerator, or vice versa, having changed the signs of that [part of the fraction] in which they are less the tangent is to be drawn in the opposite direction, that is AC is to be taken towards E.

5. And lastly if the positive terms in the numerator are equal to the negative ones, however they may be in the denominator, a will vanish to zero. Thus either AD itself is a tangent, or EA, or the tangent is parallel to it, which is easily found out from the data. This type of case may easily be explained by the equations to the circle. For let there be a semicircle, whose diameter is EB, and in it the point D given from which let fall the normal $DA = v$ [*see Fig. 3, p. 390*]. Let $BA = y$, $BE = b$. The equation will be $by - y^2 = v^2$, and having drawn the tangent DC, $AC = a = \dfrac{2v^2}{b - 2y}$. Now if b is greater than $2y$, the tangent is to be drawn towards B; if they are equal, it is parallel to EB; if b is less than $2y$, however, it is to be drawn towards E, as we have said under (1), (2), and (4) [above]. Again, given another inverted semicircle the points of which are to be understood as referred to a straight line parallel and equal to the diameter, as in the diagram [*see Fig. 4, p. 390*]. With the parts denoted as before and $NB = d$, the equation is formed $by - y^2 = d^2 + v^2 - 2dv$. Therefore $AC = a = \dfrac{2v^2 - 2dv}{b - 2y}$. As in the example we have actually supposed v to be always less than d, if $b > 2y$ the tangent is to be drawn towards E; if equal, parallel; and if $b < 2y$ then, changing all the signs, the tangent is to be drawn towards B,[2] as under (4), (5) and (3) [above]. But no tangent could be drawn, or the tangent would be EB itself, if we had supposed NB equal to the semidiameter, or $2d = b$, as under (5). Lastly, let there be another semicircle whose diameter NB is normal to the straight line BE, to which it is to be understood that its points are referred [*see Fig. 5, p. 391*]. $NB = b$, and the other parts are denoted as above; the equation $y^2 = bv - v^2$ is formed, and $a = \dfrac{bv - 2v^2}{2y}$. Now if $b > 2v$, the tangent is to be drawn towards B; if $b < 2v$ towards E, and if they are equal DA itself will be the tangent, as in (1), (4) and (5). And unless I am mistaken this is the range of all the cases that can be thought of as arising from a consideration of the equations. I need not, indeed, explain at length how the limits of equations are arrived at from the theory of tangents since I think it is obvious that the maximum or minimum ordinate, or both at once, may be determined from the parallel tangent; on which topic I have not only written to you elsewhere but touched to some extent in my *Miscellanies* Chapter   3[*sic*] where I also showed the way in which the contrary flexures of curves might be discovered from the tangents. In the same way may be found the *monachos logos* [limit ratio], as Pappus calls it,[4] and many other things which, if I meant to explain them, I should have to write a book. For the usefulness of this Rule in mathematical physics too is greater than opinion has it; for although the maxim that nature follows the shortest route may be false, yet it is most true that she follows a determinate path and where she finds none such acts haphazardly. Of this I will write more another time, if that seems fitting to you; for now I have exceeded the bounds of a letter and I am fearful lest, in striving to avoid obscurity, I have fallen into prolixity. I will only add that I have

an easy demonstration of my rule, consisting only of Lemmas well known everywhere; which will perhaps surprise you. I cannot now make any other reply to
the remaining matters contained in your letter dated the sixteenth of last month,
because of the shortage of time (for it was delivered to me but three days ago),
except to express my deep gratitude for your kindness [in writing] the things you
wished me to know. I only request that with the same kindness you will inform
me that you have received this letter immediately it reaches you, for thus you will
greatly oblige him who always professes himself full of regard and esteem for you.
Farewell most noble Sir, and present many greetings on my behalf to the famous
Mr. Collins. Liège, the seventeenth day of the year of our Lord 1673 [N.S.] which
I wholeheartedly pray may be a happy and fortunate one for you.

NOTES

Reply to Letter 2108, read to the Royal Society on 29 January.

1 Sluse's procedure is (in modern equivalent) to derive the partial derivatives Φv, Φy of
the given equation $\Phi\,(v, y) = 0$; his measure of the subtangent $a = y\dfrac{dv}{dy}$ then results
from the derivative equation $\Phi v + m\Phi y = 0$, where $m = \dfrac{dy}{dv}$ is the gradient of the tangent at D (see L. Rosenfeld, "René-François de Sluse et le Problème des Tangentes,"
Isis, 10, 1928, 416–34; and Hofmann, *Entwicklungsgeschichte*, Index, s.v. Analysis;
Tangentenmethode; Sluse).

2 Sluse inadvertently wrote a lower-case *b*.

3 Blank in original; he meant Chapter V (that is, pp. 117–30) in R. F. de Sluse, *Mesola-
bum . . . accessit pars altera de analysi et miscellanea* (Liège, 1668)—the second edition of
the *Mesolabe* with addenda.

4 See Vol. VII, p. 120, note 4. Sluse here intends the general problem of finding maxima
and minima (as the "unique" limit case where a pair of solutions coincide).

2125

Lister to Oldenburg

8 January 1672/3

From the original in Royal Society MS. L 5, no. 52
Printed in *Phil. Trans.*, no. 90 (20 January 1672/3), 5132–37

Yorke Janu. 8th 1672

Sir

We have formerly given you certain reasons for ye existence of veines (analogous to those in Animals) in all Plants whatsoever, not Mushroomes excepted: to wch we might add others of later notice; as ye skin of a plant may be cutt sheer off wth part of the Spongy parenchyma, & noe signes of milky-juice follow, yt is, noe breatch of a Vein. Again we have stript ye Plant of its skinn, by pulling it up by ye roots & exposing it to ye wett weather, untill it became flaccid as a wett Thong, without any injury to ye Veines, wch yet upon incision would freshly bleed. These experiments, I say, make against ye general opinion of one only sap loosly pervading ye whole plant, like water in a Sponge. And though we have made these & many other Experiments, to facilitate an *ocular demonstration* of these veines; yet we have not been able to effect it to our mind, & subject ym as nakedly to our Eye, as we could wish for a thorough information of their life & a minute & accurate discovery of all ye particular Accidents belonging to ym as such vessells. This, I say, is worke of much labour & patience, & yt wch renders matters very difficult, is ye infinite number, smallnesse & perplexitie of these veines.

In ye *transverse cutts* of Plants, we see as it were, a certain order & number of ye bloody Orifices of dissected veines. We observe alsoe in a Leaf, wch we take to be ye simplest part of a Plant

1. yt ye veines keep company wth ye ribbs or Nerves (as we vulgarlj call ym) & are distributed into all ye parts of ye Leaf, according to ye subdivisions of those nervous lineaments & are disposed with ym into a certain nott-worke, whether by *inosculations* or *bare contact* only, we pretend not to determin. 2 yt in a Transverse cutt of a Leaf, ye midle fibre or nerve for example, seemes to yeild one bigg drop of a *milkie-juice*, springing as it were from one Vein: yet ye Microscope plainly shews us, that there are many veines, wch contribute to ye making up of yt drop. 3. yt if a Fibre or

Nerve be carfully taken out of ye Leaf, ye Veines will appeare in it like soe many small haires or Pipes running along & striping ye nerve. 4. yt those many veines are all of an equall bignesse, for ought we have yet discerned to ye contrary. 5. yt though we seem to be more certain of ye Ramifications of ye Fibres, wherin these veines are, we yet are not soe, yt these veines doe any where grow lesse & smaller: though probably it may be soe. Yt wch makes us doubt it is ye exceeding smallnesse of these veines already, even where we might probably expect ym to be Trunk Veines & of ye largest size, and being there alsoe in very great Numbers & running in direct lines along ye Fibre, we guesse, yt one or more of ym may be distributed & fall off on either hand wth ye subdivisions of ye Fibres & not suffer any diminution in their bulke. 6. yt we cannot discern any where throughout ye whole Plant larger or more Capacious Veines then those we see adhering to ye fibres of ye leaves; wch does alsoe appeare from comparing ye bleeding Orifices in a Transverse-cutt. I have found it a difficult & labourious Taske to trace & unravel ym throughout ye whole plant. Our opinion is, yt these Veines doe still keep company wth their respective Fibres. And as all ye fibres of ye leafe are joined in ye stalke of ye leafe, & yt stalke again explicated in cloathing ye Twigg or stem of ye Plant, (wch we take to be ye reason of ye orderly breaking forth of ye leaves) soe doe we think of ye Veines their perpetual Companions. And as we have said ye fibres of ye leaves are joined in ye in ye [*sic*] Twig; soe are those of ye twiggs in ye branches; those of ye branches in ye Trunk or body of ye Tree: yt like alsoe in an inverted order we seem to observe in ye several Coates & Ramifications of ye Root. This ye several Circles of bleeding Orifices in transverse cutts seemes to confirme.

But moreover in ye Roots of Plants, if a single Coate be separated & exposed betwixt your eye & ye light, ye veines appeare to be strangely intangled & implicated & not in ye same simple order as in ye leaves. The like we thinke of ye barke of ye bodies of Trees, wch we cannot distinguish from ye roots of Plants: Though there is, indeed, something (at least at certain seasons of ye yeare) in ye root, wch is not to be found in any part of ye Plant besides.

From what hath been said it may well be doubted, whether there is any Sinus or common Trunk into wch all ye veines are gathered: but rather, yt there are a multitude of equally big Veines, each existing apart by it selfe. We, indeed, have found it very difficult soe to exhaust ye Plant of its milkie-juice, as to kill it, though we have given it very many incisions to yt purpos. Divers other instances there are, wch favour ye discontinuance of ye Veines & ye little relation & intercourse they have wth one an other; as one brantch of a Tree having faire & well grown fruit, before ye other branches of ye same Tree & fruit blossome or have leaves, from ye different situation & other circumstances of culture; ye indefinite & perpetual growth of Trees; The Cyon governing etc.

And thus far we have taken our information concerning these veines, partly by ye appearance they make in transverse-cutts & partly by ye helpe of a Microscope; wch last, indeed, has showed us something of their number, magnitude, order, distribution etc. And yet neither of these helpes in our hands has satisfactorily discovered to us other particulars belonging to these vessells, as external figure, Coates, Cavitie etc.

The substance of these Veines seemes to be as *truly membranous*, as ye Veines of Animals: A leafe will not give way & be extended, but ye Veines in a leafe, if freed of all ye woody Fibres, will be stretched out to one 3d part at least & vigourously restore ym selves again, just like a Vein, Gutt, or any other membranous Ductus of an Animal. Again those membranous Pipes are exceeding thinn & transparent, because they suddainly disappeare & subside after their being exhausted of their juice & particularly in yt, we see the liquour they hold quite through ym noe otherwise than ye blood through our Veines, or (in *Chelidonium majus* for example) a tincture of saffran in Chrystalline Pipes.

Concerning ye external Figure of these veines & Cavities, as well as other accidents, we thought, they would have been made more apparent to us, if it were possible to coagulate ye juice they hold without much srinking ye Plant. We were in great hopes Freezing would have effected this, wch, though it did not succeed, as we promised our selves, in respect of ye manifestation of these Accidents, yet it gave us some farther light into ye nature of ye juice of these Veines. In ye keenest frost, wch hapened ye other Winter, we dissected ye frozen leaves of ye *Garden* Spurge. Here we observed, yt all ye juice (besides yt wch these veines hold) was, indeed, frozen into perfect hard Ice, & to be expressed out in ye figure of ye containing pores; but ye milkie-juice, was a liquid as ever, but not soe briske as in open weather.

This Experiment we take to be good proofe of ye perfection of this milkie-juice: & that it hath within it selfe soe great a degree of Fermentation, yt it preserves it selfe & consequently ye whole Plant from ye injuries of ye weather; yt is, ye Plant owes its life to it. Thus we have seen Insects (as Hexapode Wormes etc) ly frozen upon ye Snow into very lumps of Ice; wch did not only cause ye Glasse to ring we struck ym against, but did endanger ye breaking of it: And yet put under ye Glasse & exposed to ye warmth of ye Fire, they quickly recovered their leggs & vigour to escape: wch we think could not be unlesse ye vital liquor of their Veines, as in this instance of Plants, had been untouched & little concerned in ye Frost. Further we doe hence alsoe argue ye different *Uses* as well as natures of these juices; & looke upon ye frozen Icicles or yt copious, dilute & limpid sap as Alimental; ye milkie & not frozen juice, as ye only proper venal.

As to ye *motion* of these juices, these things are certain. 1. yt ye milkie juice always moves & springs briskly upon ye opening of a Vein: ye *limpid sap* but at certain seasons & as it were by accident & not (as I judge) from any vital principal or fermentation of its owne. 2. The venal juice hath a manifest intestine motion of fermentation within it selfe; witnesse (besides what hath been just now said of it) its contributing (& ye long continuance of) yt motion to ye most insensible of liquours: & likewise its thick & troubled bleeding, like ye rising of Yeast; wch yet in a few houres after drawing falls & ye juice becomes transparent, as ye Gumm of ye Virginian Rhus etc.

I shall not desire any person to acquiesce wholly in a bare Fermentation; but endeavour a happy discovery of ye frame of all ye parts of a Plant, on wch too perhapps this motion may much depend. In ye meane time we must indeed needes thinke (according to ye knowledge we yet have of ye parts of Plants) yt these juices move by a far diffrent contrivance of parts from yt of Animals: not yet here discovering any uniting of Veines into one common Trunk, noe Plusation, noe sensible stop by a ligature, noe difference in Veines etc. All wch difficulties not withstanding may, I hope, in time be happily overcome: & ye Analogie betwixt Plants & Animals be in all things else, as well as ye motion of their juices, fully cleered. There are in Plants manifest Acts of *sense*:we instance in ye suddain srinking of some plants; ye frequent closing & opening of flowers; ye critical erecting of ye heads of Poppies from a pendulous posture; & particularly ye vermicular motion of ye veines when exposed to ye aire. Again ye veines of Plants may, indeed, be different, though at present we cannot tell wherin they are soe; ye Arteries within our heades are hardly to be known by ye eye from ye veines. Further there are Natural & spontaneous Excretions or venting of superfluous moisture in Plants, visible & constant in ye *Crowne Imperial*,[1] Rorella,[2] *Pinguicula*[3] etc. As to ye ligature, as it hath been hitherto applyed by us, it is not to be relyed on for ye discovery of this motion; ye veines only of Plants being ye parts probably distendable.

Lastly we shall not omit to tell you, yt either we must take yt away from ye other reasons given of ye necessitie of ye Circulation of ye blood in Animals, viz ye hindring of its breaking & clodding, or we must grant ye same Motion to ye venal juices in Plants. we having undeniable Experiments to shew, yt ye venal juice of ye Plants & ye blood of animals agree in this, yt they both, when they are once drawn from their respective Veines, doe forthwith breake & coagulate; & yt ye *serum* in ye one as well as in ye other becomes a stiffe gelly by a little standing.

But of ye different natures of ye juices of those veines in divers plants & their Motion we will remain your debtour & acquit our selves when we shall find it convenient: at present only acquainting you, what varietie of Experiments have taught us; yt probably more usefull preparations & certainly a truer Analysis & Separation of ye parts of Vegetable Druggs may be effected, whilst they are in bleeding & liquid, than after they are once become Concreet & have lost their natural Ferment.

Sir

I have thus redressed this letter & made it lesse positive; to ye end, yt it might give noe occasion of exception & conduce to ye designe of ye progresse of these matters: what I have added anew, is soe little yt I thinke it will be but crambe bis cocta[4] if it should appear again in ye R. S. I leave it to your disposal. I am Sir

Your most humble servant
Martin Lister

ADDRESS

For his much honoured friend
Henry Oldenburg Esquire
at his house in ye Palmal
London

POSTMARK IA 10

NOTES

This is a revision of Letter 2104, in the light of Grew's comments, sent to Lister in Oldenburg's Letter 2106. We print it in full here for comparison, although the differences are more verbal than substantive. Oldenburg has endorsed it "This letter was first written Nov. 30, 1672. and entered in ye Letterbook, as it was then: since wch time ye Author demanded it again, and altered it, as 'tis here."

1 *Fritillaria imperialis.*
2 *Rosa solis* or sundew.
3 Butterwort.
4 "twice cooked cabbage."

2126
Oldenburg to Reed
8 January 1672/3
From the memorandum in Royal Society MS. R 1, no. 28

Rec. Jan. 8.72.
Answ. yesame day.

NOTE

Reply to Letter 2123.

2127
E. Bartholin to Oldenburg
11 January 1672/3
From the original in Royal Society MS. B 2, no. 16

Vir Clarissime Nobilissime

Idoneam tibi mea officia deferendi cum Domino Trijboletio occasionem libenter amplector;[1] etsi parum habeam cujus in re literaria te certiorem faciam, cum non ita pridem tibi, ad gratissimas, cum Domino Henshaw, receptas literas, responsum miserim.[2] Optassem quidem operariorum festinationem, in Actis Academicis nostris edendis, ut una tibi mitti possem, forsan absolvenda erunt, ut cum Domino Henshaw mittantur.[3] Jus antiquum Norvegiae Aulicum jam quoque sub proelo est, nec non jus antiquum Daniae Aulicum, Latine et Danice cum annotationibus,[4] favente opportunitate tibi transmittendum. Nos summo studio desideramus eximios quos significasti tractatus, Mohuni [*sic*] de ventis Villisij de morbis Capitis, et Boyle de Gemmis, cujus multa passim indigitata scripta nondum nobis contigit videre, qualia feruntur esse de Origine formarum, de Calore et frigore, de usu Philosophiae Experimentalis, quos omnes quovis pretio redimeremus si hic prostarent. Desideramus quoque ex animo acta vestra Philosophica latine edita, ut ab omnibus legi possint.

Dolemus, permulta invidisse nobis occasionem, declarandi erga Dominos Henshaw et Trijbollet, studia nostra; profecto voluntatem, et singularem erga se amorem apertius perspexissent, nisi alijs negotijs impediti fuissent. Vale et me amare perge. Hauniae die 11 Jan. 1673

Tui studiosissimus
E. Bartholin

TRANSLATION

Most famous and noble Sir,

I gladly embrace this notable opportunity of sending you my respects by Mr. Triboulet,[1] though I have little of learned interest about which to inform you since I have recently answered your most welcome letter received from Mr. Henshaw.[2] I could wish that the printers made better speed in publishing our *Acta Academica* so that I could send a copy to you, but perhaps they will be finished in time to be sent by Mr. Henshaw.[3] The law of the ancient courts of Norway is now in press too, as also the law of the ancient Danish courts, [printed] in Latin and Danish with notes;[4] these shall be sent to you at a good opportunity. We wish with utmost eagerness for those extraordinary treatises you mention, Bohun on winds, Willis on diseases of the head and Boyle on gems; many of the latter's writings, recorded here and there, we have not yet chanced to see, such as those said to be on the *Origin of Forms, On Heat and Cold, On the Usefulness of Experimental Philosophy,* for which we would pay any price if they were on sale here. We also have a great longing for the Latin edition of your *Philosophical Transactions,* in order that everyone may read them.

We regret that a multitude of things has robbed us of the opportunity of manifesting our zeal towards Messrs. Henshaw and Triboulet; truly they would have more readily perceived our goodwill and particular affection towards them, if other business had not stood in the way. Farewell, and continue to love me. Copenhagen, 11 January 1673.

Yours most devotedly,
E. Bartholin

NOTES

1 For Triboulet, see Letters 2015 and 2141. He brought some amber which Oldenburg produced at a meeting of the Royal Society on 5 February 1672/3.

2 Bartholin's last letter was 2044 of 4 August 1672, unless some correspondence is missing.

3 The *Acta Medica et Philosophica* for 1671 and 1672 were in fact to be sent by Bartholin with Letter 2202; they only reached Oldenburg in September.

4 These are not recorded; compare note 9 of Letter 2015.

2128

Beale to Oldenburg

13 January 1672/3

From the original in Royal Society MS. B 1, no. 58
Printed in *Phil. Trans.*, no. 90 (20 January 1672/3), 5138–42

Sr·

In my last[1] I askt yu wt yu had heard from other parts of England of ye
late horrible Frost & I promised yu a considerable Accompt from a sure
hand, wch (for yr satisfaction) yu may see here inclosed, but neyther he,
nor myselfe must be named.[2] Some few words I *alter*, only to leave his
intended sense more clearly. Though we are forbidden to temper, & ragge[3]
disputations in Religion, yet we are not forbidden Religiously to acknowledge Gods Providence & Protection. Therefore I have drawe ye whole, as
on purpose, to recommend[?] my Wishes in ye last clauses. Wch I am sure
are agreable to ye ends & designes of ye RS, & may perhaps take effect, if
well handled in due place. Thus I begin

to Mr Old

The Copy of a Letter from Somersetshire Concerning a strange Frost,
wch hath lately done much hurte about Bristol & some usefull hints
upon yt occasion suggested for Ingenious Almanak Makers Prognos-
ticks of Famine, & Remedyes &c.

Sr, I have myselfe observed, & heard from others, yt much violent rayne
fell in many places of England this last Summer & Autumn, 1672. And 'tis
manifest, yt such violent showres do wash & carry away ye soyle & richest
Compost out of the common fields into ye Rivers & by them into ye Ocean
wch is ye cause of barrenes, & scarcity of Corne, & sometimes of a greate
mortality of Men & cattle, in ye following yeares as I could make appeare
by many calamitous Instances.

For a Remedy against Famine, or to prevent it, some good Men, wth
much zeale for the public wellfare, have earnestly sollicited *The Plantation
of Orchards, & Groves*; haveing received it from a Tradition pretending to
long observation & frequent Experience That in those yeares, in wch
Corne most fayles, fruite, maste, chesnuts, wallnuts, & such reliefe from
our Trees, do most abound. But there is no sufficient defense against ye
Wrath & Judgement of ye Allmighty, till we humble ourselves & returne

to our duty & obedience. That Orchards & Groves will not do it, yu may see by ye *narrative following*. The freezing raine, wch fell here ye 9th, 10th or 11th of Dec. last (for I can not confine ye Time exactly) hath made such a destruction of Trees in all ye Villages & high wayes, from Bristol towards Wells, & towards Shepton Mallet, & towards Bath & Bruton, & in other places of ye Weste, that both for ye maner & matter it may seeme incredible; & is more strange, then I have found in any English Chronicle. You will have ye prooffe, & manner, & best measure of it, in a Transcript wch I shall here give yu, from a very worthy person of unquestionable credite[4] as yu, or others of yr neere acquaintance do well knowe.

"The late prodigious Frost" (sayth he) "hath much disabled many old Orchards Exposed to ye North East. Had it concluded wth some gusts of Winde, it might have beene of sad importance. I weighed ye Sprigge of an Ashtree of iust three quarters of a pound, wch was brought to my Table the Ice on it weighed sixteene pounds, & yet neere two pounds were melted off by ye hands of them yt brought it. A bent at the same time was produced, no bigger then a small pinn, wch had an Icicle, encompassing it, of five ynches round by measure. Yet all this while, wn Trees & hedges were loaden wth Ice, there was no Ice to be seen on our Rivers, nor so much as on our standing Pooles. Now we are seriously concerned for Replanting. Dated Dec. 30. 72."

Sr, the like or worse & more strange complaints, I receive from severall other places, & from eye-Witnesses of Credite. Some Travaylers were allmost lost by ye coldnesse of ye freezing air, & freezing raine. All ye Trees, young & old, on ye high way from Bristol to Shepton, were so torne, & thrown down on both sides ye wayes, yt they were unpassable; by ye like obstructions ye carriers of Bruton were forc't to returne back. Some were affrighted wth ye noise in ye air, till they discerned yt it was ye Clatter of Icy boughes, dashed one agst another by ye Winde. Some told me, yt rideing on ye snowy downs, they sawe this freezing raine fall upon ye snowe, & immediately freeze to ice, without sinkeing at all into ye snowe; so yt the snow was covered wth Ice all along, & had been dangerous, if the Ice had been strong enough to beare them. Others were on their Journey, wn the Ice was able to beare them in some places, & they were in greate distresse. I sayd I could not punctually define ye Time wn this freezing-raine was most violent, & most apparent. Dec. 8. Much snow fell here; ye 9th much raine fell here; & all ye snow passed away, not leaving an icicle amongst us. The 10th day we had suddaine fitts of cold, & relaxing warmnesse. On Wednesday (Dec. 11) I saw a young man, who returning home from a Journey of five miles, & comeing into a warme roome, cryed out of extreame torments in all parts of his body. He affirmed, yt ye air, & ye winds (wch were then somewt high) were so unsufferably cold, yt he was in utter dispayre of comeing home alive: Yet all yt day, nothing but moist dew fell under our feete. If we say, The Earth did send foorth warme steames to keepe this freezeing raine dissolved on her Surface; whence shall we say the air & rain & winds got these freezing Icicles, wch oppressed men & plants?

Assoon as these Frosts were over, we had glowing heats, wch caused a general complaint amongt us of excessive sweating, by night & day. The bushes & many Flowers in ye garden appeared in such forwardnesse, as if it were in Aprill or May. I sawe young coleworts growing; rootes & leaves; on ye top leaves of an older Coleworte. Not far from my abode, an Apple-tree blossomed before Christmas: This I do not mention for Extraordinary. But I think tis more then ordinary, yt before Newyeares tide, this Apple-tree bore Apples perfectly knitted, & as big as ones finger end. I had some of these apples brought to me, wch I intended to send yu: But they so withered in my pocket, yt they have little resemblance of wt they were a fortnight since, wn they were greene & plumpe. As in ye foresd fickle freezing time, so nowe of late more then ever, the air seemes very aguish now very cold, then very warme by suddaine changes: Now freezing for 2 or 3 houres, then spouts of much rayne. Sometimes wth loud thunder, & much lightning; particularly on Wednesday last, about 3 in ye Morning Jan. 9. And strong feavors do rage amongst us mortally, & often bereaving ye family of more then one.

This leads me to wish yt some ingenious Almanak Makers would (instead of ye conjectures of Weather to come) give a faythfull & iudicious accompt of ye Weather, & other remarkable accidents, & phaenomena, as they fell out on the same day at ye Moneth of ye yeare foregoing. Hence we might in time examine upon sure ground how far ye positions of Planets, or other symptomes, or concomitants are indicative of Weathers. Probably we may have forewarnings of deaths, or famines, epidemicall diseases, contagions, & mortalityes of men & beasts, rot in sheepe &c: & by their causes be instructed for remedyes, & prevention. Certainly, by this methode we may learne more in fewe yeares than at random in all ye dayes of our short & brittle lives. And if such Almanaks might be had from other forreigne & remote partes, from Dantzic, Tangier, N. England, Burmudas, Barbados, Jamaica, We should make a closer chase to investigate ye cause

of heat & cold, coasting raine & coasting winds. And this diligence would
be profitable if observed from severall parts of England, Sea-coasts,
midlands &c.

Neyther would it lesse oblige posterity, if he who writes ye London-
Almanak would record at ye end of every moneth ye highest & lowest
price of wheate, rye, barley, pease, beanes, oates, as they are sold in some
chiefe mercate in London. And abstract in one page ye weekely Bills of
Births, Burials, plague, of males, & Females as is done for ye whole yeare
since his Matyes returne in compleate Catalogues of books printed. And ye
like Almanaks are to be wisht from Paris, Rome, Venice, Vienna, Madrid
since Maior Grant hath drawn us good Instructions,[4a] wt manifold uses
may be made from such informations &c.

It cannot be expected yt we should soone have it registered under every
moneth, ye Quantity, & Weight of Rayne yt falls every moneth or in greate
showers, or long lasting raine. And this would seeme a dull worke. Yet
this would signify more & to better purposes then ye hot controversyes of
some Triers who got greate names by their vexatious disputations.

In old Historyes I find, yt Earth quakes, inundations, droughts, famine,
pestilences, were each of them (in their severall Seasons, & sometimes one
close on the heeles of ye other) allmost universall over the knowne world:
sometimes rageing from place to place severall yeares together. As Meade[5]
relateth of a Pestilence, Wch in ye dayes of Gallus & Volusianus,[6] began in
Æthiopia, & for fifteene yeares wasted all ye Romane Provinces. This he
takes to be ye propheticall importance of Revel. ch. 6. v. 8.[7] Zonaras is his
Author,[8] & Lipsius his abettor.[9] As plagues, & famine, so stormes &
tempests, & (as far as I could collect) this frost, & some winds, (more in
some places then in other) did run from one place, & breake out in another
at differing times, & by short iourneys about ten miles at a time. Thunder
is not often heard above twenty miles off; except when it rolls about in a
large compass, or ye sound is assisted by ye conveyance of Woods, Forests,
Rivers or Channels. Hence Correspondence wilbe necesssary to perfect
these Rgisters.

If such a Kalendar as is here proposed, were happily begun, The leading
Example would draw on & grow to affoord us better Light, then hath
been hitherto assured by all ye remains of Astrology from ye beginning of
ye World to this day. And they may make acquaintance wth others, who
have a Genius, imployment, & opportunityes, fit to beare ye Trouble of
drawing ye Tables of Weather, & remarkable fatalityes. Forewarnings may
prepare us to consult for Preventions, or Remedyes. In ye yeare 1629 or

1630 (I am sure it was, wn a greate plague raged in Cambridge) there was a dearth in England. And much talke there was then, yt in London they had a way to knead & ferment boyled turneps wth a small quantity of meale, and yt it made better bread for whitenesse, pleasantnesse, lasting, & wholesomnes, than is made of ye finest flower of Wheate. Turneps, Rapes, carrets, parsneps, potadoes, & other rootes lye safe under ground from scorching heate, & are sayd to thrive best in ye greatest raine. Potadoes were a reliefe to Ireland in their laste famine. They yield meate & drinke. But after all diligence, & contrivances, our only Safeguard is to serve ye Ld who made & governed ye Stars, & all ye World.

Jan 13. 1672.

NOTES

These sheets (which bear evidence of having been sent to the printer) are heavily corrected by Oldenburg for printing in the *Philosophical Transactions*. We have endeavored as far as possible to restore Beale's original text. The introductory section was not printed.

1 This has not survived.

2 It seems probable that the anonymous author was in fact Beale.

3 "to tear in pieces, make ragged."

4 According to Birch, *History*, III, 74 the writer was John Buckland, for whom see Vol. II, p. 25, note.

4a John Graunt, *Natural and Political Observations upon the Bills of Mortality* (London, 1662, 1665). He was in fact a captain of the trainbands.

5 Joseph Mead (1586–1638), a biblical scholar; his chief work was *Clavis Apocalyptica* (Cambridge, 1627), translated into English as *The Key of Revelation* (London, 1643).

6 Caius Vibius Trebonianus Gallus (d. 254) was acclaimed Roman Emperor in 251; shortly afterwards he conferred the title on his son, Caius Vibius Volusianus (d. 253 or 254).

7 "And I looked, and behold a pale horse: and his name that sat on him was Death, and Hell followed with him. And power was given unto them over the fourth part of the earth, to kill with sword, and with hunger, and with death, and with the beasts of the earth."

8 Joannes Zonaras (d. *c.* 1130), Byzantine chronicler and compiler was the author of many Biblical glosses, works on ecclesiastical history, and a *Chronicle* (from the creation of the world to 1130), published at Basle in 1557.

9 This refers not to Justus Lipsius (1547–1606), the famous legal scholar, but to his great-uncle Martin Lipsius (d. 1555), a correspondent of Erasmus and a biblical scholar. Oldenburg has added here "in these words; Nec alia inquam major lues mihi lecta, spatio temporum, sive terrorum," that is, "And I have come across no greater pestilence in my reading, as to the interval of time, or the extent of the dread."

2129
Oldenburg to Huygens

13 January 1672/3

From *Œuvres Complètes*, VII, 245–50
Original in the Huygens Collection at Leiden

Monsieur

Quoyque je ne scays pas, si vous recevez ces petits traitez, que ie vous envoye de mois en mois, vous me l'ayant ainsi ordonné, ie continue neantmoins de vous les adresser voulant croire, que vos meilleures occupations ne vous permettent pas de nous escrire souvent. Je suis persuadé, que les observations, qui se trouvent dans ce Journal, faitez par Monsieur Boyle[1] ne vous desplairont pas. Vous verrez bientost quelque autre chose de sa composition, qui n'est pas vulgaire non plus.[2] Il va faire un Barometre de la facon, que vous avez descrite dans le dernier Journal de Monsieur Galloys.[3] Vous aurez vû sans doubte ce que Monsieur Boyle a publié dans la continuation de ses Experiences Physico-mechaniques. p. 68. et seqq. touchant un Barometre portatif,[4] comme aussi ce que Monsieur Hook a fait imprimer dans sa Micrographie d'un Barometre à roue, qui marque toutes les differences, mesme les plus petites, de la pesanteur de l'Air.[5] Nous esperons de voir bientost vostre Traité des Pendules, et d'entrendre de bonnes nouvelles du Pendule, que vous avez envoyé sur mer.

Je ne scaurois pas vous celer la responce de Monsieur Sluse à ce que vous m'escrivistez le 27 Sept. dernier sur sa construction du probleme d'Alhazen; vous ayant desia dit par ma lettre du 11me Novembre que i'avois pris la liberté de luy communiquer cela. Voicy ses propres paroles.

"Non tanti mihi fuerunt unquam vel sunt etiamnunc Geometria studia, ut eapropter cum quoquam contentionis funem ducere velim; nedum cum viro docto et amico, cujus ingenium et eruditionem qualibet occasione commendare soleo [. . .]" [*Here Oldenburg quotes virtually the whole of the first part of Letter 2100.*]

C'est à vous, Monsieur, de considerer comment Monsieur Sluse s'est acquitté, qui semble estre adversaire fort honeste à celuy, qui est Monsieur

Vostre tres humble et tres obeissant serviteur
Oldenburg

A Londres le 13 janvier 1673

TRANSLATION

Sir,

Although I do not know whether you are receiving the little tracts which I send you month by month, as you commanded me, I am nevertheless continuing to send them to you, wishing to believe that your more important occupations do not leave you time to write often to us. I am persuaded that the observations to be found in this journal, made by Mr. Boyle,[1] will not displease you. You will soon see something else of his composition, which is also not common.[2] He is going to make a barometer after the fashion which you have described in the latest *Journal* of Mr. Gallois.[3] You will undoubtedly have seen what Mr. Boyle has published in the *Continuation* of his *Physico-Mechanical Experiments*, p. 68 and following, about a portable barometer,[4] and also what Mr. Hooke had printed in his *Micrographia* about a wheel barometer which notes all the changes in the weight of the air, even the most minute ones.[5] We hope to see your treatise on pendulums soon, and to hear good news of the pendulum clock which you sent to sea.

I did not wish to conceal from you Mr. Sluse's reply to what you wrote to me on 27 September last [N.S.], on the construction of Alhazen's Problem, having told you already in my letter of 11 November that I had taken the liberty of communicating that to him. Here are his own words:

[*Here follows the first part of Letter 2100; for the translation see pp. 334–36, above.*]

It is up to you, Sir, to consider how Mr. Sluse has acquitted himself; he seems to have been a pretty honest adversary to he who is, Sir,

Your very humble and obedient servant
Oldenburg

London, 13 January 1673.

NOTES

1 "Some Observations about Shining Flesh," *Phil. Trans.*, no. 89 (16 December 1672), 5106–16.
2 This perhaps refers to "A New Experiment of the Noble R. Boyle, concerning an Effect of the Varying Weight of the Atmosphere upon some Bodies in the Water," *Phil. Trans.*, no. 91 (24 February 1672/3), 5156–59. The experiments were originally made in 1671.
3 See Letter 2103, note 4.
4 See Birch, *Boyle*, III, 219–24 (Experiment XXII).
5 See *Micrographia* (London, 1665), The Preface.

2130

Swammerdam to Oldenburg

14 January 1672/3

From the original in Royal Society MS. S 1, no. 120
Partly printed in *Phil. Trans.*, no. 94 (19 May 1673), 6041

Viro Clarissimo
D. D. Henrico Oldenburgh
Joh. Swammerdam S.

Non Se attolit animus meus, Vir Eruditissime, nam ut verum fatear, et Opifici meo gloriam tribuam, scopum me meum attigisse scias, quippe cum Regiam Societatem *pronis oculis et Serenissima fronte*, opera Dei nunquam satis depraedicanda, *lustrantem* viderim, quemadmodum quoque futurum satis copiose, ex anniversariis tuis philosophicis, jam ab aliquo tempore ad me datis, intellexerim; et de Dedicatione aeque ac de munere Deo gratulor.[1]

Interim ne credas quaesto[2] munus illud meum mancum tibi traditum fuisse, cum notatus a te arculae locus, virginis pudendo fuerit destinatus.

Aliud est quod metuo, nimirum contractum hinc inde ab utero aliisque partibus situm; quod facile penicillo, oleo terebinthino (in quod paululum mastiches dissolutum fuerit) intincto arcebis; atque ita levissimo negotio in longum has partes conservabis: quod ut exploratum adversus situm remedium, vobis liberaliter communico.

Noduli, qui in ramificationibus arteriarum Hepatis notantur, non naturae sed arti debentur, cum a violenta, dictorum vasorum a vena porta, post cerae injectionem,[3] instituta separatione dependeant: quod ideo noto, ne vestra Claritas contra naturae et veritatis leges, harum partium delineationum, si ita visum vobis fuerit,[4] exhiberet.

In nuperis meis sectionibus animalia quaedam ostendi, quibus licet pulmonibus uterentur, naturaliter tamen Vena arteriosa fuerit denegata, ita ut sanguis, immediate e corde, absque ulla in pulmone praevia circulatione aut conquassatione, *passus*, per totum corpus distribueretur: unde haec mea observatio pulmonis usum non tantum obscuriorem reddit, sed et anatomiam comparatam quam maxime commendat.[5]

Genitalia nasicornis scarabei,[6] Mercurio Saeri,[7] ad amussim vasorum Testiculariorum ratione, cum humanis convenire testiculis, atque ex unico tantum funiculo, longo, cavo, innumerabiliter flexo, atque, quod nondum in homine mihi visum, in principio seu apice suo caeco, constare, cum stupore lustravi;[8] ut jam nullibi non manifesta sint, divinae sapientiae et summi in abjectissimis animalibus artificii vestigia.[9] Vale vir eruditissime meque tuum crede. Dab. Amst. Ao. 1673. 24 Jan. [N.S.]

ADDRESS
Monsieur
Monsieur Grubendol
A
Londres

TRANSLATION

Jan Swammerdam greets the famous Mr. Henry Oldenburg

My mind has not been [so] transported, most learned Sir, but that I may confess the truth and assign the glory to my Maker; you know that I have attained my goal, when (to be sure) I have seen the Royal Society examining the works of God—never the object of sufficient prayer—with favor and acceptance, just as I had understood, fully enough, would be [the case] from your *Philosophical Transactions*, already presented to me for some time past; and I thank God for the presentation and the present equally.[1]

Meanwhile do not, I beg you, believe that that gift of mine was delivered to you with something missing, for that place in the box noted by you was intended for the pudenda of a virgin.

What I fear is different, namely that the uterus and other organs may grow moldy here and there, which you may easily prevent by means of a brush dipped in oil of turpentine (in which a little mastic has been dissolved); and thus you may preserve these organs for a long time with very little trouble, because I freely communicate to you the remedy against mold that I have tested.

The little lumps which may be observed in the ramifications of the hepatic arteries are due to art rather than nature, since they arise from the forceful separation of the said vessels from the portal vein after the injection of wax;[3] of which I accordingly make mention lest your exellency should present a sketch of these organs (should that seem proper to you)[4] contrary to the laws of nature and of truth.

In my recent dissections I have demonstrated some animals which, although they possessed lungs, were deprived by nature of the pulmonary artery so that the blood was distributed directly from the heart about the whole body without undergoing any previous circulation or disturbance in the lungs; this observation of mine not only makes the function of the lungs more obscure but greatly recommends [the study of] comparative anatomy.[5]

I have observed with astonishment that the genitalia of the horned-nose beetle,[6] sacred to Mercury,[7] as to the manner of the testicular vessels agrees exactly with the testes of men, consisting of no more than a single, long, hollow, innumerably inflected fine thread and (what I have never yet seen in men) at its origin or top it is blind;[8] so that everywhere and in the humblest of creatures the traces of the divine wisdom and supreme skill are made known.[9] Farewell, learned Sir, and believe me [to be] yours. Amsterdam, 24 January 1673. [N.S.]

ADDRESS

To Mr Grubendol,
London

NOTES

Reply to Letter 2111, read to the Society on 29 January, when Oldenburg was instructed to ask Swammerdam to name the animals lacking a pulmonary artery.

1 The English of this paragraph reflects Swammerdam's breathless style.
2 *Sic*; read, *quaeso*.
3 Swammerdam had employed wax injection in preparing anatomical specimens since 1667, and may have invented this technique, which he brought to a high pitch of perfection.
4 Oldenburg did not.
5 When printing these two closing paragraphs of the letter Oldenburg very much modified Swammerdam's prose for the sake of simplicity and clarity. In his next letter (Letter 2173) Swammerdam explains that his remarks are based on the frog, and that he supposes them to be also applicable to other amphibians. Although Swammerdam did in fact see the pulmonary artery of the frog, as it arises from the aorta and not directly from the heart he regarded it as undeserving of the special significance it possesses in mammals. However, his understanding of the blood supply in the frog was certainly imperfect (see Cole, *Comparative Anatomy*, 300–302).
6 The rhinocerus beetle, *Oryctes nasicornis*, according to Schierbeek, *Swammerdam*, 152.
7 Does Swammerdam mean to identify his beetle with the sacred scarab (dung beetle) of Egypt, *Scarabaeus sacer*?
8 Swammerdam prepared an elaborate account of this insect, which was printed much later and may be found in *The Book of Nature . . . By John Swammerdam . . . Translated by Thomas Flloyd* (London, 1758), I, 131–52. He was apparently wrong in supposing this blind vessel to be a testis, though it is part of the creature's reproductive system.
9 It is interesting that the author concludes his monograph on this beetle with just such another, but more elaborate, eulogy of the wisdom of God in the creation.

2131
Oldenburg to Reisel
15 January 1672/3

From the copy in Royal Society MS. O 2, no. 68

Nobilissimo et Celeberrimo Viro
Domino Salomoni Reisello Illustrissimo Com.
Hanov. Archiater Henricus Oldenburg
Salutem

Facis profecto, Vir Celeberrime: quod Virum Medicum et vere Philosophum decet, dum de Scientia physica et Arte Medica, earumque studiosis et Fautoribus, bene mereri satagis. Singulare imprimis erga Soc. Regiam studium testaris, quod Illa grato animo agnoscit, mihi iniungens, ut te ipsius nomine salutem, et de benevolentia sua certiorem reddam. Nec levem erga me affectum indicas, dum opellam meam provehendis scientiis et exstimulandis philosophis, conferre aliquid existimas. Eum equidem locum in Regia societate teneo, qui me monet, ut id quod a me expectas, valde velim; sed tenuitatis meae conscius nonnisi parcus esse possum in polliciendo dum omnes nitendo vires, ne omnino nihil egisse videar. Non sum nescius quantum valeant sociatae doctorum et solertium virorum operae in solida rerum naturalium cognitione augenda; id igitur potissimum ago, ut studia et meditata eorum longe lateque orbe polito sparsa, commercij literarij beneficio copulem, eosque si possim eo pertraham, ut observata, Experimenta, et inventa sua invicem communicent, alijque aliorum de rebus physicis et mechanicis, (quibus feracior utiliorque humanae cognitionis summa constat) sententias enquirunt, revolvant, et in vitae humanae usum convertunt, quam Tu, vir Doctissime, super literas in medio Fagi trunco latas,[1] deque Antipathia Unicornu cum obolo, ejusdem cum Mica panis sympathia commentaris,[2] haud abludere a vero videntur; quaeque de Urbibus Arcibusque ante aliquot annos ad certam distantiam non conspectis, nunc vero eadem locorum intercapedine visis, enarras, ea certe aut montium interjectorum subsidentiae, aut sylvarum interpositarum excisione tribuenda videntur. Quodvero contraversiam illam spectat circa Urinae circulum,[3] de qua sententiam nostram sciscitaris, cum sensum momentumque eius ex ijs, quae in literis tuae habentur, non assequor, veniam dabis, si de ea silem. In Curiosorum Germanorum Actis Vidi symbolas quas in Ephemerides illas contulisti, occurrunt quae de Aqua ex decollati hominis sanguine per Alebicum destilla, acrique gelido exposita annotasti.[4] Sinas me tibi commendare hac anni Tempestate Experimentum aliquod circa Plantas, in quibus sagaciores quidem Nostratium Anglorum Physici duplicia pro totidem inibi contentis liquoribus vasa, Animalium venas et fibras aemulantia,[5] deprehendere operae, inquam, precium fuerit experiendo cognoscere, num uterque ille liquor, quorum alter limpidus est, alter vero lacteus, aeque facile frigore confringatur, an vero priore congelato, posterior in fluiditatis statu; permaneat? Et dum de hoc Experimento loquor, mentem subit aliud, quod nec praeter rem fuerit Experire, Avesne scil. aliave animalcula, gelu enecta, facta dissectione, in corde alijsve visceribus mileculas glaciales contineant?

En Tibi, vir Clarissime, libertatis meae philosophicae argumentum quam pro candore tuo te in bonam partem accepturam credo, Putem innotuisse jam vobis in Germania, quae Illustrissimus Boylius nuper edidit de Gemmarum origine et Viribus,[6] quaeque exinde Doctori Henrico Moro, adversus Experimenta quaedam ejus Physico-Mechanica objicienti responderit.[7] Alia molitur idem de corporum Effluvijs, eorumque natura et effectibus meris, quae propediem quoque lucem videbunt.[8] Vos, Germaniae meae doctores, non stabilis post principia, sed pro virili philosophiam promovere et ornare non desinetis. Vale, et doctrinae et virtutis tuae cultorem amare perge. Dabam Londini d. 15. Janua. 1672

TRANSLATION

Henry Oldenburg greets the very noble and famous Mr. Salomon Reisel, Chief Physician to the most illustrious Count of Hanau

You certainly do what befits a physician and a true philosopher, famous Sir, when you strive to earn merit in the science of nature and the art of medicine, and in the eyes of those who study and encourage them. Especially you manifest a singular zeal towards the Royal Society, a fact that it acknowledges gratefully, enjoining me to greet you on its behalf and assure you of its goodwill. And you disclose no small regard for myself when you find some value in my own labors for the advancement of science and the encouragement of philosophers. For indeed I hold such an office in the Society as advises me to wish strongly for that which you expect of me; yet, being aware of my feeble powers I can, while striving with all my might, be but sparing in the promises I make lest I should seem to have achieved nothing at all. I am not unmindful of the great value of the combined efforts of learned and skilful men in advancing a sound knowledge of nature;

accordingly I do my best by means of a correspondence to compile their researches and ideas (scattered as these are up and down the civilized world) and, if I
can, induce them to communicate their observations, experiments, and discoveries
to each other [so that] some of them may investigate, consider, and turn to human
uses the opinions of others on matters of physical science and mechanics, which
are by far the most fruitful and useful [branches of knowledge] for the human
understanding[.] The notes you offer, learned Sir, on the letters hidden in the
midst of the trunk of a beech tree,[1] and on the antipathy of the unicorn for the
obulus and its sympathy for breadcrumbs[2] certainly do not seem far from the
truth; what you relate about towns and castles not being seen a few years ago at a
certain distance whereas now they are visible across the same stretch of country
must certainly be attributed either to the subsidence of intervening hills, or the
cutting down of forests lying between the places. As for that debate about the
circle of the urine,[3] upon which you solicit our opinion, as I do not understand the
meaning and significance of the [question] from the content of your letter, you will
forgive me if I am silent concerning it. In the *Miscellanea curiosa* I have seen some
contributions of your own, among them some notes on the water (distilled by the
alembic from the blood of a beheaded man) exposed to severe frost.[4] Permit me to
commend to you at this season of the year a certain experiment upon plants, in
which the shrewdest of our English naturalists have discovered vessels of two
kinds as to their fluid contents, resembling the veins and fibers of animals[.][5] It
would be worthwhile, I repeat, to find out by experiment whether both of these
fluids (of which one is clear and the other milky) will be destroyed with equal
ease by cold, or whether when the former is frozen, the latter will remain liquid?
And while mentioning this experiment another comes to mind which it would not
be irrelevant to try: namely, when birds or other small creatures are killed by frost,
does it appear on dissection that their hearts or other organs contain particles of ice?

Here you have, Sir, a token of my philosophical freedom which I believe you,
out of your sincerity will take in good part. I think that the very illustrious
Boyle's recent publication on the origin and virtues of gems is already known to
you in Germany,[6] and the reply since made to the objections raised against some
physico-mechanical experiments of the author's by the learned Henry More.[7] The
same is working on another [treatise] upon the effluvia of bodies, their nature and
their genuine effects, which will also see the light soon.[8] You, the learned men of
my German homeland, should not stand rooted behind the leaders but continue to
promote and perfect philosophy with all your might. Farewell, and continue to
love this admirer of your learning and virtue. London, 15 January 1672.

NOTES

Reply to Letter 2077 which, together with the letter addressed to the Royal Society
itself on 30 September 1672, had been read to the Society on 11 December.

1 Reisel wrote of this odd discovery of letters visible on the wood of a tree beneath the bark, to which he assigned a natural explanation, in the first part of his letter to the Society.

2 Reisel refutes this tale of Basil Valentine and others in the second part of his letter to the Society (see also *Miscellanea Curiosa*, II, 1671, Obs. no. 111). The obolus was a small Greek silver coin (one-sixth of a drachma). Reisel does not seem to doubt the existence of a unicorn, neither does he say what kind of animal it is.

3 This again is from the second part of Reisel's letter; his own words are "controversiam circa Urinae circulum seu coronam" ("the debate about the circle or crown of urine")—the point at issue seems to be optical, but (like Oldenburg) we are not clear what it is. (See also *Miscellanea Curiosa*, II, 1671, Obs. nos. 178 and 219.)

4 *Miscellanea Curiosa*, II, Obs. no. 177.

5 Compare Letter 2125.

6 One Latin version of *Gems, Exercitatio de origine et viribus gemmarum* appeared at London, and another, *Specimen de gemmarum origine & virtutibus*, appeared at Hamburg, in 1673.

7 "An Hydrostatical Discourse occasioned by the Objections of the Learned Dr. Henry More . . ." is the ninth(?) section in *Tracts . . . containing New Experiments touching the Relation between Flame and Fire . . .* (London, 1672), which were not available in Latin until 1696. (The query is inserted because of the chaotic printing history of this volume.)

8 That is, the *Essays of the* $\left\{\begin{array}{l}\textit{Strange Subtilty} \\ \textit{Great Efficacy} \\ \textit{Determinate Nature}\end{array}\right\}$ *of Effluviums* (London, 1673).

2132

F. Oswell to Oldenburg

15 January 1672/3

From the original in Royal Society MS. O 2, no. 175

Utrecht Janry 25 1672/3

Sir

However my occasions have not hitherto favoured my desires of writing unto you, yet am I not alltogether so unmindfull of your commands; or that obedience I ow them, as ye slownes of this proof of it may perhaps occasion you to suspect; and 1st as to your Enquirie what noted persons are heir, who have not addicted ymselves to peripatetick theories, in physiologicall matters I return you these, Heir in Utrecht are De Bruyn publick professor of Philosophie & Burmann of Theologie 2 through pac'd Cartesians,[1] But old Regius[2] tho he pretends to be the 1st author of yt Philosophie, does now begin to remit of his former zeal for some of it's cheif Dogmata; but especially that wch maketh brutes, to be meer mechanicall machines, & all their operations automaticall, concerning wch he did freely profess to me, that he did now rather encline to ye opinion of ye platonists, as it is exprest in thes known verses Principio caelum & terram &c.[3] Heir is also Diemerbroeck professor, whoes Anatomie is Just now comeing furth,[4] your Celebrated Kerkringius, & Velthusius a Cartesian physician,[5] & on of ye Magistrates of this city: At Leij[den] there are besides Sylvius 2 Cartesian Professors of Philosophie called Croni & Volder & on Drelincourt professor of anatomie, who passeth heir for a very Ingenious man, he wrote a tract de partu octomestri vivaci.[6] In my passage betwixt Roterdam & Leij[den] I pay'd your respects, as yow gave it me in command, to Dr De Graaf Physician at Delph, who shewed me his book De mulierum organis Generationum dicatis then unfinish'd (but now as I hear it is aprinting at Leij[den] & will come out verij shortly),[7] & his inventions viz. a new Clysterpipe far more advantageously contrived for it's proper use, yn yt wch yow have of this kind in England, as also an authenticall decision of the controversie depending betwixt Dr Clark & him & yt other concerning ye passage of ye seed from ye Vasa deferentia to the vesiculas Seminales by an ocular demonstration of what is asserted in his book,[8] If this latter discoverie of a foramen from the deferentia to the vesiculas seminales be proper to him, wherein he seems to have been prevented by Veslingius:[9] he hath lately republisht his Discourse de succo pancreatico, conteining his ingenious contrivance for its separation, wth an Epistle super added to it,[10] wherein he promiseth in his book now under ye press to deduce the whole business of our generation ab ovo;[11] But becaus the greatest Difficulty of this opinion consists in demonstrating a ductus from ye ovarium to ye Uterus, I shall heir present yow with ye best account of this matter, I have yet been able to learn; I am informed by My correspondent at Ley[den], That he was lately there present at a publick dissection in the Nosocomium,[12] where by inserting his stylus, he demonstrated a Ductus from ye Testes into ye side of ye Tuba Uterina,[13] wch being dilated by heat, he makes to transmit ye ova, in to the uterus. But Swammerdam Physician at Amsterdam conceives ye matter otherwise, for he sayes that the extremity of ye Tuba Uterina, wch is commonly called Morsus diaboli, being expanded by heat, retorquet se versus ovarium & absorbet ova:[14] Kerkringius's Explication I suppose you have seen in his printed discourse on this subject subjoyn'd to his observationes anatomicae, & he in confirmation of this opinion does shew among his many other rarities, ova a virginibus excreta:[15] But professor Diemerbroeck at a publick dissection heir of a female subject in the anatomicall Theatre where I was present doth explode all those ova muliebria as being only ye wind-eggs of their own fancy wth a sunt nugae domine, the summe of whoes reasons I shall now therefore give you & yt as near as I can in his own words;[16] haec ova sunt rejicienda 1o quia non apparet quomodo hujusmodi ova per vasa tam angusta a testibus in uterum transmitti possint 2o quia mulieres non habent ova ut vocant subventanea, 3o & praecipue quod semen in oviparis in ovarium effunditur quod hic locum habere non potest. Ipsa autem substantia testium vesiculosa, potest esse causa hujus apparentiae, cum hae vesiculae inflatae, specie quadam ovorum, spectatores illudunt, for so they doe appear to our naked eyes something lyk those vesicles wch Malpighius by his microscopes discovered the lungs to be made up of; and therfore he admitts no other eggs in this species, but that true on wch is included wthin the amnios & chorion wch 2 membranes may be sd to bear some analogie to the 2 tegum[in]a ovi:[17] And thus I have gaven yow ye best account I could procure of this matter wch is ye cheif thing under debate among physicians heir, referring yow for ye more full explication of it to ye books of ye severall authors abovementioned. To wch perhaps it may prove not unacceptable to add that Experiment lately tryed at Ley[den] wch they call after Galen Laryngotomia;[18] It is done by stopping exactly all passages wch are for inspiration of air by mouth or nostrills, & inserting a tub[e] betwixt two of the superior annulare cartilages wch are tyed hard upon at, the event whereof was this that the dog lived for 2 dayes at ye end of wch having for a further triall suck'd in 5. or 6 tymes ye flame of a wax candle, he expir'd.

As for books There are now comming furth Bartholins Anatome wth new cutts of the uterus by Swammerdam,[19] Barbetti Chirurgia translated into latine, whereof there are 2 impressions both comeing out together,[20] a New Edition of Schroder & a little peice de aphthis,[21] beside what I mention'd above. wer it not for fear of being taedious I should tell you of one who wth a plaister does wonderfull Cures upon Goutish persons. Heir was on skipper who had been troubled wth a Gout for 20 years & was now become utterly unable to walk who by ye use of it recovered his leggs again but yt For wch I cheifly mention'd was on circumstance of ye cure wch seem'd pretty odd viz yt out of his thumb did sweat a whitish matter lyk unto burnt bones in colour lightnes & consistencie but enough of this I have more need to beg your pardon for praesuming to trouble yow with

such a multitude of particulars, whereof some perhaps may appear frivo-
lous, others, may be such as yow have known very well before, for wch
all my excuse is That I was ambitious heirby to signifie in some small
measure how ready I should be if an occasion wer offered of any thing wch
might be really usefull to yow to testifie ye sense of yt obligation I ly under
to be

your most Humble & obedient servant
F. Oswell

I pray yow present my service to Mr Cooper & if yow have any service
to command me wth I live in the Wittie vrow straet at Jan Forests cleer-
maker.[22]

ADDRESS
> For
> Mr Henry Oldenbrough
> Esqr at his lodgings
> in the old Pell Mell
> London

NOTES

Except that he was an acquaintance of Peter Nelson of Durham (see Vol. VII, pp.
327, 535) we know nothing of the writer of this letter.

1 Jan van Bruyn (1620–75), at this time Professor of Logic at Utrecht, was the author
of *Defensio doctrinae Cartesianae de dubitatione et dubitandi modo* (Amsterdam, 1670).
Frans Burmann (d. 1679) had been appointed Professor of Sacred History at Utrecht
in 1671.

2 Henricus Regius (Henri le Roy, 1598–1679); see Vol. I, p. 272, note 10.

3 "In the beginning [God created?] heaven and earth."

4 Isbrand van Diemerbroeck (1609–74), Professor of Medicine and Anatomy. His
Anatome corporis humani was first published at Utrecht in 1672.

5 Lambert Velthuysen (1622–85) was educated at Utrecht. He was a prolific writer on
medical, religious, and philosophic subjects.

6 We have not identified Croni (or perhaps Oswell wrote Carom) and Volder. Charles
Drelincourt (1633–97), a French Protestant, took his M.D. at Montpellier and became
physician to Turenne, whom he accompanied to Flanders during the campaigns of
the 1650's. He went to Leiden in 1668 as Professor of Medicine and Anatomy. The
book is *De partu octimestri vivaci diatriba* (Paris, 1662; Leiden, 1668).

7 See Letter 1966, note 2.

8 The full title of De Graaf's earlier work was *De virorum organis inservientibus, de clysteri-
bus et de usu siphonis in anatomia* (Leiden and Rotterdam, 1668), which explains his interest in "clysterpipes." For the controversy with Timothy Clarke, which had begun
in 1668 and only ended with Clarke's death on 11 February 1671/2, see Vols. IV, V,
VI, and VII.

9 Johannes Veslingius (1598–1649), German anatomist, botanist, and traveler. His *Syntagma anatomicum* (Paris, 1647) went through many editions and was translated into English, German, Dutch, and Italian.

10 The second edition of De Graaf's *Tractatus Anatomico-Medicus de succi pancreatici natura et usu* was published at Leiden in 1671.

11 "from the egg" (or possibly, "from the beginning").

12 "hospital."

13 "uterine (i.e., Fallopian) tube."

14 "devil's bite . . . twists itself back towards the ovary and absorbs the egg."

15 "eggs excreted by a virgin." Theodor Kerckring, *Spicilegium anatomicum . . . nec non osteogeniam faetuum* (Amsterdam, 1670); see Vol. VI, p. 634, note 2.

16 "eggs of women . . . they are women's nensense . . . these eggs are to be rejected (1) because it is not apparent how eggs of this kind could be transmitted through such narrow vessels from the testes [ovaries] to the uterus; (2) because women do not have what are called wind-eggs; and particularly (3) because in oviparous animals the semen is poured into the ovary which cannot take place here. But the vesiculous substance of the testes itself might be the cause of this appearance, since these inflated vesicles mock the observer by simulating some kind of egg . . ."

17 "teguments of the egg." The amnion and the chorion are two membranes of the mammalian foetus; hence the meaning is, that the only true analogy is that between the egg and the foetus.

18 Galen dissected the larynx and associated structures with great care, and studied the action of this organ and its nervous supply through experiments on living animals, writing a special work "On the Voice" (compare *On Anatomical Procedures*, Book XI).

19 Thomas Bartholin, *Anatome* (Leiden, 1673).

20 Paul Barbette, *Opera chirurgico-anatomica ad circularem sanguinis motum aliaque recentiorum inventa, accommodata* (Leiden, 1672).

21 There does not, in fact, seem to have been a new edition of Johann Schroeder, *Pharmacopoeia medico-chymica, sive Thesaurus pharmacologicus* (Ulm, 1641) in the 1670's, though there were many earlier and later issues in several languages. *Aphtha* is the oral disease of infants, thrush or thrushes, but we cannot trace the tract.

22 "the street of the Woman in White at Jan Forest's the tailor."

2133
Oldenburg to Newton

18 January 1672/3

Printed in Newton, *Correspondence*, I, 255–56, from the original in CUL MS. Add. 3976, no. 1

Oldenburg begins by thanking Newton for replying to a query about cider (this correspondence no longer survives) and then quotes in French the relevant sections of Huygens' Letter 2122 dealing with Newton's theory of colors, inviting Newton's comments. In a postscript he mentions Sluse's Letter 2124 and promises to send it to Newton in his next letter to him.

2134

Oldenburg to Captain Ernetly

21 January 1672/3

From the draft in Royal Society MS. O 2, no. 102

London jan. 21. $16\frac{72}{73}$

Sir,

To give you a testimony of my hearty embraces of yr late favour in making so generous an offer to employ yrself in yr voyage to Constantinople for ye service of ye R. Society, as occasion should serve, by making Observations and Inquiries of Nature; I doe herewth send you two printed Tracts, containing many particulars both at Sea and Land, wch in our opinion, deserve to be accurately observed and curiously inquired after.[1] I am very sorry, yt yr sudden departure left us no room to furnish you wth some of those Instruments yt are annexed to these papers; wch would have served for giving a fuller Satisfaction, to you as well as to us, in these curious and usefull matters. However, set ym aside there will remaine enough for you to informe yrself about. But besides, Sr, you will very much oblige us by procuring us several seeds of ye Levant; those of Platanus[,] Barba Jovis,[2] Eschilus,[3] Castanea Equina,[4] Cedar-berries gather'd ripe in November, and sent in their Cones in perfectly baked sand, as also to be sown in Caisses there. Item ye Mastic[5] from Chio. Where inquire, whether Chio alone produces Mastic? To these add the Turky Clover, Labdanum,[6] Dictamnum Cretense,[7] Tragacanthus, Adrachne,[8] Oleander, Terebinthus Vera.[9] Item all sorts of Weeds for Dying. Endeavor also to get a good account of ye Trees of Thus and Myrrha; likewise of what *Bdellium* is, some esteeming it a Gum, others a Gem, others a kind of Pearl. As also to bring over some of ye seed of yt Poppy, wch yields opium; to learne ye time they extract it, as also its operation not only to sleep but ebriety, Venery.

It being Bellonius his opinion,[10] yt ye Cotton-plant would grow in France; it may possibly grow also here, the Experiment being made wth a litle good seed in a hot bed. But ye Gossypium perenne, or Cotton-Tree wch grows in Ægypt, we may have more hopes of, in regard our Conservatories will keep most plants, wch are not Annual, and bring ym to some perfection; whereas such as depend upon a short summer, can in England have but a short life. If ripe seed of this Tree be barrell'd up in well-dryed sand (as ye Cedar-berries and others before mention'd) and brought hither in Spring, they may doubtlesse last sound (so ordered) half a year; and not not only this Plant, but the Sycamore (wch is one of ye best greens in ye world,) ye balsamum frutescens,[11] Papyrus, Acacia, wth other noble Plants from yt place.

Inquire also upon occasion, whether all Fruits, Herbs, Earths, Fountains, are naturally saltish in ye Island of Cyprus? And what store of Amianthus[12] there is in Cyprus; and how the people work it?

Item, observe and describe ye structure and dimensions of ye Aqueducts, caused to be made by Solyman ye Magnificent in several places about Constantinople, and any other Edifices, yt have any thing considerable in ym. Endeavor also to get ye whole way of breeding and ordering their Angra-goats. And to learne ye particular dexterities and supplenesses of ye Bodies of Turks, and any other thing they excell in. Lastly be pleased to inquire, what the Turks understand by *Heiranluc*, by *Bergs*, by *Doamsamec*, by *Bangue*, and by *Asseral*?

You see, Sir, what large use I make of ye liberty, you yesterday gave me. Yr owne ingenuity will lead you to ye observation and search of many more things, yt will occur in yr voyage, wch I wish as properous to you, as you can doe yrself, being Sir

yr very humble and faithful servant

H. Oldenburg

Sir, if you shall honor me wth any letters, pray send ym by ye post, to addresse ym thus,

A Monsr

Monsr Grubendol

à Londres.

Thus they will come more safely to my hands, than if my owne name were used.

A letter to Captain Ernetly

NOTES

We can find no trace of Captain Ernetly, whose name seems to be unrecorded.

Much of this letter is a repetition of Letter 2101 to Sir John Finch, and we have not footnoted matter already dealt with there.

1 See Letter 2101, note 1.

2　Platanus is the oriental plane. Barba Jovis, mentioned by Pliny in Book XVI, ch. 18, is usually identified with Jupiter's beard, the silver bush, *Anthyllis barba jovis*.

3　Perhaps "esculus" or aesculus, the winter or Italian oak.

4　Horse chestnut.

5　Mastic is the gum exuded from the mastic tree, in this case *Pistacia Lentiscus*, found widely in the Levant.

6　Or, more correctly, Ladanum, another sort of mastic, from plants of the genus *Cistus*.

7　Dittany, *Origanum Dictamnus*

8　The strawberry tree or arbutus of the Levant.

9　The true turpentine-producing tree, *Pistacia Terebinthus*, the source of Chian turpentine.

10　Presumably Pierre Belon (1517–64), possibly in his *Portraits d'oyseaux, animaux, serpens, herbes, arbres, hommes et femmes d'Arabie* & *Egypte* (Paris, 1557). He had traveled in the Levant.

11　"fruiting balsam," a tree of the genus *Balsamodendron*.

12　A kind of asbestos.

2135
Christoph Sand to Oldenburg
24 January 1672/3
From the original in Royal Society MS. S 1, no. 128

Hambourg, ce 24. Janv.–73

Monsieur

Il y a longtemps, que j'ay cherché l'occasion de vous presenter mes services, depuisque Mrs. Boom libraires à Amsterdam m'ont commis la traduction de vostre grand'oeuvre. Et étant maintenant le Secretaire de Resident du Roy d'angleterre,[1] j'ay trouvé la plus belle commodité pour vous écrire. C'est pourqouy je vous baise treshumblement les mains par celle-cy, et vous supplie de me faire scavoir, s'il vous plaist, ce que c'est *trends*, dans vos Transactions, p. 555, qu. 15. où vous avés écrit: *How the Land trends?*[2] je devine bien que celà doit étre *tends*: mais j'en veux plutost attendre vostre explication, que changer temerairement, vos mots. P. 380. vous faites mention de deux personnes fort aagées, qui ont receu des dents nouvelles.[3] Pour celà je vous puis fournir d'autres exemples semblables. 1. Pierre Robaeijs, mourut l'an 1636. étant aagé de 66. ans. deux ans devant sa mort il receut une dent mascheliere dans la maschoire d'enhaut, où il n'avoit jamais eu auparavant une dent: et peu devant sa mort plusieurs maschelieres luy tomberent; mais cellelà tomba la premiere, sans aucune douleur, qui étoit venue la derniere. 2. Nicolas Lachtropius Pasteur Arminien étant aagé de 85. ans receut la plus interieure incissoire dans la maschoire d'enhaut, là où il n'avoit jamais eu une dent: trois ans apres il mourut à Amsteram, l'an 1670.—3. Il y a icy une femme de 75. ans, qui a aussi receu des nouvelles dents. Tous ces exemples peuvent estre confirmés par plusieurs personnes dignes de foy. 4. L'Exemple de la Comtesse de Desmond d'Irlande vous sera sans doute bien conneu.[4]—Depuis quelques semaines il est imprimé icy le livre du Sr. Robert Boyle de Origine & virtutibus Gemmarius, lequel j'ay traduit en latin, ne scachant pas qu'on faisoit, le méme en Angleterre.[5]—A Lunenbourg il y a un Escossois nommé Robert Scot Chirurgien du Regiment de Mr. Mollison, qui pretend d'avoir trouvé la longitude: laquelle invention il estime de 200000 Escus, Si quelques Rois, Princes ou Republiques en veulent avoir la conoissance: et s'il ne fait paroistre la longitude, si palpable comme la latitude, il ne veut point d'argent.[6] Pour moy je croy que cet homme-là se trompe grandement. C'est que je vous ay voulu faire sçavoir, vous priant d'excuser ma hardiesse: et si vous me jugerés digne de l'honneur de votre réponse, vous n'avés qu'à l'envoyer à Mr. Cooke Secretaire de Monsr. Coventri,[7] qui me la fera tenir. Au reste je vous asseure que je manqueray jamais à vous porter de respect, comme Monsieur

> Vostre treshumble &
> tresobeissant Serviteur
> *Chrestoffle Sand*

Mr. Oldenburg.

TRANSLATION

Hamburg, 24 January 1672/3

Sir,

For a long time I have been looking for an opportunity to present my services to you, ever since Messrs. Boom, the book sellers of Amsterdam, commissioned me to translate your great work. And being now the Secretary to the Resident of the English King,[1] I have found the most convenient method for writing to you. This is why I very humbly salute you with this letter, and beg you to let me know, if you please, what is the word "trends" in your *Transactions*, p. 555, query 15, where you have written "How the Land trends?"[2] I can readily guess that this ought to be "tends:" but I prefer to await your explanation rather than to change your words rashly. P. 380 you mention two very aged people who acquired new teeth.³ I can furnish you with other similar examples of that. 1. Pierre Robaeijs, who died in 1636 aged 66 years; two years before his death he acquired a molar tooth in the upper jaw, where he had never previously had a tooth; and a little before his death several molars fell out, and that which had come last fell out the first, without any pain. 2. Nicolas Lachtropius, Arminian minister, aged 85 acquired the inmost incisor in the upper jaw, where he had never had a tooth. Three years after, he died at Amsterdam, in 1670. 3. There is a woman here 75 years old who has also acquired new teeth. All these examples can be confirmed by several creditable people. 4. The example of the Countess Desmond of Ireland is doubtless well known to you.⁴— Some weeks ago there was printed here the Hon. Mr. Boyle's book *De gemmarum origine et virtutibus* which I translated into Latin not knowing that the same thing had been done in England.⁵—At Luneburg there is a Scotchman named Robert Scot, a surgeon in Mr. Mollison's regiment, who claims to have found [a method for determining] longitude, which invention he reckons to be worth 200,000 crowns, if any kings, princes, or republics wish to learn it; and if he does not make longitude appear as obvious as latitude he does not want any money.⁶ As for me, I think this man greatly deceives himself. This is what I wanted to let you know, begging you to excuse my boldness; and if you judge me worthy of the honor of your reply, you have only to send it to Mr. Cooke, secretary to Mr. Coventry,⁷ who will have it conveyed to me. For the rest I assure you that I shall never fail to respect you, as, Sir

Your very humble and obedient servant
Christoph Sand

Mr. Oldenburg.

NOTES

The translator is the theological writer Christoph Sand or Von Den Sand or Sandius (1644–80). His father, also Christoph, was Councillor to the Elector of Brandenburg, but lost his office as a result of adherence to Socinianism. The younger Christoph exiled himself to Holland for the same reason, where he is known to have worked as a press corrector. At this time he had already published several works on Biblical matters. It is not clear how or when he learned English, and indeed nothing is known of his education. For his relations with Henry and Theodore Boom in producing a Latin version of the *Philosophical Transactions*, see below, Letter 2171.

1 Sir William Swan (d. 1678) had been appointed English Resident at Hamburg in 1670.

2 See *Phil. Trans.*, no. 29(11 November 1667), "Inquiries for Greenland"; "trends," meaning "turning in a certain direction," is, of course, perfectly correct.

3 For this account by Samuel Colepresse, see *Phil. Trans.*, no. 21 (21 January 1666/7), and his Letter 594 (Vol. III, p. 309).

4 Katherine Fitzgerald (d. 1604), the second wife of Thomas Fitzgerald, twelfth Earl of Desmond, is said to have lived to the age of 140; the *Dictionary of National Biography* suggests this is a mistake for 104.

5 The two editions appeared with different titles: *Exercitatio de origine & viribus gemmarum* (London, 1673), and *Specimen de gemmarum origine & virtutibus* (Hamburg and Amsterdam, 1673). There is no internal indication of the translator of the London edition (probably Oldenburg); the title of the Hamburg and Amsterdam edition includes the words "Nunc Latine, interprete C.S."

6 Hooke recorded in his *Diary* under 24 January 1672/3, "In the Dutch Gazet was news from Hamborough that one Rob: Scot a Chirurgeon had found out the Longitude."

7 Henry Coventry (1619–86) was at this time Secretary of State.

2136
Oldenburg to Sluse
29 January 1672/3
From the draft in B.M. MS. Add. 28927, f. 3

Illustrissimo Viro
Domino Renato Francisco Slusio, Canonico Leodienensi
Henr. Oldenburg S.

Morem gero mandatis tuis, dum Tibi significo, Vir Illustrissime, me postremas tuas 17ᵃ januarij ad me datas recte accepisse. Legi eas summa cum voluptate, et ingenium doctrinamque tuam miratus, proximo Regiae Societatis consessui eas exhibebo.[1] Praevideo, Socios Regulae tuae Demonstrationem petituros, quam cum solis constare Lemmatibus passim notis asseras, una mecum iidem mirabuntur. Statui, Deo dante, prima quaque occasione Methodum ipsam, prout epistola tua continetur, Transactionibus Philosophicis inserere. Non ingratum interea fuerit accipere, quae Doctissimus noster Newtonus, in Academia Cantabrigiensi Mathematum Professor, de eodem argumento ad Dominum Collinium nostrum, qui Te summopere et jugiter colit, nuper perscripsit, in haec verba;[2]

"Non parum me juvat intelligere, Mathematicos exteros in eandem mecum incidisse ducendi Tangentes methodum. Qualem eam esse conjiciam, ex hoc Experimento percipies;

"Pone *CB*, applicatum ad *AB*, in quovis angulo dato terminari ad quamvis curvam *AC*, et dicatur *AB*, *x*, et *BC*, *y*; habitudoque inter *x* et *y* exprimatur qualibet aequatione; juxta $x^3 - 2xxy + bxx - bbx - y^3 = 0$, qua ipsa determinatur curva. Regula ducendi Tangentem haec est; Multiplica aequationis terminos per quamlibet Progressionem Arithmeticam juxta dimensiones y, $x^3 - 2xxy + bxx - bbx + byy - y^3$; ut ex juxta dimensiones x,

$$\overset{\text{o}}{}\quad\overset{\text{I}}{}\quad\overset{\text{o}}{}\quad\overset{\text{o}}{}\quad\overset{\text{2}}{}$$

puta $x^3 - 2xxy + bxx - bbx + byy - y^3$. Prius productum erit Numerator, et

$$\overset{\text{3}}{}\quad\overset{\text{2}}{}\quad\overset{\text{2}}{}\quad\overset{\text{I}}{}\quad\overset{\text{o}}{}\quad\overset{\text{o}}{}$$

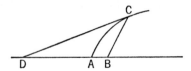

posterius, divisum per x, Denominator Fractionis, quae exprimit longitudinem BD, ad cujus extremitatem D ducenda est Tangens CD.

Est ergo longitudo $BD \dfrac{-2xxy + 2byy - 3y^3}{3xx - 4xy + 2bx - bb}$:

Hoc est unum particulare, vel Corollarium potius Methodi generalis, quae extendit se, citra molestrum ullum calculum, non modo ad decendum Tangentes ad quasvas Curvas, sive Geometricas, sive Mechanicas, vel quomodocunque rectas ilneas aliasve curvas respicientes; verum etiam ad resolvendum alia abstrusiora Problematum genera de curvitatibus, areis, longitudinibus, centris gravitatis curvarum etc. Neque (quemadmodum Huddenij Methodus de Maximis et Minimis)[3] ad solas restringitur Æquationes illas, quae quantitatibus surdis sunt immunes.

"Hanc methodum intertexui alteri isti, qua Æquationum exegesin instituto, reducendo eas ad series infinitas. Memini, me ex occasione aliquando narrasse Domino Barrovio, edendis Lectionibus suis occupato, instructum me esse hujusmodi Methodo Tangentes ducendi: Sed nescio, quo diverticulo ab ea ipsi describendo fuerim avocatus."

Hactenus Newtonus, quae ideo nunc perscribo, ut cum novissimis tuis comparare possis. Ostendi jam methodum tuum Nobilissimo Praeside Societatis nostrae, nec non Doctissimo Pellio; qui Demonstrationes Methodi exambiunt. Cum usum illius insignem innuas in Physico-Mathematicis, nec eum graveris, quaeso, in multorum nostratium gratiam communicare. Dabimus operam, ut paria suo tempore retribuamus. Vale, et, si placet, quantocyus rescribe.[4] Dab. Londini d. 29 jan. 1673.

TRANSLATION

Henry Oldenburg greets the very illustrious Mr. René François de Sluse, Canon of Liège

I am obeying your commands, most illustrious Sir, when I inform you that I have safely received your last letter to me of 17 January [N.S.]. I read it with much pleasure, and marveled at your intelligence and learning; I will present it to the Royal Society at its next meeting.[1] I foresee that the Fellows will ask for a demonstration of your rule, which will surprise them as it did me since you say that it consists only of some lemmas noted here and there. I have decided that, God willing, I will at the first possible opportunity insert the method itself, just as it is contained in your letter, in the *Philosophical Transactions.* Meanwhile, it will not be unwelcome [to you] to receive what our very learned Newton, Professor of Mathematics in the University of Cambridge, has recently written to our Mr. Collins (who is a very warm and constant admirer of yours) on this same topic, in these words:[2]

". . . it pleased me not a little to understand that the forreign Mathematicians are falln into the same method of drawing Tangents wth me. What I guess their method to be you will apprehend by this example.

Suppose *CB* applied to *AB* in any given angle be terminated at any Curve line *AC* [*see the figure, p. 428*], and calling *AB* x & *BC* y let the relation between x & y be expressed by any aequation as

$$x^3 - 2xxy + bxx - bbx + byy - y^3 = 0$$

by which the curve is determined. To draw the tangent *CD* the Rule is this. Multiply the termes of the aequation by any arithmeticall progression according to the dimensions of y suppose thus $x^3 - 2xxy + bxx - bbx + byy - y^3$, also ac-

$$\qquad\quad 0 \qquad\quad 1 \qquad 0 \qquad 0 \qquad 2 \qquad 3$$

cording to the dimensions of x suppose thus $x^3 - 2xxy + bxx - bbx + byy - y^3$.

$$\qquad\qquad 3 \qquad\quad 2 \qquad 2 \qquad 1 \qquad 0 \qquad 0$$

The first product shall be the Numerator, & the last divided by x the Denominator of a fraction wch expresseth the length of *BD* to whose end *D* the tangent *CD* must be drawn.

The length *BD* therefor is

$$\frac{-2xxy + 2byy - 3y^3}{3xx - 4xy + 2bx - bb}$$

This is one particular or rather a Corollary of a Generall Method wch extends it selfe without any troublesome calculation, not onely to the drawing tangents to all curve lines whether Geometrick or mechanick or how ever related to streight lines or to other curve lines, but also to the resolving other abstruser kinds of

Problems about the crookedness, areas, lengths, centers of gravity of curves &c. Nor is it (as Huddens method de maximis et minimis)[3] limited to aequations wch are free from surd quantities.

This method I have interwoven wth that other of working in aequations by reducing them to infinite series. I remember I once occasionally told Dr Barrow when he was about to publish his Lectures that I had such a method of drawing Tangents but some divertisment or other hindered me from describing it to him."

So far Newton, which I accordingly transcribe now so that you may compare [his letter] with your own recent one. I have already shown your method to the most noble President of our Society and also to Dr. Pell, who ask for the demonstrations of the method. As you suggest that its usefulness in mathematical physics is considerable do not, I beg you, grudge them for the satisfaction of many of our people. We will make it our business to return the like in time. Farewell, and write again as soon as possible, please.[4] London, 29 January 1673.

NOTES

Reply to Letter 2124. It is just possible that the B.M. manuscript is the original letter intended for Sluse; at any rate, Sluse never received it. Accordingly Oldenburg repeated its content later. The names of the writer and the addressee have been crudely struck out in the heading.

1 He did so on 29 January, when (as foreseen) he was instructed to ask Sluse for the demonstration.

2 Oldenburg here gives a faithful Latin rendering of the early part of Newton's letter to Collins of 10 December 1672 (Newton, *Correspondence*, I, 247–48). For the translation we have reverted to Newton's English. It is clear from Collins' own admission in a letter to Newton (dated 18 June 1673 but the original is now lost—see Newton, *Correspondence*, I, 288) that it was he who had provided this extract for Sluse.
Collins himself recognized Sluse's priority in the method of tangents described in Letter 2124, as indeed did Newton though he rightly believed his own principles—the theory of fluxions—to be more general than those of Sluse (see his letter to Oldenburg of 23 June 1673). Newton's method as conveyed to Collins was, in fact, virtually a paraphrase from his 1671 tract on fluxions, Problem 4. This was written in the winter of 1670–71 (see Newton, *Mathematical Papers*, III, 15, 120–33).

3 Oldenburg here omits the words: "& consequently Slusius his new method of Tangents as I presume"; it will be understood that Newton had not yet seen Sluse's method—indeed, in this very letter he asks Collins to send it to him when printed—although Newton's and Sluse's methods are in effect identical.

4 There was now a lapse in this interesting correspondence owing to the failure of the present letter to reach Sluse.

2137
Oldenburg to Leibniz

30 January 1672/3

From the original in Hannover MSS., f. 15
Printed in Gerhardt, pp. 73–74

Monsieur,

Me voicy en vostre logis, pour livrer à S. Exc. Monsr. de Schonborn[1] une lettre, et à vous une autre, qui me sont venues en main auiourduy sous mon couvert. Je plains mon malheur de n'avoir pas trouvé S. Excellence au logis pour luy faire la reverence, et pour rendre sa lettre en main propre. Vous me ferez la grace de la faire à ma place avec mes treshumbles baisemains.

Monsieur le Chevalier Moreland, dont vous parla hier Monsr. le Chevalier Moray, et qui est l'inventeur d'une machine Arithmetique,[2] m'ayant parlé dela vostre aujourdhuy, a dit qu'il est prest de vous monstrer la sienne demain sur les onze heures du matin, desirant aussi de voir la vostre, enfin de les conferer ensemble.[3] C'est donc, Monsr, pour vous offrir mon service de vous accompagner sur cete heure là dans le jardin de Whitehal, où il a quelques chambres, et où son dit Instrument est logé, s'il vous plait de prendre la peine m'appeller chez moy, et faire parter vostre machine avec vous. Si non, vous m'obligerez de me le faire scavoir demain matin à bonne heure, à fin que ie regle mes affaires là dessus et face scavoir à Monsr Moreland, qu'il ne nous attende pas. Je suis Monsr

vostre treshumble serviteur
Oldenburg

le 30. Janvier 1673, au soir

ADDRESS
A Monsr
Monsr Leibnitz etc.

TRANSLATION

Sir,

Here I am at your lodgings, to deliver to his Excellency, Mr. de Schönborn,[1] one letter, and another letter to you, which came today under cover to me. I feel unfortunate at not finding His Excellency at home to make my bow to him, and to give the letter into his own hand. You will be so kind as to do it for me with my very humble greetings.

Sir Samuel Morland, of whom Sir Robert Moray spoke to you yesterday, and who is the inventor of an arithmetical machine,[2] having spoken to me of yours today, has said that he is ready to show you his tomorrow at eleven o'clock in the morning, wishing also to see yours, so as to compare them together.[3] I am thus here, Sir, to offer you my services in accompanying you at that time to the garden of Whitehall, where he has rooms and where his instrument is kept, if you will take the trouble of calling at my house and bringing your machine with you. If not, you will oblige me by letting me know early tomorrow morning, so that I can organize my affairs on that basis and let Sir Samuel know not to expect us. I am, Sir,

Your very humble servant
Oldenburg

30 January 1672/3, in the evening

ADDRESS
To Mr. Leibniz, etc.

NOTES

1 This was Melchior Friedrich von Schönborn, nephew of the Elector of Mainz who had been Leibniz's employer and patron for several years, and son-in-law of Johann Christian von Boineburg, for whom see Vol. VII, p. 109. He was on a mission from the Elector to persuade Louis XIV, and failing him Charles II, to allow the interests of the Empire (now involved in the wars) to be taken into account at the forth-coming peace negotiations, which the Elector wished to be held at Cologne (as they were; see Letter 2200a, below).

2 Samuel Morland (1625–95 or 96), after a succesful diplomatic career under Cromwell, became a royalist from 1658 onwards and was made a baronet by Charles II at Breda in 1660. Soon appointed salaried "Master of Mechanicks" to the King (hence the Court apartments mentioned in the letter) he devoted all his time subsequently to instruments and engines, particularly water-raising machines. He devised two arith-metical machines, both described in *A Description and Use of two Arithmetick Instru-ments* (London, 1673), the first in 1666 (an example in Oxford bears this date), which is mentioned by Pepys ("very pretty, but not very useful") on 14 January 1667/8. They were sold by an instrument-maker named Humphrey Adamson, and were quite widely known.

3 See Letter 2122, note 8.

2138

Huygens to Oldenburg

31 January 1672/3

From the original in Royal Society MS. H 1, no. 76
Printed in *Œuvres Complètes*, VII, 252–54

A Paris ce 10 fevr. 1673 [N.S.]

Monsieur

En recevant vostre derniere du 13 Jan. j'ay estè estonnè de voir que la mienne du 14 Jan. S.N. ne vous avoit pas encore estè rendue ce jour là.[1] Toute fois comme il peut arriver des accidents qui retardent les pacquets, je veux esperer que vous l'aurez receue depuis. Je vous y ay escrit assez au long touchant ce qu'il y avoit, dans vostre penultieme journal, touchant l'Opinion nouvelle de M. Newton pour les Couleurs. Il y avoit aussi quelques remarques touchant mes barometres; comme du perpendicule qu'il faut y adjouster; et de leur position, qui ne doit pas estre perpendiculaire dans la seconde construction. Si ma lettre estoit perdue je pourrois vous repeter a peu pres les mesmes choses parce que j'en ay gardè quelque espece de minute.[2] Les barometres de la façon de Mr. Boyle et de Mr. Hook sont tresconnus icy, et l'obligation qu'on leur en doit avoir. J'eusse souhaitè que la pensee de M. des Cartes touchant le barometre composè de mercure et d'eau eust estè connue de mesme, a scavoir celle qui est mentionnee dans une lettre de M. Chanut imprimee a la fin du traité de M. Paschal de l'Equilibre des Liqueurs.[3] Car assurement je n'aurois pas donnè cette invention comme venant de moy, si ce n'est en ce que j'y puis avoir adjoustè. Mais par malheur pas un de Nostre Academie ne se souvint qu'on eust jamais pensè a telle chose, lors que j'y portay mes barometres. Et ce ne fut que 15 jours apres qu'ils eussent estè publies dans le journal, que M. Mariotte receut cet avis dans la lettre d'un de ses amis. Je feray mettre dans le prochain Journal comme je ne pretens dorenavant que tres peu de part a cette invention, n'y ayant rien que j'abhorre d'avantage que de m'attribuer ce qui appartient a d'autres.[4] Et quoyque la construction de M. des Cartes ne puisse pas reussir, a cause que l'eau fournit peu a peu de l'air dans le vuide, j'avoue pourtant qu'il n'estoit pas fort difficile, a qui auroit sceu sa pensee, de trouver l'autre construction que j'ay donnee. Je ne scay si vous aurez ouy parler d'un homme qui soustient effrontement que c'est de luy que j'ay pris ce qu'il y a de meilleur dans cette invention, et qu'il y a 2 ans qu'il l'avoit proposee dans nostre Academie.[5] Il a mesme osè le faire imprimer ayant trouvè de gens qui luy ont aidè a escrire. Et quoyque l'Intendant dela Police ait fait saisir les Exemplaires je ne doute pas qu'on n'en ait trouvè quelqu'un pour vous l'envoier. Je n'ay vu de ma vie une impudence pareille a celle de ce fol, car il est reconnu pour tel, et une quantite de propositions extravagantes qu'autrefois il nous est venu faire le tesmoignent assez. Pour le barometre qu'il proposa il y a plus de 3 ans, ce n'estoit rien que le barometre ordinaire, qu'il avoit prolongè par en haut en l'inclinant, comme scavent plusieurs de nos Messieurs, mais l'on ne trouva pas que cela deust produire grand effect, et avec raison. Que s'il avoit en des lors l'invention du barometre composè, il est bien croyable qu'il n'auroit pas manquè de la produire pendant tout ce temps, et d'autant plus que c'est le mestier de son pere de travailler a ces sortes de curiositez. Cependant des gens comme cela trouvent de personnes qui les soustienent par ce qu'il ne manque pas des envieux a Nostre Academie et a moy en particulier; Et je vois qu'il en est de mesme chez vous a l'egard de la Société Royale. La pensée du barometre qui n'est que de vif argent et dont le tuyau fait plusieurs retours par enbas, qui est dans lescrit de l'homme dont je vous ay parlè ne paroit pas mauvaise, mais elle ne reussit pas bien, parce que le vif argent se separe et laisse de grandes parties derriere. C'est pourquoy j'ay fait faire un tel tuyau serpentant a un barometre de ma seconde construction, en sorte que ces retours commencent apres la seconde boete, et cela avec de l'eau au lieu du vif argent, parce qu'elle suit parfaitement bien et se meut avec beacoup plus de libertè que le mercure.

Je vous remercie de l'extrait de la derniere lettre de M. Sluse, mais ayant enfermè quelque part les autres pieces qui appartienent a cette Exercitation sur le Probleme d'Alhazen, ou je ne scaurois les trouver a cet heure, je ne vous en diray rien, sinon que je veux croire qui M. Sluse a pleinement satisfait au doute que j'avois, Et que je serois tresfaschè s'il y a eu quelque chose dans mes precedentes lettres dont il auroit estè mal satisfait. Je ne scay ce que ce pourroit estre par ce que pour la pluspart je n'en ay pas gardè des copies, mais si la chaleur de la contention (quoyque dans cellecy je ne scache pas d'en avoir eu aucune) m'a fait avancer quelque chose qui luy ait peu deplaire je le puis assurer que cela me deplait beaucoup plus a moymesme. Car j'estime trop son amitiè pour souffrir pour des choses de si peu elle fut alteree ou diminuee en aucune facon. Vous verrez dans le livre que je fais imprimer si parmy les scavants Geometres de ce temps je ne le compte pas parmy les premiers, comme assurement il merite.[6]

Pardonnez a ma prolixitè et croiez que je suis tres veritablement Monsieur

Vostre treshumble et tresobeissant serviteur
Hugens de Zulichem

ADDRESS

A Monsieur
Monsieur De Grubendol
à Londres

TRANSLATION

Paris, 10 February 1673 [N.S.]

Sir,

When I received your last of 13 January I was astonished to see that mine of 14 January, N.S., had not yet been delivered to you on that date.[1] However as accidents may arise to slow down packages I am inclined to hope that you have received it since. I wrote to you at some length about what there was in your next to last journal concerning Mr. Newton's new opinion of colors. There were also some remarks about my barometers: for example, about the plumb line which must be added to them, and about their position, which ought not to be perpendicular in the second construction. If my letter has been lost I can repeat to you very nearly the same things, because I kept a kind of minute of it.[2]

Barometers after the fashion of Mr. Boyle and Mr. Hooke are very well known here, as is the debt which we ought to owe them for them. I could have wished that the idea of Mr. Descartes on the mercury and water barometer had been as well known—that is to say, that mentioned in a letter of Mr. Chanut printed at the end of Mr. Pascal's treatise, *De l'Equilibre des Liqueurs*.[3] For certainly I should not have given out that this invention was mine, except as regards what I might have added to it. But unfortunately not a single one of our Academy remembered that anyone had ever thought of such a thing when I brought in my barometers. And it was not until two weeks after the account of them had been published in the *Journal des Sçavans* that Mr. Mariotte received that information in a letter from one of his friends. I shall have inserted in the next *Journal* [a statement] that I do not henceforward claim more than a slight part in this invention, there being nothing I abhor more than to ascribe to myself what belongs to others.[4] And although the construction of Mr. Descartes could not work, since the water will little by little contribute air to the vacuum, I nevertheless confess that it would not be very difficult for anyone who knew of the idea to find the other construction which I gave. I don't know whether you have heard of a man who brazenly claims that it was he from whom I took whatever is best in this invention, and that it is now two years since he proposed it in our Academy.[5] He has even dared to have it printed, having found people who have helped him to write it up. And although the Intendant de la Police has had the copies seized, I do not doubt but that some-one has found some to send to you. I never in my life saw an impudence com-parable to that of this madman, for he is recognized as such, and a quantity of extravagant propositions which he formerly came to lay before us testify as much. As for the barometer which he proposed more than three years ago, it was nothing but an ordinary barometer, which he had lengthened at the top by inclining it, as several of our gentlemen know how to do, but it was not found that this ought to produce a great effect, and with reason. It is not credible that if he had then had the invention of the composite barometer he would have failed to produce it during all this time, and the more so as it is the profession of his father to work at this kind of curiosity. However people of this sort find those who will uphold them, because there is no lack of those who envy our Academy, and myself in particular. And I see it is the same with you in regard to the Royal Society. The idea of a barometer which has only mercury and whose tube has some bends at the bottom, which is contained in this man's book of which I have spoken to you is not bad, but it does not succeed well because the quicksilver separates and leaves large bits behind. This is why I had made such a serpentine tube for my barometer of the second construction, so that its bends begin after the second bulb, and that with water in place of mercury because it remains perfectly coherent and moves much more freely than mercury does.

Thank you for the extract from the last letter of Mr. Sluse, but having put away somewhere the other writings which belong to that exercise on Alhazen's Problem, and from whence I do not know how to retrieve them at this moment, I shall say nothing about it, except that I should like to think that Mr. Sluse has fully satisfied my doubts; and that I should be much annoyed if there had been any-thing in my previous letters which had not satisfied him fully. I don't know what this could be, because for the most part I kept no copies, but if the heat of the controversy (although I do not know that I displayed any) made me put forward anything which displeased him a little, I can assure him that this displeases me much more. For I esteem his friendship too much to allow such trifling matters to alter or diminish it in any way. You will see in the book I am having printed whether I do not count him in the front rank among the learned geometers of this time.[6]

Forgive me for being so prolix, and believe that I am very truly, Sir,

Your very humble and obedient servant,
Huygens of Zulichem

ADDRESS
To Mr. Grubendol
London

NOTES

Reply to Letter 2129.

1 Letter 2122, which however had arrived by 18 January, as Letter 2133 shows.

2 A summary and partial minute still exist in the Huygens collection at Leiden; see *Œuvres Complètes*, VII, 242.

3 Chanut's letters are to François Perier, who performed the Puy-de-Dôme experiment. See *Traitez de l'Equilibre des Liqueurs* (Paris, 1663; 2nd ed., 1664); they are printed in English in *The Physical Treatises of Pascal*, trans. I. H. B. and A. G. H. Spiers, Columbia University Records of Civilization, no. 28 (New York, 1937), pp. 117-20.

4 Huygens' disclaimer is printed in *Œuvres Complètes*, VII, 255-56. But it never appeared in the *Journal des Sçavans* whose publication was suspended during 1673.

5 This was René Grillet, a clockmaker of Paris, and the book *Curiositez mathematiques de l'invention du Sr G[rillet]* (Paris, 1673). Curiously Grillet was in turn to be accused of plagiarism by another Parisian instrument maker who invented a thermometer based on Huygens' barometer, in *Machines nouvellement executées, et en partie inventées par le Sieur Hubin* (Paris, 1673).

6 Huygens' praise of Sluse is to be found on p. 72 of his *Horologium oscillatorium*.

2139
Reed to Oldenburg
3 February 1672/3
From the original in Royal Society MS. R 1, no. 29

Worthy sr.

By Hereford Carrier you will receive two fagotts of grafts soe big as I suppose will supply all your Frends[1] and in case they fall short, (as you thinke) there is yet time enough to send you a further supply wch I will doe uppon intimacion from you, wth these you may gratify those that are farther of, and those that are neer may stay till ye next for any time before ye middle of March we doe graft.

I thanke you for ye papers of Dr Beale.[2] I have received papers this last week much to my Content from him, he is a great lover of this his native Country in studying yts advantage, by contreiveing Expedients for ye vending of our Liquor wthout wch in a short time we shall drowne & debauch our selves, plantations among us doe soe abound.

I remember that last yeare you desired me to give you an account of the

old men of our County:[3] I have beene for now above a yeare under infirmity
& such an one being Melancholly that it indisposeth me for any service,
but if It pleaseth God to give me some respite this spring I shall performe
yt service for you if I may be satisfyed that ye doeing thereof may be yet
acceptable to you, where of you will please to give notice to Sr

> your very faythfull servt
> *Ric Reed*

Lugwardine nere Heref[ord]
Febr. 3. 72.

ADDRESS
> To his honoured Freind
> Henry Oldenburgh Esquire
> at his house in Pell Mell neere
>   Westminster

POSTMARK FE 5

NOTES

1 On 19 February 1672/3 the Society was informed of the gift and "it was ordered,
  that such members, as had occasion to propagate this cider-fruit, should take their
  several proportion of these grafts." But these were probably those sent later; see
  Letter 2146, below.
2 Perhaps Letter 2128.
3 This letter has not survived.

2140

Leibniz to Oldenburg

3 February 1672/3

From the original in Royal Society MS. Commercium Epistolicum, no. 18
Printed in Gerhardt, pp. 74–78, from another manuscript then in the Royal Library in Berlin

Cum heri apud Illustrissimum Boylium incidissem in Clarissimum
Pellium Mathematicum insignem, ac de numeris incidisset mentio,
commemoravi ego, ductus occasione sermonum, esse mihi methodum ex
quodam *Differentiarum* genere quas voco *Generatrices*, colligendi Terminos

Seriei cujuscunque continue crescentis vel decrescentis. *Differentias* autem *Generatrices* voco: si datae seriei inveniantur differentiae, et differentiae differentiarum et ipsarum ex differentiis differentiarum differentiae etc. et series constituatur ex termino primo, et prima differentia, et prima differentia differentiarum, et prima differentia ex differentiis differentiarum etc. ea series erit differentiarum generatricium, ut si series continue crescens vel decrescens sit a.b.c.d. differentiae generatrices erunt

$$a \cdot a \pm b \cdot a \pm b, \pm, b \pm c \cdot a \pm b, \pm, b \pm c,, \pm,, b \pm c, \pm, c \pm d.$$
$$3 4$$

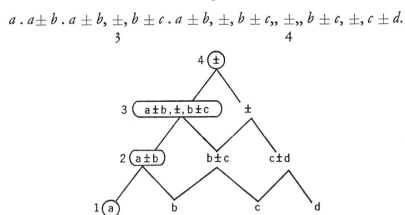

Aut in numeris, si series sit numerorum Cubicorum deinceps ab unitate crescentium, differentiae generatrices erunt numeri 1.6.6. voco autem generatrices, quia ex iis certo modo multiplicatis producuntur Termini Seriei cujus usus tum maxime apparet, cum Differentiae Generatrices sunt finitae, termini autem seriei infiniti, ut in proposito exemplo Numerorum Cubicorum.

		o		o		o		
	6		6		6		6	
6		12		18		24		30
1		7		19		37	61		91
o		1		8		27	64	125	216

Hoc cum audisset Clarissimus Pellius, respondit id jam fuisse in literas relatum a Domino Mouton Canonico Lugdunensi ex observatione Nobilissimi Viri Francisci Regnaldi Lugdunensis, dudum in literario orbe celebris in libro laudati domini Mouton de Diametris apparentibus Solis et Lunae.[1] Ego qui ex Epistola quadam a Regnaldo ad Monconisium scripta & Diario Itinerum Monconisiam inserta,[2] nomen Domini Moutoni et designata eius duo didiceram: Diametros Luminarium apparentes, & Consilium de Mensuris rerum ad posteros transmittendis; Ignorabam tamen librum ipsum prodiisse, quare apud Dominum Oldenburgium Soc. Reg. Secretarium sumtum mutuo tumultuarie percurri; et inveni verissima dixisse Pellium; sed et mihi tamen dandam operam credidi, ne qua in animis relinqueretur suspicio quasi tacito inventoris nomine alienis meditationibus honorem mihi quaerere voluissem. Et spero appariturum esse, non adeo egenum me meditationum propriarum, ut cogar alienas emendicare.

Duobus autem argumentis ingenuitatem meam vindicabo: primo si ipsas Schedas meas confusas, in quibus non tantum Inventio mea, sed et inveniendi modus occasioque apparet, monstrem; deinde si quaedam momenti maximi Regnaldo Moutonioque indicta addam, quae ab hesterno vespere confinxisse me, non sit verisimile, quaeque non possunt facile expectari a Transcriptore.

Ex schedis meis occasio inventi haec apparet, quaerebam modum inveniendi differentias omnis generis potestatum, quemadmodum constat differentias Quadratorum esse numeros impares; inveneramque regulam generalem ejusmodi: Data potentia gradus dati praecedente invenire sequentem (vel contra) distantiae datae vel radicum datarum;[3] seu invenire potentiarum gradus dati utcunque distantium differentias: multiplicetur potentia gradus proxime praecedentis radicis majoris per differentiam radicum; et differentia potentiarum gradus proxime praecedentis multiplicetur per radicem minorem, productorum summa erit quaesita differentia potentiarum quarum radices sunt datae. Eandem regulam ita inflexeram, ut sufficeret praeter radices, cujuslibet gradus etiamsi non proxime praecedentis potentias, datarum radicum, dari: ad differentias potentiarum alterius cuiuscunque, licet altioris, gradus inveniendas. et ostendi quod in Quadratis observatur, Numeros impares esse eorum differentias, id non nisi regulae propositae subsumtionem esse.

His meditationibus defixus, quemadmodum in Quadratis differentiae sunt numeri impares, ita quoque quaesivi, quales essent differentiae cuborum quae cum irregulares viderentur, quaesivi differentias differentiarum, donec invenj differentias tertias esse numeros senarios. Haec observatio mihi aliam peperit, videbam enim ex differentiis praecedentibus generari terminos differentiasque sequentes, ac proinde, ex primis quas ideo Voco Generatrices: ut hoc loco: 0.1.6.6. sequentes omnes. Hoc concluso restabat invenire quo additionis, multiplicationisve aut horum complicationis genere termini sequentes ex differentiis generatricibus producerentur. Atque ita resolvendo, exprimendoque deprehendi.[4] Primum Terminum 0. componi ex prima differentia generatrice 0. sumta semel seu vice (1)ma; secundum 1. ex prima 0 semel (1) secunda 1. semel (1)

Tertium 8. ex prima o semel (1) secunda 1. bis (2) tertia 6 semel (1), nam o(1)+1(2)+6(1) = 8. Quartum 27. ex prima o semel (1) secunda 1 ter (3) tertia 6 ter (3) quarta 6 semel (1), nam o(1)+1(3)+6(3)+6(1) = 27 etc. Idque Analysis mihi universale esse comprobavit.

· Haec fuit occasio observationis meae longe alia a Moutoniana qui cum in Tabulis condensis laboraret in hoc calculandi compendium cum Regnaldo incidit; nec vel illi vel Regnaldo adimenda laus, quod et Briggius in Logarithmicis suis jam olim talia quaedam, observante Pellio, ex parte advertit.[5] Mihi hoc superest, ut addam nonnulla illis indicta ad amoliendum transcriptoris nomen; neque enim interest Reipublicae, quis observaverit, interest quid observetur. Primum ergo illud adjicio quod apud Moutonium non extat, et caput tamen rej est, qui nam sint illi Numerj, quorum Tabulam ille exhibet in infinitum continuandam, quorum ductu in differentias generatrices, productis inter se junctis termini Serierum generentur. Vides enim ex ipso modo quo Tabula ab eo pag. 385 exhibetur, non fuisse id ei satis exploratum; alioqui enim verisimile est ita Tabulam fuisse dispositurum, ut ea numerorum connexio atque harmonia appareret, nisi quis de industria texisse dicat.

ita enim habet pars Tabulae :[6]

1	1					
2	1	1				
3	1	2	1			
(4)	1	3	3	1		
5	1	4	6	4	1	
6	1	5	10	10	5	1
7	1	6	15	20	15	6
8	1	7	21	35	35	21
9	1	8	28	56	70	56
10	1	9	36	84	126	126
11	1	10	45	120	210	252

Apparet ex hujus Tabulae constructione solam haberi rationem corresponsus numerorum generantium cum numero Termini generati, ut cum terminus est quartus (4) producitur ex prima differentia semel 1. secunda ter 3. tertia [ter] 3. quarta semel 1. ideo in eadem cum (4). linea transversa locantur: 1.3.3.1.[7] Sed vel non observavit vel dissimulavit autor corresponsum numerorum, si a summo deorsum eundo per columnas disponantur hoc modo:

1	1					
2	1 —1					
3	1	2—1				
4	1	3—3	—1			
5	1	4—6	4—1			
6	1	5—10	10	5—1		
7	1	6—15	20	15	6	
8	1	7—21	35	35	21	
9	1	8—28	56	70	56	
10	1	9—36	84	126	126	
11	1	10 45	120	210	252	

Ita enim statim vera genuinaque eorum natura ac generatio apparet, esse scilicet eos numeros quos Combinatorios appellare soleo, de quibus multa dixi in dissertiuncula de Arte Combinatoria,[8] quosque alij appellant Ordines Numericos, alii in specie primam Columnam Unitatum secundam Numerorum Naturalium, tertiam Triangularium, quartam Pyramidalium, quintam Triangulo Triangulariam etc. de quibus integer extat tractatus Pascalij sub titulo Trianguli Arithmetici, in quo tamen proprietatem numerorum ejusmodi tam illustrem, tamque naturalem, non observatam, sum miratus.[9] Sed est profecto casus quidam in inveniendo, qui non semper maximis ingeniis maxima, sed saepe etiam mediocribus nonnulla offert.

Hinc jam vera Numerorum istorum Natura et Tabulae constructio sive a Regnaldo, sive a Moutonio dissimulata intelligitur. Semper enim terminus datus columnae datae componitur ex termino praecedente columnae tam praecedentis quam datae: atque illud quoque apparet, non opus esse molesto calculo ad Tabulam a Moutonio propositam continuandam, ut ipse postulat, cum hae Numerorum series passim jam tradantur calculenturque.[10]

Caeterum Moutonius observatione ista ad interponendas medias proportionales, inter duos extremos numeros datos ego ad inveniendos ipsos numeros extremos in infinitum, cum eorum differentiis utendum censebam. Hinc ille nonnisi cum differentiae ultimae evanescunt (aut pene evanescunt) usum regulae invenit, ego detexi innumerabiles casus, regula quadam inobservata comprehendendos, ubi possum ex datis numeris finitis certo modo multiplicatis producere numeros plurimarum serierum in infinitum euntium, etsi differentiae earum non evanescant. Ex ijsdem fundamentis possum efficere in progressionibus problemata plurima, ut in Numeris singularibus, aut ut in rationibus vel fractionibus, possum enim progressiones addere subtrahereque, imo multiplicare quoque et dividere idque compendiose.

Multa alia circa hos numeros observata sunt a me: ex quibus illud eminet quod modum habeo summam inveniendi seriei fractionum in infinitum decrescentium, quarum numerator unitas, Nominatores vero Numeri istj Triangulares aut Pyramidales aut Triangulo-Triangulares etc.[11]

$$\frac{1}{3} \quad \frac{1}{4} \quad \frac{1}{5} \quad \frac{1}{6}$$

$$\frac{1}{6} \quad \frac{1}{10} \quad \frac{1}{15}$$

$$\frac{1}{10} \quad \frac{1}{20} \quad \frac{1}{35}$$

$$\frac{1}{15} \quad \frac{1}{35} \quad \frac{1}{70}$$

etc. etc. etc.

TRANSLATION

When I was yesterday at the very illustrious Mr. Boyle's I met the famous Mr. Pell, a notable mathematician, and the topic of numbers chanced to come up; I remarked, under the stimulus of the conversation, that I possessed a method of forming the terms of any continually increasing or decreasing series whatever from a certain sort of differences that I call *generative*. I call the differences generative if the differences of a given series are found, and then the differences of the differences, and then the differences of the differences of the differences, etc., and a series is formed from the first term, the first difference, and the first difference of the differences, and the first difference of the differences of the differences, etc. That series will be one of the generative differences. So if there be a continually increasing or decreasing series a, b, c, d the generative differences will be

$$a, a \pm b, a \pm 2b + c, a \pm 3b + 3c \pm d, \dots$$

[*See the figure, p. 439*]

Or, in numbers, if the series be one of cubes increasing in order from unity, the generative differences will be the numbers 1, 6, 6.

```
              o        o        o
          6        6        6        6
      6       12       18       24       30
    1        7       19       37      61      91
  o        1        8       27       64     125     216
```

I call them *generative*, because from these when multiplied in a certain way are produced the terms of the series, the usefulness of which is most obvious when the Generative Differences are finite while the terms of the series are infinite, as in the example proposed of the series of cubes. When he heard this the famous Pell answered that this was already in print, reported by Mr. Mouton, Canon of Lyons, as the discovery of the very noble François Regnaud of Lyons, formerly well-known to the learned world, in the book by the meritorious Mouton, *De diametris apparentibus solis et lunae*.[1] As for myself, though I knew of the name of Mr. Mouton, and his double purpose of transmitting to posterity the apparent diameters of the luminaries and advice on the measurement of things, from a certain letter of Regnaud's written to Monconys and inserted in Monconys' *Journal des Voyages*,[2] yet I was unaware that the book itself had appeared; for which reason, picking it up at Mr. Oldenburg's (the Secretary of the Royal Society), I ran through it hastily, and found that what Pell had said was perfectly true. Yet I believed I had to take trouble, lest any suspicion should be entertained that I had sought (under an implicit title to originality) to gain for myself credit for the thoughts of others. And I hope it will appear that I am not so lacking in ideas of my own that I go round begging for those of other men. I will vindicate the honesty of my conduct by two arguments: first by displaying my actual disordered notes in which not only my discovery appears but the occasion and manner of making it; and secondly by adding certain points of great importance not stated by Regnaud and Mouton, which it is not likely that I could have huddled together since yesterday evening, nor are they to be readily expected of a copyist.

From my notebooks the occasion of the discovery appears thus: I sought a way of finding the differences of powers of all kinds, just like the rule that the differences between [the series of] the squares form the [series of] odd numbers. And I found a general rule of this kind: given the preceding power of the given degree, to find the following one (or vice versa) of a given distance or of given roots;[3] or to find the differences of powers of a given degree of whatever distances: multiply the power of the next preceding degree of the greater quantity by the difference between the quantities; then the difference between the powers of the next preceding degree is to be multiplied by the lesser quantity, and the sum of the products will be the required difference between the powers whose quantities are given. I so modified this same rule that it sufficed to be given, besides the quantities, the powers of any degree (even though not the immediately preceding degree) of the given quantities, in order that the differences of the powers of any other degree whatever might be found, including a higher degree. And I showed that what one observes in [the series of] squares, that the differences between them are the [series of] odd numbers, is a special case of the proposed rule.

Having developed these ideas, [and knowing that] between [successive] squares the differences are the odd numbers, I sought the nature of the differences between the cubes, and as these seemed to be irregular I sought the differences of the differences and so in the end discovered that the third differences were the number six. This observation gave birth to another, for I saw that the following terms and differences were generated from the preceding differences, and hence from the first [of each rank] which I for that reason call Generative, as in this instance, o.1.6.6., all the rest following. This accomplished it remained to discover by what kind of addition or multiplication of complexity of these the following terms might be generated from the Generative Differences. And I understood them to be resolved and expressed thus:[4] the first term o is composed of the first Generative Difference o taken once, or alternatively, (1). The second, 1, from the first o [taken] once (1) [and] the second, 1, once (1). The third, 8, from the first, o, [taken once] (1), the second, 1, twice (2) and the third, 6, once (1), for o(1)+1(2)+6(1) = 8. The fourth, 27, from the first, o, [taken] once, the second, 1, three times (3), the third, 6, three times (3) and the fourth, 6, once (1), for o(1)+1(3)+6(3)+6(1) = 27, etc. And thus my analysis proved itself to me as universal.

This was the occasion of my observation, very different from that of Mouton's, who hit upon this abbreviation of calculation, with Regnaud, when he was working on the computation of tables; nor is any less praise due to him or to Regnaud because Briggs too, in part noticed something of the same kind in his *Logarithms*, according to Pell.[5] It remains for me to add some new points to these in order to relieve myself of the name of copyist: for the republic of letters is concerned not with *who* observed something, but with *what* he observed. The first thing I add, therefore, which is not to be found in Mouton and yet is the crux of the whole matter, is: what are those numbers, the table of which he displays as extending to infinity, by the multiplication of which into the Generative Differences, the combined products generate the terms of the series. You may see from the very way in which he presents the table on p. 385 that this matter was not sufficiently investigated by him; for otherwise it is likely that he would have arranged the table so that the relation and harmony between the numbers would be obvious, unless one would maintain that he has intentionally concealed this.

A part of his table runs thus:[6]

1	1				
2	1	1			
3	1	2	1		
(4)	1	3	3	1	
5	1	4	6	4	1
6	1	5	10	10	5	1
7	1	6	15	20	15	6
8	1	7	21	35	35	21
9	1	8	28	56	70	56
10	1	9	36	84	126	126
11	1	10	45	120	210	252

It is obvious from the construction of this table that attention was paid only to the correspondence of the generative numbers with the number of the generated term, so that when the term is the fourth (4) it is produced from the first difference [taken] once, 1; the second [taken] three times, 3; the third [taken three times] 3; [and] the fourth once, 1; and therefore they are placed identically with the fourth line reversed, 1. 3. 3. 1.[7]

But either the author did not observe or he concealed the correspondence of the numbers if they are arranged in this way in columns, reading from above downwards:

```
 1  │  1
 2  │  1——1
 3  │  1  2——1
 4  │  1  3——3  1
 5  │  1  4——6  4  1
 6  │  1  5——10 10  5  1
 7  │  1  6——15 20 15  6
 8  │  1  7——21 35 35  21
 9  │  1  8——28 56 70  56
10  │  1  9——36 84 126 126
11  │  1  10  45 120 210 252
```

For thus their real and true nature and generation is at once obvious: they are those numbers that I call combinatory, of which I said a good deal in that little dissertation *De arte combinatoria*,[8] and which some call numerical orders, and others [label] particularly, the first column [as] of unities, the second of natural numbers, the third of triangular numbers, the fourth of pyramidal numbers, the fifth of triangulo-triangles, etc; on this subject there exists a whole tract by Pascal under the title of *Triangle Arithmétique*, in which nevertheless I am astonished that he never noticed a property of numbers of this kind which is no less illustrious than natural.[9] But this is indeed how chance operates in making discoveries, for it does not always reserve the greatest of them for the greatest minds, but offers some, frequently, even to middling ones.

Hence may now be understood the true nature of those numbers and the construction of the table whether or no it was concealed by Regnaud or by Mouton. For invariably a given term in a given column is composed of the preceding term in both the preceding column and the given column, and it is also obvious that no tedious calculation is needed to extend the table proposed by Mouton, as he himself requires, because these series of numbers have been discussed and calculated in various places.[10]

Moreover, [whereas] Mouton proposed by that observation to interpolate mean proportionals between two given extreme numbers, I thought it might be used to discover the extreme numbers themselves with their differences, indefinitely. Thus he found a use for the rule only when the final differences vanish (or almost vanish), [but] I detected innumerable cases, comprehended by a certain unnoticed rule, whereby I can produce from given finite numbers, multiplied in a certain manner, the numbers of very many series extending to infinity, even though their differences do not vanish. Upon these fundamentals I can solve many problems in progressions consisting either of single numbers, or ratios, or fractions, for I can add, subtract, or even multiply progressions, and divide them too, and that most conveniently.

I have observed much else concerning these numbers, of which this is outstanding: that I have a way of finding the sum of a series of fractions decreasing indefinitely, whose numerator is unity and whose denominators are triangular or pyramidal or triangulo-triangular numbers, etc.[11]

$$\frac{1}{3} \qquad \frac{1}{4} \qquad \frac{1}{5} \qquad \frac{1}{6}$$

$$\frac{1}{6} \qquad \frac{1}{10} \qquad \frac{1}{15}$$

$$\frac{1}{10} \qquad \frac{1}{20} \qquad \frac{1}{35}$$

$$\frac{1}{15} \qquad \frac{1}{35} \qquad \frac{1}{70}$$

$$\text{etc.} \quad \text{etc.} \quad \text{etc.}$$

[London, 3 February 1672/3]

NOTES

The original has no heading or date; Oldenburg has endorsed it, "A Letter written by Mr Leibnitius to Mr. Oldenburg vindicating certaine Algebraicall discoveries of his from an imputation of having borroed it from an other," and added the date "Londini d. 3. Feb. 1672/3." We have therefore included it here, although it reads more like a paper handed to Oldenburg than a letter addressed to him. A transcript by Oldenburg was sent to Newton and is now in the Portsmouth Collection.

1 See Vol. VII, p. 380, note 21. François Regnaud is mentioned on p. 384 of Mouton's *Observationes* and the solution of the problem, "Given a series of numbers progressing in sequence and having their last [order of] differences equal, to find any numbers you please in the same sequence" (pp. 384–96), here at issue, is attributed to him. Regnaud is mentioned as a friend and inspirer of Mouton in the book's preface.

2 See Balthazar de Monconys, *Iournal de Voyages*, troisieme partie (Lyons, 1666), p. 38; this section contains a number of letters from Regnaud to Monconys, with several essays on mensuration.

3 We have here generally translated Leibniz's word "radix" as "quantity" rather than "root." What Leibniz means is this: given two quantities A and B $(A > B)$, and the power to which they are raised (n), then $A^n - B^n = A^{n-1}(A - B) + B(A^{n-1} - B^{n-1})$. For the early history of Leibniz's mathematical researches see Hofmann, *Entwicklungsgeschichte*; this letter is dealt with on pp. 15–17.

4 In modern notation, what Leibniz is saying may be expressed as $n^3 = 0 \cdot \binom{n}{0} + 1 \cdot \binom{n}{1} + 6 \cdot \binom{n}{2} + 6 \cdot \binom{n}{3}$, n integral, there being only three terms to the expansion because there are (in this case) only three Generative Differences. We should beware of thinking that Leibniz had yet grasped the validity of this algebraic expression for non-integral values of its binomial coefficients; he has here mastered only the feasibility of setting out the expansion of the cube of integers in a regular *table*, whose binomial pattern he goes on to define.

5 Pell referred to Henry Briggs, *Arithmetica logarithmica* (London, 1624), ch. 12, pp. 24–27, where Briggs used a simple advancing differences scheme to subtabulate

fractional values of the argument in his ensuing logarithmic table. (Compare D. T. Whiteside, "Henry Briggs: The Binomial Expansion Anticipated," *Mathematical Gazette*, *45*, 1961, pp. 9–12.)

6 It will be noticed that this is, in effect, a more complete portion of the table of binomial coefficients (note 4 above); there are here six Generative Differences.

7 Presumably Leibniz means that the array shows a bilateral symmetry, but this is of course true of all the lines (when completed).

8 See Vol. VII, pp. 64–68.

9 Blaise Pascal, *Traité du Triangle Arithmétique* (Paris, 1665). In fact Pascal did "notice" this property, as he explicitly says. In addition, Leibniz's rule is to be found in Henry Briggs, *Trigonometria Britannica* (Gouda, 1633). (D. T. W.)

10 Obviously this remark envisages the possibility of making the expansions complete (that is, of increasing the number of Generative Differences) by extending the columns of numbers (beginning with unity) indefinitely to the right.

11 The respective series are arranged in columns reading downwards (the denominators appearing in the table on p. 441); the respective sums—to infinity—of the three lefthand columnar series are $1, \frac{1}{2}, \frac{1}{3}$. Leibniz had recently been studying the summation of infinite series of fractions at Paris; see Hofmann, *Entwicklungsgeschichte*, pp. 10–12.

2141

Henshaw to Oldenburg

4 February 1672/3

From the original in Royal Society MS. H 3, no. 14

Copenhagen Feb: $4-7\frac{2}{3}$

Sr

I suppose when this comes to yu will already have seen Triboulet, whom uppon ye discharging of useles mouthes in our family I dimissed, he being of as little use as any among them,[1] he wholy spending his time in company keeping, and conversing wt his Countrimen in this towne. Wee did not speak together sometimes in two months and when he did come to me, it was always for mony, or in some unpleasing humour to complaine of some body, or to answer ye Complaints of others, or to upbraide me wth his wants of mony, and that every footman was better clothed than he, never remembring that I had advanced to him 13 lb of his 20 lb before he came out of London to discharge his Pension and put him in clothes, and a little after he came over he had 3 or 4lb more, and was always in so ill humour wth me that he could not drink his mony and have his mony still, that I never cared to see him. another of his discontents was that his quality was not enough taken notice of, when ye gentlemen of ye house had wont laughingly to say they could not imagine under what qualification he did belong to me (for he watched always to clappe on his hat as soon as mine was on though he were speaking to me) whether he were my freind my companion or my servant but that wchsoever he were he performed his part very ill: when I lent him this mony in London never having seen him but twice before, he brought me his Landlord a poore french Minister to bee cautionary for it, whom I was content to accept of though I knew he was not worth ye Tenth part of ye mony. this it seems he represented in such a manner to his father, that ye old man writ me a letter hither, full of high expressions of his gratitude and obligation to this minister and to let me know ye son of what a father I had offered to have a sample of, tells me at what expence and in what good company he had travelled ye world in his youth, but withall excuses himself for not being able to send his sonne a penny of mony, I then perceived his sonnes beggerly pride came by inheritance, but wondered to find in Swisse a humour so like an Hidalgo of Galicia. I found presently his writing nor his English would bee at all helpfull to me, and therfore desired him to designe me some of ye remarkable places heere, and for ye first 5 weeks while he lay [in] ye next chamber to me he did use to spend an houre sometimes in a day about it having not then so much acquaintance, but when wee were removed into ye Dukes house I could not get him to draw one line for me in 6 or 7 monthes though beside his lodging chamber he had a good roome allowed to himself of wch for ye most part he carryed ye Key. and a stove in it ever since it was cold wether. he knows I could say other things of him but doe for beare because I would not hinder his preferment wch truly I doe heartily wish for him, and doe beleeve there might some use bee made of him if he were strictly kept to his Employment, but I doe not love a pendantick watching of my servant if his Moralls and good nature will oblige him to nothing. so making up his wages 20 lb. for his 9 monthes taking his pleasure here, wth a good new mourning sute on his back I sent him for England.

Since ye D[uke]s death I have had an opportunity to make an acquaintance wth Erasmus Bartholinus who is a very learned man and a very civill gentleman, I presented him wth one of Mr Boyles bookes de Gemmis, and another little latine treatise of his I had by me, concerning ye Extension of Ayre &c.[2] wch he was so well pleased wth that ye next time I came to see him he gave me two fine peeces of Island Christall as they call it wch being split any way into great or little peeces they all prove Rhomboides. this I thought I had remembred to have seen Mr Hook doe wth a peece of English spar if I mistook not, and this he calls Christall is but spar, though much more transparent then any I have of that kind seen in England. but when he shewed me that looking any way through it on a small obiect such as a point or line on paper, it represented its double very distinctly wch being more then I had known observed in our sparre, made him very desirous to have some two or 3 peeces of ours sent him, and I doe not knowe any one more propper to oblige him in that then yr self, therfore I humbly begge you would oblige us both in sending some when there comes a vessell to fetch home ye Dukes body, wch yu may have information of at ye Duchesses[3] Lodgings in Whitehall, and if yu give them in a boxe or paper to one Mr Flexney one of her servants, he will take uppon him ye Care to have them conveyed to me. talking of ye peece of Ambar Monsr Hevelius writ yu he had, that was so soft on one side it would take ye impression of a seale and yet was as hard as any on ye otherside,[4] he tould me that was done by art and that he had severall times seen it done and would at my leasure shew me ye way how to doe it by any strong oyle of a vegetable and that it would ever after reteine yt softnes so far as it was touched, whether ye oyle were to bee heated or no he did not say then, but I will not bee long without this secret if his kindnes to me continue. I tould him I had a very faire large long peece of yellow Ambar sent me lately out of Holsteen by a Captain of my acquaintance that is quartered there who with it sent me a testimoniall under his hand that he stood by while that peece and some others were found by chance by some of his Souldiers as they were digging in ye earth above 30 English miles from ye sea; and that I had two large peeces more were given me by ye governor of ye Cittadelle here wch were taken out of ye Earth in digging ye Grafts[5] of that fort. he tould me that was no very strange thing here on ye Coast of ye Baltick sea, that himself had seen severall peeces taken out of ye Earth, and had been so curious as to observe that there was commonly where such peeces were found some quantity of a stuffe that looked and felt like rotten wood or Timber wch inclined him to think that yellow Ambar may bee ye Gumme of some tree. he gave me also a good piece of a substance like charkt wood which being burnt has a smell like seacole or Jet, wch he said was usually found along wth ye Ambar in ye Earth, he then brought me out of his study a great Copper tray filled wth such earth, wch when ever they find in digging, the skilfull know there is ambar not farre offe: this earth was very full of such Rotten wood and had every where small grains of Ambar mingled wth it. he hath promised me to carry me to see a peece of Ambar that is in a private mans possession in this towne that conteines a liquid part in ye middle of it wch will move up and downe as yu turne ye Ambar, wch if it bee to bee bought I intend to present ye RS with. I forgot to tell yu that he gave me a book he had published at Amsterdam anno 1670 called Experimenta Cristalli Islandici Disdiaclastici quibus mira et insolita refractio detegitur, a piece very curious and ingenious wch I suppose yu have seen before.[6] he told me farther that a priest living in ye Island of Fero had lately written a book in ye Danish Toung concerning that Island, but because it was large and not written in a language the world was acquainted wth, ye booksellers would not venture to print it, but to repaire that losse, I should shortly see in a book of his brother Thomas Bartholin now in ye presse called Acta Academica all that was worth remark in ye other, published there.[7] From Sweden they write me that Shefferus hath now finished his Relation of Lapland, according to ye Emendations of ye priest of that Country I writ yu of, but by reason there are many cuts to bee inserted in ye book it cannot bee printed at Stockholme, but will be sent to Franckford or some other place in Germany.[8]

They tell me also that there is no description of Moscovie printed there, but a Book called Historia belli suecomoscovitici decennalis wch I have seen, written by Johannes Widekindus and printed there last yeare,[9] it was written in honour, and published at ye Charge of the present Ricks Chancellour conteining ye Actions of his Father Jacobus de la Gardie.[10] if yu desire it I will send yu one of them.

The last post was the first time I had notice they had received at Court ye sad news of ye Duke of Richmonds death but they could not then tell me what ye Kings pleasure concerning my returne would bee, so I feare I shall bee deteined here longer than I desire, but I hope it shall not bee longer than Michaelmas next. So I remain Sr

Yr most affectionate humble servant
T. Henshaw

Monsr. Grubendol.

NOTES

1 Oldenburg refered to this Swiss in the Royal Society's minutes as "Mr. Henshaw's clerk." For his contact with Oldenburg, see Letter 2127, note 1.

2 Presumably *Tractatus . . . ubi 1. mira aeris . . . rarefactio detecta . . .* (London, 1670).

3 Frances Teresa Stuart or Stewart (1647–1702), a mistress of Charles II before her elopement with the Duke of Richmond in 1667, was a famous beauty, who spent most of her time at Court.

4 See Vol. VII, pp. 49–50.

5 Properly, "graffs"; that is, trenches, ditches, or moats.

6 For Oldenburg's knowledge of this book, published in 1669, see Vol. VII, p. 84, note 4.

7 The account is indeed to be found in *Acta medica et philosophica ann. 1671 & 1672*; see Oldenburg's review in *Phil. Trans.*, no. 97 (6 October 1673), 6135. See Letter 2296, notes 3 and 4 (Vol. X); the author's name was L. J. Debes.

8 Johann Scheffer's *Lapponia* was published at Frankfurt in 1673; Oldenburg reviewed it in *Phil. Trans.*, no. 102 (27 April 1674), 31–38.

9 Johan Widekindi, *Historia belli Sueco-moscovitici decennalis* was, as Henshaw says, published at Stockholm in 1672.

10 The Chancellor was Magnus Gabriel de La Gardie (1622–86); his father, Jacobus de La Gardie (1583–1652), was a Swedish general. The Chancellor's grandfather, Baron Pontus de La Gardie (d. 1585), was a Field Marshal of Sweden who came from France.

2142

Oldenburg to Vogel

6 February 1672/3

According to Vogel's acknowledgement, Letter 2170, this letter to him enclosed that for Morhof (see the next Letter) which he delivered.

2143

Oldenburg to Morhof

6 February 1672/3

From the copy in Copenhagen MSS., no. 733

Nobilissimo & Consultissimo Viro
Domino Danieli Georgio Morhofio J.V.D. & P.
Henricus Oldenburg S.P.

Invisebam Te, Vir Consultissime, epistola mea d. 20. Sept. anni super elapsi data;[1] in iisque gratias Tibi agebam tum pro munere operis Wasmuthiani, & Epistolae Clarissimi Langelotti, (quam exinde Anglice versam Transactionibus Philosophicis inserui;) tum pro gratissimo promisso, quo Celeberrimi Gudii doctas in Geoponicas Authores Notas, aliorumque ipsius MSrum Catalogum te transmissurum spoponderas. Dixeram, me idipsum significasse veris, scientiarum & artium augmenta enixe spirantibus, eosque omnes tuam & Gudii in ornanda re philosophica egregiam voluntatem unanimis praedicare, simul & efflictim rogare, ut notae istae Geoponicae, una cum Catalogo iamiam memorato, commoda occasione ad me transmittantur; caetera, nil omnino in eorum quae ab ipso proficiscentur, impressione omissum iri, quae honori ipsi debito liture poterunt. Adieceram, sub praelo, tam Graeco quam Latino, nunc apud nos sudare Jamblichum de mysteriis Ægyptiorum, nec non Pythagorae Vitam, perquam mendose hactenus editam, Lucianum insuper, Graece itidem ac Latine brevi hic imprimendum, nosque lubenter intelligere velle, ullaene Domino Gudio notae suppetant, quae ad horum scriptorum vel emendationum vel elucidationum facere possint. Ad haec rogaveram, ut si quicquam vobis de Bosii Consilio in Josepho edendo, vel de conditionibus, quibus suas circa ipsum |collationes aliis concedere cupiat, innotuerit, id quoque nobis significare dignaremini. Significaveram denique, me cum Jacobiis mercatoribus de debito illo, quod mihi commendaveras, locutum, deprehendisse, eos nil quicquam argenti hactenus potuisse impetrare, nec etiamnum posse, quamdiu Fisci regii clausura duret. Quamprimum pax rursum effulserit, siquid Ego vel seorsim, vel iunctim cum dictis mercatoribus praestare in ea re potero, nequaquam detrectabo.

Haec sunt praecipua, quae istis literis perscripseram; quas intercidisse nonnihil vereor, cum nullum ad eas responsum hactenus acceperim.

Visum igitur fuit, ea hic strictim repetere, ut, si forte perierint illae, ex his intelligas, me officio meo, quod Tibi debeo, non defuisse, & ad colendum iugiter commercium philosphicum paratissimum esse.

Unum est, quod nunc addo; nos scilicet destinare praelo Londinensi Photii Lexicon Graecum,[2] atque intellexisse, penes Clarissimum Gudium esse eius Exemplar satis nitidum. Rogamus magnopere, ut commodare nobis illud per unum saltem mensem, quo cum Manuscripto nostrate conferre id possimus, non gravetur. Ego vadimonium subibo, si ad me deferatur, me illud incolume omnino servaturum redditurumque, nec non daturum operam, ut generosus eiusmodi candor Possessoris ea qua par est gratitudine depraedicetur. Vehementer oro, Vir Amplissime, ut quamprimum fieri poterit haec in doctorum & bonorum virorum gratiam diligenter curare, & super iis responsum benevolum deproperare digneris. In eo vicissim ero, ut mandata tua hic loci pro viribus exequar. Vale & me amare perge. Dab. Londini d. 6 Februarii 1673.

P.S.

Si mihi velles sedem & titulos Clarissimi Gudii indicare, ipse eum literis meis inviserem.[3] Hac vice officiosissimam ipsi salutem dico, Te rogans, ut mihi significare etiam velis, possimne ad Te recta scribere, dummodo hic pro literis Hamburgum usque solvam; ne opus semper sit, Clarissimo Fogelio incommodum creare. Eum in finem inscriptionem, epistolis ad te scribendis debitam, ne celes. Nosti eam, ni fallor, quae convenit iis, quae ad me per tabellarios scribuntur; nempe

A Monsr.

Monsr. Grubendol, à Londres.

Nihil praeterea. Vale iterum atque iterum, Academiae Kiloniensis decus.

ADDRESS

    Clarissimo & Consultissimo Viro
      Domino Danieli Georgio Morhofio J.U.D.
        & in Academia Kiloniensi Professori dignissimo.

TRANSLATION

Henry Oldenburg sends many greetings to the very noble and wise Mr. Daniel Georg Morhof LL.D., Ph.D.

I addressed a letter to you, learned Sir, on the twentieth of September last year,[1] in which I thanked you for the gift of the writings of Wasmuth and of the *Letter* [written] by the famous Langelott (which I have since inserted in the

Philosophical Transactions, in English translation), as also for your most welcome promise to send over the learned notes of the celebrated Gude upon the geoponic writers together with a catalogue of his other manuscripts. I said that I had imparted this news to those who are truly and earnestly striving for the advancement of the arts and sciences and that they all with one voice commend your own extraordinary willingness to perfect philosophy, and that of Gude; and at the same time strongly urge you to send to me, at a convenient opportunity, those notes on the *Geoponics* and the aforesaid catalogue. Moreover, nothing whatever will be omitted in the printing of those matters that have originated with him which can be thought of as redounding to his credit. I added that we have now in press here, both in Greek and Latin, Iamblichos *On the Egyptian Mysteries* and the *Life of Pythagoras*, which has hitherto been very falsely printed; moreover Lucian is to be printed here soon, likewise in both Greek and Latin. We would gladly know whether Mr. Gude has any notes relating to either the emendation or the elucidation of these texts. Further, I asked that if anything was known to you of Bose's intention in editing Josephus or of the conditions under which he might be willing to yield to others the collations he has made concerning him, this also you would be so good as to signify to me. Lastly I informed you that I had spoken with the Jacobs, merchants, about that debt of which you gave me notice and understood from them that they could as yet obtain no money, nor would be able to so long as the Stop of the Exchequer lasts. As soon as peace returns I shall be wanting in nothing I can accomplish in that business, either alone or in conjunction with those merchants.

These are the chief things I wrote in that letter, which I rather fear has perished since I have as yet received no answer to it. So it seemed sensible to repeat them briefly here in order that you might know from this, if the other got lost, that I did not fail in my duty to you and am constantly most willing to carry on a correspondence.

One point I add now. We intend to print at London the *Greek Lexicon* of Photius,[2] and we understand that Gude possesses a rather fine copy of it. We earnestly beg him to be so good as to oblige us with it for one month at least, so that we may collate it with our manuscript. I will myself be a surety that, if it is sent to me, I will keep it safe from all harm and return it; and I will see that the generous cordiality of its owner is acknowledged with due thanks. I strongly urge you, most worthy Sir, to look into this business as soon as possible for the satisfaction of good and learned men, and to be so kind as to return a favorable reply to them. In return I will see to the carrying out of your wishes here. Farewell, and continue to love me. London, 6 February 1673.

P.S. If you will let me know the address and style of the famous Gude, I will myself address a letter to him.[3] For the present I greet him most dutifully, requesting you also to inform me whether I can write to you safely if I pay [postage] for my letter from here to Hamburg; in order not always to need to make trouble for the famous Vogel. To this end, do not conceal the address to be written on letters to yourself. If I am not mistaken you know what it is proper to write on letters for me sent by post, that is

A Monsr.

Mons. Grubendol, à Londres.

Nothing more. Again farewell and again, worthy member of the University of Kiel.

ADDRESS

To the very famous and wise
Mr. Daniel Georg Morhof LL.D.,
most worthy Professor in the University of Kiel.

NOTES

1 Letter 2068, whose contents Oldenburg here accurately summarizes.
2 Photius (d. 891) was twice patriarch of Constantinople, a noted ecclesiastical states-man and literary and theological scholar. His *Lexicon Sunagog* (probably mainly the work of his pupils) survived in only one MS., at Trinity College, Cambridge. It was first printed in 1808.
3 As he was to do on 28 April 1673 (Letter 2220).

2144

Oldenburg to Huygens

9 February 1672/3

From *Œuvres Complètes*, VII, 256–57
Original in the Huygens Collection at Leiden

A londres le 9 Fevrier 1673

Monsieur

Je m'estois proposé de vous escrire amplement par cette voye de Monsieur Leibnitz; mais il precipite tellement son voyage d'icy a Paris, qu'il m'a esté impossible dans l'estat où ie suis, estant quasi accablé d'affaires à present, d'executer mon intention.[1] Je ne scauray vous dire autre chose, sinon que i'ay receu vos deux lettres, du 14 janvier et de l'11 Fevrier, et que ie tascheray de vous y satisfaire au possible par une autre occasion. On fera icy toute justice à Monsieur Hugens, dont on conoit la doctrine et la vertu, et i'auray soin particulierement de faire scavoir à Monsieur Sluse la belle maniere dont vous usez envers luy. Vous verrez dans l'annexe² sa methode de tirer des tangents à toutes sortes de Curves Geometriques sans calcul; dont il nous envoiera, i'espere, la demonstration par sa prochaine a Monsieur

Vostre tres humble et tres obeissant Serviteur
Oldenburg

Monsieur Leibnitz a gagné beaucoup d'estime icy, comme il le merite assurement.

ADDRESS
A Monsieur
Monsieur Christian Hugens de Zulechem
dans la Bibliotheque du Roy à
Paris

TRANSLATION

London, 9 February 1673
Sir,

I had intended to write to you at length through the courtesy of Mr. Leibniz; but he has so hastened his journey from here to Paris that it is impossible for me to carry out my intention in the state I am in, being almost overwhelmed with business at present.¹ I do not know anything to tell you except that I have received your two letters of 14 January and 11 February [N.S.] and that I shall try to satisfy you as far as possible on another occasion. Everyone does Mr. Huygens all possible justice here, knowing his learning and his character, and I shall take particular care to let Mr. Sluse know the fine courtesy you display towards him. You will see in the enclosed² his method of drawing tangents to all sorts of geometric curves without calculation, of which he will, I hope, send us his demonstration by his next letter to, Sir,

Your very humble and obedient servant
Oldenburg

Mr. Leibniz has gained a great deal of esteem here, as he assuredly deserves.

ADDRESS
To Mr. Christiaan Huygens of Zulichem,
At the King's Library,
Paris

NOTES

Reply to Letters 2122 and 2138; rather curiously Oldenburg has endorsed both these letters as having been answered on 10 February.
1 Compare Letter 2145.
2 *Phil. Trans.*, no. 90 (20 January 1672/3) containing Letter 2124.

2145
Oldenburg to Leibniz
9 February 1672/3

From the original in Hannover MSS., f. 16
Printed in Gerhardt, p. 74

Monsieur,

Je vous supplie de vouloir faire mes treshumbles baisemains à S. Exce. Monsieur de Schonborn,[1] et de m'excuser aupres de luy de ne pouvoir pas iouir de l'honneur qu'il m'a destinee cejourdhuy, ayant receu ce matin à la Cour des affaires, qui demandent une despesche sans aucun delay, desorte que ie n'auray presque pas une minute de temps pour disner chez moy. Je me donneray pourtant l'honneur d'assurer son Exce. devant son depart de mes treshumbles obeissances, et de vous tesmoigner aussi, que ie suis sincerement Monsr

> Vostre tresaffectioné et
> treshumble serviteur
> *Oldenburg*

le 9. Fevr. 1673.

TRANSLATION

Sir,

I beg you kindly to give my very humble greetings to His Excellency, M. de Schönborn,[1] and to make my excuses to him, for being unable to enjoy the honor he intended me to have today, having received at the Court this morning business which must be attended to without any delay, so much so that I shall have scarcely even one minute in which to dine at home. I shall however give myself the honor to assure his Excellency before he leaves of my very humble respects, and to testify to you also that I am sincerely, Sir,

> Your very affectionate and
> very humble servant
> *Oldenburg*

9 February 1672/3

NOTE

1 See Letter 2137, and its note 1.

2146

Reed to Oldenburg

9 February 1672/3

From the original in Royal Society MS. R 1, no. 30

My worthy Frend

I am sensible that the grafts I sent last weeke[1] doe not answer in proportion the desires of your letter, wch yu may impute to ye Juice of ye tree, for sending my man to looke [out] grafts soe timely as he might have brought treble the proportion and returne in time, he met wth the Liquor & came back wth soe few & soe late that I could not exceed then, observeing ye spring to come on soe fast yt possibly ye transmitting them will not beare the delay of another week, I second them wth another Fagott, wch you will receive from ye Hereford Carrier on Fryday. If you please lett me heare from you as to my last, & if you have any further Commands for Sr

> your very respective Frend
> *Ric Reed*

Feb. 9. 72.

Sr you have them wth many good wishes from me and as my man who cartyed the last to Hereford informes me wth many hearty prayers from my neighbours who pray they may not prosper

ADDRESS
> For Henry Oldenburgh Esqr
> at his house in the Pell-Mell
>   neere
>   Westminster

POSTMARK FE 12

NOTE

1 See Letter 2139.

2147
Oldenburg to Swammerdam
10 February 1672/3
From the copies in Royal Society MS. O 2, no. 103 and Letter Book VI, 29–30

Clarissimo et Doctissimo Viro
Domino Johanno Swammerdam Med. Doctori
Henr. Oldenburgh Felicitatem

Certiorem feci Societatem Regiam quanto apud Te sit ipsius benevolentia, quamque operam jugiter naves in scientia physica, inprimis in re Anatomica magis magisque Exornanda. Praelegi etiam in publico Ejusdam consessu, quid in nuperis tuis sectionibus circa Animalia quaedam deprehendisti, quae nempe licet pulmonibus instructa sint, vena tamen arteriosa destituantur. Rogant Sodales, ut indicare Animalia illa ne graveris, in quibus rem adeo notabilem observasti. Accepimus, (id quod hac occasione narrabatur)[1] virum quendam suspensum, cultro anatomico post mortem subjectum, praebuisse apertum Foramen Ovale. Forte saepius observari id posset, si viri Anatomici frequentius animum ad eam rem adverterent.

Perquam curiosum est, quod de scarabaei nasei-cornis genitalibus annotasti. Pergas, quaesimus, vir Doctissime, naturam ejusque recessus gnaviter indagare, et nominis tui gloriam virtutis et Scientiae cultu perennem reddere. Certatim id jam agitur inter philosophos, quos inter Clarissimus Malpighius prima subsellia merito occupat, qui Plantarum

Anatomem, aeque ac Animalium, indefesso studio nobiscum excolit, quique nuper iteratas suas de ovo et Pulli Formatione observationes manuscriptas accuratissime adornatas, et prioribus, hic jam prostantibus, stabiliendis succenturiatas ad nos transmissit;[2] brevi quoque, ni admodum fallor, praelo Londinensi subjiciendas. Illustris Boylius noster novos etiam Tractatulos aliquot in publicum pronuper emisit, de Flamma vitali; de Aeris et Flammae cognatione, de positiva et relativa Corporum levitate sub aquis, una cum Diatriba Hydrostatica contra Henricum Morum &c. egregie disserentes. Pace refulgente haec et similia complura ad vos, Deo dante, curabuntur.

Interim vale, et me Tui Studiosissimum crede. Dabam Londini d. 10. Febr. 1673.

TRANSLATION

Henry Oldenburg [wishes] happiness to the very famous and learned Mr. Jan Swammerdam, M.D.

I informed the Royal Society of the great goodwill you feel towards it and that you continue to pursue knowledge of nature, especially the increasing perfection of [comparative] anatomy. I also read at its ordinary meeting what you have discovered in your recent dissection of certain animals, namely, that although they are furnished with lungs they lack a pulmonary artery. The Fellows request you to be so good as to indicate the animals in which you have observed so remarkable a fact. We have heard (the story was told on this occasion)[1] that a certain man, who had been hung and was afterwards submitted to the anatomist's knife, displayed an open *foramen ovale*. Perhaps this would be observed quite commonly if anatomists would pay attention to the point more regularly.

What you have remarked concerning the genitalia of the horned-nose beetle is very curious. Go on with your assiduous investigation of nature and her secrets, learned Sir, so as to acquire for yourself eternal distinction as a student of virtue and science. Certainly there are philosophers active in this way, among whom the merits of the famous Malpighi earn him the first place; he, with tireless zeal on our behalf, investigates the anatomy of both plants and animals, and he has recently sent us his repeated [and] most accurately perfected manuscript observations on the egg and the development of the chick, as a supplement confirming the former [series of observations] which is now on sale here.[2] Soon these too will, if I am not much mistaken, be sent to the press in London. Our illustrious Boyle has very recently published a few new essays, giving a distinguished treatment of the vital flame, the relation of fire and flame, the positive and relative levity of bodies under water, together with an hydrostatical discourse against Henry More, etc. On the

return of peace these and many similar things shall be sent to you, God willing.
    Meanwhile, farewell, and believe me most zealously yours.
London, 10 February 1673.

NOTES

Reply to Letter 2130, where the necessary notes will be found. Both copies are poor
and have been corrected by Oldenburg.
1 By Boyle
2 See Letter 2073; this second embryological study was to be printed only in 1675.

2148

Oldenburg to Sand

10 February 1672/3

Mentioned in Sand's reply, Letter 2171.

2149

Oldenburg to Reed

13 February 1672/3

Mentioned in the endorsement on Reed's Letter 2146, and in Reed's reply, Letter
2169.

2150

Oldenburg to Flamsteed

14 February 1672/3

In his reply of three days later (Letter 2154) Flamsteed notes receipt of this letter together with Hecker's ephemeris.

2151

Oldenburg to Wallis

c. 14 February 1672/3

This letter, received by Wallis on the fifteenth and acknowledged two days later in Letter 2153, contained a copy of *Phil. Trans.*, no. 90 (20 January 1672/3).

2152

Oldenburg to Williamson

16 February 1672/3

From the original in P.R.O. MS. S.P. 29/333, no. 126

Sir,

The long letter, wch you took to be highdutch, is Danish, written, as you doubtlesse found, to the K. of Denmark by his Envoy here.[1] Of yt tongue I have no further skill, than it hath affinity wth the Dutch: and therefore am not able to give you a good account of the contents thereof. How-ever I find, yt Monsr Gióe informs his Master of most of ye publique transactions here, and particularly of what hath pass'd between the King and Parlement, concerning the Election of new members, the Kings Declaration, & the Supply of money; Relating at large, how the House of

Commons annulled the Elections made before their meeting, and exagge-
rating, wth what passion the King took it: Then mentioning ye summe,
voted for carrying on the warr. Further, enlarging upon what the House of
Commons did and voted in reference to the King's Declaration; where
occurr store of numbers, wch I suppose are used for cyphers, for wch the
key is wanting; but by ye context I guesse it to be a glosse upon the vote
of the House, that notwthstanding the King had declared his power in
suspending ye penal laws about Ecclesiast. matters, yet they voted, That
there could be no such suspension of the penal laws but by act of Parlement.[2]

After this, he comments upon the Bill of Naturalising, wch is under
consideration in the H. of Lords,[3] and maketh this reflexion, that this
Nation, wch he thinks incompatible wth strangers, will never bear it. Of
all wch things he promiseth, if I mistake him not, a fuller account hereafter.

He discourses also of the Dutch prisoners here, Advocat sas etc.[4] but
the particulars of it I doe not understand.

Next he speaks of ye Duke of Neuburg,[5] wch he wrapps up in Cyphers.

He saith also something of the public ministers here, and his owne
negotation at this court.

If it be necessary, yt all the particulars of this Danish letter be interpreted, some body must be found out, yt is master of yt language.

As to ye other letters, I pressume you have already satisfied yrself as to
the contents of ym. I have sate up almost all night in finishing the Extracts
for the Mundays gazette,[6] wch will be so full from the papers I had in my
hands before the last came to me yesternight, that it will need nothing
more, unlesse it be thought fit to adde in a line or two, that ye letters by ye
last post doe all agree, that there hath been no battel fought, nor likely will
be in haste. This may be more fully mention'd in the next, together wth the
other particulars, contained in the last papers; wch therefore I shall, as you
direct, reserve as a provision for Thursday.

I hope to be at Whitehall about sermon-time

Yr humble servt
H. O.

Febr. 16. h. 7. mane

ADDRESS

    For Sir Joseph Williamson
        these

NOTES

Although we have found no remaining letters from Oldenburg to Williamson for 1671 or 1672, there is no doubt that the present letter is part of a continuous correspondence, nor that Oldenburg had worked for Williamson during all these years.

1 Marcus Gjøe (1635–98), a professional diplomat who had previously served in Paris (from 1664 to 1669) and The Hague. He had arrived in England in March, 1672 from Amsterdam, and was to remain until 1678, marrying an Englishwoman, Elisabeth Mary Thompson.

2 Parliament had voted money to continue the Anglo-Dutch War, but in return had insisted that the King withdraw his Declaration of Indulgence of the previous year; they further voted a Test Act which compelled every office holder to conform to the Church of England, thereby excluding all Catholics from office.

3 "An Act for Naturalization" had its first reading in the House of Lords on 4 February 1672/3. The Committee reported on 27 March 1673 that this "General Act" be accepted with amendments to make it conform to the provisions of the Test Act, and it was so voted. Parliament was, however, prorogued soon after.

4 Gerbrandt Zas (or Sas) had been in England in 1672 when he was in touch with Lord Arlington; he returned on 14th January 1672/3, claiming to be a member of the Prince of Orange's Privy Council, and to have come over on public affairs. He was detained at Harwich on suspicion of being a spy, and committed to the Tower on 26 January 1672/3. He was several times examined, when he claimed to have come on behalf of the Prince of Orange (apparently) to arrange a truce, and to that end had or was empowered to offer a million and a half florins. He was tried in March, and apparently convicted; in May the States-General offered to exchange him and his companion for several English prisoners. (See C.S.P.D. for 1673, where, however, many details are missing.)

5 See Vol. III, p. 135, and Vol. IV, *passim*.

6 This is the first detailed indication we have found of Oldenburg's service to the Government. Evidently he acted as a translator with a double function, working on letters intercepted at the Post Office and on printed papers from abroad containing news and rumors. Some of the material translated by Oldenburg was, obviously, secret intelligence; other material was printed in the *London Gazette*, as the *Oxford Gazette* was renamed with the issue of 5 February 1665/6. It appeared twice weekly as an official publication; Williamson, now Clerk of the Council in Ordinary, was its editor. See also Letter 2164.

2153

Wallis to Oldenburg

17 February 1672/3

From the original in Royal Society MS W 2, no. 5
Partly printed in *Phil. Trans.*, no. 95 (23 June 1673), 6060

Oxford. Febr. 17. 1672/3

Sir,

I thank you for your letter, with ye Transactions for January, which I received on Saturday night, & am reading this Munday morning.[1]

As to ye Veins of Plants, which Mr Lister observes not to be ramifyed, but rather bundles of them divaricated; they do in this represent ye Nerves, which (as in Dr Willis de Cerebro[2] is observed) goe together in that which seems ye common trunk, like a bunch of Threads which after separate & be variously divaricated; & these Nerves being cut, shrink up (as ye Veines of Plants) as much or more than do ye Veines or Arteries of Animals. Dr Willis observes allso, that there be two sorts of Nerves, one arising from ye *Cerebrum*, subservient to voluntary motions & of which we be conscious or take notice, (& which properly belong to ye Functions of ye sensitive soul, at lest to ye functions of sense;) the other from ye *Cerebellum*, subservient to ye involuntary motions, & of wch wee are not conscious or sensible, (& wch belong rather to ye functions of ye Vegetative soul (Nutrition &c) or at lest the insensible loco-motive faculty:) And to these latter seem reducible those *Acts of sense* wch Mr Lister speakes of in Plants. See Willis de Cerebro, Cap. 19. pag. (editions in 4º) 241. and Cap. 15. pag. 187. If you suggest thus much to Mr Lister, perhaps the notion may be of use to him.

The strange frost (or Freezing rather) you give account of in Somersetshire in December (though I remember not ye day) was the like wth us at Oxford; it was rather a Raining of Ice, or at lest Rain freezing as it fell: Which made strange Icicles hanging on trees, & a strange noise by ye ratling of them upon ye Bough's motion by ye Wind: But not so much as at ye places you mention in Somersetshire: Yet more in ye Country about us (as from severall relaters I have heard) than with us in Oxford. And the great warmth soon after was allso with us: in so much that not onely Blossomes, but (as was then certainly affirmed, though I was not so curious as to get a sight of any) green apples on divers trees; particularly in ye parish of Holy-well.

Slusius's Rule for Tangents, is very neat.[3] It reacheth onely to Geo-metrical Lines (as Cartes calls them) yt is such who's nature is Explicable by an Equation. It is ye result of the former of my two;[4] & of Hudde's method de Maximis & Minimis, (published by Schooten)[5] put together. His rule is from those principles demonstrable, even of mine alone. The result of his methode is precisely ye same with that of mine, but with a very neat compendium in the operation. and (I presume) his demonstration will be really done.

My latter methode he toucheth not, nor such problemes as are not re-ducible to such an AEquation.

Some small Errors of ye presse I noted as I went along:[6]

pag. 5144 l. 16. for $3^6yya-4ya^3$ read $3byya-4y^3a$

l. 19 dele[3]. l. 29 read *in latere sinistro*

p. 5145. l. 6 for $2qqa$ read $2qqya$.

p. 5146. l. 28. for b read B. p. 5149. l. 5. for Whistle, (I suppose it should be) Whiffle

My Lo. Brounckers sad Accident,[7] I am very sorry for: I heard it here ye next day; & should have written him a condoling letter, if that could have done him any good. I was glad to hear (presently upon it) that ye Bookes & papers of ye Navy were preserved; because there were not want-ing those who would pretend it to be upon design, for ye ruining of them. I would not that you should give him any trouble about my paper; yet, because he is concerned in it, it is necessary that he see it, & adde or alter what he sees fit. I hope it comes not too late for this Months Transactions.

To yt of Vectius Valens I can yet say nothing, till I have inquired further of it.[8] I am

Yr friend & servant
John Wallis

My present opinion concerning Vectius Valens, is, yt if ye Gentleman have a Coppy of it, it were better to send that hither & have it compared; than to transcribe this.

This should have come by Tuesdays Post,[9] but by a neglect it was forgotten to be carried to ye Posthouse with my other letters. I have since been seaking ye Library for Vectius Valens, but cannot yet find it. But shall inquire further after it.

ADDRESS

For Mr Henry Oldenburg
in the Palmal near St. James's
London

NOTES

1 *Phil. Trans.*, no. 90 (20 January 1672/3), contains Lister's Letter 2125, Beale's Letter 2128, and Sluse's Letter 2124.
2 Thomas Willis, *Cerebri anatome* (London, 1664); the Amsterdam editions of 1666 and 1667 were 16mo and 24mo, respectively. See *The Remaining Medical Works of . . . Dr Thomas Willis* (London, 1681), *The Anatomy of the Brain* (the fourth of *Five Treatises*, with separate title page), pp. 129–30 and p. 111, respectively.
3 See Letter 2124.
4 For Wallis's two methods for determining tangents see Letter 1949, note 4, and Letter 2078.
5 See Letter 2066, note 9.
6 These errors in *Phil. Trans.*, no. 90, were corrected in no. 91 (24 February 1672/3), 5172.
7 As Hooke records in his *Diary* under the date 29 January 1672/3, "A great fire began at L[ady] Williams closet that Burnt Navy Office and 30 other houses." Lady (or Mrs.) Williams was Brouncker's mistress. Pepys lost much of his furniture and art, but apparently most of his books, and all the Navy Office's books and papers were saved.
8 As Letter 2172 makes clear, this was Vettius Valens the astrologer, author of an *Anthology*, who lived about the middle of the second century. He was treated by Claude Salmasius in *De annis climactericis et antiqua astrologia diatribae* (Leiden, 1648) although the *Anthology* itself has been published only in modern times (edited by G. Kroll; Berlin, 1908). There are manuscripts of it in the Vatican and other Italian libraries, in the Selden collection and elsewhere. It was wanted by Huet.
9 Tuesday was the eighteenth; the letter was received on the twenty-first so it presumably went to post on Thursday.

2154
Flamsteed to Oldenburg
17 February 1672/3
From the original in Royal Society MS. F 1, no. 94

Derby: Feb: 17 16$\frac{72}{73}$

Mr Oldenburge:
Sr

I have reaceaved yrs of ye 14th wth Heckerus his admonition[1] included for which I returne yu hearty thankes but must beg yr leave to advert a little wth my wonted liberty upon it:

The Alphonsine, Prutenick, Danish & Lansbergian calculi[2] have beene a labor more troublesome yn needfull to the author. The Rudolphine has been twice observed erronious if not 3ce already in ye transits of mercurius sub sole[3] which makes mee wonder that ye ingenuous author has not given us a calculus from some tables corrected by those extant observations: it seemes ye English are in Astronomy before ye rest of ye world else should wee [have] had from them, as there are with us, more exact calculations.

The calculus from Bullialdus[4] his tables is because his tables of onely to be heeded, of all those hee hath Mercury were correct- made; by which it will appeare yt onely the be-ed by Gassendus his gining of this transit can be observeable by observation of ye transit us; But from better tables, & which have had sub sole 1631[5] ye opportunity of 2 mercuriall transits to correct them, I am persuaded yt no part of this transit will be observeable wth us much lesse at Uraniburge, I meane ye caroline, by which: in the Conjunction of ye sun & mercury 1674 Aprill 26 st. vet: will be

	h ′ ″	Lat. Mercurii Australis
the ingresse	11–05 34	12′ 29″
middle of ye eclipse	12–54–34	13 43 cent dist: 14′–01″
true conjunction	13–33–36	14 15
Central Egresse	14–43–34	14 05

Angulus viae visibilis Mercurii cum Ecliptica[6] 10° 24′ 00″

You may find this Calculus in Streets Examen Examinatum[7] pag: 27: and in pag 30 the praediction of ye the next transit of 1677 October 28 st. v.: next which will be visible to us if ye aire be serene & cleare[8] of which I could wish the Dantiscan Ephemeridist[9] were before hand, from hence, informed; that so hee may bend his mind hereafter to make truer calculations for hee supposes, for ought I can perceive yt ye visible angle of ye way of Mercury sub sole wth ye Ecliptick is the same at ye earth which it is at ye Sun, which is ye error of Hevelius;[10] or lesse, which once occasiond a Controversie betwixt Mr Wing wth Mr Street[11] & those calculations which Street has given us in his Exam. Examinat: Yu will there likewise find 2 transits of Mercury sub sole to be observed in ye next century. of all which I suppose on this occasion ye author himselfe may give yu information: I therefore forbeare any further:

I have not of late made many observations, ye heavens beeing either overclouded, when I designed them or too cold for my weake temper to beare. Some calculations I have made for my intended tract, of ye planets distances & diameters by which I find yt Mars his parallax in horizonte was not more then 15″ in my September observations[12] whence it follows that ye Suns is almost 7″; & his distance above 29000 semidiameters:[13] Mr Sargeant cannot stay let this suffice till next weeke I shall visit yu by my freind Mr Litchford,[14] I am ever

> Your obliged servant
> *John Flamsteed*

ADDRESS

> For Henry Oldenburge Esq
> these

NOTES

1 See Letter 2062, note 1.
2 The "Prutenick" calculations derive from Erasmus Reinhold, *Prutenicae tabulae coelestium motuum* (Tübingen, 1551); the Danish from Christianus Severini Longomontanus, *Astronomia Danica* (Amsterdam, 1622); the Lansbergian from *Philippi Lansbergii Tabulae coelestium motuum perpetuae* (Middelburg, 1632).
3 "Mercury across the sun."
4 In *Astronomia Philolaica* (Paris, 1645).
5 "across the sun;" Pierre Gassendi's famous and unique observation was described in his *Mercurius in sole visus et Venus invisa* (Paris, 1632).
6 "Angle of the visible path of Mercury with the ecliptic."
7 Thomas Streete, *Examen examinatum: or Wing's examination of Astronomia Carolina examined* (London, 1667).
8 It was in fact observed by Edmond Halley at St. Helena on the predicted day.
9 I.e., Hecker.
10 See Vol. II, pp. 187–89, 220, 306–7, 396–98.
11 Vincent Wing had published *Examen Astronomiae Carolinae* at London in 1665, to which Streete responded in the work cited in note 7 above.
12 See Letter 2097.
13 Flamsteed's value for the solar parallax (correctly, 8·8″ roughly) is now too small—and of course far smaller than the estimates then current.
14 William Litchford, with whom Flamsteed had been acquainted for several years on account of his knowledge of the planets (Autobiography: Baily, p. 11).

2154 bis
Reisel to Oldenburg
17 February 1672/3

According to Reisel's Letter 2246 (Vol. X) of 10 June 1673, he received Oldenburg's Letter 2131 on 12 February 1672/3, and replied five days later. He sent the letter to William Schröter (or Schröder) to be delivered by him while he was in England, but Schröter did not receive the letter before his departure from England, and it seems likely that it was lost in the post. It contained Reisel's "observations of the circulation of the urine," a paper subsequently published in *Miscellanea Curiosa* (see Letter 2131, note 3).

2155
Oldenburg to Malpighi
18 February 1672/3

From the original in Bologna University MS. 2085, VII, ff. 26–27
Printed in Pizzoli, pp. 60–61

Celeberrimo Viro
Domino Marcello Malpighio, Phil. et Med. Bononiensi
Henr. Oldenburg Salutem

Summa animorum lubentia percuriosam juxta ac perdoctam amplexata est Societas Regia Exercitationem, qua Ipsam denuo recreare et locupletare voluisti. Agnoscunt certe dotes tuas vere Philosophicas, solers ingenium, gnavam industriam, et candorem nulli secundum. Laetantur magnopere, statuisse Te indefesso studio caeptas operas urgere et provehere. Omniumque nostrum vota in valetudinis et omnigenae felicitatis tuae firmamentum augmentumque consociantur.

Commisimus curae Excellentissimi Equitis Johannis Finchij, Regis nostri ad Portam Ottomannicam constituti Legati, Exemplaria triginta Exercitationis tuae de Ovo prioris,[1] quae brevi (sic speramus) temporis spatio Tibi reddentur, Legato illo Genuam vel Liburnum usque terra iter faciente, et fortassis Aulam quoque Florentinam, unde facile et tuto ad Te transmittentur, invisuro. Quamprimum major Editionis illius Exemplarium numerus a Bibliopola, qui expensas fecit, fuerit distributus, in eo sane erimus, ut et hic ingenii et industriae tuae faetus pulcherrimus maturrime lucem videat.[2]

Videt Doctissimus Dominus Grew, quae humaniter adeo et candide de libello ejus sentis,[3] Insigne profecto videtur argumentum veritatis, quando plures viri ingenui et docti, locis et studiorum commercio licet disjuncti, in ijsdem tamen, quoad rei caput, Observatis conveniunt. Immane quantum id accendere potis est ipsorum animos, ut in laboribus et investigationibus suis alacriter pergant, eoque ipso tum Honoris Templum perenne Virtuti suae exstruant, tum uberrimam posteritati lucem in consectandis perficiendisque scientiis praeferant.

Brevi, ni fallor, ad Te mittam, quae Nobilissimus Boylius contra Henricum Morum, nonnulla in ipsius scriptis oppugnantem, doctissime commentatus est, una cum Experimentis et Observationibus circa Effluvia[e] et Flammae ponderabilitatem novis; quibus addam, Deo dante, quae Clarissimi Viri Brownius et Scharrockius nostrates (duo sc. illi, quos Dominus Grew in libello suo indigitat) de Plantis ante aliquot annos in lucem emisere.[4] Vale, et a Regia Societate plurimum Salve. Dabam Londini d. 18. Febr. 1673.

ADDRESS

All Illustrissimo Signore
Il Signor Marcello Malpighi, Dottore
et Professore Bolognese,
Patrono suo colendissime
    Bologna
    in Italia

TRANSLATION

Henry Oldenburg greets the very celebrated Mr. Marcello Malpighi, philosopher and physician of Bologna

The Royal Society has accepted with the greatest gladness of mind the very curious and learned essay with which you have recently invigorated and enriched them. They emphatically acknowledge your truly philosophical endowments: your inventive intelligence, your tireless industry, and your honesty second to none. They very much rejoice that you have decided to continue and advance with unremitting zeal the works you have begun. You have the combined wishes of every one of us for a continuance and increase of your health and every form of happiness.

We have entrusted thirty copies of your former essay on the egg to the care of the most excellent Sir John Finch, appointed as our King's ambassador to the Ottoman Porte:[1] these (we hope) will be delivered to you in a short space of time, as the ambassador is travelling by land as far as Genoa or Livorno, and perhaps to the court of Tuscany as well, whence one supposes they may be easily and safely sent on to you. As soon as a larger number of copies of this publication has been distributed by the bookseller who has borne the expense of it we confidently expect that this other fine fruit of your intelligence and industry will also see the light very speedily here.[2]

The learned Dr. Grew shall see your kind and honest opinion of his little book.[3] It is a great argument for the truth of observations when several learned and intelligent men agree upon them, as to the principal points, though separated geographically and distinct as to the manner of their research. It is a very great incentive to their pursuing their labors and researches vigorously, and thereby both building a perpetual monument of honor to their merits and affording posterity an ample guidance for the study and perfection of the sciences.

I shall soon, if I am not mistaken, send you the very noble Boyle's comments criticizing Henry More, who has opposed some things in his writings, together with [his] new experiments and observations concerning the ponderability of effluvia and flame; to which I shall add, God willing, what our famous Browne and Sharrock (the two men, that is to say, to whom Mr. Grew referred in his little book) published about plants a few years ago.[4] Farewell, with many good wishes from the Royal Society. London, 18 February 1673.

ADDRESS

To the very illustrious Mr. Marcello Malpighi,
Doctor and Professor of Bologna,
My good lord,
At Bologna in Italy

NOTES

Reply to Letter 2073.

1 See Letters 2101, note, and 2102.

2 Although John Martin made a second issue of *De formatione pulli in ovo* together with *De bombyce* in 1673, the new essay appeared only as an *Appendix iteratas et auctas . . . de ovo incubato observationes continens* to *Anatome plantarum*, issued by Martin in 1675.

3 In fact Grew wrote to Malpighi on 5 March—there is a copy in the Royal Society MS. G 1, no. 34; Malpighi never received this letter (see Adelmann, I, 699).

4 In the preface to *The Anatomy of Vegetables Begun* (London, 1672) Grew mentioned the previous neglect of his subject "except some Observations of some of our own Countrey-men," and on p. 109 refers to an observation of "the Ingenious Mr. Shar-

rock." Robert Sharrock had published *The History of the Propagation and Improvement of Vegetables by the concurrence of Art and Nature* at Oxford in 1660. Grew does not refer to Thomas Browne (who yet is presumably meant here); he wrote briefly on plants in Chapter VI of *Pseudodoxia Epidemica* (London, 1646), and more extensively in *The Garden of Cyrus* (London, 1658).

2156

Flamsteed to Oldenburg

20 February 1672/3

From the original in Royal Society MS. F 1, no. 95

Derby: Feb: 20: 1672

Mr Oldenburge
Sir

Mr Sargeants iorney hapning a day sooner then hee had informed mee I had not time to finish that letter[1] as intended in which I would have requested you to let mee know what newes yu have heard from Hevelius (from whom I doubt not but yu receaved something when Heckerus's Mercury's were sent)[2] & when wee may expect his *Machina* which yu Informed mee long since had beene some while under the presse: I therfore make bold by my freind Mr. Litchford to enquire this of yu & whether hee has finished his catalogue of ye fixed stars,[3] & if wee may not expect it in that peece: I hope yu will not thinke it a trouble to let him know this[4] from yu who is

Yr ever obliged servant
John Flamsteed

I shall want an object glasse for a 14 foot tube praecise: I wish yu would let mee know at what price I may procure one:

J: F:

NOTES

1 Letter 2154.
2 The last letter from Hevelius was dated 19 October 1672 (Letter 2083); Hecker wrote Letter 2092.

3 Hevelius' star catalogues were published after his death by his widow (*Prodromus astronomiae cum catalogo et Firmamentum Sobiescianum*, Danzig, 1690).

4 It appears from Flamsteed's letter to Collins of 19 March 1672/3 (Rigaud, II, 161–62) that this present letter was left with Collins, and Oldenburg had then not yet replied to it.

2157
Towneley to Oldenburg
20 February 1672/3

From the original in Royal Society MS. T, no. 26

Towneley Feb: 20. 1672/3

Sr

I had resolved not to have troubled you till some thing worth communicating unto you had offerd it selfe, but ye other day receiving your present[1] and your desire of hearing of my receipt of it, I can not but obey your commands though as unfurnisht as ever with anie novelties haveing not onelie had a long indisposition my selfe but allso ye sadest of afflictions ye losse of a wife,[2] wch hath not given me leave to think of anie thing of studie. I had latelie a letter from Monsr. De Sluse,[3] and in it an abridgment of his method of Tangents he signifies he hath sent you wch I shall hope to find in ye next Transactions.[4]

I know not whether it be worth acquainting you yt ye mercurie in ye Barometer hath beene verie low severall days together under 29 Inches since ye 14 of ys monethe but ye lowest on ye 17. betwixt 11. and 3 of ye clock being all yt time 28.05, after wch day it began to rise so yt at 9h at night it was 28.47, and ys day 28.97. If anie persons had ye good fortune to observe about what time it was ye lowest at London, I should be obliged to you for your information of it, as allso for an account of what is done about ye surprising experiment of ye high suspention of ye mercurie in small tubes.[5] Or for anie information of what your R. Societie is about would highlie oblige Sr

your most humble servant
Rich: Towneley

ADDRESS
    These
For Mr Henry Ouldenbourg
at his house in ye Pellmall
        Westminster

POSTMARK FE 24

NOTES

1 No doubt a copy of Hecker's *Admonitio*.
2 Towneley had married *c.* 1653 Margaret Paston, daughter of Clement Paston of Barningham Hall, Norfolk; the Pastons were another old Catholic family.
3 Compare Letter 2076 and its note 11.
4 See Letter 2124; evidently Towneley had not seen the January *Transactions*.
5 Wallis's paper on this subject was to appear in *Phil. Trans.*, no. 91 (24 February 1672/3), 5160–70; compare Letter 2072, note.

2158
Oldenburg to Lambecius
21 February 1672/3
From the copy in Royal Society MS. O 2, no. 75

Illustri Viro
Domino Petro Lambecio, Sacrae Caesaris Majestatis
Consiliario, Historiographo et Bibliothecario
Henricus Oldenburg
Salutem

Commodam hanc nactus occasionem, qua Excellentissimus Comes de Peterborough, et Amplissimus Eques Wychius, uterque e Societate Regia, Viennam proficisci statuere;[1] ambabus ulnis amplexare libuit, ut hac ratione officia mea paratissima de novo tibi offerre, inque labores tuos litterarios, quibus impraesentiarum addictus es, inquirere possum.

Vidimus Splendidissima tua volumina, quae nuper in Bibliothecae Caesareae ornamentum et decus proprium in lucem emisisti.[2] Vidimus insuper Collegij Germanorum Illustrissimi Ephemerides Phylosophicas.

Perplacet utrumque, nec dubium est ullum, quin quo caepistis pede jugiter sitis et alacriter progressuri, eoque ipso Germaniae nostrae gloriam et scientiarum utilium augmentum provecturi.

Mitto hic Cl. Heckeri Mercurium in Sole, seu admonitionem ejus ad Astronomos editam, de Mercurij in discum Solis incursu, proximi anni vere observando. Velimus utique, ut vestrates Astronomi ad curatam ejus observationem instituendam (quem in finem mature adeo prostat hoc scriptum,) excitentur, cui negotio, ut operam et curam tuam impendere ne graveris, enixe rogitamus. Vale et Tui studiosissimo favere perge. Dabam Londini die 21 Februarij 1672.

TRANSLATION

Henry Oldenburg greets the illustrious Petrus Lambecius, Councilor, Historiographer and Librarian to his Sacred Imperial Majesty

I was eager to take full advantage of the opportunity provided by the decision of the most excellent Earl of Peterborough and the very worthy Sir [Peter] Wyche, both Fellows of the Royal Society, to make a journey to Vienna,[1] so that I might in this way offer my most ready services to you afresh, and inquire as to the literary tasks you are undertaking at the present time.

We have seen those superb volumes which you lately published as an ornament to the Imperial library and an honor to yourself.[2] Moreover, we have seen the philosophical *Miscellanea* of the most illustrious German College. They have both given satisfaction, and there is no doubt but that you will continue along the path you have taken and make rapid progress, and in this way advance both the fame of our Germany and the development of the useful sciences.

I send [you] here Hecker's *Mercurius in Sole*, or notice published for the benefit of astronomers of Mercury's transit across the disk of the sun to be observed in the spring of next year. We are extremely eager that your astronomers should be urged to make careful observation of it (for which reason this paper is on sale so early); and we earnestly beg you to be so good as to devote your care and effort to this object. Farewell, and continue to favor him who is most devoted to you. London, 21 February 1672.

NOTES

1 Henry Mordaunt, second Earl of Peterborough (1624?–97), a gallant royalist, briefly governor of Tangier after the Restoration and naval commander, was appointed Groom of the Stole to the Duke of York in 1670 and, on 14 February 1672/3, ambassador extraordinary to arrange the Duke's (second) marriage with the Archduchess Claudia Felicitas of Innsbruck. He was already on his way to Vienna when informed

of the Emperor's decision to wed this lady himself. Later he inspected other possible brides, and finally (on 30 September 1673) stood in as proxy in the marriage of James to Mary of Modena, whom he escorted home to England. He was elected F.R.S. on 18 November 1663.

Sir Peter Wyche (the younger, 1628–?99) was an Original Fellow of the Royal Society, mentioned previously in the correspondence for his knowledge of Portuguese. He traveled with Peterborough as Secretary to the Embassy.

2 See Vol. VII, p. 476, note 1.

2159
Oldenburg to Julius Reichelt
21 February 1672/3
From the copy in Royal Society MS. O 2, no. 74

Clarissimo Viro
Domino Julio Reicheltio Mathematico Argentoratensi
Henricus Oldenburg salutem

Lubens equidem occasionem hanc arripio; qua Nobilissimus Comes de Peterborough et Spectatissimus Eques Wychius Argentoratum proficisci decrevere.[1] Mentem subitant illa, quae Celeberrimus Mauritius,[2] Camerae Imperialis Assessor meritissimus, de suis[3] circa de nuperrimum Cometam Observatis praeterita aestate nobis communicaverat. Prodijt ex eo tempore Doctissimi Heckeri ad Astronomos editum de Mercurij in discum solis incursu observando Monitum. Dubius, an Exemplaria ejus ad universitatem vestram pervenerint, id quod hic insertum vides transmittere ad Te volui, certus omnino, Te observationi adeo curiosae raraeque diligenter invigilaturum, nobisque observationum tuorum summam deinceps significaturum. Vides mature admodum in lucem prodijsse hanc admonitionem, ut scilicet in quasvis Mundi plagas, ubicumque harum rerum studiosi commorantur, mature possit transmitti; ijque ad sollicitas hujus Phaenomeni observationes sciscitari.[4] Vale, Vir Clarissime, et Tibi addictissimo fave. Dabam Londini d. 21. Februarij 1672.

TRANSLATION

Henry Oldenburg greets the very famous Mr. Julius Reichelt, Mathematician of Strasbourg

I gladly seize this opportunity of the decision by the very noble Earl of Peterborough and the excellent Sir [Peter] Wyche to travel to Strasbourg.[1] There comes to mind what the very celebrated Mauritius,[2] most worthy assessor of the Imperial Chamber, communicated to us last summer about his [your][3] observations concerning the most recent comet. Since that time there has appeared the published notice to astronomers of the very learned Hecker, about observing a transit of Mercury across the sun's disk. Being doubtful whether copies of it have reached your university I wished to send you that which you see enclosed here, being quite sure that you will diligently look out for so rare and strange an observation, and will afterwards impart to us a summary of your observations. You will see that this notice has appeared so very early in order that it may be sent in good time to all parts of the world where dwell those studious of such matters, and they informed [to make][4] careful observations of this phenomenon. Farewell, famous Sir, and favor him who is most devoted to you. London, 21 February 1672.

NOTES

For the recipient of this letter see Vol. VIII, p. 600, note 1.
1 See Letter 2158, note 1.
2 See Letter 1927 (Vol. VIII) and its note.
3 Or possibly "tuis" ("your"), which would be more appropriate.
4 The last sentence does not make sense, but its purport is obvious.

2160

Martel to Oldenburg

25 February 1672/3

From the original in Royal Society MS. M 1, no. 58

A Mont. de 7 Mars 1673 [N.S.]

Il me semble, Monsieur, quil y à trop de temps que nous ne scavons rien l'un de l'autre,[1] Ce n'est pas de ma part que Je ne pense souvent à Vous avec plaisir et que Vous m'amiez tousiours, mais scachant Vos occupations et Vos grandes correspondances plus utiles Je garde le silence par discretion, ce pais ne produissant rien à Vous estre communiqué pour grossier le ramas que vous faites d'Infinies belles choses, et ma philosophie ne me fournissant non plus rien dont Je desire faire estat. Mais enfin Vous demeurez bien a nostre amitté d'agreer que Je vous demande des nouvelles de Vostre estat par Mr. Ravisse, pendant que Je ne cesse de Vous le souhaiter heureux de toutes les façons, sans oublier[?] Vos progres dans la philosophie Experimentale et si le succes de Vos soins respondra à Vostre attente, que Je scache aussi si l'Incomparable Mr. Boyle à la santé assez bonne pour continuer ses recherches, et ce qu'il en faut attendre. Vous estes l'un et l'autre si necessaires à la philosophie que par cette consideration tout le monde le doibt Interesser en la santé et au repos de tout deux, ce que faict particulierement de par dessus tous

Vostre treshumble et tresobeiss. serviteur
De Martel

ADDRESS
A Monsieur
Monsieur Oldenburg
A Londres

TRANSLATION

Montauban, 7 March 1673 [N.S.]

It seems to me, Sir, that for too long a time we have learned nothing of one another.[1] It is not, on my side, that I do not think often of you and [believe] that you continue to love me, but knowing your affairs and your more useful voluminous correspondence, I discreetly keep quiet, since this part of the world produces nothing to be communicated to you to swell the collection you are making of infinitely fine things, and my philosophy furnishes me with nothing either about which I wish to make anything. But you yet remain so firmly fixed in our friendship as to permit me to ask for news of your state by Mr. Ravisse (while I never cease to wish for your happiness in all ways), not forgetting the progress you make in experimental philosophy and whether your labors attain the success you expect, and may I know also if the incomparable Mr. Boyle remains well enough to continue his researches, and what we may expect of them. You are both so necessary to philosophy that, from this consideration, everyone ought to concern himself about the health and rest of both of you, as does particularly, above all others,

your very humble and obedient servant
Martel

ADDRESS

Mr. Oldenburg
London

NOTE

1 Apparently Martel had never replied to Oldenburg's Letter 1379 of 29 January 1669/70 (see Vol. VI, pp. 453–54).

2161

Oldenburg to Lister

25 February 1672/3

From the memorandum in Royal Society MS. W 2, no. 5

Febr. 25. I sent ye Note about Veines in Plants to Mr Lister, . . .

NOTE

This memorandum is written on Wallis's Letter 2153.

2162

Oldenburg to Beale

25 February 1672/3

From the memorandum in Royal Society MS. W 2, no. 5

Febr. 25 . . . and at ye same time [I sent] ye note about Raining Ice to Dr Beale.

NOTE

This, like Letter 2161, is written on Wallis's Letter 2153.

2163

Oldenburg to Wallis

25 February 1672/3

From the memorandum in Royal Society MS. W 2, no. 5

Rec. Febr. 21
Febr. 25 . . . I answerd ye same [day] Dr Wallis and told him of my Ld. Brounckers not excepting agst his Mercurial letter.

NOTE

Reply to Letter 2153. This memorandum is a continuation of Letters 2161 and 2162.

2164
Oldenburg to Williamson
26 February 1672/3
From the original in P.R.O. MS. S.P. 29/334, no. 14

Febr. 26.
h. 8. vesp.

Sir,

The original of ye inclosed I received not till between 6 and 7 a clocke. Tis now about 8th, yt I have dispatcht it; some of wch may, I think, make part of ye gazette to morrow.

At the end of the German letter[1] I find so[me] particulars, wch I thought not fit to mingle wth the publick news; and they are;

1. That you are desired to send a pair of silk-stockings of perle-color to the son of the writer, to weare ym for yr sake.

2. That you would speak again to Monsr Lionberg,[2] that ye Tapis-series, he knows of, may be fetch't away and paid for; it being a great losse to him, saith the writer, yt he must pay for ym.

3. That in the English Post-office the Letters are sometimes visited;[3] wch may expose him, ye writer, to great danger.

4. That from the 23th of August till now he hath sent 4. letters every week; and yt he desires to know, whether he shall so continue.

Sir,

I sent this morning early what particulars I could collect out of ye papers remaining in my hands for the next gazette. I received nothing new from you since, but the Highdutch letters of March 2, here Englisht.

Yr humble servant
H.O.

ADDRESS

For Sir Joseph Williamson
these

NOTES

This letter has at some time been cut up and remounted. The enclosures (Letter 2164a) are not in Oldenburg's hand, nor in that of the Royal Society's amanuensis. Compare Letter 2152, note 6.

1 This was evidently addressed to Williamson himself, and is not among the enclosures.
2 Johann Leijonberg; see Vol. VIII, p. 383, note 2.
3 That is, intercepted.

2164a

Summaries of Letters

Enclosures with Letter 2164
From the copy in P.R.O. MS. S.P. 29/334, no. 14

No. 1 A superscription on this Cover, thus
　　For Dr. Poleman at Westminster[1]
　　　in Strutton ground,[2] In London
Containes three Papers
　　The first subscribed S de Geer (seeming to be the hand of one of the eminent Merchants in Amsterdam of that name)[3] treates of Bookes in the presse, & Manuscripts, and Comenius likely being at Dantzick & coming to Amsterdam about the Spring, except worse accidents happen[4]
　　He alludes to sad presages of Amsterdams & the whole States destruction, and advices whither best to transfer his estate & goods, not liking Emden, for the difficulty sake &c.
　　Many parts of the letter are deprecations of evill, & trust in God that the French devastations may be bridled, and desires to heare good newes & what is doing in England—.

　　The second is a Relation in High Dutch of the continuance of certain Visions of S.M. Anno 1670. consisting of 7 Articles: with Extract of a letter & writings from Poland & Hungary touching the Kings gaining upon the Malcontents. The wonderful Wormes in figure & colour fallen wth a great Snow, & living three dayes, at the end whereof the small ones devoured the bigger. The Rebels ioyned finally wth the Turkes, whence a Winter dessign feared in hand against Hungary, whereof one Count Petrozzi is named King by the Grand Signior, the Rebels leader, a stout souldier. Meanewhile the Imperiall Regiments too weake to make opposition: Lastly A short relation of the penitent death of one Nic. Drabitii: wch the writer sayes was very dangerous to be discovered, and letters narrowly search'd for.

The Third, Is a draught with a Pen of Nine of the said Wormes, being all different in shape or colour Yellow, blew & black, & mixt.

No. 2 Is a letter of Abraham de Hertogh's from Rotterdam to Mr Ger. Zas Advocat of Holland, Lodged at Sr Edw. Brets in the Pelmel London, dated 8. Febr. 1673.[5] Wherein the contents are as followeth,

That *10* dayes afore he had written under cover of one Abraham Momma, and sent a Petition with it framed by advise of Counsellor Wolfse Cousin to both, who could not iudge otherwise, but that his Maty would find reason & cause to graunt it, because it would occasion consumtion, whereby the poore inhabitants of the Hils of the Colepits might gaine a plentifull livelyhood.[6]

That the Prince at his return by Willemstadt saw & liked the draught. He forebeares to repeat the same, but desires it to be asked for, if not yet come to his hand.

That this day he spake wth Heer Kyevit[7] about it, who was of opinion it would succeede, because advantagious to the Kings Customes, his poorest subiects, and his Highnesses Towne, not disliking the use of his name to his old friends My Lo. Arlington & Sr Gabr. Sylvius,[8] & that himself would write so to them that veryday, but going to his house he had wanted time, being gone hastily to ye Hagh.

He mentions the way of trade by shipping that passe free wth unregistred Passes: and that Kyevit esteemed this busines so good, as if he (Zas) *dwelt* not now in England, he (de Hertogh) ought to have sent over his son apurpose. He hopes it wilbe done this Spring, & so time gaind to have it approved in Holland; and then to provide convenient shipping.

Also that he hath obtaind the *Action* of the West India ship together wth the former desire, or apart singly, so as to fetch it & sugar to wch he relates

That the Burgess were drawne forth in a strong body &c

No. 3 A Pacquet Superscribed thus in English:

This letter is to be delivered to my most honored friend Mr Gerbrandt Zas privy-Counseller of his Higness the Prince of Orange in his owne hands.

Containes,

A long letter from the Hagh 3 Febr. st. No. 1673. subscribed instead of a name wth 3 Adverbs—Audacter, Sapienter, Vigilanter, and beginning, Amicorum intime.[9]

It is clearly from a fellow Advocat of his, earnestly craving his good offices to the Pensionary Fagel,[10] to be preferd, for getting one foote into the styrrop, he should soone leap into the saddle. And he is glad for the receipt of his deare letter from Harwich of the 15/25 of Jany last wch he recd 1 febr. & now answers hereby, Sending wthall the Iudgement against the executed Col. Painand Vin:[11] whereby to observe how the late Secretary of *TerGou*[12] vander Tochts coate had been brushed cleene. That this was his 5th letter. Not intending other, or sooner to write, before assured under Sasses owne hand that he have well received all, whereof he sent two by *Dixon*, two by *Bolton* in St Martins-Lane, and this by Dixon: intending to observe if any miscarry'd, and then to write constantly what passeth in Holland. That he had pointed out before to him a Correspondent of Chanternels *James Burkin* being in company with one *Everson*,[13] to be easily found in London Exchange, who also hath one *William de Weerdt*, also wellknowne, besides the Widow & Eyres of *John Vermeersch*, *Adrian Beyer*, and *John Wolff*, wch last subvirgulated[14] persons doe hold close correspondence wth one Elias Marchant a Negociant in Haarlem, a *confiding* friend whom this writer serves in matters of consequence, and therefore if he (Zas) desire to write anything in *private*, he is to use *those* persons: and to the end it may be done wth more ease & secrecy, he sends him a Cifer or transposd Alphabet thus

That he had seen his wife & children & been an howre in visit wth them, being all well, but troubled this frosty weather, disswading them from apprehension

That many guesse what his (Zasses) busines in England may be, but none yet have hit on the right.

That from Colen newes is written to the States of two Munster Regiments quite cut off. He wishes it may often happen that the Bp may quickly leave armes & betake him to a Cloyster.*

*Huc spectant[15]
A letter of Zasses wife to him of kindnes & wishes
A letter from hir to the Lady Bret, to the same tune.

NOTES

1 For this man, see Vol. III, p. 34, note 14; the Polemann who was Hartlib's friend —and apparently resident in London for many years before the present time—was certainly also a friend of Comenius.

2 Still so called, in S.W.1, and scene of a street market.
3 For Oldenburg's familiarity with members of this family, see Vol. II, pp. 233, 237, note 10; and Vol. III, p. 18.
4 Possibly Oldenburg misread his source. For Comenius died at the house of Laurence de Geer in Amsterdam (and was buried in that city) on 5 November 1670. It is extraordinary that Oldenburg should be unaware of this event. However, the reference to the "French devastations" seems to indicate that the date of writing could not in any case be earlier than the summer of 1672. (We gave the date of Comenius' death incorrectly in Vol. IV, p. 389, note, and index).
5 For Zas (then in the Tower) see Letter 2152, note 4. Sir Edward Brett (knighted in 1644) was governor of York Castle 1664–66, and captain of a company in the Earl of Oxford's regiment.
6 This is all very mysterious; it *may* refer to some scheme for exporting coal to Holland, or perhaps for exporting coal free of duty elsewhere.
7 Sir Jan Kiviet or Kievit (d. 1692) had been Burgomaster of Rotterdam, but came to England about 1666, when Evelyn knew him, as a political refugee, being a supporter of the Prince of Orange. Charles II made him a baronet in 1667. He had great plans for introducing "clinker brick" (pale, hard Dutch bricks, or just possibly bricks exposed to a high temperature and partial vitrification) into English dock construction, and was interested in draining engines.
8 Sir Gabriel Sylvius (d. 1697) was another Dutch-English courtier and diplomat, also well known to Evelyn. He was knighted in 1670, and in 1677 was to marry an Englishwoman, Ann Howard, a friend of Evelyn.
9 "Boldly, wisely, carefully . . . intimate friend."
10 Kaspar Fagel (1629–88) began his career as pensionary of Haarlem; in 1670 he was clerk to the States General but, adhering to the party of the Prince of Orange he was appointed Grand Pensionary on 20 August 1672 [N.S.], the very day of the murder of the de Witts.
11 Or, possibly, "Pain and Vin."
12 Properly, "Ter Gouw," modern Gouda.
13 James Burkin and Joas Everson are mentioned several times in C.S.P.D. at this time; they were partners, and London merchants. None of the other names mentioned here can be further identified.
14 This word does not seem to be known to dictionary-makers; it probably means here "underlined."
15 "These are relevant."

2165
Leibniz to Oldenburg
26 February 1672/3

From the original in B.M. MS. Add. 4294, no. 48
Printed in Gerhardt, pp. 81–84

Paris 8. Mart. sty. nov. 1673

Amplissime Vir

Ubi primum Parisios feliciter appuli, illud inter primas meas curas fuit, ut ad Te literas grati animi indices, & commercii excultrices darem.

Ante omnia non dubito libros quos a Te mutuos habebam, recte ad Te perlatos, eos enim mane discessurus, quando perferendi spatium non supererat, Nobilissimo Schrodero[1] commendavj, adjectis ad Te literis meis,[2] quibus alias ad Illustrem Societatem Regiam incluseram voti mei, coram, Tibi expositi, et a Te approbati indicatrices.[3]

Illud certe tuto meo nomine spondere potes, daturum me operam, ne tantos viros poeniteat, hominem quantuluncumque, optime tamen animatum, benigne suscepisse.

Illustrissimo Boylio cum salute a me, obsequia & venerationem denunties oro: ita enim Illi pariter Tibique, imo amicis meis omnibus persuasum esse volo, testorque quoties occasio est, Virum esse maximis ab omni memoria hominibus coennumerandum, et cui statuas aliquando debere se agiturum sit humanum genus. Quaeso quem ille promisit mihi *Catalogum commutandorum*,[4] fac mature teneam favore Tuo, ac reciproca ei a me promitte.

Sane afflixit nos non mediocriter infelix Nuntius de Eminentissimi Electoris Moguntini morte,[5] quem Caleti offendimus, in quo Principe certum est non Rempublicam tantum, sed & Philosophiam plurimum perdidisse. Solamur nos tum successore,[6] Episcopo Spirensi, principe non sapiente tantum, sed & ad mechanica usque curioso, eidemque familiae illigato, nam frater eius Schönbornii, qui apud Vos nunc fuit,[7] sororem in matrimonio habet; tum quod literae chartaeque omnes, inprimis quae ad rem philosophicam spectare possint, in manu nostra erunt; sed *hoc non nisi ad Te scriptum volvaturque Illustrissimum Boylium.*

De caetero Illustrissimum Boylium quaeso roga, ut si placet, *menstruum stanni*, ut spem fecit, mecum communicet.[8] A Te quoque, Domine, prout promisisti, exspecto illam in *metallum impressionem*, cujus mentio fit in historia Societatis.[9] Quicquid vicissim imperabis, exequar sedulo.

In *Instrumento* meo *Arithmetico* laboratur strenue.[10] Reperi certissimam rationem in exiguum spatium, ac si placet, baculum includendi, idque sive *Elateria* sive tantum *Rotas* adhibeas : neque id ex iis quae jam habebam difficile erat praestare. Quare pro certo habeo, Clarissimum Hoockium se non mixturum inventioni alterius; ejus enim generositatis ac prudentiae esse arbitror, ut propria potius inventa, quibus non caret, poliat, quam ab alio jam publice proposita involet.[11] Sane ex relatione eius quam mihi praesente Clarissimo Hackio fecit, constabat, fundamentum constructionis idem esse cum meo : tantum ab eo compendium promitti. Nec, dicere poterit, ipsum fundamentum ei sine me in mentem venisse, cum duo constet, (1) nemini eum unquam de tali re locutem, antequam ego in Angliam cum machina mea veni, (2) machinam meam ab eo diligenter et curiose, ex proximo fuisse inspectam. Cum enim eam in Regia Societate exponerem, ipse sane proximus fuit, asserculum posticum, quo tegebatur, amovit, omnia, quae dicebam, excepit : ac proinde qua est sagacitate & rerum mechanicarum peritia, dicere non potest mea a se non percepta. Equidem omnes rotas meas non assecutum distincte, facile concessero : at sufficit in talibus homini ingenioso et mechanico ideam instituti rudem, imo exteriorem operandi modum, semel vidisse, ad aliquid de suo postea comminiscendum, quod in Rotarum tantum complicatione consistit, quae a variis varie fieri potest.

Scimus viros candidos et generosos, si quid deprehenderant, quod ad aliena inventa augenda pertineret, maluisse additamenta sua atque accessiones autoribus concedere, quam in suspicionem incurrere parum ingenuae mentis et egeni verae gloriae animi si falsum quadam inhonesta rapacitate aucuparentur. Ita Post inventa a Galilaeo sidera Medicaea Peirescius in periodos eorum observandas summo studio incubuit; at ubi autorem intellexit ad eandem curam animum appulisse longitudinum causa, sua ei omnia ultro lubens concessit, idque justitiae esse ratus est.[12] Ita Gassendus in Selenographiam quadam diligenter incuberat, multasque jam figuras Telescopio adhibito delineatas in aere sculpi curaverat; at ubi intellexit praeoccupatam esse ab Hevelio provinciam, propiusque eum a meta abesse, non destitit tantum, sed et suarum observationum participem fecit.[13] Contra inventoris est, ei quoque se obligatum publice confiteri, cuius monitis cogitate sua crevere.

Quare breviter : cum substantia inventi mea sit, aut hausta ex meo; cum quicquid Hookius tantundem ego praestiturus sim, Clarissimum Virum, qua est virtute rei meae cultum ac polituram mihi relicturum, imo si quas habet admonitiones earum mihi copiam liberaliter facturum, interventu praesertim TUO, spero; quod si faciet, publice candorem laudabo, sin minus, rem faciet neque concepta de se opinione, neque natione sua, neque Regia Societate dignam.

Caeterum cum optima quaeque sperem, hoc non nisi TIBI ac si placet Illustrissimo Boylio scriptum volui, ut, si occasio ferat, a coepto eum deducatis, imo communicationem ei persuadeatis. Quare hactenus nemini nisi Boylio TIBIque verbum de re dixi scripsive.

Locutus est mihi Dominus Boylius de quodam *praedictore ventorum*, qui et menstruas suas praedictiones mittere solebat, sic satis veraces. Interroga quaeso an novissime miserit et satisne veras.

A domino Hookio sciscitare quaeso, quid de Blondelliana circa *Trabium aequiresistentium* figuram demonstratione sentiat, quando ipsum quoque de ea re meditatum ais.[14]

Diarium homunculi Gerickiani continuatur cum successu.[15]

Oblitus sum a Domino Boylio quaerere, quid sentiat de experimento Hugeniano in Diario eruditorum aliquando relato de *duabus laminis* sive Tabulis politis,[16] in vacuo aeque ac in pleno non divulsis, cum tamen meminerim contrarium experimentum a Boylio in novissimis de vi Elastica narratum esse.[17]

De *Algebra* pervelim nosse, an aliquid circa depressiones aequationum insignes viri apud vos, Illustrissimus Brunkerus, tum viri, Clarissimus Wallisius, Pellius, Mercator, Gregorius aliique praestiterint. Parisiis est dominus Osannam juvenis in Algebra versatissimus, qui nobis aliquid in eo genere Idem Diophantum promotum dabit, reperta ratione solvendi problemata, quae neque ex Diophanto, neque ex cognita hactenus Algebra poterant solvi.[18] Ecce TIBI.

Quatuor problemata, quae, inquit, palam proposuit,
et quorum hactenus nemo dedit solutionem:

(1) Invenire infinita Triangula rectangula diversae speciei, in quorum singulis area detracta *lateri minori* circa rectum, et hypotenusae, si[n]gillatim, relinquat quadratos.

(2) Invenire infinita Triangula rectangula diversae speciei, in quorum etc. ut paulo ante, substituto *latere majore*.

(3) Invenire Triangulum rectangulum, in quo differentia quadratorum laterum circa rectum detracta alteruti eorum summae, et differentiae, sigillatim, relinquat quadratos.

(4) Invenire tres numeros ut summa duorum quorumlibet sit quadratus et differentia duorum quorumlibet etiam quadratus.

Haec problemata quae difficillima, ac taediosissima nec nisi post diuturni temporis impensas solubilia videri possent, ab illo tamen nova quadam methodo, paucis lineis, ut vidi, soluta sunt: ipse aliis solvenda consideran-daque proponit, optatque de iis sententias intelligere egregiorum apud Vos Algebristarum, ut appareat nova an trita sit methodus eius; solvit autem per speciosarij nulla numerorum consideratione.

Caeterum fac quaeso sciam, quid Clarissimus Pellius a Mengolo jam praestitum dixerit, cum schedulam ei meam monstravisses.[19] R. P. Pardies dabit dissertationem de linea Logarithmica, ejusque usu in solvendis pro-blematis graduum omnis generis: eam lineam attigit in suis Elementis Geometriae.[20] Sed ea linea describi non nisi per puncta, ni fallor potest, id est Geometrica non est. R. P. Berthet circa motum a Pardiesii libello dissentit, et ut puto aliquid de ea re edet.[21]

Prostat hic scientia Chinensium P. Intorcettae,[22] sed non videtur magna adeo mysteria continere.

Nosse distinctius velim quae circa variationem acus magneticae in Hudsons bay, item Dantisci mihi narrabas.[23] Hookiani item Catadioptrici statum et successum, inprimis an circa materiam speculi singulare aliquid praestetur, tum ut politura sit pura qualis vitri, tum ut materia ab aeris injuriis praeservetur.[24]

Plura scribam ubi in civitatem me immersero, hactenus in componendis reculis versor.

potero tunc fortasse scribere nonnihil de iis, quae dominus Mariottus de Iride contra Cartesium, et de coloribus contra Newtonium; item de aquarum proprio pondere pressarum jaculationibus, quarum leges ab iis quae autores de aequilibrio liquorum scripsere plurimum differunt; moli-tur. Construxit fonticulum, qui ubi salire desiit, emortuus videtur subito rursus incipit, simplicissimo artifico, et his ipsis quas affert legibus innixo.[25]

De Newtonii sententia scribe quaeso quid vestri sentiant; aegre certe adducentur eruditi ut eius sententiam de differente radiorum refrangibili-tate admittant.

Si Oxonii responsum accepisti circa Vectium Valentem,[26] cuius copiam sibi fieri Nobilissimus Huetius desiderat, fac ut sciam. Sumtus describendi lubens exsolvet, modo favore Tuo sit qui rem in se suscipiat.

Sed video me excedere epistolae modum, imo et moderationis, cum tot ac tanta TIBI imponere, a Te postulare audeo; quam vero rectius poenam Tuam, quam satis[factionem? *paper worn*]. Quare vicissim non patiar tantum sed et rogo, ut quaeras, jubeas, postules quidvis, quod in mea potestate est.

Quod si vero proximis literis nihil aliud quam hoc unum mihi responderis, Illustrissimam Societatem precibus meis detulisse, abunde mihi satisfactum putabo. Responsoriis mihi inscriptis operculum tale quaeso circumda, ita inscriptum: à Monsieur Monsieur le Baron de Boinebourg,[27] Paris chez Monsieur Heis rue Thibaut aux dez. Quod restat vale faveque.

Cultori Tuo
Gottfredo Gulielmo
Leibnitio, Consil. Mog.

TRANSLATION

Paris, 8 March 1673, N.S.

As soon as I arrived safely at Paris, it was among my first tasks to write you a grateful letter and take the first step towards a correspondence.

First of all, I do not doubt that the books that I had borrowed from you were duly restored to you, for on the morning when we were to leave and there was no time left to take them back I entrusted them to the very noble Schröter,[1] together with my letter to you,[2] with which I enclosed another to the illustrious Royal Society indicative of my desires and intentions, which I explained to you face to face, and you approved.[3]

You may certainly and safely promise on my behalf that I will strive to prevent such great men regretting their kind reception of so insignificant a person, though one inspired by the best intentions.

When you greet the most illustrious Boyle from me, I beg you to assure him of my dutiful respect, for I wish him and likewise yourself and indeed all my friends to be assured, and I shall be a witness whenever the occasion arises, that he is a man to be counted among the greatest of the race, and one whom humanity will one day wish to immortalize in marble. I beg that the *Catalogue of Things to be Exchanged*[4] which he promised to me may soon reach my hands by your favor, and that you will promise him a like return from me.

The unhappy news of the death of His Eminence the Elector of Mainz,[5] which we heard at Calais, has afflicted us deeply. Not only statecraft but philosophy also has suffered a great loss in this prince. We find consolation in his successor,[6] the Bishop of Speyer, a prince who is interested in mechanics as well as in learned topics and who is related to the same family, for the brother of that Schönborn who was just now among you[7] is married to [his] sister. And [we are relieved to know] also that all [the late Elector's] letters and papers, especially those concerning philosophy, are in our hands; *but this is written for your private ear and that it may be considered by the most illustrious Boyle.*

Moreover, please ask the most illustrious Boyle to be so kind as to communicate to me that *solvent of tin*, which he caused [me] to hope for.[8] And from you too, Sir, as you promised, I look for that *impression in metal*, which is mentioned in the

Society's *History*.⁹ I will carefully execute whatever you command in return.

Work continues tirelessly on my *arithmetical machine*.¹⁰ I have hit upon a most certain way of including, in little room and at pleasure, a rod that you may apply either to the [numbers to be] carried forward or to the wheels; and this was not difficult to work out from what I had already. For which reason I am certain that the very famous Hooke will not bring confusion to another's invention, for I think he is so generous and cautious that he will rather improve his own inventions (of which he has no lack) than demand possession of that which has been publicly proposed already by someone else.¹¹ Certainly from his account to the famous Haak in my presence it appeared that the basis of the construction [of Hooke's calculator] was the same as that of mine, only he promised to make it smaller. Nor could he say that this basic idea would have entered his head but for me, since two things are obvious (1) he had never spoken to anyone of such a thing before I came to England with my machine; (2) my machine was very thoroughly and carefully examined by him at close quarters. For when I explained that [machine of mine] before the Royal Society he was certainly very well forward; he removed the back plate which covered it, and absorbed every word I said; and so, such being his familiarity with mechanics and his skill in them, it cannot be said that he did not observe my machine. That he did not distinctly trace out all its wheels I readily admit. But in such cases it is enough for a man who is clever and mechanic-ally-minded to have once perceived a rough idea of the design, indeed the external manner of operation, and then for him afterwards to add to that a little of his own, consisting only of some involvement of the wheels which can be effected by different people in different ways.

We know that right-minded and decent men have preferred when they understood something that was relevant to the improvement of other persons' discoveries to ascribe their [own] improvements and additions to the [original] discoverers, rather than incur the suspicion of intellectual dishonesty and want of true magnanimity should they chase after falsehood with an unworthy kind of greed. Thus, after Galileo's discovery of the Medicean stars Peiresc embarked on the observation of their periods with the greatest zeal; but when he learned that the discoverer had applied his mind to the same subject for the sake of [the discovery of] longitudes he freely and spontaneously made over all his own to [Galileo], and this has been reckoned an act of justice.¹² Thus Gassendi at a certain time embarked upon selenography and took the trouble to have many figures drawn with the aid of the telescope engraved on copper; but when he learned that Hevelius had already taken up this task and was nearer to its conclusion, he not only desisted but imparted his own observations to [Hevelius].¹³ Conversely, it is for the discoverer also to admit before the public his obligation to anyone whose advice has caused his own ideas to prosper.

For which reason, briefly: as the substance of the invention is mine, or drawn from my own [resources, and] as whatever Hooke [may have accomplished] I myself have done as much, I hope that famous man, seeing the strength of my case, will leave the development and perfection [of the invention] to me and that if he has any advice to give on that score he will liberally impart it to me, particularly through you. If he does this I shall praise his good spirit in public; if he does not, he will do something unworthy of his own estimate of himself, unworthy of his nation, and unworthy of the Royal Society.

Moreover, as I hope all will go well, I mean this paper only for yourself and if you please the very illustrious Boyle, so that should opportunity offer you may draw [Hooke] off from what he has begun and indeed persuade him to communicate [with me]. On this account I have so far neither said nor written a word of this to anyone save Boyle and yourself.

Mr. Boyle spoke to me of a certain wind predictor, who used to put out his predictions monthly and so far pretty truthfully. Inquire, please, whether he has sent out [any] recently, and whether they were pretty truthful.

I wish to learn from Mr. Hooke his opinion of Blondel's demonstration concerning the shape of uniformly resistant beams, when you say that he too has reflected on this question.[14]

[My] daily account of Guericke's "little man" is continued successfully.[15]

I have forgotten to ask Mr. Boyle what he thinks of Huygens' experiment related somewhere in the *Journal des Sçavans* on two polished plates or tablets which do not separate either in a vacuum or in the open air,[16] which [result] I nevertheless recalled as being contrary to what Boyle says in his most recent [tract] on the elastic force.[17]

Concerning *Algebra* I very much wish to know whether anything has been set forth by those distinguished men among you, the very illustrious Brouncker, the famous Wallis, Pell, Mercator, Gregory or others concerning the reduction [of the degree] of equations. At Paris there is Mr. Ozanam, a young man highly skilled in algebra, who is to give us something of that sort (the same as was developed by Diophantus), having found a way of solving problems which could not be solved by the Diophantine or any algebraic method known hitherto.[18] And so here for you are four problems which, he says, he has posed before the public and of which no one has yet given the solution:

(1) To find infinite right-angled triangles of different types in each of which, when the shorter side adjacent to the right angle or the hypotenuse are subtracted from the area, singly, the remainders are squares.

(2) To find infinite right-angled triangles of different kinds, in each of which, etc. as before, substituting the words "longer side."

(3) To find a right-angled triangle in which, when either the sum or the difference of the two sides containing the right angle is subtracted, singly, from the difference of the squares of these sides, the remainders are squares.

(4) To find three numbers such that the sum of any two of them is a square, and the difference of any two of them is also a square.

These very difficult and tiresome problems, which seem to be soluble only after one has spent a long time on them, have nevertheless been solved by him in a few lines, using a certain novel process, as I have seen; he proposes them for consideration and solution by others and wishes to learn what the outstanding algebraists among you think of them, so that it may appear whether his method is novel or commonplace; however, he solved them without any consideration of specious numbers.

Furthermore, let me know please what the famous Pell said Mengoli had accomplished already when you showed my paper to him.[19] Father Pardies will produce an essay on the logarithmic curve and its use in solving equations of every degree; he encountered this curve in [writing] his *Elements of Geometry*.[20] But those lines can only be described by means of points, unless I am mistaken, that is they are not geometrical [in the Greek sense]. Father Bertet dissents from Pardies' little book on the subject of motion and, I think, will publish something about it.[21]

There is on sale here the *Science of the Chinese* of Father Intorcetta[22] but it seems to contain no great mysteries.

I would like to have a clearer idea of what you told me about the variation of the magnetic compass at Hudson's Bay and also at Danzig.[23] [And news of] the condition and success of Hooke's reflecting telescope, especially as to whether he has put forward anything notable concerning the material for the mirror, enabling it to take a brilliant polish as glass does and enabling it to be protected from attack by the atmosphere.[24]

I will write more when I shall have settled myself in the city; hitherto I have been busy dealing with trivialities.

Perhaps then I shall be able to write something about Mr. Mariotte's work on the rainbow, in opposition to Descartes, and on colors, in opposition to Newton; as also on the spouting of water under its own pressure, the laws of which differ markedly from what the writers on the equilibrium of fluids have said. He has constructed a little fountain which, when it has left off spouting and seems quite finished, suddenly begins again by means of a very simple trick founded on these very laws that he adduces.[25]

Please write what your people think about Newton's opinion; the learned will certainly be brought only with great difficulty to admit his opinion touching the different refrangibility of the rays.

If you have received any answer from Oxford about the Vettius Valens,[26] of which the very noble Huet wishes to receive a copy, let me know it. He would willingly pay the expense of having it transcribed, if only there is someone who, through your good offices, will undertake the task.

But I see that I trespass beyond the style and decency of a letter when I make bold to demand that you take upon yourself so many and such heavy burdens, which rather [deserves] your retribution, than satisfaction. For which reason I will not only suffer that, but beg that you ask, command and require whatever you wish that is within my power.

If you shall make no other reply to me in your next letter than that you have conveyed my wishes to the Royal Society I shall think myself abundantly satisfied. Please enclose your answer addressed to me in a cover thus addressed: To M. le Baron de Boinebourg,[27] in Paris, at Mr. Heis' house in Thibaut Street, at the [sign of the] dice. For the rest, farewell and flourish.

Your devoted,
Gottfried Wilhelm Leibniz
Councilor at Mainz

NOTES

1 See Letter 2029, note 1.

2 Letter 2140.

3 This letter, dated 10 February 1672/3, in which Leibniz desired to be elected into the Society, was read to the Society on the nineteenth, and copied into Letter Book VI, 34. Leibniz was immediately proposed candidate by Sir Robert Moray, although he was not elected until 9 April 1673.

4 No work by Boyle with this title survives, but Leibniz may mean "General Heads for a Natural History of a Countrey," *Phil. Trans.*, no. 11 (2 April 1666), 186–89; "Other Inquiries concerning the Sea," *Phil. Trans.*, no. 18 (22 October 1666), 315–16, and so on, which Boyle evidently later collected together. They were published posthumously in 1692.

5 Johann Philip von Schönborn (1605–73).

6 Johann Friedrich von Schönborn.

7 See Letter 2137, note 1.

8 This solvent is mentioned by Boyle in Experiment 47 of his *Experiments and Considerations Touching Colours* (London, 1664); see Birch, *Boyle*, I, 775. Oldenburg has noted in the margin "mixtura ex 2bus partibus Aqua fortis et una parte spiritibus salis communis" ("a mixture of two parts of aqua fortis [nitric acid] and one part spirit of common salt [hydrochloric acid]"), which is indeed a solvent for tin.

9 See Sprat, *History*, p. 197, for a reference to "a soft Metal, which hardens after it has taken off the Impression."

10 This machine was shown by Leibniz to the Society on 22 January 1672/3, in an admittedly imperfect state; he had been working on it since the previous May. For a discussion of its history, with diagrams and a photograph of the finished machine, see Ludolf von Mackensen, "Zur Vorgeschichte und Entstehung der erste digitalen 4-Spezies-Rechenmachine von Gottfried Wilhelm Leibniz," in Kurt Müller and Wilhelm Totok, eds., *Studia Leibnitia Supplementa*, Vol. II, Band II (Wiesbaden, 1969), pp. 34–68.

11 On 5 February 1672/3, Hooke "mentioned, that he intended to have an arithmetical engine made, which should perform all the operations of arithmetic, with great expedition and certainty, without making use of the rhabdology [Napier's bones], and that much more simply than that of Monsr. Leibnitz" (Birch, *History*, III, 75). He produced a machine on 5 March 1672/3 and a general discussion of such machines on 7 May 1673, which is printed in Birch, *History*, III, 86–87. There is, as Leibniz claims, no indication that Hooke had thought about calculators before this time.

12 This is recorded in Gassendi's life of Peiresc, under the year 1610; see *The Mirrour of true Nobility* & *Gentility* (London, 1657), p. 146.

13 These observations are recorded by Hevelius in *Selenographia* (Danzig, 1647), pp. 435–36. They were sent to Hevelius by Gassendi in 1644; see his letter dated at Paris 23 March 1644, N.S., printed in his *Opera omnia* (Lyons, 1658), Vol. VI. Epistolae, p. 182.

14 François Blondel (1617–86), director of the Academy of Architecture established in 1671, published *Resolution des quatre principaux problèmes d'architecture* (Paris, 1673). In the fourth problem (pp. 60–86) entitled "De la coupe des poutres également resis-tantes" Blondel examined Galileo's demonstration (*Discorsi e dimostrazioni matema-tiche*, Leiden 1638, pp. 180–81) that a beam of vertical parabolic section, fixed as a cantilever with the base embedded in a wall, has equal strength at all points along its length; that is, the parabolic is the only non-redundant profile for such a cantilever. Blondel argued that the profile should be semi-elliptical for a cantilever or elliptical for a full beam. He was wrong.

15 On 5 February 1672/3 Oldenburg had produced before the Society "a register of observations, concerning winds and weather, left with him by Monsr. Leibnitz, by whom it had been brought from Paris," where Joachim D'Alencé (d. 1707; see Vol. V, p. 88, note 6) had been using "Otto Guericke's *little man*" for wind predictions. Although D'Alencé evidently made a mystery of the instrument, it is described (to-gether with its use in weather predictions) in Guericke's *Experimenta nova* of 1672, Bk. III, Chap. XX: it is a water barometer in which the scale pointer is a little man of wood with pointing arm. Evidently Leibniz had taken up meoterological observations on his own account.

16 This is Experiment V of Huygens' paper on the anomalous suspension of mercury, for which see Letter 2058, note 1.

17 For Boyle's experiments, see above, Letter 2088 and its note 3.

18 Jacques Ozanam (1640–1717) taught mathematics first at Lyons, and then at Paris, and wrote extensively on mathematics. He wrote a treatise on Diophantine analysis which was never published, but which was known at this time.

19 Presumably Letter 2140.

20 *Elemens de Geometrie* (Paris, 1671), Book VIII, art. 24–36, esp. art. 33. Pardies did not live to publish any further mathematical work.

21 Pardies's *La Statique ou La Science des Forces Mouvantes* had only recently been publish-ed; Bertet seems never to have published on this subject.

22 Prospero Intorcetta, *La Science des Chinois ou le Livre de Cum-fu-gu* (Paris, 1673). Father Intorcetta made several translations from the Chinese.

23 For the first see Birch, *History*, III, 44, where are printed the answers to various queries provided by members of a newly returned expedition which wintered in East Hudson's Bay; the account was read to the Society on 18 April 1673. For the second, see Hevelius' Letter 1475 (Vol. VII, pp. 44–49).

24 At a meeting of the Society on 22 January 1672/3 (when Leibniz was present) "Mr. Hooke produced an essay of a reflecting objective speculum, being the segment of a sphere of thirty six feet, which he hoped, when perfectly polished, would perform as much as a refracting object-glass for an hundred foot tube. He was desired to see it brought to perfection" (Birch, *History*, III, 72). On 5 February 1672/3 he produced the speculum which he claimed was truly figured, although "not perfectly polished." Although reminded about it at later meetings, he seems never to have completed work on it.

25 Mariotte had not yet published on these subjects, but had doubtless discussed them

in the Académie Royale des Sciences. His work on colors and the rainbow was to appear in his *Traité des Couleurs,* one of the *Essais de Physique* published at Paris in 1681, and on water under pressure in *Traité du Mouvement des Eaux* (Paris, 1686), and *Regles pour les Jets d'Eaux* published in *Recueil des Ouvrages de Physique et de Mathématique de Ms. de l'Académie des Sciences* (Paris, 1693).

26 See Letter 2153 and its note 8.

27 This was not Leibniz's patron, who had died in the previous December, but his son, Philip William, (b. *c.* 1657), to whom Leibniz acted for a time as tutor in Paris and London.

2166

Oldenburg to Bartholin

27 February 1672/3

From the original in Copenhagen MSS., no. 732

Clarissimo Viro
Domino Erasmio Bartholino, M.D. et Mathematico Hafniensi
Henr. Oldenburg Salutem

Non possum non hac occasione Tibi contestari, Vir Celeberrime, animi mei gratitudinem pro affectu et studiis, quibus Amplissimum nostrum Henshavium amplexaris. Non paenitebit te, credo, officiorum, quae meritissimo viro exhibere non gravaberis. Ostendet ille Tibi Nobilissimi Slusii Methodum, Tangentes ad Curvas quaslibet Geometricas ducendi (si forte antea non vidisti;) Transactionibus Philosophicis insertum;[1] cujus Demonstrationem quoque propediem exspecto, consimiliter, ni fallor, imprimendam. Ostendet itidem Selenitis quoddam genus, quod in Anglia passim effoditur, cum Crystallo Islandico comparandum, quod duplicem refractionem admittit; cum Anglicum tale quid non patiatur.[2] Vidisti, sine dubio, Clarissimi Heckeri Admonitionem ad Astronomos de Mercurii in solem incursu, proximi anni mense Majo observando. Notat Astronomus quidam e nostratibus,[3] Calculum Rudolphinum jam bis, si non ter, observatum fuisse erroneum in transitu Mercurii sub Sole; unde nonnihil miratur; Authorem non dedisse nobis Calculum e Tabulis quibusdam per observationes extantes correctis. Adjicit idem, curam inprimis habendam esse calculi ex Tabulis Bullialdi inter omnes, quos concinnavit Author, cum

Tabulae ejus de Mercutio correctae fuerint ex observatione Gassendi, facta de transitu ejus sub Sole A. 1631; eademque ostendant, nonnisi Initium hujus Incursus (loquor de illo futuro A. 1674.) a Nobis hic terrarum visum iri. Quin addit. ex Tabulis adhuc praecisioribus (puta Carolinis, Streetii,) quaeque ex bino Transitu Mercuriali emendatae fuerint, perquam esse verisimile, nullam Transitus proximi partem Londini, multo minus Uraniburgi, conspiciendam esse; quanquam Transitus proximo proximus, (futurus scil. A. 1677. Octob. 28. st. v.) ab eodem Streetio praedicatur a Nobis in Anglia conspiciendus, caelo serenante. Quae omnia propediem, Deo dante, clarissimo Heckero perscribam.[4]

Acta vestra Academica, nec non Jus antiquum Norvegiae Daniaeque, a Te mihi amice adeo promissa, exspecto, daturus operam, ut pari officiorum genere egregia tua in nos studia compensem. Vidisti, ni fallor, Boylium de Gemmis, deque mira Aeris Rarefactione: Statui hac occasione in usum tuum transmittere ad Dn. Henshaw Bohunum de Ventis, et Willisium de Morbis capitis: novum quoque librum Domini Boylii adjecturus, si mature satis praelo exiverit.[5] Vale, Vir Doctissime, et Oldenburgium tuum amare perge. Dabam Londini d. 27. Febr. 1673.

P.S.

Hanc Epistolam signaturus accepi eximia de Caelis nova, detectionem scilicet duorum Planetarum novorum circa Saturnum, a Clarissimo Cassino factam;[6] cujus Historiam ab Amplissimo Domino Henshaw paulo fusios intelliges.

ADDRESS

  Clarissimo Viro
  Domino Erasmio Bartolino
  Mathematico Hafniensi excellentissimo
    Hafniae

TRANSLATION

Henry Oldenburg greets the famous Mr. Erasmus Bartholin M.D., mathematician of Copenhagen

I cannot but testify to you, celebrated Sir, by this opportunity, the gratitude I feel for your goodwill and the solicitude with which you have welcomed our Mr. Henshaw. You will not, I believe, regret the good offices you have been so kind as to bestow on that most worthy person. He will show you the method of the very noble Sluse for drawing tangents to any geometrical curve (if perchance you have not seen it previously) as inserted in the *Philosophical Transactions*;[1] I expect the demonstration of this soon, too, to be printed in a similar way, if I am not mistaken. He will also show you a certain kind of spar, dug up in England here and there, for comparison with the Icelandic crystal that permits a double refraction; for this the English spar will not do.[2] No doubt you have seen the famous Hecker's notice to astronomers concerning Mercury's transit across the sun, to be seen next year in May. One of our astronomers[3] remarks that the Rudolphine [Tables] have already been found in error twice, if not three times, with regard to such transits of Mercury across the sun, whence he is not a little surprised that the author has not given us a calculation from some tables corrected by the observations that have been made. The same person adds that among all the tables compiled by the author special attention should be paid to the calculation based on the tables of Boulliaud, since his tables of Mercury were corrected from the observation by Gassendi of the transit of 1631; these [tables] show that nothing but the beginning of this transit (I speak of the coming one in 1674) will be seen by us in this part of the world. And he adds that it is highly probable from still more exact tables (namely the Caroline, of Street), which were corrected by two transits of Mercury, that no part of the next transit will be observable at London, much less at Uraniburg; although the next transit after that (namely, that which will take place on 28 October 1677 O.S.) is predicted by the same Street to be visible in England, if the sky is clear. All these things, God willing, I will soon write to the famous Hecker.[4]

I shall await your academic *Acta [Hafniensia]* as also the ancient laws of Norway and Denmark, promised by you to me in so friendly a manner, and will make it my business to reward your outstanding zeal on our behalf with similar sorts of services. If I am not mistaken you have seen Boyle on gems and on extraordinary rarefaction of the air; I have decided to send to Mr. Henshaw for your use by this opportunity Bohun *On winds* and Willis *De morbis capitis*; I will add a new book of Mr. Boyle's too if it comes from the press in time.[5] Farewell, learned Sir, and continue to love your Oldenburg. London, 27 February 1673.

P.S. Just as I was about to sign this letter I received a remarkable piece of news concerning the heavens, that is the discovery of two new planets around Saturn made by the famous Cassini;[6] the narrative of this you may have a little more at length from the worthy Mr. Henshaw.

ADDRESS
    To the famous Mr. Erasmus Bartholin,
    Most excellent mathematician of Copenhagen,
    Copenhagen

NOTES

Reply to Letter 2127.
1 Letter 2124.
2 See Letter 2167.
3 Flamsteed; see Letter 2154.
4 See Letter 2168.
5 Presumably *Tracts . . . touching the Relation betwixt Flame and Air* (see Letter 1997, note 3), which was presented to the Society on 9 April 1673.
6 See Letter 2182; we do not know the source of Oldenburg's information at this early date.

2167
Oldenburg to Henshaw
27 February 1672/3

From the memorandum in Royal Society MS. H 3, no. 14

Answ. Febr. 27. sent him Selenitis scissilis,[1] and no. 88. 89. 90. 91. as also Bohun, and Willis de morbis capitis for Erasm. Bartolin, and promised Mr Boyles new Tracts, if they come time enough out of ye presse.[2]

NOTES

Reply to Letter 2141.
1 "scissile spar," properly a form of gypsum, but something else may be meant here. See also Letter 2166.
2 See Letters 2127 and 2166.

2168

Oldenburg to Hecker

27 February 1672/3

From the copy in Royal Society MS. O 2, no. 105

Clarissimo Viro
Domino Johanni Heckero, Mathematico Gedanensi
Henricus Oldenburg Salutem

Accepi tandem, Vir Celeberrime, Exemplaria omnia admonitionis tuae ad Astronomos editae de proximo Mercurij in Solem incursu observando, eaque inter Societatis Regiae consortes, aliosque Uraniae cultores distribui.[1] Jussit dicta Societas, ut plurimas tibi gratias rescriberem, deque singularis sua in te affectu certiorem te redderem. Observationi praedictae gnaviter incumbent omni dubio procul, dummodo phaenomenon illud sese his terris conspiciendum praebeat. Licet enim, ex Bullialdi Tabulis, Transitus istius initium observari apud nos possit; ex Tabulis tamen Carolinis Streetij nostri, quae ex duplicae Mercurij Transitu correctae fuerunt, nullam proximi illius incursus partem nobis hic conspectam iri, existimat nostras [*sic*] Flamstedius,[2] multo minus Uraniburgi: Etenim juxta dictas Carolinas, futura est Conjunctio solis et mercurij A. 1674, April. 26. st. v. cujus

	h	′	″	Lat ☿ Austr.
Initium	11.	5.	34	12′ 29″
Medium Ecl.	12.	54.	34	13. 43 Cent. dist. 14′ 1″
Vera conjunctio	13.	33.	36	14. 15
Central. egress	14.	43.	34	15 5

Angulus viae visibilis mercurij cum Ecliptica 10°. 24.′ 0.″
Invenitur hic Calculus in Streetij Examine Examinato p. 27; ubi etiam pag. 30. invenitur praedictio proximi dehinc Transitus Mercurij, futuri scilicet A. 1677. Octobris 28. st. v.; qui equidem Caelo serenante a Nobis hic Terrarum conspicietur.

Paucula haec circa Scriptum tuum monere te Voluimus, ut deinceps re sic ferente, similes calculos ex Tabulis per observationes emendatis instituere satagas. Ait quippe dictus Flamsteedius, Calculum Rudolphinum bis terve erroneum fuisse deprehensum in Mercurij sub sole Transitibus; proindeque maluisset eundem ea Tabulis quibusdam per observationes

correctis exhibitum fuisse. Addit idem, Bullialdi Calculum prae reliquis a
Te Examinatis esse notandum, cum ejusdem Tabulae de Mercurio cor-
rectionem, Ex Gassendi de mercurii in solem incursu observatione, su-
bierint; quamvis, iuxta eum, ut jam supradictum, nonnisi initium proximi
Transitus conspiciendum se nobis sit praebiturum. Sed de hoc satis. Velim,
si placet, Amplissimum Hevelium meo nomine plurimum salutes, eique
significes, me non dubitare, quin Jam acceperit, quae Clarissimus Hugenius
de Saturni figura, proxime praeterita aestate Parisijs observata, in Gallicis
Eruditorum Ephemeridibus, 12° Decemb. 1672. editis, est commentatus.[3]
Vale, Vir Doctissime, Tibique addictissimo favere perge. Dabam Londini
d. 27. Febr. 1673

TRANSLATION

Henry Oldenburg greets the famous Mr. Johannes Hecker mathematician of
Danzig

I have at last received, famous Sir, all the copies of your published notice to
astronomers concerning the observation of the next transit of Mercury across
the Sun, and I have distributed them among the Fellows of the Royal Society and
other lovers of astronomy.[1] The said Society ordered me to return many thanks to
you and inform you of its special favor towards you. They will doubtless take up
the predicted observation eagerly, if only the phenomenon proves to be visible in
these countries. For although the beginning of that transit can be observed by us
according to Boulliaud's tables, yet according to the Caroline tables of our Mr.
Street, which have been twice corrected by the transit of Mercury, no part of that
transit will be visible to us here and still less at Uraniburg, as our Mr. Flamsteed
thinks.[2] For according to these Caroline tables the conjunction of Mercury and
the sun will be on 26 April 1674 O.S. as follows:

	h	′	″	South Latitude of Mercury		
Commencement	11	5	34	12′	29″	
Mean eclipse	12	54	34	13	43	central distance 14′ 1″.
True conjunction	13	33	36	14	15	
Central egress	14	43	34	15	5	

The angle of the visible path of Mercury with the ecliptic, 10° 24′ 0″.

This computation is to be found in Street's *Examen examinatus*, p. 27, where also
on p. 30 is to be found the prediction of the next transit of Mercury after that, as
being on 28 October 1677 O.S., and visible to us in this part of the world if the
sky is clear.

We wished to advise you of these few details concerning your paper so that hereafter, should the occasion arise, you may labor to make such calculations from tables corrected by observations. For the said Flamsteed affirms that the Rudolphine calculus has been found inaccurate in transits of Mercury two or three times and hence he would have preferred it to be presented [to us] from some tables that have been corrected by the observations. The same person adds that the calculation of Boulliaud is to be reckoned superior among those examined by yourself, since his tables of Mercury underwent rectification by Gassendi's observation of the transit of Mercury—although, as remarked previously, according to him no more than the commencement of the next transit will be allowed to our vision. But enough of this. If you please, do salute the very worthy Hevelius on my behalf and tell him, I have no doubt that he has already received what the famous Huygens has recorded in the French *Journal des Sçavans* published on 12 December 1672 concerning the shape of Saturn as observed in Paris last summer.[3] Farewell, most learned Sir, and continue to think well of your most devoted. London, 27 February 1672/3.

NOTES

Second reply to Letter 2062.
1 Several copies were produced by Oldenburg at the Society's meeting of 19 February 1672/3.
2 See Letter 2154, where the table will also be found.
3 See Letter 2122; Huygens' account of Saturn is printed in *Œuvres Complètes*, VII, 235–37.

2169
Reed to Oldenburg
27 February 1672/3
From the original in Royal Society MS. R 1, no. 31

Worthy Sr

Yours of the 13 Instant I received. And beg yr pardon if I have glutted you wth grafts. It was my zeale to obey your former letter wch commanded me to enlarge my former proportion that caused yt,[1] I accept of yr notice of them from the hoble. society wth great acknowledgements.

your Commands of an account of ye age of our Country men I will execute this spring, if please God to give me health & ability to goe abroad: Att next sessions by ye Cheife constables of every division I shall disperse Rules for that Inquiry.

To the objection agt Late planting to wch you require my sence, I shall freely give yt, wth this, that I doe professe my self to have beene more industrious then ingenious in ye husbandry of planting; That yt was long ere I began, in ye yeare 52 being before but tenant for 3 lives I was discouraged in that husbandry that was soe long in Expectation. Then I sett to yt earnestly, but for a long time swallowed downe the Common tenetts of ye Country till my Nurseryes that I raysed of kernells came up that I might make farther Experiments. In the meane time I bought my stocks of poor men who gathered them out of woods and roughes, & sett them as they could bring them promiscuously in all seasons of ye winter. half of them dyed & I knew not ye reason. Of late yeares there upon I began to Examine in this sort of husbandry those things only wch I conceived being found out would be of Constant use & advantage (omitting Nicetyes). As mainly. The ascent & descent of ye sap & yts communication wth ye root (where in the ingenious animadversions of Dr B.[2] my Reverend & auncient frend you were please to send me doe perfectly agree wth & Justify my thoughts). And 2ly of ye nature, cause, & Cure of Cankers in trees. Wherein I would beg of you to be enformed of the sence of those yt bend their thoughts that way. for the Canker in many places destroy allmost whole Orchards, especially of some fruits as Pipins &c. & 3ly whether in planting ye roots are to be sett again at large or pruned neere to ye trunk or body of ye tree. 4thly whether early or late planting, both as to ye liveing & also the future thriveing of the tree be to be prefer'd, all benefitts & inconveniencyes of both seasons respected &c, And this last hath beene a Costly learning to me haveing destroyed more good trees by early planting before I found out the benefitt of late then would be conteyned in a Reasonable Orchard. The inconveniencyes of early planting being many as a drye season wch some times happens & is more fatall then in the spring, high winds wch shake the tree if great, much rayne or snow wch sob[3] the roots (the ground being loose to lett yt in). but especially Cold winde and hard frosts wch offer violence to trees yt are sick & weake by theyr late removeall, & are usually taken out of Nurseryes or woods where they dwell warme & are on a sudden removed & exposed to an open ayre, in a hard season, wthout ye Comfort of ye sun or supply of Nutriment from the earth for a whole winter. All these inconveniencyes are unavoydable & inreleiveable by any art or industry. Late planting is only subject to one ye drought of ye next spring. wch happens not allwayes & then the objection ceaseth, & is by a Moderate industry releiveable in great measure in the dryest Spring: ye ground about ye roots may wth little paynes or Cost be made & kept coole in ye most scorching weather. But I may assure you that ye inconvenience is not such as yt seemes & is generally complayned of to be. Cold in the winter may & does most times give the deathes wound, of wch ye tree languish and dyes in ye spring. The dry spring is accused of yt, because ye other kills secretly. And to this I offer you this late Experiment. Winter was two yeares I planted only six, these small, more apt to grow. 2 of them dyed wthout offering to put forth the next spring. The last spring I was putt of[f] planting at St Valentine as I intended untill ye midst of March, by ye frost (in wch weather I decline all removeing trees) Then I planted 42 some a little before St Mary day some after. 31 of them in a hott gravell ye rest not weeping ground: How ye spring after happened you may easily remember, a more unkind one for planting I doe not. There was not wth us I thinke a shower of rayne from Lady day till midsomer sufficient to lay the dust. There does not one of these miscarry, but all live, & are full and wch pleaseth me best preserve theyr greenesse & verdure & fullnesse & smoothnesse of barke, when trees early planted allwayes (as far as ever I could observe) shrivell, turne reddish in colour, bee barkbound & come slowly on for many yeares after. I upon ye incouragement of this & former Experiments wholy decline early planting, & have sett in ye spring trees as big as a man thigh; & have now up to be sett this day or tomorrow, trees yt ye last yeare bare above a peck of Apples, one of them, & that in ye girth are above a foot in measure. & this season I take to plant them in by choyce not of any necessity.

And as early soe planting wth much roote I recon among ye vulgar errors I have not made a full experiment hereof. But this we see by dayly experience yt a tree set of a slip wthout any root (as our Jennet Moyles) shall out grow any tree wth roots, nay a Moyle of ye same kind yt is transplanted wth ye roots. And doe thinke yt many roots below doe as well cumber the tree & hinder yts proficiency as well as many branches above, & that yt is from ye new strings or rootes yt the tree putts forth in ye spring, (wch are allwayes at ye end of ye old root where yt was cutt) that ye whole tree receives nutriment from the earth. This wilbe of use, if found true, for we here doe Covet to preserve as much of ye root as may be, thinkeing yt of great benefitt to ye future growth, in soe doeing, in our Nurseryes where ye plants are nere are forced to destroy a neighbour tree to preserve ye roots of yt wch is to be removed. Another yeare if God please to lengthen out our tranquility soe long you shall have what I find to be successfull in this Conclusion from Sr

your very affectionate servant
Ric. Reed

Febr. 27. 72.

There are some other thoughts of this sort that I intended to have added, but I have troubled you to long & indeed ye post calls on me to haste.

ADDRESS

To my honoured Frend Henry
     Oldenburgh Esquire at his house
     in the Pall Mall neere
Wesminster.

NOTES

Oldenburg has endorsed the Letter Book copy (VI, 51–54) "The original of this Letter ye Author desired to have returned to him for additions; where upon it was sent back." And a later hand has added "(: but return'd)."

Nothing further survives to explain this, but the letter was read in full to the Society on 12 March 1672/3, and the discussion (not given in the minutes) may have raised some points upon which Reed wished to reflect.

1 i.e. Oldenburg's response to the grafts sent earlier as described in Letters 2139 and 2146.

2 Beale; see Vol. VIII, pp. 53 and 55, note 2.

3 Soak or sop.

2170
Vogel to Oldenburg
28 February 1672/3
From the original in Royal Society MS. F 1, no. 39

Viro Nobilissimo & Doctissimo
HENRICO OLDENBURGIO
S.P.D.
Martinus Fogelius

Accepi, Vir Nobilissime, tum quas 2 Januar., tum quas 6 Febr. ad me misisti. Sifero & Morhofio Tuas reddidi.[1]

Clarissimo Semanno pro Scheda adjecta gratias ago maximas.[2] nondum eum possum dimittere. interrogandus adhuc mihi est, quid Turcis Cannabem Significet, & quaenam res Bozam potum constituant.[3]

Pocockio volui seorsim scribere. rogo summopere ut literas has ipsi commendes, & responsum citum procures.[4] Excusabis quam tibi facio hoc nomine molestiam. vellem, ut quam accuratissime scriptus meus libellus prodiret. neque enim a me impetrare possum, ut quiquid mihi occurrit, in chartam statim conjiciam. limam & curam semper requiro in plerisque nostratium libris. Quare denuo te obsecro, ut, annon alios viros noveris (incidit autem quotidie in varios) qui in Turcia aliquamdiu morati Nepenthis hujus Turcici cognitionem habeant, sedulo inquiras. Valde mihi placet Ricotius.[5] an hic Londini sit, & an Smithius Oxonii vivat, scire perquam cuperem.[6]

Navis, quae vehit Loencisium, jam secundo Albi mense 10br. descenderet.[7] sed cum vehemens frigus ingrueret, in portum nostrum iterum se recepit. Non dubito, quin antequam has acceperis, Martinus eum tibi tradiderit. Nauta Georgius Slos appellatur, & noster civis est.

Rauvolfium solum nondum inveni.[8] Si igitur placet, mittam integrum variorum Itinerum volumen. precium videtur aequum, cum non ita frequenter reperiatur.

Boilei opuscula uti magni aestimo, ita magnopere cupio ea quamprimum videre impressa. Literis tuis ad Siferum tantum prof[ecis—*paper torn*] ut tota hac hieme in Jungii Phoranomica digerenda occupatus fuerit. An Geoponica ad Manuscriptos Codices emendata jam Londini prodierint, pridem scire desidero.[9] Quod si ex Manuscriptis sint correcta, vellem inspici quomodo l. 20 c. 9, quod de Compositione Tarentini p[iscium] inscribitur, legatur, uti vulgo *Nauthyalia,* & an Editor quod ea voce intelligatur, noverit, interrogari;[10] item an c. 17 *Kamiae* legatur, & quod sint.[11]

Vale & me ama. Scribam Hamburgi pridie Cal. Marti 1673.

ADDRESS
>A Monsr
>>Monsr Grubendol
>>>a
>>Londres

TRANSLATION

Martin Vogel sends many greetings to the very noble and learned Henry Oldenburg

I have received [the letters] you sent me on 2 January and 6 February, noble Sir. I delivered yours to Sivers and Morhof.[1]

I offer my best thanks to the famous Seaman for his enclosed sheet.[2] I cannot yet release him, for he is still to be asked on my behalf what word the Turks use for cannabis, and what things compose the drink *boza*.[3]

I wished to write separately to Pocock. I particularly beg you to commend this letter to him and extract a speedy response.[4] You will forgive me for giving you this trouble on my account so that my little book may appear as a most accurate composition. For I cannot bring myself to throw down on paper whatever thoughts enter my head; I find a need for polish and attention in most of the books of our countrymen. For which reason, lastly, I beseech you to inquire diligently whether or not you can get acquainted with other men (one comes across various of them every day) who, having spent some time in Turkey, know something of this Turkish nepenthe. Rycaut pleases me very much.[5] I very much wish to know whether he is in London, and whether Smith lives in Oxford.[6]

The ship which carried Lonicer should have left already in December had the weather been fair.[7] But as a heavy frost assailed us it returned to our harbor again. But I do not doubt that Martin will have delivered it to you before this letter reaches you. The captain is named Georg Slos and is a citizen of this town.

Rauwolf by itself I have not yet found.[8] Accordingly, if you are agreeable, I will send [it in] a complete volume of various travels. It is equally valuable, as one does not often come across it.

I judge the little tracts of Boyle to be of great value, and so I have a strong desire to see them printed as soon as possible. You achieved so much by your letter to Sivers that he was busy all this winter digesting the *Phoranomica* of Jungius.

I long to know soon whether the *Geoponics* corrected from the manuscripts have appeared at London yet.[9] If they are corrected from the manuscripts I wish them to be examined for the reading of Book 20, Chapter 9, dealing with the Tarentine composition for fishing, where commonly *Nauthyalia* [appears], and that the Editor be asked whether he knows what is meant by this word.[10] Also whether *Kamiae* is read in Chapter 17, and what they are.[11]

Farewell, and love me. Hamburg, 28 February 1672/3.

ADDRESS

To Mr. Grubendol,
London

NOTES

Reply to Letters 2121 and 2142.

1 Letters 2120 and 2143, respectively.
2 See Letter 2048 and notes 12 and 13. Vogel had written again to Seaman on 15 November 1672, thanking him for his help; this is Royal Society MS. F 1, no. 38.
3 Vogel appears to have been confused, for "cannabis" is a Greek word, not used in Turkish. "Boza" is the Turkish for a drink made of fermented millet.
4 Vogel's letter to Pocock of 28 February 1672/3, in which he thanks him for his reply to Vogel's queries through Oldenburg's agency, is Royal Society MS. F 1, no. 40.
5 For Paul Rycaut (1628–1700), see Vol. III, p. 344, note.
6 Probably the Thomas Smith mentioned in Letter 1968, note 2.
7 See Letter 1959 for Vogel's offer to send this book.
8 This is also mentioned in Letter 1959; Oldenburg had asked for it in Letter 1934 (Vol. VIII, p. 613).
9 See Vol. VIII, p. 334, text and note 10.
10 There was at least one renaissance edition of the *Geoponica* (edited by J. A. Brassicani, Basel, 1539) which Vogel could have consulted; the first of modern editions is that by Peter Needham (1682–1731) published at Cambridge in 1704, who may conceivably have used the earlier labors implied in this correspondence. Chapter VI of Book 20 of the *Geoponica* deals with the fishing baits of the Tarentines, and Chapter IX deals with similar elaborate baits for catching huge *coracinos* (the exact species is unknown). Among the ingredients in the composition used—lentils, cummin, crowsfoot etc.— is *anthyalion* or *anthyllum*, an herb known to Dioscorides and Pliny (*Natural History*, xxi, 29) and so to the Renaissance herbalists as anthyllis.
11 Chapter XVII likewise deals with baits, in this case cooked in a pot placed in a *caminum* [κάμινον] *vitrarii* ("glassworker's furnace") for a long bake! (This chapter is numbered XVI in the modern Teubner edition.) Obviously Vogel's text—presumably Latin only—was pretty corrupt.

2171

Sand to Oldenburg

28 February 1672/3

From the original in Royal Society MS. S 1, no. 122

Hamburgi, 28 Febr.— 7⅔

Nobilissime Vir,

Accepi literas tuas 10. hujus datus. Animadversiones tuae gratiores fuissent, si citiores. Jam omnia fere sunt impressa: nec enim initium feci versionis ab anno —66.[1] Sed idem operis totius quod & versionis meae initium fuit: sic serie continua A. —67. ultra medium latine editus est, mox totus edendus. Miraris ultramarinos suspicere librorum Anglicanorum versiones. Ego vero Bibliopolae curam meam non facio. Caeterum ego operam meam loco cuivis pro argento. Pro singulis philyris latinis singuli mihi penduntur Ducatones. Quod attinet ad vocem *trends*,[2] (quam nec in Dictionariis reperire poteram; quam nec Angli in hac degentes civitate intelligere poterant, quamque Pastor Ecclesiae nostrae Anglicanae etiam sibi videri dixerat debere esse *tends*,) res adhuc salva est. Titulus operis meus non est, sed Bibliopolae ipsi contradixi, sed frustra praetendebat enim tum, annum —69. ex versione Sterpini a se denuo impressum, et toti operi inserendum, eundem ferre titulum: tum, opus ex illustriore titulo magis fore vendibile.[3] Ne quaeso ergo mihi imputes, Vir Nobilissime, culpam alienam. Ego sum quasi mercenarius Bibliopolae: opus quod facio, pro ipso facio. Si id vult corrumpere, suam corrumpat licet. Ego interea nomen meum operi non impressi, ne ego diffamarer, cui non ita opus edere licet, ut libet.[4] Nominari quoque nolim, etiamsi tota versio & Authori & Lectoribus placeret. *Stateram Orbiculatam* dixi Instrumentum illud novum *rota instructum*, vel *rotam habens*.[5] vocabulo novo vocari rem novam. Qui vero melius potui exprimere rem, cujus nec archetypum, nec figuram unquam oculis subjicere datum fuit? Interea exprimat statera Orbiculata, stateram rotam habentem. *Asserere posse confido*,[6] omnino tolerabile est, nisi elegantius, quam addito *me*: quod pronomen primae personae implicitum est in verbo ejusdem personae: prout elegantius est: *Memini legisse*, quam *Memini me legisse*. forsan tamen *mihi* omisit typographus, quae vox extat in *Ephim. lat*.[7] Porro dicis: *Vellem Hugenio praemitti voc. Clarissimo, vel saltem, Domino, prout est est in Anglico,* (ubi tantum est *Master,* quod & de sutoribus, & sartoribus dicitur,) *secus enim judicaret me studere partibus, vel magis aestimare Auzoutum, quam ipsum:* (rectius *se:*)[8] Primo equidem mirabar me contra morem meum, Viro Clarissimo Hugenio non praemisisse, vocem *Domini* itaque loco, comperi non esse verba mea, sed locum fuisse allegatum ex Ephimeridibus Gallorum. Illud *addere promittit* est Interpretis Ephimeridum:[9] cujus ceu eruditi viri elegantiam et fidelitatem in vertendo ipse Author Ephimeridum praedicat. Et est omnino Hellenismus. Ejusdem est *coronis versatilis,* ex Gallico *girouette:* qua in re habuit fidem Dictionario Duezii.[10] Et τὸ *assertionem meam,* ejusdem est, ubi in Gallico legitur *assertion.*[11] Ejusdem est, *alsiosiores homines, naturaeque debiliores:* in Gallico est: *nous devenons plus frilleux & plus foibles.* Haec primo omnium vel in Authore, vel in Interprete Ephimeridum notari deberant. Ego acta agere nolui. Ita, *infallibile in hisce:* pro, *Infallibile: In hisce. Colla:* pro, *Collo: Incumbentis nihil autem,* pro, *incumbentis. nihil autem:* vitia sunt Typographo seu correctori imputanda, non Interpreti. Illa autem *nec alterata qualitate,* item: *inventa,* pro *provecta,* festinationi Bibliopolae tribuenda videntur:[12] Eodem enim die versio mea & concepta & edita est: ex calamo statim subjecta praelo: ita ut nec semel relegere eam licuerit. Interea ubi Authori sensus inviolatus manet, & vitia Typographica facile a peritis Lectoribus emendari queunt, quid reliquum est, de quo Author jure conqueratur, aut litens moveat. Promitto tamen omnia illa monita me missurum Bibliopolae, ut corrigat secundum tuam mentem, si velit.

At sint omnia ita errata, ea tamen affatim compensata sunt emendatione plurium locorum Originalis tui: v.g.

Pag. 96 dicis: *A brass Counter was pierced, in o6",* cum tamen legendum videatur:

> *A brass Counter was pierced in 43".*
> *A little piece of Tin was pierced, in o6".*[13]

P. 172. l. 14. pro *daies* legendum *hours*[14]

P. 204. l. 10. pro *Auzout* legendum videtur *de Via.*[15]

P. 227. l. 34. pro *Stream* — — — *Steam*[16]

P. 248. l. 13. dicis: to ye States General: Author Ephemeridum habet: *à la Compagnie des Indes Orientales:*[17] Et

P. 250. l. 24 tuum *Testicles,* in Gallico est: *un amas de sang.*[18] Ex Inspectione operis Tevenoti pronum est judicare, uter aberravint.

P. 296. l. 17. & 18. dicis: *It ended at 7. h. 43'. 6". So yt its whole duration was 1 h. 58'. 14".* At author Ephemeridum legit: *Elle finit à*

7 heures, 42. min. 57. sec. & qu'ainsi sa durée entiere fut d'une heure, 58. min. 5. sec.[19] Et

P. 297. *The first contact,* &c. 5.—usque ad, *to ye Vertical & ye Ecliptick* Autor Ephim. longe aliter.[20] Hic Paijeni scriptum definiat, uter Vestrum erraveris

P. 305. l. 26. dicis: *Tropicks*: ego conjicio legendum esse, *Tropicus Cancri.*[21]

P. 315. In Tabella velocitatis Fluenti lin. 5. scripsisti 587 et lin. 17. 487. cum tamen utrobique, vel 587. vel 487 legendum sit.[22]

P. 322. l. 26. pro *Spider*: leg. *Erdshrew,* vel *Fieldmouse*[23]

P. 326. l. 24. Omissum est, close by. Nam si ex longiore distantia inspectum fuerit objectum, nulla ratione majus apparet.[24]

P. 337. l. 3. vox emissa forsan est *Shoad.*[25]

ibid. § 54. *Mundick.* al *Murdick.*[26]

P. 340. ubi § 76. & 77?[27]

P. 463. l. 27. legendum videtur ye Left Emulgent Artery[28]

P. 470. § 4. videtur legendum: *it not only not increaseth*; vel *it not only decreaseth*[29]

P. 485. l. 7. 150 *Millions of Goldcrowns*: ipse Athanasius Kircherus longe plura habet.[30]

P. 487. l. 25. pro *Pius,* leg. *Xius*[31]

P. 488. l. 17. pro *Zancut* leg. *Tanchut.*

Haec obiter reperi

Siqua in caeteris occurrant similia, nondum observavi: interea omisi quaedam contra Orthographiam Graecaricam commissa, et leviora vel manifesta errata Typographica studio praeterii. Forsan noveris etiam qua ratione Nobilissimi Viri, Domini Henshaw Observationes & Quaestiones sint editae.[32] Ubicunque porro observavi vel Authorem, vel Interpretem Ephimeridum perperam excerpta ex Collectionibus tuis vertisse, amice admonui. Toti operi praefationem meam rogatu Bibliopolae praefixi, quam vellem legisses: nec despero quin ea lecta singuli Authores, quorum observationes, &c. collegisti, excusaturi sint errata mea, quae monitus promitto me in fine libri Erratis annumeraturum.[33] Ista sunt quae te monere volui, obnixe rogans ne ea mihi vitio vertas. Interea jubeo te valere quam optime, & rogo ut faveas Nobilissime Domine,

Tibi addictissimo
C. Sandio

P.S. Inclusam ab amico meo scriptam oro cures ad Bibliopolam deferri: promitto me in subeundis mandatis huc fore promptissimum.

D. Oldenburg.

TRANSLATION

Hamburg, 28 February [16]72/3

Most noble Sir,

I have received your letter dated the tenth of this month. Your comments would have been the more welcome, if they had been quicker. Now almost everything is printed, for I have not done the beginning of the translation from the year sixty-six.[1] But the beginning of the whole work and of my translation was the same; thus it has been published in a continual series from the year sixty-seven past the halfway mark, and soon the whole will be published. You are surprised that continentals are suspicious of the translations of English books. I do not make book-selling my business. Moreover I sell my services to anyone for money. I am paid a ducat for each sheet of Latin. As for the word *trends*[2] (which I could not find in dictionaries, which English people living in this city could not understand, and which the minister of our English church also said it seemed to him ought to be *tends*) the situation is still all right. The title of the work is not mine, but I spoke against the bookseller himself; but in vain, for he claimed that, firstly, the year 1669 in Sterpin's translation recently printed by himself and to be included in the whole work, bears this same title; and secondly, that the work will be more readily saleable with a grander title.[3] Therefore please do not pin upon me, noble Sir, a fault that is not mine. I am as it were a bookseller's hack; what I do I do for him. If he wishes to spoil it, he may spoil what is his own. Meanwhile, my name is not to be printed on the work, lest I should lose my good name, not being able to publish the work as I should like.[4] I should also refuse to be named even though the whole translation should please both author and readers. I have called *stateram orbiculatam* [circle-shaped balance] that new instrument "fitted with a wheel" or "having a wheel."[5] A new thing must be called by a new name. Who could express the thing better, indeed, who was given no example or drawing to examine with his eyes? Meanwhile, let the "circle-shaped balance" be a steelyard having a wheel. *Asserere posse confido* [I am sure I can affirm][6] is quite passable, if not more elegant than with the added *me*; because the first-person pronoun is implied in the first-person verb, just as *Memini legisse* [I remember that I have read] is more elegant than *Memini me legisse*. Yet perhaps the printer omitted *mihi*, as this word exists in the Latin *Journal*.[7] You say further "I wish [the name of] Huygens to be preceded by the word *Clarissimus* or at least *Dominus*, as it is in the English" (where there is only *Master* which is aplied to cobblers and tailors too) "in case he should imagine me to take sides, or to think more of Auzout than I do of him" ([*ipsum*], but more correctly *se* [himself]).[8] In the first place I am quite surprised that, contrary to my custom, I gave the famous Huygens no prefix and so it is established that the word *Dominus* in that passage was not my own word, for that passage was cited from the French *Journal* [*des Sçavans*]. That *addere promittit* [he promises to add] is of the translator of the *Journal*,[9] whose elegance and faithfulness in translation are vouched for by the author of the *Journal* himself as those of an erudite scholar. And he is a complete Grecian. *Coronis versatilis* [movable circle] is from the same source, from the French *girouette* [weather vane], which has the authority of Duez's dictionary[10]. And as for *assertionem meam* [my assertion], it is from the same source, where one reads in French *assertion*.[11] From the same source is *alsiosiores homines, naturaeque debiliores* [men chillier, weaker in their nature]; in French it is *nous devenons plus frilleux & plus foibles*. These things ought in the first place to be remarked on either to the author or to the translator of the *Journal*. I have been reluctant to waste effort. Thus, *infallibile in hisce*, for *Infallibile: In hisce*; *Colla*, for *Collo*; *Incumbentis nihil autem*, for *incumbentis. nihil autem* are mistakes to be attributed to the printer or press corrector, not to the translator. However, that *nec alterata qualitate*, also *inventa* for *provecta* seem to be attributable to the bookseller's haste;[12] for on the same day my translation was conceived and printed, from the pen it went straight to the press, so that I was not allowed to reread it even once. Meanwhile, where the author's meaning remains unimpaired and the printer's errors can easily be emended by a knowledgeable reader what is there remaining for an author reasonably to complain about, or begin a dispute? But I promise that I will send on all those points you have noted to the bookseller to make corrections according to your wish, if he chooses.

But if all those are mistakes they are adequately compensated by the correction of many passages in your original; for example,

Page 96, you say: *A brass Counter was pierced, in 06"* when it seems, however, one should read:
    A brass Counter was pierced in 43".
    A little piece of Tin was pierced, in 06".[13]
Page 172, line 14. *hours* should be read for *daies*.[14]
Page 204, line 10. For *Auzout*, read, it seems, *de Via* [de la Voye].[15]
Page 227, line 34. For *Stream — Steam*.[16]
Page 248, line 13. You say: to ye States General. The author of the *Journal* has *à la Compagnie des Indes Orientales* [to the East India Company].[17] And

Page 250, line 24. Your *Testicles* is in French *a quantity of blood*.[18] It is easy to judge which has erred by examining the work of Thevenot.

Page 296, lines 17 and 18. You say: *it ended at 7.h. 43'. 6". So yt its whole duration was 1h. 58'. 14"* But the author of the *Journal* reads *It finished at 7 hours, 42', 57", and thus its entire duration was one hour, 58 minutes, 5 seconds.*[19] And

Page 297. *The first contact, &c* [para.] 5 — as far as, *to ye Vertical & ye Ecliptick.*

The author of the *Journal* [has it] very differently.[20] Here Payen's paper will determine which of you is in error.

Page 305, line 26. You say *Tropicks*; I conjecture that one should read *Tropic of Cancer*.[21]

Page 315. In the table of the velocity of the current you have written (line 5) 587 and in line 17, 487; whereas both should read either 587 or 487.[22]

Page 322, line 26. For *spider* read *Erdshrew* or *fieldmouse*.[23]

Page 326, line 24. *Close by* is omitted. For if the object is viewed from a considerable distance there is no reason why it should appear larger.[24]

Page 337, line 3. The omitted word is perhaps *shoad*.[25]

The same, § 54. *Mundick* or *Murdick*.[26]

Page 340. Where are §§ 76 and 77?[27]

Page 463, line 27. It would seem it should read ye *Left* Emulgent Artery.[28]

Page 470. § 4. It seems it should read: *it not only not increaseth*; or *it not only decreaseth*[29]

Page 485, line 7. *150 Millions of Goldcrowns*. Athanasius Kircher himself makes it much more.[30]

Page 487, line 25. For *Pius*, read *Xius*.[31]

Page 488, line 17. For *Zancut*, read *Tanchut*.

These I found in passing.

If there are similar things in the rest, I have not yet observed them; moreover, I have omitted certain breaches of Greek orthography and I have studiously avoided trivial or glaring printer's errors. Perhaps you will also know how the observations and questions of the most noble Mr. Henshaw have been published.[32] Wherever, moreover, I have observed that the author or translator of the *Journal* has perverted the sense of your collections, I have advised [him of it] in a friendly way. At the bookseller's request I have placed my preface before the whole work, which I would like you to read; and I hope that after reading it the individual authors whose observations etc. you have collected will forgive my mistakes, which, it is announced, I have promised to list at the end of the book.[33] These are the points of which I wished to advise you, earnestly begging you not to turn them against me. Moreover I rejoice that you are in good health, and beg you to think well of, noble Sir,

Your most devoted
C. Sand

P.S. Please see that the enclosure written by a friend of mine is delivered to the bookseller; I promise that I will be most ready in undertaking your commands here.

Mr. Oldenburg

NOTES

For the beginning of this correspondence see Letter 2135. Two volumes of Sand's translation of the *Philosophical Transactions* were issued by Henry and Theodore Boom at Amsterdam with the date 1672. The first of these, for the year 1666 (nos. 10 to 22), had evidently already been published and formed the subject of Oldenburg's comments in the lost Letter 2148; to these comments Sand replies in the first part of the present letter. The second, for the year 1667 (nos. 23–32), was still in press and is dealt with in the latter part of Sand's letter.

1 Apparently Sand means—this whole passage is somewhat obscure—that he had not yet translated *Phil. Trans.*, nos. 1 to 9, the last of which was dated 12 February 1665/6, forming the first half of Vol. I of the English edition of the *Transactions*, in which edition Vol. I concludes with no. 22.

2 See Letter 2135, note 2.

3 The errors complained of by Oldenburg, now coming up for discussion, are noted at the end of Sand's translated volume for 1667 (p. 392). Sterpin's translation of the *Transactions* for 1669, reprinted by the Booms (1671) as part of their series, bore the title *Acta Philosophica Regia anni MDCLXIXmi. Aliquam exhibentia notitiam praesentium incoeptorum, studiorum & laborum eorum, qui eruditi salutantur, in plerisque praecipuis mundi partibus.* This, apart from the added adjective *Regia* (Royal) is an exact translation of Oldenburg's English title. Sand's volume of the *Transactions* for 1666, however, was entitled *Acta Philosophica Societatis Regiae in Anglia anni MDCLXVI*, which increased the offence in Oldenburg's eyes, who was scrupulous in insisting that the *Transactions* were his own private venture, not a publication of the Royal Society. Accordingly, in the errata in Sand's volume for 1667 it is noted that the words *Societatis Regiae in Anglia* should be deleted from the title—perhaps a unique erratum in the history of bibliography! But the Booms were incorrigible, as Sand remarks; their Latin *Transactions* for 1668, dated 1674, brazenly carry the same offending title.

4 Sterpin's translated volume bears his full name; Sand's volumes simply the initials "C. S."

5 See *Phil. Trans.*, no. 10 (Latin), pp. 5 and 9; the English (pp. 164, 165) is "Wheel-Ballance."

6 See the same pages as in the previous note; the original English was: "I can say in the general . . ."

7 The Latin version of the *Journal des Sçavans* is apparently rare; the British Museum Library has no issue, and the Bibliothèque Nationale only the second edition (four volumes only): *Le Journal des sçavans, hoc est Ephemerides eruditorum . . .* (Leipzig and Frankfurt, 1671). Sand not unreasonably saved himself labor by taking from this Latin version the pieces from *Phil. Trans.* that the original *Journal* had republished in French. His misspelling *Ephimerides* is fairly consistent.

8 See *Phil. Trans.*, no. 10 (Latin), p. 21; the English (p. 171) has "M. Auzout" and "M. Hugens." Oldenburg here translated into English from the *Journal* of 22 February 1666 [N.S.]. Sand made a correction in his errata.

9 The Latin version, p. 24, has this additional paragraph, not found in the English of the *Transactions*, p. 173: "Argumenta etiam alia astronomica traduntur, plurima in literis Cassini, quibus adhuc alia nova addere promittit." ("Many other astronomical matters are touched on in Cassini's letter, to which he promises to add other novelties.")

10 In the Latin, p. 8; in the English, p. 165. Nathaniel Duez, *Dictionarium Germano-Gallico-Latinum* (Geneva, 1663).

11 Both this and the Latin expression in the next sentence appear on p. 7 in the Latin and on p. 165 in the English *Transactions*. In the former case Boyle had simply written: "and that does more confirm the indication" whereas the translator made him say: "and that rather confirms than destroys my assertion." In the second case Boyle's English reads: "our Bodies more chill, cold, and drooping."

12 All these errors are noted in Sand's list of errata.

13 Compare Oldenburg's quotation of this same account in Letter 424 (Vol. II, p. 544) whence it will be seen that Sand's correction is justified. (Oldenburg should probably have written *fer blanc* for *fer bleu*, and hence Sand's word *tin* is correct also.)

14 Sand now returns to the part of the *Transactions* already published in Latin, for the year 1666, beginning with no. 10. Oldenburg adds a comment in French or Latin, here rendered in English. (H. O.: "It can easily be corrected from the context").

15 (H. O.: "Not so, but p. 203 (1) by M. Auzout and M. delaVoye").

16 (H. O.: "It can be corrected from the context").

17 (H. O.: "To their High Mightinesses").

18 (H. O.: "If you will look at p. 27 you will see that I was not mistaken").

19 (H. O.: "I am confident that in the letter itself from which this extract was made it is as I have said, although in the *Journal* [*des Sçavans*] it is as you say"). Oldenburg received A. F. Payen's *Extrait d'une lettre de Payen à M. de Montmor contenant l'observation de l'eclipse de soleil arrivé le 2 Juillet 1666* (Paris, 1666) from Justel; see Vol. III, p. 288.

20 (H. O.: "and I say the same about p. 297, that I took it from the author's own paper").

21 (H. O.: "This applies to the regions lying between the two Tropics"). This rebuttal seems perfectly justified by the context.

22 (H. O.: "It should be 487").

23 (H. O.: "In the original it is *mesaraigne* for *mesange*"). Oldenburg means that he was misled into writing "spider" (*recte*, "araignée") for "titmouse" (a small bird)—but the French word *should* have been, as Sand conjectures, "musaraigne" ("shrewmouse").

24 (H. O.: "it would be no bad thing to add it")

25 (H. O.: "I myself don't know"). Sand might be right; *shoad* is a Cornish term applied to scattered, waterborne metallic deposits.

26 (H. O.: "Mundick"). Now spelled *mundic*, a word of Celtic origin applied by Cornish miners to pyrites.

27 (H. O.: "An error of the bookseller's").

28 (H. O.: "So it is, but it can be understood from the context since the left kidney is mentioned").

29 (H. O.: "A printer's error").

30 (H. O.: "it is enough").

31 Oldenburg simply noted by this and the next "Printer's error."

32 This sentence may refer to Thomas Henshaw's *Inquiries for Ægypt* printed in *Phil. Trans.*, no. 25 (6 May 1667), 470–72.

33 In the Preface to Vol. I (for 1665, published in 1672), Sand had apologized for possible errors. At the end of Vol. IV (for 1668) he gave (p. 454) a brief list of "errata & omissa" for the years 1666 and 1667. This was the last volume to be published.

2172

Wallis to Oldenburg

1 March 1672/3

From the original in Royal Society MS. W 2, no. 6

Oxoniae. Martij. 1. $167\frac{2}{3}$

Clarissime Vir,

Quem librum quaeris, Vettius Valens,[1] reperta difficilior erat, quoniam inter Bibliothecae Bodleianae libros Seldenianos Manuscriptos est,[2] nondum satis in ordinem redactos aut Catalogo insertos, neque potuit ipse Bibliocaria mihi indicare ubinam esset. Eos tamen evolvendo hunc tandem comperi. Est liber Astrologicus περὶ μεσουρανήματος inscriptus; Incipit Οὐετίου Οὐάλεντος Ἀντιοχείος Ἀνθολογιῶν βιβλίον A. &c. Est liber (ut loquantur) in Folio, satis grandis. Quem transcribere, laboris erit et pretij non contemnendi; et quidem eo incommodius fiet, quod extra Bibliothecam deferre non liceat, neque ad Bibliothecam pateat aditus nisi statis horis, necdum consului Curatores num transcriptiones sint permissuri; addo, non cujusvis esse, Manuscriptos Graecos (exolico[3] charactere exaratos) legere, praesertim ubi rem subjectam minime intelligunt. Author itaque essem, ut cum habeant ipsi Parisijs ejusdem Exemplar, Apographum ejus huc transmitterent, cum nostro conferendum ut quicquid diversitatis exemplarium appareat ad oram Apographi notetur, ad illos remittendi. Quaequidem Collatio facilius expedietur, quam totius transcriptio. Ego, quod in me erit, praestare non recusabo.

Tuus ad officia,
Joh: Wallis

My humble service to my Lo. Brouncker. If he thinke of any thing to be added for ye more clear or advantageous expression of his notion; pray let it be inserted accordingly.[4] Verte[5]

perhaps it may not be amiss to insert this in a proper place for ye better explication of his Lordships notion, if he please.

For if we suppose the Springy parts of ye Air to be like so many smal Haires, wrapped up (as ye Spring of a Watch) in different forms, endeavouring to expand themselves to their full length: (beyond which their Elastick or Springy power cannot operate;) the Pores of ye Glass may be too small to let them passe thus wrapped up; yet big inough to transmit them as single threads stretched out (like a body of Souldiers filing through a narrow passage) in case there be on ye other side a void space to receive them; where yet they cannot act as a Spring, till some numbers of them there recollected press one another into such crooked postures as will cause their Springs again to operate & to thrust down ye adjacent Quick-silver.

ADDRESS
    For Mr Henry Oldenburg,
    in the Pallmall
    near St James's
        London

POSTMARK MR 3

TRANSLATION

Oxford, 1 March 1672/3

Famous Sir,

The book you seek, Vettius Valens,[1] was the more difficult to discover because it is among the Selden manuscripts of the Bodleian Library[2] which are not yet arranged in order or catalogued, nor could the librarian himself tell me where it was. But by turning them over I found it in the end. It is an astrological work entitled περὶ μεσουρανήματος [*On the meridians*]; it begins Οὐετίου Οὐαλεντος Ἀντιοχείος Ἀνθολογιῶν βιβλίον A. [Book I of the *Anthology* of Vettius Valens], etc. It is a folio volume (as they say) of good size. To transcribe it would be no mean labor and expense, and the more inconvenient because it cannot be removed from the library to which access is permitted only at stated hours, and I have not yet consulted the Keepers to see whether transcriptions are allowed. And I may add that not just anyone can read Greek manuscripts written in an obsolete[3] script, especially when they have little familiarity with the subject-matter. It is my advice, therefore, that as those [who are interested in this matter] at Paris have a version of the same [text], they should send a transcript of it here for comparison with ours, so that any discrepancy between the two versions may be noted on the margin of the transcript and returned to them. This collation could be more easily effected than a transcription of the whole [Oxford MS.]. I will not refuse to do what I can in this.

Yours at your service,
John Wallis

NOTES

1 See Letter 2153, note 8.
2 The antiquary John Selden (1584–1654) had a very valuable collection of (chiefly oriental) manuscripts most of which went to the Bodleian Library at his death.
3 Read: "exoleto," which may also mean "faded."
4 This refers to Wallis's long series of letters on the anomalous suggestion of mercury in the autumn of 1672; see especially Letter 2088. As Letter 2177 indicates, this passage was never printed.
5 "Turn over." What follows is written on the back of the page.

2173

Swammerdam to Oldenburg

4 March 1672/3

From the original in Royal Society MS. S 1, no. 119
Partly printed in *Phil. Trans.*, no. 94 (19 May 1673), 6041–42

Viro Clarissimo atque Doctissimo
D.D. Henrico Oldenburg Soc: Reg. Secretario,
Joh. Swammerdam S.

Perlibenter mea studia vir benevole, in naturae ejusque recessus indagationem conferam; quare ut Clarissimi ac Dilectissimi Malpighii aliorumque vestigia persequar, ecce obsequii mei Specimen, Illustrissimis Sodalibus humanitate qua potuerim, tributum. Alias enim haud mihi animus erat, tam subito animalia illa, quae vena arteriosa destituuntur indicare; priusquam et in aliis animantibus, ubi eandem fere pulmonis conformationem observaveram, transmissam observationem[1] ad incudem revocare licuisset. Veruntamen, Societati R. cum videam, meas non displicere operas, aeque atque bene ejus desiderio e vestigio quoque obtemperare volui, eoque libentius ut etiam aliis in rem adeo notabilem inquirendi ansa daretur, atque ita naturae abdita eo citius manifestarentur.

Nemo, ut opinior, Ranis pulmones denegabit, postquam Excercitatissimus Malpighius, tam curiosa tamque notabilia de iis divulgavit;[2] atque Solertissimus Needham, pulmone manifeste eas donari atque respirare annotavit.[3] In hisce tamen Amphibiis vena arteriosa desideratur; quare nec eorum Sanguis ullo modo per pulmones circulatur, in iisque cribratur, verberatur nec comminuitur; nam mox ex simplici eorum cordis sinu per totum corpus, pulmonibus intactis relictisque dispescitur. quod si non validum haud debile saltem mihi argumentum est, quo hepati sanguificationis suum munus, inter alia restituere aliquando conabor.[4] Atque haec quidem hactenus.

Arteria tamen manifesta (bronchiali seu potius pulmonali, analoga) in Ranarum pulmonum succingente tunica adest, quae mirandum in modum, ac mirabilis retis ad instar per eorum superficiem tenditur, atque minutissimis suis propaginibus sensim ad interiores vesiculas progreditur; ubi ut ego quidem arbitror, cum vena pulmonali anastomosin patitur, etiam oculis manifestam.

Venosum illud vas, arterioso duplo majus, in pulmonum cavo ac praecique in vesicularum ejus oris ac limbis situm est, a quo omnibus cellulis, imo et ipsi tunicae succingenti, capillaribus ac fere invisibilibus ramusculis, prospicit; uti ex additis figuris [*see Plate II*][5] palam fiet: ubi fig. I. pulmonum cellularum reta, cera distentorum, graphice exprimit. fig. II. Arteriam pulmonalem in pulmonum superficie, innumeris anastomosibus gaudentem, ostendit. *A*. arteriae pulmonalis truncus *BBB*. ejusdem ramificatio triplex. *CC*. Anastomoses arteriae pulmonalis inter se. fig. III. Venam pulmonalem notat. fig. IV. Ranarum quasdam arterias exprimit. *A*. Cor cum suis auriculis. *B* principium arteriae magnae e corde assurgens, *CC* Trunci ejus ascendentes a quo coeterae oriuntur. *DD* Arteriae pulmonales. *EE*. Arteriae elegantes, ampullulae in modum dilatatae, mox iterum constrictae. *F* notabilis anostomosis ramorum descendentium e regione mesenterij. *G*. Arteriae mesenterii. *H*. rami Iliaci. *I* exiguae Glandulae in collo.

Animalia quae suspicor, eandem pulmonis structuram obtinere, sunt Bufones, Lacerti serpentes, chamaeleontes, Testudines, salamandrae aquaticae, et si quae sint alia pulmonibus membranosis instructa; et quorum structuram, cum primum hyeme instante in adumbratam inciderim observationem, non mihi licuit adhuc perquirere. Sufficit ergo indicasse animantia, virisque me longe sagacioribus viam monstrasse.

Lienem peculiari arte parenchymate exutum libenter ad vos curarem; quemadmodum quoque, pace refulgente, Illustris Boylij Dilectissimique Malpighii aliorumque libros avidissime evolverem.

Cum videam vobis gratum fuisse quae de nasi cornis scarabaei genitalibus notaveram, non alienum fore duxi, eorum delineationem Tuae Claritati hic transmittere [*see Plate II*].[6] Fig. igitur V. Nasi cornis genitalia ad vivum exprimit. *A* Scarabeus nasicornis. *B* penis pars cornea. *C*. locus quo

penis, quando erigitur, se prodit; *DD*. Testiculi ex unico funiculo, duorum pedum et sex pollicum longo, constantes. *EE*. principia seu initia
testiculorum caeca. *FF*. vasa deferentia, semen copiosissimum et album,
quando laeduntur, stillantia. *GG*. vesiculae seu potius glandulae seminales
sex, admodum elegantes. *HH*. glandularum seminalium ductus prutensi,
materiam seminalem subflavem (ut in hominibus ac brutis animantibus
quoque observatur) continentes. Vale, vir Eruditissime, meque tuum crede.
Dabam Amstelod. D. 14 Martij. Ao. 1673. [N.S.]

TRANSLATION

Jan Swammerdam greets the very famous and learned Mr. Henry Oldenburg,
Secretary of the Royal Society

I am very content, kindly Sir, to associate my studies towards the investigation
of nature and her secrets [with others'], for which reason [and] in order that I may
follow in the footsteps of the very famous and delightful Malpighi and others,
here is a specimen of my complaisance, offered to the most illustrious Fellows with
all the good will I can muster. For otherwise it was not my intention to indicate
those animals that are deprived of the pulmonary artery so hastily, before I had
had the opportunity to revise the observation I sent to you[1] by reference to other
animals also, in which I have observed almost the same structure of the lungs. But
indeed, as I see that my labors are not displeasing to the Royal Society, so equally
I wished fully to comply both with its wishes and its example, and that the more
willingly because an opportunity will thus be provided to others also for the
investigation of so notable a question and hence the byways of nature will become
known more rapidly.

No one, I think will deny that frogs have lungs after the very experienced
Malpighi has published such strange and noteworthy things about them,[2] and the
very skilful Needham has noted that they are obviously endowed with a lung, and
breathe.[3] Yet in these amphibians the pulmonary artery is wanting; for which
reason their blood is in no way circulated through the lungs, nor is it sieved in
them, nor beaten up nor comminuted; for leaving the lungs to one side untouched,
it is immediately dispersed from the single ventricle of their heart through the
whole body. And this is to me at least no weak argument, if not a conclusive one,
by which I shall try to restore to the liver its function of sanguification.[4] And thus
much so far.

However, there is a manifest artery, analogous to the pulmonary or rather the
bronchial [artery of mammals], in the tunic enclosing the lungs of frogs, which is
extended over their surface in a wonderful way, like the *rete mirabilis*, and gradually
penetrates to the interior vesicles with its minutest branches where, as I suppose,

an anastomosis with the pulmonary vein may be imagined, and is even obvious to the eye.

This venous vessel, twice the size of the artery, is situated in the hollow of the lung and especially in the margins and edges of the vesicles, whence it provides for all the cells and of course the enclosing tunic, by means of its capillaries and almost invisible ramifications. This is made plain by the annexed figures [*see Plate II*],[5] where Figure I expresses graphically the network of cells in the lung, swollen with wax. Figure II shows the pulmonary artery on the surface of the lungs, with its innumerable anastomoses: *A* is the trunk of the pulmonary artery, *BBB* its triple ramification, *CC* the mutual anastomoses of the pulmonary artery. Figure III denotes the pulmonary vein. Figure IV expresses certain arteries of the frog: *A* is the heart with its auricles, *B* the stem of the aorta springing from the heart, *CC* its ascending trunks from which the others arise, *DD* the pulmonary arteries, *EE* the elegant arteries, swelling out into a bulb and then constricting again, *F* a notable anastomosis of the branches descending from the region of the mesentery, *G* the mesenteric arteries, *H* the iliac branches, *I* small glands in the neck.

The animals in which, I imagine, the same structure of the lung obtains are toads, lizards, snakes, chameleons, tortoises, aquatic salamanders, and any others provided with membranaceous lungs whose structure I have not been able to investigate yet since I first happened on a first idea of the observation this present winter. It is enough, therefore, that I have listed the [likely] creatures and pointed the way to others far wiser than myself.

I will gladly take it on myself [to send] to you a spleen stripped of fleshy substance by a peculiar art, just, as when peace revives, I would eagerly peruse the books of the illustrious Boyle, the most delightful Malpighi, and others.

As I see that what I have noted about the genitalia of the horn-nosed beetle is welcome to you, it will not be out of the way to send you here a sketch of them [*see Plate II*].[6] Accordingly, Figure V expresses to the life the genitalia of the horn-nosed beetle. A the beetle, B the horny part of the penis, C the place from which the penis protrudes when erect, DD the testes, consisting of a single thread, two foot six inches long, EE the blind beginning or origin of the testes, FF the vasa deferentia, exuding a copious white semen when they are wounded, GG six very well contrived seminal vesicles, or rather glandules, HH the extended ducts of the seminal glandules, containing a yellowish seminal matter, as I have observed in men and brute creatures also. Farewell, most learned Sir, and believe me yours. Amsterdam, 14 March 1673 [N.S.].

NOTES

Reply to Letter 2147. Swammerdam never altered his view of the function of the heart and lungs in the frog; compare (for a fuller account) his *Book of Nature* (trans. Thomas Flloyd, London, 1758), II, 120.

1 In Letter 2130.

2 In *De pulmonibus observationes anatomicae* (Bologna, 1661). See also Letter 1630 (Vol. VII).

3 In the fifth chapter of *Disquisitio anatomica de formato foetu.*

4 In the Galenic theory, food was first transformed into chyle in the alimentary canal and the chyle in turn turned into blood in the liver. Harvey's discovery of the circulation proved that the blood did not simply flow outwards from the liver to the periphery, but it did not prove that the circulating blood was not formed in the liver, nor suggest any other site for the blood's origin. However, attempts to explain the function of the circulation by Harvey's followers suggested that the blood was perfected in the heart or lungs or both; moreover, the anatomical discoveries of Aselli, Pecquet and others rendered it certain that a large part of the chyle reached the blood stream directly from the thoracic duct. Hence Galen's account of sanguification became outmoded. If one thinks of the red cells as the most essential part of the blood, as the seventeenth-century microscopists did (the remainder being "serum"), then the origin of the blood remained a mystery until the nineteenth century.

5 The figures were not reproduced in the *Philosophical Transactions*. They are to be found in Royal Society Letter Book VI, between pp. 58 and 59. It is perhaps just worth noting that Swammerdam does not use the word "cell" in its modern biological application—he refers to the alveoli of the lung, which as they are polyhedral could aptly be called "cells" in the common sense of the word.

6 Again, a fuller account may be found in *The Book of Nature*, I, 146–47.

2174
Oldenburg to Leibniz

6 March 1672/3

From the memorandum in B.M. MS. Add. 4294, no. 48
Printed in Gerhardt, p. 84

Resp. d. 6. Martij 1672/73. misi impressionem formae in metallem, et responsa de Vectio Valente:[1] promisi me curaturum ipsius admissionem, et significaturum, quod spectat Boylium, Algebram, Osannae problemata, Pellium, spec. Catadioptricum.

TRANSLATION

Replied 6 March 1672/3. Sent [information about] the impression of form in metal, and the reply about Vettius Valens:[1] promised to take care of his admission [to the Royal Society] and to tell him, what concerns Boyle, Algebra, the problems of Ozanam, Pell, the reflecting telescope.

NOTES

Reply to Letters 2140 and 2165.
1 Letter 2172.

2175

Kirkby to Oldenburg

8 March 1672/3

From the original in Royal Society MS. K, no. 11
Partially printed in *Phil. Trans.*, no. 96 (21 July 1673), 6093

Dantzigk 18th March 73 [N.S.]

Worthy Sr

I Doubt not But ye two Bottles with the greene poisonous matter Sent yu & Mr James Pecims are come to yur hands,[1] though have not beene soe happy as of Late to heare from yu, of which studious Monsr Hevelius also complaines a Little;[2] but 'tis we Wonder the Surpriseing newes These later times have Soe plentifully affoarded should make us forgettfull; I wish & should bee glad to heare the Royall Society may make greater Conquests in Knowledge, then the Kings In Lands; Our perspective maker here is Dead Soe shall not trouble yu any further for glass plates;[3] but shall Beg of yu to gett the inclosed to Mr Boyle carefully Delivered;[4] as also the other Letter Sent to Oxford by post;—

Since I have not beene able to get a Diagram of the Speakeing Trumpet out of England I have adventured to gett one made according to the hints I mett with in the philosophical transactions, & not without Success. The utmost what it will doe I have not yett had oppertunity to try Monsr Hevelius is yett Soe Busy with his Machina Caelestis that hath not time to Examine this Experiment: which hee thinkes may bee much advanced: and of which yu shall have further accte when tryalls are made, in The interim I cannot omitt to give yu an accte of an Odd accident lately come to my Knowledge; A Minister about 50 yeares of Age beeing much indisposed and often relapseing into a Distemper accompanied with Vomitting & purgeing; His Doctor complained to mee that his cure was obstructed; by the patients beeing obliged to study; for when hee was brought by the helpe

of meanes to a Considerable State of Recovery his Studyeing for &
preacheing one Sermon would infalliblely bring a relapse; This Seemed to
mee strange, nor could I bee easily enduced to give Creditt to the Doctors
ingenious Reasons given mee to prove that Study may impaire health Soe
Visiblely as to cast a person into Violent Distempers; but one Day hee
Surprized mee (after hee had urged that The Spirits in Study beeing called
more powerfully to the braine, leaves the other faculties of the bodie more
Languid;) by Relateing what hee had seene giveing the Parson a Vissitt,
which might Confirme this his Conjecture; for the Minister falling into a
relapse after a Sermon preached; Vomitts came strongly upon him; and
amongst other matter cast out; There were many pieces (some as large as the
end of a man's finger some less) of a matter to the touch and Eye perfectly
resembling Tallow 4 peices whereof weighing above $\frac{1}{2}$ an ounce were
Showne the Doctor; how farr this may prove that heate is necessarie to
Digestion I Leave others to judge as beeing out of my Sphere to Examine;

Sr if yu chance to See Captain Kirkby please to present him with my
[*paper torn*] Service[5] & beleive that I Remaine Sr

yor Humble S[ervant]
Chri Kirkby

ADDRESS

 A Monsieur
 Monsieur Grubendol
  Presentement
   A
    Londres
per post Franco Anvers

NOTES

1 For the poisonous substance see Vol. VIII, p. 394. Kirkby had promised to send some
 in the previous summer (in Letter 1999), but there is no record of its arrival.
2 Oldenburg's last letter to Kirkby was Letter 2014, and his last to Hevelius Letter
 2050, both of the previous summer. Hevelius had doubtless expected an acknowledgement of Letters 2060 and 2060a.
3 Compare Letter 1999.
4 None of Kirkby's letters to Boyle has survived.
5 This is perhaps the relative to whom Kirkby had referred before as Colonel Kirkby;
 see Vol. VII, p. 542, and Vol. VIII, p. 395.

2176

Newton to Oldenburg

8 March 1672/3

Printed in Newton, *Correspondence* I, 262–63, from the original in private possession

In this reply to Letter 2133, and to another now lost which probably accompanied a copy of Hecker's *Mercurius in sole*, Newton thanks Oldenburg for the book and for the extract from Huygens' Letter 2122, saying that he will reply to the latter for publication if Huygens will consent. Newton also asks to be allowed to withdraw from the Royal Society "For though I honour that body, yet . . . I see I shall neither profit them, nor (by reason of this distance) can partake of the advantage of their Assemblies." Nevertheless he sent £1–6–0 for his dues.

2177

Wallis to Oldenburg

9 March 1672/3

From the original in Royal Society MS. W 2, no. 7

Oxford. March. 9. 167⅔

Sir,

This is intended you by ye hands of a Gentleman of Dantsick, who formerly came recommended to me from yourself,[1] who intends (he tells me his journey tomorrow morning. And it had like to have come onely as a letter of ordinary salutation onely, had not your packet containing ye transactions of February, & Hecker's intimation of Mercurius in sole come to my hands last night; for both which I returne you my thanks in this. In perusing the former I find these errours have scaped ye presse, to be thus amended.[2] In ye Dedication[3] *p. ult. l. 8* for Rhine read Rhosne. In ye Transactions, *p. 5160. l. 20 for* beed *read* been. *p. 5166. l. 32 for* about, *read* above. *p. 5167. l. 7. for* whatsoever, *read* what the. *p. 5168. l. 27 read* than is ordinaryly accountable for. In ye errata at ye end, instead of *yyvy³vv*, should have been *yyv—y³vv*. My last additional,[4] I find came too late: but it is not material. The numerical Problems, you mention, proposed at Paris;[5] are things I do not intend to trouble myself about, for such reasons as I have formerly mentioned. If they think they have any thing worth others knowledge, they may if they please present them without troubling others with them before hand. I am

> Your friend & servant
> *John Wallis*

ADDRESS

> These
> For Mr Henry Oldenburg
> in the Palmal near St
> James's
> London

NOTES

1 This was possibly John Bagger (see Letter 2091).
2 Some of these were corrected in *Phil. Trans.*, no. 92 (25 March 1673), 6006. For the others, see below, Letter 2185.
3 The dedication to Vol. VII (to the Earl of Anglesey) although normally prefixed to the volume in binding was, as usual, written in February at the conclusion of the volume.
4 The postscript to Letter 2172.
5 These were presumably mentioned in a letter accompanying the books, now lost; they are those of Ozanam mentioned in Letter 2165.

2178
Oldenburg to Huygens
10 March 1672/3

From *Œuvres Complètes*, VII, 258–59
Original in the Huygens Collection at Leiden

A Londres le 10 mars 1673

Monsieur

Je ne vous scauray rien dire à present si non que ie souhaite que vous voulussiez considerer ce que Monsieur Wallis a dit dans l'imprimé cyioint sur vostre discours touchant la suspension du mercure purgé, au dessus de la hauteur ordinaire.[1] Il n'a fait cela que pour vous donner l'occasion d'y penser et de vous en expliquer d'avantage.

Je ne doubte pas que vous n'ayez receu la mienne du 10 fevrier avec le nombre 90 des transactions, où il y a la methode de Monsieur Sluse pour mener des tangentes à toutes sortes de lignes courbes sans aucun calcul.² Je promis alors de respondre plus amplement à deux de vos dernieres; mais ie ne le scauray pas faire encore. J'attends le iournal, ou vous aurez mis ce que vous aviez à dire touchant le barometre, dont M. Grillet s'est attribué l'invention.³ Je suis Monsieur

Vostre tres humble et tres obeissant serviteur
Oldenburg

Monsieur, vous prendrez la peine de corriger quelques fautes de la presse dans les Transactions du mois janvier, conformement aux directions de celles-cy, que vous trouverez à la fin.⁴

ADDRESS

    A Monsieur
Monsieur Christian Hugens de Zulichem
dans la Bibliotheque du Roy à
        Paris

TRANSLATION

London, 10 March 1673

Sir,

I have nothing to tell you at present except that I should like you to reflect upon what Mr. Wallis has said in the enclosed printed work about your discourse on the suspension of mercury purged [of air] above the normal height.¹ He has written this only to give you the occasion of thinking thereon and to explain further your views.

    I do not doubt that you have received mine of 10 February with *Phil. Trans.*, no. 90, which contains Mr. Sluse's method for putting tangents to all sorts of curved lines without any calculation.² I then promised to reply more fully to two of your last, but I have not been able to do so yet. I await the *Journal* in which you have placed what you had to say about the barometer, which Mr. Grillet claims as his own invention.³ I am, Sir

Your very humble and obedient servant,
Oldenburg

Sir, you will trouble to correct some errors of the press in the *Transactions* for January, according to the directions of this month's, which you will find at the end.⁴

ADDRESS

To Mr. Christiaan Huygens of Zulichem,
    At the King's Library,
        Paris

NOTES

1 *Phil. Trans.*, no. 91 (24 February 1671/2), 5160–70, prints Wallis's revision of Letter
   2072.
2 Oldenburg's Letter 2144 was in fact dated 9 February.
3 See Letter 2138 and its note 4.
4 *Phil. Trans.*, no. 91, p. 5172.

2179
Oldenburg to Sand
11 March 1672/3

Mentioned in the endorsement on Sand's Letter 2171 of 28 February. It clearly contained Oldenburg's replies to Sand's queries about errata in the *Philosophical Transactions*. Sand acknowledged it in Letter 2191.

2180
Oldenburg to Reed
11 March 1672/3

Reed's Letter 2169 of 27 February is endorsed as received on 2 March and answered on 11 March 1672/3. In his reply Oldenburg presumably reported that he intended to read Letter 2169 to the Society on the next day, unless Oldenburg mistook the date and in fact wrote after the meeting.

2181

Oldenburg to Newton

13 March 1672/3

Printed in Newton, *Correspondence* I, 263, from the endorsement on Letter 2176

Answ. March 13 1672. Sent ye original of M. Huygens letter of Jan 14 1672/3,[1] and ye Transactions of Febr. 1672:[2] and wthall represented to him my being surprised at his resigning for no other cause, than his distance, wch he knew as well at the time of his election, offering wthall my endeavor to take from him ye trouble of sending hither his qterly payments & without any reflection.

NOTES

Reply to Letter 2176.
1 Letter 2122.
2 *Phil. Trans.*, no. 91 (24 February 1672/3), 5172, contains an entry, by title only, of Newton's edition of Bernard Varenius, *Geographia universalis* (Cambridge, 1672).

2182

Cassini to Oldenburg

15 March 1672/3

From the original in Royal Society MS. C 1, no. 57

Clarissimo Viro Dno. Henrico Oldemburg
regiae societatis a secretis
J. D. Cassinus S.P.D.

Communicavi tibi ante ante annum Vir Clarissime observationes aliquot novi Planetae prope Saturnum dephrensi.[1] nunc libellum as te mitto, in quo easdem observationes, tum alias eiusdem Planetae tum alterius novi compendiose conieci.[2] Rogo te ut haec specimina regiae societati impertiares.[3] Vale. Parisijs die 25 Martij 1673. [N.S.]

TRANSLATION

J. D. Cassini sends many greetings to the famous Henry Oldenburg, Secretary of the Royal Society

I communicated to you more than a year ago, famous Sir, a few observations I had made of a new planet adjacent to Saturn.[1] Now I send you a little book in which I have succinctly expressed the same observations as well as others of the same planet and of another new one.[2] I beg you to convey this copy to the Royal Society.[3] Farewell. Paris, 25 March 1673 [N.S.]

NOTES

1 See Letter 1848, Vol. VIII, pp. 423–26.
2 *Découverte de deux nouvelles planetes autour de Saturne* (Paris, 1673), a pamphlet of twenty pages. Oldenburg published "A Discovery of two New Planets about Saturn, made in the Royal Parisian Observatory by Signor Cassini, Fellow of both the Royal Societies, of England and France; English'd out of French" in *Phil. Trans.*, no. 92 (25 March 1673), 5178–85. The two satellites were Japet and Rhea.
3 This was done at the meeting of 26 March 1673.

2183
Oldenburg to Gornia
15 March 1672/3
From the copy in Royal Society MS. O 2, no. 106

Clarissimo et Doctissimo Viro
Domino Joh. Baptistae Gornia Phil. et Medo. Florento.
Henr. Oldenburg S.

Accepimus literas tuas, quae dum feralem Caroli Fracassati obitus nuncium afferunt, funestum Episcopi nostratis[1] casum atrociorem reddunt. Quo plura subruuntur reipublicae literariae columina, eo graviore sensu genuini illius alumni percelluntur. At sic fata voluere, quibus philosopho, Christiano inprimis, aequo animo parendum.

Cognovit Regia Societas, quae in in Episcopi Cestransis morbum mortemque es commentatus.[2] Agnoscit ingenium tuum, simul et modestiam,

quae pari passu in Te ambuare videntur. Sperat omnino, Te, rebus ferentibus, celebraturum frequentius commercium literarium, nobisque ea
communicaturum, quae per Italiam vestram sagacissimam in re philosophica passim occurrunt, quaeque inprimis Tu ipsa, tum Franciscus Redi,
Bellinus, Mengolus, De gl'Angeli, Borrellus, et similia Italiae lumina nuper
produxissis. Quae Malpighius meditatur et concinnerat, vir inter caeteros
cedro dignissimus, sua ipsius manu innotescere Societati nostrae assolet.
Egregia multa denuo edidit lingua Anglica Illustrissimus Boylius, brevi in
sermonem latinum vertenda; spectant illa tum cognationem, Aeri et
Flammae intercedentem, Tum Flammam vitalem Animantium; adhaec,
Positivam et Relativam Corporum sub aquis levitatem; Elaterij Aeris in
corpora sub Aquis demersa pressionem, nec non differentem gravium
solidorum et Fluidorum pressionem; Adjecit ijs omnibus Diatribam quandam Hydrostaticam, qua Henrici Mori objectiones quasdam, ab ipso in
Enchiridio Metaphysico adversus Boylij Experimenta nonnulla Physico-
Pneumatica vibratas retundit.[3] vidisti sine dubio, quae idem Boylius edidit
de Gemmis, cujus Exemplaria duo, ad Dn Magalotti unum, ad Dn. Malpighium alterum, per amicos in Italiam profectos transmisi.[4] Attolitur
Willisius noster Tractatum de Medicamentorum in corpore humano
operationibus, quem libris ipsius jam editis inferiorem haud fore auguramur.[5]

Latere Te non potest scriptum, quod Dn. Swammerdam de miranda
Uteri humani Fabrica Societati Regiae non ita pridem consecravit.[6]
Author ille in eo jam videtur esse, ut sanguificationis munus possessori
pristino vindicet restituatque;[7] quod quam feliciter exequatur, videre docti
avent. Tu interim Vale, et me Tibi devinctissimum crede. Dabam Londini d. 15. Martij 1673.

TRANSLATION

Henry Oldenburg greets the very famous and learned Mr. Giovanni Baptista
Gornia, philosopher and physician of Florence

We have received your letter which, as it brings the dreadful news of the death
of Carlo Fracassati, renders the grievous case of our bishop[1] the more
dreadful. As many leading lights of the world of learning fade out, the more
grievous is the blow suffered by their disciples. But such is the will of Fate, to
which the philosopher, the Christian philosopher especially,[1] must submit with
equanimity.

The Royal Society has learned of your remarks on the sickness and death of the

Bishop of Chester.[2] It acknowledges both your intelligence and your modesty, which you seem to possess in equal proportion. It is very hopeful that you will as opportunity permits conduct a more frequent correspondence and will communicate to us the philosophical news arising here and there among you very astute Italians, particularly of your own recent productions and those of Francesco Redi, Bellini, Mengoli, degl'Angeli, Borelli, and similar Italian luminaries. What that man most worthy among all others of immortality, Malpighi, thinks and writes he himself is accustomed to impart to our Society in his own hand. The very illustrious Boyle has recently published in English some very remarkable things, soon to be translated into Latin; they are concerned with the relation between air and flame as well as the vital flame of animals; further, the positive and relative levity of bodies under water; the pressure of the air's spring on bodies under water, and the differing pressure of heavy solids and fluids; he has added to all these a certain hydrostatical essay in which he rebuts some objections raised by Henry More in his *Enchiridion metaphysicum* against several of Boyle's *Experiments physico-mechanical*.[3] You have no doubt seen what the same Boyle has published concerning gems, of which I transmitted two copies by friends traveling to Italy, one for Mr. Magalotti, the other for Mr. Malpighi.[4] Our Willis has brought out a treatise on the operations of medicine in the human body, which book we predict will be not inferior to his already published works.[5]

You cannot be ignorant of the paper on the wonderful structure of the human uterus which Mr. Swammerdam dedicated to the Royal Society not long ago.[6] That writer seems now to be engaged in vindicating and restoring to the liver its ancient function of sanguification,[7] and it seems that the learned wish him a happy issue in this. Meanwhile, farewell, and believe me most devoted to you. London, 15 March 1673.

NOTES

Reply to Letter 2113.
1 John Wilkins; see Letter 2105, note 12.
2 The note on Wilkins' illness mentioned in Letter 2113 (it was in the form of a letter to Sir Theodore de Vaux) was read to the Society on 12 March 1672/3.
3 These *Tracts* (London, 1672), were not translated into Latin until 1696.
4 See Letter 2056.
5 Willis's *Pharmaceutice rationalis; sive diatriba de medicamentorum operationibus in corpora humano* was published at Oxford in 1674.
6 See Letter 1938 (Vol. VIII, pp. 617–19).
7 See Letter 2173 and its note 4.

2184
Oldenburg to De Graaf

15 March 1672/3

Mentioned in De Graaf's reply, Letter 2209.

2185
Oldenburg to Wallis

20 March 1672/3

From the draft in Royal Society MS. O 2, no. 107

London March 20. 1672.

Sir,

I am now to give you my thanks for two of yrs, March 1. and 9. The Contents of ye former, concerning Vectius Valens and yr advise about him, I have sent to Paris; but ye addition to ye notion of MyLd Brouncker, touching ye suspension of ye Mercury, came a litle too late. The *Errata* you noted in the latter, I have annexed to ye book, now in the presse for this month; though of ym I find not in ye original, what you take notice of p. 5168 l. 22. I mean ye word *ordinarily*; wch yet is very fit to be added, as you have advertised. As for yt, wch you note in ye *Errata* at ye end, videl. *yyvy³vv*, it was first of all printed as you would have it, wth a — between (as appears in p. 5144. no. 90) but an other good Algebraician here thought it was to be alter'd as is done in the *Errata* before-mention'd; though, when I lookt again upon the original itself of Slusius, it seem'd to me, yt there was a —, as you understood it, wch yet was not cleerly marked.

Sir, I presume to send you herein inclosed a duplicate of yt letter, wch was formerly lost, between London and Oxford.[1] It came thus open from Hamburg under a cover to me, and I now take the liberty again to trouble you wth it, believing, both yt you would not be displeased to read such a letter and also not be unwilling to procure a speedy and full answer to it from ye worthy Dr Pocock, whose humble servant I am, as I am also

Yrs

H. Oldenburg

NOTES

There is no heading, but internal evidence clearly shows this to be addressed to Wallis in reply to Letters 2172 and 2177.

1 See Letter 2114 and its note 2.

2186
Oldenburg to Towneley

22 March 1672/3

From the memorandum in Royal Society MS. T, no. 26

Rec. le 14 Febr. 1672/73.
Answ. March 22. 73.

Written about new planets,[1] and Dr Wallis's discourse ab. Suspen[sion] of [mercury] printed,[2] etc.

NOTES

Reply to Letter 2157.

1 See Letter 2182, note 2.

2 See Letter 2072, note.

2187
Huet to Oldenburg
26 March 1673
From the original in Royal Society MS. H 1, no. 100

Clarissimo viro
D. OLDENBURGIO
S.P.D.
Petr. Dan. Huetius

Gothofredus Leibnitius Moguntinus attulit ad me epistolam sibi a te scriptam,[1] qua significabas de Vettii Velentis Oxoniensi codice ea scripsisse ad te Clarissimum Wallisium,[2] quibus ejus fruendi spes omnis tolleretur: nec enim Bibliotheca efferri eum fas esse, nec in eam admitti quemquam, nisi statis horis, proindeque librum exscribi non posse propter molem operis; praeterea paucorum esse codices Manuscriptos evolvere, eosque praesertim quibus argumentum per se obscurum contineatur; cujusmodi est Astrologicum illud in quo Vettius versatus est, notis quibusdam antiquis ad hanc artem pertinentibus, et vulgo ignorabilibus expressum: si tamen apographum meum transmittatur illuc, daturum se operam, ut cum nostro conferatur, et discrepantiae accurate ad oram adnotentur. Accipio conditionem, clarissime Vir; sed cum hoc flagrante bello, quo viae omnes terra, marique sunt infestae, tuto ad vos perferri codex meus minime possit, expectandus est vel aureae pacis reditus, vel Legati alicuisque ad vos profectio, cui liber sine periculi metu tradi possit. Interim sic habeto, vigere apud me amicitiam inter nos, ut spero, conflatam, nec me commissurum, ut ulla unquam temporis diuturnitate extabescat. Plurimam meis verbis salutem nunties velim, gratesque meo nomine referas clarissimo Wallisio, cujus lucubrationes, summae profecto eruditionis et subtilitatis, cum fructu, & voluptate legendo contrivi. Vale, clarissime vir, & humanissime. Sangermani, Nonis Aprilibus MDCLXXIII [N.S.].

TRANSLATION

Pierre Daniel Huet presents many greetings to the famous Mr. Oldenburg

Gottfried Leibniz of Mainz brought me your letter to him,[1] in which you informed [him] of what the famous Wallis had written to you about the Oxford codex of Vettius Valens;[2] by which all hope of using it is destroyed. For it may not be removed from the library, nor is anyone admitted to the library save at stated hours, and so the book cannot be transcribed because of its size; moreover, there are few who can decipher manuscript codices, especially those dealing with an obscure topic such as that astrology in which Vettius was skilled is, expressed in certain ancient annotations upon this art unintelligible to the ordinary person. Yet if my copy may be sent there, he will make it his business to collate it accurately with ours, and note the variant readings in the margin.

I accept the condition, famous Sir; but as this war is raging which besets all routes by land or sea it is impossible to send my codex to you safely; we must await either the happy return of peace or the journey of some ambassador to [London], who could carry the book without fear of damage. Meanwhile be assured that the settled (I hope) friendship between us is thriving on my side nor shall it ever die away through however long a time by any act of mine. I wish many greetings to be presented on my behalf and offer my thanks to the famous Wallis whose studies, which are indeed of great learning and subtlety, I have contrived to read with both pleasure and profit. Farewell, kind and famous Sir. St. Germain, 5 April 1673 [N.S.].

NOTES

This Letter was enclosed by Leibniz with Letter 2208.
1 Letter 2174.
2 See Letter 2172.

2188
Oldenburg to Hevelius
26 March 1673
From the original in BN MS. N.a.L. 1641, ff. 23–24

Illustrissimo Viro
Domino Johanni Hevelio, Gedanensium Consuli dignissimo
Henr. Oldenburg Salutem

Mitto Tibi, Vir Celeberrime, partem librorum illorum, quos praeterita aestate sub autumnum transmittebam[1] quo tempore hic fasciculus nondum ad manus meas pervenerat. Diu quippe asservatus fuit a quodam Anglo, qui eum Parisiis Londinum secum asportaverat, sed una cum aliis suis reculis ita convasaverat, ut iis omnibus Oxonium, ubi nunc commoratur, delatis, hunc fasciculum non prius huc remitteret, quin jam praeclusa esset per hyemem navigatio.

Prima navi, quae in Balticum hinc navigat, nunc transmitto, satis securus, Te hanc moram, quae extra meam culpam est, haud aegre laturum. Doleo magnopere, naves vestras captas a Scotis etiamnum detineri,[2] quin vehementer metuo, eas nunquam restitutum iri, quicquid Ego et Amici summa cura et sollicitudine flagitaverimus. Mars confundit omnia, et jus in vim plaerumque, proh dolor! convertit. Spes est, pacem brevi refulsuram, damnaque hactenus tolerata amplissimo lucro per libera commercia compensaturam.

Sunt adhuc penes me quaedam Cometographiae tuae, nec non reliquorum librorum tuorum Exemplaria, quae quando volueris ad Te remittam. Speramus, Machinam tuam brevi temporis spatio exituram praelo, et bibliothecas nostras locupletaturum.

Accepimus Clarissimi Heckeri Admonitionem de Mercurii in Solam incursu, anni proximi vere observando. Distribui Exemplaria ab Authore transmissa inter Astronomos nostros, perque varias etiam Mundi partes, ubi commercium nostrum literarium viget, dispersi: id quod jam ante meis literis doctissimo Heckero significavi,[3] cui nunc quoque plurimam salutem dico. Vale, Vir Amplissime, et me Tibi addictissimum amare perge. Dabam Londini, d. 26. Martij 1673.

P.S.

Hanc epistolam obsignaturus accepi Parisiis a Domino Cassino eximia de Caelis nova, detectionem scilicet duorum Planetarum novorum circa Saturnum,[4] quos interjacet Planeta Hugenianus,[5] qui cum 16 dierum spatio periodum suam conficiat, alter ex Cassinianis duobus, intimus nempe, cursum suum conficit $4\frac{1}{2}$ dierum (circiter) spatio, alter vero, extimus, suum absolvit spatio dierum circiter 80, multo longius a Saturno distans, quam reliqui duo.[6] Non dubito, quin Cassinus ipse brevi Tibi sit exemplar transmissurus totius Historiae. Nonnisi unum exemplar mihi suppetit; si plura habuissem, lubentissime Tibi unum alterumve communicassem.

ADDRESS
    Amplissimo et Celeberrimo
    Viro, Domino Johanni Hevelio
    Gedanensium Consuli et
    Astronomo dignissimo
            Dantz[ig]
    avec un pacquet de livres

TRANSLATION

Henry Oldenburg greets the very illustrious Mr. Johannes Hevelius, most worthy senator of Danzig

I send you, famous Sir, a part of those books which I was [in the act of] sending last summer, towards autumn,[1] at which time the package had not yet come to my hands here. In truth it was retained for a long time by a certain Englishman who had carried it with him from Paris to London, but he had so packed them up among trifles of his own that they were all conveyed to Oxford, where he lives now; and he did not return the package here before the winter season had put an end to navigation.

I now send it by the first ship sailing hence for the Baltic, being pretty confident that you will not take this long delay very ill, as it was no fault of mine. I greatly regret that your vessels captured by the Scots are still detained,[2] and I have the gravest fears that they will never be restored, whatever demands I and [my] friends make with great care and solicitude. War upsets everything and more often than not, alas, takes might for right. It is to be hoped that peace will soon be restored and that the damage suffered up to now will be recompensed by very ample profits from free trade.

I have in my possession some copies of your *Cometographia* and of your other books, which I will return to you when you please. We hope that your *Machina* [*coelestis*] will soon come from the press to the enrichment of our libraries.

We have received the *Admonitio* of the famous Hecker concerning the transit of Mercury which is to be observed next spring. I have distributed the copies sent by the author among our astronomers and also dispersed it into various parts of the world where our correspondence thrives, as I have already informed the very learned Hecker in my letter to him;[3] whom I now also greet many times. Farewell, most worthy Sir, and continue to love him who is most devoted to you. London, 26 March 1673.

P.S. As this letter was about to be sealed I received from Paris, from Mr. Cassini, extraordinary news of the heavens, that is the discovery of two new planets [circling] around Saturn,[4] between which is the Huygenian planet;[5] this completes its period in sixteen days whereas one of the Cassinian pair, the innermost, completes its course in about four and a half days and the other, the outermost, performs its round in about eighty, being much further from Saturn than the other two.[6] I do not doubt that Cassini himself will soon send you a copy of his full narrative. I have only one copy for myself; if I had many I would very gladly have passed on one or two to you.

ADDRESS
   To the very worthy and celebrated
   Mr. Johannes Hevelius, most worthy Senator
   and Astronomer of Danzig.
          Danzig
   with a package of books

NOTES

1 See Letter 2050.
2 See Letter 2050, note 3.
3 Letter 2168.
4 See Letter 2182 and its note 2.
5 Titan.
6 Rhea, the nearer and smaller of the new satellites, has a period of four and a half days;
  that of Japet is seventy-nine days.

2189
Oldenburg to Cassini
26 March 1673

From the copy in Royal Society MS. O 2, no. 108

Illustri Viro
Domino Johanni Dominico Cassino,
Reg. Acad. Paris. Astrono.
Henricus Oldenburg Soc. Reg. Ang. Secr.
Salutem

Perquam gavisa est Societas Regia, vir Celeberrime, cum eximium adeo industriae et ingenij fructum, non singulum quidem sed geminum, conspiceret, quem utriusque Academiae,[1] Angliae non minus quam Galliae, Sodalis, in duplici retegendo Planeta, produxit. Gratulatur illa Tibi ex animo, gratulatur Galliae, quin imo toti orbi philosphico, de tam ubere curarum tuarum successu, ac uberiorem usque et usque in excolendis tot residuis Naturae latifundis messem exoptat. Geminum profecto utriusque Societatis alumnum Te praebes, dum indefesso studio, Collegarum operis

Sociato, feracem naturam pertinaciter scrutaris, cumulatisque observationibus Philosophicum penu identidem locupletas. Perennem hoc pacto praestabis Cassiniani nominis gloriam, cui laudes accinet sera posteritas nunquam equidem intermorituras. Vale, Vir Clarissime et Consimilia e Caelis nova crebro nobis impertiri allabora. Dabam Londini d. 26 Martij. 1673.

TRANSLATION

Henry Oldenburg, Secretary of the English Royal Society, greets the illustrious Mr. Giovanni Domenico Cassini, Astronomer of the Royal Academy at Paris

The Royal Society is highly delighted, famous Sir, when it perceives no single outstanding fruit of industry and intelligence but a double one which a Fellow of both the Academies,[1] the English as well as the French, has produced by disclosing twin planets. It congratulates you wholeheartedly, it congratulates France, not to say the whole world of learning on such an ample reward for your diligence and prays for still richer harvests as we go on and on in the cultivation of the rest of Nature's broad fields. You show yourself to be a complete pupil of both societies when, with indefatigable zeal and by combining your labors with your colleagues', you tirelessly examine the fruitful works of Nature and time and again return your gleanings to the philosophical garner. In this way you attach immortal renown to the name of Cassini, whose undying praises even a remote posterity will sing. Farewell, famous Sir, and toil on to bring us continually such news from the heavens. London, 26 March 1673.

NOTES

Reply to Letter 2182.
1 For Cassini's election to the Royal Society in May 1672 see Vol. VIII, p. 501 and p. 502, note 12.

2190
Fermat to Oldenburg
29 March 1673

From the original in Royal Society MS. F 1, no. 51

A Thoulouse le 8me Avril [N.S.]

Monsieur

La lettre que vous m'aves faict l'honneur de m'escrire[1] ne m'aiant esté rendue que depuis peu a cause du retardement du messagér ches qui elle avoit demeurè quelque temps sans que ie le sceusse, ie n'ai peu vous remercier plustost des nouvelles marques de vostre souvenir et de cet ouvrage que vous avés eu la bontè de m'envoiér de Monsieur Boyle.[2] Il m'a pareu digne de l'autheur dont l'esprit et le sçavoir sont assès cogneus, ie ne doubte pas qu'un philosophe de qualité comme luy ne soit fort exact a faire ses experiences et a racontér celles qu'il a faictes, il me semble qu'il y en a dans ce petit livre quelques unes qui sont bien remarquables. Je souhaitte que la relation du canal que vous pourrés lire dans une lettre qui a esté imprimée icy il n'y a pas longtemps vous agrée, aussi bien que la description poetique qui l'accompagne,[3] ie voudrois bien avoir quelque chose qui meritast de vous estre presenté, c'est vous, Monsieur, qui pourrés nous faire part, quand il vous plairra, des belles descouvertes que vous faictes si souvent dans la physique, si Mr Baile[4] qui a tousiours beaucoup de respect pour vous en faict quelqu'une qui soit considerable vous le sçaurès bientost, Je vous coniure de croire que ie suis autant qu'on le peut estre Monsieur

Vostre treshumble et tres
obeissant serviteur
Fermat

ADDRESS
A Monsieur
Monsieur Oldenbourg
A Londres

TRANSLATION

Toulouse, 8 April [N.S.]

Sir,

The letter which you did me the honor to write[1] not having been delivered to me until recently, because of the delay of the messenger in whose hands it remained for some time without my knowledge, I could not thank you sooner for the fresh tokens of your recollection [of me] and for the work by Mr. Boyle which you were good enough to send me.[2] It seemed to me worthy of the author, whose intelligence and knowledge are pretty well known; I have no doubt that a philosopher of his caliber is very careful in performing his experiments and in describing those he has made; it seems to me that some of those in this little book are very remarkable. I hope that the description of the canal which you can read in a letter recently printed here is acceptable to you, as well as the poetic description which accompanies it;[3] I should like to have something worthy of being presented to you, it is you, Sir, who can share with us, when you wish, the fine discoveries which you so often make in natural philosophy; if Mr. Bayle[4] who always has such great respect for you makes any considerable discovery you will know it soon. I adjure you to believe that I am, as far as it is possible to be so, Sir,

Your very humble and obedient servant
Fermat

ADDRESS

Mr. Oldenburg,
London

NOTES

The manuscript is endorsed by Oldenburg as having been received on 30 April 1673.

1 This can hardly be Letter 1881 (Vol. VIII) as Oldenburg then sent a book by Morland, not one by Boyle; evidently some correspondence is missing.

2 Probably *An Essay about the Origine & Virtues of Gems.*

3 This was presumably Louis de Froidour, *Lettre à M. Barrillon Damoncourt contenant la relation et la description des travaux qui se font en Languedoc pour la Communication des deux mers* (Toulouse, 1672), which actually contains three letters. But there is no poetry in the two copies in the British Museum. Oldenburg had already published a translation in *Phil. Trans.*, no. 84 (17 June 1672), 4080–86, with a summary of two other letters by Froidour.

4 See Vol. VI, p. 100, note, for this inventor of Toulouse.

2191

Sand to Oldenburg

31 March 1673

From the copy in Royal Society MS. S 1, no. 126

Nobilissime Vir.

Hodie tradita mihi fuit epistola tua responsoria 5. Id. Mart. data. Iam notam feci Bibliopolae indignationem tuam ob tituli immutationem: responsum vero ejus necdum accepi.[1] Operam suam pro argento locare, non nisi ingenuis datum est: vernis & mancipiis herorum suorum mercenariis esse n[on: *paper torn*] licet.[2] Eadem licentia uti in meis scriptis Bibliopola sibi non praesumpsit: ne[c: *paper torn*] vero si praesumpsisset, patienti id tulissem animo. At Domino rem suam si corrumpere libet, sane licet. Si operam ei meam negassem, alius Bibliopolae magis gratificans laboris mercede accepta stultitiae meae illusisset. Pag. 322. lin. 36. non ita legendum, ut suspicaris.[3] Non enim in Gallico mentio est avis, latine dictae *Pari* Gallice *mesange*, Anglice *Tidmouse*. Sed agitur ibi de animali quadrupede Gallice vocato *mesaraigne*, al. *musaraigne*, Latine *Mure Araneo*, Anglice *Fieldmouse* vel *Erdshrew*, quod me docuit Merrettus in Pinace rerum naturalium, p. 167. Eandem vocem Interpres Ephemeridum perperam reddidit *Soricem*. Pag. 562. lin. 20 dicis *Lambsbloud*, at in Gallicis Ephemeridibus est *du sang de veau* quod nosti esse calves-blood. Pag. 580. line. 12. pro 5. videtur leg. 6. Errata postica non tantum Num. 16.[4] sed & alias semper observavi, neque enim sivi Acta priora perperam inprimi, ubicunque admonitio errorum in sequentibus fuit exhibita. Praefationem meam in Acta Philosophica reor te jam accepisse traditam a Domino Cooke.[5] Quod ad Dominum Martyn epistolam prioribus meis inclusam deferri curasti, opus [*paper torn*][6] gratissimum fecisti, pro quo tibi gratias ingentes ago, qui sum &c.

P.S. Festinationi tabellarii publici tribuendum, quod supra non admonui, me Pag. 3. ex antecedentibus & consequentibus firmiter concludere legendum *Tropicum Cancri*. nullum enim verborum sensum perspicio, si *Tropici* legantur.[7] Considera quaeso verba, & me non aberasse comperies. Vale.

TRANSLATION

Most noble Sir,

Your answering letter of 11 March was delivered to me today. I have already reported to the bookseller your indignation at the change of the title, but I have as yet received no reply from him.[1] Only the freeborn can hire their labor out for money, it is not possible for slaves and bondsmen to be their masters' hirelings.[2] The bookseller did not allow himself the same freedom with regard to my own writings, and if he had so indulged himself I would not have patiently borne with him. But if an employer wishes to spoil his own property, he may. If I had refused him my labor, another person more compliant to the bookseller in his work would, by taking his pay, have made fun of my folly.

Page 322, line 36. It is not to be read as you suppose.[3] For in the French there is no mention of the bird called in Latin *parus*, in French *mésange*, in English *titmouse*. But what is in question there is the quadruped animal called in French *mesaraigne* or *musaraigne*, in Latin *mus araneus*, in English fieldmouse or earth shrew, as I learn from Merret in the *Pinax rerum naturalium*, p. 167. The translator of the *Journal* [*des Sçavans*] incorrectly rendered the same word as *sorex* [shrew mouse].

Page 562, line 20 you say *lambsblood*, but in the French *Journal* it is *sang du veau*, which you know to be calves' blood.

Page 580, line 12. For 5, it seems, read 6. I have taken note of the subsequent errata always, not only in Number 164 but elsewhere too, for I have not allowed the earlier *Transactions* to be printed incorrectly, whenever notice of errors was given in subsequent ones. I reckon you have already received my preface to the *Philosophical Transactions* delivered by Mr. Cooke.[5] As for your taking the trouble to have the letter, enclosed in my former to you, carried to Mr. Martin you have done something for which I am most grateful,[6] for which I return hearty thanks, who am, etc.

P.S. You must attribute to hastening to catch the public post that I did not advise you that I definitely conclude from the antecedents and the consequences on page 3 that one should read *Tropic of Cancer*.[7] For I see no sense in the words if *Tropics* be read. Reflect on the words, I beg you, and you will find I have not gone astray. Farewell.

NOTES

This letter, sent in a packet to the Mr. Cooke mentioned in it, was lost in the post; however, Sand sent a copy of it in his later letter of 10 November 1673, which we have extracted to print here.

1 Compare Letter 2171, and its note 3.
2 Presumably Sand means: "I am no man's slave, but ..."
3 Compare Letter 2171, note 23.

4 Errors in no. 16 are corrected at the end of no. 17, p. 310.
5 We do not know when this was sent. See Letter 2171, note 33.
6 Perhaps the word "mihi" (to me) has been lost here.
7 Compare Letter 2171, note 21.

2192

Hill to Oldenburg

31 March 1673

From the original in Royal Society MS. H 3, no. 7

Lixa.[1] 10th Aprill 1673 [N.S.]

Sr

By the last shipps I received yours of the 9th October[2] as I hope you have one from mee with an inclosed from Padre Valentin Estansen, ye Jesuite, at the Bahia in Brazeel.[3] I understand by my Correspondent there, That ye Father, had prepared a Large answer to your Quaeries, but thought it necessary to review them wch. could not bee done time enough for the Last shipps, but by the next, in November, you may depend on them. Somuch I suppose you have heard from himself if my Letter of the first of December L[ast] wch. accompanied his, bee received.[4]

I have made strict inquiry about ye Herb of Paraguay, but without Succes, nor can I give you any hopes of obtaining it because the Spaniards do not permitt any of this Nation to trade at Buenos Ayres, where you intimate the Herb growes. However I shall write to ye Father about it, who probably may do you the Service you desire. If in any thing I can serve you, I shall do it most readily. I am Sr

your most humble servant
Mr. Oldenburgh Esq. *Tho Hill*

ADDRESS

For Henry Oldenburgh Esq
Secretary to ye Royal Society
London

By Capt. Jenifer POSTMARK MA 26

NOTES

1 Lisbon.

2 Letter 2080, of which no copy survives.

3 The *Giornale de' Letterati* was to publish some astronomical observations made in 1668 by Father "Valentino Estancel" in the issue of 20 September 1673 [N.S.].

4 In Letter Book VI, 81, where this letter is copied out is written "Note, that neither of ye letters above-mentioned did ever come to my hands." Compare Letters 1780 and 1780a (Vol. VIII), for Oldenburg's queries.

2193
Collins to Oldenburg
c. 1 April 1673
From the copy in Royal Society Letter Book VI, pp. 75–80

An Answer to the letter of Mr. Leibnith of Febr. 3. 1673

Sr

Your letter concerning the doctrine of interpolations, & about the discourse you had with Dr. Pell concerning the same, and what Monsr. Mouton had performed therein, I imparted to Mr Collins a member of the Society who gave me a synopsis of Mr. Kersy's Algebra now half finished,[1] with a narrative concerning what may be the argument of another volume to be fitted for the presse, which gives an account in some measure of the advancement and application of the Analytick doctrine here.[2] As for the doctrine of interpolations,[3] he saith, it is farr more generall and easy to doe, and that by two severall methods, by fitting an aequation to the ranke proposed, than by ayd of tables of figurated numbers; and, for instance, the hardest rankes in Mouton's booke:[4] in relation to either of which if you take the number of Termes to be the root or t, and out of the aequation raise the resolvend, you shall light upon any number or intermediate number in either of these rankes:

The former hath this aequation proper to it

$$\left.\begin{array}{l} 3 \\ 5 \\ 8 \\ 18 \\ 45 \\ 105 \end{array}\right\} \quad \tfrac{1}{60}t^5 - \tfrac{1}{12}t^4 + \tfrac{3}{4}t^3 - 3\tfrac{5}{12}t^2 + 7\tfrac{11}{15}t - 2 = N$$

The other is,

$$\left.\begin{array}{l} N \\ 3 \\ 18 \\ 222 \\ 1317 \\ 4977 \end{array}\right\} \quad \text{The aequation is } 4\tfrac{1}{20}t^5 - 20\tfrac{1}{4}t^4 + 56\tfrac{1}{4}t^3 - 101\tfrac{1}{4}t^2 + 103\tfrac{2}{10}t - 39 = N$$

For instance, if I take the 4th terme,

$$
\begin{array}{l}
+4 \times 103\tfrac{2}{10} = \;+\;412{,}8 \\
-16 \times 101\tfrac{1}{4} = \qquad\qquad\quad -1620 \\
+64 \times 56\tfrac{1}{4} \;= +3600 \\
-256 \times 20\tfrac{1}{4} \;= \qquad\qquad\quad -5184 \\
\underline{+1024 \times 4\tfrac{1}{20} = +4147{,}2 \quad - \quad 39} \\
\qquad\qquad\qquad\quad +8160 \quad -6843 \\
\qquad\qquad\qquad\quad \underline{-6843} \;\cdots \\
\qquad\qquad\qquad\quad +1317
\end{array}
$$

And in any aequation of the 5th. degree (the like for other degrees) it is easy by 4 Multiplications out of the roots to raise the Resolvends, without raising the powers of the roote. Monsieur Leibnitz saith, he hath a Method, that will add these rankes of fractions, whose denominators are figured numbers, viz.

$$
\begin{array}{cccc}
\tfrac{1}{3} & \tfrac{1}{6} & \tfrac{1}{10} & \tfrac{1}{15} \\[4pt]
\tfrac{1}{4} & \tfrac{1}{10} & \tfrac{1}{20} & \tfrac{1}{35} \\[4pt]
\tfrac{1}{5} & \tfrac{1}{15} & \tfrac{1}{35} & \tfrac{1}{70}
\end{array}
$$

There rankes (if we much mistake not) Mengolus in his booke de additione fractionum sive quadraturae Arithmeticae, printed at Bononia in 1658.[5] hath already taught to add. But when he comes to speake of a Musicall progression in fractions, or, which is all one, the Reciprocall of an Arithmeticall progression with the squares and cubes thereof, as

$$\frac{1}{2} \quad \frac{1}{3} \quad \frac{1}{4} \quad \frac{1}{5} \quad \frac{1}{6}$$
$$\frac{1}{4} \quad \frac{1}{9} \quad \frac{1}{16} \quad \frac{1}{25} \quad \frac{1}{36}$$

Mengolus confesseth, he could not add those rankes, saying, *ditioris ingenij adminiculum postulant.*[6]

Our method extends to the adding of these, and if that of Leibnitz doth the like I conceive they must be the same: for a Tryall whereof this usefull question many be putt. One that hath a lease of 100 lbs per annum to continue 100 years, desires to know the present worth of it, discounting 6 per cent per annum simple interest, the payments being yearly.

It is the summe of 100 Tearms in this ranke.

$\frac{10000}{106} \quad \frac{10000}{112} \quad \frac{10000}{118} \quad \frac{10000}{124}$ &c. which according to our computation is 3200 lbs and not a penny more or lesse.[7]

What is the summe of any other or greater number of Termes in the said ranke?

If Monsr. Leibnitz can helpe us to Mengolus booke intituled, *Via regia ad scientias Mathematicas*, and his late Musick,[8] it will be very acceptable to us; as will likewise be Griembergerus *de Speculo Ustorio Elliptico una cum nova Caeli perspectiva et praxi sectionum conicarum et consectarijs, circulorum contactus et sectiones angulares concernentibus.*[9]

As to Pere Pardies designe of finding the roots of aequations by ayd of the Logme. Curve, it is a Method here well known, and is only proper for aequations of two Nomes,[10] aequall to ye resolvend, like those cubickes, to which Cardan applyes his rules, which are or may be rendred generall, notwithstanding the difficulty by reason of the root of a negative quantity, at wch writers have hitherto stumbled; and for these Kinds of aequations, tables of square roots & Cube roots &c. would mightily facilitate the worke.

Dulaurens, a late writer, in the preface to his *specimina*[11] promised a method of takeing away all the midle powers in any aequations, and consequently leave none but the highest and lowest power aequall to an absolute (of which doubtlesse Monsr. Frenicle can give an account:) If this could always be done, we should confesse, that the Logme. Curve might serve for the construction of all aequations; if you can procure this Notion, or any other, of Monsr. Hozanna,[12] about the divideing of aequations into their components &c; they will come as a seasonable supplement of our designes, and the Authour shall have an honorable mention with thankes.

There came lately to our view and perusall a folio Treatise of perspective written by Monsr. Heuret,[13] wherein he censures and rejects the Conickes of Monsr. Desargues, intituled, *Leçons de tenebres*, whereof we understand, there were but 50 Coppies in all printed, and it will be extreame difficult to procure one of them;[14] if the Authors intention be well minded, the doctrine deserves applause and accessions to be made thereto, rather than dispraise. Now his designe was, to treate of Conick Sections as projected from lesser Circles situated on the surface of the sphere; for explication whereof, suppose the Eye be at the Center of a sphere which is touched by a plaine at the Zenith, and beholds the plaine of a segment of the sphere, the said plaine is the base of a Cone whose vertex is the Eye: If the said circle be above the Horizon, and Parallel thereto, ye section on the touching plaine is a circle; but if not Parallel to the Horizon, it is an Ellipsis, if it toucheth the Horizon, and all other parts of it be above the same, it is a Parabola; &c. seing many such elevated circles may touch the Horizon in the same point, their projection will be all *congruentes Parabolae*; but if one or more circles be partly above and partly beneath the Horizon, their projections are hyperbolas; & if they have the same common Chord in the Horizon, their projections are *congruentes hyperbolae*; if they be quite beneath the horizon, they cannot be projected at all. From diverse circles the conick-sections being thus supposed to be projected, if the Eye be likewise supposed to be removed to the Nadir, and to project the same circles again, it will follow that what was before determined by the intersections of these Conick-sections, may now be found & determined by circles that are sub-contrarily projected or placed to those circles on the sphere that are bases of the visuall cones; so that it leads to the consideration, in what cases problemes determined by conick-sections may be solved by plaine Geometry. Whereas Mersennus saith concerning Paschall the Son, *quod unica propositione universalissima, 400 Corollarijs armata, totum Apollonium complexus est*;[15] we understand that this treatise is yet unprinted, but proceedes in Desargue's Method (whose scholar he was;) and Monsr. de Prex a Bookseller in Paris hath informed, that the manuscript of it remaines with one of the brothers of him the said de Prex at Auvergne.[16]

You see we are promised Fermats remaines, but these or some of them, with Desargue's Treatise and a MS of Robervalls *de Locis planis solidis Linearibus et ad superficiem*,[17] we believe are already and have long beene in England in the hands of a Learned man, that does not thinke fitt to impart them, who hath thoughts of writing a Treatise *de canone Mathematico* or Table of sines, shewing what strange difficult Problemes and aequations may be solved thereby. As to Descartes's solution of Pappus's probleme,[18] he saith there is much paines bestowed, where little would have served; and indeed, to say the truth; if there be 5 points in a Conick-section, or 4 in a parabola given, innumerable other points may be described by aid of moveable Angles without Knowing either the figure at all, or its Axes, foci, Asymptotes, ordinates, whence Trigonometricall supputations doe likewise ensue.

If it be not our good Luck to be partakers of these things, may we not at least hope to meet with them in the cursus Mathematicus of the Learned Pere Claudius Millet de Chales now aprinting if not finished at Lyons.[19]

Monsr. Picart received from Bartholinus the Treatise of the late Monsr. de Beaune, *de Angulo Solido*, with an intention to gett it printed at paris.[20] May we ere long expect it?

NOTES

The copy bears the marginal note "This letter was made latin, haveing been drawn up as tis here in English by Mr. Collins." For the Latin version see Letter 2196. It is a reply to Leibniz's Letter 2140. For clarification and assistance in the mathematical problems we are once again indebted to Dr. D. T. Whiteside.

1 See Letter 2093, note 4. The first two books are mentioned as published in *Phil. Trans.*, no. 95 (23 June 1673), 6073.

2 The second part of Kersey's work is described as on sale in *Phil. Trans.*, no. 108 (23 November 1674), 192. These references to Kersey are included in Letter 2196a.

3 Besides his knowledge of Pell's investigations, Collins had learned of the single advancing-differences formula of interpolation from his correspondence with Gregory. See particularly the latter's letter to him of 23 November 1670 (Turnbull, *Gregory*, 118-33; Newton, *Correspondence*, I, 45-49).

4 Book III, Chapter 3, of Gabriel Mouton's *Observationes diametrum solis et lunae* . . . (Lyons, 1670), is entitled "De nonnulis numerorum proprietatibus" and is concerned with tabular interpolation by the "Stirling" function $f_n = A + nB + \binom{n}{2}C + \binom{n}{3}D +$ . . . The examples chosen by Collins appear on pp. 384-89. However, Collins prefers for the expression the "Newton" function, $f_n = A + Bn + Cn^2 + Dn^3 + $ . . . which really is less elegant in use. Although Collins fails to recognize the fact, his two examples are in fact the same—in the first $n = t - 1$, in the second $n = 3(t-1)$.

5 See Vol. VI, p. 236, note 3. The correct date of publication is 1650. In this work Mengoli does indeed deal with the addition of infinite series of the reciprocals of triangular numbers, pyramidal numbers and so on.

6 "they demand the assistance of a more splendid intelligence." Strictly speaking, in his preface (** 3) which Collins quotes, Mengoli only says that he has failed to sum the reciprocals of the series of squares. A musical or harmonical progression, the reciprocals of whose terms are in arithmetical progression, has the general form $\frac{a}{b}, \frac{a}{b+c}, \frac{a}{b+2c}, \ldots$

7 A summation of four terms of the same example is given by Newton at the end of his letter to Collins of January 1669/70 (Newton, *Correspondence*, I, 16-19). Collins' "not a penny more or lesse" seems a strangely inappropriate comment, especially as it is

likely that he had not used any method for arriving at this sum, but had worked out (approximately) and added the terms mechanically.

8 Pietro Mengoli, *Via regia ad mathematicas per arithmeticam, algebram speciosam et plano-metriam* was published at Bologna in 1655; it is in verse. For his *Speculazioni di musica*, see Letter 1984, note 2.

9 This work by Christoph Grienberger is said in the *Neue Deutsche Biographie* to have been published at Rome in 1613. See also Vol. VI, p. 231, note 16.

10 Monomial terms. Collins refers obliquely to Newton's manuscript notes on Kinckhuysen's *Algebra* (Newton, *Mathematical Papers*, II, 376–94, 418–22).

11 For the *Specimina mathematica* (Paris, 1667) of François Dulaurens, see Vol. III, pp. 335–37.

12 Ozanam.

13 Grégoire Huret, *Optique de portraiture et peinture* (Paris, 1670 and 1672); both editions are in folio. Collins lent a copy of this book to Newton in May, 1673. There is a review (almost certainly by Collins) of the 1670 edition in *Phil. Trans.*, no. 86 (19 August 1672), 5048–49, which mentions his criticisms of Desargues. For Collins's earlier interest in the work of Desargues, see Vols. IV–VI. The relevant passage from Huret is quoted in R. Taton, *L'œuvre mathématique de Desargues* (Paris, 1951), p. 46. It seems that Collins is largely paraphrasing Huret here.

14 For this lost pamphlet by Desargues see Vol. IV, p. 324, note 5. Collins confuses the *Leçons de ténèbres* with Pascal's *Essay pour les Coniques* of 1640 and perhaps also with Desargues' *Brouillon-proiect d'une atteinte aux evenemens des rencontres du cone avec un plan* (Paris, 1639; reprinted in Taton, *L'œuvre mathématique de Desargues*, pp. 99–180). The lost *Leçons*, though much more succinct, seems from Huret's and other contemporary references to have dealt with much the same questions as the *Brouillon-proiect*.

15 See Vol. VIII, p. 510 (the same quotation) and p. 511, note 9; also Vol. IV, p. 324, note 5.

16 Collins was thoroughly confused. The brothers Etienne and Louis Perier of Clermont-Ferrand in Auvergne were certainly not booksellers, although they did attempt to persuade the Paris booksellers to publish Pascal's manuscript works. The brothers sent the mathematical manuscripts of Blaise Pascal which they owned to Leibniz at Paris in 1676, among them a copy of the (privately printed) *Essay pour les coniques*. (See R. Taton, "L'Essay pour les Coniques' de Pascal," *Revue d'Histoire des Sciences*, VIII, 1955, pp. 1–18.)

17 No such manuscript by Roberval exists; very probably Collins means Fermat, *Ad locos planos et solidos isagoge* (*Varia opera mathematica*, Toulouse, 1679, pp. 1–8, and *Œuvres de Fermat*, ed. Charles Henry and Paul Tannery, Paris, 1891–1912, I, 91 f) and *Isagoge ad locos ad superficiem* (*Œuvres de Fermat*, I, 279 ff). Perhaps the "learned man" below might be John Pell, or Thomas Hobbes.

18 That is, Descartes's analytical reduction of the Greek three or four locus to a general conic in *Géometrie*, Book II. Below, Collins refers to the construction Newton had sent to him on 20 August 1672 (see Newton, *Correspondence*, I, 230–31, and *Mathematical Papers*, II, 156–58).

19 As already noted, this book appeared only in 1674.

20 See Letter 2044, note 11, and P. Costabel, "Le traité de l'Angle solide de Florimond de Beaune," *Actes du XIe Congrès internationale d'histoire des sciences*, 1968, pp. 189–94.

2194
Beale to Oldenburg
early April 1673

According to Birch (*History*, III, 83) this letter, dated "April 1673" was read to the Society at the meeting on 9 April 1673. It contained an account of a pear tree whose fruit, although inedible, produced especially fine perry, and Beale was requested to procure some grafts of it for Mr. Charles Howard.

2195
Newton to Oldenburg
3 April 1673

Printed in Newton, *Correspondence* I, 264–66, from the original in private possession

In this reply to Letter 2181, Newton replied very patiently in detail to the points raised by Huygens in Letter 2122.

He begins by remarking that the best way to understand the nature of colored light is "by resolving light into colours as far as may be done by Art" and examining the colored light, combining various colors and resolving them again. He comments dryly, "This will prove a tedious & difficult task to do it as it ought to be done but I could not be satisfied till I had gone through it. However I onely propound it, and leave every man to his own method."

He then explains why he does not think that yellow and blue will make up the colors of the spectrum, and declares that it is no "easier to frame an Hypothesis by assuming onely two originall colours rather than an indefinite variety," adding "But to examin how colours may be thus explained Hypothetically is besides my purpose. I never intended to show wherein consists the nature and difference of colours, but onely to show that *de facto* they are originall & immutable qualities of the rays wch exhibit them, & to leave it to others to explicate by Mechanicall Hypotheses the nature & difference of those qualities; wch I take to be no very difficult matter."

He goes on to insist that Huygens is mistaken in supposing that all colors are not required to produce white light, for if two colors do give white light it will be found that these are compound, not simple, colors.

He finally explains away Huygens' criticism of his experiments on refraction with the object glasses of telescopes.

2196
Oldenburg to Leibniz
6 April 1673

From the original in Hannover MSS., ff. 18–19, 51–52
Printed in Gerhardt, pp. 85–89, 239–40

Amplissimo et Consultissimo Viro
Domino Gothofredo Gulielmo Leibnitio J.U.D. etc.
Henr. Oldenburg S.P.

Londini die
6 April 1673.

Promiseram, Vir Amplissime, in literis meis, 6to Martii novissimi ad Te datis, me ampliorem ad tuas responsionem adornaturum, quamprimum edoctus forem de iis, quae porro ex me scire desideraveras.[1] Datam itaque fidem liberaturus, hanc priori epistolam succenturiare volui, ut intelligas eo luculentius, nolle me tibi in ulla re deesse, quae quidem a mea proficisci tenuitate poterit. Scias itaque primo, me scriptum illud tuum de Interpolationum doctrina,[2] deque tuo cum Clarissimo Pellio circa id argumentum et Moutonum colloquio, impertiise Doctissimo nostro Collinio, similiter e Societate Regia, qui in hac est sententia, dictam Interpolationum doctrinam multo posse latius extendi, longeque reddi faciliorem, idque binae methodi adminiculo, Aequationem seriei propositae accommodando, quam numerorum figuratorum Tabulas adhibendo. Ut exemplis rem ostendat, duas omnium difficillimas in Moutoni libro series sub incudem vocat, dicitque, si respectu alterutrius earum sumas numerum terminorum esse radicem, sive t atque ex Aequatione eruas Homogeneum, inventum iri quemlibet numerum vel numerum intermedium in alterutra harum serierum:

Prior series

$$
\left.\begin{array}{r} 3 \\ 5 \\ 8 \\ 18 \\ 45 \\ 105 \end{array}\right|
$$

Hujus prioris haec est Aequatio ipsi accommoda;

$$\tfrac{1}{60}t^5 - \tfrac{1}{12}t^4 + \tfrac{3}{4}t^3 - 3\tfrac{5}{12}t^2 + 7\tfrac{11}{15}t - 2 = N$$

Altera series

$$\left.\begin{array}{l} N \\ 3 \\ 18 \\ 222 \\ 1317 \\ 4977 \end{array}\right\} \text{Aequatio haec est:}$$

Aequatio haec est:

$$4\tfrac{1}{20}t^5 - 20\tfrac{1}{4}t^4 + 56\tfrac{1}{4}t^3 - 101\tfrac{1}{4}t^2 + 103\tfrac{2}{10}t - 39 = N$$

Ex. gr. sumo terminum quartum:

$$
\begin{array}{rll}
+4 \times 103\tfrac{2}{10} &= + 412,8 & \\
-16 \times 101\tfrac{1}{4} &= & -1620. \\
+64 \times 56\tfrac{1}{4} &= +3600 & \\
-256 \times 20\tfrac{1}{4} &= & -5184. \\
+1024 \times 4\tfrac{1}{20} &= +4147,2 & - \quad 39. \\
\hline
& +8160 & -6843 \\
& -6843 & \\
\hline
& +1317 &
\end{array}
$$

Adjicit in quavis Aequatione quinti gradus (quod et extendit ad alios gradus) facile esse, per 4 Multiplitiones e Radicibus excitare Homogenea, ita ut non sit opus radicis excitare Potestates.

Deinde quod commemorabas, Methodum tibi suppetere, qua addere possis eas Series Fractionum, quarum Denominatores numeris constant Figuratis; putat idem Collinius, Mengolum in libro suo de Additione Fractionum sive Quadraturae Arithmeticae, Bononiae impresso A. 1658, docuisse nos modum summae harum serierum inveniendae.

$$
\begin{array}{cccc}
\tfrac{1}{3} & \tfrac{1}{6} & \tfrac{1}{10} & \tfrac{1}{15} \\
\tfrac{1}{4} & \tfrac{1}{10} & \tfrac{1}{20} & \tfrac{1}{35} \\
\tfrac{1}{5} & \tfrac{1}{15} & \tfrac{1}{35} & \tfrac{1}{70}
\end{array}
$$

At quando idem Mengolus pergit ad Progressionem Musicam in Fractionibus, vel, quod idem est, ad Reciproca Progressionis Arithmeticae, cum Quadratis et Cubis eorum, puta,

$$
\begin{array}{ccccc}
\tfrac{1}{2} & \tfrac{1}{3} & \tfrac{1}{4} & \tfrac{1}{5} & \tfrac{1}{6} \\
\tfrac{1}{4} & \tfrac{1}{9} & \tfrac{1}{16} & \tfrac{1}{25} & \tfrac{1}{36},
\end{array}
$$

Fatetur ille, non potuisse se harum serierum summam invenire, ditiorisque ingenii adminiculum in eo postulat.[3]

Methodus nostra, ait Collinius, ad harum quoque summam inveniendam se porrigit, atque si illa methodus idem praestat, eas coincidere arbitratur. Ad quod experiundum, utilem hanc quaestionem proponit;

Quidam habet domum fundumve sibi locatum pro censu annuo 100 librarum, spatio 100 annorum: scire cupit praesentem ejus valorem, accisis 6 libris in 100 pro simplici faenore annuo, solutione annuatim facienda.

Valor ille est summa 100 terminorum, hac serie:
$\frac{10000}{106}$ $\frac{10000}{112}$ $\frac{10000}{118}$ $\frac{10000}{124}$ etc. Quod juxta computum nostrum facit 3200 lb. quam proxime.[4] Quaeritur, quae sit summa cujusvis alterius vel majoris numeri Terminorum in dicta serie?

Si procurare nobis potes eum Mengoli librum, cui titulus: *Via Regia ad Scientias Mathematicas*, ejusdemque *Musicam* novissime editam; adhaec, *Griembergerum de Speculo Ustorio Elliptico*, una cum ejusdem *Nova Caeli Perspectiva*, nec non *Praxi Sectionum Conicarum*, et Consectariis, circulorum contactus et sectiones angulares concernentibus; rem omnino gratam nobis es praestiturus, quam, re ferente, demereri annitemur.

Reverendi Patris Pardies institutum quod attinet de Inveniendis AEquationum radicibus, Curvae Logarithmicae beneficio; laudatus Collinius ait, Methodum ejusmodi probe inter nos esse cognitam, eamque accommodam non esse nisi AEquationibus duarum potestatum, aequalium Numero Resolvendo sive Homogeneo Aequationis, quales sunt illae Cubicae, quibus suas Cardanus regulas applicat, quae sunt, vel saltem reddi possunt, generales, obstante nequicquam difficultate ex negativae quantitatis radice orta; id quod omnibus hucusque Authoribus crucem fixit. Atque in hoc genus AEquationibus conficiendis, Tabulae equidem radicum quadraticarum, cubicarum etc. operationes sane tales apprime faciliores redderent.

Dn. Laurentius Gallus, in praefatione ad *Specimina* sua, methodum pollicebatur, omnes Potestates medias in quibusvis AEquationibus auferendi, proindeque relinquendi nullas nisi Potestatem supremam infimamque, Homogeneo aequalem, (qua de re doctissimus Freniclius haud dubie edocere harum rerum curiosos poterit:) Hoc si fieri semper posset, fateremur profecto, Curvam Logarithmicam inservire omnium AEquationum constructioni posse. Atque si hanc obtinere poteris Notionem ullasve alias a Dno. Osanna, in nuperrimis literis tuis a Te celebrato, circa Aequationum in sua componentia divisionem etc; supplemento erunt institutis nostris tempestivo, quae in lucem edita doctissimum Authorem debita laude cumulabunt.

Vidimus non ita dudum Perspectivam *Heureti*, in qua perstringuntur rejiciunturque Dni. Des Argues Conica, *Leçons de Tenebres* nuncupata; quorum nonnisi 50 Exemplaria fuisse impressa dicuntur, adeo ut perdifficile sit, vel unum ex tam paucis procurare. Sentit Dn. Collinius, siquidem mens et scopus Authoris probe attendatur, doctrinam illam applausum potius et augmentum mereri, quam vituperium; Consilium quippe ipsius fuisse, Agere de Sectionibus Conicis ceu projectis e circulis minoribus, in Sphaerae superficie sitis: In cujus rei Explicationem,

Suppone (cum dicto Collinio) Oculum in centro sphaerae, quam tangit Planum Zenithi, eumque spectare Planum Segmenti Sphaerae; dictum Planum est basis Coni, cujus vertex est in Oculo; si quidem supra Horizontem fuerit, eique Parallelus, dictus Circulus, Sectio in Plano tangente erit Circulus; si vero non fuerit Horizonti parallelus, erit Ellipsis; si Horizontem tangat, omnesque ejus partes reliquae fuerint supra Horizontem, erit Parabola; cumque complures ejusmodi Circuli elevati tangere in eodem puncto Horizontem possint, Projectiones eorum omnes erunt congruentes Parabolae: At si unus pluresve Circuli partim supra Horizontem fuerint, partim infra eum, Projectiones eorum, Hyperbolae erunt; atque si eandem habuerint chordam communem in Horizonte, Projectiones eorum erunt congruentes Hyperbolae: si plane fuerint infra Horizontem, projici nullatenus possunt. Supposito, ex diversis Circulis Sectiones Conicas istum in modum projici, si supponatur consimiliter oculum transferri ad Nadir, eosdemque circulos denuo projici, sequetur, quod prius fuit per Conicarum harum Sectionum Intersectiones determinatum id inveniri jam posse et determinari per Circulos projectos positosve subcontrarie ad istos in Sphaera circulos, qui Conorum visualium Bases constituunt. Adeo ut exinde in eam deducamur considerationem, in quibusnam scilicet Casibus Problemata per Sectiones Conicas determinata solvi Geometriae planae beneficio queant?

Sed pergo ad alia.[5] Commemorat alicubi Mersennus de Paschali filio, Eum unica Propositione universalissima, 400 Corollariis armata, totum Apollonium fuisse amplexum. Inaudivimus, hunc Tractatum hactenus esse ineditum; insistere autem methodo Des-Argueanae (quam forte ceu viri illius discipulus imbiberat;) edoctique fuimus a Bibliopola Parisiensi de Prex, manu-scriptum id esse penes fratrem quendam suum (Prexii) in Auvernia. Utinam id protrahi in lucem posset![6]

Videre est in Scripto hic sociato, promissa nobis fuisse Residua Fermati. Credimus interim, haec ipsa vel saltem nonnulla eorum, nec non Tractatum Dni. Des Argues, ut et MS Clarissimi Robervallii de Locis Planis, Solidis, Linearibus, et ad Superficiem, jam esse diuque fuisse in Anglia, penes virum quendam doctum, qui scripta illa hactenus premit, quique Tractatum molitur de Canone Mathematico, sive Tabulam Sinuum, qua ostendatur, quam difficilia Problemata et Æquationes solvi illius beneficio possint. Quoad Cartesianam Problematis Pappi solutionem, ait idem, multum operae fuisse impensum ubi parum suffecisset. Atque, ut verum fateamur, inquit Collinius, si 5. puncta in sectione conica, aut 4. in Parabola, dentur, alia puncta innumerabilia describi possunt angulorum mobilium ope, absque ulla cognitione vel figurae, vel ipsius Axium, Focorum, Asymptotων, Ordinatarum; unde supputationes Trigonometricae similiter consequuntur.

Interim si non fiat nobis horum copia aliunde, sperandumne saltem, ea nos inventuros esse in Claudii Milleti de Chales Cursu Mathematico, Lugduni Galliarum sub praelo nunc sudante?

Denique, accepit ab Erasmio Bartolino Picardus Dni. de Beaune tractatum de Angulo solido, ea scilicet lege ut Parisiis imprimendum curaret. Lubenter sciremus, num praelo jam commissum sit opus, et quanto temporis spatio proditirum in lucem credatur?

Ob varia complurium Societatis Regiae membrorum negotia publica raro adeo fuerunt a discessu tuo conventus, ut Electio nulla fieri hactenus potuerit. Nec ipse professor Astronomiae Oxoniensis, Dn. Bernhardus, eandem ob causam cooptari potuit. Quamprimum numerus debitus convenerit, vos ambo simul, ni fallor admodum, cooptabimini.[7]

Polliceor mihi properam ad binas meas responsionem. Lubeat, tuas ad me litteras sic inscribi, siquidem per tabellarium expediantur;

A Monsieur

Mons. Grubendol

à

Londres

Nil praeterea. Vale.

Sum Tui studiosissimus

H. Oldenburg

P.S.

Non obstante tam enormi prolixitate petiit Dn. Collinius, ut sequentia haec prioribus subjicerem; nempe

1. Nonnisi post sex mensium lapsum secundum volumen Algebraicum Dni. Kersy praelo commissum iri: sperare se proinde, Clarissimi Freniclii opus interea proditurum, quod suppeditaturum nobis credit complures breves intermediatasque responsiones in istis Inventi novi Fermatiani Problematibus:[8] quodipsum licet et hic praestitum a viro quodam docto fuerit, non tamen ipse nos hactenus edocuit, qua methodo. Addit, nos percipere, Fermatum, Wallisium et Kersium, omnes (consiliis haud com-

municatis,) in idem Theorema incidisse, dividendi sc. summam duorum Cuborum in duos Cubos, neminem vero eorum posse beneficio ejus invenire parvos illos numeros, quos Dn. Freniclius nobis dedit in quadam epistola sua in Wallisii Commercio Epistolico.[9]

2. Narrationi illi de Constructione ad dividendum Aequationem Biquadraticam in duas Quadraticas, subjungit idem Collinius; Hoc praestari citra opem Aequationis Cubicae, quando Biquadratica aequatio fit per multiplicationem duorum Quadraticorum: Subtilitatem consistere ait in determinando, quando fieri non possit absque ope Aequationis ejusmodi Cubicae, et quando non item.[10]

3. Ad Cartesii Solutionem Problematis Pappi ait idem, Virum quendam doctum in Operatione sive Processu Problematis, semper eam continebat intra duas AEquationes quadraticas, quae multiplicatae per se invicem producebant AEquationem illam bi-quadraticam, quae solvebat Problema, poteratque dividi in duas AEquationes Quadraticas citra opem Cubicae.

Jungo hic summam eorum, quae destinantur secundo Volumini Algebraico, quod meditantur Angli lingua vernacula;[11] eamque mitto Anglice, prout acceperam ab amico, satis compertum habens, Te linguam hanc satis callere ad haec intelligendum. Vale iterum atque iterum a Tibi addictissimo

H.O.

TRANSLATION

Henry Oldenburg [sends] many greetings to the very worthy and wise Mr. Gottfried Wilhelm Leibniz LL.D. etc.

London, 6 April 1673

In my letter to you, worthy Sir, of 6 March last I promised that I would prepare a fuller reply to yours as soon as I should have informed myself on those points concerning which you desired to learn more from me.[1] In order to fulfill my promise I mean this letter to serve as a substitute for the former one so that you may have a firmer grasp of my wish to fail in nothing that my feeble powers can accomplish. Know, then, in the first place that I have imparted to our learned Collins, who is likewise a Fellow of the Royal Society, that paper of yours on the theory of interpolation[2] and on your conversation with the famous Pell concerning that subject and Mouton; he [Collins] is of the opinion that: "it is farr more generall and easy to do . . ."

[*Oldenburg has now begun to translate Collins' Letter 2193, see pp. 549–53, above*]

Because of the variety of public concerns affecting many members of the Royal

Society [its] meetings have been infrequent since your departure, so that no election could be made up to this time. Not even the professor of astronomy at Oxford himself, Dr. Bernard, could be elected for the same reason. As soon as the proper number is assembled we shall elect you both unless I am very much mistaken.[7]

I promise myself a speedy answer to my two letters. Please address your letters to me thus, if they are sent by the post:

To Mr Grubendol,
at London

Nothing more. Farewell.

I am yours most zealously,
H. Oldenburg

P.S. Despite such enormous prolixity Mr. Collins has asked me to add these following [points] to the former ones, viz:

1. Only after an interval of six months will the second volume of Mr. Kersey's *Algebra* be committed to the press; whence he [Collins] hopes that in the meantime the work of the famous Frénicle will appear which (he believes) will supply us with many brief and intermediate answers to those problems of Fermat's new discovery;[8] because although that was done here also by a certain learned person, yet he himself has not hitherto told us by what method [they were solved]. He adds, that we observe Fermat, Wallis, and Kersey all to have hit upon the same theorem (without any sharing of ideas between them), which is that of dividing the sum of two cubes into two [other] cubes, [though] indeed no one among them can by that means discover those small numbers which Mr. Frénicle gave us in a certain letter of his in Wallis's *Commercium Epistolicum*.[9]

2. The same Collins appends to that account of the construction for dividing a biquadratic equation into two quadratics that this may be done without the aid of cubic equation, when the biquadratic is formed from the multiplication of two quadratics; the subtlety consists (he says) in determining when it cannot be done without the aid of a cubic equation of this kind, and when it may not be so done.[10]

3. As regards Descartes's solution of Pappus's problem, he says that a certain individual learned in the process or procedure of Pappus always contained it within a pair of quadratic equations which, multiplied together, produced that biquadratic equation that solved the problem, and could be divided into two quadratic equations without appealing to a cubic.[11]

I annex here a summary of the matters intended for the second volume of the *Algebra* which the English are thinking about [for publication] in English;[12] and this I send to you in English, just as I received it from a friend, having sufficiently discovered that you follow this language well enough to understand it. With a renewed farewell from your most devoted

H.O.

NOTES

The postcript begins on a new sheet, and has become separated from this letter. Gerhardt erroneously printed it with Oldenburg's letter of 2 May 1677; as was first pointed out by Hofmann (*Entwicklungsgeschichte*, p. 21), it clearly belongs with this letter. The whole document is in Oldenburg's hand.

1 See Letter 2174.
2 Letter 2140.
3 Collins wrote, "postulant."
4 Collins wrote, "and not a penny more or lesse," but compare Letter 2193, note 7.
5 "But I turn to other things," an addition by Oldenburg.
6 "Would that it might be brought to light!"—an addition by Oldenburg.
7 As they were to do on 9 April 1673; see below, Letter 2202.
8 Collins refers to the *Inventum novum* of Jacques de Billy; see Vol. VIII, p. 127 and p. 128, note 8. For Frénicle's book see Letter 2103, note 5.
9 The problem was raised first by Fermat, in relation to a lost porism of Diophantus. See Fermat to Kenelm Digby, 5 August 1657; Brouncker to Wallis, 3 October 1657; and Frénicle to Digby, ?10 February 1658, these letters being printed in John Wallis, *Commercium epistolicum* (1658), see *Opera mathematica*, II (Oxford, 1693), pp. 770–72, 768–69, and 820–23 respectively, and for an explanation Hofmann, *Entwicklungsgeschichte*, p. 23.
10 The first "not" has been added ("n̄" with a caret) before *possit*, but Oldenburg forgot to cross out the second "not" before *item*. This paragraph and the next allude to developments of Descartes's graphical resolution of a biquadratic equation by the intersection of a parabola and a circle.
11 According to Dr. Whiteside, this was almost certainly Pell, whose claim, however, cannot be taken seriously.
12 See Letter 2196a.

2196a

Mathematical Report

Enclosure with Letter 2196
From the original in Hannover MSS., ff. 72–73

Contenta secundi voluminis Algebrae, lingua Anglica edendae a Domino Kersey, cujus volumen primam jam sub praelo versatur, ut ex iis patet, quae No. 90 Transact. philosoph. inseruimus. Cum haec mihi communicata fuerint sermone Anglico, eodem illa Tibi, hujus linguae satis perito, transmittere volui.[1]

A Collection out of de Beaune, Hudden, Bartholinus, Du Laurens, Brasser, and Ferguson: Of ye Constitution, Depression and Limits of

Æquations, wth the dividing of them into their Components, whereby to find ye Roots of Æquations, when they are either mixt numbers, fractions, or surds, either simple, or binomial: Of wch doctrine we have nothing yet in the English tongue. To wch end a construction of Dr Pells in the High-dutch Algebra of his Schollar Rhonius deserves remarke.[2]

This Doctrine to be illustrated wth Schemes and Numeral Examples: To which purpose we have already Mr Merrys Explication of Hudden's rules, shewing from what Æquations he invented and derived thesame.[3] Hudden de Maximis et Minimis exceeds much those methods of Bartholinus; so that from his doctrine 'tis easy to assume what roots you please, and thence to raise such aequations, that the Homogenea to those roots, shall be the greatest Ordinates in those indented Curves that are the loca[4] of Æquations. Wch loca wth the aid of Slusius his method of Tangents, afford most excellent easy approaches, majus et minus,[5] by Logarithmes, for finding the rootes: To wch may be added Methods for fitting Æquations to innumerable series's of numbers; ye ready summing up of such series; the interpoling and filling up of Tables: as also Mr Collins's Paper of Interest printed A. 1664,[6] shewing, how to carry on a rank of continual proportionals by meer substraction, and from any such rank or any assum'd one of a smal ratio, wthout any extraction of roots, to derive any other, to solve problems about Compound interest, and Annuities, and to raise ye Logarithmes and the Converse, wth a Method of adding the Reciprocals of and Arithmet[ical] progression, or of ye Squares or Cubes thereof.

Hereto may be annex'd from ye pains of Dr Wallis ye problemes of his enlarged Commerc[ium] Epistolicum; his method of putting a large Decimal fraction into others, that shall best expresse thesame according to any number of given figures; his Treatise de Section[ibus] Angularibus, for the making of Sphaerical Trigonometry accurately, wth what also he shall either adde or advise; wth 105 Theoremes about Sines, Chords, Tangents, Secants etc. in Rhonius.

As to ye remains of Fermat, we are promis'd his Euclidis Porismata restituta,[7] his Treatises de Contactibus Sphaericis, et de Locis planis, solidis, Linearibus, et ad superficiem.[8]

We have an Euclides Analyticus, written by Mr Merry; another I presume done by Mr. Strode;[9] and a third (as Mr Bernard affirmes) by van Schooten, whereof he thinks he can procure a copy, perchance wth some enlargements of Hudden.[10]

Much of this kind is ready done; as ye 2d and 5th book by Dr Wallis, and in Fosters Miscellanies.[11] See also the Elemens Nouveaux de Geometrie.[12] The 10th Book well done by Mr Oughtred and le Sieur le Tan-neur.[13] Part of ye 6th book is handled by Camillus gloriosus.[14] To ye 9th might be subjoined what Broschius hath de numeris perfectis;[15] and to ye 13th, some excellent properties of a number divided in extreme and mean proportion; a Table made by addition for doing thereof; wth the Consequences ensuing, as ye carrying on of a rank of continual Proportionals by meer addition or substraction. Dibaudius hath illustrated all the propositions in the 10 Books wth examples in Numbers, or Surds,[16] and Henrion the last.[17] Those about the 5 regular Bodies are done by Diggs etc.[18]

The great advantage and ease there is in inventing of Demonstrations by Ayde of Algebra, is handsomely treated of by Bartolinus in his Book de Arte Analytica inveniendi omnia Problemata Proportionalium maxime harmonicorum.[19] A Discourse about the Methods of bringing problems to an Æquation, is exspected from Mr Newton, being by him promised[20].

As to ye Conicks, Mr Strode hath collected an Analytical Body thereof from his own knowledg, ye two Books of Kinkhuysen and all other good Authors extant.[21]

Dr Barrow hath written and put into my hands an Exercitation about Conical and Mechanical Constructions for AEquations; of wch good use may be made; Mr Newton hath done the like.[22]

To compleat ye Conical doctrine, 'tis fit (in regard we find in divers Authors diverse constructions wthout any AEquations or Calculations suited to them) that this Probleme be considered, viz.

Any two given Conick sections being drawn in any position at pleasure, to find, which Æquation is solved by Ordinates falling from their Intersections on the Diameters or Axes of either Figure. E.g. Mydorgius gives Conical Constructions (but no Calculations) for these Problemes;[23]

On an Ellipsis (or Hyperbola) giving [*sic*] the Axes *AB*, *CD* to find the situation of those Conjugates that shall make an Angle wth each other, equal to ye angle *A*.

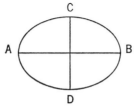

And how from ye Locus of an Æquation to derive Conical or other Constructions for Æquations, seems a pretty consideration; for in their natural locus, the roots lye all in one right line, and being found by a construction wth a circle and a parabola, the inquiry may be, whether the Incurvation of that right line hath any habitude of the Arches of the quadrilateral figure of the Circle; or, if the 4 roots be made perpendiculars, viz. ye first of them on the Resolvend of the Biquadratick Æquation; another, on the Resolvend of the inferiour Cubick Æquation, that serves for finding the next root, and the remaining two on the Resolvend or Absolute of the quadratick aequation that serves for their discovery; or, if they be made all Perpendiculars on the roots of ye respective pure powers of these Resolvends, the Quaere's may then be, whether their extremities being joined shall make a quadrilateral figure inscriptible in a Circle, and such an one as may have its Diameters and or Axes parallel to the line of Resolvends; or whether, in such a construction, the parallel distances of the rootes be alter'd from what they had in their Locus, and, if so, in what habitude?

Mr Newton solves all Æquations not exceeding the 9th degree,[24] by the aid of a constant cubick parabola, wch being once described never varies, either by ye Intersections of another cubick parabola, or of conick sections; And yesame solves those not exceeding ye 16th degree, by two Biquadratick parabolasters, or Curves of a lower nature, as ye cubick parabola, or the conick sections. And he hath given Mechanick constructions for those of ye 3d and 4th degree, wch ad libitum may be solved by Conical constructions.

The Censure of Monsr Huret (a Censurer of all Perspective-writers) in a Treatise of yesd Argument, on the doctrine of Des-Argues and Paschall about the Conicks seems not to deserve much regard.[25] If those Speculations be duely heeded, the Intersections of Conick sections may be calculated Trigonometrically. We believe, Copies of ye Book, wch he censures, may be procured and are worth having.

As to solid or Curvi-linear Geometry, Mr Newton hath invented (before Mercator publish't his Logarithmotechnia)[26] a general method of ye same kind for ye quadrature of all Curvilinear figures, the straightening of Curves, the finding of ye Centers of gravity and solidity of all round solids and of their second segments;[27] ye area's of their surfaces albeit inclined; yea, any sine, tangent, or secant, Logarithmical or Natural, being given, to find the Arch and the Converse, viz. from the Arch to raise the Logarithmical sines, tangents or secants, without first finding the natural, wth infinite series's for ye roots of affected Æquations, easily composed out of those, for pure powers; so that one series shall be fitted for all Cubicks, another for all Biquadraticks etc.

Wch doctrine, I hope, Mr Newton is a publishing wth Kinkhuysen's Introduction.[28] Thesame is likewise fully understood by Mr Gregory, who hath suited it to many Mechanick problems, as yt of Kepler, and ye Tangents of innumerable Mechanique Curves.[29]

To all wch may be subjoined some Practical Algebraical problems for Gauging by Mr Dary;[30] wth a solution or explication of those Ingenious problems of Kepler at the end of his Stereometria about the Diagonal line.[31]

Also divers Geometrical problems applied to the Dioptricks wth their Analytical Calculus and Construction.[31a]

The Tactions of Circles are handled by Camillus Gloriosus,[14] and Griembergerus (in speculo Ustorio Elliptico mention'd by Blancanus in Chronologia Mathematicorum wch we cannot procure;[32] since both by Ghetaldus, and Vieta in his Apollonius Gallus;[33] on wch Des-Cartes hath likewise touched in some of his Epistles: And many considerable propositions there are in Pappus and in those Pieces of Geometry restored by Snellius.[34]

Lastly an Exercitation De Arte Combinatoria[35] will be very usefull and pleasant; a specimen whereof Mr Merry hath afforded concerning ye variety of Problems that may be put about a right-angled Triangle, divided into two right Triangles by a perpendicular falling from the right Angle in the Hypothenuse, shewing yt meerly from thesd parts and from their sums and differences there may arise 629 distinct Problems, and no more. And Mr Strode having tryed above 500 Conclusions in oblique Plaine Triangles, did light upon some, wch by reason of their great toyle and difficulty he could not bring to any Æquation; others, yt mounted very high. The making out the severall varieties of all cases possible in respect to ye *Data* in these, may be a good Example for the like induction in others. This kind of skill Dr P[ell] calls *Cribrum syntheticum*.[36]

NOTES

For the discovery and placing of this *Report* we are again indebted to Professor Hofmann, who has given a full analysis of it in his *Entwicklungsgeschichte*, p. 21 *et seq*. It is (as he writes) an extraordinary document, which Leibniz was at the time of receiving it "too inexperienced to appreciate fully"; but he studied it carefully later. Since it represents Collins's review of all the most interesting work in English mathematics a full commentary upon it would demand a large treatise; it seems to us, however, that while Collins was certainly keen to impress Leibniz he was also genuinely eager to help him, and that his desire to protect English priority-rights (on which Professor Hofmann insists) was only a small factor. It is true that Collins's comments are vague, so that to reconstruct the methods of which he speaks from them alone would be almost impossible, but this was Collins's way, equally evident in his letters to James Gregory which contain closely similar passages.

1 "Contents of the second volume of the algebra to be published in the English language by Mr. Kersey, of which the first volume is already in the press as is obvious from what we have inserted in no. 90 of the *Philosophical Transactions*. As these [contents] were communicated to me in English I decided to send them on to you in the same language, since you are well enough skilled in it." In *Phil. Trans.* no. 90 (20 January 1672/3), pp. 5152–53, Oldenburg took the unusual step of inserting a long "Advertisement" for Kersey's *Algebra*, then in press, as a book recommended by some Fellows of the Royal Society, for copies of which many had already subscribed. There is no mention here of a second volume, but the announcement of the actual publication of the book (*Phil. Trans.*, no. 95 (23 June 1673), pp. 6073–74) states that two "books" of a proposed four are on sale, and recommends them in order to promote the printing of mathematical works in England, and hints that the last part of the work will no appear if the former does not sell. There is a bare notice of the appearance of this final part in *Phil. Trans.*, no. 108 (23 November 1674), p. 192. John Kersey (1616–77) kept a mathematical school near Covent Garden.

2 All these mathematical writers have been mentioned before, some many times; for further details see the Index. *Rhonius* is, of course, J. H. Rahn.

3 Collins frequently refers to Mr. Merry's commentary on Hudde in his correspondence. He told Pell of it and of possessing the MS. in 1667 (see Rigaud, I, 127), and in 1672/3 sent a copy to Wallis (Rigaud, II, 587, 560, 592), presumably that now with Wallis's papers under the title "Mr. Merry's Invention and Demonstration of Hudden's Rules for Reducing Equations," in Bodleian Library MS. Savile 33. His first name is nowhere given; there were several Oxford and Cambridge graduates of this name, several of whom were at this time country clergymen. It is tempting to suppose that he might have been Richard Merry who matriculated at Christ Church in 1653, M. A. St Mary Hall 1659, at this time Rector of Earnshill in Somerset, about twenty miles from John Beale at Yeovil, who might have put him in touch with Collins as he was later to do for Thomas Strode (see Letter 2027a).

4 This is a correct Latin form for the now more familiar form *loci*.

5 "the greater and the less." Collins had written all this before in "Concerning the Resolution of Equations in Numbers" (*Phil. Trans.*, no 46 (12 April 1669), 929–32).

6 Compare, for Collins's concern with this matter, Vols. IV, p. 483, V, pp. 212–13, and VI, p. 274. The bibliographical history of Collins's work on interest is obscure and complex, and the evidence often contradictory. Despite the positive statement here, the second of these references and another allusion in Rigaud, II, 482, indicate pretty conclusively that "the paper of interest" was destroyed in the Fire of London. Collins published ultimately two separate versions, *An Introduction to Merchants-Accompts* (London, 1674) and *Doctrine of Decimal Arithmetic, Simple Interest* &c. (London, 1685) which have survived. Of earlier editions the only ones clearly traced are: (1) "An introduction to Merchants accounts compiled by J. Collings," appended to Gerard de Malynes, *Consuetudo vel Lex Mercatoria, or, the Ancient Law Merchant*; part IV appeared in 1653; and (2) a copy of *Doctrine of Decimal Arithmetic* dated London, 1665 which was in the possession of John Wallis, and may be that which Collins sent to Wallis.

7 Pappus records and describes a lost work in three books on higher geometry by Euclid dealing with *Porisms* (see John Murdoch's summary in *DSB*, IV, 426–27; the *locus classicus* is Michel Chasles, *Les trois livres de Porismes d'Euclide*, Paris, 1860). Fermat attempted to "restore" this lost treatise in his *Porismatum Euclideorum renovata doctrina*, published in *Varia opera mathematica* (Toulouse, 1679), pp. 116–19, and in *Œuvres de Fermat* (ed. Charles Henry and Paul Tannery, Paris, 1891–1912), I, 76–84.

The substance of Fermat's tract had been sent by him to Sir Kenelm Digby (for Wallis) in a letter of 13 June 1658, printed by Wallis in his *Commercium epistolicum* (Oxford, 1658), Appendix, pp. 187–88.

8 The former appeared in the *Varia opera* of 1679, but the second was only published in modern times in the *Œuvres de Fermat*.

9 Compare Letter 2027a; for his work on Euclid, see Rigaud, II, 449–50; it was not published.

10 We have not come across other definite indications about this.

11 The references are to John Wallis, *Mathesis universalis* (Oxford, 1657), chap. XXIII, "Euclidis elementum secundum, arithmetice demonstratum," and chap. XXXV, "Euclidis elementum quintum, arithmetice demonstratum," and Samuel Foster, *Miscellanea* (London, 1659).

12 Probably Antoine Arnauld, *Nouveaux Elemens de Geometrie* (Paris, 1667).

13 William Oughtred's *Elementi Euclidis declaratio* was appended to his *Clavis mathematicae* (London, 1648 and subsequent editions); for Tenneur's, see Vol. VII, p. 380, note 19.

14 Giovanni Camillo Glorioso, *Exercitationum mathematicarum Decas prima . . . secunda* (Naples, 1627–35).

15 Joannes Broschius, *De numeris perfectis disceptatio* (Amsterdam, 1638).

16 Christophorus Dibaudius published *In geometriam Euclidis prioribus sex elementorum libris comprehensam demonstratio linealis* (Leiden, 1603) succeeded by a *demonstratio numeralis* in the same year; further works on Euclidean rationals and irrationals appeared in 1605.

17 Denis Henrion, *Les quinze livres des Elements d'Euclide* (Paris, 1615).

18 This essay was appended by Thomas Digges to Leonard and Thomas Digges, *A Geometrical Practise named Pantometria* (London, 1571).

19 See Vol. V, p. 212 (when Collins had not yet seen this book), and *ibid*, p. 214, note 13.

20 See Newton's letter to Collins of 25 May 1672 in Newton, *Correspondence*, I, 161. The "discourse" is printed in Newton, *Mathematical Papers*, II, 422–44.

21 See Letter 2027a; Strode's studies of conics were not published. For Kinckhuysen's two books, see Letter 1974, notes 6 and 7.

22 For Barrow's manuscript, see Vol. VI, p. 230, note 6; as for Newton, Collins was probably thinking of Newton's tract on "Problems for construing Aequations" sent to him on 20 August 1672 (see Newton, *Mathematical Papers*, II, 450–517, and compare Newton, *Correspondence*, I, 231). Although Collins copied the manuscript Newton lent him, the tract was first published only in 1968; however, Newton incorporated substantial portions of it into his contemporaneous Lucasian lectures on algebra, edited by William Whiston as *Arithmetica universalis* (Cambridge, 1707).

23 Presumably Claude Mydorge, *De sectionibus conicis libri iv* Paris, 1631), unless Collins was thinking of Mersenne's description of Mydorge's now lost works given in *Universae geometriae mixtaeque mathematicae synopsis* (Paris, 1644).

24 In the tract mentioned in note 22 above (*Mathematical Papers*, II, 499 ff).

25 See Letter 2193, note 13.

26 Nicholas Mercator, *Logarithmotechnia* (London, 1668).

27 This paragraph is based on Collins' knowledge of Newton's *De analysi* (Newton, *Mathematical Papers*, II, 206–46) and passages in some of Newton's letters to him—he wrote very similar summaries of Newton's achievements to other correspondents (*ibid.*, III, 21–23).

28 See Letter 1974, note 6, and Newton, *Mathematical Papers*, II, 277–90.

29 See the Collins-Gregory correspondence in Turnbull, *Gregory*.

30 Michael Dary had published *Gauging epitomised* at London in 1669 (*Phil. Trans.*, no. 52, 17 October 1669, 1053–54) and subsequently engaged in computational researches which led him into correspondence with Newton in 1674 (for which see Newton, *Correspondence*, I, 319–20, 326, 332–33).

31 *Nova stereometria doliorum vinariorum* (Linz, 1615); "diagonal lines" are measuring rods calibrated to give the volume of a barrel directly.

31a Presumably Collins was thinking of the early part of Newton's (as yet unpublished) *Lectiones opticae*.

32 For this work by Christopher Grienberger, see Letter 2193, note 9. Josephus Blancanus (Giuseppe Biancani) published "Clarorum mathematicorum chronologia" in his *Aristotelis loca mathematica ex universis ipsius operibus collecta & explicata* . . . (Bologna, 1640).

33 Collins presumably refers to Marinus Ghetaldus, *Apollonius redivivus seu restituta Apollonii Pergaei inclinationum geometria* (Venice, 1607, 1613), reprinted in his *Opera omnia* (Zagreb, 1968), pp. 173–351; this contains nothing on "tactions," but Collins may never have seen it. François Viète, *Apollonius Gallus* (Paris, 1600) is certainly earlier than Grienberger's book.

34 Willebrord Snel, *Apollonius Batavus* (Leiden, 1608) is his main work of "restoration" of Apollonius, but there is also *Apollonii Pergaei de determinata sectione geometria*, published in Pierre Hérigone, *Cursus mathematicus*, I (Paris, 1634); Snel's work is described by Schooten in his *Exercitationes* of 1657, p. 198.

35 "On the art of combinations."

36 "synthetic sieve."

2197

Oldenburg to Huygens

7 April 1673

From *Œuvres Complètes*, VII, 264
Original in the Huygens Collection at Leiden

A Londres le 7me Avril 1673

Monsieur

Pour executer la promesse que ie vous fis dans ma lettre du 10 Fevrier dernier[1] ie vous envoye la responce de Monsieur Newton sur les considerations, que vous aviez la bonté de mettre dans la vostre du 14 janvier touchant sa nouvelle theorie des couleurs.[2] Je veux croire, que vous ne la lirez pas sans plaisir, et qu'elle vous donnera occasion de mediter davantage sur cete belle et importante matiere. Je vous puis assurer, que

Monsieur Newton est une personne de grande candeur, comme il est homme qui ne dit légerement des choses qu'il avance.

Je ne doubte pas que vous n'ayez aussi receu la mienne du 10 Mars[3] avec le nombre 91. des Transactions, où il y a entre autres choses, la methode de Monsieur Sluse pour tirer des tangentes à toutes sortes de lignes courbes sans calcul; dont i'attends tous les iours la demonstration. Je ne veux pas vous interrompre davantage a present, mais vous assurer que ie suis tousiours Monsieur

Vostre treshumble et tresobeissant serviteur
Oldenburg

Monsieur Newton a esté plusieurs semaines absent de Cambridge;[4] sans cela vous eussiez bien plustost receu sa responce.

ADDRESS
    A Monsieur
      Monsieur Christian Hugens de Zulichem,
dans la Bibliotheque du Roy à
                Paris

TRANSLATION

London, 7 April 1673

Sir,

In order to carry out the promise I made to you in my letter of the tenth of February last,[1] I am sending you Mr. Newton's reply to the thoughts on his new theory of colors which you were so good as to put in yours of the fourteenth January [N.S.].[2] I like to think that you will read it not without pleasure, and that it will give you the opportunity of meditating further on this fine and important matter. I can assure you that Mr. Newton is a man of great candor, as also one who does not lightly put forward the things he has to say.

I do not doubt but that you have also received mine of the tenth of March[3] with number 91 of the *Transactions*, where there is, among other things, Mr. Sluse's method for drawing tangents to all sorts of curved lines without calculation, of which I expect the proof any day. I do not wish to disturb you any further at present, except to assure you that I am always, Sir,

Your very humble and obedient servant,
Oldenburg

Mr. Newton has been absent from Cambridge for several weeks,[4] or you would have received his reply much sooner.

ADDRESS

To Mr. Christiaan Huygens of Zulichem,
     The King's Library,
          Paris

NOTES

1 Letter 2144, actually dated the ninth.
2 For Newton's reply to Huygens' Letter 2122, see Letter 2195.
3 Letter 2178.
4 In Letter 2176 Newton had told Oldenburg that he would "be henceforth absent from Cambridge for about a month"; in fact he was absent from Trinity College from 10 March 1672/3 to 1 April 1673.

2198

Sluse to Oldenburg

8 April 1673

From the original in Royal Society MS. S 1, no. 76
Printed in Boncompagni, p. 677

Nobilissimo et Clarissimo Viro
D. Henrico Oldenburg Regiae Societatis Secretario
Renatus Franciscus Slusius
S.P.D.

Ante tres menses ad te scripsi, Vir Clarissime, misique methodum meam ducendarum ad curvas quaslibet geometricas tangentium,[1] rogans ut statim monere me velles, cum meas accepisses. Cum autem a te nihil abinde literarum acceperim, notaque nihilominus mihi sit ac plurimis experimentis perspecta humanitas tua singularis, vereri cogor ne aut meae in itinere perierint, aut tuae.[2] Fac igitur me certiorem quid tandem acciderit, meque sollicitudine libera. Nam si meae ad te non pervenerint, alias in eundem sensum scribam: sin autem responsum tuum perierit, multum tibi debebo si iterata scriptione ea scire me volueris, quae non ignorari a me, plurimum mea interesse existimo.[3] Nihil addam de studiis nostris, quandoquidem incertum sim, num has sis accepturus. Faciam porro, si ita tibi visum fuerit, cum meas certo tibi redendas intellexero. Vale, Vir praestantissime, meque tui observatissimum solito semper favore prosequi perge. Dabam Leodii XVIII Aprilis MDCLXXIII [N.S.]

TRANSLATION

René François de Sluse presents many greetings to the very noble and famous Mr. Henry Oldenburg Secretary of the Royal Society

More than three months ago I wrote to you, famous Sir, and sent you my method of drawing tangents to any geometrical curve,[1] asking you to please to advise me at once when you had received mine. However, as I have received nothing by way of a letter from you since then, and as your singular kindness is nevertheless well known to me and tried by many tests, I am compelled to fear that either your letter or mine has been lost *en route*.[2] Tell me, therefore, what has happened in the end and release me from my worry. For if my letter did not reach you, I will write another having the same content; if on the other hand it was your reply that was lost I shall be very much in your debt if you will kindly inform me by a repeated writing [of your letter] of those things which, I believe, it very much concerns me to be aware of.[3] I add nothing of our studious affairs since I am uncertain whether this will be received by you. Farewell, most excellent Sir, and continue to favor me with your ever customary good will, who am most devoted to you. Liège, 18 April 1673 [N.S.].

NOTES

1 Letter 2124 of 7 January 1672/3.
2 Oldenburg's reply was Letter 2136; for its failure to reach Sluse, see its note. Compare also Letter 2217, below, which deals further with Sluse's distress at Oldenburg's apparent failure to reply.
3 This Oldenburg presumably did in Letter 2204, now lost.

2199
Oldenburg to Williamson

8 April 1673

From the original in P.R.O. MS. S.P. 29/335/1, no. 21
Printed in C.S.P.D. 1673, p. 125

Sir,

I am apt to believe, you will be much surprised at some passages in these letters,[1] especially yt, wherein your person is abused and dangerously defamed. I doubt not but you know the man, yt hath written these Letters, so yt I need not name him here.[2] Mean time he hath subscribed his name so confusedly and scurvily (on purpose doubtlesse,) that 'twill be very hard for any man to discover it except either the writer be very well known to him, or the decypherer well versed in the Highdutch Character.

Sir, when any thing coms from you to me, I sett all other business aside, till yrs be dispatch't. I hope it will be considered, that I have spent many a day, and sometimes a good part of ye night too, in such work, as concerns the kings service; and yt I am very ready to goe on so upon all occasions, and particularly to be Sir

Yr faithful servant
H.O.

April 8. 73.

ADDRESS

For Sir Joseph Williamson
these

NOTES

1 Letter 2199a.
2 Oldenburg also omitted his name from the translations and summaries.

2199a

Translations and Summaries of Letters

Enclosures with Letter 2199
From the originals in P.R.O. MS. S.P. 29/335/1, no. 21
Printed in C.S.P.D. 1673, pp. 126–27

No. 1

To his Highnesse Prince Herman
Marquesse of Baden Hochberg[1] at
Brussels

London
March 28. 1673.

May it please yr Highnesse,

All things have been hitherto uncertain in the Parlement. In their last addresse to the king they moved,[2] 1. That the monies to be raised might not be trusted in ye hands of ye Lord Treasurer. 2. That, in case his Majty should dye wthin the 18 months, wherein the 120000 lbs, at ye rate of 70000 lbs per mensem, were to be paid, ye remainder not yet paid, in yt case, should not be paid to the successor. 3. If ye Parlement should not sit in October next, that from that time no more mony should be paid. 4. That ye King should strictly execute the Lawes against the Papists in Ireland. 5. They used some menaces against several Ministers of the king, whom they would impeach as guilty of High treason. Some such other strange propositions were made by the House of Commons; to whom the King declared himself so graciously, yt he would doe all what they should think fit for the good of the kingdom: Whereby matters have been so composed, that the Mony-bill was yesterday sent up to ye House of Lords, where it will be dispatch't this day, together wth the Bill agst Popery;[3] in respect of wch latter, the King and the Duke of York will be obliged to putt away all Roman-Catholick servants, and those yt are suspected of Popery must abjure ye doctrine of Transubstantiation, if they will hold their places and employments. Mean time the Queen is allowed to keep a certain number of Catholique servants.[4] The King was heard to say by way of raillery, that he would purge his Court from all Catholiques, except his barber, whom he meant to keep in despight of all their bills, for he was so well accustomed to his hand.

But then, this Parlement hath resolved to doe a very good and usefull thing, wch were to be wish't yt all Princes would imitate, viz. That they will give ye king yearly a certain summ of money, wth wch his Majty is to entertain and defray ye charges of the Mint, wthout laying ym upon ye monies coined, whereby such monies will have their full intrinsique value, and every body, yt shall bring any silver or gold into the mint, shall have the full value in coined mony for it wthout allowing any thing for the coynage.[5] The revenue wch they allow the king for this purpose, is an Excise, viz. 5 shill. for every Ohme of Wine, and 10 sh. for every Ohm of Brandy, yt shall be imported into England.[6]

There was brought in an other bill, to prevent the setting up a military government, wch was, that every man may accuse every common souldier before the Civil Magistrat, arrest him and proceed against him wthout acquainting his officer therewth; wch is a bill of great consequence.[7]

For the rest, the House of Commons in their last Address represented unto the King, that his goodnes and generosity had made ym desist from pressing any further at this time the rest of their grievances, his Majty having been pleased to assure them, yt himself would take great care of redressing ym. Whereupon the King thanked them for the confidence they reposed in him, of wch they would not find cause in their next session to repent.[8] So yt this day 'tis hoped all the bills will be passed.[9]

I have been all along of opinion, that in the present conjuncture none of the great ministers would be willing to be absent from this Court: Whence also none of them would undertake the Commission for Collen; so yt for it have been chosen the Earle of Sunderland, who hath been hitherto in France, a person not capable enough for this busines.[10] 2. The Secretary of the privy Counsell, Sir Joseph Williampson: wch two are mercenaries to France.[11] 3. Sir Jenkins, an Advocat and ye Judge of the Court of ye Admiralty, a Learned and Discreet man, not very good French.[12]

Tis here said, that the King of France raiseth new difficulties about the Place for the Treaty, because there is an Imperial Garrison in Collen, commanded by a Minister of ye Emperors.[13]

Monsieur de Schomberg[14] hath lately written to a friend of mine, who is a favorite of the king, that an Express was arrived from the Emperour, signifying ye death of the Empresse, and wthall the Emperors resolution of marrying the Arch-Dutchesse of Inspruck himself;[15] though it seems very improbable, that the Emperour should certify by one and yesame Messenger ye death of the Empresse and the marriage of another.

The 26th instant I took my leave of his Majty; but am yet detained by reason of some letters; so yt I am not yet certain, whether or no I shall begin to morrow my voyage for Germany. I remaine

Yr Highnesses

To the same

London April
$\underline{3}$. 1673.
$\overline{13}$

The day before the Parlement was adjourned,[16] some whose interest it was did so manage the business, that the king passed a General act of pardon, extending itself to all and every one, yt are not therein excepted by name, whereby all the kings ministers were freed from all accusation for things past; wch was a good advice.

A book was sent out of Holland for London, but seized on by ye way and confiscated, and the Master of the ship, to whom it was committed, put in prison. The Title of the book is, An Appeal from the Cabale of ye king to the Parlement of England. Printed in English, and containing ye particulars of ye Alliance between the two Crowns of England and France. This book vexeth the English extreamly. The Author of it is said to be Isola, who caused it to be translated into English.[17]

Besides this, there is litle publique news; only they laugh at and make sport wth the brave actions of the Confederate Army, wch certainly hath been the cause that our whole German nation have lost their esteem.[18]

Tis not yet known when the Plenipotentiaries shall goe to ye Place of Treaty. The English Ambassader designed for Vienna is still at Paris, exspecting letters from Sr Bernard Gascon.[19] Some have proposed a marriage between the Duke of York and the Emperors sister; but I know not who it is, that hath interposed, and given out, yt the Emperors sister was no fit person, as being very sickly and infirme. I remaine etc.

No 2. Is to Count Zinzendorf,[20] one of ye Emperors privy Counsel at Vienna; containing ye self same particulars wth those of No. 1.
No 3. Is to ye Count of Hohenloh, first Minister of the Elector of Mayence.
No 4. To ye Baron de Meyersberg, the Emperors Envoy at Mayence.
No 5. To the Baron Paul Vohern, one of the Emperors privy Counsell at Vienna.

All these letters are of yeselfsame import, and so many severall Copies directed to as many different persons.

NOTES

1 Baden-Hochberg was a younger branch of the Baden-Baden line; "Marquesse" is an English version of "Margraf."
2 Not surprisingly, none of this is to be found in the House of Commons *Journal*, although it is certainly an accurate reflection of the spirit of the House. The hated ministers were all crypto- or pro-Catholics.
3 The Supply Bill was passed by the Commons on 26 March 1673 and by the Lords on 29 March 1673. The address of the Commons to the King against Catholics was voted in the Commons early in March and presented on 7 March 1672/3. All public servants and officers of the crown were obliged to swear that they did not hold to the doctrine of Transubstantiation.
4 This was insisted upon by the Lords at the session on 25 March 1673.
5 The Coinage Bill passed the Lords on 25 March 1673.
6 An "ohm" is an old German measure equivalent to approximately forty gallons.
7 This was discussed in the Commons on 25 March 1673.
8 All this occurred on 26 March 1673.
9 They received the Royal Assent on 29 March 1673.
10 Robert Spencer, Earl of Sunderland (1640–1702), had been educated partly in France. His first political employment had been when he was sent to Madrid in September 1671 to try to neutralize Spain in the anticipated Dutch Wars, in which he was unsuccessful. He had then gone to Paris in March of the next year as ambassador extraordinary. He was indeed appointed one of the plenipoteniaries to Cologne charged with negociating a general peace—which was not achieved.
11 Williamson did go to Cologne; doubtless this is the expression which Oldenburg thought so insulting.
12 Sir Leoline Jenkins (1623–85), a successful lawyer who had been knighted in 1670, and was at this time a Member of Parliament. He also went to Cologne.
13 Cologne was a Free Imperial City.
14 Presumably either Duke Frederick Herman (1615–90), the great general, whose mother was English, and who was briefly in the English service under Prince Rupert in 1673, although normally in the French service, or his son Charles (1645–93).
15 See Letter 2158, note 1.
16 It was adjourned on 29 March 1673.
17 We have found no trace of this obscure pamphlet; Baron Isola was later reported to be at the negociations at Cologne, furthering the Spanish interest.
18 The Empire had declared war on France in 1672, but there had been little effective action. There was at this time no standing Imperial Army; the various states within the Empire furnished troops, although the Confederation of the Rhine technically existed only from 1658 to 1667.
19 See Letter 2158, note 1. Sir Bernard Gascoigne (1614–87), originally Bernardo Guasconi, was a Florentine soldier who came to England to serve in the Royalist armies about 1644. After a ten-year residence in Italy he returned at the Restoration, and in 1661 was granted a patent of denization under the name of Sir Bernard Gascoigne. He was elected F.R.S. in 1667. In Florence during these years he organized an intelligence service for Lord Arlington. He eventually went to Vienna for the marriage embassy and while there wrote "A Description of Germany" for Charles II, published posthumously.
20 This was a well-known Austrian and German military and diplomatic family.

2200

Borelli to Oldenburg

10 April 1673

From the original in Royal Society MS. B 1, no. 115

Praeclaro Viro
Domino Henrico Oldenburg Regiae Anglicanae
Societatis Secretario Joh. Alphonsus
Borellus S.P.

S erius quam optaveram epistola tua, Vir Clarissime, cum plurimis libris Doctissimorum virorum, quibus me locupletare dignatus es, ad manus meas pervenere; et quod maxime doleo non licuit itinere iam agresso tam eruditis lucubrationibus frui, ut avide cupiebam. Nec scio an Romae, ubi quietem nactus fuero, quod poscis de Clarissimi Leibnitii Hypothesi physica tradere potero iudicium. Agnosco temeritatem meam, cum nunquam ausus fuerim totius aedificii naturalis philosophiae Architectonicam structuram exponere. Laudo tamen Viri ingenium et solertiam, qua ex optimis Authoribus meliora selegit. Multa conformia meis placitis in eo invenio, licet in aliquibus ab eo dissentiam, in quibus forsan ipse sum qui decipior; quod patebit, quando idem author methodice demonstrabit ea quae cursim in suo opusculo vel innuit, vel historice pronunciat. Caeterum opuscula Illustris et Eruditissimi Boylii libentissime amplexus sum, sicuti tertiam partem Mechanices Clarissimi Wallisii, quos plurimum meo nomine salutes velim, una cum caeteris doctissimis viris istius Regiae Societatis. Scito praeterea post editionem mei opusculi me incredibili labore ad summitatem Ætnei Montis ascendisse, et multa, quae prius conieceram vera esse autopsia comprobavit; nonnulla nova et praeter expectationem meam reperi, de quibus cum Romae fuero ad te scribam: interim, Vir eruditissime Vale, et ad me, si quid novi societas vestra ediderit, scribere digneris obsecro Romae agentem. Haec scripsi expotitus ob tempestates in littore Brutio, 20 Aprilis 1673.

ADDRESS
Praeclaro Viro
Domino Henrico Oldenburg Regiae
Anglicanae Societatis secretario dignissimo etc.
Londini

TRANSLATION

Giovanni Alphonso Borelli presents greetings to the exceedingly famous Mr. Henry Oldenburg, Secretary of the English Royal Society

Your letter, famous Sir, with many books of learned authors with which you were so good as to enrich me, came to my hands later than I could have wished, and what I chiefly regret is that as I had already embarked on a journey I could not enjoy such erudite studies, as I eagerly wished to do. And I do not know whether I shall be able to deliver the judgment of the famous Leibniz's *Hypothesis physica nova* that you ask for [even] at Rome, where I shall have some peace. I admit my rashness, since I have never dared to explain the architectonic structure of the whole fabric of natural philosophy. Yet I praise the intelligence and diligence by which he has chosen the best from many excellent authors. I find many things agreeable to my own opinions, though in some matters I disagree with him, in which perhaps I am myself the one who is deceived; this will become clear when the same writer shall demonstrate methodically the matters that he touches on cursorily in his essay or delivers as a matter of history. Moreover I have very willingly received the little works of the illustrious and very learned Boyle, as also the third part of the *Mechanics* of the famous Wallis, to [both of] whom I wish many greetings on my behalf, together with the remaining learned men of that Royal Society. Note that after the publication of my little book[1] I ascended by incredible labors to the summit of Mount Etna, and proved by personal examination many things which I had formerly conjectured to be true. I found several that were new to me and beyond my expectation, of which I will write to you when I shall be at Rome. Meanwhile, farewell, learned Sir, and be so good, I beg you, as to write to me while I am in Rome if your Society publishes anything new. I have written this while disembarked because of storms on the shores of southern Italy, 20 April 1673 [N.S.]

ADDRESS
     To the exceedingly famous
     Mr. Henry Oldenburg
     Most worthy secretary of the English Royal Society etc.
          London

NOTES

Reply to Letter 1812 (Vol. VIII) of 2 November 1671.
1 *Historia et meteorologia incendii Aetnaei anni 1669* (Reggio Julio, 1670).

2201

Bartholin to Oldenburg

10 April 1673

From the original in Royal Society MS. B 2, no. 18

Nobilissime et Clarissime Domine

Promissi ante facti a me memoria,[1] mitto tibi Acta Medica et Philosophica a fratre edita; quibus symbolam me contulisse videbis.[2] Utriusque conatus obsecro aequi bonique consulas. In Gallia duos Circum-Saturniales Planetas novos nuper detectos cognovi ex literis et tractatulo mihi a Domino Picart misso.[3] Eos detexerunt ope tubi longitudine 35 et 45 pedum, Divini, et alio 36 pedum Campani. In Jove quoque maculas varias observatas nuntiat alius amicus.[4] Ipsos satellites in facie Jovi, adeoque simul umbram et satellitem apparere in facie. Sensibilem praeterea notari diametrum Satellitum Jovis. Haec raptim non potui non tibi significare, tuumque amorem ut mihi conserves obnixe rogare. Vale. Hauniae die 10 Aprilis 1673

T[uus]. S[tudiosissimus].
E Bartholin

TRANSLATION

Very noble and famous Sir,

Remembering the promise I formerly made to you,[1] I send you the *Acta medica et philosophica* edited by my brother [Thomas], to which you will see I have made my contribution.[2] I beg you to think well of both our endeavors. From a letter and a little treatise sent me by Mr. Picard I have learned that two satellites of Saturn have been discovered in France recently.[3] They detected them by means of a [telescope] tube of 35 and 45 feet long, by Divini, and with another of 36 feet by Campani. Another friend sends me news of varied spots observed in Jupiter also.[4] [And that] the satellites themselves [are observed] on the face of Jupiter, and so both the satellite and its shadow appear at once upon his face. [And that] moreover the diameter of the satellites of Jupiter is to be observed as measurable. I could not but let you know these things hastily, and earnestly beg you to maintain your affection for me. Farewell. Copenhagen, 10 April 1673.

Most zealously yours,
E. Bartholin

NOTES

1 In Letter 2127.
2 Erasmus Bartholin has eight papers in this number of the *Acta*, on a variety of subjects, mostly astronomical and geographical.
3 See Letter 2182.
4 In the *Journal des Sçavans* for 21 March 1672 [N.S.] was printed "Relation du retour d'une grande tache permanente dans la Planete de Jupiter," reprinted in English translation in *Phil. Trans.*, no. 82 (22 April 1672), 4039–42. In spite of the title the contents of Cassini's "relation" are as described by Bartholin.

2202

Oldenburg to Leibniz

10 April 1673

From the original in Hannover MSS., ff. 20–21
Printed in Gerhardt, pp. 89–90

Amplissimo et Consultissimo Viro
Domino Gothof. Guil. Leibnitio J.U.D. celeberrimo etc.
Henr. Oldenburg Salutem

Voti tui, quod relictis mecum litteras[1] exposueras, compos jam es factus, dum Regia Societas hesterno die, conspirantibus omnium suffragiis, in sodalium suorum Album Te cooptavit, idque eodem tempore, quo Doctissimum Astronomiae in Oxoniensi Universitate Professorem Savilianum, Dn. Edwardum Bernhardum, unanimi similiter consensu elegit. Negotia publica, negotiosa hac rerum facie accumulata, aliquam Electioni huic moram injecere, eo quod complures Societatis nostrae consortes, gravibus occupationibus tum in Aula tum in Regni Comitiis involuti, conventus nostros philosophicos infrequentiores reliquerunt: unde factum, ut requisitus Electioni numerus ad usque diem hesternum nobis defecerit. Exinde vero rebus tuis ex animi sententia transactis, tuum jam erit, genuinum Te Societatis hujus Philosophicae alumnum praestare, inque medium ea conferre, quae vel Tutemet in Physicis Mechanicisve meditando et experiundo fueris consecutus, vel alii per Germaniam in eadem re philosophica excogitaverint. Germana id fide Te praestiturum nulli dubitamus, ad similia vicissim officia Tibi exhibenda ex animo parati.

Lubens haec addere iis volui, quae jam uberiori epistola, die 6. Aprilis ad te data, conscripseram.² Vale, deque litteris hisce bene traditis quantocius Tui studiosissimum Oldenburgium certiorem redde.
Dabam Lond. die 10. April. 1673.

ADDRESS
Amplissimo et Consultissimo
Viro Domino Gothofredo Guilielmo
Leibnitio, J.U.D. et Consilario Moguntino
Parisiis

TRANSLATION

Henry Oldenburg greets the very worthy and wise Mr. Gottfried Wilhelm Leibniz, most celebrated LL.D. etc.

The desires you expressed in the letter left with me¹ are now fulfilled, since yesterday the Royal Society unanimously elected you into its register of Fellows at the same time as the very learned Dr. Edward Bernard, Savilian Professor of Astronomy in the University of Oxford, was similarly chosen by a unanimous vote. Public concerns, made the more pressing by this [present] state of affairs, have imposed some delay upon this election in that many Fellows of our Society being involved in the serious undertakings of both the Court and committees of the realm have left our philosophical meetings the less well attended, so that it came about that we lacked the requisite number for an election until yesterday. And so with your business done to your heart's content it is now for you to prove yourself a true alumnus of this philosophical society, and to bring before the public those matters which either you shall have yourself pursued by reflection and experience in physics or mechanics, or others in Germany shall have thought out on the same philosophical topics. That you, with Germanic trustworthiness, will so prove yourself we do not doubt, being ready to make a sincere return of similar services to you.

I would have been happy to add these sentences to a more copious letter that I have already written to you on 6 April.² Farewell, and as soon as possible inform your most zealous Oldenburg that this letter has been safely delivered.
London, 10 April 1673.

ADDRESS
To the very worthy and wise Mr. Gottfried Wilhelm Leibniz LL.D.,
Councilor of Mainz,
at Paris

NOTES

1 Read (with Gerhardt), "litteris." For Leibniz's letter declaring his desire of being made F.R.S., see Letter 2165, note 3.
2 Letter 2196.

2203

Swammerdam to Oldenburg

11 April 1673

From the original in Royal Society MS. S 1, no. 117

Doctissimo Viro
Domino Henrico Oldenburg Regiae Societatis Secretario
Joh. Swammerdam Salutem

Quod de Leoniceno sentis, et voce et mente censentio, sed quid dicam 1 : acrimonis et salis plurimum habet.[1] Amo ego ingenium, amo eruditionem et raras in illa aetate (nam Pechlinum[2] autorem referunt) animi et corporis dotes; at optandum esset ut unus quisque ipsum semel tali lixivio probe perfunderet. non enim nosti inconsideratissimam Apollinis pancreatici temeritatem, que se natricem futurum quendam venditabat, si modo Klark se diabolum anses fuisset asserere.[3]

Non dubito quin jam acceperis delineationes quas de Animalibus vena arteriosa destitutis ad te dedi.[4] In praesentiarem haec sociabunt quae ad piscium pancreas subinde notavimus, de quibus vestrum expectamus Judicium perpolitum.[5] Mirum est quod addendum hebeo, nimirum pancreas in Salmone ex plurimis appendicibus compositum, secundum intestini longitudinem affabre situm esse, cujus orificia amplo hiatu singulatim et ordine pulcherrimo disposita, in ecphysin aperiuntur:[6] *A*. ventriculus. *B* intestinum. *C* pancreas sive appendices.[7] *D* vesica fellea una cum ductibus hepaticis. *E* insertio ductus bilaris. *F* intestinum apertum pancreatis orificia exhibens. [*For Swammerdam's drawing, see the frontispiece.*]

Acipenseris pancreas prae aliis omnibus cum humano convenit, quia ejus appendices seu ductus, in unum corpus colliguntur, atque communi gaudent membrana.[8]

Ante tres quatuorve dies Clarissimus Ruyschius⁹ in publico theatro anatomico demonstravit conceptum humanum recentissimum nondum coalito testiculo dextro, cujus lateris tuba manifestissime adaucta erat, ut ut Uterus ejusque vasa ac orificium internum, quod tamen apertum cernebatur; at circa arterias spermaticas secus¹⁰ atque venas vix observabilis quaedam mutatio lustrabatur.

D. Grandi Chirurgus Romanus¹¹ faetum humanum inter ovarium et tubam, suis involucris naturaliter contentum, ostendit, cujus descriptionem simul ac delinationem (referente mihi D. Huyberts) meditatur Romae. Vale, vir Eruditissime, et me ama. Dab. Amstel. 21 April 1673.

TRANSLATION

Jan Swammerdam greets the very learned Henry Oldenburg, Secretary of the Royal Society

With word and thought I agree with what you say of Leonicenus, but what I say 1. has much of acrimony and salt.¹ I myself love intelligence, I love learning and the gifts of mind and body rare at that age (for they report Pechlin² [as] the author); but it would be preferable for each person to drench himself thoroughly once with such a lye. For you do not know the very thoughtless boldness of the pancreatic Apollo, who was proclaiming himself a future scourge, if only Clarke were to have claimed that the devil . . .³

No doubt you have already received the sketches I sent you of the animals deprived of a pulmonary artery.⁴ Now they may be combined with this which we have noted in the pancreas of fishes immediately afterwards, and on which we await your well-considered judgment.⁵ There is an extraordinary thing which it amazes me to add, namely that in salmon the pancreas, composed of many appendixes, is most ingeniously placed along the length of the intestine, the orifices of it singularly arranged and in a most beautiful order with a wide aperture opening into the intestine.⁶ *A* is the stomach, *B* the gut, *C* the pancreas or appendixes,⁷ *D* the gall-bladder with the hepatic ducts, *E* the insertion of the bile duct. *F* the gut opened to show the apertures of the pancreas. [*For Swammerdam's drawing, see the frontispiece.*]

The "pancreas" of the sturgeon agrees with the human better than any other, because its appendixes or ducts are united into a single structure and possess a common membrane.⁸

Three or four days ago the famous Ruysch⁹ demonstrated in the public anatomy theatre a very late human foetus with the right testicle [ovary] still not knit together, the lateral tube of which was manifestly enlarged so that the uterus and its vessels and its internal orifice, which was open, could be perceived; but about the spermatic arteries . . .[10] and veins hardly any observable change was displayed.

Mr. Grandi, a Roman surgeon,[11] showed a human foetus between the ovary and the [Fallopian] tube, naturally contained within its teguments; the description and sketch of this are (Mr. Huyberts tells me) under consideration at Rome. Farewell, learned Sir, and love me. Amsterdam, 12 April 1673.

NOTES

1 Janus Leonicenus, *Metamorphis Aesculapii et Apollinis Pancreatici* (Leiden, 1673) was a satire on the work of Sylvius and De Graaf on pancreatic anatomy and chemistry. Oldenburg must have referred to him in a letter now totally lost. We do not know what the "1." signifies.

2 Jan Nicolaus Pechlin (1646–1706), a Dutch medical writer who was to become a correspondent later in 1673, was indeed the author of the work just cited.

3 Although we have not been able to make out his exact meaning, undoubtedly Swammerdam here refers to De Graaf. For the latter's long dispute with Dr. Timothy Clarke, see Vols. IV–VI. Disputes between Swammerdam and De Graaf were of equally long standing, and now reached their height. One was relatively trivial. According to Boerhaave's *Life* of Swammerdam (in the work cited in Letter 2173, note) it was in 1668 that Swammerdam was led, by discovering a large "pancreas" (note 7, below) in a sturgeon, to investigate this organ and conclude that Sylvius and his pupil De Graaf were mistaken in describing the pancreatic juice as acid. Although Swammerdam's dissection of the sturgeon was published only in 1673 in the *Observationum anatomicarum Collegii privati Amstelodamensis, pars altera*, it was undoubtedly well known. The irony of his refutation of Sylvius and De Graaf is that the "pancreas" of Swammerdam in the sturgeon is a peculiar form of the pyloric caeca. (See Cole, *Comparative Anatomy*, 334–35).

Far more serious was their rivalry for the discovery of the mammalian egg; the correspondence through which its development may be traced was printed by De Graaf in the book referred to in Letter 2209. There were four chief contenders for this honor, all Dutch: Van Horne, De Graaf, Swammerdam, and Kerckring. The latter, whose work was of a fanciful quality, need not concern us. Like De Graaf, Johann van Horne had published a brief *Prodromus* on the human organs of generation (see Vol. IV, p. 369, notes 23 and 24). It was mainly concerned with the male, and problems of male anatomy were at issue between Van Horne and De Graaf; but the former also addressed himself to the "testes" of the female, of which he wrote that "the testes in women are what the ovary is in the ovipara, namely they contain perfect eggs." However, this bare statement of a startlingly anti-traditional theory, which is quoted by De Graaf in his *Defensio* (*Opera omnia*, Amsterdam 1705, p. 334), is a very different matter from its demonstration by a complete anatomical investigation. At the end of his treatise on the male reproductive system (1668; see Vol. IV, p. 523) De Graaf promised to publish such a study, "time and opportunity permitting."

As a student at Leiden Swammerdam had studied under Van Horne and Sylvius, and formed a friendship with De Graaf. On his return from Paris (1665?) Swammerdam resumed dissection with Van Horne, though he was also a most active member of the "Private College" in Amsterdam. Boerhaave makes two claims that are difficult to reconcile: that on 22 January 1667 "in Van Horne's own house, Swammerdam first injected the uterine vessels of a human subject with a ceraceous matter"; and (three pages later) that before 21 January 1667 all the "curious pieces" on the organs of generation that Swammerdam was later to send to the Royal Society had been sketched out in Van Horne's house, "though not finished or illustrated with proper explanations till" 7 May 1671. Thus, if one would read Boerhaave literally (which is impossible) Swammerdam had completed his rough sketches before applying his famous method to the female system!

As De Graaf pursued his study of the female reproductive organs he was (he reports) visited by Swammerdam, who saw his anatomical plates, and even wrote (in 1671) to urge De Graaf into print, warning him of Kerckring's forthcoming book (see Vol. VIII, pp. 39, 611) dealing with the same subject. Shortly after, De Graaf learned to his surprise that Swammerdam had supplied to another Amsterdam anatomist, Gerard Blasius, for the edition of Bartholin's *Anatome* to be published at Leiden in 1673, a plate of the female reproductive system and another of the intestines (see Letter 2132 and its note 19). De Graaf begged Swammerdam to refrain from so doing, on the ground that his own work was to appear shortly. Swammerdam maintained that it was now out of his power to refuse, and to strengthen his position further, sent his plate to the Royal Society. The coincidence of two dates is striking and obviously not fortuitious; on 7 May 1671 (according to Boerhaave, as we have seen) Swammerdam finished all three of his plates, and on 30 May 1671 De Graaf wrote an epistle *De partibus genitalibus mulierum* addressed to Lucas Schacht, which he attached to the second edition of his *De succo pancreatico* (*Opera omnia*, 108–12); this was despatched to the Royal Society in mid-June 1671 (Vol. VIII, p. 114).

Swammerdam's first published plate, that dedicated to Dr. Tulp which was to be the third in his series, probably reached the Society some months later, in November 1671 (Vol. VIII, xxvii); on 26 March 1672 he followed it up with two more plates (Vol. VIII, pp. 617–19) and later a set of prepared anatomical specimens which was received by Oldenburg only in December 1672 (Letter 2111); meanwhile, on 4 June, Swammerdam had also despatched to the Royal Society a copy of his *Miraculum naturae*, dedicated to the Royal Society (Letter 1996), which contained all three plates.

Meanwhile, De Graaf's much heralded book, *De mulierum organis generationi inservientibus*, was long in the press; he sent it off to London about 21 March 1671/2 (Vol. VIII, p. 610) and Oldenburg had received it by mid-April (Letter 1966). In his epistle to Schacht De Graaf had made no mention of Swammerdam, nor did he in *De mulierum organis*. Whatever his private thoughts of his former friend and present rival, he had at the time of writing, of course, no fore-knowledge of the *Miraculum naturae*, nor of Swammerdam's dealings with the Royal Society. Swammerdam, however, took offence at De Graaf's failure to assign to him by name any part in the new anatomy of reproduction, and in a letter printed by De Graaf (*Opera omnia*, 341–42) charged him with failure to ascribe discoveries to their true inventors, particularly as regards reproduction in the rabbit; and when he examined the *Miraculum naturae* De Graaf found it to contain repeated accusations of plagiary and incompetence against himself. Accordingly, he prepared his own *Defensio*, for which see Letter 2209.

What did each man claim? There can be no doubt that Swammerdam claimed absolute technical superiority for his method of dissection and preparation, and priority in the discovery of the mammalian egg. After the death of Van Horne (1670) he maintained in the *Miraculum naturae* that Van Horne's *Prodromus* was all his own work, that is, that he (not Van Horne) first identified the female gonad as an ovary. This claim—which may be just and is accepted by writers on Swammerdam—could not have been known to De Graaf as he prepared his own study of female anatomy. De Graaf claimed only that his careful and detailed anatomical work was his own, and that his plates illustrating it had been prepared by at least the beginning of the year 1670 (*Opera omnia*, p. 108). De Graaf did *not* claim that the identification of the gonad with the ovary was his; on the contrary, he declared in Chapter XII of *De mulierum organis*, speaking of "vesicles" in the mammalian ovary: "others call them hydatids; but the famous Mr. Van Horne calls them 'eggs' in his *Prodromus*; as we preferred this employment of a word above the others we have taken up that name as being the more convenient, and we will, with that famous man, denominate them eggs" (*Opera omnia*, p. 228).

Even if Swammerdam was the unacknowledged first discoverer of the mammalian "egg"—really the follicle, of course—it was highly unjust of him to calumniate De Graaf for not acknowledging the discovery to him, when it had been published over the name of Van Horne, and it was reasonable for De Graaf to seek to exonerate himself by appeal to the tribunal of the Royal Society.

4 See Letter 2173 and its note 5. The letter was read to the Society on 19 March 1672/3.
5 The figure is to be found in Royal Society Letter Book VI between pages 91 and 92.
6 The word looks like *ecphysin* (Greek, "shoot" or "outgrowth"), but the meaning "intestine" or "gut" is required.
7 The structures in teleost fish called by Swammerdam the "pancreas" are, in fact, the pyloric caeca, which are very well drawn by him in the figure. On this point see Cole, *Comparative Anatomy*, pp. 334–35, 253, 352; the caeca were (imperfectly) represented by later anatomists like Grew, but Cole was not aware of Swammerdam's earlier drawing. The real pancreas in *Salmo* species, though it may be more visible in the young fish, is in the adult a diffuse and obscure organ of little physiological importance.
8 Swammerdam dissected the sturgeon about 1668 or 1669; his correct observation of the peculiar form of the caeca was printed in 1673 (see the first part of note 3, above).
9 For Frederik Ruysch (1638–1731), see Vol. VII, p. 136, note 5.
10 The original word is illegible; the Letter Book copy has "secus" which makes no sense.
11 Giacopo Grandi (1646–91) was an acquaintance of Malpighi's.

2204

Oldenburg to Sluse

13 April 1673

We know of this letter, a reply to Letter 2198, only from Sluse's answer to it, Letter 2215. However, it very clearly contained a repeat of Letter 2136 (which, as already noted, was lost en route) briefly describing Newton's method of tangents. Presumably because its substance was repetitive Oldenburg kept no copy.

2205
Oldenburg to Leibniz
14 April 1673

From the original in Hannover MSS., f. 33
Printed in Gerhardt, pp. 93–94

Monsieur

Jeudy dernier ie vous envoyay un pacquet assez large,[1] l'addressant selon vostre ordre[2] à vous sous le couvert de Monsr Boineburg chez M. Heis. Ayant desia vous adressé une autre lettre dela mesme maniere, sans avoir receu aucune responce lá dessus,[3] i'ay voulu prendre cete voye pour vous dire derechef, que vous fustez eleu le 9. de ce mois dans la Societé Royale nemine contradicente;[4] et que ie vous ay respondu sur toutes les particularitez, si ie ne me trompe, que vous m'aviez proposées dans vostre lettre escrite de Paris; y ayant adjousté d'autres choses, que vous ne serez pas mary d'entendre. Je seray bien aise de recevoir promptement vostre responce comme Monsieur

Vostre treshumble et tres obeissant
serviteur
Oldenburg

le 14. Avril 1673

ADDRESS
    A Monsieur
        Monsieur Leibnitz etc.
            à
                Paris

TRANSLATION

Sir,

Last Thursday I sent you a pretty large packet,[1] addressing it as you requested[2] to you under cover to Mr. Boineburg care of Mr. Heis. Having already sent you another letter in the same way, without having received any reply to it,[3] I wanted to take this means of letting you know once again that you were elected unanimously to the Royal Society on the ninth of this month;[4] and that I had

replied, unless I am mistaken, to all the points which you raised in your letter
written from Paris; and added other things which you will not be sorry to hear.
I should be very glad to receive your reply promptly, as, Sir

> Your very humble and obedient
> servant
> *Oldenburg*

14 April 1673

ADDRESS

>   To Mr. Leibniz, etc.
>   Paris

NOTES

>   Further reply to Letter 2165.
> 1 Letter 2202, of 10 April 1673.
> 2 In Letter 2165.
> 3 As Oldenburg could not have expected a reply yet to Letter 2196 he must refer to
>   Letter 2174.
> 4 This news, of course, he could not have sent before Letter 2202.

2206

Oldenburg to Huygens

14 April 1673

From *Œuvres Complètes*, VII, 268
Original in the Huygens Collection at Leiden

A londres le 14 Avril 1673

Monsieur

N'y ayant que huit iours que ie vous escrivis amplement, y joignant la
responce de Monsieur Newton a vos considerations sur sa theorie des
couleurs,[1] ie ne vous eusse pas sitost importuné de nouveau n'eust esté que
vous voulez que ie continue de vous faire tenir mes journaux de temps en
temps. Vous trouverez dans celuy-cy[2] la version Angloise de la description
faite par Monsieur Cassini de ses nouvelles descouvertes,[3] que i'ay voulu

traduire en nostre langue, à fin de donner la satisfaction à tous les curieux du pais de s'informer de toutes les particularitez observees dans cete matiere.

Mesmes vous ne serez pas marry de voir les chefs des nouveaux traitez de Monsieur Boyle, en attendant que vous receviez les traitez mesmes.[4] C'est tout ce que i'avois a vous dire à present, si ce n'est que ie vous prieray de faire voir à Monsieur Cassini cette traduction, avec mes baisemains. Je suis sincerement Monsieur

Vostre treshumble et tresobeissant serviteur
Oldenburg

ADDRESS

A Monsieur
Monsieur Christian Hugens de Zulichem
dans la Bibliotheque de Roy à
Paris

TRANSLATION

London, 14 April 1673

Sir,

As it is only a week since I wrote to you at length, adding Mr. Newton's reply to your reflections on his theory of colors,[1] I should not have importuned you again were it not that you wish me to continue to have my journal conveyed to you from time to time. You will find in this one[2] an English version of the description made by Mr. Cassini of his new discoveries,[3] which I wanted to translate into our language in order to permit all those in this country who are interested to inform themselves of all the details observed in this business.

In the same you will not be sorry to see the heads of the new tracts by Mr. Boyle, while waiting to receive the tracts themselves.[4] This is all I have to tell you at this time, except that I beg you to let Mr. Cassini see this translation, with my respectful greetings. I am sincerely, Sir,

Your very humble and obedient servant,
Oldenburg

ADDRESS

To
Mr. Christiaan Hugens of Zulichem
The King's Library
Paris

NOTES

1 Letter 2197, enclosing Letter 2195.
2 *Phil. Trans.*, no. 91 (25 March 1673).
3 See Letter 2182, note 2.
4 See Letter 2089, note 6.

2207

Bernard to Oldenburg

15 April 1673

From the original in Royal Society MS. B 2, no. 8

Sr!

I beseeche you to commend my most humble service to ye Right Honble ye President & ye Fellowes of ye Royall Society, assuring ym yt I receive wth all humble Thankfulnesse ye great honour they have done mee in rechoning mee in ye number of their assembly,[1] & shall be glad to understand how I may here serve either ye worthy Designe of ye whole body or ye desire of any particular member, especially your selfe, whose kindnesse is more ancient, yn yt I should now be carefull at large to persuade yt I am

> your most obliged servant
> *E. Bernard*

St Johns Oxon.
Apr. 15. 1673.

Pray advise me of ye duty & observances belonging to one newly Elected, yt I may performe ym. as alsoe recommend my most humble service to ye Honble Mr Boyle, to Mr Hooke, Revd Mr Haake, & my very good freind Mr Collins, &c

I hear of ye goodluck of Cassini, & hope shortly to reade it out of French or Latine[2]

ADDRESS

　　　　These
For his hond Freind Henry
Oldenburgh Esq att his
Lodgeings in ye Pallmell
near St. James's
　　　　　　London

NOTES

1 Bernard was elected F.R.S. on 9 April 1673, together with Leibniz. It is not known
who informed Bernard of this.
2 See Letter 2182, note 2.

2208
Leibniz to Oldenburg

16 April 1673

From the copy in Royal Society Letter Book VI, 101–6
Printed in Gerhardt, pp. 90–93, from the draft in the Hannover MSS.

Amplissimo Viro
Henrico Oldenburgio, Societatis Regiae Secretario
Gottfredus Guilielmus Leibnitz S.P.D.

Obligatissimus favori tuo, rescripsissem dudum, sed promissas a Clarissimo Huetio literas indies exspectanti, quas fluxio quaedam oculi ejus
incommoda, distulerat, tempus elapsum est; Eas nunc ubi primum accepi,
statim mitto.[1] Sententiam ejus facile intelliges: Ea viri eruditio est, ut
publici; ea humanitas, ut obligantis intersit, eum beneficio ejusmodi obli-
gari. Ea vero promptitudo officiositatis tuae, ut ab ea quidvis sibi polli-
ceantur eruditi. Huetium fortassis non ignoras Delphini Studijs admotum;
scis Gubernatorem esse Montauserium ducem, in quo cum aulica prudentia
doctrinae profunditas certat;[2] studiorum ejus Rector primarius, Epis-
copus Condomensis[3] proximus ab hoc Huetius. Iussu Montauserij, rec-
tore Huetio, caepta res est, ad amaeniores literas, fugientemque antiqui-
tatis eruditionem velut revocandum, perutilis. Certis enim hominibus doctis
id negotij datum est, ut scriptores veteres latinos, quos classicos vocant,

alio quam hactenus more tractent; adjecta quadam velut paraphrasi, ubi
opus est lucida ac brevi, ut facilis juventuti reddatur veterum lectio: Rejectis in notas, quae ad autoris intelligentiam ex historia scientijsve repeti
debent.[4] Inter caeteros, Vitruvius quoque et Celsus ea lege tractabuntur.[5]
Sed Huetius ipse alia agitat, utilia sane etiam ad scientias severiores, nec
vobis ingratas. Nam praeter Vectium Valentem, hactenus ineditum, habet
Heronis Spiritalia acceptiora multo, quam exstant: Naumachiam item, non
Leonis tantum sed et Basilij cujusdam patricij: εἰκόνας item Philostrati
cum scholiis hactenus ineditis, ut alia non memorem.[6]

Celeberrimum Wallisium, cui ego jam bis obligatus sum,[7] rogo, ut a me
officiosissime salutes, eique promptitudinem meam denunties, si quid ille
exquiri in Gallia Germaniaque, aut alibi etiam cupit, aut si qua alia occasio
offertur utendi opera mea. Id fortasse libenter intelliges, mox proditurum
esse tractatum Cl. Mariotti *du Choc des Corps*,[8] in quo sententia, quam ille
fovit dudum, et quam Wallisius in tractatu de Motu pulchre expressit,
quamque ego, nulla horum conscientia, in hypothesi illa mea[9] attigeram
breviter, (Reflexionem ab Elaterio esse) multis experimentis elegantibus
praeclare admodum confirmatur: unde satis appariturum arbitror, phaenomena Hugenio-Wrenniana ex abstractis motus principijs explicari non
posse.[10] Ego, supposito itidem Elaterio, modum reperi explicandi mechanica claritate cur Lumen in densioribus refringatur *ad* perpendicularem, in
rarioribus *a* perpendiculari; cum contrarium evenire debere videbatur.
Scis explicationem ejus rei visam difficillimam, et Cartesianam hypothesin,
pororum assumtione innixam, vix ullis nisi qui in verba Magistri jurarunt,
satis fecisse. Cum Ego praesertim tum rationibus, tum experimentis evinci
posse putem, perspicuitatem a porositate non pendere. Solutio phaenomeni
manifesta est in hypothesi mea, si tanti putas, tibi mittam. Caeterum, rem
tibi haud dubie ingratam invitus nuntio, P. Pardies aliquot abhinc diebus
obijsse;[11] doleo jacturam viri docti, et diligentis, et a quo non pauca utilia
poterant exspectari. Tria ab eo opuscula sub praelo sunt, sed quae sint,
nondum explicatum habeo:[12] ubi intellexero, faxo, ut scias. Credo, Op-
ticam ejus inter caetera fore, quod vellem sane. Scio enim id argumentum
ab eo tractatum diligenter.

Memini Te quaerere, cum apud vos essem, nossemne, quid Dn. de St.
Hilaire circa magnetem novi haberet.[13] Ego nunc ita accepi: Repertam ab
eo rationem ope magnetis, a dato baculo ferreo, utrimque inaequali,
abscindendi partem ponderis datam, ut sextam, quartam, tertiam; Magnete
scilicet determinante punctum sectionis. Magnam id lucem utique philosophiae magneticae afferet.

Clarissimus Mariotus rem quandam perutilem agitat, sine ulla Aere-
ometria, aut virgula Stereometrica determinare, quantum liquoris vas
aliquod datum figurae cujuscunque contineat. Ubi Experimentis satis
multis, ut solet, stabiliverit artem suam, non dubito quin sit juris publici
facturus.

Clarissimi Cassini observationes circa Systema Saturnicum et maculas
solares, haud dubie jam sunt in manibus vestris.[14] Extimus Satelles jam
inde ab anno 1671. ab eo observatus, octoginta diebus periodum absolvit,
intimus hoc demum anno detectus 5 et dimidio, medius, Hugenianus,
diebus sedecim. Accessere observationes de Macularum solarium, quibus
illud concluditur, Revolutionem solis circa proprium axem absolvi circiter 26 diebus cum dimidio. Sed haec Te dudum habere puto.

Hoc interea tuo favore nosse desidero: scis aestate praeterita publi-
catum illustris Hugenij experimentum, de duabus Tabulis vel laminis
politis, in vacuo sive Recipiente exhausto suspensis, ac ne pondere quidem
inferiori appenso dissolutis;[15] At ego me legere memini, in experimentorum Elasticorum Boylianorum editione novissima, ubi sub finem, nisi
fallor, in Tabulis politis institutum experimentum recensetur, referri
contrarium: Tabulas nimirum exhausto recipiente fuisse dilapsas. Librum
hic non reperio, ut eam dubitationem mihi adimere possim: quare rogo, ut
librum, imo ipsum Ill. Boylium data occasione consulas; id enim nosse
interest philosophiae.

An, ut audio Cl. vir Isaac Vossius musicos veteres aut musicam veterem,
aut aliquid simile editurus sit, Tu optime noveris.[16] Audio, Oxonij nescio
quem Geometras veteres publicaturum:[17] Optem Wilkinsij Characterem
Latinum prodire quamprimum; visum enim est mihi opus utilissimum.[18]
Ill. Boylium quaeso, data occassione meis verbis saluta, eique cultum a me
perennem denuntia: nihil est quod malim, quam continuatam ejus erga me
benevolentiam, cujus indicium habebo, si quod coram pollicitus est,
Catalogum commutandorum mihi miserit.[19] Ego eo non aliter utar, nec
apud alios quam ipse volet, satis enim in istis mihi cautelae est ac circum-
spectionis.

Desiderium meum, quod illustri Societati Regiae per literas exposueram,
ubi occasio se obtulerit, exitum expectat.

Machina mea arithmetica, officium suum plane factura, uti absente me
coepta erat, nunc ad finem decurrit, et magno, ut video, applausu generatim excipitur. Spero alia, momenti non minoris, mox secutura.

Attuli mecum Barrovij Lectiones opticas; sub libri calcem doctissimus
autor phaenomenon exhibet, cujus rationem reddere posse negat, aliosque

ut inquirant hortatur; aut ut, si possint causam sibi communicent, rogat; dubitat vero ut id facile praestari possit.[20] Hugenius tamen et Mariottus ejus Solutionem se habere dixere.

Cum hoc scripsissem, exspectatissimas a Te literas accepi,[21] quibus Illustrem Societatem Regiam desiderio meo locum dedisse, nuntias. Regiae Societati gratias rebus ipsis habebo, eique studia mea probare conabor.

Ad caetera literarum tuarum, profunda rei Algebraicae eruditione refertarum, justis literis respondere, et quae jubes, quae postulas, inquirere ac praestare conabor. Subtilissimo Collinio tam praeclara communicanti, obligatum me profiteor. Caeterum quod Mengolum aiunt praestitisse, quod ego promiseram, summam fractionum quarum nominatores sunt numeri triangulares et pyramidales etc. id fortasse ex promisso meo non satis recte percepto profectum est:[22] quanquam enim nondum mihi inquirendi in Mengolum otium fuerit, conjicio tamen ex illis ipsis, quae in literis tuis repraesentas, Mengolum summas quidem inijsse serierum ejusmodi, $\frac{1}{3} \frac{1}{6} \frac{1}{10} \frac{1}{15} = \frac{1}{4} \frac{1}{10} \frac{1}{20} = \frac{1}{5} \frac{1}{15} \frac{1}{35} \frac{1}{70}$, sed finitarum, seu ad aliquem Terminum usque, qualiscunque tamen ille sit, continuatarum. At Ego totius seriei in infinitum continuatae summam invenio Methodo mea, $\frac{1}{3} \frac{1}{6} \frac{1}{10} \frac{1}{15} \frac{1}{21} \frac{1}{28}$ etc. in infinitum; quod jam publice praepositum esse, vel ideo non credidi, quia Nobilissimo Hugenio mihi primum propositum est hoc problema in numeris Triangularibus; Ego vero id non in Triangularibus tantum, sed in pyramidalibus, etc. et in universum in omnibus eius generis numeris solvi, ipso Hugenio mirante. Dominum Collinium autem de his infinitarum Serierum summis non loqui vel inde conjicio, quia exemplum hujus seriei affert $\frac{1}{2} \frac{1}{3} \frac{1}{4} \frac{1}{5} \frac{1}{6}$, quae si in infinitum continuetur, summari non potest, cum summa ista, non ut numerorum triangularium sit finita, sed infinita.[23] Sed nunc literarum spatio excludor.

Dominus Agar[24] hic de frigore experimenta memorabilia fecit, figurasque in varijs congelescentibus summa diligentia observavit miras et curiosas; si quid distinctius ab ipso, ut spero; impetravero, Te participem reddam. Interea vale ac homini Tui studiosissimo fave.

Paris $\frac{16}{26}$ April. 1673.

TRANSLATION

Gottfried Wilhelm Leibniz sends many greetings to the very worthy Henry
Oldenburg, Secretary of the Royal Society

Being much obliged by your favor, I should have replied some little while since,
but time has elapsed while I was daily expecting a letter [to be sent to you]
from the famous Huet, which he postponed [writing] because he was inconve-
nienced by some kind of discharge from his eye; I send it at once, just as soon as I
have received it.[1] You will easily perceive his meaning. His learning is such that
it should be published; and his kindness is such that it concerns those who are
under obligation for it, to oblige him with a like kindness. And such is the readiness
of your courtesy that the learned expect all things of it. Perhaps you know that
Huet is taking a hand with the Dauphin's education; you will know that his
Governor is the Duc de Montausier, in whom depth of learning contends with a
courtier's shrewdness;[2] his principal tutor is the Bishop of Condom,[3] and next
to him is Huet. By order of Montausier and with Huet as director, something has
been begun which will be most useful to the lighter kind of learning and for
recapturing the fleeing learning of antiquity. For certain learned men have been
entrusted with the business of dealing with the ancient Latin authors, whom they
call *classical*, in a different way from that used hitherto, by adding as it were some
paraphrase where it is necessary to be lucid and brief so that the reading of ancient
authors is made easy for young people. What should be related from history or the
sciences for the understanding of the author['s text] is inserted into notes.[4] Among
others, Vitruvius and Celsus too will be treated in this way.[5] But Huet himself is busy
with other things more useful to serious branches of study and not unwelcome to
yourselves. For besides Vettius Valens, hitherto unpublished, he has a far more
acceptable [version of] the *Spiritalia* of Hero than is available [now]; as also the
Naumachia not only of Leo but of a certain patrician, Basil; also the *Eiconas* of
Philostratus with hitherto unpublished scholia, and other things I don't remember.[6]

I ask you to salute the very famous Wallis most courteously on my behalf, to
whom I am now doubly obliged,[7] and assure him of my readiness if he wishes
anything of me in France or Germany or anywhere else even, or if any other
opportunity presents itself of employing my services. You will perhaps be glad to
know that the famous Mariotte's treatise *Du choc des corps* will soon appear,[8] in
which the opinion which he has lately advocated, and which the famous Wallis
expressed elegantly in his treatise on motion and which I, in ignorance of all this,
touched on briefly in that hypothesis of mine,[9] that reflection arises from springiness, is very thoroughly confirmed by a multitude of elegant experiments. Whence
I think it will appear clearly enough that the Huygens-Wren phenomena cannot be
explained by the abstract principles of motion.[10] I, postulating this springiness,
have found a way of explaining with mechanical clarity why light [entering] into a

denser medium is refracted *towards* the perpendicular and in rarer ones *away from* the perpendicular; as it seemed that the contrary ought to happen. You know that the explanation of this matter has been seen as a difficulty and the Cartesian hypothesis, based on the assumption of pores, gave satisfaction to hardly any but devotees of the master's word. Whereas I particularly think it may be shown, both by experiments and by reason, that transparency does not depend on porosity. The solution of the phenomenon is manifest upon my hypothesis, and if you think it worth-while I will send it to you. For the rest, I reluctantly give you the doubtless unwelcome news that P. Pardies died a few days ago;[11] I grieve at the death of a learned and hard-working man, from whom no slight number of useful things was to be expected. There are three short works of his in the press but I have no account yet of what they are;[12] when I find out, I will see to it that you know. I believe his *Optics* will be among the rest, and certainly hope so. For I know he labored diligently upon that topic.

I remember your asking, when I was among you, whether I knew what novelty concerning magnetism Mr. de St. Hilaire possessed.[13] I have now heard this: He has discovered a method, by means of a magnet, of cutting off from a given iron rod, unequal as to its two ends, a given part of the weight—that is, a sixth, a quarter or a third, determining the point of cutting by means of the magnet. This must surely throw a great light on the philosophy of magnetism.

The famous Mariotte is busy with a very useful thing, determining how much fluid any given vessel of any shape whatever will contain, without any aereometry or stereometric rod. I do not doubt that he will publish his method when he shall have confirmed it by many trials, as is his wont.

No doubt the observations of the famous Cassini on the system of Saturn and sunspots are in your hands.[14] The outermost satellite, observed by him since 1671, completes its period in eighty days, the innermost one, discovered this year, in five and a half days, and that in between, the Huygenian, in sixteen days. He has added observations on sunspots from which it is concluded that the sun revolves about its own axis in a period of twenty-six and a half days. But I expect you have known these things for some time.

Meanwhile, by your favor I wish to know this; you are aware that last summer there was published the experiment of the illustrious Huygens on two polished plates or sheets, suspended in a vacuous or exhausted receiver, which do not separate even when a weight is hung on the lower one.[15] But I recall having read in the most recent edition of the Boylian experiments on elasticity, that towards the end, if I mistake not, where the performance of the experiment on polished plates is recounted, he reports the contrary effect, that is to say the plates fell apart when the air was exhausted. I cannot find the book here in order to remove my doubt, hence I ask you to look into the book and indeed consult the illustrious Boyle himself when opportunity occurs; for you know this is of concern to philosophy.

You should know best of all whether, as I hear, the famous Mr. Isaac Vossius is to publish something on ancient music, or ancient musicians, or something similar.[16] I hear that some ancient geometers or other are to be published at Oxford;[17] I wish that Wilkins' [*Real*] *Character* would come out in Latin as soon as possible, for it seems to me a work of the greatest utility.[18] When opportunity serves please present words of greeting from me to the illustrious Boyle, and announce my undying regard for him; I wish for nothing more than the continuance of his goodwill towards myself, of which I shall have a token if he will send me, as he promised in my presence, his *Catalogue of Things to be Exchanged*.[19] I will make no other use of it, nor in relation to other people, than he himself shall choose, for I am pretty cautious and circumspect in such matters.

My arithmetical machine, which will do its work perfectly, as it was begun while I was away has now been brought to a conclusion and as I see wins great applause generally. I hope that other things, of no less importance, will soon follow.

I brought with me Barrow's *Lectiones opticae*; at the end of the book the very learned author reports a phenomenon which he says he cannot explain, and exhorts others to investigate it, so that (he asks) they may, if they can, impart its cause to him; but he doubts whether this can easily be discovered.[20] Yet Huygens and Mariotte say they possess the solution of [the difficulty].

When I had written thus far I received you long awaited letter,[21] in which you announced that I had been granted my place in the Royal Society, according to my desire. I shall be most grateful to the Royal Society on that account and will endeavor to prove my zeal towards it.

I will try to reply in just terms to the rest of your letter, devoted to algebraic profundities, and to inquire after and to furnish what you command and demand. I profess myself much obliged to the very subtle Collins, so distinguished in communication. Furthermore, as to Mengoli's having performed, as they say, what I myself promised, that is the summation of fractions whose numerators are triangular or pyramidal numbers, etc., I am not fully satisfied that he has done this;[22] for although I have not yet had leisure yet to look into Mengoli, yet I guess from the very things you say concerning him in your letter that Mengoli had actually gone into the sums of series of this kind $\frac{1}{3}, \frac{1}{6}, \frac{1}{10}, \frac{1}{15} = \frac{1}{4}, \frac{1}{10}, \frac{1}{20} = \frac{1}{5}, \frac{1}{15}, \frac{1}{35}, \frac{1}{70}$, but [only as] finite series or ones continued up to some certain term, whatever that may be. But by my method I find the sum of the whole series continued to infinity, $\frac{1}{3}, \frac{1}{6}, \frac{1}{10}, \frac{1}{15}, \frac{1}{21}, \frac{1}{28}$ etc.; indeed, I do not believe this to have been laid before the public previously for the reason that the very noble Huygens first proposed this problem to me, with respect to triangular numbers, and I solved it generally for numbers of all kinds much to the surprise of Huygens himself. I conjecture that Mr. Collins himself does not speak of these summations of infinite series because he brings forward the example of this series $\frac{1}{2}, \frac{1}{3}, \frac{1}{4}, \frac{1}{5}, \frac{1}{6}$, [. . .] which if it is continued to infinity cannot be summed because that sum is not finite, like the sum of triangular numbers, but infinite.[23] But now I am cramped by the space on my paper.

Mr. Agar[24] has made memorable experiments on cold here and has observed the strange and wonderful shapes in a variety of congealing substances with great diligence; if, as I hope, I can get anything more precise from him I will share it with you. Meanwhile, farewell and cherish as a person must zealous for yourself

[*Leibniz*]

Paris, 16/26 April 1673

NOTES

Reply to Letters 2196, 2202 and perhaps 2205.
1 Letter 2187.
2 Charles de Sainte-Maure (1610–90) became Marquis de Montausier by the death of his elder brother in 1635, and was made *duc et pair* by Louis XIV in 1664. Born a Huguenot, he abjured before his marriage, remaining a loyal servant of the Crown during the Fronde and afterwards. He was the Dauphin's governor from 1668 to 1679; although primarily a soldier, he was an eager associate of men of letters. His direction of the Dauphin was harsh in the extreme.
3 Jacques-Bénigne Bossuet (1627–1704), the great Catholic apologist, had particularly won the King's esteem by his funeral orations, first for Henrietta Maria and then for Madame Henriette, Duchesse d'Orleans. He was appointed Bishop of Condom (Gers) in September 1669 but resigned his see not long after being appointed tutor to the Dauphin. The bishopric of Condom was suppressed in 1790.
4 This was the series of editions of texts *ad usum Delphini* ("for the Dauphin's use"), in which Huet was the prime mover. See further Letter 2239.
5 Claude Perrault's edition of Vitruvius was published at Paris in 1673.
6 Hero's *Pneumatics* was first published in Greek in Thevenot's *Veterum mathematicorum* (Paris, 1693). The *Naumachia* of Leo VI, the Wise (866–912), who came to the throne in 886 as the second Macedonian Emperor, formed chapter 19 of his work on military and naval tactics. To this was later joined that ascribed to Basil the Patrician who was at the Court of Constantine Porphyrogenesis, Nicephoros Phoca and Basil II in the later tenth century; in fact it was not written by him but dedicated to him by its anonymous author. The whole collection of works is known in a number of manuscripts; an Italian translation was first printed at Venice in 1541, a Latin translation at Basle in 1554, and the Greek text at Leiden in 1612. (Professor J. M. Hussey, who has kindly drawn our attention to Alphonsus Dain's edition of the *Naumachia*, Paris, 1943, pp. 15–18, 57–59, and Gyula Moravcsik, *Byzantino-Turcica*, I, Berlin, 1958, pp. 400–406). Huet's copy of Flavius Philostratus the Elder (3rd century) *Opera quae extant* (Paris, 1608) with his marginal notes is in the Bibliothèque Nationale.
7 For his information on Vettius Valens, see Letter 2153, and for his earlier comments on Leibniz's *Hypothesis physica nova*, see Vol. VIII, Index, s.v. "Wallis."
8 Edmé Mariotte, *Traité de la Percussion, ou Chocq des Corps* (Paris, 1673).
9 Oldenburg has noted in the margin (in Latin) "This refers to the Hypothesis Physica nova, which Leibniz formerly dedicated to the Royal Society."
10 Compare the discussions of the laws of impact motion published in Vol. V (see index, s.v. "Mechanics").
11 See further, Letter 2211, below.

12 In fact, two works by Pardies were shortly to be published: *Deux machines propres à faire les quadrans* and *La statique*. A third, *Globi coelestis*, was to be published in 1674.

13 It is impossible to tell whether this is the man (often referred to in previous volumes) who was in the suite of the French Ambassador to London, or not.

14 See Letter 2182.

15 Leibniz appears to have forgotten that he had brought this matter up in Letter 2165, where he also mentioned Boyle's experiments; see Letter 2165, notes 16 and 17.

16 This appears to be a mistake.

17 See Vol. VIII, p. 93.

18 See Vol. V, p. 281, note 7.

19 Already mentioned in Letter 2165; see its note 4.

20 Barrow in *Lectiones opticae* (London, 1669), Lectio XVII, § xiii, pp. 125–26, poses the following problem: suppose a point to be placed before a lens or concave mirror, and the eye to be placed between the image-point and the focus of the lens or surface of the mirror, where does the eye perceive the point to be? The difficulty in the question is that since the point has no magnitude only a single ray reaches the eye; the radiation from it does not converge, but is all parallel. Therefore, Barrow says, the point should appear to be at infinity though in practice it seems to be more or less remote according to the position of the eye. Barrow's highly abstract problem arises from his taking a purely geometrical point of view; it would of course be open to Leibniz and those whom he had consulted to discuss estimation of distance while invoking physical considerations.

21 Letter 2196.

22 On this point Leibniz was mistaken; see Letter 2193, note 5.

23 Leibniz makes the point that this series of the type $\frac{1}{1^n}+\frac{1}{2^n}+\frac{1}{3^n}+\ldots$ (where $n = 2$, 3, 4, ...) is convergent whereas Collins' harmonic series $\frac{1}{1}+\frac{1}{2}+\frac{1}{3}+\frac{1}{4}+\ldots$ is divergent; he means to emphasize the point (to which Collins seems obtuse) that the former converges to finite values while the latter does not.

24 The only plausible person of this surname we have come across is Jacques Agar (1640–1715), a painter; but there is no evidence in favor of identifying him with Leibniz's acquaintance.

2209
De Graaf to Oldenburg
18 April 1673

From the original in Royal Society MS. G 1, no. 11

Clarissimo Viro Henrico Oldenburgio
Regiae Societatis Secretario
S.P.

G rata et accepta mihi fuit epistola vestra 15 martis ad me missa eo que magis cum sub praelo haberem tractatulum quemdam Regiae Socie-tati dicatum cuius exemplar modo ad vos mitto:[1] spero fore tractatulum illum vobis non ingratum fore, cum non ad inferendas sed ad retorquendas iniurias, et veritatem confirmandam illum publici iuris fecerim. Edidit nuper etiam tractatum satis amplum (in 4 fredricus Deckers de exercitatio-nibus Medicinae Practicis),[2] in quo multa remedia ab aliis proposita et circa medendi methodum notata diligenter congessit. Ut vero adhuc magis vobis pateat necdum exulare hic propter armorum strepitum studi huma-niora et philosophica, vobis in praesentiarum communicabo quod vir qui-dam ingeniosissimus nomine *Leewenhoeck* excogitaverit microscopia, quae longe superant ea quae ab eustachio Divino et aliis hactenus fabrefacta vidimus, cuius specimen vobis dabit adiunxta eius epistola,[3] in qua nonnulla a se accuratius quam ab aliis autoribus observata refert, quae si vobis arrideant et diligentissimi illius viri dexteritatem promovere et experiri velitis epistolam aliquam vernacula conscriptam de modo propositis ad illum scribite et difficiliora quaedam circa illam materiam occurrentia ei proponite. hisce valete et amore pristino diligite

Vestrum Famulum
Regnerum De Graaf

Raptim Delphis
28 Aprilis 1673

ADDRESS
A Monsieur
Monsieur Grubendol
A Londres

POSTMARK AP 26

TRANSLATION

Many greetings to the famous Henry Oldenburg Secretary of the Royal Society

Your letter to me of 15 March was the more welcome and acceptable to me because I had in press a certain little tract dedicated to the Royal Society of which I now send you a copy;[1] I hope this little tract will not be unwelcome to you as I have set it before the public not in order to wrong anyone but to repair wrongs done and vindicate the truth. There has lately been published, too, a pretty ample treatise (in Frederick Deckers' four essays on medical practice)[2] in which many remedies proposed by others and notes on the method of effecting cures have been diligently compiled. So that it may be clear to you that humane and philosophical studies are not yet banished from this place by the din of war, I will communicate to you at this present time what a certain very ingenious person named Leeuwenhoek has achieved by means of microscopes which far excel those we have seen hitherto made by Eustachio Divini and others, of which his enclosed letter (in which he reports several things observed more accurately by himself than by other writers) will give you a specimen.[3] If you bless this, and wish to encourage and try out the dexterity of this most diligent person write him a letter in the vernacular about the [matters] now proposed and propound to him some pretty hard [questions] that crop up in that subject. With this, farewell and favour with your former affection

Your servant
Regnier De Graaf

In haste, at Delft.
28 April 1673

ADDRESS
To Mr. Grubendol
London

NOTES

1 De Graaf's *Partium genitalium defensio* (Leiden, 1673) was produced by Oldenburg at a meeting of the Society on 7 May 1673 (see Letter 2203, note 3). It was given to Drs. Walter Needham, Croone, and King to examine and report upon. De Graaf prefaced this work with an open letter to the Royal Society inviting its judgment.
2 Frederick Deckers (or Dekkers), *Exercitationes medicae practicae circa medendi methodum, observationibus illustratae* (Leiden and Amsterdam, 1673).
3 See Letter 2209a.

2209a

Antoni Leeuwenhoek's Observations

Enclosure with Letter 2209
Printed in Leeuwenhoek, *Letters*, I, 28–36, from *Phil. Trans.*, no. 94 (19 May 1673), 6037–38
Copy in Royal Society Letter Book VI, 99–100

These observations (made, as Oldenburg, following De Graaf, observed in the *Philosophical Transactions* with "Microscopes excelling those that have been hitherto made by Eustachio Divini and others") are on mold, the sting of a bee, the head of a bee, the eye of a bee, and a louse; it is not, as the editors of his *Letters* suggested, a letter, but a paper drawn up for transmission by De Graaf. The Dutch original is lost.

Antoni Leeuwenhoek or Leeuwenhoeck (1632–1723)—the familiar "van" he adopted only in 1680—was a native of Delft, his home during all his life except for half a dozen years in Amsterdam, where he learned the trade of linen draper. He set up as an independent linen draper in Delft, and was apparently successful. In 1660 he was appointed Chamberlain to the "Sheriffs" of Delft (town officials), the first of several municipal appointments. In 1669 he was admitted by the Court of Holland as a Surveyor. There is no information about his work in microscopy before this paper.

2210

Flamsteed to Oldenburg

19 April 1673

From the original in Royal Society MS. F 1, no. 97
Partly printed in *Phil. Trans.*, no. 94 (19 May 1673), 6033

Derby Aprill 19th. 1673

Mr Oldenburge
Sr

The included paper[1] conteines some observations of Jupiter which being made [at] a more convenient station then I commonly have used are more accurate then my former ones, & the planet being in a fit place of his orbite they are the most usefull for the determineing its inclination to the Ecliptick that wee can againe expect this 6 yeares or perhaps before hee returnes againe to this place. had the latitudes of the fixed star[2] of Tychoes constitution beene exact & coherent, wee should easily have determined the praecise quantity of this inclination, and those regular inequalityes wee find in this and in all the other planets which are found irrepresentable by numbers, onely by reason of some latent errors in ye places & latitudes of ye fixed: wee can expect no great effect from Hevelius his endeavors since hee uses no glasses. It would be a taske deserveing ye paines & accuracy of Cassinus, & of all others, worthy the French observatory, to endeavor ye restoreing of these fixed stars especiall those which lie neare ye ecliptick. had I onely a large 7 foot Wall quadrant, a Sextans or octans of the same radius, a convenient place for observeing, one good pendulum clocke & a ready assistant, I should not doubt in a few nights to rectifie a many of Tychos errors and add some stars to his cataloge as well visible to ye bare eye, yet omitted, as Telescopicall: but this apparatus being beyond my facultys, I can onely, as it were, dreame of; and wonder that amongst so many ingenious persons of large estates there should be none that dares adventure at so small charges, as this provision requires, to undertake this worke whereby hee may raise him a selfe a name greater then Tychos, and a monument wth posterity—aere perrenius:[3]

I have made lately some observations of the utmost elongations of the 3 inmost Satellits which I find greater then Cassinus states them but almost the very same wth Mr Towneleys. but I have just cause to suspect some excentricity in the 3d. for I find its elongation greater on one hand Jupiter then the other, except I mistooke, as I thinke I could not possibly in my Measures. When I have another opportunity I shall make some more carefull trialls. either to confirme or destroy this conceite in the meane time I would transmit an Evenings observations or two to Cassinus if yu can convey them. but first I shall wait ye answer to this & yr thoughts whether it may be convenient.

I want an object glasse for my longer tube of 14 foot but would have it ground of much thinner glasse then my old one which is more then $\frac{1}{4}$ of an inch thick, for I always thought, & now find it true by a 7 foot Glasse which Mr Collins procured Mr Cocks to grind thiner then usually, which is a very excellent one, that the thicknesse of the glasse hindred a many rais theire passage. my said seven foot glasse cost me but 6 shillings I hope one for a tube of double length will not be above double rate. Mr Sargeant comes up to London after Whitsentide I will then send further directions for one & put monys into yr hands to pay for it, or into Mr Collins his. if I have erred any where in my latine pray correct & pardon a blurd place or two I had not time to mend by transcription So yu will more oblige:

Your affectionate & obliged Servant
John Flamsteed

ADDRESS

For Henry Oldenburge Esquire
at his house in the middle of
the pellmell neare St Jamese's
Westminster these

I have just now rec yr transactions wth a letter & Ruler from Mr Collins
I give yu many thankes:[4]

J F

NOTES

Oldenburg has edited this letter heavily for publication, striking out the reference to
Hevelius, shortening some sentences, and, naturally, omitting the final paragraph.

1 This is Royal Society MS. F 1, no. 96, printed in *Phil. Trans.*, no. 94 (19 May 1673),
   6034–36, giving in Latin Flamsteed's extended observations of Jupiter in March, and
   as usual comparing his results with published tables. These were republished in his
   Historia coelestis Britannica, Vol. I (1725).
2 *Sic* in original; Oldenburg correctly printed "Stars."
3 "more lasting than bronze."
4 *Phil. Trans.*, no. 91, was dated 25 March 1673. Flamsteed thanked Collins personally
   for his letter and the "box ruler" on 5 May 1673 (see Rigaud, II, 162–63).

2211
Duhamel to Oldenburg
19 and 21 April 1673
From the original in Royal Society MS. H 1, no. 112

Monsieur

Nous avons perdu depuis 8 iours le P. Pardies; il est mort d'une fievre
maligne, avec un transport au cerveau; on croit qu'il á esté trop
seigné á la mode de Paris: Il est regretté de tous ceux qui le connoissoient
Je vous avoue que cette mort m'á touché sensiblement; i'avois contracté
amitié avec Luy; tout ce que ie Vous puis dire est que vous avez perdu une
personne qui avoit bien de l'estime pour Vous.
Je suis bien aise que nos livres sont arrivés á Londres; Mais Nous

n'avons aucune nouvelle de ceux que Mr Martin á du envoyer á Mr Petit.[1]
Je Vous prie, Monsieur d'avoir la bonté de Luy dire, quand Vous le verrez,
afin qu'il en écrive á son correspondant á Rouen Je vois que l'on demande
souvent chez les libraires des livres de Monsieur boyle, et de Monsieur
Willis. Il y'en á peu á Paris. on attend icy avec impatience les derniers
imprimés de Mr Boyle

J'ay commencé l'impression de corpore animato,[2] i'espere qu'il sera
achevé dans 3 mois. Le livre des pendules de Mr hugens est achevé.[3] Je ne
doute point, qu'il ne Vous en envoye par la premiere occasion; cest un
petit in fol. on ne se presse pas d'imprimer dautres ouvrages de LAcademie.
Le livre de Mr frenicle est prest á imprimer.[4] Mr Mariotte nous donnera
bientost, comme ie crois, son traitté de la percussion;[5] Nous attendions
plusieurs ouvrages du p. pardies, ie ne sçais en quel estat, il les á laissez. Il y
avoit un Optique, un traitté latin de quadrans, qu'il alloit mettre sous la
presse.[6] Je ne sçais ce que sa compagnie en fera.

Pour Mr bienaise, c'est un homme d'esprit, adroit dans son mestier:
comme i'ay veu, qu'il n'avoit pas dessein de Nous donner son pretendu
secret, i'ay prié un de mes amis, dr de medicine, qui la vû travailler, de me
donner par escrit ce que c'est; il me la envoyé en latin que vous trouverez
dans cette lettre.[7] Il m'a asseuré qu'il n'y a pas d'autre mystere ie crois qu'il
ne reussit pas tousiours.

on fist il y a huict jours une experience assez considerable, chez Mr
denis;[8] on coupa l'artere crurale d'un chien, et avec une certaine eau, on
arresta aussitost le sang, en sorte que le chien n'en á resenti aucun mal; et
j'ay vû celuy qui á le secret;[9] Il parloit d'aller en Angleterre dans peu de
temps on m'á dit qu'il a esté depuis á St germain, et fait la mesme experience, cette eau n'est point corrosive, il pretend recompense de ce secret, et
ie crois qu'il la merite bien; car il seroit de grand usage. on m'a dit depuis,
que d'autres personnes pretendent l'avoir decouvert, ou un semblable.
Il nous dist chez Mr de Launay,[10] que cette eau laissoit dans la playe un
petit noeud, qui n'empeschoit point le mouvement du sang. voila tout ce
que iay pu apprendre de nouveau. Nous sommes dans limpatience de
recevoir les livres d'Angleterre que Mr Martin á envoyé.

Je suis de tout mon coeur Monsieur

Vostre tres humble et tres obeissant serviteur
J. b. du hamel pr. de s. l.

de paris ce 29
d'Apvril 1673. [N.S.]

depuis cette lettre escritte, iay appris que le pacquet de Mr Martin est
arrivé á Rouen; il est peutestre déja a Paris. ce 1. de Mai [N.S.]

Je vis hier le sr. hubin, qui fait à present des thermometres avec du vif
argent et de l'eau, comme ie pense, presque de la maniere du barometre de
Mr hugens.[11] quand les autres thermometres marquent 2 lignes de difference, celuyci marque pres d'un pied. je n'en ay pas encore vu, il n'en á
encore fait qu'un à Orleans.

ADDRESS
    A Monsieur
    Monsieur grubendol
        á Londres

TRANSLATION

Sir,

We lost Father Pardies a week ago; he is dead of a malignant fever, with a
brain seizure; it is thought that he was bled too much, in the Paris fashion;
he is regretted by all those who knew him. I confess to you that this death has hit
me hard; I had formed a friendship with him; all that I can say to you is that you
have lost a person who had a great respect for you.

I am very glad that our books have arrived in London; but we have had no
news of those which Mr. Martin was to have sent to Mr. Petit.[1] I beseech you, Sir,
to be so good as to tell him, when you see him, so that he may write to his agent
at Rouen about them. I see that the books of Mr. Boyle and of Mr. Willis are in
frequent demand at the booksellers. There are few in Paris. The latest published
works of Mr. Boyle are awaited with impatience here.

I have begun the printing of *De corpore animato*;[2] I hope it will be finished in
three months. Mr. Huygens' book on pendulums is finished.[3] I do not doubt but
that he will send you some by the first opportunity; it is a small folio. They are in
no hurry to print the other works of the Academy. Mr. Frénicle's book is ready to
print.[4] Mr. Mariotte will, I think, soon give us his treatise on percussion.[5] We have
been expecting several works from Father Pardies; I don't know what state he
left them in. There was an optics [and] a Latin treatise on sundials which he was
going to publish.[6] I do not know what his Society will do with them.

As for Mr. Bienaise, he is a clever man, skilful in his profession: as I saw that
he did not intend to give us the secret he claimed, I asked one of his friends, a
doctor of medicine who has seen him at work, to give it to me in writing; he has
sent me the Latin which you will find in this letter.[7] He has assured me that there
is no other mystery; I think he does not always succeed.

A week ago a pretty important experiment was performed at Mr. Denis's house:[8] the crural artery of a dog was cut, and the blood quickly staunched with a certain water, so that the dog felt no ill effects, and I saw the man who has the secret.[9] He spoke of going to England soon; I have been told that he has since been to St. Germain and made the same experiment. This water is not in the least corrosive. He claims a reward for the secret, and I think he richly deserves it, for it would be of great use. I have since been told that others claim to have discovered this or something similar. He told us at Mr. de Launay's[10] that this water left a little knot in the wound, which did not at all hinder the flow of blood. This is all the news I could learn. We are very impatient to receive the books from England sent by Mr. Martin.

I am, with all my heart, Sir

Your very humble, obedient servant,
J. B. Duhamel, Prior of St. Lambert

Paris, this 29 April 1673 [N.S.]

Since this letter was written I have learned that Mr. Martin's package has arrived at Rouen; it is perhaps already at Paris. 1 May [N.S.]

I saw the Sieur Hubin yesterday, who is now making thermometers with mercury and water, very like the barometer of Mr. Huygens.[11] When other thermometers only show a difference of two lines, this one shows nearly a foot. I have not yet seen one, he has only made one at Orleans.

ADDRESS
    Mr. Grubendol
        London

NOTES

1 See Letter 2103.
2 See Letter 2103, note 9.
3 The dedication is dated 25 March 1673 [N.S.].
4 See Letter 2103 note 5.
5 See Letter 2208, note 8.
6 The treatise on optics was never printed but *Deux machines propres à faire les quadrans* did appear in this year.
7 See Letter 2211a.
8 See further Letter 2212.
9 According to Duhamel's letter of 11 June 1673 his name was Vivons.
10 For Gilles de Launay see Vol. III, p. 580, note 4, and Vol. VIII, p. 19.
11 See note 5 of Letter 2138. For Huygens' barometer, see Letter 2103, note 4.

2211a

Morand to Duhamel

20 April 1673

Enclosure with Letter 2211
From the original in Royal Society MS. M 1, no. 78

Cum nihil habeam antiquius quam tibi morem gerere, tendinis consuendi rationem, quam a me descriptam quaesivisti, quemadmodum ab eo qui hanc nuper instauravit, non semel vidi susceptam, tibi paucis trado. Transversa paenitusque secti tendinis extrema quamprimum (si datur) ad se invicem adducantur, et ea componantur arte, ut fibrae fibris correspondentes coeant. mox sutura quam intercisam vocant) acu semel, bis, vel amplius pro tendinis mole adacta connectantur. Verum quoniam haec, praesertimque magnis in musculis quibus impetus sese contrahendi maior inest, a vulnere longe remota et revulsa saepe numero delitescunt, coniungi nequeunt, nisi forficibus aut scalpello sectis communibus involucris, atque hinc inde dissecando membranas, huius novae plagae diductis oris prorsus detecta, ope manuum apponantur et copulentur.

Nec iuncta diu cohaererent quin lacerata se retrahentis musculi nisu brevis dissilirent, quamobrem sutura, filo per tegumenta praedicta, simulque per transversum tendinem, semel, bis terve, (si huius robur et proceritas postulant,) traiecto, continenda sunt. His peractis vulnus suendum, glutinandum et sanandum est, ea methodo, quae partibus nervosis congruens est; hac praesertim adhibita cautione; ut violata pars apta ligatura et accomoda collocatione placidissimae quieti tradatur, ne tendo divellatur atque dissolvatur. sic illa cura perficitur nihil habens aliud peculiare nisi quod sit crudelissima. Dolorem tamen utilitate rependit; hac enim vidi motum integre restitutum, quamquam obscurum inutilemque saepe superesse observetur. de illa Guido de Cauliaco disserit trac. 3. doct. 1. cap. 4. de nervis incisis

haec scribebat 2 Kal. Mai. an.
r.s.h. m.dclxxiii. Tuus
humillimus et obsequentissimus
Morand

ADDRESS
Clarissimo Doctissimoque
Viro D.D. du Hamel
Priori Sti Lamberti

TRANSLATION

As I hold nothing more settled than obedience to yourself, I will deliver to you in a few words the manner of stitching tendons together, which you asked me to describe, as I have seen it done more than once by the recent founder of this [art]. The transverse and wounded ends of the cut tendon are brought together as soon as possible and skilfully disposed so that the fibers join the corresponding fibers. Then they are firmly linked together by the suture which is called "interrupted," with the needle, once, twice, or more according to the size of the tendon. But in truth since these oftentimes lie hidden, pulled away to a great distance from the wound, particularly in large muscles in which the force of contraction is the stronger, they cannot be joined together unless you have with the scissors or scalpel (after cutting through the usual bandages and after dissecting the membranes here and there and opening the mouths of this new wound [so that the tendons] are quite uncovered) applied them to each other and joined them with your hands.

And they would not long adhere when joined together without the injured parts soon bursting apart, being drawn back by the muscular tension, for which reason they are to be restrained by passing the thread once, twice or three times (if the strength and length of the tendon demand it) through the aforesaid teguments and at the same through the tendon. When this has been done the wound is to be sutured, closed up, and healed using that method which is appropriate for the tendinous parts; observing particularly this precaution: that the injured part is to be kept very still by means of a proper ligature and a suitable support, lest the tendon become disjointed and loosened. And so that cure may be perfected, without any extraordinary feature except that it may be very agonizing. However, its painfulness is repaid by its utility; for I have seen movement completely restored in this way, although [the part] is often observed to remain dull and useless. On that Gui de Chauliac has written in treatise 3, doctrine 1, chapter 4, about cut tendons.

Your humble and obedient servant wrote this on 30 April [N.S.] in the year of Our Lord 1673.

Morand

ADDRESS
To the famous and learned
Reverend Mr. Duhamel
Prior of St. Lambert

NOTE

Gui de Chauliac, *Chirurgia* (1363) went through many editions. The section on "De incisione nervorum" in which he remarks that severed tendons often leave the part without motion (because, he says, the wound heals without leaving pores for the penetration of spirits) is on p. 153 of *Chirurgia magna Guidonis de Gauliaco* [*sic*] (Leiden, 1585).

The medical terminology is highly ambiguous; *tendo* could bear the meaning "nerve," and indeed this letter is headed by Oldenburg "A letter written to Mr Du Hamel concerning ye healing of Nerves by M. de Bienaise"; but then the English *nerve* could, of course, bear the meaning *sinew*. We have taken the word *tendo* in this latter sense, and not as signifying a nerve in the modern sense. This interpretation seems to fit the whole context better, even though Gui de Chauliac seems to be talking about nerves, rather than tendons.

2212

Denis to Oldenburg

21 April 1673

From the original in Royal Society MS. D 1, no. 5

de paris ce 1er May 73 [N.S.]

Monsieur

Jay creu vous avoir envoyé ma neuvieme conference.[1] Mais je vois par vostre derniere Lettre que vous ne L'avez pas. cest pourquoy ie vous La renvoye par ceste ordinaire avec La dixieme.[2] Nous sommes occupez presentement par ordre du Roy a faire des experiences dont tout le monde recevra de grands avantages;[3] il n'est pas necessaire de vous y preparer en vous faisant souvenir de La peine qu'on a d'arrester le sang des arteres quand elles sont picquées ou coupées. Cependant nous avons trouvé une essence merveilleuse La quelle estant appliquée sur quelque artere que ce soit, arreste à linstant mesme le sang sans qu'il soit besoin d'aucun bandage à la partie. Nous L'avons experimentée sur des chiens aux quels nous avons couppé les arteres crurales et carotides, et la cuisse mesme et le sang s'est arresté en moins de temps qu'il n'en faut pour Lire cette lettre c'est un remede qui n'est point scarrotique ou corrosif; car la playe se guerit sans escarre, ny suppuration, ny Cicatrice.[4] Nous avons fait des experiences sur des hommes aux quels on avoit ouvert des arteres temporales, sur dautres qui avoient esté couppez aux mains et au visage et la chose nous a reussy aussi bien que sur les animaux. Vous pouvez juger combien ceste essence sera utile dans les armées où la pluspart meurent faute de pouvoir arrester le sang soit dans les coups tranchans, soit lorsque lescarre tombe dans les coups de feu. Nostre essence agit non seulement exterieurement, mais encore audedans quand on en boit, car elle arreste les pertes de sang des femmes, les fluxs de sang inusites, les hemoroides ouvertes et autres hemoragies. A present que ce Remede a esté bien esprouvé aux yeux de toutte la cour et de tout ce qu'il y a de scavans medicins et chirurgiens qui L'ont admiré, le Roy nous a donné privilege pour la rendre dans ses armées et par tout le Royaume. J'avois pensé qu'on en pourroit faire quelque chose en Angleterre, et que si quelqu'un y en portoit on en tireroit bien de l'argeant.⁵ Mandez moy si vous jugez plus apropos que J'y envoye quelqu'un pour la debiter, ou bien s'il ny a personne en Angleterre qui vueille en achepter le secret pour en tirer ensuite le profit. Si l'on avoit un privilege du Roy d'Angleterre il y auroit quelque chose a faire, car pour une pistole de despense on en tireroit plus de mille, et cest une chose dont tout le monde aura a faire tant a l'armée que dans tous les menages. Je suis en attendant vostre responce Monsieur

Vostre tres humble serviteur
Denis

TRANSLATION, partly from *Phil. Trans.*, no. 94 (19 May 1673), 6039

[Paris, 1 May 1673 N.S.]

Sir,

[I thought I had sent you my ninth *Conference*.¹ But I see by your last letter that you do not have it, which is why I am sending it to you again by this post, with the tenth.]²

We are now busie, by the King's order, in making Experiments, whence the world is like to receive great benefit.³ 'Tis needless to prepare you for it by putting you in mind of the difficulty there is in stopping the Blood of Arteries, prickt or cut. Mean time here hath been found out an admirable Essence, which being applied to any Artery whatever, stops the blood instantly without any need of binding up the wound. We have first experimented it upon Dogs, of whom we cut the Crural and Carotid arteries and the Thigh it self; and the blood stopp'd in less time than needs to read this Letter. 'Tis a remedy which is not corrosive [nor scarifying]; the wound healing without any scar [scab], suppuration, or cicatrice.⁴

We have also made Tryals upon Men, of whom the Temporal arteries were open'd; and upon others, whose hands and face had been cut: And it succeeded with them as well as it did upon dogs.

You may judge, how useful this Essence is like to prove in Armies, where most men dye for want of a good remedy to stop the blood [in slash wounds, or when the scab falls off gunshot wounds]. The Liquor works not only outwardly, but also being taken inwardly; for it stops the Loss of blood *in faeminis* [in women], Inveterate fluxes of blood, open Hemorrhoides, and other Hemorrhagies.

Now that this Remedy hath been well tryed in the presence of all the Court, and of many of our best Physicians and Chirurgions, that have admired it; the King hath given [us] a priviledge to sell it in his Armies and throughout the whole Kingdome.

[I should have thought that something could be done with it in England, and if someone were to bring some of it there much money could be made from it.5 Let me know if you think it more suitable for me to send someone to sell it, or if there is rather some person in England who would like to buy the secret in order to draw a profit from it later. If a license could be obtained from the King of England it would be worthwhile, since for an expenditure of one pistole it would be possible to make more than a thousand, and it is a thing which everyone will find useful, both in the army and at home. I am Sir, while awaiting your reply,

> Your very humble servant
> *Denis*]

NOTES

The letter to which this is a reply is missing. The passages in square brackets have been translated by the editors.

1 Denis's *Neuviéme Conference* is dated 28 February 1673 [N.S.] and is concerned with "the changing of chyle into blood, which occurs in the heart."

2 The *Dixiéme Conference* is dated 31 March 1673 [N.S.] and is entitled "A Continuation of the description of the parts which make up the heart."

3 These experiments are fully described in Denis, *Onzieme Conference*, dated 30 April 1673 [N.S.].

4 As Denis explains in his *Onzieme Conference*, the ordinary methods involve ligaturing, cauterization, or treatment with corrosive materials like vitriol. All, even when successful, leave undesirable scars. In addition there is a danger that when the large scab provoked by cauterization or application of corrosives falls off, uncontrollable bleeding may again take place. Hence the advantage of the new method.

5 Denis came to England himself shortly after this and demonstrated "his" styptic liquid successfully before the Royal Society on 13 June 1673. (It is not clear whether this is the original liquid described by Duhamel in Letter 2211, or a separate invention.) Interest was widely aroused, and many trials were made with the liquid of Denis as well as with liquids proposed by others. Although most reports were favorable, interest seems to have died out by the end of the year to revive (to judge by the *Philosophical Transactions*) only in the eighteenth century.

2213
Oldenburg to Henshaw
22 April 1673

Mentioned in Henshaw's reply of 9 August 1673, as being a covering letter for a "bundle" to be sent on to Hevelius.

2214
Nelson to Oldenburg
22 April 1673
From the original in Royal Society MS. N 1, no. 33

Honoured Sr

The maine business of this is to give you thanks for your last, wch I doo wth all the reallity and affection that can be, as also to your worthie friend Mr Collins for his share in it.[1] They tell us from Northumberland of a Cow that had within her 50 Calves at once, (or little kinde of animalcula) some of wch the Spectatours fancyed to be about the Shape & Size of Ratts, 13 of them came from her alive the rest found within her after she was dead: this is very credibly told but not wth absolute certaintie, if I thought it worth as much I could endeavour a further information. But much more strange is it (if true) wch is written from Leeds (as I remember they call it) or Liege in the Border of Germany,[2] of a man transpeciated into a Dog, saving only his head wch remaines as before; this was done they say upon the pronounceing of a certaine prodigious blasphemies and execrations, by him uttered agt God. This is testified by severall Young Schollers, (who are at a Place of Education there about) to their Parents in this Countie, who are of the other Kirk; but if it prove true I expect to hear of it in your Philosophicall Paper's,[3] only I thought good to mention it, that in case you had not yet heard of it, you might enquire of it when you have occasion to write to some of your Fellows or Correspondents in those Parts. I am heartily glad both of Mr Boile's health and of those Productions of his finished and designed.

I observe you wave mentioning the name of the Transproser,[4] and indeed I begun to think (before I received yours) yt that enquiry was not proper for you; only, a discourse being remarkable, whether wth or against one's judgement, it is commonlie wisht to know the Author. And here I cannot choose but mention to you 2 things wch I have sometimes observed and wonder'd at. One is that many learned men, who have ingenuity enough to approve and contribute to your Designe of Advanceing Naturall Knowledge, have so little compassion or moderation towards their fellow christians, in case of some difference in matters of Religion; that men should be so treatable in humane things, yet so fierce and savage in Divine: as if there were no grounds of doubting in these things, as well as in the other; or as if men affected to be Christians in Philosophie, and Bruits in Christianitie. The other is, that many men of good learning, ingenious mindes, ample fortunes, and (pretended) moderation, have so little care for the comerces of Philosophie & the Improvement of knowledge, as if the world were so wise already that nothing further needs to be enquired after. But I begin to be troublesome, therefore wth reiterated thanks and service recomended I remaine Worthy Sir

> Your most humble Servt
> *Peter Nelson*

Durham
Apr 22th
1673

ADDRESS
    For my honoured friend
    Henry Oldenburg Esquire
    Secretary to the
          Royal Society
    At his house in the Pellmell
    in St James's fields
           London
per a friend

NOTES

The references in this letter are the only indication that Oldenburg's correspondence with Nelson, active in 1670 and 1671 (see Vol. VII), had continued uninterruptedly during 1672 and early 1673.

1 There is no reference to Nelson in the correspondence of Collins as published so far.

2 There is some confusion here. Liège (Flemish Luik) is certainly on the borders of Germany, but it was not a center for the education of English Catholic youth, unlike Douai; this latter is only about twenty miles from Lille (on the river Deûle) which had only passed into French hands in 1667. Nelson may mean either Lille or Douai.

3 Needless to say, it did not appear in the *Philosophical Transactions*.

4 "One who turns into prose."

2215

Sluse to Oldenburg

23 April 1673

From the original in Royal Society MS. S 1, no. 77
Printed in *Phil. Trans.*, no. 95 (23 June 1673), 6059 and in Boncompagni, pp. 678–79

Nobilissimo et Clarissimo Viro
D. Henrico Oldenburg Regiae Societatis Secretario
Renatus Franciscus Slusius Salutem

Pareo mandatis tuis, Vir Clarissime, et prima occasione respondeo literis tuis idibus aprilis datis quas heri demum accepi. De Clarissimi Newtoni methodo nihil aliud dicere possum nisi mihi videri meam esse, qua nempe tot ante annos usus sum, et cuius ope flexus curvarum contrarios ac Problematum limites ostendi tum in Miscellaneis meis tum etiam in literis, si recte memini, olim ad te datis. Qua via in illam inciderit, et quomodo illam demonstret Vir doctissimus ab ipso intelligere poteris. Ego sane paucis, ut alias ad te scripsi, et vulgo notis lemmatibus rem absolvo. atque ut candide tecum agam, ecce ipsa lemmata.

1um Differentia duarum dignitatum eiusdem gradus applicata ad differentiam laterum, dat partes singulares gradus inferioris ex binomio laterum. Ut $\dfrac{y^3 - x^3}{y - x} = yy + yx + xx$. Legitur hoc apud plerosque et facile ostenditur.[1]

2 Tot sunt partes singulares ex binomio in gradu quolibet, quot unitates habet exponens dignitatis immediate superioris tres nimirum in quadrato, quatuor in cubo etc et hoc vulgo notum est.

3 Si quantitas eadem applicetur ad duas alias quarum ratio data sit, quotientes erunt reciproce in eadem ratione data. Quod quidem evidens est vel cuilibet Arithmetice candidato.

His lemmatibus methodus mea demonstratur: et si bene te novi, non multum temporis tibi erit impendendum ut demonstrationem ex illis concinnes, cum eo ordine a me disposita sint qui ad illam quasi manu ducit.[2]

Expectabo, quando ita iubes, ab Excellentissimo Domino Legato transactionum vestrarum exemplar, ac pro eo, in antecessum humanitati tuae gratias ago. Plura scribere me vetat temporis brevitas. Vale igitur Vir Nobilissime meque ut soles ama. Dabam Leodii 3 Maii MDCLXXIII [N.S.].

Clarissimo Viro Domino Collinio ut plurimam a me salutem dicas enixe rogo.

TRANSLATION

René François de Sluse greets the very noble and famous Mr. Henry Oldenburg, Secretary of the Royal Society

I obey your commands, famous Sir, and reply at the first opportunity to your letter, dated 13 April, which I at last received yesterday. I can say nothing else of the famous Newton's method than that it seems to me to be my own, which to be sure I have used for so many years now and by means of which I determined the contrary flexures of curves and the limits of problems, both in my *Miscellanea* and in letters addressed to you in the past, if I remember rightly. You will be able to learn from that very learned person himself by what track he came upon it, and how he demonstrates it. I myself do the business in a few lemmas, as I wrote to you another time, and those few well known to all. And to be plain with you, here are these very lemmas:

1. The difference between two powers of the same degree divided by the difference of their roots yields undivided terms of a lower degree from the binomial of the roots. Thus $\frac{y^3 - x^3}{y - x} = y^2 + xy + x^2$. This is to be read in most [authors] and is easily proved.[1]

2. There are as many individual terms [arising] from a binomial of any degree as there are units in the exponent of the immediately next higher power, that is to say three terms for the square, four for the cube, etc., and this is common knowledge.

3. If the same quantity be divided by two others whose ratio is given, the quotients will be reciprocally in the same given ratio. Which is surely evident to any student of arithmetic.

My method is demonstrable from these lemmas; and if these are thoroughly familiar to you, you will not take much time in thinking out how to contrive the demonstration from them for I have arranged them in such an order that, as it were, they lead you by the hand to it.[2]

I shall when you instruct me look out for the copy of your *Transactions* from his excellency the Ambassador and in advance I return you thanks for your kindness. Shortness of time prevents my writing more. So farewell, most noble Sir, and love me as usual. Liège, 3 May 1673 [N.S.]

I earnestly beg you to convey a grand salute from me to the famous Mr. Collins.

NOTES

Reply to Letter 2204, (that is, Letter 2136).

1 Dividing y^n by $y-x$, the quotient is $y^{n-1}+xy^{n-2}+x^2y^{n-3}+\ldots x^{n-2}y+x^{n-1}$ with the remainder x^n. Hence the n terms in the expression resulting from $\dfrac{y^n-x^n}{y-x}$ have the sums of their indexes always equal to $n-1$.

2 Despite Sluse's calm assurance, the application of his three lemmas in the theory of tangents is far from transparent: see L. Rosenfeld (Letter 2124, note 1), pp. 422–25. Dr. Whiteside writes: "The important point is that Sluse's three lemmas relate not to the tangent problem specifically, but to the *derivative* of an arbitrary power x^n, where n is a positive integer. It is in this general sense that he refers to "Newtoni methodus [tangentium]" (with "methodus tangentium inversa" = integration). *Lemma 1* mostly states (note 1) $\dfrac{y^n-x^n}{y-x}=\displaystyle\sum_{1\le i\le n} y^{n-i}\,x^{i-1}$, in the typical case $n=3$. *Lemma 2* specifies that the right-hand side has n terms $y^{n-i}\,x^{i-1}$ ($i=1,2,3,\ldots n$). *Lemma 3* states, so far as I can see, that since

$$\frac{y^{n-i}x^i}{x}=y^{n-i}x^{i-1} \text{ and } \frac{y^{n-i}x^i}{y}=y^{n-i-1}x^i$$

then the ratio of the two successive terms $y^{n-i}\,x^{i-1}$ and $y^{n-i-1}\,x^i$ on the right-hand side is *inversely* as the denominators (x and y) in the respective fractions; that is,

$$y^{n-i}\,x^{i-1} : y^{n-i-1}\,x^i = y : x.$$

On putting the three together, $\dfrac{y^n-x^n}{y-x}=\displaystyle\sum_{1\le i\le n} y^{n-i}\,x^{i-1}$, where the ratio of each term on the right to that following it is as y to x. The application of this to derivation comes by letting y decrease to x: in the limit it follows that the derivative of x^n is

$$\lim_{y\to x}\left(\frac{y^n-x^n}{y-x}\right), \text{ that is, } \lim_{y\to x}\left(\sum_{1\le i\le n} y^{n-i}x^{i-1}\right)$$

where *now* each term has the ratio of (y to x or) equality to its successor, and hence

$$\lim_{y\to x}\left(\sum_{1\le i\le n} y^{n-i}\,x^{i-1}\right) \text{ is } \left(\sum_{1\le i\le n} x^{n-i}\,x^{i-1}\right) \text{ or } \sum_{1\le i\le n} x^{n-1} = nx^{n-1}.$$

More generally, now using Leibnizian notation,

$$\frac{d}{dx}\left(\sum_i a_i\,x^i\right) = \sum_i i\,a_i\,x^{i-1}.$$

Sluse's method is structurally identical with one developed by Fermat in the mid 1660s (letter to Torricelli, late 1646; *Œuvres*, II, 338) and the more finished MS. published in *Œuvres*, I, 255–85; see also Hofmann, *Entwicklungsgeschichte*, p. 128."

2216
Oldenburg to Williamson
23 April 1673

From the original in P.R.O. MS. S.P. 29/335, no. 71
Partly printed in C.S.P.D. 1673, p. 165

London April 23.
1673.

Sir,

I only give you here the English of what is of a publick nature in ye letters, you sent this morning.[1] The other letters of Ostende contain nothing but private concerns of particular marchands, about freighting some ships wth wine and brandy; wch, I suppose, you care not to know the particulars of.

Sr, I hope still, you will remember my concern, and let me know, when I shall see the effect of it, who make it a scruple to importune you in person, at a time when you are so crowded wth business;[2] but who am faithfully Sir

Yr very humble servt
H.O.

ADDRESS
For Sir Joseph Williampson

NOTES

1 Oldenburg's summaries are no longer with the letter.
2 Williamson was about to depart for the peace negotiations at Cologne (see Letter 2199a, note 11); Oldenburg was evidently seeking some personal advancement.

2217

Towneley to Oldenburg

24 April 1673

From the original in Royal Society MS. T, no. 27

Towneley Ap: 24 1673

Sr

I am asham'd still to be forced to use ye same cause and laying ye fault of my not complying with your obligations upon others, but since tis a truth I dare relie upon your goodnesse howsoever I think it not amisse to lett you know yt I am inform'd yt there are severall persons in this countie much above 100 years ould,[1] but yt wch to mee seemd verie strange was what I heard latelie yt at one triall at Yorke assises 2 witnesses were producd ye one above 150 and ye other 130.[2] if you desire further information I shall endeavour to procure it but for our parts I am informd of verie manie above 80. I am much obliged unto you for yr newse from ye heavens,[3] but am afraid my tubes will not be able to show mee those wonders, but probably in some of yr Transactions wee may learne, what others in towne shall doe. howsoever it fairs with us, who are as grate wellwishers as others and to all sort of improvement of Learning. And 'tis upon this score yt I think I am obliged to acquaint you that at ye same time yt Monsr. de Sluse sent you his method of Tangents with wch you since obliged ye world,[4] yt he did me ye honour to send me an abstract of it, for wch flaterye anie thing but so sad an accident as yt which then befell me could be excuse[5] differd my thanks, and yett it seemes yt yt letter miscarried, for about a monethe since I had an other from him, desiring to know whether either you or I had received what he sent, and by ye last post I had ye honour of an other from him dated Ap: 22. signifieing yt he had my last in wch I gave him an account of yr. haveing printed his Method, and yt my former letter had not onelie miscarried, but that he had not heard from you in 3 monethes, so yt I doubt not but some from you to yt most worthie person miscarried,[6] and with them our hopes at least so soone of receiveing from him ye demonstration of his method he promiseth and ye other particulars, wch I doubt not but you will obtaine for us from him, who since you last heard from him was Elected Abbie of Amay,[7] some 4 howers (as they count) from Liege upon ye Maise, and is therby ye heade of some Cannons and ye disposall of ye vacant places. In yt letter of mine wch was lost I gave him an account of some particulars of Mr. Newtons Theorie of light wch obligation he had laid on me but did it but verie rudelie in french and shall be forc'd to doe it againe except I could procure it from a better hand in some language he is better acquainted with yn ours, though I perceive he hath some little knowledge of it. Sr. whether anie such thing may be expected both for his satisfaction and of others abroade is yt wch I must expect from you, and I hope you will give me Leave to say yt Mr Newtons thoughts of Coulours are so admirable in my opinion yt a short account of them in Latin would much oblige ye world, and add much to ye honour of ours, for wch you are so much concern'd. Howsoever I hope you will pardon yt freedome in

Your most humble servant
Rich Towneley

I have long expected to hear from Mr Collins about some books I writ for, and such as both you and he put us in hopes of haveing from France.

ADDRESS

    These
For Mr. Henry Ouldenbourg
at his house in ye Pellmell
     London

POSTMARK AP 28

NOTES

Reply to Letter 2186.
1 There is no surviving trace of Oldenburg's asking Towneley for a list of "aged persons," but compare Letter 2045 and its note 4, and Letter 2076 (from Towneley).
2 This seems to have been a recurrent tale; Lister gave another version of it in March 1670/1 (Vol. VII, p. 521).
3 That is, Cassini's account of Saturn's satellites, for which see Letter 2182.
4 Letter 2124.
5 The last three words are interlineated; read; "befell me could excuse my deferring thanks."
6 As already noted, Letter 2136 from Oldenburg never reached Sluse; compare Letter 2198.
7 There is some confusion here. Sluse had been Abbé of Amay since 1666, and no other change in his ecclesiastical status seems to have occurred at this time.

2218

Duhamel to Oldenburg

24 April 1673

From the original in Royal Society MS. H 1, no. 113

Monsieur

Je me suis donné l'honneur de Vous écrire par la poste,[1] celle cy est pour Vous recommandez trois gentishommes de la France qui vont veoir l'Angleterre, dont l'un qui s'appele Monsieur de la garde est de mes amis, fils d'un president du parlement de provence, et Nepveu d'un de mes intimes amis, et illustre pour sa grande Science, qui s'appele le p. Thomassin de l'oratoire.[2] Ces Messieurs auront peutestre besoin de vostre credit pour entrer dans la Societé Royale, ou veoir quelques experiences chez Monsieur Boyle, ou enfin veoir les raretes du repositoire, Je Vous prie Monsieur, d'avoir la bonté de leurs donner quelqun qui prenne la peine de leurs faire veoir ce qu'il sera de plus rare.

Monsieur hugens me fist la grace de m'envoyer il ý à deux iours son livre du mouvement des pendules;[3] Jen ai leu quelques choses je trouve fort beaux ce que je puis comprendre; mais je ne sçaurois à present m'appliquer a cette geometrie épurée.

Je ne doute point qu'il ne vous en envoye au plustost;[4] si vous le souhaitez ie vous en enverai une et mesme si vous iugez à propos que je parle au librarie, qui est de mes amis, pour en envoyer à Mr Martin, je le ferai. Je crois que les livres qu'il á envoyé á Rouen pour Mr Petit sont arrives á Paris, dont je suis bien rejoui: car je craignois quelque mauvais rencontre sur la mer.[5]

S'il ý á quelques livres nouveaux de Monsieur Boyle, ou si la dissertation de Monsieur Malpighi touchant les plantes est achevée, Je Vous prie de me l'envoyer par ces Messieurs, quand ils retourneront en France. Je suis avec respect Monsieur

Vostre tres humble et
tres obeissant Serviteur
j. b. du hamel p. d. St. L.

de paris ce 4 de
May 1673 [N.S.]

ADDRESS
A Monsieur
Monsieur Oldembourg
Secretaire de la Societé
Royal á Londres

TRANSLATION

Sir,

I had the honor of writing to you by the post,[1] this letter is to introduce to you three gentlemen of France who wish to see England; one of them, who is named Mr. de La Garde, is a friend of mine, son of a President of the Parlement of Provence and nephew of one of my intimate friends, notable for his great learning who is called Father Thomassin, an Oratorian.[2] These gentlemen will perhaps need your influence to attend the Royal Society or to see some experiments at Mr Boyle's, or indeed to view the rarities in the [Society's] repository. I beg you, Sir, to be so good as to find them someone who will take the trouble to let them see whatever is most curious.

Mr. Huygens did me the favor of sending me his book on the motion of pendulums two days ago;[3] I read in it several things I find very fine which I can understand; but I cannot at present apply myself to this rarefied geometry.

I do not at all doubt that he will send you some as soon as possible;[4] if you wish I will send you one, and if you judge it convenient even for me to speak to the bookseller, who is a friend of mine, to send some to Mr. Martin I will do it. I think that the books he sent to Rouen for Mr. Petit have arrived in Paris at which I rejoice, for I feared some mishap at sea.[5]

If there are any new books by Mr. Boyle or if Mr. Malpighi's treatise on plants is finished, I beg you to send them to me by these gentlemen when they return to France. I am, Sir, with respect

Your very humble and obedient servant,
J. B. Duhamel, Prior of St Lambert

Paris, 4 May 1673 [N.S.]

ADDRESS
To Mr. Oldenburg
Secretary of the Royal Society
London

NOTES

1 Letter 2211.
2 Louis de Thomassin (1619–95) came of an old Burgundian family. In his youth he taught literature in Provence, and later came to Paris to teach history and theology at the bidding of his Order. His early publications, in which he attempted to reconcile Jansenism and orthodox Catholicism, caused his Order to stop his teaching, after which he devoted himself to writing prolifically. His nephew seems not to have made any stir in the world, and there is no trace of his visiting the Royal Society.
3 See Letter 1951, note 11.
4 A dozen copies arrived in late May, and were acknowledged by Oldenburg in a letter dated 2 June 1673.
5 See the postscript of Letter 2211 and, earlier, Letter 2103.

2219

Oldenburg to Sluse

26 April 1673

From the copy in Royal Society MS. O 2, no. 110

Illustrissimo viro
Dno Renato Francisco Slusio,
Canonico Leodiensi et Serenissimo
Electori Coloniensia consilijs etc
Henr. Oldenburg
ευπραγειν

Cum in more sit positum Regiae Societati, vir Illustrissime, quotiescunque sociorum aliquis in oras exteras, sive publico sine privato nomine, proficiscitur, rei philosophiae augmentum curae ejus commendare, sitque Amplissimus Eques Dn. Josephus Williamson, Legatorum ad Tractatum Aquisgranensem[1] ab Augustissimo Rege nostro amandatorum unus; laudatae Societatis membrum dignissimorum, isque operam suam in instituto nostro, etiam apud exteros, pro viribus ornando augendoque cordate obtulerit, cohibere me equidem non potui, quin has litterulas. Quaesitis illis philosophicis, circa res per Regionem vestram notatu dignas, ipsi jam concreditis, sociarem, Teque per inclitam nostram consuetudinem impensius rogarem, ut, si forte per civitatem vestram transiverit vir spectatissimus, Tibique philosophia nostra ζητημάτα exhiberi curaverit, in ijs elucidandis pro ingenito tuo candore adesse ipsi ne graveris.² Egregie profecto hac ratione de provehenda scientia naturali mereri perges; simul et virum Tibi obstringes ejusmodi dotibus praeditum, unde praeclara aliquando emolumenta scientiae et liberales artes sibi pollicentur. Vale, vir Celeberrime et Tui observantissimum favore solito prosequi ne desine. Dabam Londini VI Kal. Maji. MDCLXXIII.

TRANSLATION

Henry Oldenburg sends good wishes to the very illustrious Mr. René François de Sluse, Canon of Liège and Councilor of the most Serene Elector of Cologne, etc.

As it is the custom of the Royal Society, most illustrious Sir, whenever one of its Fellows travels abroad either on public or private business to commend to him responsibilities for the improvement of philosophy, and as the very worthy Sir Joseph Williamson is one of the plenipotentiaries sent by our most august King to the negotiation at Aix-la-Chapelle,¹ who is one of the most worthy members of that Society and is one who has applied his labors wholeheartedly and with all his might to the perfection and development of our purpose, even among foreigners, I could not but combine this little letter with those philosophical queries concerning the noteworthy things in your part of the world which have already been committed to him, and sincerely beg you (on the basis of our excellent correspondence) that if this distinguished gentleman should pass through your city, perhaps, and take the trouble to show our philosophical queries to you, you will not begrudge him assistance in elucidating them, out of your inborn goodness of heart.² You will continue, truly, in this manner to win repute for your outstanding development of natural science and will at the same time place under an obligation to yourself a man endowed with talents for this kind of thing, whence the sciences and the liberal arts may assure themselves of great advantages some day. Farewell, famous Sir, and do not cease to bless your most devoted [Oldenburg] with your customary favor. London, 26 April 1673.

NOTES

1 Corrected to "Coloniensem" (Cologne) in Letter Book VI, p. 92. For Williamson's diplomatic appointment, see Letters 2199a, note 11, and 2216, note 2. The Society was told by Oldenburg on 9 April that Williamson had offered it his services "for inquiries after philosophical matters in those parts," and that he himself had drawn up a paper of queries which, with some additions, was then approved for transmission to Williamson.
2 See Letter 2219a.

2219a
Enquiries for Sir Joseph Williamson

Enclosure with Letter 2219
From the copy in Royal Society Letter Book VI, 94–97

Quaesita commendata Amplissimo Viro Domino Joseph
Williamson Equiti, Tractatus Coloniensis Legatorum uni etc.

1. Inquirat minutim in aesificium et εγχειριαν Aquisgrani per-frequen-
tem, Aeris scil, ex Cupro conficiendi, lapidis Calaminaris beneficio, numque ipsum Aquisgranense solum Lapidis illius ferax sit, et si sit, qua
copia?

2. Circa Thermas Aquisgranenses exploret; Quaenam substantiae Metalli-
cae Saliave in iis dominentur?[1] Quisbusnam illae aegritudinibus imprimis
medeantur? Verumne sit, i. Calculum humanum excretum, si harum
Thermarum aqua maceretur, paucorum dierum spatio non tantum emol-
lescere, sed et in phlegma penitus abire? ii. Aquas has, e fonte primum
scaturientes, albicare; postquam vero aliquamdiu constiterint et frigefactae
fuerint, virescere. iii. Ipsas, dum frigefiunt, cremorem quendam nitrosum
in superficie sua progignere. iiii. Easdem, a marcere conservare Rosas
aliosve flores iis immissos. Denique, vapores earum sursum evectos Argentum denigrare; cum e contra, vapores Thermarum in pago vicino
Boreet scaturientium, quae salso-aluminoso-nitrosae perhibentur, Argentum
dealbent?[2]

3. Observet rationes potiores conservandi vina Rhenana; et sciscitetur,
ante omnia, causam odoris illius enormis, vina quaedam Baccharacensia
inficientis, quo hircum olent; unde vinum ejusmodi, lingua Germanis
vernacula, *Brountzer* nuncupatur.[3] Inquirat, debeaturne ingratus hic odor
solo peculiari, an culturae, fimo forsan caprino factae; an viti cuidam
singulari, an vitibus incineratis etc?

4. Si Leodium forte invisat, salutet Illustrissimum Slusium, ipsique tradat
Exemplar Methodi ipsius jam editae, nobis non ita dudum scripto com-
municatae, Tangentes scil. ad quasvis lineas Curvas ducendi absque calculo; ipsique una innuat, nos Demonstrationem ejus methodi avide ab
ipso expectare?

Porro inquirat ibidem,

i. In ea, quae observatu ibi digna sunt circa fodinas Carbonarias; puta,
in earum profunditatem, sitne ea 150 ulnarum, ut fertur; nec non in artem

qua donantur Aere, quaque Aquis excuuntur; item, in Exhalationes, earumque qualitates etc.

ii. In fontes Spadanos: De quibus licet multa jam sint praelo edita, inprimis in Spada-crene Henrici ab Heers,[4] superesse tamen videntur, quae confirmationem requirant, quam ab Excellentissimi Slusii candore et peritia nobis pollicemur; qualia sunt

Num Fontes illi omnibus illis viribus revera polleant, quae ipsis a laudato Domino Ab Heers aliisque tribuuntur; Quod scil. abstergunt inciduntque humores viscidos et tartareos; omnia viscera venasque mesaraicas infarctu expediunt; inflammationes restingunt; ventriculum roborant, insignemque orexin cient; Colica Iliacaque tormina sedant; nervos reficiunt; sanguinem depurant, serumque sanguinis et humores excrementitios non una via exturbant, his multum mingentibus, illis magna copia sordes, atro colore infectas, deponentibus, aliis vomentibus, aliis sudantibus. Porro, quod Febres pellunt, oculorum fluxus sistunt; cutis infectiones pustulasque et scabiem lotione auferunt; morphaeam lepramque recentem fugant; verminosis presunt; conceptum juvant; catharres, paralysin, apoplexiam, epilepsiam, impediunt; tonsillarum affectionibus gargarizatu medentur; hydropen, leuco-phlegmaticam maxime, et ascitem incipientem exhauriunt. Inprimis vero, an fide sua testari Dominus Slusius possit, non-nullos Spadani fontis beneficio a calculo, adhuc friabili, fuisse curatos, alios etiam Aquae hujus potu Calculos excrevisse; nominatim, Italum quendam, Rhinbergae stipendia merentem, ante aliquot annos, Spadanae usu sedecim calculos, pisis recentibus majores, eminxisse? Adhaec, an emaciatos et exsuccos, Spadanorum fontium usu carnosum corporis habitum induisse noverit? Insuper, an harum aquarum Accolae aliis hominibus sint longaeviores, ac plaerosque morbos, quibus laborant advenae, ignorent; capite, pulmonibus, praecordiis, renibus etc. valeant; paucissimi cephalalgia, cardialgia, calculo, obstructionibus renum, hepatis, lienis, mesaraicarum, laborent; nulli Icterici, Hydropici, Podagrici, Scabiosi, Epileptici, inveniantur? Praeterea, num aquae hae potae insuetos inebrient? Num rustici, e *Savenirio*, Spadanorum fontium uno, aquam haurientes, pluviam saepe, idque biduo ante, praesagiant, dicentes caelo etiam serenissimo, *Pluet quia fons cecinit*? Num revera spiritus viresque Savenirii fontis translatione minuantur; quidque de eo sentiendum, quod *Frambesarius* Medicus scribit,[5] se bidui itinere absentem, 48 lagenas fontis *Pouhontii*, et 12 lagenas *Savenirii* asserendas curasse; *has* vero posteriores nihil ab aquis communibus tunc discrepasse, ejusque lagenis singulis aquae vitrum decessisse, cum aquae Pouhontiana acidissimum servaverint gustum, earumque lagenae plenissimae remanserint, eodem licet homine utrasque lagenas apud suum fontem picante et obturaculis subereis obserante? Insuper, an in locis Spadae vicinis, prope Franchemontium, magnae sint fodinae, unde Vitriolum et Sulphur insigni copia Eburones eruant? Praeterea, num harum rerum periti etiamnum Sal ex his aquis Spadanis eliciant, uti Elichmannus olim factitavit,[6] qui (ut a viro docto et fide digno accepimus) ejusdem beneficio praecipuas suas morborum medelas perfecit?

Denique, occasione data, in viros doctos, Naturalium inprimis rerum, Medicinae, Chymiae, Matheseos et Mechanices scientia praecellentes, in transitu inquirat, eorumque nobiscum in re Philosophica commercium procuret.

TRANSLATION

Queries commended to the very worthy Sir Joseph Williamson, one of the plenipotentiaries for the negotiations at Cologne, etc.

1. Let him inquire minutely into the very widespread copper workings and manufacture at Aix-la-Chapelle, that is to say the making of brass from copper with the aid of calamine; and whether the ground at Aix yields that mineral, and if so how plentifully?

2. Let him explore the hot springs at Aix; do metallic substances or salts preponderate in them?[1] For what diseases are they highly curative? Is it true that (i) if an excreted human [urinary] calculus is macerated in the water of these springs, it will not only soften in the course of a few days but will quite dissolve into a phlegm? (ii) when these waters first gush from the spring they are whitish [in color]; but after they have stood for a while and grown cold, they become greenish; (iii) they generate some sort of nitrous scum on the surface as they cool; (iv) they keep roses and other flowers dipped into them from withering. And lastly, that the vapors arising from them blacken silver, whereas on the contrary the vapors from the hot springs welling up in the neighboring parish of Boreet and yielding an aluminous-nitrous salt make silver whiter?[2]

3. Let him observe the most effective ways of preserving Rhenish wine, and let him discover above all else the cause of that very strong smell spoiling a certain wine made at Bacharach which stinks of goats, whence that kind of wine is called in the German tongue *Brountzer*.[3] Let him inquire whether this unpleasant smell is due to a peculiar soil, or to its cultivation (perhaps involving goat manure), or to a particular vine, or to the burning of the vines, etc.?

4. If he should perhaps visit Liège, let him greet the very illustrious Sluse and deliver to him a copy of his own *Method of drawing tangents to any curved lines without calculation*, communicated to us not long ago and now published, and at the same

time drop a hint to him that we are eagerly awaiting his demonstration of this method.

Let him make further inquiries in the same place:

i. As to what is noteworthy concerning coalpits; for example their depth, is it down to 150 fathoms, as is reported; and also as to the arts by which they are ventilated and freed from water; also, as to their damps, their qualities etc.

ii. As to the springs at Spa: concerning which, although much has been printed already, especially in the *Spadacrene* of Heinrich ab Heer[4] yet there seem to remain many requiring confirmation, such as we promise ourselves from the skill and frankness of the very excellent Sluse; among such things are:

Do those springs really act with such vigor as Mr. ab Heer and others attribute to them? Namely, do they cleanse and remove viscid and tartarous humors; drive all constipated matter from the viscera and mesaraic veins; quench inflammations; strengthen the stomach and stimulate a keen appetite; calm the colic and the iliac passion; restore the nerves; purify the blood, and expel the watery serum and excrementitious humors from the blood not by one route only, some [patients] passing great quantities of water and others copious stools tainted with a blackish color, others vomiting, and others still sweating [as a means to their cure]? Further, do they drive away fevers and staunch discharges from the eyes; do they [when used] as a lotion take away skin infections, pimples and scabies; drive away recent morphew and leprosy; suppress worms; aid conception; prevent paralysis, apoplexy, epilepsy; when used as a gargle cure ailments of the tonsils; draw away dropsy especially that of the white-phlegmatic kind and incipient ascites? Particularly, can Mr. de Sluse affirm on his own authority that a number of patients have been cured of the stone (while it was still friable) by use of the Spa water and that yet others by drinking this water have caused their stones to increase? To take a special case, did a certain Italian living on a pension at Rhijnburg a few years ago pass sixteen stones as big as fresh peas after using the Spa water? Has he known Spa water to restore a fleshy build to those who were emaciated and dried up? Moreover, are those living near to these springs longer lived than other men, unfamiliar with many diseases under which aliens suffer? Being healthy as to the head, lungs, diaphragm, kidneys etc., suffering very little from diseases of the head or the heart, or from the stone, or obstructions of the kidneys, liver, spleen, or mesariac [vessels]; so that no jaundiced, dropsical, gouty, scabious or epileptic cases are found [among them]? Moreover, do these waters when drunk by those unaccustomed to them make them drunk? Do the countrypeople drawing water from one of the Spa springs, at Sauvenière, often foretell rain as much as two days ahead, saying (even when the sky is perfectly clear): "It will rain because the spring has been singing"? Are the spirit and strength of the Sauvenière spring really diminished by transportation, and what is to be thought of what the physician Frambesarius writes,[5] that when he was distant two days' travel he had 48 flasks of Pouhontian [water] and 12 of Sauvenierian brought to him, the latter then differed in no way from ordinary water, and its level had receded down the glass in each of the flasks, whereas the Pouhontian water had preserved its very acid taste and its flasks had remained quite full although both [lots of] flasks were well filled by the same man from his spring and well stopped with cork and pitch? Moreover, are there near Franchemont in the neighborhood of Spa great pits whence the Liègeois dig out great quantities of vitriol and sulfur? Furthermore, do those skilled in such things still extract a salt from these Spa waters such as Elichmann once used to do, who by this resource perfected his extraordinary cures for diseases, as we have heard from a learned and trustworthy person?[6]

Lastly, should opportunity arise, let him in his travels inquire after learned men, especially those who are outstanding in knowledge of natural history, medicine, chemistry, mathematics and mechanics; and obtain from them a correspondence with us.

NOTES

1 The waters at Aachen are highly sulfurous.
2 Perhaps Burtscheid, now a suburb of Aachen but also containing hot wells, is meant.
3 There is no such word in modern German, and the association with goats seems highly improbable. Bacharach, on the Rhine, nevertheless is an old center for the wine trade of that region. Possibly the real explanation lies in the use of the fumes of burning sulfur (sulfur dioxide) to prevent the corruption of wines by mold spores; the word *brountzen* might derive from *brennen*, to burn. Sweet white wines can receive a disagreeable taste and smell from treatment with sulfur.
4 See Vol. VIII, p. 151, note 16.
5 The falsity of this tale had been pointed out by Sluse already (see Vol. VIII, p. 149). For de Framboisière, see Vol. VI, p. 279, note 4.
6 Possibly Johann Elichmann (d. 1639), a physician who practised at Leiden; but his writings are on oriental medicine only.

2220

Oldenburg to Marquard Gude

28 April 1673

From the original in B.M. MS. Harleian 4934, ff. 25–26

Nobilissimo et Consultissimo Viro
Domino Marquardo Gudio, Serenissimo Principi Holsatiae
a Consiliis et Cancellariae etc.
Henricus Oldenburg Felicitatem

Eruditio et humanitas tua singularis facile pelliciunt quosvis, ejusmodi virtutum amantes, tuam ambiendi consuetudinem, tuique thesauri litterarii et philosophici usura fruendi. Ad nos, perinde atque ad alios, doctae tuae opulentiae fama percrebuit. Aditum mihi ad Te patefacit Clarissimus Morhofius, dum, sollicitante me, de MStis quisbusdam rarioribus apud Te nuper inquisivit, quorum nobis copiam fieri, si commodum esset, quam maxime optamus.¹ At quia difficillima haec tempora id nunc prohibentur, rem ad meliora et tutiora remittere oportet. His literis commercium saltem litterarium aperire volui, quod utrique nostrum, in scientiarum et artium decus et augmentum, gratissimum fore confido. Quae Tu deinceps, Vir Amplissime, impertiri nobis de gaza tua non gravaberis, ea nos omni officiorum genere, quae proficisci a nobis possunt, redhostire annitemur.

Caeterum Geoponica quod attinet, quae Graece Latine sub praelo nostro jam per biennium labor[are—*paper torn*] credere videris, id profecto se ita non habet; et ne quidem ullum eorum folium hactenus commissum praelio fuit; nec committetur, credo, quin prius Manuscripta insigniora (inter quae Tua palmam praeripere reliquis putamus,) accurate et diligenter comparata inter se fuerint. Paramus quoque Photii Lexicon emendatius, et Jamblichi Lucianique editionem correctiorem.² Quid Tu, Vir Optime, in haec opera ex tuis conferre velis, reflorescent scilicet pace, scire perquam avemus. Vale, et me, Doctrinae et Virtutis tuae cultorem studiosissimum ama. Dabam Londini d. 28. April. 1673.

Responsionem tuam, si quam dare velis, inscribis, quaeso, hoc modo;

A Monsieur
Monsr Grubendol à
Londres

Nil [praeterea—*paper torn*]. Haec ratione litterae tuae, siquidem per tabellionem ordinarium mittantur, certius mihi tradentur, quam si nomini proprio inscribantur.

Mittendae per Antwerpium vel Amstelodamnum; unde tuto Londinum referentur.

ADDRESS

Nobilissimo et Consultissimo
Viro, Domino Marquardo Gudio
Serenissimi Principis Holsatiae
a Consiliis et Cancellariae etc.
Slesviga

TRANSLATION

Henry Oldenburg wishes happiness to the very noble and wise Mr. Marquard Gude, Councilor and Chancellery Officer to the most serene Prince of Holstein

Your singular learning and kindness readily entice all who are lovers of the same virtues to solicit your acquaintance and to enjoy your literary treasury and philosophical capital. The fame of your wealth of learning has spread to us and hence to others also. The famous Morhof opened up an approach to yourself for me when, at my request, he recently made some inquiries about some rather rare manuscripts in your possession, of which we greatly desire full information, if that should be convenient.[1] But because the difficulties of the present times prevent that being done now, we must postpone that to safer and better days. I wanted at least to begin a correspondence with this letter, believing it will be most welcome to both of us as making for the improvement and growth of the arts and sciences. We shall strive to recompense you for what you will be good enough to impart to us from your treasure house with every kind of service we can afford you.

Furthermore, as to the *Geoponica* which you have seemed to believe to be in press here for the last two years, in a Greek and Latin [text], the matter is indeed not so at all; for no single page of it has been entrusted to the printer as yet, nor will it be, I think, until the more notable manuscripts (of which we suppose yours to be pre-eminent above all the rest) have been accurately and diligently compared one with another. We are also preparing an improved [edition of] Photius' *Lexicon* and a more correct one of Iamblichus and Lucian.[2] We are very eager to learn what you, best of men, can contribute to these tasks from your own resources, when peace returns once more. Farewell, and love me as a most zealous devotee of your learning and virtue. London, 28 April 1673.

If you wish to make a reply, please address it in the following way:

A Monsieur
Monsr Grubendol à
Londres

Nothing more. In this way your letter will reach me more safely, if it be sent by the ordinary post, than it would if inscribed with my own name.

It should be sent either by Antwerp or by Amsterdam, it will be safely conveyed to London.

ADDRESS

To the very wise and noble Mr. Marquard Gude,
Councillor and Chancellery Officer to the most
Serene Prince of Holstein,
Schleswig

NOTES

The manuscript is a holograph original intended for the post, with the address properly written, but never sent. For the first mention of the addressee, see Vol. VIII, p. 332; Marquard Gude (1635–89) was the son of the burgomaster of Rensburg (Holstein) and educated at Jena in law. His lifelong interest, however, was in classical learning. In 1658 he began years of travel and study in Holland, France, Italy, England and Germany, his particular interest being in Greek and Latin inscriptions. In 1671, after having refused several professorships, he accepted the post of Councilor and Librarian to the Duke of Holstein-Gottorp. In 1678, having lost favor with his Duke, he migrated to the Danish Court. Most of his work was published posthumously, but he carried on a large correspondence with other classical scholars, not always without acrimony.

1 For an extract of Morhof's remarks, see Letter 2057; Oldenburg replied and asked for information from Gude in Letters 2068 and 2143.

2 See Letters 2143, note 2, and 2068, notes 5 and 6, respectively.

2221

Oldenburg to Martel

28 April 1673

From the memorandum in Royal Society MS. M 1, no. 58

Rec. le 27. Avril.
Resp. le 28. envoyé par le couvert de M. Justel, et prié de me respondre par la mesme voye.

TRANSLATION

Received 27th April. Replied the twenty-eighth. Sent under cover to Mr. Justel, and asked him to reply by the same route.

NOTE

Reply to Letter 2160, on which this memorandum is written.

2222

Bernard to Oldenburg

28 April 1673

From the original in B.M. MS. Add 4294, f. 47

Sr!

I hope you received my humble Acknowledgment to ye most worthy Royall Society for chuseing me into their Number[1] & alsoe for your many favours to mee, for wch I againe thanke you: And desire to know my duty at present to ye Society & to ye secretary to ym belonging yt in all matters I may satisfye as farr as in me lyeth. In enclose a specimen of ye Arabe Proverbs, wch in all will amount to a good folio.[2] This I pray you upon occasion to shew to Mr Haake with my humble service. This is all at present

From your Everobliged freind
E. Bernard

Aprill. 28. 1673.

ADDRESS
    These
  For his honoured Freind Henry
    Oldenburgh Esq att the
      Pallmell near st
       Jameses
        London

NOTES

1 See Letter 2207.
2 No edition of proverbs edited by Bernard ever appeared; it was perhaps to be a revision of Joseph Scaliger and Thomas Erpenius, [*Kitab al-amthāl*] *Seu proverbiorum Arabicorum centuriae duae* (Leiden, 1614), often reprinted. But see Birch, *Boyle*, VI, 585, for a further reference to this projected edition proposed by the bookseller Scott.

2223
Malpighi to Oldenburg
30 April 1673
From the original in Royal Society Malpighi Letters, no. 19
Printed in Pizzoli, pp. 61–62

Praeclarissimo et Eruditissimo Viro
Domino Henrico Oldenburg Regiae Societatis Angliae Secretario
Marcellus Malpighius S.P.

Laetor postremam meam de Pullo exercitatiunculam te recepisse, et commissa Excellentissimo Equiti Finchio Legato vestro exemplaria libentissime recipiam: interim eximiae tuae humanitati, quae me perpetuo honoribus cumulare non desinit, quas possum retribuo gratias. Ego licet valetudinarius circa Plantarum anatomen mea prosequor studia. Clarissimus Mengolus brevi evulgabit Solarem annum non exiguae molis opus,[1] quod ad Te subito opportuna occasione transmittam. Praeclarissimus Borrellius brevi Romae moram trahet et typis tradet tertium librum de Motu animalium,[2] et Maurolicam traductionem Archymedis de insidentibus aquae, additis proprijs cogitatis et inventis.[3]

Concivis quidam noster, qui in praeparando Bononiensi lapide[4] multum insudavit, elapsis diebus statuas et picturas flammeo, ceruleo, et lacteo colore in tenebris rutilantes mihi ostendit. Bellorum impetus hisce regionibus debacchantes adeo rempublicam literariam turbant, ut nullus liber, nullaque vestrorum inventorum notitia (quorum copiosa perpetuo extat messis) ad nos perveniat. Valeas, et si otium permittit, tui addictissimum humanissimis fovere ne desinas epistolis.

Dabam Bononiae d. 10. Maij 1673 [N.S.].

ADDRESS

Praeclarissimo et Eruditissimo Viro D. Henrico
Oldenburg Regiae Societatis Angliae Secretario
Londini

TRANSLATION

Marcello Malpighi greets the very famous and learned Mr. Henry Oldenburg,
Secretary of the English Royal Society

I am happy that you have received my latest little essay on the chick, and I shall
most willingly receive the copies entrusted to your most excellent ambassador,
Sir John Finch; meanwhile, I return what thanks I can for extraordinary kindness
which ceases not to overwhelm me continually with honors. For myself, though
in weak health I continue my studies on the anatomy of plants. The famous
Mengoli will soon publish a work of no small bulk on the solar year[1] which I will
be sending to you immediately by a convenient opportunity. The most excellent
Borelli will soon move his residence to Rome and deliver to the press the third
volume of *De motu animalium*[2] and Maurolyco's translation of Archimedes' *On
Floating Bodies*, with the addition of his own reflections and discoveries.[3]

A certain fellow citizen of ours, who has labored much on the preparation of
the Bononian stone,[4] showed me during the last few days statues and pictures
glowing in the dark with a flame-red, blue, or milky color. The violence of war
raging into these parts has so upset the world of learning that no book, no announcement of your discoveries (whose harvest is invariably so copious) reaches
our ears. Farewell, and if leisure permits, do not cease to cherish your most
devoted [admirer] with your very kind letters. Bologna, 10 May 1673 [N.S.]

ADDRESS

To the very famous and learned Mr. Henry Oldenburg,
Secretary of the English Royal Society,
London

NOTES

Reply to Letter 2155.
1 *Anno di Pietro Mengoli priore* . . . (Bologna, 1673).
2 Published in two volumes at Rome in 1680 and 1681; perhaps Malpighi means
"third volume on motion, [that] of animals."
3 For Borelli's use of Maurolyco's translations of Archimedes and his own work on
the same author, see Volume VI, p. 423, note 13.
4 See Vol. V. p. 403, note 3.

2224
Oldenburg to Bernard
1 May 1673

Bernard's Letter 2222 is endorsed as having been answered on this date.

2225
Oldenburg to Lister
1 May 1673

From the original in Bodleian Library MS. Lister 34, ff. 94–95

London May 1. 73.

Sir,

I must breake silence, if you will not;[1] and this I doe by sending you a Quaere about ye truth of an information I received lately out of Lancashire concerning two persons, yt were produced as witnesses at one Tryal, ye one of 150, and ye other of 130 years of age.[2] I intreat you, if it be so, to favour me wth the particulars, adding the regiment of their life. I understand from Paris,[3] yt Monsr Bullialdus, ye famous Astronomer, had a Letter out of Poland, informing him, yt there dyed lately a Cosac of 117 years of age, who for the last 7 years of his life had taken no other sustenance but *L'eau de Vie.*

I doe promise myself some new Observations from yr curious researches. I have litle to acquaint you wth from hence, safe what is contained in the late Transactions. In those yt are now in the Presse, you'l find a good description of ye Cacao-Tree, and ye way of its husbandry and curing; presented us by ye Intelligent Governor of Jamaica.[4]

Mr Henshaw, the king's Envoy in Denmark, and an ingenious member of ye R. Society, sent me lately Olaus Wormius his discourse *de Mure Norvagico*; to wch he hath prefixed wth his owne hand this Note;[5]

"Memorandum, quod 10 junii 1672. Excellentissimus Dn. Uldaricus Fredericus Guldenlow, filius naturalis Serenissimi Regis Daniae Frederici

III. defuncti, Prorex Norvagiae, affirmavit mihi cum juramento, aliquando in Norvagia aliquos ex istis Muribus, quos Incolae *Lemming* vocant, super galerum suum depluisse; quod antea et sibi accidesse ibidem mihi affirmaverat Dn. Crous, Telonarius Regis Daniae in Norvagia.

Thom. Henshaw."

If ye matter of fact be true, those animals must have been by ye violence of ye wind carried up into the Air from some high place, and thence fallen down: wch may be confirm'd wth what is said to have been observ'd in ym, viz. yt in their bowels were found herbs and corn yet un-digested. Fides esto penes authores.[6]

I have not seen Mr Brooks[7] these 2 or 3. meetings at ye R. Society; nor doe I know, whether he be returned to York; if he be, I beseech you my humble service to him from Sir

Yr very humble and faithf. servt
Oldenburg

ADDRESS

To his honored friend
Dr Martyn Lyster at his
house in Stone-Gate at
York

NOTES

1 Lister had never replied to Oldenburg's Letter 2161 of 25 February 1672/3, Lister's last letter having been Letter 2125 of 8 January 1672/3.

2 See Letter 2217, and its note 2; evidently Oldenburg had quite forgotten Lister's previous account.

3 Perhaps from Justel, none of whose letters survives in this period.

4 See *Phil. Trans.*, no. 93 (21 April 1673), 6007–9, where the description is said to be "by an Intelligent person now residing in Jamaica." Sir Thomas Lynch (d. 1684?) was Governor of Jamaica in 1673, and the account had been produced before the Society by Moray on 22 May 1672.

5 "Memorandum, that on 10 June 1672 the excellent Mr. Uldaricus Fredericus Guldenlow, natural son of the most serene King of Denmark, Frederick III deceased, Viceroy of Norway, affirmed to me on oath, that once in Norway certain of those mice which the natives call "Lemmings" rained down upon his hat; which that it formerly happened to him was affirmed to me by Mr. Crous, Tollmaster to the Danish king in Norway." For the book, Ulrik Frederick Gyldenløve, and Mr. "Crous," or "Cruys," see Letter 2015, notes 9, 10, and 11. (The affidavit is also printed in Birch, *History*, III, 85).

6 "You must take the writers' word for it."

7 For John Brooke (*c.* 1635–91), see Vol. VIII, p. 302, note 6.

2226

Oldenburg to Towneley

1 May 1673

From the memorandum in Royal Society MS. T, no. 27

Rec. April 28. 73.
Answ. May 1. to every particular.

NOTE

Reply to Letter 2217, on which this endorsement is found.

2227

Oldenburg to Nazari

5 May 1673

From the copies in Royal Society MS. O 2, no. 111 and Letter Book VI, 112–13

Clarissimo Viro
Domino Francisco Nazari
Henricus Oldenburg Salutem

Multum Tibi debemus, Vir Clarissime, quod uti ab amicissimo Justello Parisiensi nuper intelleximus,[1] memor nostrum viris, quin et commercium philosophicum, ante hac caeptum, locorum vero intercapedine fere exolitum, instaurari expetis.[2] Ambabus id equidem ulnis amplector, meaque ex parte nihil amittam, quod ad strictum frequentemque ejus cultum facere ullatenus possit.

Ante hac per Amplissimum Dodingtonium miseram ad Te fasciculum, quem rite curatum fuisse nequaquam dubito. Incluseram, ni fallor Transactiones aliquot philosophicas, rationemque certam et commodam ex Te sciscitabar, consuetudinem nostram literarium perpetuandi.[3] Idem etiamnum a Te peto; cum absque eo si fuerit, in metu semper de rerum invicem transmittendarum Jactura versaturi simus; ex qua causa nil quicquam hac vice, nisi has litterulas, ad Te expedio, paratissimus profecto, quamprimum has Tibi traditas fuisse cognovero, ampliora erga Te studij mei testimonia exhibere. Si Tu Judices, litteras nostras posse tuto per Mantuam hac illac commeare, lubentissime viam illam Tecum insistam. Si vero per Lutetiam Parisiorum, Legati Veneti⁴ vel Justelli nostri favore, rem confici melius posse existimas, et ibi vestigia tua sequar; Utrum horum mavis, quantocijus rescribe, quaeque hinc a me expectes, significia. Vale vir Doctissime, et viros Romae praecellentes Olivam, Corvinum, Riccium, Johannem Alphonsum Borelli, Auzoutum, Malpighium, Honoratum Fabri etc,⁵ nomine meo officiocissime saluta. Dabam Londini d. 5 Maij 1673.

TRANSLATION

Henry Oldenburg greets the famous Mr. Francisco Nazari

We are much obliged to you, famous Sir, because (as we have just heard from our great friend Justel at Paris)¹ memory of us is still fresh with you and because you ask for a restoration of our philosophical correspondence begun long ago but almost fallen into desuetude because of the distance between the two places.² I embrace this [proposal] most eagerly and for my part will let slip nothing that can in any way make its development more regular and frequent.

Before this time I have sent you by the worthy Dodington a package which beyond all doubt, was properly taken care of. If I mistake not I included a few *Philosophical Transactions* and I asked you for a safe and convenient way of establishing regularly our customary correspondence.³ I ask the same of you still, since without that being done we shall live perpetually in fear of the loss of anything exchanged between us; for which reason I send you nothing this time but this little note being quite prepared, as soon as I shall know that this has been safely delivered to you, to present you with more ample testimonies to my zeal. If you judge that our letters can safely pass to and fro through Mantua, I will most cheerfully apply myself to that route with you. If you think instead that the thing can best be done via Paris, through the good offices of the Venetian Ambassador⁴ or of our [friend] Justel, there too I will follow in your footsteps. Write back as soon as possible which of these two you prefer, and let me know what you expect of me henceforth. Farewell, learned Sir, and salute most dutifully in my name those outstanding persons at Rome: Oliva, Corvinus, Ricci, Giovanni Alphonso Borelli, Auzout, Malpighi, Honoré Fabri etc.⁵ London, 5 May 1673.

NOTES

The Letter Book copy has been corrected by Oldenburg.
1 This letter is missing, as are all Justel's letters for this period.

2 Nazari had initiated the correspondence in 1669, about a year after undertaking to edit the *Giornale de' Letterati*; see Letter 1295 (Vol. VI, pp. 258–60). Oldenburg replied to this in Letter 1367 (Vol. VI, p. 429), and there the exchange appears to have stopped.

3 See Letter 1296 (Vol. VI, pp. 260–62), written on the same day as Nazari's Letter 1295.

4 Dodington had been recalled to London six months previously (see Letter 2023, note 5) and so could no longer provide postal service.

5 For a similar list, see Vol. V, p. 299, and p. 301, note 1.

2228

Oldenburg to Denis

8 May 1673

From the memorandum in Royal Society MS. D 1, no. 5

resp. le 8. May. 73, demandé une phiole de cete essence l'experience reussissante i'auray soin d'en debiter une bonne quantité sans dem—[ander] privilege ou sans envoyer un homme expres.

TRANSLATION

Replied 8 May 1673; asked for a phial of that essence. If the experiment succeeds I will take care to sell a good quantity of it, without asking for a privilege and without sending a man for the purpose.

NOTE

Reply to Letter 2212, on which it is written. The "essence" is Denis's blood-staunching liquor.

2229

Oldenburg to Huygens

8 May 1673

From *Œuvres Complètes*, VII, 277–78
Original in the Huygens Collection at Leiden

A Londres le 8. May 1673

Voicy, Monsieur, les Transactions du mois d'Avril[1] je ne doubte pas, que vous n'ayez receu toutes mes dernieres lettres, particulierement celles du 7 et 14 Avril;[2] celle du 7me contenant la responce de Monsieur Newton à la vostre du 14me janvier.[3] J'espere, que nous aurons bientost icy vostre Traité des Pendules, qui, à ce qu'on m'a dit, est achevé d'estre imprimé. Je crois, que vous aurez vû les petits traitez de Monsieur Boyle, nouvellement sortis de la presse; dont on a envoyé quelques Exemplaires à Paris.[4] Vous ayant assez importuné cy-devant des longes lettres, ie feray court icy, n'y adjoustant rien si non que ie demeure Monsieur

Vostre treshumble et tresobeissant serviteur
Oldenburg

ADDRESS
A Monsieur
Monsieur Christian Hugens de Zulechem
a la Bibliotheque du roy à
Paris

TRANSLATION

London, 8 May 1673

Here, Sir, are the *Transactions* for April.[1] I have no doubt but that you have received all my last letters, especially those of 7 and 14 April [1673],[2] that of the seventh containing Mr. Newton's reply to yours of the fourteenth of January [N.S.].[3] I hope that we shall have here soon your *Treatise on Pendulums* which, by what I have been told, is now printed off. I hope you have seen the little tracts of Mr. Boyle which have recently come from the press, of which several copies have been sent to Paris.[4] Having formerly importuned you sufficiently with long letters I shall be brief here, adding nothing except that I remain, Sir

Your very humble, obedient servant,
Oldenburg

ADDRESS
    Mr. Christiaan Huygens of Zulichem,
        The King's Library,
           Paris

NOTES

1 *Phil. Trans.*, no. 93 (21 April 1673).
2 Letters 2197 and 2206.
3 Letters 2195 and 2122, respectively.
4 Presumably the work described in Letter 2089 and its note 6, reviewed in *Phil. Trans.*, no 92 (25 March 1673), 5197–6001).

2230

Oldenburg to Leibniz

8 May 1673

From the original in Hannover MSS., f. 23
Printed in Gerhardt, p. 94

Consultissimo Viro
Domino Gotofredo Guil. Leibnitio J.U.D. etc.
H. Oldenburg S.

Hac ipsa hora gratissimas tuas, d. 16. April. datas, accepi, plurimorum argumentorum, mihi pergratorum, copia refertas. Noli ad singula hac vice responsum exspectare. Plane enim hoc tempore, ut fuse scribam, non vacat. Remitto hoc ad alium diem, quo de omnibus rationem Tibi reddere, quantumpote, conabor; simul et Amplissimo Huetio ea qua par est observantia respondere. Duo duntaxat nunc seligo, de quibus amice te moneam. Prius est, ut Epistola, ad ipsam R. Societatem data, gratias ipsi agas pro Electione.[1] Alterum, ut promissi tui, publice in Caetu R. Societatis dati, memor, organum tuum Arithmeticum, quamprimum fieri id commode et tuto poterit, ad nos transmittas: qua ratione honori tuo imprimis consules, et majorem Invento tuo plausum apud nos conciliabis. Paucula haec, in rem tuam, Te raptim volui: de caeteris brevi tempore fusius agam. Vale, et has lineolas Tibi redditas esse quantocius rescribe. Dabam Londini d. 8. Maji 1673.

Jacturam feci notae, quae indicabat locum hospitii tui Parisiis; iterato mihi significare eundem ne graveris, rogo.[2]

TRANSLATION

Henry Oldenburg sends greetings to the very wise Mr. Gottfried Wilhelm Leibniz, LL.D.

Within this very hour I have received your very welcome [letter] dated 16 April, well filled with many matters of discussion highly welcome to me. Do not expect a reply to each point on this occasion. For clearly I do not have time, at present, to write at length. I am putting this off to another day, when I shall try as much as I can to give you a rational account of every particular; and at the same time I will reply to the very worthy Huet with proper respect. I choose two matters now only, of which to give you friendly notice. The first is that you should write to the Royal Society itself a letter of thanks for your election.[1] The other is, that you should remember your promise, publicly made at a meeting of the Royal Society, to send your arithmetical machine to us as soon as this may be done with convenience and safety. In this way you will particularly preserve your own honor, and will win the greater praise here for your invention. I wished [to write] these few words hastily to you, in your own interest; in a little while I will deal with the other things at greater length. Farewell, and write back as soon as possible that these few lines have been delivered to you. London, 8 May 1673.

I have thrown away the note indicating the place of your lodging in Paris; please be so good as to let me know the same once more.[2]

NOTES

First reply to Letter 2208. The tone and style of this letter indicate the degree of familiarity that had grown up between Leibniz and Oldenburg.

1 Leibniz did so on 1 June and the letter was read on 11 June. There is a copy in Royal Society Letter Book VI, 137, and it is printed in Gerhardt, p. 99, from another copy.

2 See Letter 2165, *ad fin*; Oldenburg must have forgotten that he had given this letter (now in the British Museum) to someone else—perhaps Collins, or Boyle.

2231

Oldenburg to Duhamel

9 May 1673

Duhamel's Letter 2211 bears an endorsement to the effect that it was answered on this date.

2232

Oldenburg to Kirkby

14 May 1673

From the copy in Royal Society MS. O 2, no. 113

Answer to Mr Kirkby's Letter of March 18. 1673. [N.S.]

London May 14. 73

Sir

I have received the two botles with the odd greenwater and produced them before the R. Society; who return you their hearty thankes, and have taken care to recommend it to be examined: which when done, I intend to give you an account of the examiner's opinion about it.[1] I cannot but commend your curiosity and care in makeing a tryall of the Loud-speaking Trumpet, and am very glad to understand, you have not made it without successe. I also thanke you for the relation of that odd case concerning the sicknesse of the minister, and shall be glad to be further informed of his condition, since he vomited that Tallowy matter, which perhaps had lain a good while in the debilitated stomach, that was unable to digest fatt meat, which the patient possibly had eaten, and wanted vigour to concoct, as being a substance of harder digestion than other alimentary matter.

I doubt not but that Monsr. Hevelius is considerably advanced in printing of his Machina Caelestis. I pray give him my humble service, and let him know, that I have lately written to him by long sea, sending him att the same time a large pacquet, containing some printed bookes recommended to me for him by Monsr Bullialdus.[2] In the same I gave him notice of the two new planets about Saturn, lately discovered by Signor Cassini. before that time, I had written also to Monsr Heckerus,[3] giving him thankes from the R. Society for presenting them with his printed advertisement of de *Mercurij in Solem incursu,* to be seen in May 1674, and intimating to him some considerations of an Astronomer of ours upon that advertisement.

I suppose you have seen, ere this, Mr Boiles discourse of the Origin and vertues of Gems, which is now in latin as well as in English, as also Dr. Willis's Booke *de Anima Brutorum, et Morbis cerebrum et genus nervosum afficientibus.* The same is now writing I hear, a treatise, *de medicamentorum operationibus in corpore humano,*[4] as Mr Boile is publishing a dissertation *de Effluviorum subtilitate et efficacia* etc.[5]

I hope, Sir, you will let me know by the first, that this is come to your hands from

Yr affectionate friend
& humble Servant
H. Oldenburg

NOTES

Reply to Letter 2175.
1 There is no record of this in Birch, *History.*
2 Letter 2188.
3 Letter 2168.
4 This is the work noted in Letter 2183, note 5.
5 The first Latin edition of Boyle's *Essays . . . of Effluviums* (see Letter 1997, note 3) was published under the title *Exercitationes de atmosphaeris corporum consistentium* (London, 1673).

2233

Leibniz to Oldenburg

14 May 1673

From the copy in Royal Society Letter Book VI, 115–17
Printed in Gerhardt, pp. 95–97, from another copy then in the Royal Library in Berlin

Vir Amplissime,

Non satis mirari possum literas, quas nuper ad Te dedi satis grandes, semipagulam qualis haec est, presse scriptam, implentes, tibi non fuisse redditas. Scripseram earum partem, ut de Societatis Regiae voluntate denuo sciscitarer; interea Tuae advenere prolixae, et multis rebus memorabilibus, ad Algebram imprimis et Geometriam pertinentibus, graves; quibus nonnihil statim respondi, relinquamque partem earum, quas jam ante caeperam, literarum absolvi, easque altero ex quo Tuas acceperam die Tabellario publico commisi.

Quod summas attinet fractionum, quarum Nominatores sunt numeri triangulares, pyramidales, aliterve figurati, quas a Mengolo initas indicas, ita respondi: Cum Mengoli liber non sit ad manus, videri ex relatione vestra, Mengolum summam tantum iniisse seriei talium fractionum finitae, v.g. $\frac{1}{3}+\frac{1}{6}+\frac{1}{10}+\frac{1}{15}$; me vero summam invenire totius seriei infinitae $\frac{1}{3}+\frac{1}{6}+\frac{1}{10}+\frac{1}{15}+\frac{1}{21}$ etc. Quod praestitum esse vel ideo non puto, quia Illustris Hugenius eam quaestionem mihi proposuit, in Nominatoribus tantum Triangularibus, a se occasione eorum, quae de alea inquisiverat, determinatam. Ego vero solutionem reperi universalem, qua summam non tantum infinitarum fractionum Triangularium, sed et infinitarum Pyramidalium et Triangulo-Triangularium etc. ineo; ipso Hugenio mirante. Si tamen idem et Mengolus praestitit, non miror; saepe enim concurrere solent diversi.

Quod vero subtilissimus Collinius (cui salutem a me officiosam nunties rogo) non de summa serierum infinitarum, sed certo terminorum numero constantium loquatur, vel id me credere fecit, quod de summa fractionum hujusmodi, $\frac{1}{1}\frac{1}{2}\frac{1}{3}\frac{1}{4}$ (cujus termini sunt progressionis harmonicae) loquitur. Certum enim est seriem istam in infinitum productam, non esse (ut aliae plurimae fractionum infinitarum series) finitam, nec summabilem. At vero hujus seriei in infinitum productae $\frac{1}{1}\frac{1}{4}\frac{1}{9}\frac{1}{16}$ etc. summam nondum, fateor, reperi; sed et necdum inquirendi satis diligenter, otium habui.[1] Theorema aliquod reperi nuper alia quaerendo, satis memorabile, ni fallor. Si sint series, quas vides, infinities infinitae, fractionum omnium quadratarum, cubicarum, quadrato-quadraticarum, simul summa omnium aequabitur unitati. Seu, si a quantitate data auferas, primum quartam partem, deinde nonam, postea decimam sextam: item octavam, 27mam, 64mam; rursus decimam sextam, 81tam, 256tam etc. et ita porro in infinitum, quantitas data praecise exhaurietur.[2]

$$\left. \begin{array}{ccc} \frac{1}{4} & \frac{1}{9} & \frac{1}{16} \text{ etc.} \\ \frac{1}{8} & \frac{1}{27} & \frac{1}{64} \text{ etc.} \\ \frac{1}{16} & \frac{1}{81} & \frac{1}{256} \text{ etc.} \\ \text{etc.} & \text{etc.} & \text{etc.} \end{array} \right\} = 1$$

Obtulere se nuper mihi Geometrica nonnulla, quae ubi nonnihil expolivero perscribam. At prolixiores tuas sumto tempore ample respondebo, et quae jussisti praestare conabor. Scripseram Tibi jam in praecedentibus literis, R. P. Pardies obiisse; magno dolore meo. En tibi quae ab eo expectabamus: La statique (dont il nous a donné une petite partie seulement), L'Optique, L'Algebre, l'Arithmetique, le comput Ecclesiastique, l'horologe Thaumantique, des Eclypses, la Cosmographie, la Geographie, l'hydrographie, Recueil de quelques Experiences modernes remarquables, du mouvement des corps pesants, des Liqueurs, de l'ondulation et libration, de Arte militari, militiaque Graecorum, Romanorum, et hodierna. Claudius Millet de Chales, ejus cursus Mathematicus, et tuae quoque literae meminere, Lugduni prodit, est ex Societate Jesu. Accepi, eum post introductionem generalem purae matheseos, Elementa mathematice tractata, Terram, Aquam, Aerem, Ignem, nobis exhibiturum: quae sane Methodus non videtur contemnenda, cum plerasque artes mechanicas comprehendat.

Est hic vir eruditus, et in Experimentis egregie versatus Monsr. Agar, qui circa gemmas, rem vitrariam, colores, frigus, putredinem, multa magno studio annotavit: habet inprimis experimenta notabilia de Sympathia et antipathia colorum qui scilicet in eadem Tabula picta, mixti, se mutuo destruunt, deprimunt, attollunt: quod magni in artem pictoriam est momenti. Sed quae de varijs figuris liquorum, frigore concrescentium, annotavit, plane insignia sunt. Sed vir est paulo morosior, ac lentior in producendis suis. Si placet fac, quaeso, honorificam ejus mentionem in ijs quas mihi rescribes literis; id eum excitabit fortasse, ad colendum vobiscum commercium.

In Machina mea arithmetica multa mutare coactus sum, ut, (quod antea non poterat) additionem, multiplicationem, eundo, subtractionem, divisionem redeundo, exhibere possit. Alioquin enim hoc inest incommodi, ut in catena operationum super eundem numerum aut productum ex eo, subinde mutanda sit machina, quod plurimum temporis perdit: idque mutari; hic quoque non a viris tantum doctis, sed et alijs spectatoribus illustribus ad perfectionem machinae, valde est desideratum. Nunc tandem superata est ea difficultas, et machinam mox dabimus absolutam. Alias fusius, nunc ideo tantum scribo, ne aut de diligentia mea aut de literarum tuarum curatione sinistre suspiceris; interea vale, faveque Vir Amplissimo

Tibi obligatissimo
Gotfredo Guilielmo Leibnitio

Paris $\frac{14}{24}$ Maji 1673

TRANSLATION

Very worthy Sir,

I cannot sufficiently marvel that the rather large letter I wrote to you recently, filling up a half sheet like this closely written, was not delivered to you. I had written a portion of it in order to learn the Royal Society's will afresh; meanwhile your letter arrived, which was lengthy and heavy with a multitude of noteworthy matters relating to geometry and algebra in particular; to which I at once replied at some length, completing the remaining part of that letter which I had begun previously; and the day after I had received your letter I entrusted mine to the public post.

As to the sums of fractions the nominators of which are triangular, pyramidal or otherwise figurate numbers, which you suggest were begun by Mengoli, I replied thus: As Mengoli's book is not to hand, it seems from your account that Mengoli only gave the sum of such fractions in a finite series, for example, $\frac{1}{3}+\frac{1}{6}+\frac{1}{10}+\frac{1}{15}$; whereas I had actually found the sum of the whole infinite series $\frac{1}{3}+\frac{1}{6}+\frac{1}{10}+\frac{1}{15}+\frac{1}{21}$ etc. which I do not think to have been furnished [by him] because the illustrious Huygens propounded the problem to me (with triangular nominators only) as resolved by himself in connection with things he had been looking into concerning dice. I actually found a universal solution by which, to the surprise of Huygens himself, I gave the sums of not only infinite triangular fractions but also infinite pyramidal and triangulo-triangular ones, etc. Yet if Mengoli has done the same thing I shall not be astonished because different people commonly fall into agreement.

That the very subtle Collins (whom I ask you to greet dutifully from me) spoke not of the sums of infinite series but of terms limited to a certain number I was the more led to believe by his speaking of the sum of fractions of this kind $\frac{1}{1}, \frac{1}{2}, \frac{1}{3}, \frac{1}{4}$

(whose terms are in harmonic progression). For it is certain that that series extended to infinity is not (as many other series of infinite fractions are) finite, nor can it be summed. But I confess I have not actually found the sum of this series $\frac{1}{1}, \frac{1}{4}, \frac{1}{9}, \frac{1}{16}$ etc extended to infinity as yet, nor have I so far had leisure to look into it diligently enough.[1] I recently discovered a certain theorem when searching for other things which is pretty remarkable, if I mistake not. If there are series (such as you see [below]), infinitely infinite, of the reciprocals of all the squares, cubes, fourth powers and so on, the sum of all of them [added] together is equal to unity. Or, if you subtract from a given quantity first the fourth part, then the ninth, then the sixteenth [etc.] and also the eighth, twenty-seventh, sixty-fourth [etc.] and again the sixteenth, eighty-first, two hundred and fifty-sixth etc. and continue thus to infinity, the given quantity will be precisely exhausted.[2]

$$\left.\begin{array}{ccc} \frac{1}{4} & \frac{1}{9} & \frac{1}{16} \text{ etc.} \\ \frac{1}{8} & \frac{1}{27} & \frac{1}{64} \text{ etc.} \\ \frac{1}{16} & \frac{1}{81} & \frac{1}{256} \text{ etc.} \\ \text{etc.} & \text{etc.} & \text{etc.} \end{array}\right\} = 1$$

Certain geometrical points presented themselves to my notice lately, of which I may write when I have polished them considerably. But I will make a full answer to your longer letter when I can take the time and try to furnish what you command. In my preceding letter I had written to you that the Rev. Fr. Pardies has died, much to my grief; here for you is what we looked for from him: his *Statics* (of which he has given us a small portion only); *Optics*; *Algebra*; *Arithmetic*; ecclesiastical computation; thaumantic clock; on eclipses; cosmography, geography, hydrography; a collection of some noteworthy modern experiments; on the movement of heavy bodies; on fluids; on undulation and oscillation; on the military art and armed forces of the Greeks and Romans and of today. Claude [François] Milliet de Chales, whose *Cursus mathematicus* (also mentioned in your letter) has appeared at Lyons, is a Jesuit. I have heard that in a general introduction to pure mathematics he will give us an account of the [four] elements, Earth, Water, Air and Fire, mathematically treated—indeed, it seems no bad scheme, as it would embrace many mechanical arts.

There is here a learned man well versed in experiments, Mr. Agar, who has with great zeal noted down many things concerning gems, glass-making, colors, frost, putrefaction; particularly he has notable experiments on the sympathy and antipathy of colors which, when painted upon the same board, and [thus] mixed, do destroy each other mutually, or reduce or diminish each other; which is of great moment in the art of painting. But what he has recorded concerning the varied figures of fluids congealing through cold is truly remarkable. But this gentleman is rather reserved and reluctant to bring his things forward. Please, do as I ask and make some flattering mention of him in the letter you write me in reply; perhaps this will egg him on to develop a correspondence with you.

I have been compelled to modify many features of my arithmetic machine so that it can perform (as it could not before) addition and multiplication by going forwards or subtraction and division by going backwards. For otherwise there is this inconvenience, that in a sequence of operations upon the same number or product, from time to time an alteration must be made to the machine, which wastes much time; and that this [state of affairs] should be changed for the further perfection of the machine is very much desired not by learned persons only but by other illustrious spectators also. Now that difficulty is overcome at last and we shall soon present the machine [to the public] as quite complete. More at another time, for I am only writing now lest you should have any disagreeable suspicions concerning my diligence or the attention devoted to your letters. Meanwhile farewell, worthy Sir, and cherish

Your most obliged,
Gottfried Wilhelm Leibniz

Paris, 14/24 May 1673

NOTE

Evidently Leibniz had not yet received Letter 2230, which was probably waiting for him in Justel's hands. The contents of this letter are more or less a repetition of those of Letter 2208.

1 The sum of this series, $\dfrac{\pi^2}{6}$, was first stated by Euler in 1734.

2 "Notice here," writes Dr. Whiteside, "the ingenuity with which Leibniz sets a bound

to $\displaystyle\sum_{2 \le i \le \infty} \frac{1}{i^n}$, $n = 2, 3, 4, \ldots$ by showing

$$\text{that } \sum_{2 \le n \le \infty}\left(\sum_{2 \le i \le \infty} \frac{1}{i^n}\right) = \sum_{2 \le i \le \infty}\left(\sum_{2 \le n \le \infty} \frac{1}{i^n}\right) =$$

$$\sum_{2 \le i \le \infty}\left(\frac{1/i^2}{1 - 1/i}\right) = \sum_{2 \le i \le \infty}\left(\frac{1}{i(i-1)}\right) = \sum_{2 \le i \le \infty}\left(\frac{1}{i-1} - \frac{1}{i}\right) = 1;$$

in the seventeenth century it would have been impossible to *compute* the same expression exactly (as an infinite sum)."

2234
Oldenburg to De Graaf
15 May 1673
From the copy in Royal Society MS. O 2, no. 112

Clarissimo viro
Domino Regnero De Graaf Med. Dri.
Henr: Oldenburg S.P.

Exhibui libellum tuum Societati Regiae, quae Serena fronte eum excepit, mihique, ut pro eximio tuo in ipsam studio et affectu gratias maximas Tibi agerem, in mandatis dedit.

Comisit Eadem rem tuam et Swammerdamianam, quorundam ex socijs suis virorum doctorum curae et Examini, qui quando sententiam suam de hoc negotio nobis exposuerint, operam dabo, ut ea tibi quantocius communicetur.[1]

Rem insuper pergratam nobis praestitisti; quod quae ingeniosus vester Leewenhoeckius circa Microscopia excogitavit, atque beneficio eorundem observavit, impertiri nobis voluisti.[2] Praelegi observata, in sermonem Anglicum ex Belgico versa, deprehendique probare nostrates viri diligentiam et ἀκρίβειαν singularem, et optare omnino, et aculeorum trium in Ape observatorum, nec non artuum in eodem insecto notatorum, figuras conspicere ipsis detur. Adhaec, Microscopio illo novo attentius, te duce lustrari velimus ovi faecundi, necdum incubati; Cicatriculam et chalazam prout eam Malpighius et Croonius lustravere, repertis in eo primis pulli formandi staminibus. Alia quamplurima vobismet ipsis, etiam non monitis, observanda succurrant, circa plantarum scilicet insectorum et similium structuram, inprimis vero circa corporum variorum poros, et figuras, unde permultorum in physicis magni momenti phaenomenon explicatio deprehendere videtur. Haec sunt, vir doctissime, quae hac vice Te volui, suo tempore significaturus, quae nostrates de libello tuo referent. Vale, et tui studiosissimum amare perge. Dabam Londini d. 15. Maij 1673.[3]

TRANSLATION

Henry Oldenburg greets the very famous Mr. Regnier De Graaf M.D.

I presented your little book to the Royal Society, which received it kindly and ordered me to return you its best thanks for your remarkable zeal and goodwill towards it.

The Society entrusted the affair between yourself and Swammerdam to the care and scrutiny of certain learned persons among its Fellows and when they have laid their opinion of this business before us I will be sure to communicate it to you as soon as possible.[1]

Moreover, you have done something that was extremely welcome to us in that you decided to impart to us the reflections of your countryman Leeuwenhoek concerning microscopes and the results he has achieved with their aid.[2] I read over [to the Society] a translation of his observations made into English from the Dutch language and I gathered that our people approved of the man's diligence and outstanding precision, and were extremely anxious to be able to examine figures of the triple sting observed in the bee and of the limbs noted in the same insect. Moreover, we desired that he would under your direction look more attentively through that new microscope upon the cicatricula [blastoderm] and chalaza of a fertilized but unincubated egg just as Malpighi and Croone examined it, discovering in it the first signs of the embryonic chick. Many other things will occur to you both (without need of advice) as being worthy of observation, concerning the structure of plants, insects and the like that is to say, especially matters concerning the pores and forms of various bodies upon which the explanation of very numerous phenomena of great importance in physical science seems to depend. These are the points I intended for you this time, learned Sir; in due course I shall let you know what our Fellows report concerning your little book. Farewell, and continue to love him who is most zealously yours. London, 15 May 1673.[3]

NOTES

Reply to Letter 2209.

1 The *Defensio* was assigned at the meeting on 7 May to Walter Needham, William Croone, and Edmond King "who were desired to give the Society an account of it." At the next meeting Needham reported that he had not yet shown the book to his colleagues in committee; that for his own part he thought the question of priority concerning the discovery of the mammalian egg was best left to each reader's judgment; that on the anatomical technicalities in dispute he thought De Graaf sometimes right, and Swammerdam right on other occasions, and that more observations were needed to settle these questions. He was asked to make them. On 15 August 1673 Drs. Croone, Needham, and King wrote a report which is printed in Birch, *History*, III, 102–7, in which they gave credit and criticism about equally to De Graaf and Swammerdam.

2 See Letter 2209a.

3 There is no further correspondence with De Graaf, who died on 7 August 1673.

2235

Oldenburg to Huet

19 May 1673

From the original in Laurenziana Huet MSS. Cassata 27, no. 1920

Amplissimo Viro
Domino Petro Danieli Huetio
Henr. Oldenburg S.P.

Juvat me intelligere ex tuis, 5° Aprilis [N.S.] ad me datis, Vir Amplissime, nostram Tibi de Vettio Valente, ex bibliothecis nostris augendo, sententiam probari. Operam dabimus, ut Codice vestro ad nos transmisso datam fidem liberemus. Resalutat Te Clarissimus Wallisius officiosissime, et suas Tibi lucubrationes non displicuisse gaudet. Me quod attinet, impense laetor, amicam nostram consuetudinem Tibi aeque ac mihi cordi esse, nec Te commissurum unquam, ut edaci rerum tempore exolescat. Persuasissimum Tibi esse velim, me in eo totum fore, ut amicitiae nostrae vinculum semper adstringatur arctius, tuque rebus ita ferentibus plane sentias, perspectam mihi esse indolem et virtutem Amici, eaque nihil a me in rerum natura sanctius existimari.

Accepi non ita pridem, Viris quibusdam doctis in Gallia id datum esse negocii, ut Scriptores veteres Latinos alio quam hactenus factum more versent, adjecta quadam velut paraphrasi, ubi opus est, lucida ac brevi, ut facilis Juventusti reddatur Veterum lectio; rejectis in Notas, quae ad Authoris intelligentiam ex historia scientiisve repeti debent.[1] Scire velim, num ita se res habeat, numque speciatim Vitruvius et Celsus ea lege sint tractandi. Fertur insuper, moliri Teipsum Heronis Spiritalia, multo quam extant auctiora; Leonis item et Basilij cujusdam Patricij Naumachiam, etsim. Fac, si placet, sciam, sintne haec studia tua jam praelo matura; quaeque alia in usum publicum adornare cogites? Si quae a Nostratibus agitantur, vicissim cognoscere aves, audacter impera. Commisit praelo Nob. Boylius Dissertationem unam de Subtilitate, Efficacia et Natura determinata Effluviorum; aliam, de Positiva vel Privativa indole Frigoris; tertiam, de Ponderabilitate Flammae: quae omnia, cum aliis nonnullis ab eodem Authore paratis, brevi lucem videbunt.[2]

At non ausim Virum, Serenissimi Delphini studia curantem, pluribus interpellare. Vale igitur et me Tibi addictissimum crede. Dabam Londini. XIV Cal. junij MDCLXXIII.

Quandocunque vacaverit mihi scribere, inscribantur, quaeso, omnes tuae literae, per tabellionem ordinarium ferendae, hoc modo;

A Monsieur

Monsr Grubendol à Londres.

Nihil praeterea; multo tutius hac ratione literae ad me datae curabuntur, quam si nomini meo proprio inscribantur, ob rationes, quas hic commemorare nil attinet.

ADDRESS
    Amplissimo Viro
    Dn. Petro Danieli Huetio
    Amico suo plurimum colendo.
        Parisiis

TRANSLATION

Henry Oldenburg sends many greetings to the very worthy Mr. Pierre Daniel Huet

I am delighted to learn from your letter to me of 5 April [N.S.], worthy Sir, that you approve our opinion [expressed] to you concerning the improvement of the Vettius Valens from our libraries. We take it on ourselves to see that the promise we have made shall be performed, when your manuscript has been sent to us. The famous Wallis returns your greeting most dutifully and rejoices that his studies have by no means displeased you. As for myself I am very glad that our friendly intercourse is as dear to you as it is to me, and that you will never do anything to cause time's corrosion of things to destroy it. I mean you to be quite sure that I shall be wholly eager to strengthen the bonds of our friendship and you shall plainly perceive if things develop in this way that when I have learned the character and virtue of a friend I hold nothing in the whole natural world more sacred to me.

I heard not long since that a responsibility for treating the ancient Latin writers in a different way from that used hitherto, adding some paraphrase that is clear and short where the need arises so as to render reading the ancients easy for young people, and resigning to the notes what needs to be rehearsed from ancient history or the sciences in order to understand the author, had been entrusted to certain scholars.[1] I would like to know whether this is indeed the case, and whether in particular Vitruvius and Celsus are to be dealt with by this rule. Moreover, it is reported that you yourself are laboring upon [an edition of the] *Spiritalia* of Hero much more accurate than those we have; the *Naumachia* of Leo too, and of a certain patrician Basil, and so forth. Let me know, please, whether these studies of yours are now ripe for printing and whether you think of improving any other text for the public good? If there is anything which any of our people has in hand of which in return you wish more knowledge, ask for it boldly. Recently the noble Boyle sent to the press an essay on the *Subtility, Efficacy and Determinate Nature of Effluviums*; another, on the positive or privative character of cold and a third on the ponderability of flame;[2] all of which things together with some others prepared by the same author will soon see the light.

But I should not have been so bold in troubling one charged with direction of the Dauphin's education with so many matters. So farewell, and believe me most devoted to you. London, 19 May 1673.

Whenever you shall have leisure to write to me, please let all your letters to be conveyed by the ordinary post be addressed in this way:

> A Monsieur
> Monsieur Grubendol à Londres

Nothing more: letters addressed to me in this fashion will be much better taken care of than if they were addressed with my own name, for reasons which it would be pointless to record here.

ADDRESS

> To the very worthy Mr. Pierre Daniel Huet,
> his most dear friend
> Paris

NOTES

Reply to Letter 2187.
1 See Letter 2208.
2 This work has been mentioned previously (Letter 1997, note 3) and was published in 1673 by Moses Pitt. However, the second essay mentioned here by Oldenburg, on cold, did not come out in this book; instead, it was published together with *The Saltness of the Sea* in 1674. Another strange point about the *Essays of Effluviums* is that the third English issue contained Oldenburg's translation of Steno's *Prodromus to a Dissertation concerning Solids naturally contained within Solids*—this issue being exceptionally rare.

2236
Lister to Oldenburg
21 May 1673

From the original in Royal Society MS. L 5, no. 53
Partly printed in *Phil. Trans.*, no. 95 (23 June 1673) 6060–65

Yorke May 21st 1673

Sir

I am your thankfull debtour, for your two last: you will pardon my
silence & beleeve me much diverted from my inclinations, by necessary
attendance upon my imployment. I know not whether, I formerly omitted[1]
(to begin wth ye particulars of your last letter) ye relation of ye age of two
men, fathar & sonne said to have been produced as witnisses at an Assize
at ye Castle of Yorke, about 8 yeares since; ye sonn above 100 yeares old:
perhapps I might omit it, for though I had it affirmed to me by more than
one person, who than saw ym & spoake wth ym; yet because it was accompanied wth soe strange & romantiq Circumstances, I did not enquire
further: but its possible, ye Relation sent you out of Lanchashire & this,
may both be meant of ye same persons. they are, as I remember, said to
live in Dent a small valley in ye western mountains of Yorkshire.[2] but I
will endeavour to satisfy your curiositie herein.

I much wonnder at ye confirmation Mr Henshaw gives you of ye falling
of ye Norway Ratts out of ye Aire; I have sometime read what Wormius
has writ concerning ym in his *Musaeum*.[3] and found not any thing more
strange, yn ye particulars of this fall: for, for their suddain over running
whole feilds & countreys, & their generation, I conceive it would be noe
difficult matter to find out ye reasons if an unprejudiced person had ye
opportunity of making ye Observation. In ye meane time, I little doubt but
yt ye manner of their generation is by ye ordnary course of Nature.

I have been twice surprised in England wth such like suddain appear-
ances of vast troopes of Animals, but of ye Insect kind.

The first was of ye small Catterpillar, observed in ye ripe Corne in
Cambrigshire 1666. of wch you had my notes some yeares since.[4]

The other, as followeth. August 2d 1667 riding over from Hull to
Barton on a very calme Evening, I observed in our passage, ye whole
surface of Humber for some miles togathar so looke black & foule, as tho

dust had been cast upon it: &, indeed, ye boat-men told me, it was dust raised by ye Tide coming in; but when I tooke some of it upon an Oare, it proved Pismires with-wings of divers Species; most of ye black kind, yet were there many amongst ym wth large russet-tailes.

I come to your first Letter, where ye Analogie betwixt ye Veines in Plants & ye Nerves in Animals hinted by Dr Wallis[5] is a considerable Notion & I shall sett my selfe a taske e're long to examine ym both again on purpos & give you my thoughts.

In ye meane time, I will entertain you if you please wth some Anatomical Observations & Experiments.

It has been long in my thoughts & desire to have discovered ye actual Passage of ye Chyle into ye lacteous veines; of wch yet I never doubted, as I find some doe at this day. The difficulty lyes in ye certain, constant & unalterable character of ye chyles whitenesse, espeacially when received into those veines. And yet it is as certain yt in a Diabetes ye Urine retains all ye qualities of ye liquour drunk: also in yt famous instance of those who eat ye fruit called ye prickle Pear (if I remember aright,) their Urine has affrighted ye eater wth ye colour of blood, yt is wth ye not-altered-colour of ye juice of ye fruit. in those instances at least, we cannot doubt but ye Chyle, even in ye lacteous veines, was qualifyed according to ye food & drinke.

To effect than something to this purpos, we have formerly & yt very often repeated ye Experiment of injecting highly tinged liquours into ye Gutts of a live Animal. it would be too tedious & impertinent to writ downe ye circumstances of many different tryalls, we will only breifly tell you ye manner of performing it & ye successe.

We laced ye skin of ye abdomen loosly for a hands breadth & than opening it underneath ye stitches, we tooke out either ye duodenum or any other part of ye tenuia intestina;[6] the Gutt tooke out we opened wth a very small Orifice & having ready ye tinged liquour luke-warme, we injected it upwards & downwards; carfully stitching up ye Gutt & than drawing ye lace, we unloosed 2 of his feet, laying ye Dog on his side for what time we thought convenient. The tinged liquours we used were good Barbados indigo in fair water & filtrated; alsoe lumps of Indigo thrust down his throat good broth (as they call it) of a blew fatt:[7] Indigo in milke: saffran in milke: Again we tryed in some Doggs fed before hand & injected ye liquors in ye very height of chyles distribution: into others yet fasting & yt for a longer or shorter time.

The successe was constant, yt we cannot say, yt we ever did find ye least discolouring of ye chyle on ye other side ye Gutts, yt is, within ye lacteous veines, but ever white & uniforme. Whence we judge it not very feasable to tinge ye Venal Chyle in a well & sound Animal. And he yt would dem-onstrate ye matter of fact to ye dye, must, probably doe it by giving him some such thing in his food as shall cause a Diabetes or some distemper equivalent to it.

Though we have observed many odd things in ye several exercises of this Nature, yet we shall not trouble you at present wth any other particu-lars, than what we have further observed in ye Gutts, to wch we shall con-fine our Paper. Of these we shall proceed to tell, tho possibly they may be better known to you already: As of ye Glandules miliares[8] of ye small Gutts, wch may alsoe in some Animals be well called fragi-formes from ye figure of ye one halfe of a strawberry,[9] & wch yet I take to be excretive glandules, because conglomerate.

The use of ye intestinum caecum, subservient to yt of ye colon & rectum; manifest in such Animals where nature intends a certaine & deter-minate figure to ye excrements.

Of some sorts of Vermin we found in ye Gutts. And first of ye lumbricj latj or Tape-wormes. of these I say, we found in ye Gutts of one Dogg, perhapps more than 100 in all: the duodenum was exceedingly stuffed out & extended wth ym (wch alsoe well agrees wth an other observation I made in a Mouse, where I found ye Duodenum to be far bigger than ye stomack it selfe, by reason of ye great number of these Wormes for kind, wch were contained in it, for kind, I say, for these Tape-wormes, were of a quite different shape from those of ye Dog, or any that I have yet seen) to proceed, we found ym alsoe in ye jejunum & ileon, but not any one lower than ye valvula colj, nor any higher than ye duodenum or within ye Pilorus: below ye duodenum they lay at certain distances one from an other, though sometimes by paires or more of ym twisted togathar: neer ym was con-stantly to be observed an Excrement of their owne distinct for colour (more grey) & consistance from ye chyle (ye observation was made in Dogs plentifully fed for other purposes) just as we find in worme eaten tracks of wood, where ye Cossi[10] leave behind ym ye wood wch has passed through their bodies: these wormes lay mostly wth ye small ends upwards as feeding upon & expecting ye Chyle in its discent. These lumbrici latj were none of ym above one foot long & most of ym of an equall length & bignesse. ye one end was as broad as my litle finger nail & pointed like a lancet, ye other end, coming small gradually for ye 3d part of ye whole length of ye Animal, was knotted or ended in a small button like a pin head: they were every where & in all parts of ym a like milke white, of a flat & thin substance like fine Tape, divided into infinite rings or incisures; each incisure having sharpe angles on both sides, looking to ye broader end standing out beyond each other; from wch alsoe I take ye small end to be ye head, els ye sharpe corners of ye Annulj would necessarily hinder ye Ascent of ye Animal, wheras if ye contrary be tru they serve to keep it up: each ringe has alsoe on ye one side only & yt alternatively one small protuberance, much like ye midle feet of ye body of some Catterpillars.

After I have thus described ym to you, I desire you to view ye cutt of Tulpius in ye last-yeares edition of his *Medic. Observat.* lib. 2. cap. 42, where he retracts ye first figure given us, in ye edition of yt booke in ye yeare 1652:[11] & yet I cannot say, yt all in this last is tru, for to me ye rictus & eye in ye there supposed head of ye Animal seem to be ye meer fancies of ye Painter; not to say, yt probably ye smaller end is ye head, wch, indeed, is in this Cutt wholly neglected. comparing our Animals wth yt cutt of Tulpius it was not very easie for me to observe because of ye great resemblances ye specifick differences of ye lumbricj latj of men & those of this Animal. I was not soe happy as to discover any motion in any part of ym, in water or out of it: nor did they seem (if pricked or otherwise injured), much (if at all) to contract ym selves or shorten ye Annulj, soe yt they than appeare to me as things without motion or sense.

There are an other sort of lumbricj lati to be mett wth very frequently alsoe in Doggs; called cucurbitinj from ye likenesse each annulus or linck hath to a coucumber seed. Ihave found of ym about halfe a foot long, but more often broaken into shorter peices. The former by us described is undoubtedly a compleat & entire Animal; but there is great reason of suspicion, yt this is a chain of many Animals linked togathar. These Animals for kind have been observed to have been voided by men enclosed in a Gutt of Membrane of a prodigious length. And wch yet is more notable, a person of great integritie & worth Mr F. J.[12] affirmed to me, yt he once assisted at ye opening of a Dog, in wch one of ye kidneys was observed to be quite wasted & become a perfect blather & in yt blathar they found something like an Animal of a monstrous shape, wch being dissected, was nothing else, but a skin full of these lumbricj cucurbitinj. it were to be desired, yt such as have ye opportunity of such rare phaenomena as of snakes, lizards, Beetles, Catterpillars, Toades & such like things as we read off in medical Histories to have been voided or found in any part of ye body, would carfully examine whether they are not ye like disguises of this sort of wormes, much assisted by ye surprised fancys of ye first observers.

And because these sort of Worms are sometimes said to be found out of ye Gutts their most proper place, we shall conclude wth a very recent Observation of ye last month in this Cittie. A surgeon brought me about 20 Wormes wch he had just than taken out of an ulcerated Ankcle of a Girle of about 8 yeares old I had ye curiositie to goe my selfe & see it: I found ye legg sound, alle but ye anckle wch was vastly swolled, & ye Girle otherwise harty & well coloured: she had been in great miserie for some months: had been sent up to London, where she was touched & dressed for ye Evil: sometime after her returne her pain continuing a yong Puppie was opned & applyed to ye Soares. ye surgeon who took off ye Puppie found it to his great admiration full of Wormes, at least 60 in number what those he found in ye body of ye Puppie, & what he drew out of ye soar Anckle; into wch he said they crawled down as wormes doe into ye ground. ye same Puppie was again applyed, & it was than (at ye 2d taking off of ye Puppie) yt I made ye visite, and saw only one worme, gott out into ye Puppie, but a very live and stirring one; many were afterwards killed by injections. These wormes I affirme, according to my best knowledge (& I had ye opportunity of comparing ym) were of ye very Species of ye Lumbrici teretes[13] wch children familiarly void from ye Gutts. they were betwixt 3 & 4 intches long; all about ye matter of an equall bignesse, as of one brood; something thicker than a Ducks quill; very sharpe at both ends; stiffe; & exactly round, without incisures visible at least, & yet could move & twist ym selves readily enough. All ye difference was in ye colour, these being much whiter, than any I have seen from ye Gutts. vide Barth. *Hist. 63. cent. 5.*[14] where neer 20 wormes, as long as my finger, were found in a Ladys arme, probably of this species too.

Sir I begg pardon for my long silence. I have been forc't to writ this letter by intervalls, I have been much busied & called away into remote parts since ye receipt of yours. this might have been shorter, if I had had more leisure. for all apologie, I am sincere & tru to my power in all circumstances. I am Sir

Your most humble servant
Martin Lister

P.S.

In ye Papers Mr Brookes[15] is pleased to pleasure me wth, I find an Expt brought in, of mixing Oil of Vitriol wth water & of their taking up lesse roome mixt than single. I am apt to suspect, yt soe much may be lost in ye ebullition. for I consider Oil of Vitriol, as a thing made by great stresse of fire & therfore participating of ye nature of a calx viva,[16] wch consiquently will heat wth water. but it is my doubt only suggested to ye Exp[*page torn*]

I am glad the Table of Snailes is not yet published:[17] I hope to send you it improved after this summer is over; having now seen ye spawn of both land & fresh-water snailes, & alsoe by good Expt found, yt ye scarlet juice of our snailes is a saliva of yt colour, & noe venall juice, as ye Ancients believed.

I pray let me trouble you to get me ye description of tongue grafting: wch a curious person desires to learn.[18]

ADDRESS
For my honoured friend
Henry Oldenburgh
Esquire
at his house in ye Palmal
London

POSTMARK MA 23

NOTES
Reply to Letters 2161 and 2225.
1 In Letter 1656; see Vol. VII, pp. 521–22.
2 Dentdale, ten miles long, is near the meeting point of Yorkshire, Westmorland, and Lancashire. There is both a parish and a village called Dent.
3 See Letter 2105, note 5.
4 See Vol. VII, p. 342; Lister's account was sent on 23 December 1670.
5 In Letter 2153.
6 "small intestine."
7 That is, "a strong decoction from a blueing vat."
8 "miliary glands."
9 The Latin for strawberry is "fraga," whence the modern genus is *Fragaria*.
10 Used by Pliny for larvae found under the bark of trees; Lister presumably is using the word as a generic name for woodworms.
11 Nicholas Tulp's *Observationum medicarum libri tres* was first published at Amsterdam in 1641; there were also editions in 1652, 1672, and 1685.
12 Probably Francis Jessop (1638–91); see Vol. VII, p. 149.
13 "round worms."
14 Thomas Bartholin, *Historiarum anatomicarum rariorum centuriae I ... VI* (3 vols., Copenhagen, 1654–61).
15 For John Brooke (*c.* 1635–91) see Vol. VIII, p. 302, note 6.
16 "quicklime."
17 See Letter 2085, and its note.
18 On 12 March a paper by Israel Tonge (for whom, see Vol. VI, p. 564, note, and Vol. VII, Index) had been read describing a way of grafting on the roots of trees which he called (humorously or not) "tongue grafting."

2237

Oldenburg to Bernard

22 May 1673

From the original in Bodleian Library MS. Smith 45, f. 69

London May 22. 73.

Sir,

I shall begin this wth answering the import of yr post-script, concerning the way of printing copies according to Mr Hugenius.[1] But I must first informe you, yt Mr Hugens never sent over his way otherwise, than by telling us, it was thesame wth yt of Mr Surveyor, Dr Wren;[2] wch is this following:

"Take a thin Bras-plate, as thin as paper; cover it wth Etching vernish, and let it be etched upon wth a hand carefull not to close any letter. The Aqua fortis must be so strong as to corrode the plate quite through. Then turne this plate, and lay it upon another thick plate, cover'd all over wth Printers Ink, and so after the usual manner pass it through the rolling presse."

Sir, As I communicate this frankly to you, so I desire you would keep it to yrself, and by no means divulge it. I never saw the practise of it, though I saw an effect thereof produced by M. Hugens sending us the figure of the Alhazenian problem resolv'd by himself.[3]

As for yr Admission-mony, it will be time enough to pay it, when you come to towne, yt so you may put yr name to the book at yesame time.

Signor Malpighi writes me word, yt Mengolus is ready to print *Solarem annum, non exiguae molis opus*: And yt Borellius of Sicily intends to be shortly at Rome, and there to publish *Maurolycam traductionem Archimedis de Insidentibus aquae, additis propriis cogitatis et inventis*.[4]

One of my Parisian Correspondents informs me thus of Claudius Millet de Chales, "quod Cursus ejus Mathematicus jam imprimatur Lugduni Galliarum quodque idem Author, post Introductionem generalem purae matheseos, Elementa Mathematice tractata, Terram scilicet, Aquam, Aerem, Ignem, nobis sit exhibiturum."[5]

Monsr Hugens his book de *Motu Pendulorum* is not only abroad, but also

come into England; so yt I exspect the person, yt hath brought over one
for me from the Author, every day to come and to deliver it to Sir,

> Yr very affectionate friend
> and humble servt
> *Oldenburg*

ADDRESS

    To his honored friend
    Mr Edward Bernard, Savi-
    lian Professor of Astronomy,
        in St Johns College in
            Oxford

                        POSTMARK MA 22

NOTES

    The letter to which this is a reply is missing.
1 See Vol. V, p. 558, note 2.
2 See Vol. V, p. 583; Wren's method is described in the Royal Society's minutes for
  2 December 1669, when Hooke produced an example (see Birch, *History*, III, 409).
3 Sent by Huygens with Letter 1213 (Vol. VI, pp. 42–46); it is reproduced in facsimile
  in *Œuvres Complètes*, VI, facing p. 462.
4 See Letter 2223, notes 1 and 3.
5 Leibniz; see Letter 2233; Oldenburg has paraphrased the original.

2238
Oldenburg to Leibniz
26 May 1673

From the copy in Royal Society Letter Book VI, 121–23
Printed in Gerhardt, pp. 97–98

An Answer to Mr Leibnitius his letter of April 26 1673

Clarissimo et consultissimo Viro
Domino Gottfredo Gulielmo Leibnitio JU.D.
Henr. Oldenburg S.P.

Jam antea paucis significavi, traditas mihi fuisse tuas d. 26. April. [N.S.] ad me datas.[1] Exinde alteras accepi $\frac{14}{24}$ Maji exaratas. Gaudeo imprimis, feliciter adeo superasse Te difficultatem in machina tua Arithmetica objectam, ut eam brevi numeris omnibus absolutam sis daturus. Suaserim omnino, ut datam Societati nostrae in consessu publico fidem quamprimum liberare satagas. Interest existimationis tuae, ut id facias; interest mea, ut ad id praestandum Te stimulem.

Respondi Huetio de Vectii Valentis codice Oxoniano, et opellam meam Praestanti Viro paratissimam obtuli:[2] velim ipsum urgeas, ut Heronis Spiritalia (quae multo auctiora ipsum habere, quam quae extant, asseris) nec non Leonis et Basilii Patritii Naumachiam juris publici faciat; ad haec Vitruvii Celsique novam editionem maturet. Spero, ex ejusmodi lucubrationibus, quales sunt Wallisii, Hugenii, Leibnitii, Mariotti, Wrenni et similium, doctrinam de Motu tandem perspectam fore. Rem omnino gratam feceris, si quae Tu de porositate, Cartesiana hypothesi abludentia, meditatus es, mihi transmiseris.

Quod tu ex Domini St. Hilarii sententia circa Magnetem annotas, eget explicatione, quam proinde proximis tuis literis a te exspecto. Modum determinandi capacitatem vasis cujuscunque figurae sine ulla stereometria aut virgula stereometrica non capio; Ut eam Clar. Mariottus, quem ex me plurimum salvere velim, stabiliat et in lucem emittat, impense opto.

Necdum vidimus Celeberr. Hugenii de Pendulorum motu Tractatum: Interim nobilis quidam Anglus ex occasione demonstrationis, a Rev. Domino Pardies ad libelli sui statici calcem exhibitae, suam de vibrationum in cycloide peractarum synchronismo demonstrationem Transactionibus Philosophicis,[3] jam sub praelo sudantibus, et per tabellarium proximum Parisios mittendis, commisit.

Experimentum illud Boylianum de duabus Laminis politis, in recipiente exhausto ab invicem dilapsis, bona fide a se enarratum ait Boylius; de aliorum Experimentis respondere non potest.

Lubentissime accipiam Barroviani in Lectionibus Opticis phaenomeni solutionem, ab Hugenio et Mariotto, ut ais, inventam. Quod ad series illas Fractionum attinet, quarum denominatores sunt numeri figurati, sive finiti illi sint sive infiniti, Dn. Collinius ait, Mengolum in libro suo de Additione fractionum, sive quadraturis Arithmeticis,[4] ostendere modum eos addendi omnes; at quando ad illam accedit Fractionum seriem, quarum denominatores sunt in progressione Arithmetica, demonstrare Mengolum, quamlibet ejusmodi seriem infinitam majorem esse quovis numero assignabili; atque idem eum facere de cujusvis ejusmodi seriei quadratis et cubis, affirmantem, tentatum a se fuisse, finiti terminorum numeri in seriebus modo dictis additionem, at imparem se operi comperisse, idque ditioris ingenii adminiculum postulare. Quaerit itaque Collinius, an Methodus tua ad id praestandum se extendat; nostram, inquiens, id praestare, infinitamque approximationem praebere. Addit idem Collinius, cum assignaverit tibi summam 100 terminorum in serie fractionum musicalium, atque ut significes petierit, methodusne tua potis sit majorem minoremve numerum simul addere, manifestum satis fuisse, ipsum (Collinium puto) non potuisse de infinitae seriei summa intelligi.[5]

Quod Theorema tuum attinet, in posteriori tua epistola commemoratum, Collinius ait, non sibi novum videri, Fractiones illas, a Te positas, addere deorsum, cum denominatores earum in continua tunc proportione se habeant; at si separatim et lateraliter eas sumas, $\frac{1}{4}$ $\frac{1}{9}$ $\frac{1}{16}$ etc. quaerit idem, an eo casu addere eas possis. Spero, quae elaboravit nuper denatus Dn. Pardies, lucem suo tempore visura, et Societatem illam in eo futuram, ne viri docti lucubrationes pereant. Videre aveo, quae D. de Chales circa elementa mathematica methodo tractavit: Inprimis vero Eruditissimum Dn. Agar sollicitari et urgeri velim, ut eximia, quae ipsum habere intelligo, de Frigore, putredine, gemmis, re vitriaria, Coloribus, iisque quae ad ornandam augendamque pictoriam artem faciunt, meditata et experimenta in lucem emittat; maxime hoc pacto sibi devinciet universum doctorum orbem, et nostrates praesertim Anglos, et prae aliis omnibus, Nobilissimum Boylium et Oldenburgium tuum. Hoc ipsi ex me, addita salute officiosissima significare ne graveris oro. Vale. Dabam Londini d. 26 Maji 1673.

TRANSLATION

Henry Oldenburg presents many greetings to the famous and wise Mr. Gottfried Wilhelm Leibniz LL.D.

I have already told you a few days since that your letter addressed to me on 26 April [N.S.] was delivered to me.[1] Since then I have received another written on 14/24 May. I am particularly pleased that you have so successfully overcome the difficulty raised against your arithmetical machine that you are confident of having it perfected soon for all numbers. I am quite sure that you will try earnestly to redeem your promise given to our Society at an ordinary meeting as soon as possible. It concerns your reputation to do so and it concerns mine to urge you to lay it before [us].

I have answered Huet about the Vettius Valens manuscript at Oxford and have offered my very ready assistance to that exceptional person.[2] I would like you to incite him to publish the *Spiritalia* of Hero (which you say he has much increased over what is available) as well as the *Naumachia* of Leo and Basil the Patrician; moreover, let him bring to fruition a new edition of Vitruvius and Celsus. I hope that the theory of motion will stand out clearly at last as a result of the studies in that field by Wallis, Huygens, Leibniz, Mariotte, Wren, and so forth; you will do something entirely welcome if you send me your reflections on porosity, differing from the Cartesian hypothesis.

Your comments on Mr. St. Hilaire's opinion concerning magnetism demand an explanation, which I shall accordingly look forward to in your next letter. I do not understand the way of determining the volume of a vessel of any shape without any stereometry or stereometrical rods; I very much hope that the famous Mariotte (to whom I send a grand salute) may define and publish [the method].

We have not yet seen the famous Huygens' treatise on the motion of pendulums; meanwhile a certain noble Englishman has, upon the occasion of the demonstration presented by the Reverend Mr. Pardies at the end of his book on statics, entrusted his own demonstration of the synchronism of oscillations made in a cycloid to the *Philosophical Transactions*,[3] which is now in press and is soon to be sent by post to Paris.

Boyle says that that experiment of his on two polished plates, which fell apart from each other in the exhausted receiver, was related by himself in good faith; he cannot answer for the experiments of others.

I shall very cheerfully receive the solution of that phenomenon of Barrow's in *Lectiones opticae* discovered, as you say, by Huygens and Mariotte. As for those series of fractions whose denominators are figurate numbers (whether finite or infinite), Mr. Collins says that Mengoli has shown the method of summing them all in his book on the addition of fractions or arithmetical quadratures;[4] but that when he comes to that series of fractions whose denominators are in arithmetical progression Mengoli demonstrates that any infinite series of that sort is greater than any assignable number; and that he does the same concerning the squares and cubes of any series of that sort, affirming that he had attempted the addition of a finite number of terms in series of the type just mentioned but found himself unequal to that task, and demanded assistance from some richer genius. Accordingly Collins inquires whether your method extends to yielding that [sum], saying that ours does yield it and furnishes an infinite approximation. The same Collins adds that when he assigned you the sum of one hundred terms in a series of harmonic fractions, and asked you to let him know whether or not your method was good enough for the summation of a greater or less number of terms, it was pretty obvious that he (Collins, I mean) could not be supposed to speak of the sum of an infinite series.[5]

As to your theorem, recorded in your later letter, Collins says that it does not seem new to him to add those fractions postulated by yourself downwards, when their denominators arrange themselves in continual proportion; but if you take them separately and laterally, as $\frac{1}{4}$, $\frac{1}{9}$, $\frac{1}{16}$, etc., then he asks whether in that case you can summate them. I hope that the works completed by the recently defunct Mr. Pardies will see the light in due course and that that Society [of Jesus] will take steps to prevent that learned man's researches being lost. I long to see the way in which Mr. de Chales treats the elements of mathematics; and I particularly wish the very erudite Mr. Agar to be besought and incited to make public the excellent reflections and experiments I understand he has, on cold, putrefaction, gems, glassworking, colors, and what relates to the development and perfection of the art of painting; in this way he will place a great obligation on the whole learned world and we English particularly, among them the very noble Boyle and your Oldenburg. I beg you to be so good as to let him know this from me, with a most dutiful greeting. Farewell. London, 26 May 1763

NOTES

Reply to Letters 2208 and 2233.
1 In Letter 2230.
2 See Letter 2235.
3 On contemporary researches into cycloidal motion, see D. T. Whiteside's note in Newton, *Mathematical Papers*, III, 391–401. "'Nobilissimi cujusdam Angli Demonstratio Synchronismi Vibrationum peractarum in Cycloide . . .'" was published in *Phil. Trans.*, no. 94 (19 May 1673). As Oldenburg was later to make explicit in letters to Huygens (Vol. X), the author was Viscount Brouncker. There was a review of Pardies's *La Statique* in the same number, pp. 6042–46 (compare Vol. VIII, Letter 1859). Brouncker's terse, even cryptic "demonstration" is a précis of the second proof of the isochronism of cycloidal motion which he had sent to Huygens in 1662 (the first involving a misapprehension) and laid before the Royal Society on 22 January 1661/2 (see Vol. VIII, p. 489, and Birch, *History*, I, 70–74). In Whiteside's view (Newton, *Math. Papers*, III, 399) Brouncker's proof was not so incomprehensible or

even false as Huygens later declared it to be, since it is "structurally identical" with that produced by Pardies—hence Brouncker's anxiety to claim priority, even though it was clear to all that the real distinction for discovering and proving the isochronal property of the cycloid must belong to Huygens.

4 Pietro Mengoli, *Novae quadraturae arithmeticae, seu de additione fractionum* (Bologna, 1650).

5 Presumably all these comments of Collins were written, but we have not so far come across the sheet of paper that may contain them.

2239

Jacques Moisant de Brieux to Oldenburg

26 May 1673

From the original in Royal Society MS. B 2, no. 21

Monsieur

Jay estés de puis quelque temps tourmenté dune cruelle disurie qui graces a Dieu est a present un peu diminuee mais qui ne me laisse pas encore la liberté de Vous pouvoir escrire moy mesme; Je suis donc forcé demprunter la main dautruy pour vous confirmer les asseurances de mes treshumbles services et vous remercier des lettres dont il vous en plu mhonorer; elles me furent rendues par M. Le Bas des le lendemain du iour de son arrivee en ceste ville et elles mont causé en mesme temps bien de la Joye et bien de la douleur.[1] car elles mont apris a mesme temps que vous maimies tousiours et que M. Vrooth estoit mory.[2] Si Jen avois su plustost la nouvelle je naurois pas manque d'en Tesmoigner mon desplaisir a M. son fils et si Josois je vous prirois bien humblement Monsieur de le luy vouloir tesmoigner; Mais sur le sujet de ce jeune gentilhomme que iay cognu et que Je cheris souffrez moy de vous dire que cest quelque chose d'asses estonnant qu'une personne de sa qualité de son bien de sa taille et de son âge demeure a la Campagne les bras croisez pendant que tous vos braves aussi bien que les nostres courent aux occasions qui se presentent de servir leur prince et de moissoner des Lauriers; C'est trop mingerer et donner des conseils et des avis que lon ne me demande point en des affaires domestiques dont les interests quoy qu'ils me soient tres chers ne me sont pas assez cognus. Il me donc suffire de satisfaire a ce que vous me demandez touchant les affairès de nos Academies; Mrs Justel et Huet vous auront plainement informé de ce qui se passe a celle de Paris et sur tout de la descouverte que M. denis et un autre Provençal ont faite sans sestre communiqués l'un lautre dune eau qui a la Vertu darrester le sang des arteres coupées et dont on a fait diverses experiences sur des chiens et dautres animaux,[3] on aura beau la faire sur des hommes dans l'armee de nostre grand Monarque sil est vray ce qu'on mescrit qu'il a fait porter dans son camp quantité de cet eau dont on iuge que le vitriol fait le corps; Pour ce qui est de nostre petite Societé de cette ville M. Graindorge vous aprendra ce qui se fait dans ce qui regarde les choses de la fisique;[4] et en ce qui regarde les belles lettres ie vous diray que M. de Touroude[5] homme fort versé en la Geographie l'histoire et la Langue Grecque va nous donner bien tost la premiere partye de sa Grece antienne et nouvelle avec des Cartes dautant plus exactes qu'il a voullu faire une Voyage de deux ans pour voir les Isles de Larchipel et conferer avec tous les habilles qu'il a trouves en ce pays la et a Venise; M. de la Roque a mis depuis peu au iour une disertation touchant Les Armoiries de France en attendant son grand Armorial qui sera un Volume In folio fort gros et fort curieux;[6] M. de Graindorge et M. Piron travaillent de leur costé a faire des nottes et des explications courtes et claires. Le premier Sur Lucrece Lautre sur Claudian. cela par Lordre de Monsr le Duc de Montauzier et par lavis de M. Huet, qui dans les autres villes donne a chacun des plus habilles gens qu'on y peut trouver un Autheur a esclaircir et cela pour l'usage de Monseigneur Le Dauphin nostre Jeune Prince qui fait de merveilleux progres dans la carriere des vertus et des sciences.[7]

Jallois finir cette lettre qu'and iay apris que vous honories de vostre bien veillance M. le Bourgeois[8] l'un de nos citoyens et qui mest cher par bien des raisons; son pere est mon hoste Il a esté mon camarade dans ma Jeunesse et dans ma derniere maladie Il ma asisté avec autant de soin que de suffisance; Son fils que Vous avez a present en vostre ville est un jeune homme bien fait de corps et desprit de bonnes moeurs cr[a]ignant Dieu qui a joint la chirurgie avec la medicine et qui est fort bon Philosophe et Jen parle ainsy pour lavoir ouy non seulement dans les conversations particulieres mais aussi dans des disputes publiques de sorte que les Illustres personnes qui lont mis aupres de Monsieur leur fils ne pouvaient iamais Lay trouver dans ses voyages ou dans ses Etudes de meilleur guide et de meilleure compagnye.

Cest tout ce que la petite treve que me donnent mes maux me permet de vous dire a cette heure et ie nay rien a vous ajouster sinon que ie suis avec toutte sorte de passion et de respect vostre treshumble et tres obeissant serviteur

de Brieux

a Caen ce 5e Juin 1673 [N.S.]

TRANSLATION

Sir,

I have for some time been tormented by a cruel dysury which, thanks be to God, is now a little diminished, but which does not yet leave me sufficient liberty to allow me to write to you myself. I am therefore forced to borrow the hand of another to confirm to you the assurance of my very humble service and to thank you for the letters with which you were pleased to honor me.[1] They were delivered to me by Mr. Le Bas as soon as the day after his arrival in this town, and they gave me much joy and at the same time much pain. For they told me both that you still love me and at the same time that Mr. Wroth was dead.[2] If I had known the news sooner I should not have failed to testify my regret to his son, and if I dared I should very humbly beg you, Sir, to be so kind as to represent it to him. But on the matter of this young gentleman whom I knew and loved, permit me to say to you that it is a pretty surprising thing that a person of his quality, wealth, figure, and age should rest in the country with his arms folded while all your brave men, as well as ours, jump at all opportunities to serve their prince and to reap laurels; [but] this is meddling and giving advice and counsel which I am not asked for in domestic affairs, with whose concerns, although they are very dear to me, I am not sufficiently well acquainted. It is therefore enough for me to answer what you ask of me concerning the affairs of our Academies. Messrs. Justel and Huet will have informed you fully of what goes on in that at Paris, and above all of the discovery that Mr. Denis and another man from Provence have made, without having had any communication with each other, of a liquid which possesses the ability of staunching the blood of a severed artery, and of which various experiments have been made on dogs and other animals.[3] There will be a good opportunity to try it on men in the army of our great monarch if it is true what I have had in writing, that he has had a quantity of this liquid carried in his camp; it is judged that vitriol composes the body of it. As for our little Society in this town, Mr. Graindorge will instruct you about what goes on in scientific matters.[4] As to literary subjects, I will tell you that Mr. de Touroude,[5] a man very well informed in geography, history, and Greek, will soon give us the first part of his "Ancient and Modern Greece," with maps so far exact that he was willing to make a two-year voyage to see the islands of the archipelago and to confer with all the skilled men whom he has found in that country and in Venice. Mr. de la Roque has recently published a dissertation on the armorial bearings of France, while waiting for his great armorial, which will be a very large and interesting volume in folio.[6] Mr. de Graindorge and Mr. Pyron for their part are at work on making notes and short and clear explanations, the first on Lucretius, the other on Claudian, all by order of the Duke of Monstausier and on the advice of Mr. Huet, who in other towns gives to each of the ablest men that he can find an author to illuminate, this for the use of the Dauphin, our young prince, who makes marvellous progress in the realms of ethics and learning.[7]

I was finishing this letter when I learned that you honor with your benevolence Mr. le Bourgeois,[8] one of our citizens, who is dear to me for a variety of reasons: his father is my landlord, he was my companion in my youth, and in my last illness tended me with equal care and thoroughness. His son, who is at present in your city, is a young man of both bodily and mental fitness, with good manners, and Godfearing, who has combined medicine and surgery and is very much of a good philosopher. I can speak thus not only from having heard him in private conversations but also in public debates. This is so much the case that the illustrious personnages who have placed him near their son could never find for him in travel or study a better guide or better companion.

This is all that the short truce granted me by my ills permits me to tell you at present, and I have nothing to add except that I am, very passionately and respectfully, your very humble and obedient servant

de Brieux

Caen, 5 June 1673 [N.S.]

NOTES

For Jacques Moisant de Brieux (1614–74), see Vol. VI, p. 356, note 3.

1 There is now no trace of these letters, nor of the traveler who brought them.

2 For Oldenburg's cousin by marriage, Sir John Wroth (d. 1671), and his travels, see Vol. VI, pp. 21–23, 113, and 355, where his son is also mentioned.

3 See Letters 2211 and 2212.

4 Probably André Graindorge (1616–76), for whom see Vol. VII, p. 209, note 4; there is no record of his corresponding with Oldenburg. Huet in his autobiographical *Commentarii de rebus ad eum pertinentibus* (Paris, 1718) also mentions a Jacques Graindorge de Prémont, who was a member of Brieux's academy. According to Harcourt Brown ("L'Académie de Physique de Caen," *Mémoires de l'Académie des Sciences Arts et Belles-Lettres de Caen*, N.S. IX, 1938, 117–208) the scientific academy virtually ceased to exist from December 1672, after the ending of royal subventions. The present letter was not known to Professor Brown. Graindorge had been the principal figure in this academy since Huet's departure from Caen.

5 Huet mentions "Louis Touroude" as a member of Brieux's academy, but the book does not seem to have appeared.

6 Gilles André de la Roque de La Lontière, *Traité singulier du blason, contenant les règles des armoiries* (Paris, 1673), in octavo; the great folio work was apparently not published, but a quarto, *Traité de la noblesse*, was to appear at Paris in 1678.

7 For these editions "ad usum Delphini," see Letter 2208. Graindorge seems never to have completed his edition of Lucretius. Guillaume Pyron published both an edition

of Claudian (*Cl. Claudiani opera quae extant*, Paris, 1677, which is number 33 of "Collectio ad usum Delphini") and *Ad serenissimum Delphinum, oblato ipsi Claudiano interpretatione et notis illustrato epigramma* (n.p., n.d.).

8 For Esaie le Bourgeois, see Letter 1810 (Vol. VIII, pp. 325–30).

2240

Huygens to Oldenburg

31 May 1673

From the original in Royal Society MS. H 1, no. 77
Printed in *Œuvres Complètes* VII, 302–3

A Paris ce 10 Juin 1673 [N.S.]

Monsieur

Il y a desia quelque temps que je vous ay envoyé une douzaine d'Examplaires de mon livre de l'Horloge.[1] Monsieur Vernon a eu la bontè de vous adresser le pacquet, en ayant chargè un de ses amis qui partoit pour Angleterre.[2] Mais comme les Voiageurs ne vont pas si viste que la Poste, je ne me suis pas hastè de vous en donner avis, et de vous prier de vouloir avoir le soin de faire la distribution de tous ces livres suivant les inscriptions que j'y ay mises. Que si vous avez peutestre desia pris cette peine je vous en rends treshumbles graces. Je seray bein aise d'apprendre ce qu'en disent tous ces sçavants geometres, qui sont en plus grand nombre en ce pais là qu'en aucun autre de l'Europe.

J'ay receu toutes celles que vous m'avez fait l'honneur de m'escrire, dont la derniere estoit avec le Numero 93 de vos Transactions. Pour ce qui est des solutions de M. Newton aux doutes que j'avois proposez touchant sa Theorie des couleurs,[3] il y auroit de quoy y respondre et former encore de nouvelles difficultez, mais voyant qu'il soustient son opinion avec tant de chaleur, cela m'oste l'envie de disputer. Que veut dire, je vous prie, qu'il assure que quand mesme je luy aurois montrè que le blanc se peut composer de deux seules couleurs primitives, je n'en pourrois pourtant rien conclure contre luy; et cependant il a dit pag. 3083 des Transactions[4] que pour composer le blanc toutes les couleurs primitives sont necessaires. Apres cela il n'a garde de demeurer court a aucune objection qu'on luy puisse faire.

Quant a la maniere dont il concilie l'effect des verres convexes a assembler si bien les rayons, avec ce qu'il establit touchant la differente refrangibilité, j'en suis satisfait, mais aussi doit il avouer que cette abstration des rayons ne nuit donc pas tant aux verres qu'il semble avoir voulu faire accroire quand il a proposè les miroirs concaves comme la seule esperance de perfectionner les telescopes. Son invention assurement estoit tresbelle, mais a ce que j'ay y pu connoistre par l'experience, le defaut de la matiere la rend presque aussi impossible d'executer, que la difficultè de la forme repugne aux Hyperboles de M. Des Cartes. de sorte qu'a mon avis il en faudra demeurer a nos verres spheriques aux quels nous avons desia tant obligation, et qui peuvent recevoir encore plus grande perfection tant par l'augmentation de la longueur des lunettes que par la correction de la matiere du verre mesme. Hier on essaya un verre de 62 pieds a l'Observatoire qui parust bon pendant le jour, mais comme je n'y pus rester jusqu'au soir, je ne scay pas encore ce qu'on en aura trouvè pour ce qui est des astres. L'on commence a revoir Saturne le matin, mais il est encore trop proche du soleil pour pouvoir voir les 2 nouveaux satellites, dont le periode du plus distant n'est pas encore si bien verifiè que celuy du plus proche. N'aton pas encore chez vous des lunettes par les quelles on les puisse decouvrir? Je suis Monsieur

Vostre treshumble et tresobeissant serviteur
Hugens de Zulichem

ADDRESS
    A Monsieur
    Monsieur de Grubendol
        à Londres.

TRANSLATION, partly from *Phil. Trans.*, no. 97 (6 October 1673), 6112

[Paris, 10 June 1673 N.S.]

Sir,

It is now already some time ago that I sent you a dozen copies of my book on the clock.[1] Mr. Vernon was so kind as to address the package to you and to charge with it one of his friends who was leaving for England.[2] But as travelers don't go as quickly as the post does, I was in no hurry to advise you of it, and to request you kindly to take care of the distribution of all the books following the inscriptions which I have put in them. If you have perhaps already taken this trouble I send you my very humble gratitude for it. I should be very pleased to learn what is said about it by all these learned geometers, who are more numerous in that country han in tany other in Europe.

I have received all those [letters] which you have done me the honor of writing me, of which the last was with number 93 of your *Transactions*.] Touching the Solutions, given by M. Newton to the scruples by me propos'd about his Theory of Colors,[3] there were matter to answer them, and to form new difficulties; but seeing that he maintains his opinion with so much concern, I list not to dispute. But what means it, I pray, that he saith; *Though I should shew him, that the White could be produced of only two Un-compounded colors, yet I could conclude nothing from that.* And yet he hath affirm'd in p. 3083 of the *Transactions*,[4] that to compose the White, all primitive colors are necessary. [After that, he is not in a position to deal abruptly with any objection that one may raise against him.]

As to the manner, whereby he reconciles the effect of Convex glasses for so well assembling the rays, with what he establishes concerning the different refrangibility, I am satisfied with it; but then he is also to acknowledge, that this aberration of the rays is not so disadvantagious to Optic glasses as he seems to have been willing to make us believe, when he proposed *Concave speculums* as the only hopes of perfecting Telescopes. His invention certainly was very good; but, as far as I could perceive by experience, the defect of the Matter renders it as impossible to execute, as the difficulty of the Form obstructs the use of the *Hyperbola* of M. Des-Cartes: So that, in my opinion, we must stick to our Spheric Glasses, whom we are already so much obliged to, and that are yet capable of greater perfection, as well by increasing the length of Telescopes, as by correcting the nature of Glass it self. [Yesterday at the Observatory they tried a glass of sixty-two feet, which seemed good during the day, but as I could not remain until the evening I do not yet know what will be found out about it as far as the stars are concerned. Saturn begins to be visible in the morning, but it is still too near the sun for the two new satellites to be visible; the period of the more distant one is not yet as well determined as that of the nearer one. Are there not yet any telescopes with you by which they could be made out? I am, Sir,

Your very humble and obedient servant
Huygens of Zulichem

ADDRESS

Mr. Grubendol,
London

NOTES

Reply to Letters 2144, 2178, 2197, 2206, and 2229. Huygens had not written to Oldenburg since the end of January (Letter 2138).

1 I.e., *Horologium oscillatorium*.
2 Vernon was presumably back in Paris on his way to the Middle East, a long journey that ended with his murder.
3 In Letter 2195, sent to Huygens by Oldenburg with Letter 2197.
4 See *Phil. Trans.*, no. 80 (19 February 1671/2), Letter 1891 (Vol. VIII).

Index

Boldface figures indicate Letter numbers. Both originals and translations have been indexed.

DESIGNED BY WILLIAM NICOLL OF EDIT, INC.

COMPOSED AND PRINTED BY

KONINKLIJKE DRUKKERIJ G. J. THIEME B.V., NIJMEGEN, NETHERLANDS

BOUND BY BOEHM BINDERY CO., MILWAUKEE, WISCONSIN

TEXT AND DISPLAY LINES ARE SET IN GARAMOND

Library of Congress Cataloging in Publication Data
Oldenburg, Henry, 1615?–1677.
Correspondence.
Some of the letters in Latin, French, or German
with translations into English.
CONTENTS: —v. 1. 1641–1662. with the collaboration
of E. Reichmann.—v. 2. 1663–1665.—v. 3. 1666–1667.—[etc.]
I. Hall, Alfred Rupert. 1920–   ed. and tr.
II. Hall, Marie (Boas) 1919–   ed. and tr.
Q143.04A4   509'.24   65–11201
ISBN 0–299–06390–9